SECOND CANADIAN EDITION

Economics Today The Macro View

Roger LeRoy Miller
Institute for University Studies, Arlington, Texas

Brenda Abbott
Northern Alberta Institute of Technology

Sam Fefferman
Northern Alberta Institute of Technology

Ronald K. Kessler
British Columbia Institute of Technology

Terrence Sulyma
Northern Alberta Institute of Technology

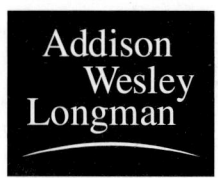

Addison
Wesley
Longman

Toronto

National Library of Canada Cataloguing in Publication Data

Main entry under title:

Economics today: the macro view

2nd Canadian ed.
First ed. written by: Roger LeRoy Miller, Nancy W. Clegg.
Includes index.
ISBN 0-201-71616-X

1. Macroeconomics.   2. Economics   I. Miller, Roger LeRoy.

HB172.5.M54 2002   339   C2001-930214-2

ISBN 0-201-71616-X

Vice President, Editorial Director: Michael Young
Acquisitions Editor: Dave Ward
Director of Marketing: Michael Campbell
Developmental Editor: Laurie Goebel
Production Editor: Marisa D'Andrea
Copy Editor: Edie Franks
Production Coordinator: Janette Lush
Page Layout: Nelson Gonzalez
Photo Research: Alene McNeill
Art Director: Mary Opper
Interior Design: Monica Kompter
Cover Design: Monica Kompter
Cover Image: FPG/Justin Pumfrey

2 3 4 5   06 05 04 03 02

Printed and bound in USA.

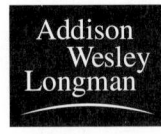

Statistics Canada information is used with the permission of the Minister of Industry, as Minister responsible for Statistics Canada. Information on the availability of the wide range of data from Statistics Canada can be obtained from Statistic Canada's Regional Offices, its World Wide Web site at http://www.statcan.ca, and its toll-free access number 1-800-263-1136.

Photo Credits
Page 1, 14, Ronald Zack/AP Photo–Canadian Press; page 18, 35, SuperStock; page 49, 62, Ryan Remiorz/Canadian Press; page 69, 92, "These materials have been reproduced with permission of eBay Inc." COPYRIGHT © EBAY INC. All rights reserved; page 99, 117, Ernest Doroszuk/ISOTR Sun/Canadian Press; page 122, 144, © H&R Block Tax Services; page 149, 170, Dick Hemingway; page 175, 196, Mark Antman/The Image Works; page 201, 217, Stray Light Pictures/Greg Locke; page 222, 244, Ryan Remiorz/Canadian Press; page 249, 261, National Archives of Canada; page 265, 289, Dick Hemingway; page 295, 311, Dick Hemingway; page 318, 338, Jiang Jin/SuperStock; page 342, 354, © Grant LeDuc/Stock Boston; page 357, 371, Courtesy of VanCity Credit Union; page 375, 401, Dick Hemingway; page 408, 431, Bank of Canada; page 436, 455, © Corel Corporation; page 460, 482, Dick Hemingway; page 488, 502, Courtesy of UNICEF/United Nations Children's Fund.

Dedicated to my parents, George and Lilli, who always understood the true value of a good education.
R.K.K.

To Andrea, Drew, and Vanya; for their love, support, and patience in my "booking."
T.J.S.

CONTENTS IN BRIEF

CONTENTS

companion Website . . .

Your Internet companion to the most exciting, state-of-the-art educational tools on the Web!

T he Pearson Education Canada Companion Website is easy to navigate and is organized to correspond to the chapters in this textbook. The Companion Website comprises these distinct, functional features:

Customized Online Resources

Online Interactive Study Guide

Interactivities

Communication

Explore these areas in this Companion Website. Students and distance learners will discover resources for indepth study, research, and communication, empowering them in their quest for greater knowledge and maximizing their potential for success in the course.

A NEW WAY TO DELIVER EDUCATIONAL CONTENT

Course Management

Our Companion Websites provide instructors and students with the ability to access, exchange, and interact with material specially created for our individual textbooks.

- **Syllabus Manager** provides instructors with the option of creating online classes and constructing an online syllabus linked to specific modules in the Companion Website.

- **Grader** allows the student to take a test that is automatically marked by the program. The results of the test can be e-mailed to the instructor and then added to the student's record.

- **Help** includes an evaluation of the user's system and a tune-up area that makes updating browsers and plug-ins easier. This new feature will facilitate the use of our Companion Websites.

Instructor Resources

This section features modules with additional teaching material organized by chapter for instructors. Downloadable PowerPoint Presentations, Electronic Transparencies, and an Instructor's Manual are just some of the materials that may be available in this section. Where appropriate, this section will be password protected. To get a password, simply contact your Pearson Education Canada representative or call Faculty Sales and Services at 1-800-850-5813.

General Resources

This section contains information that is related to the entire book and that will be of interest to all users of the site. A Table of Contents and a Glossary are just two examples of the kind of information you may find in this section.

The General Resources section may also feature *Communication facilities* that provide a key element for distributed learning environments:

- **Message Board** – This module takes advantage of browser technology to provide the users of each Companion Website with a national newsgroup to post and reply to relevant course topics.

- **Chat Room** – This module enables instructors to lead group activities in real time. Using our chat client, instructors can display website content while students participate in the discussion.

Want some practice before an exam?

The Student Resources section contains the modules that form the core of the student learning experience in the Companion Website. The modules presented in this section may include the following:

- Learning Objectives
- Self-Check Questions
- Exercises
- Lecture Slides
- Net Applications
- Web Destinations
- Net Search
- Glossary

The question modules provide students with the ability to send answers to our grader and receive instant feedback on their progress through our Results Reporter. Coaching comments and references to the textbook may be available to ensure that students take advantage of all available resources to enhance their learning experience.

Objectives

Key Terms

Glossary

Net Search

Lecture Slides

Self-Check

Exercises

Net Applications

Web Destinations

News Room

Instructor Resources

General Resources

Message Board

Live Chat

Feedback

Site Search

Here are just some of the student resources you will find at Economics Place:

- Actual past exams for download
- Online lessons for tough topics
- E-mail help through the online tutor

PEARSON EDUCATION CANADA

26 Prince Andrew Place
Toronto, Ontario M3C 2T8

To order:
Call: 1-800-567-3800
Fax: 1-800-263-7733

For samples:
Call: 1-800-850-5813
Fax: (416) 299-2539
E-mail:
phabinfo_pubcanada@pearsoned.com

The Companion Website for this text can be accessed through Economics Place at:

www.pearsoned.ca/economics

PREFACE

From the Authors

When we were asked to work on the second edition of this book, we knew it would be a tough job to continue the good work done by our predecessor, Nancy Clegg. Guided by the helpful suggestions and comments provided by adopters and reviewers of the first edition, we proceeded to make some major revisions. We were careful to ensure that any changes we made to the first edition would maintain the straightforward and approachable style that made this book so popular in its first edition in Canada. As instructors with extensive teaching experience in both college and university settings, we want to continue to present a text that students can relate to, based on their personal, social, and career interests. We also hope that this book will encourage students to broaden their interests to include local, national, and global economic issues. Many of our students will not take subsequent economics courses; in that case, we want them to be ready for the world, and not just ready for intermediate economics courses.

The approach used in *Economics Today: The Macro View*, Second Canadian Edition, is based on the belief that students learn more when they are involved and engaged in the material they are studying. The presentation of issues and applications in a Canadian setting is a major strength of this text. Each chapter begins with an issue that introduces certain economic principles; those principles are presented throughout the chapter, and at the end of the chapter an Issues and Applications section explains how those principles can be applied to that issue. This section ends with For Critical Analysis questions, which help to reinforce the theory at hand and encourage the students to reflect on economics in the "real" world—their world. In addition, each chapter contains numerous short examples that further illustrate the points being made in the text. Thinking Critically About The Media boxes in each chapter look carefully at what the real economics of the reportage suggest.

In writing the second Canadian edition, we have been mindful of Canada's reliance on global events for our economic well being. Accordingly, we have used many examples and issues that connect Canada with the rest of the world. In keeping with today's "wired world," each chapter includes a Netnomics example, which illustrates how the theory in the chapter can be applied in cyberspace. At the end of every chapter, Economics on the Net encourages the student to use the Internet as a research tool in order to answer chapter-related questions.

Over the years, we have found that more of our students are heading for degrees in business rather than economics. In recognition of this trend, the accompanying Study Guide includes a Business Section in each chapter, providing business applications that apply economic theory to accounting, marketing, finance, management, and small business. The Web site that accompanies this text presents additional business applications and exercises. In the text, business students will find more examples than ever that apply economic theory to business situations.

In the end, we believe that *Economics Today: The Macro View* and the Study Guide will provide college students with a relevant and interesting book, one that will provide students with a "window on the world" that will help them in their personal lives as citizens and professionals. We hope that you will enjoy this book and begin to appreciate the many ways in which economics can be a part of your day-to-day activities.

What's New in the Second Canadian Edition?

This edition includes changes in the sequencing of various chapters; changes in chapter content; updated issues, applications, and example boxes; and pedagogical revisions.

Compared to the first Canadian edition, the sequencing of many of the first six chapters has been changed. Specifically, the demand and supply chapters were reorganized to introduce the discussion of elasticity earlier in the book. It now appears as Chapter 5, "Elasticity," and is included in the six chapters common to both Micro and Macro. The rest of Chapters 1-6 have been reorganized as follows:

Chapter 1: The Nature of Economics (same as the first Canadian edition)

Chapter 2: Scarcity and the World of Trade-Offs (same as the first Canadian edition)

Chapter 3: Economies in Transition (Chapter 6 in the first Canadian edition)

Chapter 4: Demand and Supply (Chapter 3 in the first Canadian edition)

Chapter 5: Elasticity (Chapter 8 in the first Canadian edition)

Chapter 6: The Public Sector (Chapter 5 in the first Canadian edition)

In addition, Chapters 15–17 (the money and banking chapters) have been reorganized so that the discussion moves from a single bank (Chapter 15) to the banking system (Chapter 16), and then to the Bank of Canada (Chapter 17).

Changes in content include the following:

- A new section entitled "Making Decisions at the Margin" has been added to the discussion about rationality in Chapter 1.
- Chapter 1 in the new edition places more emphasis on the role that theory plays in policy analysis.
- Chapter 3, "Economies in Transition," has been significantly streamlined, making room for a more complete description of pure capitalism.
- More information about the natural rate of unemployment, the GDP deflator, and business fluctuations has been added to Chapter 7.
- Chapter 8 now includes a discussion of the limitations of using GDP as a measure of economic well-being.
- The discussion of the costs and benefits of economic growth has been expanded in Chapter 9.
- Material on aggregate demand and supply has been moved from Chapter 11 to Chapter 10. In addition, much of what remains in Chapter 10 has been rewritten to improve the clarity of the explanations.
- In Chapter 12, several definitions and relationships are now presented algebraically as well as textually for those who wish to integrate more algebra into the discussion of consumption, income, and the multiplier.
- Chapter 14 has been updated to discuss why we have budget surpluses instead of deficits.
- Material on supply-side economics has been added to Chapter 18.
- Chapter 20 now includes a section on fixed versus floating exchange rates.

In completing the second Canadian edition, many applications and example boxes have been changed to reflect current events and issues. What follows is just a sample of some of the new issues discussed:

- The Brain Drain: It Works Both Ways (Example 1-1)
- For-Profit Health Care in Canada? (Issues and Applications, Chapter 3)
- Structural Unemployment in Europe Never Seems to Go Away (International Example 7-1)
- How Does Productivity Affect Our Standard of Living in Canada? (Thinking Critically About the Media 9-1)
- The Internet is Making Investment a Fuzzier Concept (Netnomics, Chapter 12)
- Monetary Policy: Where Are We Now? (Policy Example 17-2)
- Can Foreign Exchange Rates Be Fixed Forever? (International Policy Example 20-1)

Many enhancements were made to the pedagogical elements for this edition. They include the following:

- Each chapter has a new Netnomics box, illustrating how the chapter's economic principles can be applied to cyberspace and e-commerce activities.
- A new feature entitled Economics on the Net is presented at the end of every chapter. This pedagogical tool encourages the student to use the Internet as a research tool in order to answer chapter-related questions.
- In many of the chapters, the Preview Questions have been modified and expanded to ensure a more comprehensive coverage of all the topics in the chapter.
- All example boxes are now numbered and referenced in the text; students will know when to read them in order to associate their content with the appropriate theory.
- The Concepts in Brief and Summary sections have been fine-tuned to ensure that they comprehensively summarize the essential points covered in the chapter.
- Many end-of-chapter Problems have been modified to cover the main points in the chapter in a more comprehensive way. In chapters that are predominantly technical in nature, additional numeric and graph problems have been added to the Problems section.

Economic Principles in Practice

CHAPTER OPENING ISSUES.   Each opening issue motivates student interest in the key chapter concepts. The issue presented is revisited in the Issues and Applications section at the culmination of the chapter.

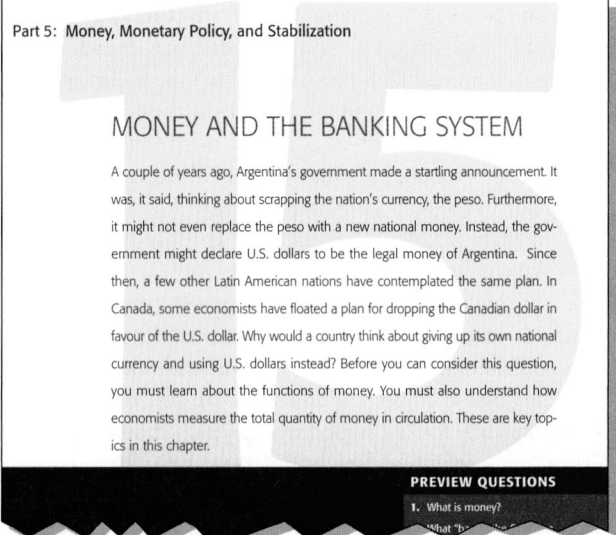

Part 5: **Money, Monetary Policy, and Stabilization**

MONEY AND THE BANKING SYSTEM

A couple of years ago, Argentina's government made a startling announcement. It was, it said, thinking about scrapping the nation's currency, the peso. Furthermore, it might not even replace the peso with a new national money. Instead, the government might declare U.S. dollars to be the legal money of Argentina. Since then, a few other Latin American nations have contemplated the same plan. In Canada, some economists have floated a plan for dropping the Canadian dollar in favour of the U.S. dollar. Why would a country think about giving up its own national currency and using U.S. dollars instead? Before you can consider this question, you must learn about the functions of money. You must also understand how economists measure the total quantity of money in circulation. These are key topics in this chapter.

PREVIEW QUESTIONS

1. What is money?

ISSUES AND APPLICATIONS. The Issues and Applications feature is designed to encourage students not just to apply economic concepts, but also to think critically about them. Each begins with the concepts being applied in this instance, and is followed by two For Critical Analysis questions that could be used to prompt in-class discussions. Suggested answers to these questions are given at the back of the text (p. 521), as well as in the Instructor's Manual along with the relevant chapter.

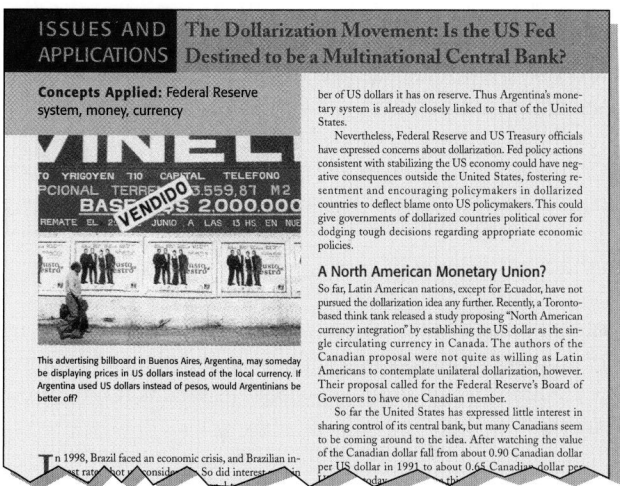

This advertising billboard in Buenos Aires, Argentina, may someday be displaying prices in US dollars instead of the local currency. If Argentina used US dollars instead of pesos, would Argentinians be better off?

THINKING CRITICALLY ABOUT THE MEDIA. These boxed items keep students abreast of recent newsmaking issues, while at the same time offering a "twist" on typical media coverage. They encourage students to think critically about, rather than simply accept, what they hear and read in the news.

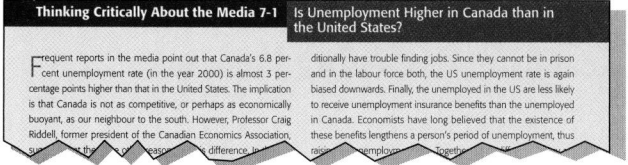

POLICY EXAMPLES. Many of the economic debates reported in the media involve important policy issues. Here, students are presented with various key policy questions on both the domestic and international fronts. Each Policy Example and International Policy Example is followed by a For Critical Analysis question that encourages students to consider exactly what is involved in the discussion, and what the further ramifications might be. Suggested solutions to these questions are provided in the Instructor's Manual, at the end of the appropriate chapter. In addition, students will find hints and suggested answers with each chapter in the Study Guide.

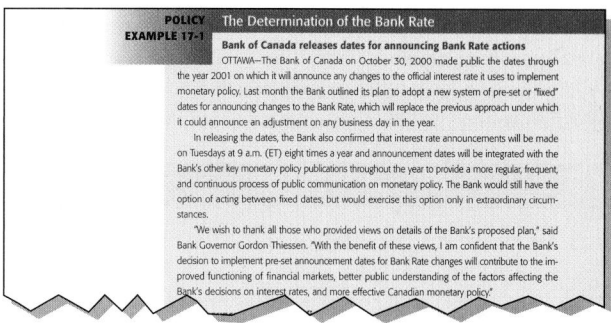

A WORLD OF GLOBAL EXAMPLES. International examples emphasize today's global economy. The issues presented in them, and the For Critical Analysis question which follows each, help students to understand the worldwide economy and Canada's place in it. Suggested answers to the questions are given in the Instructor's Manual and in the Study Guide.

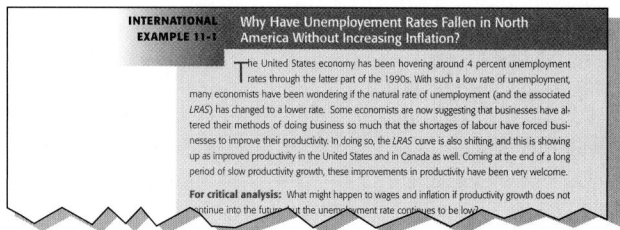

EXAMPLES CLOSER TO HOME. Many thought-provoking and relevant examples highlight Canadian events and demonstrate economic principles. For Critical Analysis questions with each encourage students to apply the knowledge and information gained from the example. Possible answers to the questions are provided in the Instructor's Manual and in the Study Guide.

NETNOMICS. This new feature applies the economic theory in each chapter to cyberspace. The Netnomics examples illustrate the relevance of economic principles to current online activities, including the e-commerce boom and bust.

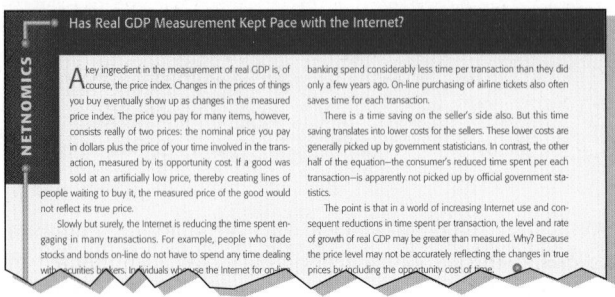

ECONOMICS ON THE NET. At the end of every chapter, students are presented with a structured online activity in the form of Economics on the Net, which is suitable for individual or group assignments. This activity encourages students to use the Internet as a research tool.

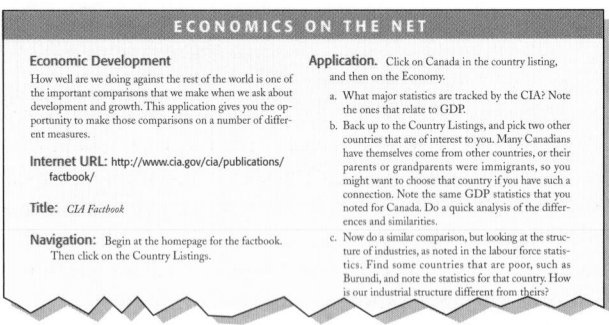

Pedagogy With a Purpose

This second Canadian edition of *Economics Today* is loaded with the same highly regarded pedagogy of the first Canadian edition. It helps students apply what they learn.

FOR CRITICAL ANALYSIS. At the end of each example, students are asked to reflect on real-world problems by answering For Critical Analysis questions. The answers to the questions are found as follows:

- Issues and Applications—at the end of the student text (p. 521)
- Examples, International Examples, Cyberspace Examples, Policy Examples, International Policy Examples—in the student Study Guide, at the end of the relevant chapter
- All For Critical Analysis questions (i.e., all of the above)—in the Instructor's Manual, in the appropriate chapter

DID YOU KNOW THAT...? Each chapter starts with a provocative question to engage students' interest and lead them into the content of the chapter.

PREVIEW QUESTIONS. On the first page of each chapter, several questions are posed, giving purpose and focus for the chapter. These are then fully answered at the end of the chapter. Students are also directed through marginal prompts to try answering the preview questions as the topic of each is covered in the text.

GRAPHS. Articulate and precise, the four-colour graphs illustrate key concepts.

KEY TERMS. Key terms are printed in bold type, and are defined in the margin of the text the first time they appear. These terms are also reproduced alphabetically in the Glossary in the Study Guide.

CONCEPTS IN BRIEF. At the end of each major section in each chapter, Concepts in Brief summarizes the main points, thus reinforcing students' knowledge as well as testing their learning.

CHAPTER SUMMARY. Every chapter ends with a concise but thorough summary of the important ideas of the chapter.

PROBLEMS. A variety of problems support each chapter, and answers for all odd-numbered problems are provided at the back of the textbook. The complete set of problem answers (both even- and odd-numbered) appears in the Instructor's Manual.

Teaching/Learning Package

For the Instructor

INSTRUCTOR'S MANUAL. The Instructor's Manual has been adapted by Haldun Sarlan (University of Northern British Columbia) for this second Canadian edition of *Economics Today*. Features include:

- Chapter overviews, objectives, and outlines
- Points to emphasize, including more theoretical issues for those who wish to stress theory
- Suggested questions for further class discussion
- Answers to the For Critical Analysis questions that follow each example in the chapter
- Answers, with detailed step-by-step solutions, to all end-of-chapter problems
- Selected references

TEST ITEM FILE. The Test Item File contains over 4000 questions with answers. There are over 2500 multiple choice questions as well as short answer questions in the test bank. This supplement has been adapted by Elizabeth Evans (Nova Scotia Community College, Akerley Campus).

PEARSON EDUCATION TEST MANAGER. This supplement is a computerized version of the Test Item File described above. This package allows instructors to custom design and generate tests in PC Windows format. Questions and figures can be edited, created, or deleted to suit each instructor's needs.

POWERPOINT PRESENTATIONS. PowerPoint Presentations are available for each chapter of the text. The slides highlight and illustrate important ideas in the text and contain animation that shows students how to build key graphs.

TRANSPARENCY MASTERS. This hardcopy supplement contains copies of the figures and tables from the text that can be used as transparency masters for each chapter.

www.pearsoned.ca/economics. This site for introductory economics students and professors contains a wealth of online resources to help you study or teach economics. You will also find the following features at this site:

- an instructor newsletter;
- actual exams from previous years for students to use as practice tests;
- online lessons for topics students often find challenging;
- links to breaking economic news around the world;
- an online tutor accessible through e-mail;
- tutorials on math and graphing;
- and lots more!

In addition, from this site you can go directly to our Companion Website created specifically for *Economics Today*. Just follow the links! This site contains self-test questions, Internet assignments, links, and a glossary, all of which are tied directly to the second Canadian edition of *Economics Today*.

ONLINE LEARNING SOLUTIONS. Pearson Education Canada supports instructors interested in using online course management systems. We provide text-related content in WebCT, Blackboard, and our own private label version of Blackboard called CourseCompass. To find out more about creating an online course using Pearson content in one of these platforms, contact your local Pearson Education Canada representative.

For the Student

STUDY GUIDE. Available in Micro and Macro versions, the Study Guides have been adapted by the text authors. Each includes the following:

- Putting the chapter into perspective
- Learning objectives
- Chapter outlines
- Key terms and concepts
- Completion questions
- True-or-false questions
- Multiple-choice questions
- Matching questions
- Problems
- Working with Graphs
- A Business Section, giving applications and problems that relate to economic theory in accounting, marketing, finance, management, small business, and entrepreneurship
- Answers to the problems and questions that are included in the Study Guide
- Answers to the For Critical Analysis questions that follow examples in the textbook
- Glossary of terms, defined exactly as in the textbook

ACKNOWLEDGEMENTS

We began work on the second Canadian edition of this text with the understanding that there was a lot of work to do in a short time. We could not have held to our challenging schedule without the help of a terrific team of professionals at Pearson Education Canada. Thanks to Dave Ward, Executive Editor, for giving us this opportunity! Laurie Goebel, Developmental Editor, was a constant source of timely advice and encouragement. Marisa D'Andrea, Production Editor, guided the book through the final stages with a calm and sure hand. Edie Franks, Copy Editor, juggled four authors and four different writing styles with great dexterity.

We would also like to thank the following professors who helped with the development of this text by offering us their insightful comments and constructive criticisms:

Ian Wilson, St. Lawrence College
Peter Peters, University College of the Cariboo
Peter MacDonald, Cambrian College
Rafal Kosztirko, Mount Royal College
Haldun Sarlan, University of Northern British Columbia
Martin Moy, University College of Cape Breton
Ibrahim Hayani, Seneca College
Dan Otchere, Concordia University
Elizabeth Evans, Nova Scotia Community College
Dennis McGuire, Okanagan University College

John Saba, Champlain Regional College
Lucas Rosnau, University of Calgary

In addition, Susan Kamp of the University of Alberta provided us with numerous reviews, a user diary, and feedback from her students, all of which helped us shape this new edition.

In completing this work, we sincerely appreciate the support and patience which we received from each of our families.

Finally, we would like to thank our colleagues and students at Northern Alberta Institute of Technology and British Columbia Institute of Technology for their valuable advice and support during the writing of this book.

In keeping with the cyber-age, and because we would appreciate suggestions about what to do in future editions, you and your students can contact us via e-mail. Visit the *Economics Today* Companion Website by following the links at www.pearsoned.ca/economics to contact us. We look forward to hearing from you!

Brenda Abbott
Sam Fefferman
Ronald K. Kessler
Terrence Sulyma

THE NATURE OF ECONOMICS

Woody Allen once said, "Money is better than poverty, if only for financial reasons."
Yet who has not heard or even said that "money cannot buy happiness"? Such a
statement seems to pose problems for the study of economics. As you will see, economics does deal with people's quest for money or, more correctly, for wealth. Is
it useful to study economics even if "money doesn't buy happiness"? You will find
out as you read about the nature of economics in this introductory chapter.

PREVIEW QUESTIONS

1. What is the definition of
   economics?

2. What is the difference
   between microeconomics
   and macroeconomics?

3. What role does rational
   self-interest play in
   economic analysis?

4. Why is the study of
   economics a science?

5. What is the difference
   between positive and
   normative economics?

6. What are the primary
   socio-economic goals that
   form the basis of policy?

DID YOU KNOW THAT... between 1987 and 1997, the number of fax machines in Canadian offices and homes increased by over 10,000 percent? During the same time period, the number of bike messengers in downtown Toronto *decreased* by over 50 percent. The world around us is definitely changing. Much of that change is due to the dramatically falling cost of communications and information technology. In the late 1990s, the computers inside video games cost only a few hundred dollars, yet had 50 times the processing power that a US$10 million IBM mainframe had in 1975. It's not surprising that since the start of the 1990s, Canadian firms have been spending more on communications equipment and computers than on new construction and heavy machinery.

Cyberspace, the information superhighway—call it what you want, but your next home (if not your current one) will almost certainly have an electronic address on it. Close to 100 percent of Canadian households have at least one telephone, and more than 80 percent have video recorders. Almost 30 percent of homes have personal computers, and about half of those machines are set up to send and receive information via phone lines. Your decisions about such things as when and what type of computer to buy, whether to accept a collect call from a friend travelling in Europe, and how much time you should invest in learning to use a new multimedia system involve an untold number of variables: where you live, the work your parents do, what your friends think, and so on. But, as you will see, there are economic underpinnings for nearly all the decisions you make.

The Power of Economic Analysis

Knowing that an economic problem exists every time you make a decision is not enough. You also have to develop a framework that will allow you to analyze solutions to each economic problem—whether you are trying to decide how much to study, which courses to take, if you should finish school, or if Canada should send peacekeeping troops abroad or raise tariffs. The framework that you will learn in this text is based on the *economic way of thinking*.

Economists believe that economic analysis can help you make better decisions concerning your career, your education, financing your home, and other important issues. In the business world, the power of economic analysis can help you increase your competitive edge as an employee or as the owner of a business. As a voter, for the rest of your life you will be asked to make judgments about the policies advocated by a particular political party. Many of these policies will deal with questions related to international economics, such as whether the Canadian government should encourage or discourage immigration, prevent foreigners from investing in domestic TV stations and newspapers, or restrict other countries from selling their goods here. Finally, just as taking an art, music, or literature appreciation class increases the pleasure you receive when you view paintings, listen to concerts, or read novels, taking an economics course will increase your understanding when watching the news on TV, listening to it on radio, or reading the newspapers.

Defining Economics

What is economics exactly? Some cynics have defined *economics* as "common sense made difficult." But some common sense, by definition, is within everyone's grasp. In the following pages you will encounter numerous examples which show that economics is, in fact, pure and simple common sense.

Economics is one of the social sciences and, as such, seeks explanations of real events. All social sciences analyze human behaviour. The physical sciences, on the other hand, generally analyze the behaviour of electrons, atoms, and other non-human phenomena.

Economics A social science that studies how people allocate limited resources to satisfy unlimited wants.

Economics is a social science that studies how people allocate their limited resources to satisfy unlimited wants.

To understand this definition fully, we need to explain the terms *wants* and *resources*. **Wants** refers to the goods and services people would consume if they had unlimited income. **Resources** are items used to produce goods and services. While resources will be discussed in more detail in the next chapter, they include things such as skilled and unskilled labour, land, machinery, and entrepreneurial talent.

Resources are limited relative to wants—consumers, managers, business owners, citizens, and politicians must continually make choices among alternative courses of action. For example, as a consumer, you choose how to spend your limited income on a vast array of goods and services. If you manage an organization or own a business, you will have to decide what resources to hire and what goods and services to produce and sell while working with a limited budget. Finally, as a citizen and potential politician, you make decisions that affect how limited tax dollars are used to better society. Economics helps us study how such choices can be made.

Wants refers to the goods and services people would consume if they had unlimited income.

Resources are items used to produce goods and services.

Try Preview Question 1:
What is the definition of economics?

Microeconomics Versus Macroeconomics

Economics is typically divided into two types of analysis: **microeconomics** and **macroeconomics**.

> Microeconomics is the part of economic analysis that studies decision making undertaken by individuals (or households) and by firms. It is like looking through a microscope to focus on the small parts of our economy.

> Macroeconomics is the part of economic analysis that studies the behaviour of the economy as a whole. It deals with economy-wide phenomena such as changes in unemployment, the general price level, and national income.

Microeconomic analysis, for example, is concerned with the effects of changes in the price of gasoline relative to that of other energy sources. It examines the effects of new taxes on a specific product or industry. If price controls were to be re-instituted in Canada, how individual firms and consumers would react to them would be in the realm of microeconomics. The raising of wages by an effective union strike would also be analyzed using the tools of microeconomics.

By contrast, issues such as the rate of inflation, the amount of economy-wide unemployment, and the yearly growth in the output of goods and services in the nation all fall into the domain of macroeconomic analysis. In other words, macroeconomics deals with **aggregates**, or totals—such as total output in an economy.

Microeconomics The study of decision making undertaken by individuals (or households) and by firms.

Macroeconomics The study of the behaviour of the economy as a whole, including such economy-wide phenomena as changes in unemployment, the general price level, and national income.

Try Preview Question 2:
What is the difference between microeconomics and macroeconomics?

Aggregates Total amounts or quantities; aggregate demand, for example, is total planned expenditures throughout a nation.

The Economic Person: Rational Self-Interest

Economists assume that individuals act as *if* motivated by self-interest and respond predictably to opportunities for gain. This central insight of economics was first clearly articulated by Adam Smith in 1776. Smith wrote in his most famous book, *An Inquiry into the Nature and Causes of the Wealth of Nations*, that "it is not from the benevolence of the butcher, the brewer, or the baker that we expect our dinner, but from their regard to their own interest." Otherwise stated, the *typical* person about whom economists make behavioural predictions is assumed to look out for his or her own self-interest in a rational manner. The word *typical* is very important. Economists know that not all people respond in the same way when faced with the same circumstances. If offered a free trip to

Hawaii for participating in a marketing experiment, for example, most people will take part. There inevitably will be some who don't want to go to Hawaii, perhaps because they don't like traveling, so they won't participate in the study. But, *on average*, the promised trip to Hawaii will be sufficient to attract participants because people behave in a predictably self-interested way.

Because monetary benefits and costs of actions are often the most easily measured, economists most often make behavioural predictions about individuals' responses to ways to increase their wealth, measured in money terms. Refer to Example 1-1, below, to see if we can apply the theory of rational self-interest to explain the much touted brain drain to the United States.

| **EXAMPLE 1-1** | The Brain Drain: It Works Both Ways |

Much has been made recently of the number of highly educated Canadians moving to the United States. Doctors, nurses, university professors, and engineers are among those heading south for more money, or better working conditions, or both. However, the "brain drain" works both ways: for every university graduate who leaves for the US, Canada receives from the rest of the world four immigrants with university degrees, including one with a post-graduate degree. Is it rational for highly trained workers to be leaving Canada at the same time as other highly trained workers are arriving?

Take nurses, for example. The average Canadian general-duty nurse will make about $50,000 per year before overtime. The average general-duty nurse in the US will make about $72,000 while an equivalent job in the United Kingdom pays only $38,000. Thus, it does make economic sense to see Canadian nurses leaving for the US at the same time as British nurses are heading for Canada. Both are acting in their own self-interest to increase their personal well-being.

For critical analysis: Who can we predict will be filling the nursing void in the United Kingdom?

The Rationality Assumption

Rationality assumption The assumption that people do not intentionally make decisions that would leave them worse off.

The **rationality assumption** of economics, simply stated, is as follows:

> We assume that individuals do not intentionally make decisions that would leave them worse off.

The distinction here is between what people may think—the realm of psychology and psychiatry and perhaps sociology—and what they do. Economics does *not* involve itself in analyzing individual or group thought processes. Economics looks at what people actually do in life with their limited resources. It does little good to criticize the rationality assumption by stating, "Nobody thinks that way" or "I never think that way" or "How unrealistic! That's as irrational as anyone can get!"

Take the example of driving. When you consider passing another car on a two-lane highway with oncoming traffic, you have to make very quick decisions: You must estimate the speed of the car you are going to pass, the speed of the oncoming cars, the distance between your car and the oncoming cars, and your car's potential rate of acceleration. If we were to apply a model to your behaviour, we would use the laws of calculus. In actual fact, you and most other drivers in such a situation do not actually think of using the laws of calculus, but we could predict your behaviour *as if* you understood the laws of calculus.

Responding to Incentives

If it can be assumed that individuals never intentionally make decisions that would leave them worse off, then almost by definition they will respond to different incentives. We define **incentives** as the potential rewards available if a particular activity is undertaken. Indeed, much of human behaviour can be explained in terms of how individuals respond to changing incentives over time.

Incentives Potential rewards available if a particular activity is undertaken.

School students are motivated to do better by a variety of incentive systems, ranging from gold stars and certificates of achievement when they are young, to better grades with accompanying promises of a "better life" as they get older. There are, of course, negative incentives that affect our behaviour, too. Students who disrupt the class are given after-school detentions or sent to the vice-principal for other punishment.

Implicitly, people react to changing incentives after they have done some sort of rough comparison of the costs and benefits of various courses of action. The linked concepts of incentive and costs and benefits can be used to explain seeming anomalies in the world around us. International Policy Example 1-1 illustrates what can happen when the benefits of an action far exceed the costs.

INTERNATIONAL POLICY EXAMPLE 1-1

Chinese Smuggling

Recently, China's leaders announced the formation of a new anti-smuggling police force to try to stop the annual flow of tens of billions of dollars in illegal contraband.

One example of "illegal contraband" is cigarettes. Domestic taxes on cigarettes are so high that many Chinese cigarette manufacturers export half of their output, which they then smuggle back into China. Another example is diesel oil. The Chinese government sets the price of diesel oil at levels above prices elsewhere in the world. This gives consumers of diesel oil an incentive to smuggle foreign-produced diesel oil into the country.

Why does China need an anti-smuggling police force when it already has an army of border guards and customs inspectors? The answer is that the returns on smuggling are so high that many existing border guards and customs inspectors have become smugglers themselves. Thus, the government feels that new police are needed in part to watch over the existing cadre of "law enforcers."

For critical analysis: What actions could the government take to remove the incentives to smuggle cigarettes and diesel oil?

Making Decisions at the Margin

As you progress through this text, you will be reminded frequently that, in order to rationally evaluate a possible course of action, you must compare the action's **marginal benefit** with its **marginal cost**. The marginal benefit refers to the all the *extra* benefits that one receives in pursuing a course of action while the marginal cost refers to the all the *extra* costs or sacrifices incurred. To better understand this notion of making decisions at the margin, we refer you to Example 1-2: "What Does a Year at College Really Cost?"

Making decisions at the margin will often reveal that there can be too much of a good thing! As an example, suppose that at a time when marijuana use is at an all-time low, one of the contenders for prime minister, in a federal election campaign, proposes a policy of eliminating all marijuana use in Canada. While this type of zero tolerance policy proposal can win votes, if implemented it can result in the transfer of a massive amount of policing resources away from the prevention of serious violent crimes in order to achieve a very small reduction in marijuana use. In other words, the marginal cost of the zero tolerance policy far exceeds the marginal benefit!

EXAMPLE 1-2   What Does a Year at College Really Cost?

Jane Sanders is currently earning $1,100 per month working full-time in Hamilton, Ontario. She lives in a one-bedroom apartment and pays $300 per month in rent. Her monthly food, personal care, and entertainment expenses are $320 per month. Since she does not own a vehicle, she pays $45 per month for a bus pass.

Jane is in the process of estimating the extra cost related to the decision to enroll full time in the first year of a business program at a college in the Hamilton area. If she enrolls, she will give up her full-time job for the eight-month period of the first-year program. If Jane goes to college, she plans to continue to live in her one-bedroom apartment, take the bus to the college campus, and maintain her current lifestyle. Jane estimates that her decision to enroll in college for the first year (eight-month period) will cost $7,900, estimated as follows:

Rent	$300 × 8 =	$2,400
Food, Personal Care, Entertainment	$320 × 8 =	$2,560
Public Transportation	$ 45 × 8 =	$360
Tuition, Books, College Fees		$2,580
Total Cost		**$7,900**

For critical analysis: Did Jane correctly determine the extra cost related to the decision to enroll in college full time for eight months? What else must Jane try to estimate in order to make a rational decision? Explain.

Defining Self-Interest

Self-interest does not always mean increasing one's wealth as measured in dollars and cents. We assume that individuals seek many goals, not just increased monetary wealth. Thus the self-interest part of our economic-person assumption includes goals relating to prestige, friendship, love, power, helping others, creating works of art, and many other matters. The giving of gifts can be considered a form of charity that is nonetheless in the self-interest of the giver. As Example 1-3 explains, donors may even expect to get some of their giving back.

CONCEPTS IN BRIEF

- Economics is a social science that studies how people allocate limited resources to satisfy unlimited wants.
- Microeconomics, the study of the decision-making processes of individuals (or households) and firms, and macroeconomics, the study of the performance of the economy as a whole, are the two main branches into which the study of economics is divided.
- In economics, we assume that people do not intentionally make decisions that will leave them worse off. This is known as the rationality assumption.
- Making rational choices among alternatives involves comparisons of marginal costs and marginal benefits.
- Self-interest is not confined to material well-being but also involves any action that makes a person feel better off, such as having more friends, love, power, affection, or providing more help to others.

EXAMPLE 1-3   Giving Charity to Oneself?

Economists have long recognized that charitable giving is in the self-interest of the donors. It makes them feel that they are contributing to society, helping the less fortunate and, more pragmatically, saving on the income tax they pay. But perhaps there are other reasons as well. Let's look at some of the evidence from 1995, the most recent year for which this data is available.

	Quintile of Households				
	1	2	3	4	5
Average income	$13,365	$27,278	$43,111	$62,363	$111,151
Average donation	$615	$1,228	$1,423	$1,933	$3,223
Percent of income to charity	4.60%	4.50%	3.30%	3.10%	2.90%

Source: Adapted from Statistics Canada

The first quintile of households contains the 20 percent of households with the lowest average incomes, while the fifth quintile contains the 20 percent with the highest incomes. Notice that those with the lowest incomes gave the highest proportion of their income to charity, while those with the highest incomes gave the lowest proportion. Can this be rational, especially on the part of the poorest households?

One explanation that would make the giving pattern rational is that the poorer households are those most likely to have used charity in the past or to need it in the future. Perhaps these households, unable to build large savings accounts to help them through periods of economic misfortune, look to public charity as a kind of insurance, and to their donations as the premiums they pay for it.

For critical analysis: Can you devise an explanation for the pattern of giving using the notion of costs and benefits?

Try Preview Question 3:
What role does rational self-interest play in economic analysis?

Economics as a Science

Economics is a social science that makes use of the same kinds of methods used in other sciences such as biology, physics, and chemistry. Similar to these other sciences, economics uses **models**, or **theories**. Economic models, or theories, are simplified representations of the real world that we use to help us understand and predict economic phenomena in the real world. There are, of course, differences between sciences. The social sciences—especially economics—make little use of laboratory methods in which changes in variables can be explained under controlled conditions. Rather, social scientists, and especially economists, usually have to examine what has already happened in the real world in order to test their models, or theories.

Models, or theories Simplified representations of the real world used as the basis for predictions or explanations.

Models and Realism

At the outset it must be emphasized that no model in *any* science, and therefore no economic model, is complete in the sense that it captures *every* detail or interrelationship that exists. Indeed, a model, by definition, is an abstraction from reality. It is conceptually impossible to construct a perfectly complete realistic model. For example, in physics we cannot account for every molecule and its position, nor every atom and subparticle. Not only would such a model be prohibitively expensive to build, but also working with it would be impossibly complex.

The nature of scientific model building is such that the model should capture only the essential relationships that are sufficient to analyze the particular problem or answer the particular question with which we are concerned. *An economic model cannot be faulted as unrealistic simply because it does not represent every detail of the real world.* A map of a city that shows only major streets is not necessarily unrealistic if, in fact, all you need to know is how to pass through the city using major streets. As long as a model is realistic in terms of shedding light on the *central* issue at hand or forces at work, it may be useful.

A map is the basic model. It is always a simplified representation, always unrealistic. But it is also useful in making (refutable) predictions about the world. If the model—the map—predicts that when you take Campus Avenue to the north, you always reach the campus, that is a (refutable) prediction. If our goal is to explain observed behaviour, the simplicity or complexity of the model we use is irrelevant. If a simple model can explain observed behaviour in repeated settings just as well as a complex one, the simple model has some value and is probably easier to use.

Assumptions

Every model, or theory, is based on a set of assumptions. Assumptions define the conditions under which a model is to meant to apply. By eliminating detail that is not considered to be essential to the economic phenomena under investigation, assumptions help to simplify a model.

In the theory of the firm, we assume that, typically, firms attempt to maximize profits when deciding how much of a product to produce in an industry. This assumption leads to an economic model of the firm that provides numerous predictions about how the firm will react to various events and incentives. As an example, one prediction would be that, if the firms can sell their product at a higher price, they will tend to produce more of this product. Another prediction would be that if a major cost of producing this product increases, such as energy costs, the firms will likely reduce the level of production of this product. Finally, this model would predict that if the government lowered the taxes imposed on the firms in this industry, this would entice firms to increase their supply of this product.

While the owners of the firms in the industry under investigation may well have a variety of other motives for producing the product, the profit-maximizing assumption model is valid to the extent that it consistently provides accurate predictions of real-world behaviour.

THE *CETERIS PARIBUS* ASSUMPTION: ALL OTHER THINGS BEING EQUAL. Constructing a model typically involves making generalizations of how variables in our environment relate to each other. It would be impossible to isolate the effects of changes in one variable on another variable if we always had to worry about the many additional variables that might also enter the analysis. As in other sciences, economics uses the ***ceteris paribus* assumption**. *Ceteris paribus* means "other things constant" or "other things equal."

Ceteris paribus
[KAY-ter-us PEAR-uh-bus] assumption
The assumption that nothing changes except the factor or factors being studied; "other things constant," or "other things equal."

Consider an example taken from economics. One of the most important determinants of how much of a particular product a family buys is how expensive that product is relative to other products. We know that in addition to relative prices, other factors influence decisions about making purchases. Some of them have to do with income, others with tastes, and yet others with custom and religious beliefs. Whatever these other factors are, we hold them constant when we look at the relationship between changes in prices and changes in how much of a given product people will purchase. Researchers at an American university used the *ceteris paribus* assumption in their experiment in the animal world, as explained in International Example 1-1.

| INTERNATIONAL EXAMPLE 1-1 | Incentives Work for Pigeons and Rats, Too |

Researchers at Texas A&M University in Houston, Texas, did a series of experiments with pigeons and rats. They allowed them to "purchase" food and drink by pushing various levers. The "price" was the number of times a lever had to be pushed. A piece of cheese required 10 pushes, a drop of root beer only one. The "incomes" that the animals were given equaled a certain number of total pushes per day. Once the income was used up, the levers did not work.

The researchers discovered that holding income constant, when the price of cheese went down, the animals purchased more cheese. Similarly, they found that when the price of root beer was increased, the animals purchased less root beer. These are exactly the predictions we make about human behaviour.

For critical analysis: What were the animals doing when they changed their "purchasing" behaviour?

Deciding on the Usefulness of a Model

We generally do not attempt to determine the usefulness, or "goodness," of a model merely by evaluating how realistic its assumptions are. Rather, we consider a model good if it yields usable predictions and implications for the real world. In other words, can we use the model to predict what will happen in the world around us?

Once we have determined that the model does predict real-world phenomena, the scientific approach to the analysis of the world around us requires that we consider evidence. Evidence is used to test the usefulness of a model. This is why we call economics an **empirical** science, *empirical* meaning that evidence (data) is looked at to see whether we are right. Economists are often engaged in empirically testing their models.

Consider two competing models for the way students act when doing complicated probability problems to choose the best gambles. One model predicts that, based on the assumption of rational self-interest, students who are paid more for better performance will in fact perform better on average during the experiment. A competing model might be that students whose last names start with the letters A through L will do better than students with last names starting with M through Z, irrespective of how much they are paid. The model that consistently predicts more accurately is the model that we would normally choose. In this example, the "alphabet" model did not work well: The first letter of the last name of the students who actually did the experiment was irrelevant in predicting how well they would perform the mathematical calculations necessary to choose the correct gambles. The model based on rational self-interest predicted well, in contrast.

Empirical Relying on real-world data in evaluating the usefulness of a model.

Models of Behaviour, Not Thought Processes

Take special note of the fact that economists' models do not relate to the way people *think*; they relate to the way people *act*, to what they do in life with their limited resources. Models tend to generalize human behaviour. Normally, the economist does not attempt to predict how people will think about a particular topic, such as a higher price of oil products, accelerated inflation, or higher taxes. Rather, the task at hand is to predict how people will act, which may be quite different from what they say they will do (much to the consternation of poll takers and market researchers). The people involved in examining thought processes are psychologists and psychiatrists, who are not usually economists.

An Economic Model: The Circular Flow of Income

A simple model economists use to explain the workings of the economy is the Circular Flow of Income. Figure 1.1 shows the basic form of the Circular Flow model.

FIGURE 1.1 The Circular Flow of Income

Firms go to the labour market to hire workers for production. They pay workers a wage, represented by the flow of income from the firms through the labour market to the households. The households spend part of their income purchasing goods and services in the product market. The money they pay for the goods and services flows back to the firms in the form of revenues. If households save any of their income, they put it in the financial market where firms go to borrow money for production purposes. This flow is represented by the arrow from the households through the financial market to the firms.

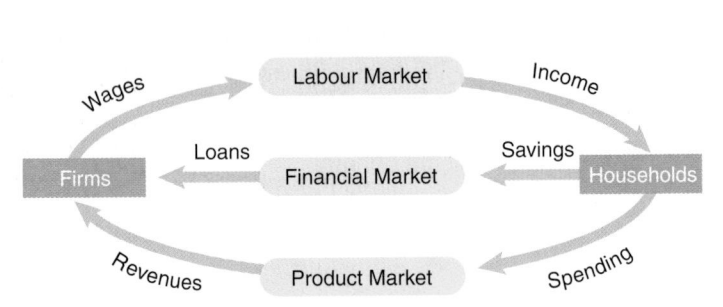

When using the Circular Flow model, we make two main assumptions. The first is that households—people like you and me—produce nothing, but *own* everything in the economy. This makes sense when you think that we own our own labour, and we also own all the firms—whether as shareholders or as entrepreneurs. Firms own nothing, since the shareholders own it all, but they *produce* everything in the economy. As soon as someone produces a good or a service to be sold in the economy, we call that producer a firm.

A good place to start thinking about this model is with the firms. The firms go to the labour market and hire workers to produce their output. In exchange, the firms pay the workers a wage, and income flows *from* the firms *to* the households. Households need food, shelter, and clothing, so they go to the product (or output) market to purchase goods and services. In exchange for the goods and services, the households give the firms a part of their incomes, and income flows *from* the households *to* the firms. So the flow of income in the economy is circular; it flows from firms to households and back to firms again.

We can complicate our model to make it a little more realistic. Most households wish to save part of their income. That part therefore does not flow through the product market, but instead flows to the financial market—to savings accounts with banks, credit unions, and trust companies. These financial institutions hold the households' savings, which they lend to firms that need funds for investment. Thus the income paid out by firms to workers still returns to them via the product market and the financial market.

Whether this is a useful model depends on how well it predicts real-world events. For example, what would happen to the economy if the government decided to put a tax (or an additional tax) on household incomes? Households would have less money to spend and/or save. The Circular Flow model predicts that households would purchase less and save less, and the flows to the firms would diminish. If the flows to the firms diminished, the firms would produce less, and hire fewer workers—thus compounding the problem of shrinking incomes. We could test this prediction by looking at Canada's, and other similar countries', experiences when taxes have risen. We would almost certainly find a slowing in the growth of the economy; our model would represent this as a slowing of the flows between the households and the firms.

If we ask what would happen to our economy if the Americans asked Canadian firms to produce twice as many automobile parts for them than in the past, what will our model predict? We have not included the foreign sector in our simple model, but we could look at the opportunity to increase our sales to the United States as a large injection of income into the firms. The firms would go to the labour market and hire more workers to produce the extra output. Increased income would flow from the firms to the households, and, *ceteris paribus*, back to the firms again. The economy would grow with the increased economic activity.

Try Preview Question 4:

Why is the study of economics a science?

Positive Versus Normative Economics

Economics uses *positive analysis*, a value-free approach to inquiry. No subjective or moral judgments enter into the analysis. Positive analysis relates to statements such as "If *A*, then *B*." For example, "If the price of gasoline goes up relative to all other prices, then the amount of it that people will buy will fall." That is a positive economic statement. It is a statement of *what is*. It is not a statement of anyone's value judgment or subjective feelings. For many problems analysed in the hard sciences such as physics and chemistry, the analyses are considered to be virtually value-free. After all, how can someone's values enter into a theory of molecular behaviour? But economists face a different problem. They deal with the behaviour of individuals, not molecules. That makes it more difficult to stick to what we consider to be value-free or **positive economics** without reference to our feelings.

Positive economics Analysis that is strictly limited to making either purely descriptive statements or scientific predictions; for example, "If *A*, then *B*." A statement of *what is*.

Normative economics Analysis involving value judgments about economic policies; relates to whether things are good or bad. A statement of *what ought to be*.

When our values are interjected into the analysis, we enter the realm of **normative economics**, involving *normative analysis*. A positive economic statement is "If the price of gas rises, people will buy less." If we add to that analysis the statement "so we should not allow the price to go up," we have entered the realm of normative economics—we have expressed a value judgment. In fact, any time you see the word *should*, you will know that values are entering into the discussion. Just remember that positive statements are concerned with *what is*, whereas normative statements are concerned with *what ought to be*.

Each of us has a desire for different things. This fact means that we have different values. When we express a value judgment, we are simply saying what we prefer, like, or desire. Because individual values are diverse, we expect—and indeed observe—people expressing widely varying value judgments about how the world ought to be.

Try Preview Question 5:

What is the difference between positive and normative economics?

A Warning: Recognize Normative Analysis

It is easy to define positive economics. It is quite another matter to catch all unlabelled normative statements in a textbook such as this one (or any other), even though authors go over the manuscript many times before it is printed. Therefore, do not get the impression that a textbook's authors will be able to keep all personal values out of the book. They will slip through. In fact, the very choice of which topics to include in an introductory textbook involves normative economics. There is no value-free, or objective, way to decide which topics to use in a textbook. The authors' values ultimately make a difference when choices have to be made. But from your own standpoint, you might want to be able to recognize when you are engaging in normative as opposed to positive economic analysis. Reading this text will help equip you for that task.

Economic Policy

As we noted above, economic models will enhance your ability to understand and predict behaviour. In chapters to come, we'll illustrate how these models prove useful in formulating, assessing, and reacting to government policies that affect you as a consumer, an employee, an investor, a business owner, and a concerned citizen.

Most government economic policies are action plans designed to achieve commonly accepted socio-economic goals. The major goals are listed here. We discuss them in more detail in Chapter 6.

1. Full Employment: an economy in which people looking for work find jobs reasonably quickly.
2. Efficiency: an economy in which resources are allocated to the production of goods and services in a way that achieves maximum benefit for society.
3. Economic Growth: an economy with the ability to increase its rate of production over time to enhance society's well-being.
4. Price Stability: an economy in which prices remain relatively stable over time.
5. Equitable Distribution of Income: an economy in which no particular group of people lives below or near the poverty level.

Theory and Policy

Economic theory plays a useful role in helping us understand how existing and proposed policies relate to major socio-economic goals. As you progress through this text, you will be surprised at the frequency with which a proposed policy is shown to conflict with the very goals it is meant to promote, once you employ the relevant economic model.

For example, a local politician may propose a rent control policy aimed at reducing apartment rents in order to make housing more affordable to the poor. That is, the rent control policy is aimed at promoting a more equitable distribution of income. However, once you become familiar with the demand and supply model presented in Chapter 4, you will see that this policy will more likely conflict with the goal of an equitable distribution of income because of the resulting shortages in livable accommodation. Moreover, this same policy will also conflict with the goal of full employment to the extent that construction workers are laid off as less new apartments are being built.

We hope that you will enjoy the challenge of using economic models to formulate superior alternative policies. A superior policy refers to a plan of action that promotes as many socio-economic goals as possible with minimal goal conflict. In the rent control example, you may find that relevant economic theory suggests that a policy of increasing competition in the apartment construction and rental industries may prove to be the superior policy. By increasing the supply of affordable, quality housing units, the goals of full employment and equitable distribution can both be promoted!

Try Preview Question 6:

What are the primary socio-economic goals that form the basis of policy?

CONCEPTS IN BRIEF

- A model, or theory, uses assumptions and is by nature a simplification of the real world. The usefulness of a model can be evaluated by bringing empirical evidence to bear on its predictions.
- Models are not necessarily deficient simply because they are unrealistic and use simplifying assumptions. Every model in every science requires simplification compared to the real world.
- Most models use the *ceteris paribus* assumption, that all other things are held constant, or equal.
- Positive economics is value-free and relates to statements that can be refuted, such as "If *A*, then *B*." Normative economics involves people's values, and normative statements typically contain the word should.
- Economic models play a useful role in understanding how policies relate to major socio-economic goals.

NETNOMICS

Is It Irrational for People to Pay Amazon.com More for a Book They Can Buy for Less at Books.com?

To try to understand how consumers respond to changing incentives they face now that they can purchase goods and services on the Internet, business professors Erik Brynjolfsson and Michael Smith gathered more than 10,000 observations of the prices charged by traditional brick-and-mortar bookstores and Internet booksellers. What they found was what most economists would predict: The lower costs faced by Internet booksellers allowed them to charge about 8 percent less for a given book than traditional bookstores. Furthermore, the cost advantage of Internet booksellers allowed them to gain market share at the expense of traditional bookstores. (Indeed, some brick-and-mortar bookstores initially included in the study went out of business before the study ended.)

One finding seemed surprising, however. Amazon.com, which garnered an 80 percent share of all Internet-based book sales, charged an average of $2.40 more per book than Books.com, another Internet bookseller (now part of barnesandnoble.com). Yet Books.com could not seem to push its market share much above

2 percent during the period of the study. On the surface, this seemed to imply irrational consumers. After all, wouldn't everyone want to choose Books.com and save $2.40 per book?

As Brynjolfsson and Smith point out, this would be true only if the *ceteris paribus* assumption had been satisfied. In their study, however, it was not. For one thing, Amazon.com spent a considerable amount on advertising and got a jump-start on its Internet competitors. Indeed, even today, a great many Internet users have heard of Amazon.com but are unfamiliar with its competitors. This made Brynjolfsson and Smith wonder if perhaps people felt confident that Amazon.com really would deliver but might not have as much faith in less well known Internet companies. Thus, part of the $2.40 difference in the average price of a book might amount to a "trust premium." Furthermore, Brynjolfsson and Smith's study did not take into account differences in features of the two companies' Web sites. If people already knew how to use the Amazon.com Web site, then a legitimate question to ask is, would the average person consider $2.40 enough to compensate for having to learn how to order a book from another Web site?

ISSUES AND APPLICATIONS

Does Money Buy Happiness?

Concepts Applied: Rational self-interest, the rationality assumption, incentives, models, realism

Despite all his wealth, Frank Stronach is probably no happier than you. However, because people act rationally, we can assume that Frank Stronach would not choose to give away all his wealth.

One of the major criticisms of economics is that it seems to posit that more money (wealth) is better than less. In other words, economic theory appears to assume that people act in such a way as to make higher and higher incomes. People are assumed always to act so as to maximize their incomes, even if "money cannot buy happiness." A recent study in the *Journal of Personality and Social Psychology* presents evidence to support the notion that seeking ever-higher wealth does not lead to any greater level of happiness.

What Researchers Have Found

The researchers of this study randomly selected 100 very wealthy individuals identified as such in popular business magazines. Each wealthy person in the study filled out a detailed inquiry, which included the question, "How do you feel about how happy you are?" to which the answer choices ranged from "delighted" to "terrible." The same questionnaire was given to a randomly selected set of individuals who were not rich. The average happiness score for the rich was only slightly above the non-rich. Indeed, one-third of the super-rich scored below the average group.

The conclusion the researchers reached was that an increase in income is like a martini: It induces optimism and raises the spirits, but only temporarily. The researchers argued that only recent life events (occurring within the past three months) have any influence on one's feelings of subjective well-being.

International Confirmation

The researchers discovered that international data confirmed their findings. Only residents of the poorest countries (India and Bangladesh) had below-average happiness ratings. Happiness in all the others appeared about the same. Moreover, neither Canadian nor Japanese residents showed any rising trend in reported subjective well-being over the past few decades despite rising average household incomes.

But Asking Gets You Nowhere

Do the research results summarized here contradict the methodology we use in economics? Hardly. Economics is a science of *revealed* preferences. We find out virtually no useful information by asking people to rate their happiness on a scale of 1 to 10. We assume that people act rationally. In other words, they will not knowingly do things that make them worse off. We can predict that given the choice between a lower-paying job and an otherwise identical yet higher-paying job, people will choose the latter. We make no assumptions about their thought processes.

One Can Always Become Poorer

Finally, if indeed additional income typically makes people worse off, the rich and the very rich always have an option—they can dispose of their wealth at any time. No one is forced to keep wealth. Because we rarely see individuals routinely giving away a significant portion of their wealth, we can infer that higher income is preferred to lower income.

For Critical Analysis

1. Even if you choose not to spend additional income that you earn on yourself, what other options do you have?

2. Let us view the statement "On average, individuals behave as if higher income is preferred to lower income" as an economic model. How might this model be used to devise effective policies in the following situations?

   a. A politician wishes to propose popular policies in an election campaign.

   b. Hospital management needs to "convince" more nurses to live in its remote region.

   c. A newly established bank needs to attract households' savings.

CHAPTER SUMMARY

1. Economics as a social science is the study of how individuals make choices to satisfy wants. Wants are defined as what people would buy if their incomes were unlimited.

2. Economics is usually divided into microeconomic analysis, which is the study of individual decision making by households and firms, and macroeconomics, which is the study of nationwide phenomena, such as inflation and unemployment.

3. The rationality assumption is that individuals never intentionally make decisions that would leave them worse off. This is achieved by making decisions at the margin.

4. We use models, or theories, to explain and predict behaviour. Models, or theories, are never completely realistic because by definition they are simplifications using assumptions that are not directly testable. The useful-

ness of a theory, or model, is determined not by the realism of its assumptions but by how well it predicts real-world phenomena.

5. An important simplifying assumption is that all other things are held equal, or constant. This is sometimes known as the *ceteris paribus* assumption.

6. No model in economics relates to individuals' thought processes; all models relate to what people do, not to what they think or say they will do.

7. Much economic analysis involves positive economics; that is, it is value-free. Whenever statements embodying values are made, we enter the realm of normative economics, or how individuals and groups think things ought to be.

8. Economic models play a useful role in understanding how policies relate to socio-economic goals.

DISCUSSION OF PREVIEW QUESTIONS

1. What is the definition of economics?

Economics is a social science that studies how people allocate limited resources to satisfy unlimited wants. Wants refer to the goods and services people would consume if they had unlimited income. Resources are items used to produce goods and services such as skilled and unskilled labour, land, machinery, and entrepreneurial talent.

2. What is the difference between microeconomics and macroeconomics?

Microeconomics is concerned with the choice-making processes of individuals, households, and firms, whereas macroeconomics focuses on the performance of the economy as a whole.

3. What role does rational self-interest play in economic analysis?

Rational self-interest is the assumption that individuals behave in a reasonable (rational) way in making choices to further their interests. In other words, we assume that individuals' actions are motivated primarily by their self-interest, keeping in mind that self-interest can relate to monetary and nonmonetary objectives, such as love, prestige, and helping others.

4. Why is the study of economics a science?

Economics is a science in that it uses models, or theories, that are simplified representations of the real world to analyse and make predictions about the real world. These predictions are then subjected to empirical tests in which real-world data are used to decide whether to accept or reject the predictions.

5. What is the difference between positive and normative economics?

Positive economics deals with what is, whereas normative economics deals with what ought to be. Positive economic statements are of the "if ... then" variety; they are descriptive and predictive and are not related to what "should" happen. Normative economics, by contrast, is concerned with what ought to be and is intimately tied to value judgments.

6. What are the primary socio-economic goals that form the basis of policy?

The primary Canadian socio-economic goals that guide policy decisions include: full employment, efficiency, economic growth, price stability, and equitable distribution of income.

PROBLEMS

(Answers to the odd-numbered problems appear at the back of the book.)

1-1. Categorize the following issues as either a microeconomic issue or a macroeconomic issue.

a. The national unemployment rate increases.

b. The wage increases of nurses do not keep up with the wage increases of doctors.

c. The price of cigarettes increases due to a tax imposed on cigarette manufacturers.

d. The annual inflation rate exceeds the average annual increase in wages.

e. The nation's total annual rate of production declines.

f. In response to strong retail competition, Eaton's corporation files for bankruptcy.

1-2. In order to spend a winter in Victoria, B.C., Paul Dafoe rents out his Montreal condo, as well as his car, to a married couple attending university. Paul estimates that the total cost associated with his decision to winter in Victoria for the eight-month period is $15,000. He calculates this total cost by adding the following costs: round trip plane fare; eight months rental fees for a Victoria condo; estimated total grocery, personal care, and entertainment expenses while staying in Victoria; and total rental car expenses incurred in Victoria. Is $15,000 the correct marginal cost associated with Paul's decision to winter in Victoria? Explain.

1-3. The council of a Canadian city justifies the construction of a beautiful new city hall on the basis of there being sufficient tax dollars available to pay for this project. Is the mayor's decision to construct the city hall a rational one? Explain.

1-4. Since health care is an essential service, all health care services should be provided free of charge. Moreover, the government should continue to increase the resources to health care until all hospital wait lists across the nation disappear. Is this view consistent with making decisions at the margin? Explain.

1-5. Give a refutable implication (one that can be tested by evidence from the real world) for each of the following models:

a. The accident rate of drivers is inversely related to their age.

b. The rate of inflation is directly related to the rate of change in the nation's money supply.

c. The wages of professional basketball players are directly related to their high school grade-point averages.

d. The rate at which bank employees are promoted is inversely related to their frequency of absenteeism.

1-6. Consider the following statements, based on positive economic analysis that assumes *ceteris paribus*. List one other thing that might change and thus alter the outcome stated.

a. Increased demand for laptop computers will drive up their price.

b. Falling gasoline prices will result in additional vacation travel.

c. A reduction in corporate income tax rates will result in more people working.

1-7. Identify which of the following statements use positive economic analysis and which use normative analysis.

a. Increasing the minimum wage will reduce employment opportunities for young people.

b. A teacher should earn a higher salary than a hockey player, as the teacher's job is far more valuable to society.

c. Everyone should enjoy free access to dental care.

d. If the price of admission to each NHL hockey game is reduced, there will be an increase in ticket sales for each NHL game.

1-8. Identify which socio-economic goal(s) may be promoted and which goal(s) may be conflicted with, for each policy listed below.

a. Policy: In order to provide free public-health services, the government severely taxes Canadian corporation profits.

b. Policy: The government raises the rate of income tax on all employees. The extra tax dollars raised are used to compensate upper-income investors who were swindled by fraud schemes.

c. Policy: The government increases the monthly benefits (payments) to those collecting welfare. These people immediately spend the extra income on new goods and services.

d. Policy: The government levies a special tax on all luxury goods. The taxes collected are used to keep college and university tuition fees relatively low.

ECONOMICS ON THE NET

The Usefulness of Studying Economics

This application helps you see how accomplished people benefited from their study of economics. It also explores ways in which these people feel others of all walks of life can gain from learning more about the economics field.

Internet URL: http://woodrow.mpls.frb.fed.us/pubs/region/98-12/quotes.html

Title: Economists in *The Region* on Their Student Experiences and the Need for Economic Literacy

Application: Read the interviews of the six economists, and answer the following questions.

a. Based on your reading, what economists do you think other economists regard as influential? What educational institutions do you think are the most influential in economics?

b. Which economists do you think were attracted to microeconomics and which to macroeconomics?

SCARCITY AND THE WORLD OF TRADE-OFFS

The traditional family in our society consists of a married man and woman and their children. Because children used to share the family workload and provide for their parents in their old age, couples had a strong incentive to have children. In most developed countries, however, this incentive for having children has largely disappeared. Even on today's "family farms," many tasks are mechanized and even automated.

At the same time, the costs of raising children have increased. Of course, parents have always housed, fed, and clothed their children. In addition, they have sacrificed to provide "quality time" with their children. For many people today, the value of that time is greater than it was in years past. In this chapter you will learn how to put a value on time spent with children. This will help you understand why children are a more costly "commodity" than they used to be.

PREVIEW QUESTIONS

1. Why are individuals forced to consider opportunity costs?

2. What assumptions are made when drawing a specific production possibilities curve?

3. Why is a production possibilities curve bowed out?

4. What socio-economic goals can be illustrated with a production possibilities curve?

5. What is the difference between absolute advantage and comparative advantage?

Scarcity A situation in which unlimited wants exceed what can be produced with limited resources.

Production Any activity that results in the conversion of resources into products that can be used in consumption.

Land The natural resources that are available from nature. Land as a resource includes location, original fertility and mineral deposits, topography, climate, water, and vegetation.

DID YOU KNOW THAT... some people make a profit out of standing in line? Prior to a recent *Tragically Hip* concert in Toronto, several "professional line waiters" set up camp at the ticket booth the night before tickets went on sale. When the box office opened the next morning, they bought tickets, not for themselves, but for the many young people who paid them $20 in addition to the price of the ticket to stand in line for them. What were those young people doing? They were working at jobs that paid them more than $20 for the day. They did not want to miss the opportunity to make that income. After all, those young people do not have an unlimited amount of time to work and to stand in line. Time is scarce to them.

Scarcity

Whenever individuals or communities cannot obtain everything they desire simultaneously, choices occur. Choices occur because of *scarcity*. **Scarcity** is the most basic concept in all of economics. Scarcity means that we do not and cannot have enough income or wealth to satisfy our *every* desire. Scarcity exists because human wants always exceed what can be produced with the limited resources that nature makes available.

What Scarcity Is Not

Scarcity is not a shortage. When flooding forced many people in southern Manitoba to leave their homes, TV newscasts showed those evacuated crowding into the local high school gymnasium or community centre common room for the night. A news commentator noted that this crowding was caused by a scarcity of short-term housing. But housing is always scarce—we cannot obtain all we want at a zero price. The flood victims were not facing a scarcity of short-term housing, rather there was a shortage of it. Do not confuse the concept of scarcity, which is general and all-encompassing, with the concept of shortages which are more specific short-term situations.

Scarcity is not the same thing as poverty. Scarcity occurs among the rich as well as the poor. Even the richest person on earth faces scarcity because available time is limited. Low income levels do not create more scarcity. High income levels do not create less scarcity.

Scarcity is a fact of life, like gravity. And just as physicists did not invent gravity, economists did not invent scarcity—it existed well before the first economist ever lived. It exists even when we are not using all of our resources.

Scarcity and Resources

The scarcity concept arises from the fact that resources are insufficient to satisfy our every desire. Resources are the inputs used in the production of the things that we want. **Production** can be defined as virtually any activity that results in the conversion of resources into products that can be used in consumption. Production includes delivering things from one part of the country to another. It includes taking ice from an ice tray to put in your soft-drink glass. The resources used in production are called *factors of production*, and some economists use the terms *resources* and *factors of production* interchangeably. The total quantity of all resources that an economy has at any one time determines what that economy can produce.

Factors of production can be classified in many ways. Here is one such classification:

1. **Land** encompasses all the nonhuman gifts of nature, including timber, water, fish, minerals, and the original fertility of the land. It is often called the *natural resource.*

Labour Productive contributions of humans who work, involving both mental and physical activities.

Physical capital All manufactured resources, including buildings, equipment, machines, and improvements to land that is used for production.

Human capital The accumulated training and education of workers.

Entrepreneurship The factor of production involving human resources that perform the functions of raising capital, organizing, managing, assembling other factors of production, and making basic business policy decisions. The entrepreneur is a risk taker.

2. **Labour** is the human resource, which includes all productive contributions made by individuals who work, such as steelworkers, ballet dancers, and professional baseball players.

3. **Physical capital** consists of the factories and equipment used in production. It also includes improvements to natural resources, such as irrigation ditches.

4. **Human capital** is the economic characterization of the education and training of workers. How much the nation produces depends not only on how many hours people work but also on how productive they are, and that, in turn, depends in part on education and training. To become more educated, individuals have to devote time and resources, just as a business has to devote resources if it wants to increase its physical capital. Whenever a worker's skills increase, human capital has been improved.

5. **Entrepreneurship** is actually a subdivision of labour and involves human resources that perform the functions of organizing, managing, and assembling the other factors of production to make business ventures. Entrepreneurship also encompasses taking risks that involve the possibility of losing large sums of wealth on new ventures. It includes new methods of doing common things, and generally experimenting with any type of new thinking that could lead to making more money income. Without entrepreneurship, virtually no business organization could operate.

Goods Versus Economic Goods

Goods All things from which individuals derive satisfaction or happiness.

Economic goods Goods that are scarce.

Goods are defined as all things from which individuals derive satisfaction or happiness. Goods therefore include air to breathe and the beauty of a sunset, as well as food, cars, and CD players.

Economic goods are a subset of all goods—they are goods derived from scarce resources about which we must constantly make decisions regarding their best use. By definition, the desired quantity of an economic good exceeds the amount that is directly available from nature at a zero price. Virtually every example we use in economics concerns economic goods—cars, CD players, computers, socks, baseball bats, and so on. Weeds are a good example of *bads*—goods for which the desired quantity is much *less* than what nature provides at a zero price.

Services Mental or physical labour or help purchased by consumers. Examples are the assistance of doctors, lawyers, dentists, repair personnel, housecleaners, educators, retailers, and wholesalers; things purchased or used by consumers that do not have physical characteristics.

Sometimes you will see references to "goods and services." **Services** are tasks that are performed for someone else, such as laundry, cleaning, hospital care, restaurant meal preparation, car polishing, psychological counselling, and teaching. One way of looking at services is to think of them as *intangible goods*.

Wants and Needs

Wants are not the same as needs. Indeed, from the economist's point of view, the term *needs* is objectively indefinable. When someone says, "I need some new clothes," there is no way of knowing whether that person is stating a vague wish, a want, or a life-saving necessity. If the individual making the statement were dying of exposure in northern Quebec during the winter, we might argue that indeed the person does need clothes—perhaps not new ones, but at least some articles of warm clothing. Typically, however, the term *need* is used very casually in most conversations. What people usually mean is that they want something that they do not currently have.

Humans have unlimited wants. Just imagine if every single material want that you might have were satisfied. You can have all of the clothes, cars, houses, CDs, tickets to concerts, and other things that you want. Does that mean that nothing else could add to your total level of happiness? Probably not, because you might think of new goods and services that you could obtain, particularly as they came to market. You would also still be lacking in fulfilling all of your wants for compassion, friendship, love, affection, prestige, musical abilities, sports abilities, and so on.

In reality, every individual has competing wants but cannot satisfy all of them, given limited resources. This is the reality of scarcity. Each person must therefore make choices. Whenever a choice is made to do or buy something, something else that is also desired is not done or not purchased. In other words, in a world of scarcity, every want that ends up being satisfied causes one or more other wants to remain unsatisfied or to be forfeited.

CONCEPTS IN BRIEF

- Scarcity exists because human wants always exceed what can be produced with the limited resources that nature makes available.
- We use scarce resources, such as land, labour, physical and human capital, and entrepreneurship, to produce economic goods—goods that are desired but are not directly obtainable from nature to the extent demanded or desired at a zero price.
- Wants are unlimited; they include all material desires and all nonmaterial desires, such as love, affection, power, and prestige.
- The concept of need is difficult to define objectively for every person; consequently, we simply consider that every person's wants are unlimited. In a world of scarcity, satisfaction of one want necessarily means nonsatisfaction of one or more other wants.

Scarcity, Choice, and Opportunity Cost

The natural fact of scarcity implies that we must make choices. One of the most important results of this fact is that every choice made (or not made, for that matter) means that some opportunity had to be sacrificed. Every choice involves giving up another opportunity to do or use something else.

Consider a practical example. Every choice you make to study one more hour of economics requires that you give up the opportunity to do any of the following activities: study more of another subject, listen to music, sleep, browse at a local store, read a novel, or work out at the gym. Many more opportunities are forgone also if you choose to study economics an additional hour.

Because there were so many alternatives from which to choose, how could you determine the value of what you gave up to engage in that extra hour of studying economics? First of all, no one else can tell you the answer because only you can *subjectively* put a value on each alternative. Only you know the value of another hour of sleep, or of an hour looking for the latest CDs. That means that only you can determine the highest-valued, next-best alternative that you had to sacrifice in order to study economics one more hour. It is you who come up with the *subjective* estimate of the expected value of the next-best alternative.

Opportunity cost The highest-valued, next-best alternative that must be sacrificed to attain something or to satisfy a want.

The value of the next-best alternative is called **opportunity cost**. The opportunity cost of any action is the value of what is given up—the next-highest-ranked alternative—because a choice was made. When you study one more hour, there may be many alternatives available for the use of that hour, but assume that you can do only one thing in that hour—your next-highest-ranked alternative. What is important is the choice that you would have made if you hadn't studied one more hour. Your opportunity cost is the *next-highest-ranked* alternative, not *all* alternatives.

In economics, cost is always a forgone opportunity.

Try Preview Question 1:
Why are individuals forced to consider opportunity costs?

One way to think about opportunity cost is to understand that when you choose to do something, you lose. What you lose is being able to engage in your next-highest-valued alternative. Thus, the cost of your choice is your next-highest-valued alternative. This is your opportunity cost.

Let's consider the opportunity cost of protecting wilderness areas in northern British Columbia (refer to Policy Example 2-1, below).

POLICY EXAMPLE 2-1

The Multi-Million Dollar Park

In October 1997, the British Columbia government established the Muskwa Kechika land use area, a wilderness area larger than Switzerland. If you visit its Web page (http://www.luco.gov.bc.ca/nrockies/home.htm) you will learn all about this park which is home to herds of caribou, elk, and moose.

What the Web page does not tell you is that 1.7 million of the 4.4 million hectares in the park lie above huge oil reserves worth, according to an industry spokesman, hundreds of millions of dollars—reserves that will now never be used.

For critical analysis: Recall that opportunity cost is the value of the next best alternative. What does this tell us about the social value of the Muskwa Kechika land-use area?"

The World of Trade-Offs

Whenever you engage in any activity using any resource, even time, you are *trading off* the use of that resource for one or more alternative uses. The value of the trade-off is represented by the opportunity cost. The opportunity cost of studying economics has already been mentioned—it is the value of the next-best alternative. When you think of any alternative, you are thinking of trade-offs.

Let's consider a hypothetical example of a one-for-one trade-off between the results of spending time studying economics and accounting. For the sake of this argument, we will assume that additional time studying either economics or accounting will lead to a higher grade in the subject studied more. One of the best ways to examine this trade-off is with a graph. (If you would like a refresher on graphical techniques, study Appendix A at the end of this chapter before going on.)

Graphical Analysis

In Figure 2.1, the expected grade in accounting is measured on the vertical axis of the graph, and the expected grade in economics is measured on the horizontal axis. We simplify the world and assume that you have a maximum of 10 hours per week to spend studying these two subjects, and that if you spend all 10 hours on economics, you will get an A in the course. You will, however, fail accounting. Conversely, if you spend all of your 10 hours studying accounting, you will get an A in that subject, but you will flunk economics. Here the trade-off is a special case: one-to-one. A one-to-one trade-off means that the opportunity cost of receiving one grade higher in economics (for example, improving from a C to a B) is one grade lower in accounting (falling from a C to a D).

The Production Possibilities Curve (PPC)

The graph in Figure 2.1 illustrates the relationship between the possible results that can be produced in each of two activities, depending on how much time you choose to devote to each. This graph is a representation of a **production possibilities curve (PPC).**

Consider that you are producing a grade in economics when you study economics and a grade in accounting when you study accounting. Then the graph in Figure 2.1 can

Production possibilities curve (PPC) A curve representing all possible combinations of total output that could be produced assuming (1) a fixed amount of productive resources of a given quality, and (2) the efficient use of those resources.

FIGURE 2.1 Production Possibilities Curve for Grades in Accounting and Economics (Trade-offs)

We assume that only 10 hours can be spent per week on studying. If the student is at point x, equal time (5 hours a week) is spent on both courses and equal grades of C will be received. If a higher grade in economics is desired, the student may go to point y, thereby receiving a B in economics but a D in accounting. At point y, 2.5 hours are spent on accounting and 7.5 hours on economics.

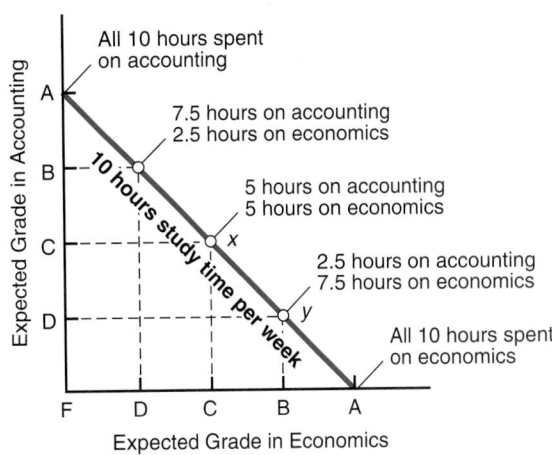

be related to the production possibilities you face. The line that goes from A on one axis to A on the other axis therefore becomes a production possibilities curve. It is defined as the maximum quantity of one good or service that can be produced, given that a specific quantity of another is produced. It is a curve that shows the possibilities available for increasing the output of one good or service by reducing the amount of another. In the example in Figure 2.1, your time for studying was limited to 10 hours per week. The two possible outputs were grades in accounting and grades in economics. The particular production possibilities curve presented in Figure 2.1 is a graphical representation of the opportunity cost of studying one more hour in one subject. It is a *straight-line production possibilities curve*, which is a special case. (The more general case is discussed next.) If you decide to be at point x in Figure 2.1, five hours of study time will be spent on accounting and five hours will be spent on economics. The expected grade in each course will be a C. If you are more interested in getting a B in economics, you will go to point y on the production possibilities curve, spending only two-and-a-half hours on accounting but seven-and-a-half hours on economics. Your expected grade in accounting will then drop from a C to a D.

Note that these trade-offs between expected grades in accounting and economics are the result of *holding constant* total study time as well as all other factors that might influence a student's ability to learn, such as computerized study aids. Quite clearly, if you wished to spend more total time studying, it would be possible to have higher grades in both economics and accounting. In that case, however, we would no longer be on the specific production possibilities curve illustrated in Figure 2.1. We would have to draw a new curve, farther to the right, to show the greater total study time and a different set of possible trade-offs. Read Example 2-1 to find out about a trade-off most Canadian teenagers are making every day.

| EXAMPLE 2-1 | Teenagers Trade Off TV Time to Surf the Net |

A recent survey conducted for Montreal-based Youth Culture Inc. found that 85 percent of Canada's 2.4 million teenagers are spending an average of 9.3 hours per week on the Internet. While some of that time is homework-related, most is spent in online chat rooms like ICQ.com and listening to songs at MuchMusic.com.

The survey also discovered that teenagers are finding time to surf the Net mostly by watching less television. As the director of consumer intelligence for Youth Culture noted, "TV is definitely in a long-term generational decline." Now television advertisers who spend $2.3 billion annually face their own trade-off decision: how much of that budget to move over to advertising on the Internet.

For critical analysis: Would the teenage production possibilities curve for television watching and Internet use be a straight line or bowed out?

CONCEPTS IN BRIEF

- Scarcity requires us to choose. When we choose, we lose the next-highest-valued alternative.
- Cost is always a forgone opportunity.
- Another way to look at opportunity cost is as the trade-off that occurs when one activity is undertaken rather than the next-best alternative activity.
- A production possibilities curve (PPC) graphically shows the trade-off that occurs when more of one output is obtained at the sacrifice of another. The PPC is a graphical representation of, among other things, opportunity cost.

The Choices Society Faces

The straight-line production possibilities curve presented in Figure 2.1 can be generalized to demonstrate the related concepts of scarcity, choice, and trade-offs that Canada faces. As you will see, the production possibilities curve is a simple but powerful economic model because it can demonstrate these related concepts. The example we will use is the choice between the production of automobiles and newsprint. We assume for the moment that these are the only two goods that can be produced in Canada. Part (a) of Figure 2.2 gives the various possible combinations of automobiles and newsprint. If all resources are devoted to auto production, 3 million per year can be produced. If all resources are devoted to newsprint production, 12 million tonnes per year can be produced. In between are various possible combinations. These combinations are plotted as points *A*, *B*, *C*, *D*, *E*, *F*, and *G* in part (b) of Figure 2.2. If these points are connected with a smooth curve, Canada's production possibilities curve is shown, demonstrating the trade-off between the production of automobiles and newsprint. These trade-offs occur *on* the production possibilities curve.

Notice the major difference in the shape of the production possibilities curves in Figures 2.1 and 2.2. In Figure 2.1, there is a one-to-one trade-off between grades in economics and in accounting. In Figure 2.2, the trade-off between newsprint production and automobile production is not constant, and therefore the production possibilities curve is a *bowed* line. To understand why the production possibilities curve for a society is typically bowed outward, you must understand the assumptions underlying the PPC.

FIGURE 2.2 Society's Trade-Off Between Automobiles and Newsprint

The production of automobiles is measured in millions of units per year, while the production of newsprint is measured in millions of tonnes per year. The various combinations are given in part (a) and plotted in part (b). Connecting the points A–G with a relatively smooth line gives the production possibilities curve for automobiles and newsprint. Point R lies outside the production possibilities curve and is therefore unattainable at the point in time for which the graph is drawn. Point S lies inside the production possibilities curve and therefore represents an inefficient use of available resources.

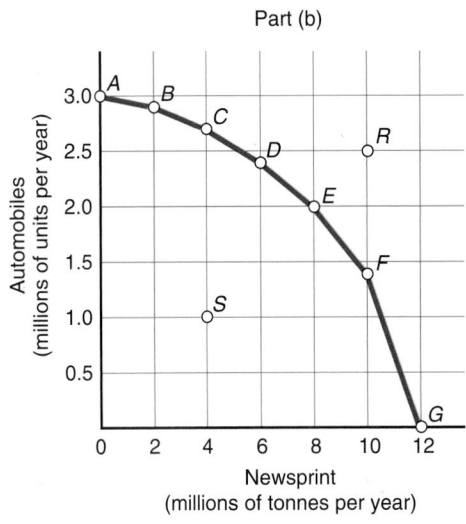

Part (a)

Combination	Automobiles (millions of units per year)	Newsprint (millions of tonnes per year)
A	3.0	0
B	2.9	2
C	2.7	4
D	2.4	6
E	2.0	8
F	1.4	10
G	0	12

Assumptions Underlying the Production Possibilities Curve

When we draw the curve that is shown in Figure 2.2, we make the following assumptions:

1. That resources are fully employed.
2. That we are looking at production over a specific time period—for example, one year.
3. That the resource inputs, in both quantity and quality, used to produce automobiles or newsprint are fixed over this time period.
4. That technology does not change over this time period.

Technology Society's pool of applied knowledge concerning how goods and services can be produced.

Technology is defined as society's pool of applied knowledge concerning how goods and services can be produced by managers, workers, engineers, scientists, and craftspeople, using land and capital. You can think of technology as the formula (or recipe) used to combine factors of production. (When better formulas are developed, more production can be obtained from the same amount of resources.) The level of technology sets the limit on the amount and types of goods and services that we can derive from any given amount of resources. The production possibilities curve is drawn under the assumption that we use the best technology that we currently have available, and that this technology doesn't change over the time period under study.

Try Preview Question 2:

What assumptions are made when drawing a specific production possibilities curve?

Being off the Production Possibilities Curve

Look again at part (b) of Figure 2.2. Point R lies *outside* the production possibilities curve and is *impossible* to achieve during the time period assumed. By definition, the production possibilities curve indicates the *maximum* quantity of one good given some quantity of the other.

It is possible, however, to be at point S in Figure 2.2. That point lies beneath the production possibilities curve. If the nation is at point S, it means that its resources are not being fully utilized. This occurs, for example, during periods of unemployment. Point S and all such points within the production possibilities curve are always attainable but are usually not desirable.

Efficiency

The production possibilities curve can be used to define the notion of efficiency. Whenever the economy is operating on the PPC at points such as *A*, *B*, *C*, or *D*, we say that its production is efficient. Points such as *S* in Figure 2.2, which lie beneath the production possibilities curve, are said to represent production situations that are not efficient.

Efficiency can mean many things to many people. Even within economics, there are different types of efficiency. Here we are discussing efficiency in production, or **productive efficiency**. An economy is productively efficient whenever it is producing the maximum output with given technology and resources.

A simple commonsense definition of productive efficiency is getting the most out of what we have as an economy. Clearly, we are not getting the most that we have if we are at point *S* in part (b) of Figure 2.2. We can move from point *S* to, say, point *C*, thereby increasing the total quantity of automobiles produced without any decrease in the total quantity of newsprint produced. We can move from point *S* to point *E*, for example, and have both more automobiles and more newsprint. Point *S* is called a **productively inefficient point**, which is defined as any point below the production possibilities curve.

The concept of **allocative efficiency** is concerned with producing the mix of goods and services most valued by consumers. An allocatively efficient economy is one in which people who place relatively the most value on specific goods end up with those goods. If you own a vintage electric Fender guitar, but I value it more than you, I can buy it from you. Such trading benefits both of us. Maximum allocative efficiency is achieved when all such mutual benefits through trade have been exhausted. In terms of the product possibility curve in Figure 2.2 part (b), an allocatively inefficient situation would result if the economy produced combination *F*, yet consumers prefer to have combination *C* produced.

Productive efficiency The case in which a given level of inputs is used to produce the maximum output possible. Alternatively, the situation in which a given output is produced at minimum cost.

Productively inefficient point Any point below the production possibilities curve at which resources are being used.

Allocative efficiency Producing the mix of goods and services most wanted by society.

The Law of Increasing Relative Cost

In the example in Figure 2.1, the trade-off between a grade in accounting and a grade in economics is one-to-one. The trade-off ratio was fixed. That is to say, the production possibilities curve was a straight line. The curve in Figure 2.2 is a more general case. We have re-created the curve in Figure 2.2 as Figure 2.3. Each combination, *A* through *G*, of automobiles and

FIGURE 2.3 The Law of Increasing Relative Cost

Consider equal increments of newsprint production, as measured on the horizontal axis. All of the horizontal arrows—*aB*, *bC*, and so on—are of equal length (2 million tonnes). The opportunity cost of going from 10 million tonnes of newsprint per year to 12 million (*Ff*) is much greater than going from zero tonnes to 2 million tonnes (*Aa*). The opportunity cost of each additional equal increase in newsprint production rises.

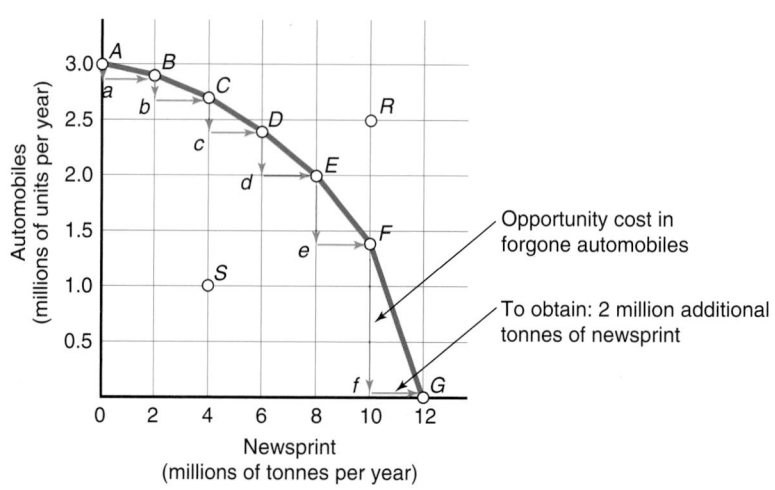

newsprint is represented on the production possibilities curve. Starting with the production of zero newsprint, Canada could produce 3 million automobiles with its available resources and technology. When we increase production of newsprint from zero to 2 million tonnes per year, we have to give up the automobile production represented by that first vertical arrow, *Aa*. From part (a) of Figure 2.2 you can see that this is 0.1 million autos a year (3.0 million − 2.9 million). Again, if we increase production of newsprint by 2 million tonnes per year, we go from *B* to *C*. In order to do so, we have to give up the vertical distance *Bb*, or 0.2 million automobiles a year. By the time we go from 10 million to 12 million tonnes of newsprint, to obtain that 2 million tonne increase we have to forgo the vertical distance *Ff*, or 1.4 million automobiles. In other words, the opportunity cost of the last 2 million tonnes of newsprint is 1.4 million autos, compared with 0.1 million autos, the opportunity cost for the first 2 million tonnes of newsprint (starting at zero production).

What we are observing is called the **law of increasing relative cost**. When society takes more resources and applies them to the production of any specific good, the opportunity cost increases for each additional unit produced. The reason that, as a country, we face the law of increasing relative cost (which causes the production possibilities curve to bow outward) is that certain resources are better suited for producing some goods than they are for others. Resources are generally not *perfectly* adaptable for alternative uses. When increasing the output of a particular good, producers must use less efficient resources than those already used in order to produce the additional output. Hence the cost of producing the additional units increases. In our hypothetical example here, at first the mechanical technicians in the automobile industry would shift over to producing newsprint. After a while, though, upholstery specialists and windshield installers would also be asked to help. Clearly, they would be less effective in making newsprint.

As a rule of thumb, the more *specialized the resources, the more bowed the production possibilities curve*. At the other extreme, if all resources are equally suitable for newsprint production or automobile production, the curves in Figures 2.2 and 2.3 would approach the straight line shown in our first example in Figure 2.1.

> **Law of increasing relative cost** The observation that the opportunity cost of additional units of a good generally increases as society attempts to produce more of that good. This accounts for the bowed-out shape of the production possibilities curve.

> **Try Preview Question 3:**
> Why is a production possibilities curve bowed out?

CONCEPTS IN BRIEF

- Trade-offs are represented graphically by a production possibilities curve (PPC) showing the maximum quantity of one good or service that can be produced, given a specific quantity of another, from a given set of resources over a specified period of time—for example, one year.
- A PPC is drawn holding the quantity and quality of all resources fixed over the time period under study.
- Points outside the production possibilities curve are unattainable; points inside are attainable but represent an inefficient use or under-use of available resources.
- Because many resources are better suited for certain productive tasks than for others, society's production possibilities curve is bowed outward, following the law of increasing relative cost.

Economic Growth and the Production Possibilities Curve

Over any particular time period, a society cannot be outside the production possibilities curve. Over time, however, it is possible to have more of everything. This occurs through economic growth. Figure 2.4 shows the production possibilities curve for automobiles and newsprint shifting outward. The two additional curves represent new choices open to an economy that has experienced economic growth. Such economic growth occurs because of many things, including increases in the number of workers and productive investment in equipment. As Example 2-2 illustrates, economic growth can also take place just because workers work harder.

EXAMPLE 2-2 Economic Growth Due to Harder Working Workers

Economies grow when they put more labour and more productive equipment to work. But they also grow when their labour and equipment work harder or faster. Labour productivity is the term we use to describe output per worker-hour. It can increase when workers have better machinery to work with, or even when tasks are rearranged so that the work process becomes more efficient.

Part of Canada's economic growth in most years is due to improvements in labour productivity. Over the period 1978-1999, labour productivity grew by an average of one percent per year, although in 1996 it decreased by 0.1 percent and in 1999 it grew by 1.4 percent.

For critical analysis: In 1996, would labour productivity have caused production possibilities curves in Canada to shift inward or outward? Suppose that in 1999, while labour productivity increased, the number of people unemployed also increased. Describe this 1999 situation graphically, using a production possibilities curve.

Try Preview Question 4:

What socio-economic goals can be illustrated with a product possibilities curve?

Scarcity still exists, however, no matter how much economic growth there is. At any point in time, we will always be on some production possibilities curve; thus we will always face trade-offs. The more we want of one thing, the less we can have of others.

If a country experiences economic growth, the production possibilities curve between automobiles and newsprint will move outward, as is shown in Figure 2.4. This takes time and does not occur automatically. One reason it will occur involves the choice about how much to consume today.

FIGURE 2.4 Economic Growth Allows for More of Everything

If the country experiences economic growth, the production possibilities curve between automobiles and newsprint will shift out, as shown. This takes time, however, and it does not occur automatically. This means, therefore, that we can have more automobiles and more newsprint only after a period of time during which we have experienced economic growth.

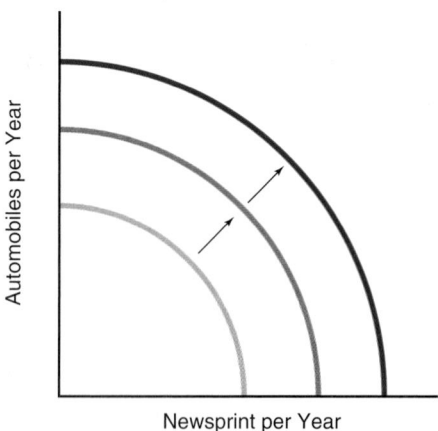

The Trade-Off Between the Present and the Future

Consumption The use of goods and services for personal satisfaction.

The production possibilities curve and economic growth can be used to examine the trade-off between present **consumption** and future consumption. When we consume today, we are using up what we call consumption or consumer goods—food and clothes, for example. And we have already defined physical capital as the manufactured goods, such as machines and factories, used to make other goods and services.

Why We Make Capital Goods

Why would we be willing to use productive resources to make things—capital goods— that we cannot consume directly? For one thing, capital goods enable us to produce larger quantities of consumer goods or to produce them less expensively than we otherwise could. Before fish are "produced" for the market, equipment such as fishing boats, nets, and poles are produced first. Imagine how expensive it would be to obtain fish for market without using these capital goods. Catching fish with one's hands is not an easy task. The price per fish would be very high if capital goods weren't used.

Forgoing Current Consumption

Whenever we use productive resources to make capital goods, we are implicitly forgoing current consumption. We are waiting until some time in the future to consume the fruits that will be reaped from the use of capital goods. In effect, when we forgo current consumption to invest in capital goods, we are engaging in an economic activity that is forward-looking—we do not get instant utility or satisfaction from our activity. Indeed, if we were to produce only consumer goods now and no capital goods, our capacity to produce consumer goods in the future would suffer. Here we see a trade-off situation.

The Trade-Off Between Consumption Goods and Capital Goods

To have more consumer goods in the future, we must accept fewer consumer goods today. In other words, an opportunity cost is involved here. Every time we make a choice for more goods today, we incur an opportunity cost of fewer goods tomorrow, and every time we make a choice of more goods in the future, we incur an opportunity cost of fewer goods today. With the resources that we don't use to produce consumer goods for today, we invest in capital goods that will produce more consumer goods for us later. The trade-off is shown in Figure 2.5. On the left in part (a), you can see this trade-off depicted as a production possibilities curve between capital goods and consumption goods.

Assume that we are willing to give up $1 billion worth of consumption today. We will be at point *A* in the left-hand diagram of part (a). This will allow the economy to grow. We will have more future consumption because we invested in more capital goods today. In the right-hand diagram of part (a), we see two goods represented, food and recreation. The production possibilities curve will move outward if we collectively decide to restrict consumption each year and invest in capital goods.

In part (b), we show the results of our willingness to forgo more current consumption. We move to point *C*, where we have many fewer consumer goods today, but produce a lot more capital goods. This leads to more future growth in this simplified model, and thus the production possibilities curve in the right-hand side of part (b) shifts outward more than it did in the right-hand side of part (a).

In other words, the more we give up today, the more we can have tomorrow, provided, of course, that the capital goods are productive in future periods and that society desires the consumer goods produced by this additional capital.

FIGURE 2.5 Capital Goods and Growth

In part (a), the nation chooses not to consume $1 billion, so it invests that amount in capital goods. In part (b), it chooses even more capital goods. The PPC moves even further to the right on the right-hand diagram in part (b) as a result.

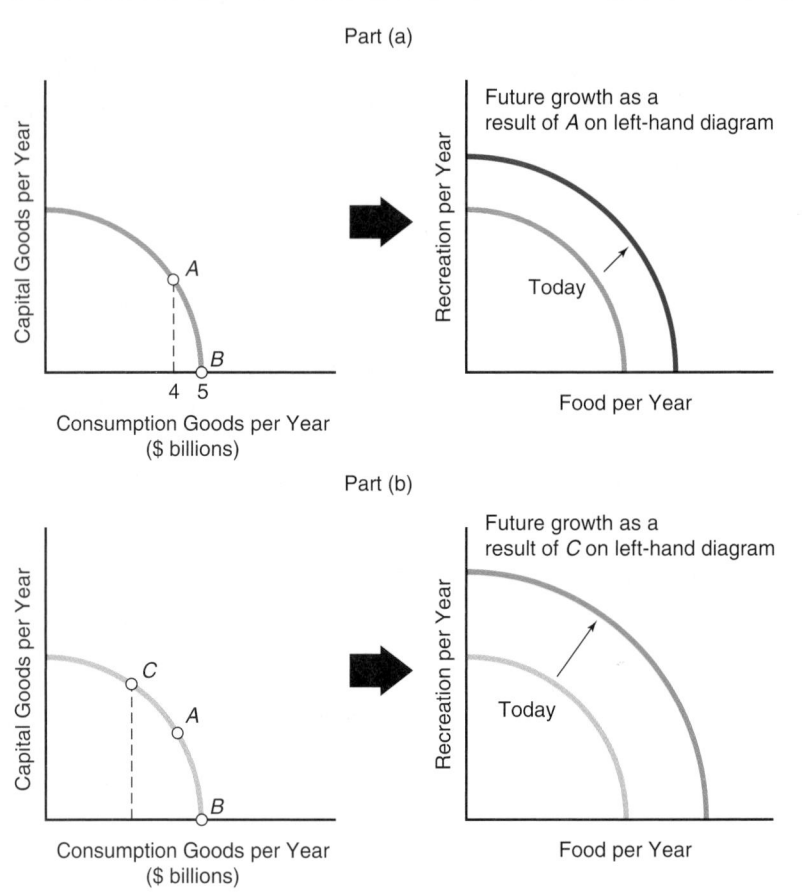

CONCEPTS IN BRIEF

- The use of capital requires using productive resources to produce capital goods that will later be used to produce consumer goods.
- A trade-off is involved between current consumption and capital goods or, alternatively, between current consumption and future consumption. This is because the more we invest in capital goods today, the greater the amount of consumer goods we can produce in the future, and the smaller the amount of consumer goods we can produce today.

Specialization and Greater Productivity

Specialization The division of productive activities among persons and regions so that no one individual or area is totally self-sufficient. An individual may specialize, for example, in law or medicine. A nation may specialize in the production of lobsters, computers, or cameras.

Specialization involves working at a relatively well defined, limited endeavour, such as accounting or teaching. It involves a division of labour among different individuals and regions. Most people, in fact, do specialize. For example, you could probably change the oil in your car if you wanted to. Typically, though, you take your car to a garage and let the mechanic do it. You benefit by letting the garage mechanic specialize in changing the oil and in completing other repairs on your car. The specialist has all the proper equipment to do the work, and will likely get the job finished sooner than you could. Specialization usually leads to greater productivity, not only for each individual but also for the country.

Specialization pays off for companies around the globe. This has often proved true in the automotive industry as International Example 2-1 explains.

INTERNATIONAL EXAMPLE 2-1   **Why the Light Turned Green Once the Trabi Was Parked**

Among residents of eastern Germany, one of the best-recalled failures of communist rule was a little automobile known as the "Trabi." Years after the reunification of Germany, people still joke about the car. For instance, "Why didn't the Trabi move when the light turned green? Because its tire got stuck on a piece of gum." Or, "Why do deluxe Trabis have heated rear windows? To keep your hands warm as you push it." Another goes, "How do you double a Trabi's value? Fill the gasoline tank."

Today the punch line is different, however. The company that once manufactured Trabis now has a booming business. The key to its success is that it no longer builds cars. Instead, it supplies auto parts to General Motors, Volkswagen, and DaimlerChrysler. What the company learned was that it was better off specializing in making auto parts and leaving assembly of the parts to someone else.

For critical analysis: How do General Motors, Volkswagen, and DaimlerChrysler gain from specialization?

Absolute Advantage

Specialization occurs because different individuals and different nations have different skills. Sometimes it seems that some individuals are better at doing everything than anyone else. A president of a large company might be able to type better than any of the typists, file better than any of the file clerks, and wash windows better than any of the window washers. The president has an **absolute advantage** in all of these endeavours— by using fewer labour hours for each task than anyone else in the company. The president does not, however, spend time doing those other activities. Why not? Because a president is paid the most for undertaking managerial duties and specializes in that one particular task despite having an absolute advantage in all tasks. Indeed, absolute advantage is irrelevant in predicting how the president's time is spent; only *comparative advantage* matters.

Absolute advantage The ability to produce a good or service at an "absolutely" lower cost, usually measured in units of labour or resource input required to produce one unit of the good or service.

Comparative Advantage

Comparative advantage is the ability to perform an activity at the lowest opportunity cost. You have a comparative advantage in one activity whenever you have the lowest opportunity cost of performing that activity. Take the example of a lawyer and her secretary who can both review law cases and type legal opinions. Suppose the lawyer can review two law cases or type one legal opinion in one hour. At the same time, her secretary can review one law case or type one legal opinion in one hour. Here the lawyer has an absolute advantage in reviewing law cases, and seemingly is just as good as her secretary at typing legal opinions. Is there any reason for lawyer and her secretary to "trade"? The answer is yes, because such trading will lead to higher output.

Comparative advantage The ability to produce a good or service at a lower opportunity cost compared to other producers.

Consider the scenario of no trading. Assume that during each eight-hour day, the lawyer and her secretary devote half of their day to reviewing law cases and half to typing legal opinions. The lawyer would review eight law cases (4 hours × 2 per hour) and type four legal opinions (4 × 1). During that same period, the secretary would review four law cases (4 × 1) and type four legal opinions (4 × 1). Each day the combined output for the lawyer and her secretary would be 12 reviewed law cases and eight typed legal opinions.

If the lawyer specialized only in reviewing law cases and her secretary specialized only in typing legal opinions, their combined output would rise to 16 reviewed law cases (8 x 2) and eight typed legal opinions (8 × 1). Overall, production would increase by four law cases per day.

The lawyer has a comparative advantage in reviewing cases. In the time it takes her to review one case (1/2 hour) she could have typed one-half of a legal opinion. Her opportunity cost of reviewing the law case is therefore one-half of a legal opinion. The secretary, however, gives up typing an entire legal opinion each time she reviews a case. Since the lawyer's opportunity cost of reviewing law cases is less than her secretary's, she has the comparative advantage in reviewing law cases. See if you can work out why the secretary has a comparative advantage in typing legal opinions.

You may be convinced that everybody can do everything better than you. In this extreme situation, do you still have a comparative advantage? The answer is yes. To discover your comparative advantage you need to find a job in which your *disadvantage* relative to others is the smallest. You do not have to be a mathematical genius to figure this out. The market tells you very clearly by offering you the highest income for the job for which you have the smallest disadvantage compared to others. Stated differently, to find your comparative advantage no matter how much better everybody else can do the jobs that you want to do, you simply find which job maximizes your income.

The coaches of sports teams are constantly faced with determining each player's comparative advantage. Former Blue Jay Dave Winfield was originally one of the best pitchers in college baseball, winning the most valuable player award for pitching for the University of Minnesota Golden Bears in the 1973 College World Series. After he was drafted by the San Diego Padres, the coach decided to make him an outfielder even though he was one of the best pitchers on the roster. The coach wanted Winfield to concentrate on his hitting. Good pitchers do not bring in as many fans as home-run kings. Dave Winfield's comparative advantage was clearly in hitting homers rather than practising and developing his pitching game.

Scarcity, Self-Interest, and Specialization

In Chapter 1, you learned about the assumption of rational self-interest. It says that for the purposes of our analyses we assume that individuals are rational in that they will do what is in their own self-interest. They will not consciously carry out actions that will make them worse off. In this chapter, you learned that scarcity requires people to make choices. We assume that they make choices based on their self-interest, and attempt to maximize benefits net of opportunity cost. In so doing, individuals choose their comparative advantage and end up specializing. Ultimately, when people specialize, they increase the money income they make and therefore become richer. When all individuals and businesses specialize simultaneously, the gains are seen in greater material well-being. With any given set of resources, specialization will result in higher output.

Try Preview Question 5:

What is the difference between absolute advantage and comparative advantage?

The Division of Labour

Division of labour The segregation of a resource into different specific tasks; for example, one automobile worker puts on bumpers, another doors, and so on.

In any firm that includes specialized human and nonhuman resources, there is a **division of labour** among those resources. The best-known example of all time comes from one of the earliest and perhaps most famous economists, Adam Smith, who in *The Wealth of Nations* (1776) illustrated the benefits of a division of labour in the making of pins: "One man draws out the wire, another straightens it, a third cuts it, a fourth points it, a fifth grinds it at the top for receiving the head; to make the head requires two or three distinct operations; to put it on is a peculiar business, to whiten the pins is another; it is even a trade by itself to put them into the paper."

Making pins this way allowed 10 workers without very much skill to make almost 48,000 pins "of a middling size" in a day. One worker, toiling alone, could have made perhaps 20 pins a day; therefore, 10 workers could have produced 200. Division of labour allowed for an increase in the daily output of the pin factory from 200 to 48,000! (Smith did not attribute all of the gain to the division of labour according to talent, but credited also the use of machinery and the fact that less time was spent shifting from task to task.)

What we are discussing here involves a division of the resource called labour into different kinds of labour. The different kinds of labour are organized in such a way as to increase the amount of output possible from the fixed resources available. We can therefore talk about an organized division of labour within a firm leading to increased output.

Thinking Critically About the Media 2-1   International Trade

If you watch enough news on TV or frequently read the popular press, you get a distinct impression that international trade is somehow different from trade within our borders. At any given time, Canada is either at economic war with the United States over our exports of softwood lumber, or we are fighting with the European Union over whether Canadian furs caught using leg-hold traps should be allowed into the EU. International economics is just like any other type of economics; trade is just another economic activity. Indeed, one can think of international trade as a production process that transforms goods that we sell to other countries (exports) into what we buy from other countries (imports). International trade is a mutually beneficial exchange that occurs across political borders. If you imagine a world that was just one country, trade would still exist worldwide, but it would not be called international trade.

Comparative Advantage and Trade Among Nations

Though most of our analysis of absolute advantage, comparative advantage, and specialization has dealt with individuals, it is equally applicable to countries. First consider Canada. The Prairie provinces have a comparative advantage in the production of grains and other agricultural goods. Ontario and Quebec in Central Canada tend to specialize in industrialized production, such as automobiles and newsprint. Not surprisingly, grains are shipped from the Prairies to Central Canada, and automobiles are shipped in the reverse direction. Such specialization and trade allow for higher incomes and standards of living. If both the Prairies and Central Canada were politically defined as separate countries, the same analysis would still hold, but we would call it international trade. Indeed, Europe is smaller than Canada in area, but instead of one nation, Europe has 15. What in Canada we call *interprovincial trade*, in Europe is called *international trade*. There is no difference, however, in the economic results—both yield greater economic efficiency and higher average incomes. See the Thinking Critically About the Media box, above, for further discussion.

Political problems that do not normally arise within a particular nation often do between nations. For example, if Nova Scotia crab fishers develop a cheaper method of harvesting crabs than fishers in British Columbia, British Columbia fishers will lose out. They cannot do much about the situation except try to lower their own costs of production. If crab fishers in Alaska, however, develop a cheaper method, both Nova Scotia and British Columbia fishers can (and likely will) try to raise political barriers to prevent Alaskan fishers from freely selling their product in Canada. Canadian crab fishers will use such arguments as "unfair" competition and loss of Canadian jobs. In so doing, they are only partly right: Crab-fishing jobs may decline in Canada, but jobs will not necessarily decline overall. If the argument of Canadian crab fishers had any validity, every time a region in Canada developed a better way to produce a product manufactured somewhere else in the country, employment in Canada would decline. That has never happened and never will.

When countries specialize where they have a comparative advantage and then trade with the rest of the world, the average standard of living in the world rises. In effect, international trade allows the world to move from inside the global production possibilities curve towards the curve itself, thereby improving worldwide economic efficiency.

CONCEPTS IN BRIEF

- With a given set of resources, specialization results in higher output; in other words, there are gains to specialization in terms of greater material well-being.
- Individuals and nations specialize in their areas of comparative advantage in order to reap the gains of specialization.
- Comparative advantages are found by determining which activities have the lowest opportunity cost—that is, which activities yield the highest return for the time and resources used.
- A division of labour occurs when different workers are assigned different tasks. Together, the workers produce a desired product.

NETNOMICS

Allocating Scarce Space on the Web

Nearly half of all users of the World Wide Web visit fewer than 10 Internet sites per month. Companies that want to sell their products on the Internet know this. They also know that when individuals access the Internet, their homepage is typically that of their Internet service provider (Netscape, Explorer) or a search engine such as Yahoo! Consequently, many companies advertise on those Web pages.

This is why each time you access the Net, you see advertising—banners, buttons, keywords, hot links, and other promotions. Some of the biggest advertisers on the Web are Microsoft, Toyota, General Motors, Disney, IBM, and American Express. Internet-based companies, such as Amazon.com, are also major Web advertisers. It is estimated that by 2005, advertisers will be spending more than $300 million a year on the Web.

The owner of any Web page that carries advertising faces an opportunity cost. For example, advertisers widely consider the opening page of the Yahoo! search engine "prime real estate" because so many people see it each day. But there is relatively little space on the screen. Thus when Yahoo! allocates space to promote its own services and products, it gives up space it could sell. But if it fills up too much of the screen with ads, some users will switch to a less cluttered search engine. That fact makes Web page design a crucial economic concern.

ISSUES AND APPLICATIONS   The Costs of Raising a Child

Concepts Applied: Rational self-interest, scarcity, choice, opportunity cost

This family is probably unaware of all the costs of raising their son.

The Government of Manitoba's Agriculture Department has estimated the costs of raising a child. These include explicit expenses parents incur in providing the child with housing, food, clothing, daycare, recreation, health care, and transportation. Figure 2-6 shows estimates of the expenses that typical working Canadian parents will incur in raising a male child to age 18. All in all, it comes to $155,562. (The cost of raising a female child is $155,074. While girls' clothing is typically more expensive than boys', girls eat less than boys, and thus cost less to raise.)

Manitoba Agriculture used average prices for food and clothing and included only basic needs in the recreation expenses—no music lessons or hockey leagues for this child. As you might expect, higher-income parents incur greater expenses than lower-income parents; they are more likely to buy high-tech toys and trendy clothing for their children.

"Quality Time" With Kids Has a Market Value

Another key component of the cost of raising a child, however, is the wages that parents forgo when they spend time taking kids to school, the doctor, soccer games, and so on. In some families, one spouse stays home most of the time to provide these services. In others, both parents work but take turns allocating some of their time each day to these duties. No matter how they choose to balance the time, parents forgo wages they otherwise could have earned if they had allocated their time to income-generating activities. Once again, the forgone wages of higher-income parents will be greater than those of lower-income parents.

Forgone Wages and the Opportunity Cost of Raising a Child

The total cost of raising a child would be the sum of the explicit expenses and the forgone wages of the parents. In most cases, the forgone wages far outweigh the explicit costs. For example, the average earned income of a woman in 1998 was $32,553. If she stayed at home with her child until he reached age 12, she would have forgone almost $400,000 in wages. If the father had stayed home, he would have forgone over $500,000 in wages. For higher-income earners, these lost wages would be greater.

We can infer an important fact from this discussion. When people acquire more training and education and move into higher-wage occupations, the opportunity cost of raising a child rises significantly. Other things being equal—for instance, if we assume that parents derive roughly the same satisfaction from raising children irrespective of their income—this is likely to induce higher-income people to have fewer children.

FIGURE 2-6 The Explicit Cost of Raising a Male Child

The explicit cost of raising a male child from birth to age 18 is initially almost $10,000 per year, falling to about $7,000 per year by the time the child turns 18.

Source: Based on information from the Manitoba Government, Manitoba Agriculture and Food.

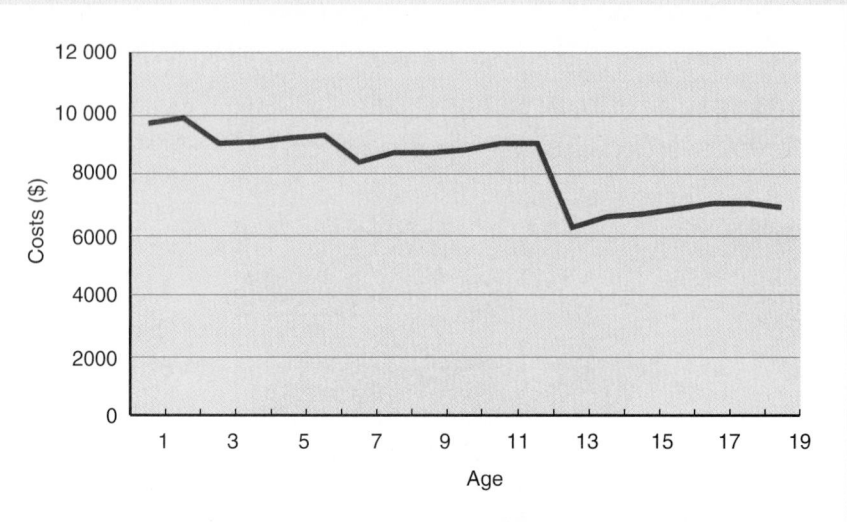

For Critical Analysis

1. Notice that in Figure 2-6, the cost of raising a child drops at age 6 and again at age 12. What institutional factors do you think might account for this pattern?

2. In recent decades, population growth in lower-income countries has exceeded population growth in higher-income countries. Based on our current discussion, can you provide a hypothesis explaining why?

CHAPTER SUMMARY

1. All societies at all times face the universal problem of scarcity because we cannot obtain everything we want from nature without sacrifice. Thus scarcity and poverty are not synonymous. Even the richest persons face scarcity because they also have to make choices among alternatives.

2. The resources we use to produce desired goods and services can be classified into land, labour, physical and human capital, and entrepreneurship.

3. Goods are all things from which individuals derive satisfaction. Economic goods are those for which the desired quantity exceeds the amount that is directly available from nature at a zero price. The goods we want are not necessarily those that we need. The term *need* is indefinable in economics, whereas humans have unlimited *wants*, which are defined as the goods and services on which we place a positive value.

4. We measure the cost of anything by what has to be given up in order to have it. This cost is called opportunity cost.

5. The trade-offs we face as individuals and those we face as a society can be represented graphically by a production possibilities curve (PPC). This curve shows the maximum quantity of one good or service that can be produced, given a specific quantity of another, from a given set of resources over a specified period of time, usually one year.

6. Because resources are specialized, production possibilities curves bow outward. This means that each additional increment of one good can be obtained only by giving up more and more of the other goods. This is called the law of increasing relative cost.

7. It is impossible to be outside the production possibilities curve, but we can be inside it. When we are, we are in a situation of unemployment, inefficiently organized resources, or some combination of the two.

8. There is a trade-off between consumption goods and capital goods. The more resources we devote to capital goods, the more consumption goods we can normally have in the future (and less currently). This is because more capital goods allow the economy to grow, thereby moving the production possibilities curve outward.

9. You find your comparative advantage by looking at the activity that has the lowest opportunity cost. That is, your comparative advantage lies in the activity that generates the highest income. By specializing in that comparative advantage, you are assured of reaping the gains of specialization.

10. Division of labour occurs when workers are assigned different tasks.

DISCUSSION OF PREVIEW QUESTIONS

1. Why are individuals forced to consider opportunity costs?

Scarcity forces individuals to consider opportunity costs. Because resources are limited and wants are unlimited, a choice which commits resources to one good or activity will result in other desirable goods or activities being forgone. In order to rationally choose one course of action, one must always be aware of the opportunity cost or the highest valued next best alternative that must be sacrificed.

2. What assumptions are made when drawing a specific production possibilities curve?

The assumptions being made include: full employment of resources; the production possibilities relate to a specific period (i.e. year); the quantity and quality of resources are fixed over this period of time; technology is fixed over this time period.

3. Why is a production possibilities curve bowed out?

Typically, resources are specialized. Thus, when society allocates additional resources to producing more and more of a single good, it must increasingly employ resources that would be better suited for producing other goods. As a result, the law of increasing relative costs holds. Each additional unit of a good can be obtained only by giving up more and more of other goods, which means that the production possibilities curve that society faces is bowed out.

4. What socio-economic goals can be illustrated with a production possibilities curve?

When the full employment goal or the productive efficiency goal is not achieved, the economy ends up being inside its production possibilities curve. If the economy is on its production possibilities curve, but producing a mix of goods not desired by consumers, the goal of allocative efficiency is not being promoted. Over time, the goal of economic growth is illustrated by an outward shift in the production possibilities curve.

5. What is the difference between absolute advantage and comparative advantage?

A person has an absolute advantage if she can produce more of a specific good than someone else who uses the same amount of resources. This also means that she can produce the same amount of that good using fewer resources. Nevertheless, the individual may be better off producing a different good if she has a comparative advantage in producing the other good, meaning that she can produce the other good at a lower opportunity cost than someone else. By specializing in producing the good for which she has a comparative advantage, she assures herself of reaping gains from specialization in the form of a higher income.

PROBLEMS

(Answers to the odd-numbered problems appear at the back of the book.)

2-1. The following table illustrates the marks a student can earn on examinations in economics and biology if the student uses all available hours for study.

Economics	Biology
100	40
90	50
80	60
70	70
60	80
50	90
40	100

Plot this student's production possibilities curve. Does this PPC illustrate increasing or decreasing opportunity costs?

2-2. Based on the information provided in Problem 2-1, what is the opportunity cost to this student of allocating sufficient additional study time on economics to move her grade from a 90 to a 100?

2-3. Consider a change in the table in Problem 2-1. The student's set of opportunities is now as follows:

Economics	Biology
100	40
90	60
80	75
70	85
60	93
50	98
40	100

Plot this student's production possibilities curve. Does this PPC illustrate increasing or decreasing opportunity costs? What is the opportunity cost to this student of allocating sufficient additional study time on economics to move her grade from a 60 to a 70? From a 90 to a 100?

2-4. The following sets of numbers represent hypothetical production possibilities for a country in 2001. Plot these points on graph paper.

Cheese	Apples
4	0
3	1.6
2	2.4
1	2.8
0	3.0

Does the law of increasing relative cost seem to hold? Why? On the same graph, plot and draw the production possibilities curve that will represent 10 percent economic growth.

2-5. Construct a production possibilities curve for a country facing increasing opportunity costs for producing food and video games. Show how the PPC changes given the following events.

a. A new and better fertilizer is developed.

b. There is a surge in labour that can be employed in both the agriculture sector and the video game sector.

c. A new programming language is invented that is less costly to code and is more memory-efficient, enabling the use of smaller games cartridges.

d. A heat wave and drought results in a decrease of 10 percent in usable farmland.

2-6. The president of a university announces to the local media that the university was able to construct a sports complex at a lower cost than it had previously projected. The president argues that the university can now purchase a yacht for the president for no additional cost. Explain why this statement is false using the concept of opportunity cost.

2-7. If, by going to college, you give up the chance to work in your mother's business for 35 hours per week at $7.00 per hour, what would be your opportunity cost of earning a two-year college diploma? What incentives exist to make you incur that opportunity cost? What are you giving up today in order to have more in the future? Assume that you will need to spend 60 weeks in college to earn a diploma.

2-8. You can wash, fold, and iron a basket of laundry in two hours and prepare a meal in one hour. Your roommate can wash, fold, and iron a basket of laundry in three hours and prepare a meal in one hour. Who has an absolute advantage in laundry and who has an absolute advantage in meal preparation? Who has a comparative advantage in laundry and who has a comparative advantage in meal preparation?

2-9. Based on the information in Problem 2-8, should you and your roommate specialize in a particular task? Why? And if so, who should specialize in which task? Calculate how much labour time you save if you choose to "trade" an appropriate task with your roommate as opposed to doing it yourself.

2-10. Two countries, Workland and Playland, have similar populations and identical production possibilities curves but different preferences. The production possibilities combinations are as follows:

Point	Capital Goods	Consumption Goods
A	0	20
B	1	19
C	2	17
D	3	14
E	4	10
F	5	5

Playland is located at point *B* on the PPC, and Workland is located at point *E*. Assume that this situation continues into the future and that all other things remain the same.

a. What is Workland's opportunity cost of capital goods in terms of consumption goods?

b. What is Playland's opportunity cost of capital goods in terms of consumption goods?

c. How would the PPCs of Workland and Playland be expected to compare to each other 50 years in the future?

ECONOMICS ON THE NET

Production Possibilities and the Canadian Economy

The size of our economy is measured by its gross domestic product (GDP). When the GDP is measured in "constant" dollars—that is, using a dollar measure that does not include any inflation—any increase or decrease represents a change in the quantity of output the economy produces. This application looks at the size of the Canadian economy and the mix of output we produce.

Internet URL:

http://www.statcan.ca/english/Pgdb/Economy/Economic/econ41.htm

Title: Gross Domestic Product at Factor Cost

Application: Look at the values for 1995 and 1999 for All Industries, Goods Producing Industries, and Services Producing Industries.

a. Draw production possibilities curves for the Canadian economy for the years 1995 and 1999. Put goods producing industries on the vertical axis and services producing industries on the horizontal axis. (Assume there was no unemployment in the economy during those years.)

b. Calculate the ratio of goods to services for 1995 and 1999. Show where the economy was producing on your PPCs from part (a).

c. Has there been a trade-off between goods and services between 1995 and 1999? Explain.

A PPENDIX A

READING AND WORKING WITH GRAPHS

Independent variable A variable whose value is determined independently of, or outside, the equation under study.

Dependent variable A variable whose value changes according to changes in the value of one or more independent variables.

A graph is a visual representation of the relationship between variables. In this appendix, we'll stick to just two variables: an **independent variable,** which can change freely in value, and a **dependent variable,** which changes only as a result of changes in the value of the independent variable. For example, if nothing else is changing in your life, your weight depends on the amount of food you eat. Food is the independent variable and weight the dependent variable.

A table is a list of numerical values showing the relationship between two (or more) variables. Any table can be converted into a graph, which is a visual representation of that list. Once you understand how a table can be converted to a graph, you will understand what graphs are and how to construct and use them.

Consider a practical example. A conservationist may try to convince you that driving at lower highway speeds will help you conserve gas. Table A-1 shows the relationship between speed—the independent variable—and the distance you can go on a litre of gas at that speed—the dependent variable. This table does show a pattern of sorts. As the data in the first column get larger in value, the data in the second column get smaller.

TABLE A-1

Gas Consumption as a Function of Driving Speed

Kilometres per Hour	Kilometres per Litre
70	11
80	10
90	9
100	8
110	7
120	6
130	5

Now let's take a look at the different ways in which variables can be related.

Direct and Inverse Relationships

Direct relationship A relationship between two variables that is positive, meaning that an increase in one variable is associated with an increase in the other and a decrease in one variable is associated with a decrease in the other.

Inverse relationship A relationship between two variables that is negative, meaning that an increase in one variable is associated with a decrease in the other and a decrease in one variable is associated with an increase in the other.

Two variables can be related in different ways, some simple, others more complex. For example, a person's weight and height are often related. If we measured the height and weight of thousands of people, we would surely find that taller people tend to weigh more than shorter people. That is, we would discover that there is a **direct relationship** between height and weight. By this we simply mean that an increase in one variable is usually associated with an increase in the related variable. This can easily be seen in part (a) of Figure A-1.

Let's look at another simple way in which two variables can be related. Much evidence indicates that as the price of a specific commodity rises, the amount purchased decreases—there is an **inverse relationship** between the variable's price per unit and quantity purchased. A table listing the data for this relationship would indicate that for higher and higher prices, smaller and smaller quantities would be purchased. We see this relationship in part (b) of Figure A-1.

FIGURE A-1 Relationships

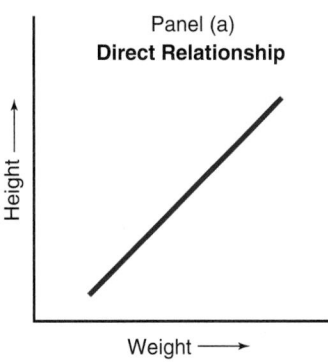

Panel (a)
Direct Relationship

Height ⟶

Weight ⟶

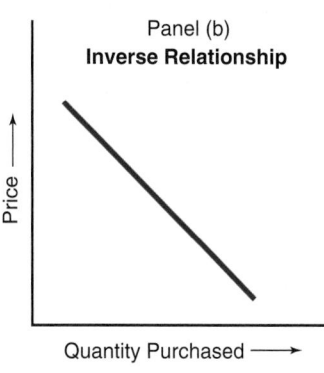

Panel (b)
Inverse Relationship

Price ⟶

Quantity Purchased ⟶

Constructing a Graph

Let us now examine how to construct a graph to illustrate a relationship between two variables.

A Number Line

Number line A line that can be divided into segments of equal length, each associated with a number.

The first step is to become familiar with what is called a **number line.** One is shown in Figure A-2. There are two things that you should know about it.

1. The points on the line divide the line into equal segments.
2. The numbers associated with the points on the line increase in value from left to right; saying it the other way around, the numbers decrease in value from right to left. However you say it, what we're describing is formally called an *ordered set of points.*

On the number line, we have shown the line segments—that is, the distance from 0 to 10 or the distance between 30 and 40. They all appear to be equal and, indeed, are equal to 13 mm. When we use a distance to represent a quantity, such as barrels of oil, graphically, we are scaling the number line. In the example shown, the distance between 0 and 10 might represent 10 barrels of oil, or the distance from 0 to 40 might represent 40 barrels. Of course, the scale may differ on different number lines. For example, a distance of 1 cm could represent 10 units on one number line but 5,000 units on another. Notice that on our number line, points to the left of 0 correspond to negative numbers and points to the right of 0 correspond to positive numbers.

Of course, we can also construct a vertical number line. Consider the one in Figure A-3. As we move up this vertical number line, the numbers increase in value; conversely, as we descend, they decrease in value. Below 0 the numbers are negative, and above 0 the numbers are positive. And as on the horizontal number line, all the line segments are equal. This line is divided into segments such that the distance between −2 and −1 is the same as the distance between 0 and 1.

FIGURE A-2 Horizontal Number Line

−20	−10	0	10	20	30	40

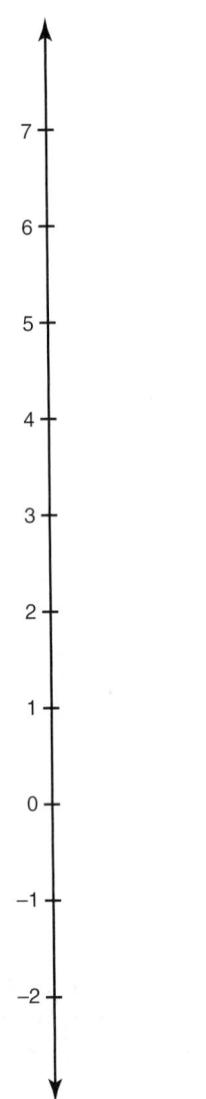

Combining Vertical and Horizontal Number Lines

By drawing the horizontal and vertical lines on the same sheet of paper, we are able to express the relationships between variables graphically. We do this in Figure A-4.

We draw them (1) so that they intersect at each other's 0 point and (2) so that they are perpendicular to each other. The result is a set of coordinate axes, where each line is called an axis. When we have two axes, they span a plane.

For one number line, you need only one number to specify any point on the line; equivalently, when you see a point on the line, you know that it represents one number or one value. With a coordinate value system, you need two numbers to specify a single point in the plane; when you see a single point on a graph, you know that it represents two numbers or two values.

The basic things that you should know about a coordinate number system are that the vertical number line is referred to as the **y axis,** the horizontal number line is referred to as the **x axis,** and the point of intersection of the two lines is referred to as the **origin.**

Any point such as *A* in Figure A-4 represents two numbers—a value of *x* and a value of *y*. But we know more than that; we also know that point *A* represents a positive value of *y* because it is above the *x* axis, and we know that it represents a positive value of *x* because it is to the right of the *y* axis.

Point *A* represents a "paired observation" of the variables *x* and *y*; in particular, in Figure A-4, *A* represents an observation of the pair of values $x = 10$ and $y = 1$. Every point in the coordinate system corresponds to a paired observation of *x* and *y*, which can be simply written (x, y)—the *x* value is always specified first, then the *y* value. When we give the values associated with the position of point *A* in the coordinate number system, we are in effect giving the coordinates of that point. *A*'s coordinates are $x = 10$, $y = 1$, or $(10, 1)$.

Graphing Numbers in a Table

Consider Table A-2. Column 1 shows different prices for T-shirts, and column 2 gives the number of T-shirts purchased per week at these prices. Notice the pattern of these numbers. As the price of T-shirts falls, the number of T-shirts purchased per week increases. Therefore, an inverse relationship exists between these two variables, and as soon as we represent it on a graph, you will be able to see the relationship. We can graph this rela-

FIGURE A-4 A Set of Coordinate Axes

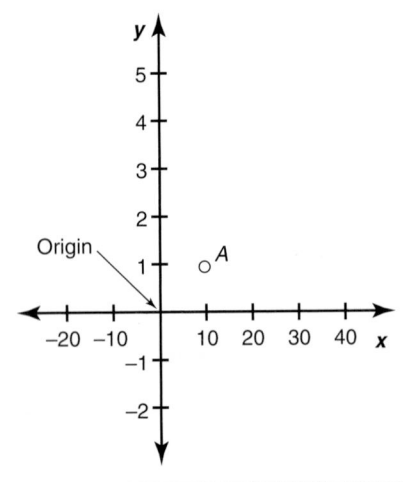

TABLE A-2
T-Shirts Purchased

(1) Price of T-Shirts	(2) Number of T-Shirts Purchased per Week
$10	20
9	30
8	40
7	50
6	60
5	70

tionship using a coordinate number system—a vertical and horizontal number line for each of these two variables. Such a graph is shown in part (b) of Figure A-5.

In economics, it is conventional to put dollar values on the *y* axis. We therefore construct a vertical number line for price and a horizontal number line, the *x* axis, for quantity of T-shirts purchased per week. The resulting coordinate system allows the plotting of each of the paired observation points; in part (a), we repeat Table A-2, with a column added expressing these points in paired-data (*x*, *y*) form. For example, point *J* is the paired observation (30, 9). It indicates that when the price of a T-shirt is $9, 30 will be purchased per week.

If it were possible to sell parts of a T-shirt ($\frac{1}{2}$ or $\frac{1}{20}$ shirt), we would have observations at every possible price. That is, we would be able to connect our paired observations, represented as lettered points. Let's assume that we can make T-shirts perfectly divisible. We would then have a line that connects these points, as shown in the graph in Figure A-6.

In short, we have now represented the data from the table in the form of a graph. Note that an inverse relationship between two variables shows up on a graph as a line or curve that slopes downward from left to right. (You might as well get used to the idea that economists call a straight line a "curve" even though it may not curve at all. Much of economists' data turn out to be curves, so they refer to everything represented graphically, even straight lines, as curves.)

FIGURE A-5 Graphing the Relationship Between T-Shirts Purchased and Price

Part (a)

Price per T-Shirt	T-Shirts Purchased per Week	Point on Graph
$10	20	*I* (20, 10)
9	30	*J* (30, 9)
8	40	*K* (40, 8)
7	50	*L* (50, 7)
6	60	*M* (60, 6)
5	70	*N* (70, 5)

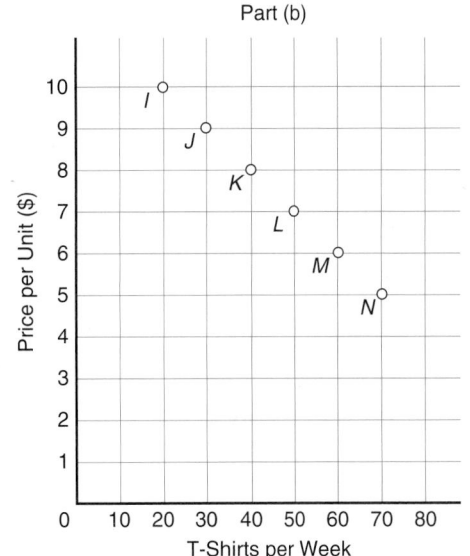

Part (b)

FIGURE A-6 Connecting the Observation Points

The Slope of a Line (A Linear Curve)

An important property of a curve represented on a graph is its *slope*. Consider Figure A-7, which represents the quantities of shoes per week that a seller is willing to offer at different prices. Note that in part (a) of Figure A-7, as in Figure A-5, we have expressed the coordinates of the points in parentheses in paired-data form.

The **slope** of a line is defined as the change in the *y* values divided by the corresponding change in the *x* values as we move along the line. Let's move from point *E* to point *D* in part (b) of Figure A-7. As we move, we note that the change in the *y* values, which is the change in price, is +$20, because we have moved from a price of $20 to a price of $40 per pair. As we move from *E* to *D*, the change in the *x* values is +80; the number

FIGURE A-7 A Positively Sloped Curve

Part (a)

Price per Pair	Pairs of Shoes Offered per Week	Point on Graph
$100	400	A (400, 100)
80	320	B (320, 80)
60	240	C (240, 60)
40	160	D (160, 40)
20	80	E (80, 20)

of pairs of shoes willingly offered per week rises from 80 to 160 pairs. The slope calculated as a change in the y values divided by the change in the x values is therefore

$$\frac{20}{80} = \frac{1}{4}$$

It may be helpful for you to think of slope as a "rise" (movement in the vertical direction) over a "run" (movement in the horizontal direction). We show this abstractly in Figure A-8. The slope is measured by the amount of rise divided by the amount of run. In the example in Figure A-8, and of course in Figure A-7, the amount of rise is positive and so is the amount of run. That's because it's a direct relationship. We show an inverse relationship in Figure A-9. The slope is still equal to the rise divided by the run, but in this case the rise and the run have opposite signs because the curve slopes downward. That means that the slope will have to be negative and that we are dealing with an inverse relationship.

Now let's calculate the slope for a different part of the curve in part (b) of Figure A-7. We will find the slope as we move from point B to point A. Again, we note that the slope, or rise over run, from B to A equals

$$\frac{20}{80} = \frac{1}{4}$$

FIGURE A-8 Figuring Positive Slope

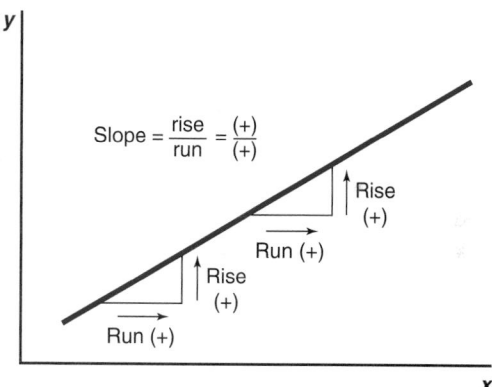

FIGURE A-9 Figuring Negative Slope

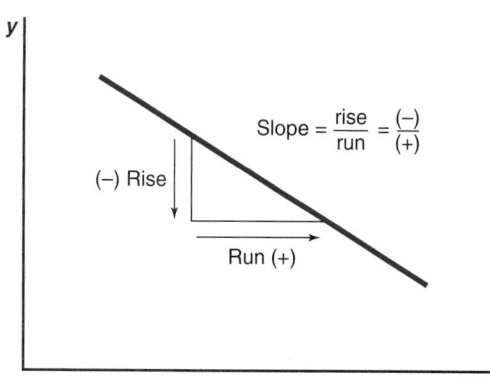

A specific property of a straight line is that its slope is the same between any two points; in other words, the slope is constant at all points on a straight line in a graph.

We conclude that for our example in Figure A-7, the relationship between the price of a pair of shoes and the number of pairs of shoes willingly offered per week is linear, which simply means "in a straight line," and our calculations indicate a constant slope. Moreover, we calculate a direct relationship between these two variables, which turns out to be an upward-sloping (from left to right) curve. Upward-sloping curves have positive slopes—in this case, it is $+\frac{1}{4}$.

We know that an inverse relationship between two variables shows up as a downward-sloping curve—rise over run will be a negative slope because the rise and run have opposite signs as shown in Figure A-9. When we see a negative slope, we know that increases in one variable are associated with decreases in the other. Therefore, we say that downward-sloping curves have negative slopes. Can you verify that the slope of the graph representing the relationship between T-shirt prices and the quantity of T-shirts purchased per week in Figure A-6 is $-\frac{1}{10}$?

Slopes of Nonlinear Curves

The graph presented in Figure A-10 indicates a *nonlinear* relationship between two variables, total profits and output per unit of time. Inspection of this graph indicates that at first, increases in output lead to increases in total profits; that is, total profits rise as output increases. But beyond some output level, further increases in output cause decreases in total profits.

Can you see how this curve rises at first, reaches a peak at point *C*, and then falls? This curve relating total profits to output levels appears mountain-shaped.

Considering that this curve is nonlinear (it is obviously not a straight line), should we expect a constant slope when we compute changes in *y* divided by corresponding changes in *x* in moving from one point to another? A quick inspection, even without specific numbers, should lead us to conclude that the slopes of lines joining different points in this curve, such as between *A* and *B*, *B* and *C*, or *C* and *D*, will *not* be the same. The curve slopes upward (in a positive direction) for some values and downward (in a negative direction) for other values. In fact, the slope of the line between any two points on this curve will be different from the slope of the line between any two other points. Each slope will be different as we move along the curve.

Instead of using a line between two points to discuss slope, mathematicians and economists prefer to discuss the slope *at a particular point*. The slope at a point on the curve,

FIGURE A-10 The Slope of a Nonlinear Curve

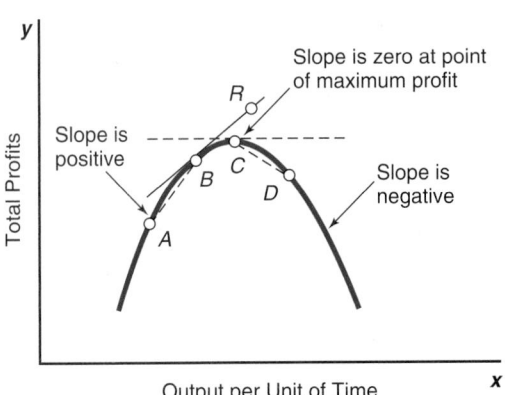

such as point B in the graph in Figure A-10, is the slope of a line *tangent* to that point. A tangent line is a straight line that touches a curve at only one point. For example, it might be helpful to think of the tangent at B as the straight line that just "kisses" the curve at point B.

To calculate the slope of a tangent line, you need to have some additional information besides the two values of the point of tangency. For example, in Figure A-10, if we knew that the point R also lay on the tangent line and we knew the two values of that point, we could calculate the slope of the tangent line. We could calculate rise over run between points B and R, and the result would be the slope of the line tangent to the one point B on the curve.

APPENDIX SUMMARY

1. Direct relationships involve a dependent variable changing in the same direction as the change in the independent variable.

2. Inverse relationships involve the dependent variable changing in the opposite direction of the change in the independent variable.

3. When we draw a graph showing the relationship between two economic variables, we are holding all other things constant (the Latin term for which is *ceteris paribus*).

4. We obtain a set of coordinates by putting vertical and horizontal number lines together. The vertical line is called the y axis; the horizontal line, the x axis.

5. The slope of any linear (straight-line) curve is the change in the y values divided by the corresponding change in the x values as we move along the line. Otherwise stated, the slope is calculated as the amount of rise over the amount of run, where rise is movement in the vertical direction and run is movement in the horizontal direction.

6. The slope of a nonlinear curve changes; it is positive when the curve is rising and negative when the curve is falling. At a maximum or minimum point, the slope of the nonlinear curve is zero.

APPENDIX PROBLEMS

(Answers to the odd-numbered problems appear at the back of the book.)

A-1. Explain which is the independent variable and which is the dependent variable in the following examples.

a. Once you determine the price of a notebook at your college bookstore, you will decide how many notebooks to buy.

b. You will decide how many credit hours to register for this semester once the university tells you how many work-study hours you will be assigned.

c. You are anxious to receive your Economics exam grade because you studied many hours in the weeks preceding the exam.

A-2. For the following items, state whether a direct or indirect relationship exists.

a. The number of hours you study for an exam and your exam mark

b. The price of pizza and the quantity purchased

c. The number of games your college basketball team won last year and the number of season tickets sold this year

A-3. Complete the schedule and plot the following function:

$y = 3x$

y	x
	4
	3
	2
	1
	0
	−1
	−2
	−3
	−4

A-4. Review Figure A-4, and then state whether the following paired observations are on, above or below the x axis and on, to the left of or to the right of the y axis.

a. (−10,4)

b. (20, −2)

c. (10,0)

A-5. Calculate the slope for the function you graphed in Problem A-3.

A-6. Complete the schedule and plot the following function:

$y = x^2$

y	x
	4
	3
	2
	1
	0
	−1
	−2
	−3
	−4

A-7. Indicate at each ordered pair whether the slope of the curve you plotted in Problem A-6 is positive, negative or zero.

A-8. State whether the following functions imply a positive or negative relationship between x and y.

a. $y = 5x$

b. $y = 3 + x$

c. $y = -3x$

ECONOMIES IN TRANSITION

Hospital and bed closures, crowded emergency rooms, health-care worker strikes, physician emigration to the U.S., and growing queues for a variety of medical treatments have all become part of the daily news across Canada.

To address these reported problems, politicians, academics, and concerned citizens are debating the merits of recent moves towards a market economy approach in the provision of health care in Canada.

The concepts presented in this chapter will enhance your ability to understand and evaluate these recent trends in health care.

PREVIEW QUESTIONS

1. What are the three basic economic questions that arise due to the scarcity problem?

2. What are the differences between a pure command economy and a pure capitalist economy?

3. How does a pure capitalist system answer the three basic economic questions?

4. What are the differences between consumer and frontier capitalism?

Economic system The institutional means through which resources are used to satisfy human wants.

Resource allocation The assignment of resources to specific uses by determining what will be produced, how it will be produced, and for whom it will be produced.

Try Preview Question 1:
What are the three basic economic questions that arise due to the scarcity problem?

Pure command economy An economic system characterized by public ownership of all property resources. The three basic economic questions are answered in a centralized manner by government.

Pure capitalist economy An economic system characterized by private ownership of all property resources. Households and firms interacting through a system of markets answer the three basic economic questions in a decentralized manner. This is also called a market economy or the price system.

DID YOU KNOW THAT... there used to be a country called the Soviet Union, whose chief of state in 1950 took off his shoe at the United Nations and pounded it on the desk while shouting, "We will bury you"? That person was Nikita Khrushchev; he died in 1971. It took quite a few more years for his country to die, but die it did. The Soviet Union is no more. The 74-year experiment in trying to run an economy without using the price, or market, system will go down in history as one of the greatest social and economic failures of all time. But just because the Soviet Union dissolved itself at the end of 1991 does not mean that the entire world economy automatically became like that of Canada. In particular, the 15 republics of the former Soviet Union, the Soviet "satellite" countries of Eastern Europe, and other nations, including China, are what we call *economies in transition.*

At any point in time, every nation has its own **economic system,** which can be defined as the institutional means through which resources are used to satisfy human wants. No matter what institutional means—marketplace or government—a nation chooses to use, three basic economic questions must always be answered due to the scarcity problem explained in Chapter 2.

The Three Basic Economic Questions

In every country, no matter what the form of government or type of economic system, who is running the government, or how poor or rich the country is, three basic economic questions must be answered. They concern the problem of **resource allocation,** which is simply how resources are to be allocated. As such, resource allocation answers the three basic economic questions of *what, how,* and *for whom* goods and services will be produced.

1. *What and how much will be produced?* Literally billions of different things could be produced with society's scarce resources, but not all at the same time. Some mechanism must exist that causes some things to be produced and others to remain as either inventors' pipe dreams or individuals' unfulfilled desires.
2. *How will it be produced?* There are many ways to produce a desired item. It is possible to use more labour and less capital or vice versa. It is possible to use more unskilled labour and fewer units of skilled labour. Somehow, in some way, a decision must be made as to the particular mix of inputs, the way they should be organized, and how they are brought together at a particular place.
3. *For whom will it be produced?* Once a commodity is produced, who should get it? In a modern economy, individuals and businesses purchase commodities with money income. The question then is what mechanism is there to distribute income, which then determines how commodities are distributed throughout the economy.

Economic Systems

Not long ago, in response to the problem of scarcity, textbooks presented two extreme economic systems as possible polar alternatives for industrialized nations to consider—the **pure command economy** versus the **pure capitalist economy**. Despite the fact that many countries have recently moved away from a command economy, it is appropriate to review both types of economic systems. This is because many informed citizens within Canada and other capitalist economies feel that elements of the command economy should prevail in the provision of important services such as health care, education, and national security.

Pure Command Economy

Public (government) ownership of all property resources characterizes a pure command economy. The three basic economic questions: What, How, For Whom, are answered in a very centralized manner by the government or the "state." Detailed five-year plans are formulated by the central authorities, in order to respond to the three basic economic questions.

Until recently, nations such as Russia and China used the pure command economy to make their resource-allocation decisions. In the past, depending on the economics text one reviewed, this type of system has typically been associated with nations practising communism or socialism.

Pure Capitalist Economy

In contrast to the pure command economy, resources are privately owned in pure capitalism. Moreover, the three basic economic questions: What, How, For Whom, are answered in a very decentralized manner by households and firms with the aid of an elaborate system of markets and prices. The pure capitalist economy goes by other names such as *capitalism*, *market economy*, or *price system*.

Since there has been a global trend away from pure command economies towards capitalist economies, we will describe pure capitalism in more depth below. In explaining the pure capitalist economy, we will periodically refer to the Circular Flow Model presented in Figure 3-1.

Key features of pure capitalism include:

1. *Private ownership of resources:* Individual households and individual firms own the productive resources in pure capitalism. As described in Figure 3-1, households have two essential roles in capitalism—they supply resources to firms and they demand goods and services with the income received from supplying resources. Firms, in turn, demand or hire resources in order to supply goods and services to households.
2. *Self-interest:* The primary motive underlying decisions made by households and firms in pure capitalism is the pursuit of self-interest. More specifically, firms attempt to maximize their own profit, when deciding what resources to demand or hire and what products to supply. Similarly, households are assumed to attempt to maximize individual wealth and other personal goals when deciding on where to supply their resources. When demanding goods and services, households attempt to maximize self-satisfaction or utility.

FIGURE 3.1 Circular Flow Model

This model describes how households and firms interact through both product and factor markets in a pure capitalist economy. In the product markets the households demand goods and services, while the firms supply the goods and services. In the factor markets these roles are reversed. That is, households supply the resources and the firms demand the resources.

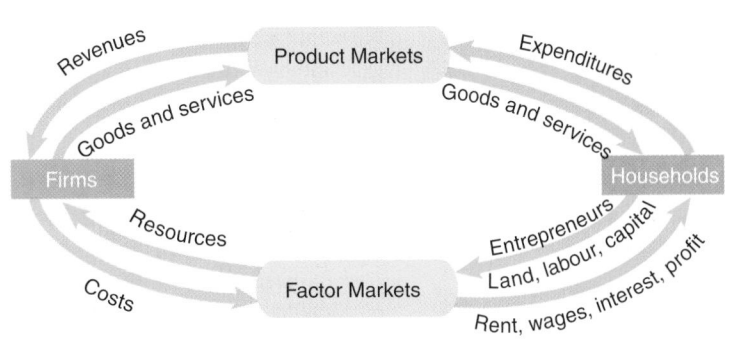

3. *Consumer sovereignty:* The pure capitalist system is to serve the household in its consumer role. Operationally, this means that capitalism is to produce the mix of goods and services that consumers desire, at the lowest possible prices.

4. *Markets and Prices:* The Circular Flow Diagram in Figure 3-1 indicates the two broad types of markets that exist in pure capitalism—product markets and factor (resource) markets. When consumer demand changes or resource availability changes, this sets off changes in relative prices in affected product and factor markets. These price changes ultimately reallocate resources in line with the change in consumer demand or resource availability. While we will examine how prices are determined in individual markets in the chapters that follow, we will provide a simple example below.

   Suppose that consumer demand for red wine increases and consumer demand for cigarettes decreases. Referring to the product markets in Figure 3-1, the price of red wine will increase while the price of cigarettes will decrease. The higher price for red wine serves as a signal to firms that red wine is now relatively more profitable to produce than cigarettes.

   Driven by the profit motive, the red wine firms will increase their demand to hire resources, while the cigarette firms will decrease their demand for resources, to reduce their losses. Prices will now change in the factor markets in Figure 3-1. Prices (i.e., wages) of resources (i.e., employees) that engage in the production of red wine will increase relative to the prices offered resources in the cigarette industry. Resources, guided by self-interest, will move out of cigarette production and into the production of red wine. Eventually, red wine production will increase. Note how this system of markets and prices operates to reallocate resources in line with changes in consumer demand, thus promoting consumer sovereignty.

5. *Competition:* In order to ensure that the self-interests of firms and resources work to the best interests of consumers, it is necessary that many independent sellers and buyers compete in each market. This will be more fully explained in subsequent chapters of this text.

6. *Limited government:* To the extent that competition exists in each market, the "invisible hand" of self-interest will serve to promote consumer sovereignty. Hence, allocating resources to meet changes in consumer demand does not require the "heavy hand" of government. The French have termed this feature of capitalism "**laissez-faire**" which means that the government should leave it (the economy) alone or "let it be."

One way to remember some of the important attributes of the market economy is by thinking of capitalism's **Three P's**: Private property, Profits, and Prices.

Laissez-faire French term for "leave it alone." This term is used to describe the limited government feature of pure capitalism.

Three P's Private property, Profits, and Prices inherent in capitalism.

Try Preview Question 2:

What are the differences between a pure command economy and a pure capitalist economy?

Pure Capitalism and the Three Economic Questions

Now that we have reviewed the essential features of pure capitalism, we can proceed to examine how this economic system operates to answer the three basic economic questions—What, How, For Whom.

What and How Much Will Be Produced?

Since firms can enhance profits by producing what consumers are willing to buy, we can see that consumer demand plays an important role in deciding what goods and services are produced. In more formal terms, the profit motive and competition lead firms to promote allocative efficiency—that is, firms will produce the mix of goods and services most wanted by society. However, we must keep in mind that if the highest price that consumers are willing to pay for a good is less than the lowest resource cost at which the good can be produced, no profit will result, and none of this good will be produced. In other words, resource availability also plays a role in determining what goods and services are produced.

How Will It Be Produced?

The question of how output will be produced in a pure capitalist system relates to the efficient use of scarce inputs. Consider the possibility of using only two types of resources, capital and labour. A firm may have the options given in Table 3.1. It can use various combinations of labour and capital to produce the same amount of output.

Two hypothetical combinations are given in Table 3.1. How then is it decided which combination will be used? Under pure capitalism the least cost combination (technique B in our example) will be chosen by firms because it will maximize profits. In other words, in pure capitalism, competition and the profit motive encourage firms to achieve productive efficiency.

For Whom Will It Be Produced?

This last question involves how households share in the consumption of the goods and services produced. This, in turn, is based on the distribution of money incomes and wealth among households. Households with higher levels of income and wealth will get to purchase and consume a greater portion of the goods produced in the economy.

What determines the distribution of wealth and money income among different households? This distribution is based on the quantities, qualities, and types of the various human and non-human resources that different households own and supply to the marketplace.

Try Preview Question 3:

How does a pure capitalist system answer the three basic economic questions?

Mixed Economics

The pure command and the pure capitalist systems are extreme economic systems. Real world economies which typically fall somewhere between these two extreme systems are called **mixed economies**. In mixed economies decisions about how resources are used are made partly by the private sector and partly by the public sector. As an example, Canada is referred to as a mixed capitalist system. This is because, while the majority of products are produced in the private sector, there are other goods and services provided by the government. These mixed economies can be regarded as the different faces of capitalism.

Mixed Economy An economic system in which decisions about how resources should be used are made partly by the private sector and partly by the government.

TABLE 3.1

Production Costs for 100 Units of Product X

Technique A or B can be used to produce the same output. Obviously, B will be used because its total cost is less than A's. Using production technique B will generate a $2 savings for every 100 units produced.

Inputs	Input Unit Price	A Production Technique A (input units)	Cost	B Production Technique B (input units)	Cost
Labour	$10	5	$50	4	$40
Capital	8	4	32	5	40
Total cost of 100 units			82		80

CONCEPTS IN BRIEF

- The three basic economic questions arising from the problem of scarcity are: What and how much will be produced? How will it be produced? For whom will it be produced?
- The pure command economy is one in which all property resources are owned by the government. The three basic economic questions are answered through central government planning.
- The pure capitalist economy is characterized by private ownership of all resources. The three basic economic questions are determined in a decentralized manner by individual households and firms interacting in markets.
- The key features of pure capitalism include private ownership of resources, self-interest, consumer sovereignty, markets and prices, competition, and limited government. In short, think of the three P's—private property, profits, and prices.
- In capitalism, consumer demand and resource availability determine what goods and services will be produced. Due to the profit motive, the least cost method of production will be chosen when deciding how the goods will be produced. Who gets what is based on each consumer's level of wealth and income. This, in turn, depends on the degree to which households own marketable resources.

The Different Faces of Capitalism

With the recent decline in command economic systems, one can view the world as being left with a single economic system that, thanks to the diversity of human cultures, has a variety of faces. Table 3.2 presents one way to categorize today's economic systems.

TABLE 3.2
Four Faces of Capitalism

Type of Capitalism	Examples	Characteristics	Problem Areas
Consumer	Canada, United States, New Zealand, Australia, United Kingdom	Borders are relatively open; focus is on profit maximization and laissez-faire.	Low saving and investment rates; income inequality
Producer	Japan, France, Germany	Production is emphasized over consumption; employment is a major policy issue; state controls a relatively large part of the economy.	Consumer dissatisfaction; potential slow future growth rates; inertia within the economy
Family	Indonesia, Malaysia, Thailand, Taiwan	Extended clans dominate business and capital flows.	Lack of modern corporate organizations; lack of money markets
Frontier	Russia, China, Ukraine, Romania, Albania	Many government enterprises pursue for-profit activities; new entrepreneurs emerge every day.	Difficulty of crossing borders; rising criminal activity

Source: Based on, in part, "21st Century Capitalism," *Business Week*, February 23, 1995, p. 19.

The Transitional Phase: Frontier Capitalism

Frontier capitalism describes economies in transition from state ownership and control of most of the factors of production to a system of private property rights in which the price system is used to answer the basic economic questions. Table 3.3 presents theoretical stages in the development of frontier capitalism. Two aspects appear to be the most important: developing the legal system and selling off state-owned businesses.

TABLE 3.3
How Frontier Capitalism Develops

Stage	Characteristics
I	The central government, as the controller of all economic activities, collapses and starts to disappear. The black market, typically involving government enterprises still owned by the state, expands enormously. Many former state factory managers and other bosses become involved in criminal activities using the state's resources. Government corruption occurs more than before.
II	Small businesses start to flourish. Families pool funds in order to become entrepreneurs. The rules of commerce are not well understood because there is not yet a well-established commercial law system, nor are property rights well defined or protected by the state.
III	The economy is growing, but much of its growth is not measured by government statisticians. Small financial markets, such as stock markets, begin to develop. Foreigners cautiously invest in the new stock markets. The government attempts to develop a clear set of commercial laws.
IV	Foreign corporations are more willing to invest directly in new factories and stores. The state gets serious about selling all businesses that it owns. More resources are devoted to suppressing criminal activity. Commercial law becomes better established and better understood.

Development of the Legal System

In Canada and many other countries, we take a well-established legal system as a given. That does not imply the total absence of a legal system in countries where we are now seeing frontier capitalism. To be sure, the former Soviet Union had a legal system, but virtually none of it had to do with economic transactions, which were carried out by state dictates. Individuals could not own the factors of production, and therefore there were no legal disputes over property rights involving them. Consequently, the legal system in the former Soviet Union and its Eastern European satellites consisted of many volumes of criminal codes—laws against robbery, murder, rape, and theft, as well as so-called economic crimes.

Enter the new world of private property rights and unrestricted exchange of those rights among buyers and sellers. Now what happens when a buyer claims that a seller breached a particular agreement? In Canada, lawyers, courts, and established contract law can be used to settle the dispute. Yet until recently in the frontier economies of the former Soviet Union, there was nothing even vaguely comparable. The rule of law in Canada (and Great Britain—from where much of Canada's law is evolved) has developed over hundreds of years; we cannot expect countries in transition towards full capitalism to create an entire body of law and procedure overnight.

Privatization

Privatization The sale or transfer of state-owned property and businesses to the private sector, in part or in whole. Also refers to contracting out—letting private business take over government-provided services such as garbage collection.

The transition towards capitalism requires that the government reduce its role in the economy. This transition involves what has become known as *privatization*. **Privatization**

FIGURE 3.2 The Trend Towards Privatization

Privatization worldwide has been on the upswing since 1985, as shown in part (a). Nationalizations (the opposite of privatizations) reached their peak in about 1970 as is shown in part (b).

Source: Adapted from *OECD* and *The Economist,* August 21, 1993, p. 19.

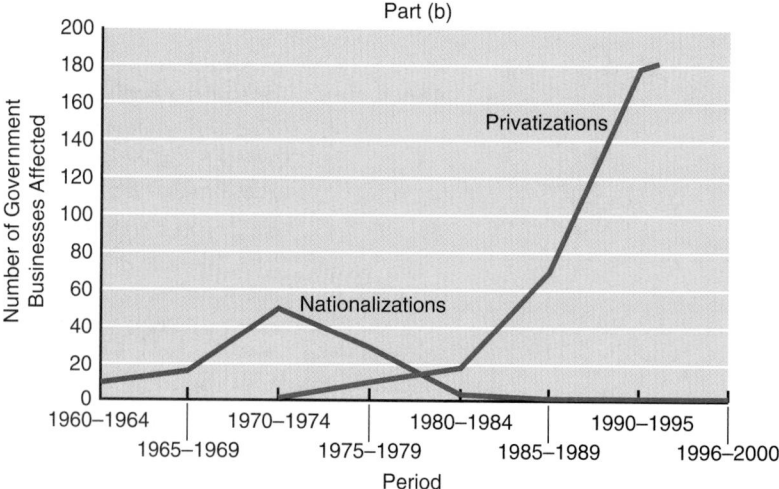

is the transfer of ownership or responsibility for businesses run by the government, so-called *state enterprises,* to individuals and companies in the private sector. Even in capitalist countries, the government has often owned and run various parts of the economy. During and after World War II, it became the norm for many European governments to "nationalize" different industries. This was particularly true in the United Kingdom, where the steel industry was nationalized, for example. In the early 1980s, France nationalized its banking industry. The opposite of nationalization is privatization. Late in 1996, Canada privatized air traffic control and sold it to Nav Canada for $1.5 billion.

In the early 1980s, Turkey and Chile were the first capitalist countries to start mass privatization of government-owned businesses. Under Margaret Thatcher, the United Kingdom pioneered the mass privatization of state industry, including the huge road haulage company (NFC), a health care group (Amersham International), telephone services (British Telecom), British Petroleum, and British Aerospace.

A country must employ some method to put government-owned businesses into the hands of the private sector; government-owned businesses are not simply given away to the first party who asks. Imagine if the Canadian government said that it wanted to sell Canada Post. How would it do so? One way is to sell it outright, but there might not be any buyers who would be willing to pay to take over such a giant money-losing corporation. An alternative would involve selling shares of stock to anyone who wanted to buy them at the stated price. This latter technique is indeed the way in which most privatizations have been carried out in established capitalist countries throughout the world over the past 15 or 20 years.

In the former Soviet Union and in Eastern Europe, alternative systems have been devised. For example, citizens, at various times, have been given vouchers granting them the right to purchase a specified number of shares in particular government-owned companies that were being sold off.

The trend in privatization versus nationalization is shown in part (b) of Figure 3.2. The cumulative worldwide sales of state-owned enterprises can be seen in part (a). In Europe, privatization will probably continue into the next century at the rate of over $50 billion a year. Privatization in Latin America will go on for much longer. Finally, privatization in the former Soviet Union and Eastern Europe has in a sense just begun, and may take a long time indeed.

Political Opposition to Privatization

There is often strong political pressure to slow down or even prevent the privatization of state-owned businesses. The political pressure to prevent privatization is derived from simple economics: Managers of state-owned businesses typically have had lifetime job security, better working conditions than they could obtain elsewhere, and little threat of competition. In other words, life for a manager is usually better in a state-owned firm than in that same firm once it has been privatized.

Workers in state-owned firms also believe, often rightly, that their lot in life will not be quite so good if the state-owned firm is sold to the private sector. State-owned firms tend to pay their workers higher wages and give them better fringe benefits, including much better pension plans, than similar firms that are privately owned. For example, an examination of state-owned phone companies in France and Germany shows that they have two to three times as many workers per telephone customer as the private telephone companies in Canada. This comparative overuse of labour in state-owned firms is even more obvious in the republics of the former Soviet Union and in Eastern Europe.

Economists cannot say whether privatization of state-owned firms is good or bad. Rather, economists can simply state that the rigours of a competitive market will generally cause resources to be used more efficiently after privatization occurs. In the process, however, some managers and workers may be made worse off.

Is There a Right Way to Go About the Transition?

Ever since the fall of the Berlin Wall in 1989, economists have debated whether there is a "right" way for former socialist and communist countries to move towards capitalist systems. The once-communist nations have, indeed, embarked on a social experiment in how to move towards a market economy. Basically, they have chosen two methods— a slow one and a fast one. Romania, Russia, and Ukraine have only gradually privatized their economies, whereas the Czech Republic and, to a lesser extent, Poland and Estonia, opted for a "shock treatment."

The rapid move towards a market economy, though not free of problems, has seemed to work better than the go-slow approach. The more slowly the transition occurs, the more the former entrenched bureaucrats in the state-owned businesses have been able to maintain their power over the use of resources. In the meantime, the state-owned businesses continue to use valuable resources inefficiently in these developing countries.

In contrast, the Czech Republic used a voucher system to privatize over 2,000 state-owned enterprises. All citizens were given *vouchers*—legal rights evidenced on printed certificates—which could be used to purchase shares of stock in state-owned businesses.

A stock market quickly developed in which shares of hundreds of companies are now traded every day. After an initial period of transition to a market economy, the Czech Republic has now achieved one of the lowest unemployment rates in Europe.

We will next examine Russia's economic system which is in the throes of frontier capitalism.

CONCEPTS IN BRIEF

- Today there are four types of capitalism: consumer, producer, family, and frontier. The last begins when a centralized economy starts collapsing and black markets thrive. Eventually small businesses flourish, and then financial markets develop. Finally, foreign investment is attracted, and state-owned businesses are privatized.
- The development of a well-functioning legal system is one of the most difficult problems for an economy in the frontier capitalism stage. Such economies do not have the laws or courts to handle the new system of property right transfers.
- Privatization, or the turning over to the private sector of state-owned businesses, is occurring all over the world in all types of economies. There is much political opposition, however, whenever managers in soon-to-be privatized businesses realize that they may face harder times in a private setting.

Russia and Its Former Satellites, Yesterday and Today

Russia was the largest republic in the former Soviet Union. The economic system in place was at times called communism and at other times called command socialism. There is no question that it was a command economy in which there was centralized economic leadership and planning. All economies involve planning, of course; the difference is that in capitalist societies, most of the planning is done by private businesses rather than the government. Leaders in the former Soviet Union believed that its economic planners in Moscow could micromanage an economy that spanned 11 time zones, involved millions of consumers and producers, and affected vast quantities of goods and services.

Imagine trying to run a single business that big! Perhaps more importantly, state ownership in such a large country resulted in unintended consequences throughout the economy. For example, when the government issued production quotas for glass based on the number of panes, the glass produced was almost paper thin and shattered easily. Managers of the glass factories found it took less time to make thin panes of glass which allowed them to produce the required number in the time allotted. In an effort to correct the problem, the government changed its quotas to weight. However, the resulting glass panes were so thick that they were useless. Once again managers found it took less time to meet their quotas if they produced very heavy panes of glass. In short, former Soviet citizens responded rationally to their incentives every time central planners figured out a new way to set production quotas. In the process, untold resources were inefficiently used or completely wasted.

By the time the Soviet Union collapsed in 1991, it consisted of a society in which perhaps one or two percent of the population (the communists, privileged bureaucrats, athletes, and artists) enjoyed a comfortable lifestyle and the rest of the citizens were forced to scrape by. The standard of living of the average citizen prior to the Soviet Union's breakup was at best a quarter, but more realistically one-tenth, of that in Canada. The same was true perhaps to an even greater degree in the former East Germany, Romania, Poland, Hungary, Czechoslovakia (now the Czech Republic and Slovakia), and Albania. For a discussion of Russia's reduction in national output, see the Thinking Critically About the Media box on the next page.

Thinking Critically About the Media 3-1   Taking Russia's Pulse

When economists and journalists discuss the transition from the centralized Soviet economy to its current market orientation, they lament the tremendous reduction in national output. Official estimates for the period 1989 to 1995, for example, claim that national output dropped by over 50 percent. True though it may be that output dropped during this time, it is not clear what the actual value of that output was to the population. Much of the reduction was in military hardware, such as missiles. How much did the average citizen lose when that output shrank? Also, fewer television sets and radios were produced during this time period—but the ones produced earlier either never worked properly or tended to explode. Steel mills have been shut down in Russia, but they had been using technology that was 45 years old. Further, the official Russian state agency that measures the economy, Goskomstat, has none of the sophistication that Statistics Canada has for measuring a nation's output. Even if Goskomstat had better computers and more refined techniques, it would still miss a vast off-the-books black market economy that won't be counted by government statisticians for years to come. All in all, Russia's 150 million people earn more and live better than what Goskomstat statistics say.

Privatization During Transition

The fact that a former state-owned business in Russia is now privatized does not mean that shareholders control it the way they do in, say, Canada. In Canada, shareholders elect a board of directors, which then chooses upper management. Shareholders can force out directors who have acted improperly, and can also show their disapproval by selling their shares of stock and purchasing shares in another company. It will be some time before the same system of control operates in all recently privatized Russian businesses. Many such businesses are actually controlled by their managers and workers, not by shareholders. One might use the analogy of a divorced couple still sharing the same house and the children.

In some former Soviet satellite countries, one arm of government sells a state-owned firm and another reappears as its owner. This has happened a lot in Poland, for example, where the government's Industrial Development Agency is managing one of the 15 funds that were set up to take over 440 formerly state-owned enterprises.

In the businesses that are being run by worker cooperatives, there is little incentive to fire the least efficient workers or to seek more highly qualified workers. Manager-owners do not often do much better. Manager-owners of recently privatized firms in Russia clearly do not want to surrender control.

The Persistence of Old Ways

The more an economy tends towards pure market capitalism, the less place there is for a government élite that is able to seize economic power and, more importantly, economic privileges. In Russia today, some of the old Communist Party bases of economic power are being redeveloped. Although newspapers and television stations are now privately owned, their owners are increasingly afraid of angering powerful government interests.

Just a few years ago, President Boris Yeltsin created a new political party named "Our House—Russia." The party was and continues to be backed by wealthy banking and business interests. It consists almost entirely of state bureaucrats and provincial governors and administrators, most of whom are former communists. Prior to the downfall of communism, the political élite were able to use special clinics and hospitals. Today the same persons have the same privileges, although the names of the hospitals have changed. Even a new, special food store was built for officials with parliamentary identification cards. Under communism, special food stores served to provide Communist Party élite with low-cost, high-quality food without their having to wait in lines. Why such a special food store has cropped up again in Russia's now more capitalistic system remains something of a mystery.

The Inevitable Crime Wave

The shift to a market economy in Russia has brought with it a major increase in crime, particularly organized crime. Currently, virtually every small business pays protection money to some gang. Moscow boasts at least a million unregistered firearms, and the country as a whole has over 30 million of them. According to former *Toronto Star* Moscow reporter Stephen Handelman, "The second Russian revolution of this century is awash in corruption, opportunism, and crime."

One needs to examine the crime statistics more carefully, though, to get a real feeling for what is happening in this nation in transition. Street crime is certainly greater than it used to be under the Soviet régime. But Moscow is still probably safer than many American cities. With respect to "breaking the law," the legal system is in such a state of flux that probably everyone is breaking the law at one time or another. Because the legal system is in its infancy for facilitating private enterprise, business people have had to resort to extralegal methods to collect debts and enforce contracts. Unfortunately, some of these methods involve firearms and violence.

A good analogy for what is happening in Russia today is the violence associated with the illegal production and sale of alcoholic beverages during the United States' experiment with Prohibition (1920–1933) and what is happening in Russia today. The violence associated with the business of illegal booze disappeared with the repeal of Prohibition. It will not disappear so quickly in Russia, but it certainly will eventually fade out as property rights become better established, the legal system increasingly facilitates trade, and the court system gains enough experience to handle legal problems from the business world.

One must also look at what used to exist under the old system. Because everything belonged to "the people," there was little in the way of communications, credit, banking, and computerization. Money was less important than connections and rank in the Communist Party. People who were adept at thriving in such an environment—the Communist Party élite—have had a comparative advantage in the initial stages of transition to a market economy. They maintain their connections with the state bureaucrats who controlled resources. It is not surprising that many of those in power today are the same communists who were in power a decade ago.

All of this is simply a transition. The incidence of certain crimes in Russia has actually fallen, as can be seen in Figure 3.3.

CONCEPTS IN BRIEF

- Russia and its former satellite states in Eastern Europe operated under a system of command socialism with much centralized economic planning. The end result was a declining economy in which a small percentage of the population lived extremely well and the rest very poorly.
- Russia and Eastern Europe are privatizing at varying speeds, depending on the level of political opposition.
- Russia has experienced a crime wave during its transition to capitalism. As property rights and the legal system become more efficient, much of the crime associated with illegal economic activities will probably disappear.

Try Preview Question 4:

What are the differences between consumer and frontier capitalism?

FIGURE 3.3 Crime in Russia

While crime increased after the fall of communism in Russia, its rate has recently stabilized or fallen.

Source: Interior Ministry of Russia.

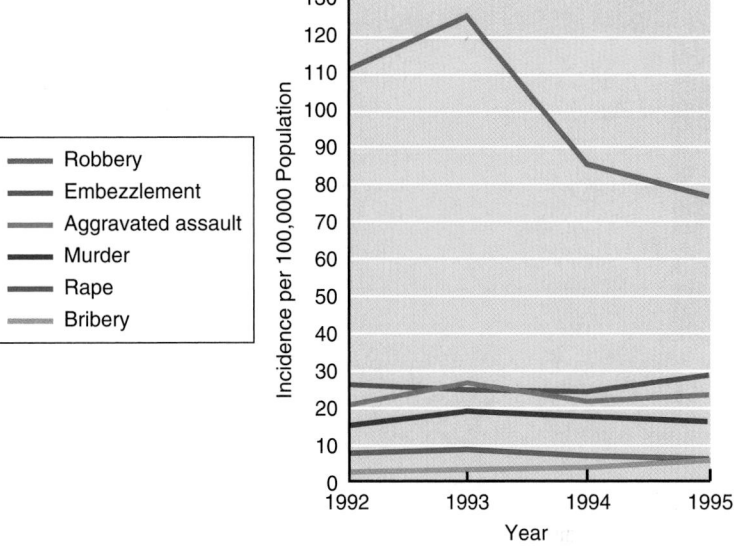

INTERNATIONAL POLICY EXAMPLE 3-1

A Booming Business in Facelifts by Russian Plastic Surgeons

One of the beneficiaries of Russia's economic system in transition is the facelift industry. There is as yet no legal procedure in Russia for imposing liability on physicians for malpractice. Consequently, a patient who desires a facelift or other cosmetic surgery has no consent forms to sign, and the physician has no malpractice (liability) insurance to purchase. People are travelling from outside Russia to take advantage of the resulting relatively inexpensive plastic surgery. According to one of Russia's best-known plastic surgeons, Igor A. Volf, "Surgeons in the West work in a very rigid frame. They are afraid of being sued by their patients—they fear complications. I do the big, bold operations Western doctors are afraid to do." As word of mouth travels, the demand for Russian plastic surgeons continues to increase.

For critical analysis: What are the costs that a Canadian contemplating a facelift in Moscow would have to include in making a rational decision about going there?

Thinking Critically About the Media 3-2   Rich Industrial Nations—Really?

Virtually all news commentators and research organizations continue to classify countries such as Canada, the United States, the United Kingdom, and France as industrial economies. Such an appellation today is a misnomer. In the industrial economies of today, less than one-third of the output is from "industry." Two-thirds of the jobs in so-called industrial economies are from services—doctors, lawyers, computer programmers, and Internet facilitators. Indeed, it might be more appropriate to call the richer countries knowledge economies because that is where the primary source of growth will lie—the storage, processing, and distribution of knowledge.

NETNOMICS

Will Innovation in Asia Rocket its Net Economy?

A group of renowned executives, entrepreneurs, and asset managers convened at the sixth Annual Wharton Asian Business Conference in Philadelphia to discuss the changing face of Asia and its transition to the new economy.

Despite the negative impact of the economic crisis of the late 1990s, experts at the Nov. 17, 2000 forum note that further development of the Internet, construction of a technology and telecommunications infrastructure, and institutional reform are all signs that a second East Asian miracle—powered largely by foreign capital and investments—will be taking place in the region soon.

Development of the Internet and e-commerce has had a slow start in Asia, according to speakers at the forum. Asia's Internet lag has been attributed to four factors: the Asian financial crisis; language barriers; an insufficient IT infrastructure; and tight regulatory practices of local governments.

Despite these roadblocks, the region continues to develop its Web savvy, anchored by the Internet's enormous potential as an engine for economic growth. The Internet has significantly penetrated Singapore, Hong Kong, Taiwan, and Korea, contributing to the growth of those respective economies. The mobile communications sector carries enormous promise and is an example of the investment opportunities available to companies that want to do business in East Asia.

Both the Internet and the emergence of mobile communications have caused the traditional barriers to entry to fall in Asia, creating an environment characterized as "the new entrants' paradise," in which existing companies that had been operating inefficiently are now forced to specialize while new competition emerges.

The potential for profound growth in Asia is contingent upon the emergence of globally competitive Asian businesses in high-growth sectors that are managed and marketed well. The growth potential is enormous, particularly in China. In 1999, China became the second largest economy in the world, after the United States.

ISSUES AND APPLICATIONS   For-Profit Health Care in Canada?

Concepts Applied: Mixed, capitalist, and command systems; allocative efficiency; productive efficiency; and equity

On May 30, 2000, the Alberta government passed the Alberta Health Care Protection Act, Bill 11. This new legislation permits for-profit medical clinics to provide surgical procedures that involve overnight stays. Before this legislation, only for-profit day surgery services were allowed.

Bill 11 was the most debated bill in Alberta history. The Alberta government defended this legislation by suggesting that contracting out surgical procedures to private clinics would improve the cost effectiveness of these health services as well as reduce waiting lists in the public system.

Bill 11 has renewed a national debate over which type of economic system best suits the provision of health care serv-

Is for-profit health care the way to eliminate scenes like this?

ices—a capitalist or command system. To appreciate the differing views, we will begin by examining Canada's existing system of providing health care services.

Canada's Current Medicare Policy

Canada has a predominantly publicly financed, privately delivered health-care system that consists of ten provincial (and three territorial) government health insurance plans. This mixed system of providing health-care services is frequently referred to as "Medicare."

The federal government's role in health care involves using financial incentives to ensure that each province provides equal access to universal, comprehensive coverage for medically necessary hospital, in-patient, and outpatient physician services.

Typically, each province makes each of its working residents pay into the medicare insurance fund through compulsory taxation (or compulsory monthly premiums). When a Canadian consumer (patient) visits a physician (or hospital), monies from the medicare fund pay for the visit. This means that the patient does not incur any additional out-of-pocket expense each time he or she makes another visit to a physician or hospital.

In the Canadian medicare system, physicians typically operate their own private practices and are compensated from the medicare insurance fund on a "fee-for-service" basis. In other words, a doctor can enhance his or her monthly income by providing more services per month either through seeing more patients or encouraging the same patient to incur repeat visits in any given month. Since the majority of acute-care Canadian hospitals are operated on a non-profit basis, the only pressure to contain hospital costs is the annual hospital budgets determined by government authorities.

In the early 1990s, faced with public debt concerns, federal and provincial governments cut back the growth in government spending despite the aging population. As a result we have witnessed through the Canadian media, if not personally, emergency treatments conducted in hospital hallways, nurses on picket lines, Canadian-trained doctors practising in the US, and lengthy waits for medical tests and surgical procedures. To address these reported problems, politicians, academics, medical practitioners, and concerned citizens have debated the merits of adopting a more capitalist approach in the provision of health care in Canada.

A Capitalist Oriented Health-Care Model?

In the United States, health-care services are predominantly provided in the for-profit private sector. As Table 3.4 indicates, public expenditures constitute a much smaller portion of total health expenditures in the US when compared to Canada.

In order to finance their health-care costs, many US consumers voluntarily pay monthly premiums to private health insurance companies. In addition, consumers may have to pay a co-payment out of his or her pocket each time he or she visits a physician or hospital. Some private insurance plans may involve an experience rating which is a situation where those who make more frequent visits to physicians may end up paying higher insurance premiums. Some private insurance companies may not insure consumers with certain pre-existing conditions.

In some cases, US physicians are paid employees in large profit-oriented health maintenance organizations (HMOs). These organizations are paid an annual fee for each consumer (patient) registered in them. In return, the registered patient is provided with managed care plans which restrict the range of services provided as well as the patient's choice of physician(s).

In theory, one would expect to see a given quality of health care provided more efficiently in the United States, when compared to Canada. Since US health consumers may pay each time they visit the doctor, they are less likely to make trivial visits. As well, it is in the interests of HMOs to contain the costs of providing health care, as this would enhance profits. However, the data displayed in Tables 3.4 and 3.5 suggest that although Canada spends less of a percentage of GDP (national income) on health care, Canada manages to achieve a higher level of health achievement in terms of life expectancy and infant mortality rates.

Source: Based on "Premier Explains Why Alberta Needs Bill 11."March 18, 2000. *Health Facts, Government of Alberta.* Sept. 10, 2000. <http://www2.gov.ab.ca/healthfacts/index.cfm?PgNm=ContentDetail&Id=147>

	Total Health Expenditure as a Percent of GDP	Public Expenditures as a Percent of Total Health Expenditures
Country		
Canada	8.6%	72%
United States	13.7%	44.1%

TABLE 3.4
Annual National Health Expenditures: Canada and the United States, 1997

Source: Based on "Annex Table 8: Selected National Health Accounts Indicators for All 191 Members States," *World Health Report 2000.* June 28, 2000. World Health Organization. Sept. 10, 2000.<http://www.who.int/whr/2000/en/statistics.htm>

Country	Life Expectancy at Birth (Years)	Infant Mortality Rate	Disability Adjusted Life Expectancy at Birth (Years)
Canada	79.43	5.08 deaths per live 1000 births	72 (world rank of 12)
United States	77.12	6.82 deaths per live 1000 births	70 (world rank of 24)

Source: The Revenue Outlook. Budget Plan 2000. Finance Canada. Reproduced with the permission of the Minister of Public Works and Government Services Canada, 2000.

For Critical Analysis

1. What aspects of the Canadian medicare system would encourage allocative inefficiency? Briefly explain. Hint: Allocative inefficiency relates to situations where resources are either overallocated or underallocated to the production of a good or service.

2. Briefly explain how the US system of health-care delivery might promote productive efficiency.

3. What aspects of the capitalist health-care model would conflict with equity (fairness) as perceived by a lower-income family or an individual who is born with a chronic illness? Briefly explain.

4. How might one explain the data described in Tables 3.4 and 3.5?

CHAPTER SUMMARY

1. The pure command system is characterized by public ownership of all property resources. The basic economic questions: What, How, and For Whom, are answered in a centralized manner through government planning.

2. In the pure capitalist system all resources are privately owned. Households and firms interacting in product and factor markets answer the basic economic questions: What, How, and For Whom, in a decentralized manner. This system is often called the price system or the market economy.

3. The essential features of pure capitalism include: private ownership of resources, self-interest, consumer sovereignty, markets and prices, competition, and limited government. A quick description of pure capitalism is in terms of the three P's—Private property, Profits, and Prices.

4. In pure capitalism, the economic question, What and How Much Will Be Produced, is based on consumer demand and resource availability. The question, How Will It Be Produced, is answered by firms who will choose the most efficient or least cost method of production. For Whom Will It Be Produced is decided based on the quantities, qualities, and types of human and property resources owned by the different households in the capitalist system.

5. In mixed economies the basic economic questions are answered partly in the private sector and partly in the public sector. Canada is classified as a mixed capitalist economy.

6. Today there are four types of capitalism: consumer, producer, family, and frontier. The last emerges when a centralized economy starts collapsing and black markets thrive. Eventually, small businesses flourish and financial markets develop. Finally, foreign investment is attracted, and state-owned businesses are privatized.

7. The development of a well-functioning legal system is one of the most difficult problems for an economy in the frontier capitalism stage. Such economies do not have the laws or courts to handle property right protection and transfers.

8. Privatization, or turning over state-owned businesses to the private sector, is occurring all over the world in all types of economies. There is much political opposition, however, whenever managers in soon-to-be-privatized businesses realize that they may face harder times in a private setting.

9. Russia and its former satellite states in Eastern Europe operated under a system of command socialism with much centralized economic planning. The end result was a declining economy in which a small percentage of the population lived extremely well and the rest very poorly.

10. Russia has experienced a crime wave during its transition to capitalism. As property rights and the legal system become more efficient, much of the crime associated with illegal economic activities will probably disappear.

DISCUSSION OF PREVIEW QUESTIONS

1. **What are the three basic economic questions that arise due to the scarcity problem?**

   Scarcity exists for a society because people want more than their resources will allow them to have. Because of this scarcity, each nation must decide What and How Much Will Be Produced. Since resources are limited, nations must try to answer the question, How Will It Be Produced, in an efficient manner. Finally, since not all wants can be satisfied, a country must devise a way to ration the limited output among its households, which relates to the question, For Whom Will It Be Produced.

2. **What are the differences between a pure command economy and a pure capitalist economy?**

   The pure command system is characterized by public ownership of all property resources. The basic economic questions of What, How, and For Whom are answered in a centralized manner through government planning. In the pure capitalist system all resources are privately owned. The basic economic questions are answered in a decentralized manner by households and firms interacting in product and factor markets. This system is often called the price system or the market economy. A quick description of pure capitalism is in terms of the three P's—Private property, Profits, and Prices.

3. **How does a pure capitalist system answer the three basic economic questions?**

In pure capitalism, the economic question, What and How Much Will Be Produced, is based on consumer demand and resource availability. The question of How Will It Be Produced is answered by firms who will choose the most efficient or least cost method of production. For Whom Will It Be Produced is decided based on the quantities, qualities, and types of human and property resources owned by the different households in the capitalist system.

4. **What are the differences between consumer and frontier capitalism?**

Consumer Capitalism: National borders are relatively open in terms of the flow of resources and the trade of goods and services. The focus is on profit maximization and laissez-faire. When making resource allocation decisions, due to intense global competition, firms are forced to put the consumer first. Property rights, the legal system, and financial markets are well established.

Frontier Capitalism: This stage is the beginning face of capitalism. Many government organizations pursue for-profit activities. As well, new entrepreneurs emerge every day. There is still difficulty in the crossing of borders. The legal system which establishes and protects property rights and enforces the laws of contract is in an infant stage. As a result, a lot of criminal activity surrounds the organizations pursuing for profit-activities.

PROBLEMS

(Answers to the odd-numbered problems appear at the back of the book.)

3-1. Suppose that you are an economic planner and you have been told by your country's political leaders that they want to increase automobile production by 10 percent over last year. What other industries will be affected by this decision?

3-2. Some argue that prices and profits automatically follow from well-established property rights. Explain how this might occur.

3-3. A business has found that it makes the most profits when it produces $172 worth of output of a particular product. It can choose from three possible techniques, A, B, and C, to produce the desired level of output. The table gives the amount of inputs these techniques use along with each input price.

a. Which technique will the firm choose, and why?

b. What would the firm's maximum profit be?

c. If the price of labour increases to $4 per unit, which technique will be chosen, and why? What will happen to profits?

		Production Technique		
Input	Input Unit Price	A (units)	B (units)	C (units)
Land	$10	7	4	1
Labour	2	6	7	18
Capital	15	2	6	3
Entrepreneurship	8	1	3	2

3-4. Answer the questions on the basis of the accompanying graph.

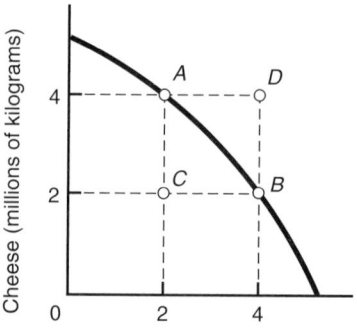

a. A switch to a decentralized, more market-oriented economy might do what to the production possibilities curve, and why?

b. What point on the graph represents an economy with unemployment?

3-5. The table gives the production techniques and input prices for 100 units of product X.

| | Production Technique | | | |
| | Input Unit | A | B | C |
Input	Price	(units)	(units)	(units)
Labour	$10	6	5	4
Capital	8	5	6	7

a. In a market system, which techniques will be used to produce 100 units of product X?

b. If the market price of a unit of X is $1, which technique will lead to the greatest profit?

c. The output of X is still $1, but the price of labour and capital changes so that labour is $8 and capital is $10. Which production technique will be used?

d. Using the information in (c), what is the potential profit of producing 100 units of X?

3-6. The table gives the production techniques and input prices for one unit of product Y.

| | Production Technique | | | |
| | Input Unit | A | B | C |
Input	Price	(units)	(units)	(units)
Labour	$10	1	3	2
Capital	5	2	2	4
Land	4	3	1	1

a. If the market price of a unit of product Y is $50, which technique generates the greatest potential profit?

b. If input unit prices change so that labour is $10, capital is $10, and land is $10, which technique will be chosen?

c. Assuming that the unit cost of each input is $10 and the price of a unit of Y is $50, which technique generates the greatest profit?

3-7. Visit the World Bank's Selected World Development Indicators website at http:// www.worldbank.org/html/ iecdd/wdipdf.htm. Open Table 1, Basic Indicators. Notice that the countries are arranged by the size of their economies (GNP per capita) from small to large.

a. Find Canada. What income level group of countries is Canada in?

b. Select one of the low-income economies. Compare its per-person GNP with that of Canada. How much larger, in percentage terms, is Canada than your low-income country?

c. Compare the life expectancy at birth in your low-income country with that of a middle-income country and with that of Canada. What conclusions can you draw about health as a country develops? Why do you think this happens?

Producer Face of Capitalism vs. Consumer Face of Capitalism

Before going to the Internet URL listed below, briefly review the differences between the producer face and the consumer face of capitalism as outlined in Table 3.2 of this chapter. The purpose of this exercise is to encourage you to use the CIA *World Factbook* on the Internet to review an updated description of one of the producer-face countries listed in Table 3.2.

Internet URL: http://www.odci.gov/cia/ publications/factbook/

Title: Economy-overview, Country Listing, *CIA World Factbook*

Application: After you have selected the Country Listing link at the URL site listed above, select one of the producer-face nations displayed in Table 3.2. Once the specific country page displays, choose the Economy link. After reading the Economy-overview section of the country you selected, answer the following:

1. What aspects of the Economy overview are consistent with the text's description of the producer face of capitalism?

2. Is there anything in the Economy overview that suggests a transition from the producer face of capitalism towards the consumer face of capitalism? Explain.

DEMAND AND SUPPLY

Auctions have been around for centuries. Farmers first used auctions to sell their grains to people who would use the grains to make flour and other food products. Today, some of the best-publicized auctions involve fine art at Sotheby's and Christie's. In addition to the normal auction scene, however, a whole new revolution in auctioneering is taking place. Hundreds, if not thousands, of auctions are taking place on the Internet as you read this sentence. To understand better how auctions work, whether online or elsewhere, you will need the tools of demand and supply.

PREVIEW QUESTIONS

1. Why are relative prices important in understanding the law of demand?

2. How can we distinguish between a change in *demand* and a change in *quantity demanded*?

3. Why is there normally a direct relationship between price and quantity supplied (other things being equal)?

4. Why will the market clearing price occur at the intersection of the supply and demand curves rather than at a higher or lower price?

5. What are the four distinct ways that market equilibrium can change?

Market All of the arrangements that individuals have for exchanging with one another. Thus we can speak of the labour market, the automobile market, and the credit market.

DID YOU KNOW THAT... more than 20 million people worldwide currently own portable cellular phones? Two million Canadians have purchased them since their introduction in 1985. Over the last decade, sales outside Canada have grown between 45 to 50 percent every year. Marketing consultants expect cell phone ownership to increase by 10 to 15 percent per year for the next several years. There are many reasons for the growth in ownership of cellular phones, not least being the dramatic reduction in both price and size thanks to improved and cheaper computer chips used in making them. There is something else at work, though. It has to do with security. In a recent survey, 46 percent of new cellular phone users said that personal safety was the main reason they bought a portable phone. In the case of an automobile breakdown, for example, they would be able to call a garage or tow truck for help.

We could attempt to explain the phenomenon simply by saying that more people like to use portable phones. But that explanation is neither satisfying nor entirely accurate. If we use the economist's primary set of tools, *demand and supply,* we will have a better understanding of the cellular phone's explosion in popularity, as well as many other phenomena in our world. Demand and supply are two ways of categorizing the influences on the price of goods that you buy, and the quantities available. As such, demand and supply form the basis of virtually all economic analysis of the world around us.

As you will see throughout this text, the operation of the forces of demand and supply take place in *markets*. A **market** is an abstract concept referring to all the arrangements individuals have for exchanging with one another. Goods and services are sold in markets such as the automobile market, the health food market, and the compact disc market. Workers offer their services in the labour market. Companies, or firms, buy workers' labour services in the labour market. Firms also buy other inputs in order to produce the goods and services that you buy as a consumer. They purchase machines, buildings, and land. These markets are in operation at all times. One of the most important activities in them is the setting of the prices of all of the inputs and outputs that are bought and sold in our complicated economy. To understand the determination of prices, you first need to look at the law of demand.

The Law of Demand

Demand A schedule of how much of a good or service people will purchase at any price during a specified time period, other things being constant.

Law of demand The observation that there is a negative, or inverse, relationship between the price of any good or service and the quantity demanded, holding other factors constant.

Demand has a special meaning in economics. It refers to the quantities of specific goods or services that individuals, either singly or as a group, will purchase at various possible prices, other things being constant. We can therefore talk about the demand for microprocessor chips, French fries, compact disc players, and children.

Associated with the concept of demand is the **law of demand**, which can be stated as follows:

> When the price of a good goes up, people buy less of it, other things being equal. When the price of a good goes down, people buy more of it, other things being equal.

The law of demand tells us that the quantity demanded of any commodity is inversely related to its price, other things being equal. In an inverse relationship, one variable moves up in value when the other moves down. The law of demand states that a change in price causes the quantity demanded to change in the *opposite* direction.

Notice that we tacked onto the end of the law of demand the statement "other things being equal." We referred to this in Chapter 1 as the *ceteris paribus* assumption. It means, for example, that when we predict that people will buy fewer CD players if their price goes up, we are holding constant the price of all other goods in the economy as well as people's incomes. Implicitly, therefore, if we are assuming that no other prices change when we examine the price behaviour of CD players, we are looking at the *relative* price of CD players.

The law of demand is supported by millions of observations of how people behave in the marketplace. Theoretically, it can be derived from an economic model based on rational behaviour, as was discussed in Chapter 1. Basically, if nothing else changes and the price of a good falls, the lower price induces us to buy more over a certain period of time. This is because we can enjoy additional net gains that were unavailable at the higher price. For the most part, if you examine your own purchasing behaviour, you will see that it generally follows the law of demand.

Relative Prices Versus Money Prices

Relative price The price of a commodity expressed in terms of another commodity.

Money price The actual price that you pay in dollars and cents. Also called the *absolute, nominal,* or *current price.*

The **relative price** of any commodity is its price in terms of another commodity. The actual price that you pay in dollars and cents for any good or service at any point in time is called its **money price.** Consider an example that you might hear quite often around older friends or relatives. "When I bought my first new car, it cost only $1500." The implication, of course, is that the price of cars today is outrageously high because the average new car might cost $20,000. But that is not an accurate comparison. What was the price of the average house during that same year? Perhaps it was only $12,000. By comparison, then, given that houses today average about $150,000, the current price of a new car doesn't sound so far out of line, does it?

The point is that money prices during different time periods don't tell you much. You have to find out relative prices. Consider an example of the price of CDs versus the price of cassettes from last year and this year. In Table 4.1, we show the money price of CDs and cassettes for two years during which both have gone up. That means that we have to pay out more for each in today's dollars and cents. If we look, though, at the relative prices of CDs and cassettes, we find that last year, CDs were twice as expensive as cassettes, whereas this year they are only 1.81 times as expensive. Conversely, if we compare cassettes to CDs, last year they cost only half as much as CDs, but today they cost about 55 percent as much. In the one-year period, while both prices have gone up in money terms, the relative price of CDs has fallen (and, equivalently, the relative price of cassettes has risen). Refer to the Thinking Critically About the Media box on the next page for another example of relative price.

Try Preview Question 1:

Why are relative prices important in understanding the law of demand?

CONCEPTS IN BRIEF

- The law of demand states that there is an inverse relationship between the quantity demanded of a good and its price, other things being equal.
- The law of demand applies when other things, such as income and the prices of all other goods and services, are held constant.
- Relative prices give the price of a good in terms of the price of another commodity.

TABLE 4.1

Money Price Versus Relative Price

The money price of both compact discs (CDs) and cassettes has risen. But the relative price of CDs has fallen (or conversely, the relative price of cassettes has risen).

	Money Price		Relative Price	
	Last Year	This Year	Last Year	This Year
CDs	$18	$20	$18 / $9 = 2.0	$20 / $11 = 1.81
Cassettes	$ 9	$11	$9 / $18 = 0.5	$11 / $20 = 0.55

Thinking Critically About the Media 4-1   The Real Price of Stamps

The press is fond of pointing out the rise in the price of a particular good, such as a stamp for first-class mail. In the 1940s, a first-class stamp in Canada cost only 4 cents, but by the late 1990s, it had climbed to 46 cents. That is the absolute price of postage, however. What about the relative price, the price relative to the average of all other prices? The relative price of postage is actually lower today than when it reached its peak in 1975. Many other relative prices have fallen over the years, ranging from gasoline prices to

the prime minister's salary. Indeed, relatively speaking, the prime minister's current $155,000-a-year salary is peanuts compared to what Prime Minister William Lyon Mackenzie King earned in 1946. In relative terms (dollars in 1947), the current prime minister earns only about 78 percent of Mr. King's salary, even though in absolute terms, the current prime minister makes more. Remember, everything is relative.

The Demand Schedule

Let's take a hypothetical demand situation to see how the inverse relationship between the price and the quantity demanded looks (holding other things equal). We will consider the quantity of computer diskettes demanded *per year* by one person. Without stating the *time dimension*, we could not make sense out of this demand relationship because the numbers would be different if we were talking about the quantity demanded per month, or the quantity demanded per decade.

In addition to implicitly or explicitly stating a time dimension for a demand relationship, we are also implicitly referring to *constant-quality* units of the good or service in question. Prices are always expressed in constant-quality units in order to avoid the problem of comparing commodities that are in fact not truly comparable.

In part (a) of Figure 4.1, we see that if the price were $1 per diskette, 50 of them would be bought each year by our representative individual, but if the price were $5 per diskette, only 10 would be bought each year. This reflects the law of demand. Part (a) is

FIGURE 4.1 The Individual Demand Schedule and the Individual Demand Curve

In part (a), we show combinations *A* through *E* of the quantities of diskettes demanded, measured in constant-quality units at prices ranging from $5 down to $1 per disk. In part (b), we plot combinations *A* through *E* on a grid. The result is the individual demand curve for diskettes.

Part (a)

Combination	Price per Constant-Quality Diskette	Quantity of Constant-Quality Diskettes per Year
A	$5	10
B	4	20
C	3	30
D	2	40
E	1	50

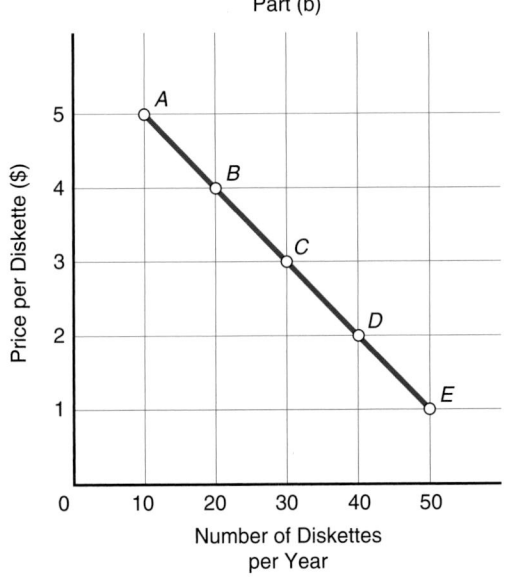

Part (b)

also called simply demand, or a *demand schedule*, because it gives a schedule of alternative quantities demanded per year at different possible prices.

The Demand Curve

Tables expressing relationships between two variables can be represented in graphical terms. To do this, we need only construct a graph that has the price per constant-quality diskette on the vertical axis, and the quantity measured in constant-quality diskettes per year on the horizontal axis. All we have to do is take combinations *A* through *E* from part (a) of Figure 4.1 and plot those points in part (b). Now we connect the points with a smooth line, and *voilà*, we have a **demand curve**[1]. It is downward-sloping (from left to right) to indicate the inverse relationship between the price of diskettes and the quantity demanded per year. Our presentation of demand schedules and curves applies equally well to all commodities, including toothpicks, hamburgers, textbooks, credit, and labour services. Remember, the demand curve is simply a graphical representation of the law of demand.

Demand curve A graphical representation of the demand schedule; a negatively sloped line showing the inverse relationship between the price and the quantity demanded (other things being equal).

Individual Versus Market Demand Curves

The demand schedule shown in part (a) of Figure 4.1 and the resulting demand curve shown in part (b) are both given for one individual. As we shall see, determining price in the marketplace depends on, among other things, the **market demand** for a particular commodity. The way in which we measure a market demand schedule and derive a market demand curve for diskettes or any other commodity is by adding the individual demand at each price for all those in the market. Suppose that the market for diskettes consists of only two buyers: buyer 1, for whom we've already shown the demand schedule in Figure 4.1, and buyer 2, whose demand schedule is displayed in Figure 4.2, part (a), column 3. Column 1 of Figure 4.2, part (a) shows the price, and column 2 gives the quantity demanded by buyer 1 (data taken directly from Figure 4.1). Column 4 states the total quantity demanded at each price, obtained by adding columns 2 and 3. Graphically, in part (d) of Figure 4.2, we add the demand curves of buyer 1 [part (b)] and buyer 2 [part (c)] to derive the market demand curve.

Market demand The demand of all consumers in the marketplace for a particular good or service. The summing at each price of the quantity demanded by each individual.

There are, of course, literally millions of potential consumers for diskettes. We'll assume that the summation of all of the consumers in the market results in a demand schedule, given in part (a) of Figure 4.3, and a demand curve, given in part (b). The quantity demanded is now measured in millions of units per year. Remember, part (b) in Figure 4.3 shows the market demand curve for the millions of users of diskettes. The "market" demand curve that we derived in Figure 4.2 assumed that there were only two buyers in the entire market. This is why that demand curve is not a smooth line, whereas the true market demand curve in part (b) of Figure 4.3 is, and has no kinks.

Now consider some special aspects of the market demand curve for CDs in International Example 4-1.

---

[1] Even though we call them "curves," for the purposes of exposition we often draw straight lines. In many real-world situations, demand and supply curves will in fact be lines that do curve. To connect the points in part (b) with a line, we assume that for all prices in between the ones shown, the quantities demanded will be found along that line.

FIGURE 4.2 The Horizontal Summation of Two Demand Schedules

Part (a) shows how to sum the demand schedule for one buyer with that of another buyer. Column 2 shows the quantity demanded by buyer 1, taken from part (a) of Figure 4.1. Column 4 is the sum of columns 2 and 3. We plot the demand curve for buyer 1 in part (b) and the demand curve for buyer 2 in part (c). When we add those two demand curves horizontally, we get the market demand curve for two buyers, shown in part (d).

Part (a)

(1) Price per Diskette	(2) Buyer 1 Quantity Demanded	(3) Buyer 2 Quantity Demanded	(4) = (2) + (3) Combined Quantity Demanded per Year
$5	10	10	20
4	20	20	40
3	30	40	70
2	40	50	90
1	50	60	110

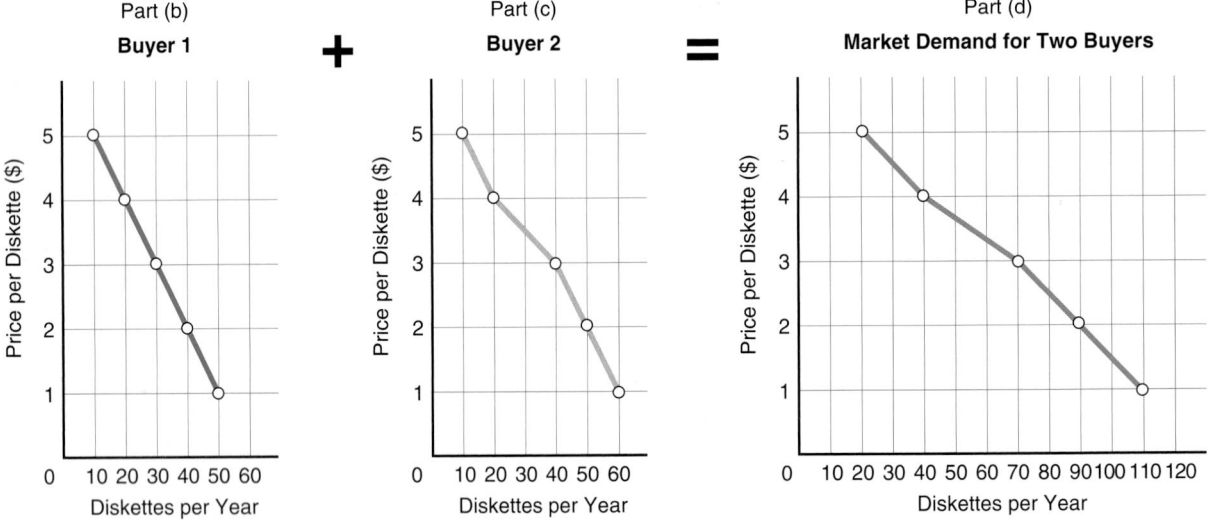

Part (b) Buyer 1 **+** Part (c) Buyer 2 **=** Part (d) Market Demand for Two Buyers

FIGURE 4.3 The Market Demand Schedule for Diskettes

In part (a), we add up the millions of existing demand schedules for diskettes. In part (b), we plot the quantities from part (a) on a grid; connecting them produces the market demand curve for diskettes.

Part (a)

Price per Constant-Quality Diskette	Total Quantity Demanded of Constant-Quality Diskettes per Year (millions)
$5	2
4	4
3	6
2	8
1	10

Part (b)

INTERNATIONAL EXAMPLE 4-1

Garth Brooks, Used CDs, and the Law of Demand

A few years ago, country singer Garth Brooks tried to prevent his latest album from being sold to any retail chain or store that also sells used CDs. His argument was that the used-CD market deprived labels and artists of earnings. His announcement came after a giant American retailer started selling used CDs side by side with new releases, at half the price. Brooks, along with the distribution arms of Sony, Warner Music, Capitol-EMI, and MCA were trying to quash the used-CD market. By so doing, it appears that none of these parties understands the law of demand.

Let's say the price of a new CD is $15. The existence of a secondary used-CD market means that to people who choose to resell their CDs for $5, the net cost of a new CD is, in fact, only $10. Because we know that quantity demanded is inversely related to price, we know that more of a new CD will be sold at a price of $10 than of the same CD at a price of $15. Taking only this force into account, eliminating the used-CD market tends to reduce the sale of new CDs.

But there is another force at work here, too. Used CDs are substitutes for new CDs. If used CDs are not available, some people who would have purchased them will instead purchase new CDs. If this second effect outweighs the incentive to buy less because of the higher effective price, then Brooks is behaving correctly in trying to suppress the used-CD market.

For critical analysis: Can you apply this argument to the used-book market, in which both authors and publishers have argued that used books are "killing them"?

CONCEPTS IN BRIEF

- We measure the demand schedule both in terms of a time dimension and in constant-quality units.
- The market demand curve is derived by summing the quantity demanded by individuals at each price. Graphically, we add the individual demand curves horizontally to derive the total, or market, demand curve.

Shifts in Demand

Assume that the federal government gives every student registered in a Canadian college, university, or technical school a personal computer that uses diskettes. The demand curve shown in part (b) of Figure 4.3 is no longer an accurate representation of the total market demand for diskettes. There will now be an increase in the number of diskettes demanded *at each and every possible price*. What we have to do is shift the curve outward, or to the right, to represent the rise in demand. The demand curve in Figure 4.4 will shift from D_1 to D_2. Take any price, say, $3 per diskette. Originally, before the federal government giveaway of personal computers, the amount demanded at $3 was 60 million diskettes per year. After the government giveaway, however, the quantity demanded at $3 is 100 million diskettes per year. What we have seen is a shift in the demand for diskettes.

The shift can also go in the opposite direction. What if colleges uniformly outlawed the use of personal computers by students? Such a regulation would cause a shift inward—to the left—of the demand curve for diskettes. In Figure 4.4, the demand curve would shift to D_3; the amount demanded would now be less at each and every possible price.

FIGURE 4.4 A Shift in the Demand Curve

If some factor other than price changes, the only way we can show its effect is by moving the entire demand curve, say, from D_1 to D_2. We have assumed in our example that the move was precipitated by the government's giving a free personal computer to every registered college student in Canada. That meant that at all prices, a larger number of diskettes would be demanded than before. Curve D_3 represents reduced demand compared to curve D_1, caused by a law prohibiting computers on campus.

The Other Determinants of Demand

The demand curve in part (b) of Figure 4.3 is drawn with other things held constant, specifically all of the other factors that determine how much will be bought. There are many such determinants. The major ones are income; tastes and preferences; the prices of related goods; expectations regarding future prices, future incomes, and future product availability; and population (market size). Let's examine each determinant more closely.

INCOME. For most goods, an increase in income will lead to an increase in demand. The phrase *increase in demand* always refers to a comparison between two different demand curves. Thus for most goods, an increase in income will lead to a rightward shift in the position of the demand curve from, say, D_1 to D_2 in Figure 4.4. You can avoid confusion about shifts in curves by always relating a rise in demand to a rightward shift in the demand curve, and a fall in demand to a leftward shift in the demand curve. Goods for which the demand rises when income rises are called **normal goods**. Most goods, such as shoes, computers, and CDs, are "normal goods." For some goods, however, demand *falls* as income rises. These are called **inferior goods**. Beans might be an example. As households get richer, they tend to spend less and less on beans and more and more on meat. (The terms *normal* and *inferior* are merely part of the economist's terminology; no value judgments are implied by or associated with them.)

Remember, a shift to the left in the demand curve represents a fall in demand, and a shift to the right represents a rise, or increase, in demand. The changing demand for dental services is illustrated in Example 4-1.

TASTES AND PREFERENCES. A change in consumer tastes in favour of a good can shift its demand curve outward to the right. When Frisbees® became the rage, the demand curve for them shifted outward to the right; when the rage died out, the demand curve shifted inward to the left. Fashions depend to a large extent on people's tastes and preferences. Economists have little to say about the determination of tastes; they have no "good" theories of taste determination or why people buy one brand of a product rather than others. Advertisers, however, do have various theories that they use in trying to make consumers prefer their products to those of competitors.

Normal goods Goods for which demand rises as income rises. Most goods are considered normal.

Inferior goods Goods for which demand falls as income rises.

EXAMPLE 4-1 Is Dental Care Becoming an Inferior Good?

A British health minister once claimed that the demand for health care is infinite because in the end everyone is in a losing battle against death. This is not so for Canadian dentistry, however. As aggregate Canadian income levels have risen during the past 25 years, overall spending on dental-care services has declined.

It isn't that fewer Canadians are seeing dentists each year. They just do not require as many fillings or extractions. As incomes rose across the country, people purchased more expensive and effective toothpastes. More municipalities began to fluoridate their water as the relative price of the anticavity agent declined; thus, changing relative prices has also played a role. And higher incomes of their residents have permitted more municipalities to purchase fluoridation systems.

At every age, the average Canadian now has about two more teeth than 25 years ago. Unfortunately for dentists who specialize in treating decaying and diseased teeth, Canadians' teeth are healthier than ever before.

For critical analysis: Many new dentists have been specializing in "cosmetic dentistry" desired by patients with healthy but less than beautiful teeth. Compared to traditional dental care services, is cosmetic dentistry more or less likely to be a normal good?

PRICES OF RELATED GOODS: SUBSTITUTES AND COMPLEMENTS. Demand schedules are always drawn with the prices of all other commodities held constant. In other words, when deriving a given demand curve, we assume that only the price of the good under study changes. For example, when we draw the demand curve for butter, we assume that the price of margarine is held constant. When we draw the demand curve for stereo speakers, we assume that the price of stereo amplifiers is held constant. When we refer to *related goods*, we are talking about goods for which demand is interdependent. If a change in the price of one good shifts the demand for another good, those two goods are related. There are two types of related goods: *substitutes* and *complements*. We can define and distinguish between substitutes and complements in terms of how the change in price of one commodity affects the demand for its related commodity.

Substitutes Two goods are substitutes when either one can be used to satisfy a similar want—for example, coffee and tea. The more you buy of one, the less you buy of the other. For substitutes, the change in the price of one causes demand for the other to shift in the same direction as the price change.

Butter and margarine are **substitutes**. Let's assume that each originally cost $4 per kilogram. If the price of butter remains the same and the price of margarine falls from $4 to $2 per kilogram, people will buy more margarine and less butter. The demand curve for butter will shift inward to the left. If, conversely, the price of margarine rises from $4 to $6 per kilogram, people will buy more butter and less margarine. The demand curve for butter will shift outward to the right. An increase in the price of margarine will lead to an increase in the demand for butter, and an increase in the price of butter will lead to an increase in the demand for margarine. For substitutes, a price change in the substitute will cause a change in demand *in the same direction*.

Complements Two goods are complements if both are used together for consumption or enjoyment—for example, coffee and cream. The more you buy of one, the more you buy of the other. For complements, a change in the price of one causes an opposite shift in the demand for the other.

For **complements**, the situation is reversed. Consider stereo speakers and stereo amplifiers. We draw the demand curve for speakers with the price of amplifiers held constant. If the price per constant-quality unit of stereo amplifiers decreases from, say, $500 to $200, that will encourage more people to purchase component stereo systems. They will now buy more speakers than before at any given price. The demand curve for speakers will shift outward to the right. If, by contrast, the price of amplifiers increases from $200 to $500, fewer people will purchase component stereo systems. The demand curve for speakers will shift inward to the left. To summarize, a decrease in the price of amplifiers leads to an increase in the demand for speakers. An increase in the price of amplifiers leads to a decrease in the demand for speakers. Thus for complements, a price change in a product will cause a change in demand *in the opposite direction*.

Are new learning technologies complements or substitutes for college instructors? Read Example 4-2 for further discussion.

EXAMPLE 4-2   Getting Your Degree Via the Internet

In this class and in others, you've probably been exposed to some of the new (and old) instructional technologies such as films and videos, interactive computer software, and interactive CD-ROM learning systems. Your professors have used these as a complement to their teaching, but in the future those technologies may in fact become a substitute for what your professors do in the classroom.

Televised and audio-taped lectures mean that more and more Canadian institutions can offer distance education courses, thus allowing a given number of professors to teach a greater number of students. Athabasca University in Alberta and Simon Fraser University in British Columbia offer enough distance education courses that a student can earn a university degree in business administration, history, or education without ever attending a class. Mount Saint Vincent University in Nova Scotia and CJRT Open College in Ontario offer diplomas entirely through distance education. Now consider interactive CD-ROM learning systems. In theory, virtually every college course could be put on CD-ROM, thereby entirely eliminating the need for instructors. Going one step further, institutions of higher learning are now using the Internet to provide instruction. The University of Western Ontario and Queen's University currently bring their programs to western Canada, offering an executive MBA through a combination of interactive video classroom instruction, high-speed Internet connections, e-mail, and shared application computing.

For critical analysis: What do you predict will happen to the demand curve for college professors in the next decade?

EXPECTATIONS. Consumers' expectations regarding future prices, future incomes, and future availability may prompt them to buy more or less of a particular good without a change in its current money price. For example, consumers getting wind of a scheduled 100 percent price increase in diskettes next month may buy more of them today, at today's prices. Today's demand curve for diskettes will shift from D_1 to D_2 in Figure 4.4 on page 76. The opposite would occur if a decrease in the price of diskettes were scheduled for next month.

Expectations of a rise in income may cause consumers to want to purchase more of everything today, at today's prices. Again, such a change in expectations of higher future income will cause a shift in the demand curve from D_1 to D_2 in Figure 4.4. Finally, expectations that goods will not be available at any price will induce consumers to stock up now, increasing current demand.

POPULATION. An increase in the population in an economy (holding per capita income constant) often shifts the market demand outward for most products. This is because an increase in population means an increase in the number of buyers in the market. Conversely, a reduction in the population will shift most market demand curves inward because of the reduction in the number of buyers in the market.

Changes in Demand Versus Changes in Quantity Demanded

We have made repeated references to demand and to quantity demanded. It is important to realize that there is a difference between a *change in demand* and a *change in quantity demanded*.

Demand refers to a schedule of planned rates of purchase, and depends on a great many nonprice determinants. Whenever there is a change in a nonprice determinant, there will be a change in demand—a shift in the entire demand curve to the right or to the left.

A quantity demanded is a specific quantity at a specific price, represented by a single point on a demand curve. When price changes, quantity demanded changes according to the law of demand, and there will be a movement from one point to another along the same demand curve. Look at Figure 4.5 below. At a price of $3 per diskette, 60 million diskettes per year are demanded. If the price falls to $1, quantity demanded increases to 100 million per year. This movement occurs because the current market price for the product changes. In Figure 4.5, you can see the arrow pointing down the given demand curve *D*.

When you think of demand, think of the entire curve. Quantity demanded, in contrast, is represented by a single point on the demand curve.

> A change or shift in demand causes the *entire* curve to move. The *only* thing that can cause the entire curve to move is a change in a determinant *other than its own price*.

In economic analysis, we cannot emphasize too much the following distinction that must constantly be made:

> A change in a good's own price leads to a change in quantity demanded, for any given demand curve, other things held constant. This is a movement *along* the curve.

Try Preview Question 2:

How can we distinguish between a change in *demand* and a change in *quantity demanded*?

> A change in any other determinant of demand leads to a change in demand. This causes a shift *of* the curve.

FIGURE 4.5 Movement Along a Given Demand Curve

A change in price changes the quantity of a good demanded. This can be represented as movement along a given demand schedule. If, in our example, the price of diskettes falls from $3 to $1 apiece, the quantity demanded will increase from 60 million to 100 million units per year.

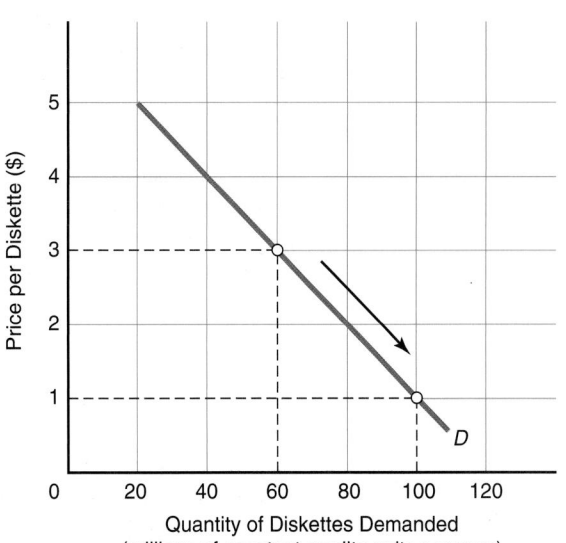

- Demand curves are drawn with determinants other than the price of the good held constant. These other determinants are (1) income; (2) tastes and preferences; (3) prices of related goods; (4) expectations about future prices, future incomes, and future availability of goods; and (5) population (number of buyers in the market). If any one of these determinants changes, the demand schedule will shift to the right or to the left.
- A change in demand happens only when there is a change in the other determinants of demand. This change in demand shifts the demand curve to the left or to the right.
- A change in the quantity demanded occurs when there is a change in the price of the good (other things held constant). Such a change in quantity demanded involves a movement along a given demand curve.

The Law of Supply

The other side of the basic model in economics involves the quantities of goods and services that firms are prepared to *supply* to the market. The **supply** of any good or service is the amount that firms are prepared to sell under certain conditions during a specified time period. The relationship between price and quantity supplied, called the **law of supply**, can be summarized as follows:

> At higher prices, a larger quantity will generally be supplied than at lower prices, all other things held constant. At lower prices, a smaller quantity will generally be supplied than at higher prices, all other things held constant.

There is generally a direct relationship between quantity supplied and price. For supply, as the price rises, the quantity supplied rises; as the price falls, the quantity supplied also falls. Producers are normally willing to produce and sell more of their product at a higher price than at a lower price, other things being constant. At $5 per diskette, 3M, Sony, Maxell, Fuji, and other manufacturers would almost certainly be willing to supply a larger quantity than at $1 per unit, assuming, of course, that no other prices in the economy had changed.

As with the law of demand, millions of instances in the real world have given us confidence in the law of supply. On a theoretical level, the law of supply is based on a model in which producers and sellers seek to make the most gain possible from their activities. For example, as a diskette manufacturer attempts to produce more and more diskettes over the same time period, it will eventually have to hire more workers and overutilize its machines. Only if offered a higher price per diskette will the manufacturer be willing to incur these extra costs. That is why the law of supply implies a direct relationship between price and quantity supplied.

The Supply Schedule

Just as we were able to construct a demand schedule, we can construct a *supply schedule*, which is a table relating prices to the quantity supplied at each price. A supply schedule can also be referred to simply as *supply*. It is a set of planned production rates that depends on the price of the product. We show the individual supply schedule for a hypothetical producer in part (a) of Figure 4.6. At $1 per diskette, for example, this producer will supply 200,000 diskettes per year; at $5, it will supply 550,000 diskettes per year.

Supply A schedule showing the relationship between price and quantity supplied for a specified period of time, other things being equal.

Law of supply The observation that the higher the price of a good, the more of that good sellers will make available over a specified time period, other things being equal.

The Supply Curve

We can convert the supply schedule in part (a) of Figure 4.6 into a **supply curve**, just as we created a demand curve in Figure 4.1. All we do is take the price-quantity combinations from part (a) of Figure 4.6 and plot them in part (b). We have labelled these combinations *F* through *J*. Connecting these points, we obtain an upward-sloping curve that shows the typically direct relationship between price and quantity supplied. Again, we have to remember that we are talking about quantity supplied *per year*, measured in constant-quality units.

The Market Supply Curve

Just as we had to add the individual demand curves to get the market demand curve, we need to add the individual producers' supply curves to get the market supply curve. Look at Figure 4.7, in which we horizontally sum two typical diskette manufacturers' supply curves. Supplier 1's data are taken from Figure 4.6; supplier 2 is added. The numbers are presented in part (a). The graphical representation of supplier 1 is in part (b), of supplier 2 in part (c), and of the summation in part (d). The result, then, is the supply curve for diskettes for suppliers 1 and 2. There are many more suppliers of diskettes, however. The total market supply schedule and total market supply curve for diskettes are represented in Figure 4.8, with the curve in part (b) obtained by adding all of the supply curves such as those shown in parts (b) and (c) of Figure 4.7. Notice the difference between the market supply curve with only two suppliers in Figure 4.7 and the one with a large number of suppliers—the entire true market—in part (b) of Figure 4.8. There are no kinks in the true total market supply curve because there are so many suppliers.

Observe what happens at the market level when price changes. If the price is $3, the quantity supplied is 60 million diskettes. If the price goes up to $4, the quantity supplied increases to 80 million per year. If the price falls to $2, the quantity supplied decreases to 40 million diskettes per year. Changes in quantity supplied are represented by movements along the supply curve in part (b) of Figure 4.8.

FIGURE 4.6 The Individual Producer's Supply Schedule and Supply Curve for Diskettes

Part (a) shows that at higher prices, a hypothetical supplier will be willing to provide a greater quantity of diskettes. We plot the various price-quantity combinations in part (a) on the grid in part (b). When we connect these points, we find the individual supply curve for diskettes. It is positively sloped.

Part (a)

Combination	Price per Constant-Quality Diskette	Quantity of Diskettes Supplied (thousands of constant-quality units per year)
F	$5	550
G	4	400
H	3	350
I	2	250
J	1	200

Part (b)

FIGURE 4.7 Horizontal Summation of Supply Curves

In part (a), we show the data for two individual suppliers of diskettes. Adding how much each is willing to supply at different prices, we arrive at the combined quantities supplied in column 4. When we plot the values in columns 2 and 3 on grids in parts (b) and (c) and add them horizontally, we obtain the combined supply curve for the two suppliers in question, shown in part (d).

Part (a)

(1) Price per Diskette	(2) Supplier 1 Quantity Supplied (thousands)	(3) Supplier 2 Quantity Supplied (thousands)	(4) = (2) + (3) Combined Quantity Supplied per Year (thousands)
$5	550	350	900
4	400	300	700
3	350	200	550
2	250	150	400
1	200	100	300

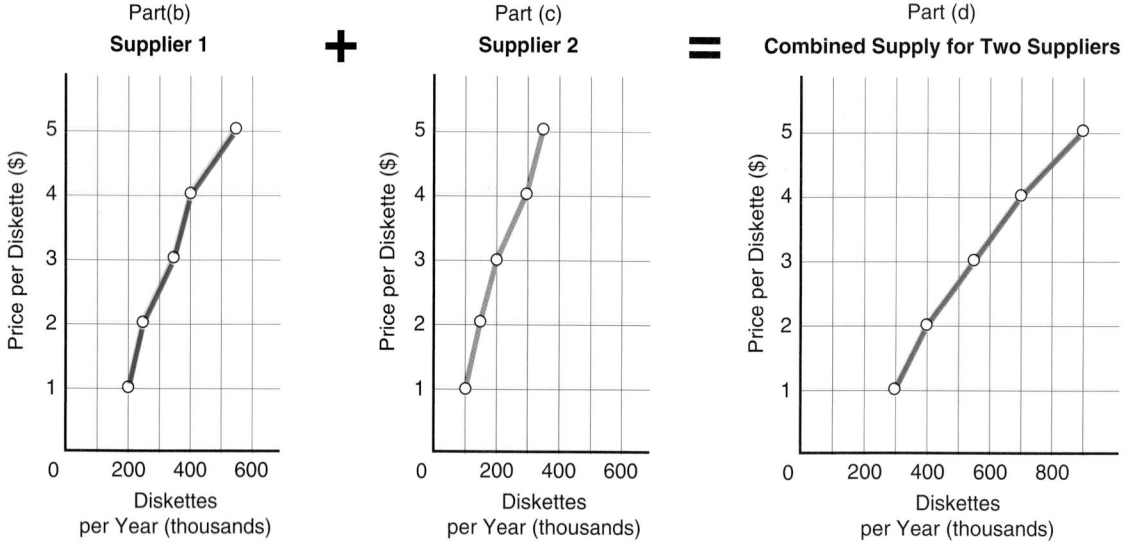

Part(b) **Supplier 1** ＋ Part (c) **Supplier 2** ＝ Part (d) **Combined Supply for Two Suppliers**

FIGURE 4.8 The Market Supply Schedule and the Market Supply Curve for Diskettes

In part (a), we show the summation of all the individual producers' supply schedules; in part (b), we graph the resulting supply curve. It represents the market supply curve for diskettes and is upward-sloping.

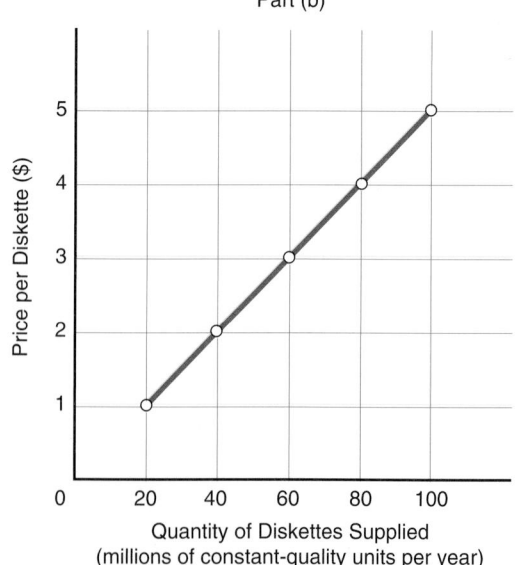

Part (b)

Part (a)

Price per Constant-Quality Diskette	Quantity of Diskettes Supplied (millions of constant-quality units per year)
$5	100
4	80
3	60
2	40
1	20

- There is normally a direct, or positive, relationship between price and the quantity of a good supplied, other things held constant.
- The supply curve normally shows a direct relationship between price and quantity supplied. The market supply curve is obtained by horizontally adding individual supply curves in the market.

Shifts in Supply

When we looked at demand, we found out that any change in anything relevant other than the price of the good or service caused the demand curve to shift inward or outward. The same is true for the supply curve. If something relevant changes apart from the price of the product or service being supplied, we will see the entire supply curve shift.

Consider an example. A new method of putting magnetic material on diskettes has been invented. It reduces the cost of producing a diskette by 50 percent. In this situation, diskette producers will supply more product at all prices because their cost of so doing has fallen dramatically. Competition among diskette manufacturers to produce more at every price will shift the supply schedule of diskettes outward to the right from S_1 to S_2 in Figure 4.9. At a price of $3, the quantity supplied was originally 60 million diskettes per year, but now the quantity supplied (after the reduction in the costs of production) at $3 a diskette will be 90 million diskettes a year. (This is similar to what has happened to the supply curve of personal computers and fax machines in recent years as computer memory chip prices have fallen.)

Now consider the opposite case. If the cost of the magnetic material needed for making diskettes doubles, the supply curve in Figure 4.9 will shift from S_1 to S_3. At each price, the number of diskettes supplied will fall due to the increase in the price of raw materials.

The Other Determinants of Supply

When supply curves are drawn, only the price of the good in question changes, and it is assumed that other things remain constant. The other things assumed constant are the costs

FIGURE 4.9 A Shift in the Supply Schedule

If the cost of producing diskettes were to fall dramatically, the supply schedule would shift rightward from S_1 to S_2 such that at all prices, a larger quantity would be forthcoming from suppliers. Conversely, if the cost of production rose, the supply curve would shift leftward to S_3.

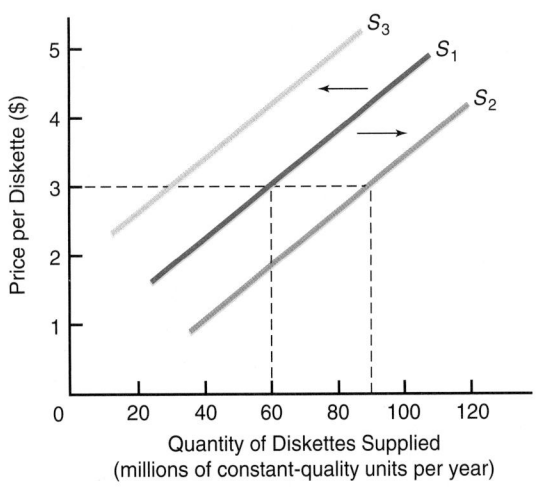

of resources (inputs) used to produce the product, technology and productivity, taxes and subsidies, producers' price expectations, and the number of firms in the industry. These are the major nonprice determinants of supply. If any of them changes, there will be a shift in the supply curve.

COST OF INPUTS USED TO PRODUCE THE PRODUCT. If one or more input price falls, the supply curve will shift outward to the right; that is, more will be supplied at each price. The opposite will be true if one or more inputs becomes more expensive. For example, when we draw the supply curve of new cars, we are holding the cost of steel (and other inputs) constant. When we draw the supply curve of blue jeans, we are holding the cost of cotton fixed.

TECHNOLOGY AND PRODUCTIVITY. Supply curves are drawn by assuming a given technology, or "state of the art." When the available production techniques change, the supply curve will shift. For example, when a better, cheaper, production technique for diskettes becomes available, the supply curve will shift to the right. A larger quantity will be forthcoming at every price because the cost of production is lower.

TAXES AND SUBSIDIES. Certain taxes, such as a per-unit tax, are effectively an addition to production costs and therefore reduce the supply. If the supply curve were S_1 in Figure 4.9, a per-unit tax increase would shift it to S_3. A **subsidy** would do the opposite; it would shift the curve to S_2. Every producer would get a "gift" from the government of a few cents for each unit produced.

Subsidy A negative tax; a payment to a producer from the government, usually in the form of a cash grant.

PRICE EXPECTATIONS. A change in the expectation of a future relative price of a product can affect a producer's current willingness to supply, just as price expectations affect a consumer's current willingness to purchase. For example, diskette suppliers may withhold part of their current supply from the market if they anticipate higher prices in the future. The current amount supplied at all prices will decrease.

NUMBER OF FIRMS IN THE INDUSTRY. In the short run, when firms can only change the number of employees they use, we hold the number of firms in the industry constant. In the long run, the number of firms (or the size of some existing firms) may change. If the number of firms increases, the supply curve will shift outward to the right. If the number of firms decreases, it will shift inward to the left. However, as International Example 4-2 explains, in some instances an increase in the number of producers can lead to a decrease in supply.

Changes in Supply Versus Changes in Quantity Supplied

We cannot overstress the importance of distinguishing between a movement along the supply curve—which occurs only when the price changes for a given supply curve—and a shift in the supply curve—which occurs only with changes in other nonprice factors. A change in price always brings about a change in quantity supplied along a given supply curve. We move to a different coordinate on the existing supply curve. This is specifically called a *change in quantity supplied*. When price changes, quantity supplied changes, and there will be a movement from one point to another along the same supply curve.

When you think of *supply*, think of the entire curve. Quantity supplied is represented by a single point on the curve.

A change in supply causes the entire curve to shift. The *only* thing that can cause the entire curve to shift is a change in a determinant *other than price*.

INTERNATIONAL EXAMPLE 4-2

Caviar Poaching is Making a Pricey Delicacy Even Pricier

You've probably heard that caviar is nothing but fish eggs. That is true, but the best caviar comes from a fish called the sturgeon, which thrives in the waters of the Caspian Sea and the Volga River in Russia. Caviar is a big but dwindling business. The reason is that in years past, poachers have removed so many sturgeon from their watery home that their population today is lower than in prior years.

The immediate effect? A leftward shift in the market supply curve. The market outcome? A big increase in the market price of caviar. In 1998, an ounce of prized caviar from a particular sturgeon, the beluga, sold for $55 US in New York caviar boutiques. Since then, the market price has steadily risen, and within a few years it is expected to top $80 US per ounce.

For critical analysis: The Russian government is trying to beef up its fisheries police force that patrols the Volga River, and countries bordering the Caspian Sea are working on a way to enforce the ban on poaching. If successful, how are these policies likely to affect the market price of caviar?

Consequently,

A change in the price leads to a change in the quantity supplied, other things being constant. This is a movement *along* the curve.

A change in any other determinant of supply leads to a change in supply. This causes a shift *of* the curve.

CONCEPTS IN BRIEF

- If the price changes, we *move along* a curve—there is a change in quantity demanded or supplied. If some other determinant changes, we *shift* a curve—there is a change in demand or supply.
- The supply curve is drawn with other things held constant. If other determinants of supply change, the supply curve will shift. The other major determinants are (1) input costs, (2) technology and productivity, (3) taxes and subsidies, (4) expectations of future relative prices, and (5) the number of firms in the industry.

Putting Demand and Supply Together

In the sections on supply and demand, we tried to confine each discussion to supply or demand only. But you have probably already realized that we can't view the world just from the supply side or just from the demand side. There is an interaction between the two. In this section, we will discuss how they interact and how that interaction determines the prices that prevail in our economy. Understanding how demand and supply interact is essential to understanding how prices are determined in our economy and other economies in which the forces of supply and demand are allowed to work.

Let's first combine the demand and supply schedules and then combine the curves.

Demand and Supply Schedules Combined

Let's place part (a) from Figure 4.3 (the market demand schedule) and part (a) from Figure 4.8 (the market supply schedule) together in part (a) of Figure 4.10. Column 1

FIGURE 4.10 Putting Demand and Supply Together

In part (a), we see that at the price of $3, the quantity supplied and the quantity demanded are equal, resulting in neither an excess in the quantity demanded nor an excess in the quantity supplied. We call this price the equilibrium, or market clearing, price. In part (b), the intersection of the supply and demand curves is at *E*, at a price of $3 per constant-quality diskette and a quantity of 60 million per year. At point *E*, there is neither an excess in the quantity demanded nor an excess in the quantity supplied. At a price of $2, the quantity supplied will be only 40 million diskettes per year, but the quantity demanded will be 80 million. The difference is excess quantity demanded at a price of $2. The price will rise, so we will move from point *A* up the supply curve and point *B* up the demand curve to point *E*. At the other extreme, $5 elicits a quantity supplied of 100 million but a quantity demanded of only 20 million. The difference is excess quantity supplied at a price of $5. The price will fall, so we will move down the demand curve and the supply curve to the equilibrium price, $3 per diskette.

Part (a)

(1) Price per Constant-Quality Diskette	(2) Quantity Supplied (diskettes per year)	(3) Quantity Demanded (diskettes per year)	(4) Difference (2) − (3) (diskettes per year)	(5) Condition
$5	100 million	20 million	80 million	Excess quantity supplied (surplus)
4	80 million	40 million	40 million	Excess quantity supplied (surplus)
3	60 million	60 million	0	Market clearing price—equilibrium (no surplus, no shortage)
2	40 million	80 million	−40 million	Excess quantity demanded (shortage)
1	20 million	100 million	−80 million	Excess quantity demanded (shortage)

Part (b)

shows the price; column 2, the quantity supplied per year at any given price; and column 3, the quantity demanded. Column 4 is merely the difference between columns 2 and 3, or the difference between the quantity supplied and the quantity demanded. In column 5, we label those differences as either excess quantity supplied (a surplus), or excess quantity demanded (a shortage). For example, at a price of $2, only 40 million diskettes would be supplied, but the quantity demanded would be 80 million. The difference is 40 million, which we label as excess quantity demanded (a shortage). At the other end of the scale, a price of $5 per diskette would elicit 100 million in quantity supplied, but quantity demanded would drop to 20 million. This leaves a difference of 80 million units, which we call excess quantity supplied (a surplus).

What do you notice about the price of $3? At that price, the quantity supplied and the quantity demanded per year are both 60 million. The difference, then, is zero. There is neither excess quantity demanded (shortage) nor excess quantity supplied (surplus). Hence the price of $3 is very special. It is called the **market clearing price**—it clears the market of all excess supply or excess demand. There are no willing consumers who want to pay $3 per diskette but are turned away by sellers, and there are no willing suppliers who want to sell diskettes at $3 who cannot sell all they want at that price. Another term for the market clearing price is the **equilibrium price**, the price at which there is no tendency for change. At that price, consumers are able to buy all they want and suppliers are able to sell the quantity that they desire.

Equilibrium

We can define **equilibrium** in general as a point from which there tends to be no movement unless demand or supply changes. Any movement away from this point will set in motion certain forces that will cause movement back to it. Therefore, equilibrium is a stable point. Any point that is not at equilibrium is unstable and cannot be maintained.

The equilibrium point occurs where the supply and demand curves intersect. The equilibrium price is given on the vertical axis directly to the left of where the supply and demand curves cross. The equilibrium quantity demanded and supplied is given on the horizontal axis directly underneath the intersection of the demand and supply curves. Equilibrium can change whenever there is a *shock*.

A shock to the supply-and-demand system can be represented by a shift in the supply curve, a shift in the demand curve, or a shift in both. Any shock to the system will result in a new set of supply-and-demand relationships and a new equilibrium; forces will come into play to move the system from the old price-quantity equilibrium (now a disequilibrium situation) to the new equilibrium, where the new demand and supply curves intersect.

Part (b) from Figure 4.3 and part (b) from Figure 4.8 are combined as part (b) in Figure 4.10 on page 86. The only difference now is that the horizontal axis measures both the quantity supplied and the quantity demanded per year. Everything else is the same. The demand curve is labelled *D*, the supply curve *S*. We have labelled the intersection of the two curves as point *E*, for equilibrium. That corresponds to a market clearing price of $3, at which both the quantity supplied and the quantity demanded are 60 million units per year. There is neither a surplus nor a shortage. Point *E*, the equilibrium point, always occurs at the intersection of the supply and demand curves. This is the price towards which the market price will automatically tend to gravitate.

Shortages

The demand and supply curves in Figure 4.10 represent a situation of equilibrium. But a non-market-clearing, or disequilibrium, price will bring into play forces that cause the price to change, and move towards the market clearing price. Then, equilibrium is again

---

Market clearing, or equilibrium, price The price that clears the market, at which quantity demanded equals quantity supplied; the price where the demand curve intersects the supply curve.

Equilibrium The situation when quantity supplied equals quantity demanded at a particular price.

Try Preview Question 4:
Why will the market clearing price occur at the intersection of the supply and demand curves rather than at a higher or lower price?

sustained. Look once more at part (b) in Figure 4.10 on page 86. Suppose that instead of being at the market clearing price of $3 per diskette, for some reason the market price is $1 per diskette. At this price, the quantity demanded (100 million), exceeds the quantity supplied (20 million). We have a situation of excess quantity demanded at the price of $1. This is usually called a **shortage**. Consumers of diskettes would find that they could not buy all that they wished at $1 apiece. But forces will cause the price to rise: Competing consumers will bid up the price, and suppliers will raise the price and increase output, whether explicitly or implicitly. (Remember, some buyers would pay $5 or more rather than do without diskettes. They do not want to be left out.) We would move from points *A* and *B* towards point *E*. The process would stop when the price again reached $3 per diskette.

> **Shortage** A situation in which quantity demanded is greater than quantity supplied at a price below the market clearing price.

At this point, it is important to recall a distinction made in Chapter 2:

> Shortages and scarcity are not the same thing.

A shortage is a situation in which the quantity demanded exceeds the quantity supplied at a price *below* the market clearing price. Our definition of scarcity was much more general and all-encompassing: a situation in which the resources available for producing output are insufficient to satisfy all wants. Any choice necessarily costs an opportunity, and the opportunity is lost. Hence we will always live in a world of scarcity because we must constantly make choices, but we do not necessarily have to live in a world of shortages.

Surpluses

Now let's repeat the experiment with the market price at $5 per diskette rather than at the market clearing price of $3. Clearly, the quantity supplied will exceed the quantity demanded at that price. The result will be an excess quantity supplied at $5 per unit. This excess quantity supplied is often called a **surplus**. Given the curves in part (b) in Figure 4.10, however, there will be forces pushing the price back down towards $3 per diskette: Competing suppliers will attempt to reduce their inventories by cutting prices and reducing output, and consumers will offer to purchase more at lower prices. Suppliers will want to reduce inventories, which will be above their optimal level; that is, there will be an excess over what each seller believes to be the most profitable stock of diskettes. After all, inventories are costly to hold. But consumers may find out about such excess inventories and see the possibility of obtaining increased quantities of diskettes at a decreased price. It benefits consumers to attempt to obtain a good at a lower price, and they will therefore try to do so. If the two forces of supply and demand are unrestricted, they will bring the price back to $3 per diskette.

> **Surplus** A situation in which quantity supplied is greater than quantity demanded at a price above the market clearing price.

Shortages and surpluses are resolved in unfettered markets—markets in which price changes are free to occur. The forces that resolve them are those of competition: In the case of shortages, consumers competing for a limited quantity supplied drive up the price; in the case of surpluses, sellers compete for the limited quantity demanded, thus driving prices down to equilibrium. The equilibrium price is the only stable price, and all (unrestricted) market prices tend to gravitate towards it.

Changes in Equilibrium

When a non-price determinant of demand or supply changes, this will result in a shift in the demand or the supply curve for the product under study. In turn, this will cause the product's equilibrium price and equilibrium quantity to change. In certain situations, it

FIGURE 4.11 **Shifts in Demand and Supply**

In part (a) the supply curve is stable at S. The demand curve shifts outward, or increases, from D_1 to D_2. The equilibrium price increases from P_1 to P_2 and the equilibrium quantity increases from Q_1 to Q_2. In part (b), with the supply curve stable, the demand curve shifts to the left or decreases. In this case the equilibrium price decreases from P_1 to P_3, while the equilibrium quantity decreases from Q_1 to Q_3. In part (c) the demand curve is stable at D. Now the supply curve shifts to the right or increases. This results in a decrease in the equilibrium price from P_1 to P_2 but an increase in equilibrium quantity increases from Q_1 to Q_2. In part (d) with the demand curve stable at D, there is a leftward shift, or a decrease in the supply. While this causes the equilibrium price to increase from P_1 to P_3, the equilibrium quantity decreases from Q_1 to Q_3.

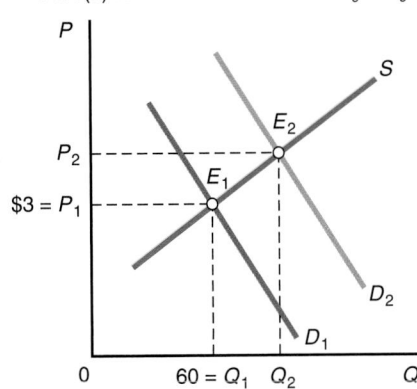

Part (a) An increase in demand: $P_e \uparrow Q_e \uparrow$

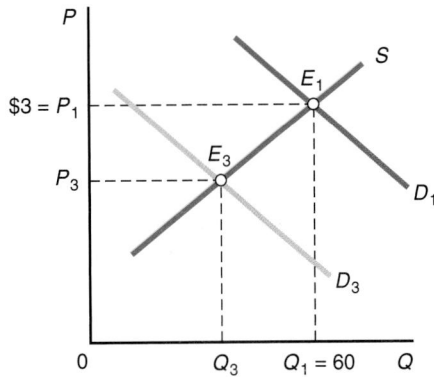

Part (b) An decrease in demand: $P_e \downarrow Q_e \downarrow$

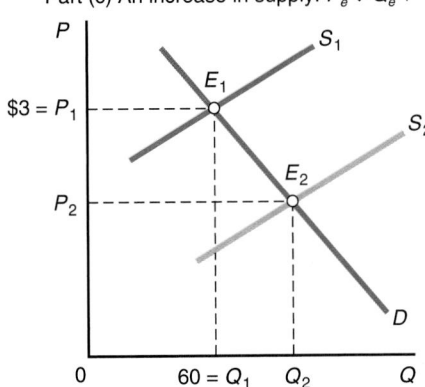

Part (c) An increase in supply: $P_e \downarrow Q_e \uparrow$

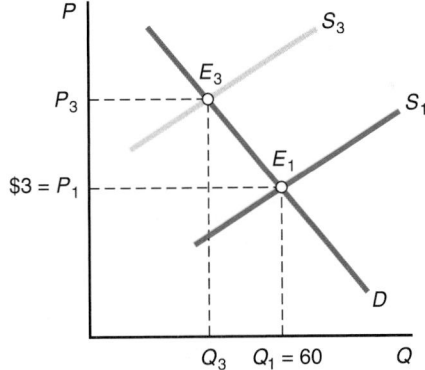

Part (d) An decrease in supply: $P_e \uparrow Q_e \downarrow$

is possible to predict in which direction the equilibrium price and equilibrium will change. Specifically, whenever one curve is stable while the other curve shifts, we can tell what will happen to price and quantity. Consider the four possibilities in Figure 4-11. Each possibility starts with the equilibrium price of diskettes equal to $3.00 ($P_1$) and the equilibrium quantity equal to 60 million diskettes (Q_1).

In part (a), the supply curve remains stable but demand increases from D_1 to D_2. Note that the result is both an increase in the market clearing price of diskettes from P_1 to P_2 and an increase in the equilibrium quantity from Q_1 to Q_2. In part (b), there is a decrease in demand from D_1 to D_3. This results in a decrease in both the relative price of diskettes and the equilibrium quantity. In part (c), the demand curve remains stable but supply increases. The relative price of diskettes falls; the equilibrium quantity increases. In part (d), supply has shifted to the left—there has been a supply decrease. The diskette's relative price increases; the equilibrium quantity decreases.

Try Preview Question 5:

What are the four distinct ways that market equilibrium can change?

When Both Demand and Supply Shift

The examples given in Figure 4-11 each showed a unique outcome of a shift in either the demand curve holding the supply curve constant, or the supply curve holding the demand curve constant. When both supply and demand curves change, the outcome is indeterminate for either equilibrium price or equilibrium quantity.

When both demand and supply increase, all we can be certain of is that equilibrium quantity will increase. We do not know what will happen to equilibrium price until we determine whether demand increased relative to supply (equilibrium price will rise) or supply increased relative to demand (equilibrium price will fall). The same analysis applies to decreases in both demand and supply, except that in this case equilibrium quantity falls.

We can be certain that when demand decreases and supply increases, the equilibrium price will fall, but we do not know what will happen to the equilibrium quantity unless we actually draw the new curves. If supply decreases and demand increases, we can be sure that equilibrium price will rise, but again we do not know what happens to equilibrium quantity without drawing the curves. In every situation in which both supply and demand change, you should always draw the graphs to determine the resulting change in equilibrium price and quantity. That is what we have done to portray the babysitting market in Example 4-3.

EXAMPLE 4-3   Why Babysitters Are Earning More

Though good data are hard to come by, parents today agree that the market price of babysitting is way up. Two factors have worked together to bring this about. To see how, take a look at Figure 4-12. There you see the original supply and demand curves for babysitting services in 1980, labelled S_1 and D_1. The market price is P_1, and the equilibrium quantity is Q_1. Now let's think about two events that occurred in the two decades between 1980 and 1999.

First, there was a population shift. In 1980, there were about 4.4 million Canadians aged 10 to 19, the typical age of babysitters. By 1999, there were almost 7 percent fewer people in this age group. Thus, the number of suppliers of babysitting services declined at any given price; the market supply schedule shifted leftward from S_1 to S_2.

At the same time, the number of children younger than 10 rose from 3.6 million in 1980 to almost 3.9 million in 1999. Furthermore, Canadian incomes rose, so more parents desired to eat out and be entertained without their children in tow. These two factors together increased the demand for babysitting services. That is, at any given price, the quantity of babysitting services demanded rose, and the demand curve shifted from D_1 to D_2.

As you can see in Figure 4-12, the net effect of these two shifts is an unambiguous rise in the market price of babysitting services from P_1 to P_2. The equilibrium quantity of babysitting service may

FIGURE 4-12 The Changing Price of Babysitting Services

Simultaneous shifts in the demand curve for babysitting services from D_1 to D_2 and in the supply curve for babysitting services from S_1 to S_2 will cause the equilibrium price of babysitting services to rise from P_1 to P_2. The equilibrium quantity may increase, decrease, or, as illustrated, remain unchanged.

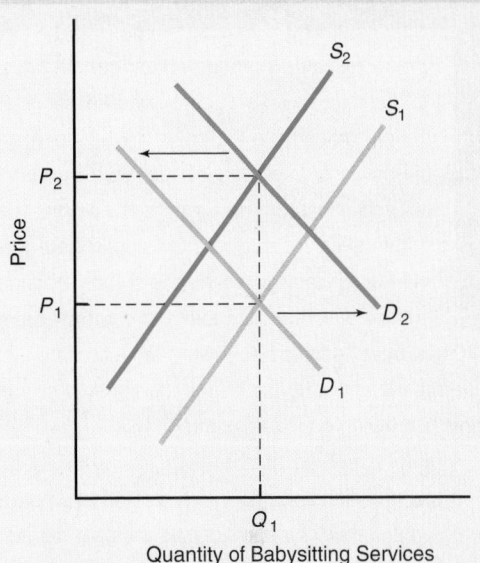

increase or decrease. We have illustrated a situation in which it does not change. That is, it is entirely possible that parents in 1999 are paying a lot more for exactly the same amount of babysitting services that parents purchased at a lower price in 1980.

For critical analysis: Suppose that, in a few years, retiring baby boomers decide to earn extra income by offering to spend some of their time babysitting. What would happen to the equilibrium price of babysitting services? Why?

CONCEPTS IN BRIEF

- The market clearing price occurs at the intersection of the market demand curve and the market supply curve. It is also called the equilibrium price, the price from which there is no tendency to change unless there is a change in demand or supply.
- Whenever the price is greater than the equilibrium price, there is an excess quantity supplied (a surplus). Whenever the price is less than the equilibrium price, there is an excess quantity demanded (a shortage).
- When the demand curve shifts outward or inward with a stable supply curve, equilibrium price and quantity increase or decrease, respectively. When the supply curve shifts outward or inward given a stable demand curve, the equilibrium price moves in the opposite direction to equilibrium quantity.

Stealth Attacks by New Technologies

Successful new products often get off to a slow start. Eventually, however, consumers substitute away from the old products to the point at which demand for the old products effectively disappears. Consider handwritten versus printed manuscripts. For several years in the mid-fifteenth century, printed books were a rarity, and manuscript-copying monks and scribes continued to turn out the bulk of written forms of communication. By the 1470s, however, printed books were more common than handwritten manuscripts. By the end of the fifteenth century, manuscripts had become the rare commodity.

A more recent example involves train engines. Just before 1940, after the diesel-electric engine for train locomotives was invented, an executive of a steam-engine company declared, "They'll never replace the steam locomotive." In fact, it only took 20 years

to prove the executive wrong. By 1960, steam engines were regarded as mechanical dinosaurs.

Some observers of the software industry think the same sort of thing could happen to a powerhouse of the present: Microsoft Windows. Today the code for this program is on most personal computers on the planet. Competing operating system applications offered by Sun Microsystems's Java software and others currently run more slowly than Windows. But they consume many fewer lines of computer code and hence promise swift accessibility via the Internet. It is conceivable that someday people may log on to the Internet and pay by the minute to use such software to run their computers, thereby freeing up their hard drives for other uses. Thus, today's dominant operating system may someday look a lot like a handwritten manuscript does to a generation accustomed to reading printed books instead of handwritten ones.

ISSUES AND APPLICATIONS
Online Auctions: Reaching Equilibrium Price on the Web

Concepts Applied: Demand and supply, shifts in demand and supply, equilibrium

At online auctions on sites such as eBay, we can watch the market find the equilibrium price.

In the absence of constraints, the equilibrium price of just about anything tends toward where the demand curve intersects the supply curve. Notice the word *tends*. As with everything, reaching an equilibrium price takes time. A shift in demand or supply normally does not immediately result in a change in price to its equilibrium level. Where we see the equilibrium price determined rapidly, though, is at auctions. Certain commodities in certain quantities are offered for sale at auctions, typically to the highest bidder. The equilibrium price becomes obvious when the auctioneer pounds the gavel and says something like "Going once, going twice, gone."

Enter the Internet Auction

Nowadays, you can auction off just about anything on the Internet. Indeed, one of the fastest-growing activities on the Internet is the online auction. For example, the Web-based auctioneer company eBay started up in 1995. Now it lists over 450,000 new items every day in 4,320 categories, from Beanie babies to computer equipment to automobiles. When you register to sell an item through eBay, you set a minimum price and choose to participate in a 3-, 5-, 7-, or 10-day auction. The highest bidder at the end of the specified time wins the auction. Then you and your buyer arrange directly for payment and shipping.

As of year 2000, there are over 400 online auction sites. Auction seekers can gain access by using BidFind (www.vsn.net/af/). This is a search engine that allows you to type in the item you would like to purchase. BidFind will display for you a list of matches on the product or service and the names of online auctioneers who have it for sale. There are "hot links" (instant transfers) directly to those sites.

Online Auctions Are Different, Though

Notice the difference between online auctions and traditional auctions. At a traditional auction, you have to go or send a representative who is physically present (although for fine art auctions, you can sometimes do your bidding over the telephone). The auction process for each item takes only a few minutes. On the Internet, in contrast, auctions may last for a day or a week or even longer.

Reverse, or Dutch, Auctions

Rather than the normal "selling to the highest bidder" type of auction, there are also reverse, or Dutch, auctions on the Internet. Klik-Klok Online Dutch Auction (www.klik-klok.com) reverses the normal bidding process. Klik-Klok's gardening tools and jewellery are offered with a clock ticking and prices dropping every few seconds. The first registered user who clicks her computer's mouse gets the product at the currently displayed price.

A very successful reverse auction system has been used by Internet Liquidators. Every five minutes, the prices of offered goods decline. Bidders time their move to get the best price before the goods they wish to buy sell out.

Buying and Selling Electronic Parts Over the Internet

One of the fastest growing online auction markets involves electronics parts. Electronics manufacturing managers routinely end up with too few or too many parts. They do not want to disclose anything about their business to rivals, however. Therefore, they need an anonymous way to auction parts. Today, they use FastParts, which started in 1996. About 300 electronics firms trade their surplus parts at an Internet auction that FastParts holds three times a week. Prices typically average about two-thirds of the original manufacturing cost of the parts.

Getting a Cheap Round Trip to Anywhere

Airlines sometimes find themselves with excess inventory, just as electronics manufacturers do. Many airlines have turned to the Internet to auction off their excess seats. They offer silent auctions and also last-minute fare deals handled via e-mail.

Canadian Airlines has turned to auctions to lure its customers to spend their Canadian Plus frequent-flyer points before its final merger with Air Canada. The airline offers specific round-trip flights for Canadian Plus members to bid on within a 5-day period. For example, two business class tickets between Toronto and Vancouver return normally cost 80,000 frequent-flyer points, but one lucky bidder won the seats for 55,000 points. Table 4-2 highlights some of the auction deals that Canadian Airlines has provided.

TABLE 4-2

Buying a Cheap Round-Trip Ticket on the Internet

Here you see the prices (in Canadian Plus points) of a pair of round-trip tickets obtained via the Canadian Airlines Internet auction compared with the usual value of the tickets.

Route Round trip from a Canadian destination to:	Auction Price	Usual Price
Dallas/Fort Worth, Business Class	62,000	80,000
Chicago, Canadian Class	41,000	50,000
Rome, Business Class	157,000	160,000
Beijing, Canadian Class	122,000	150,000

Source: Based on information from Canadian Airlines

The Future of Online Auctioning

The future of online auctions is limited. Not everyone wants to purchase overstocked, discontinued, or reconditioned items. Even for airline flights and holiday offers, many online auctions attract no bids at all. Nonetheless, some people enjoy the "thrill of the chase" that an auction provides. Online auctions have found their niche.

For Critical Analysis

1. If buyers compete for auctioned products by bidding up the price, what can you conclude about the available supply of those products?

2. Will a successful bid for a particular product set the equilibrium price for other auctions of the same product? Why or why not?

CHAPTER SUMMARY

1. The law of demand says that at higher prices, individuals will purchase less of a commodity and at lower prices, they will purchase more, other things being equal.

2. Relative prices must be distinguished from absolute, or money, prices. During periods of rising prices, almost all prices go up, but some rise faster than others.

3. All references to the laws of supply and demand refer to constant-quality units of a commodity. A time period for the analysis must also be specified.

4. The demand schedule shows the relationship between various possible prices and their respective quantities purchased per unit time period. Graphically, the demand schedule is a demand curve and is downward-sloping.

5. The nonprice determinants of demand are (a) income, (b) tastes and preferences, (c) the prices of related goods, (d) expectations, and (e) population, or market, size. Whenever any of these determinants of demand changes, the demand curve shifts.

6. The supply curve is generally upward-sloping such that at higher prices, more will be forthcoming than at lower prices. At higher prices, suppliers are willing to incur the increasing costs of higher rates of production.

7. The nonprice determinants of supply are (a) input costs, (b) technology and productivity, (c) taxes and subsidies, (d) price expectations, and (e) entry and exit of firms.

8. A movement along a demand or supply curve is not the same thing as a shift of the curve. A change in price causes movement along the curve. A change in any other determinant of supply or demand shifts the entire curve.

9. The demand and supply curves intersect at the equilibrium point, marking the market clearing price, where quantity demanded just equals quantity supplied. At that point, the plans of buyers and sellers mesh exactly.

10. When the price of a good is greater than its market clearing price, an excess quantity is supplied at that price; it is called a surplus. When the price is below the market clearing price, an excess quantity is demanded at that price; it is called a shortage.

11. With a stable supply curve, a rise in demand leads to an increase in equilibrium price and quantity; a decrease in demand leads to a reduction in equilibrium price and quantity. With a stable demand curve, a rise in supply leads to a decrease in equilibrium price and an increase in equilibrium quantity; a fall in supply leads to an increase in equilibrium price and a decrease in equilibrium quantity.

12. When both demand and supply change at the same time, indeterminate results occur. We must know the direction and the degree of each change in order to predict the change in equilibrium price and quantity.

DISCUSSION OF PREVIEW QUESTIONS

1. **Why are relative prices important in understanding the law of demand?**

People respond to changes in relative prices rather than changes in absolute prices. If the price of CDs rises by 50 percent next year, while at the same time the prices of everything else, including your wages, also increase by 50 percent, the relative price of CDs has not changed. If nothing else has changed in your life, your normal quantity demanded of CDs will remain about the same. In a world of generally rising prices (inflation), you have to compare the price of one good with the average of all other goods in order to decide whether the relative price of that one good has gone up, gone down, or stayed the same.

2. **How can we distinguish between a change in demand and a change in quantity demanded?**

Use the accompanying graphs to aid you. Because demand is a curve, a change in demand is equivalent to a *shift* of the demand curve. Changes in demand result from changes in the other determinants of demand, such as income, tastes and preferences, expectations, prices of related goods, and population. A change in quantity demanded, given demand, is a movement along a demand curve and results only from a change in the price of the commodity in question.

A Change in
Demand

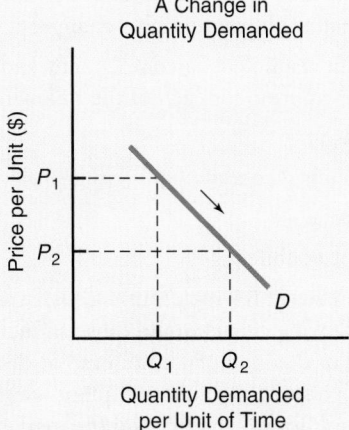

A Change in
Quantity Demanded

3. **Why is there normally a direct relationship between price and quantity supplied (other things being equal)?**

In general, businesses experience increasing *extra* costs as they expand output in the short run. This means that additional units of output, which may be quite similar in physical attributes to initial units of output, actually cost the firm more to produce. Consequently, firms often require a higher and higher price as an incentive to produce more in the short run; this "incentive" effect implies that higher prices, other things being constant, lead to increases in quantity supplied.

4. **Why will the market clearing price occur at the intersection of the supply and demand curves rather than at a higher or lower price?**

Consider the graph above. To demonstrate that the equilibrium price will be at P_e, we can eliminate all other prices as possibilities. Consider a price above P_e, \$8 per unit. By inspection of the graph, we can see that at that price, the quantity supplied exceeds the quantity demanded for this product ($B > A$). Clearly, sellers cannot sell all they wish at \$8, and they therefore find it profitable to lower price and decrease output. In fact, this surplus situation exists at *all* prices above P_e. Sellers, competing for sales, will reduce prices if a surplus exists.

Consider a price of \$4 per unit, where the quantity demanded exceeds the quantity supplied ($F > C$); a shortage of this commodity exists at a price of \$4 per unit. Buyers will not be able to get all they want at that relatively low price. Because buyers are competing for this good, buyers who are willing to give up more of other goods in order to get this one will offer higher and higher prices. By doing so, they eliminate buyers who are not willing to give up more of other goods. An increase in price encourages sellers to produce and sell more. A shortage exists at *any* price below P_e, and therefore price will rise if it is below P_e.

At P_e, the quantity supplied equals the quantity demanded, Q_e, and both buyers and sellers are able to realize their intentions. Because neither group has an incentive to change its behaviour, equilibrium exists at P_e.

5. What are the four distinct ways that market equilibrium can change?

The four distinct ways market equilibrium can change are:

a. An increase in demand will cause equilibrium price and quantity to increase.

b. A decrease in demand will cause equilibrium price and quantity to decrease.

c. An increase in supply will cause equilibrium price to decrease and equilibrium quantity to increase.

d. A decrease in supply will cause equilibrium price to increase and equilibrium quantity to decrease.

PROBLEMS

(Answers to the odd-numbered problems appear at the back of the book.)

4-1. Suppose that, in a recent market period, an industry-wide survey determined the following relationship between the price of rock music CDs and the quantity supplied and demanded.

Price	Quantity Demanded	Quantity Supplied
$ 9	100 million	40 million
$10	90 million	60 million
$11	80 million	80 million
$12	70 million	100 million
$13	60 million	120 million

a. What is the equilibrium price and equilibrium quantity?

b. If the industry price is $13, is there a shortage or a surplus of CDs? How much is the shortage or surplus? Will the price stay at $13? Explain.

c. If the industry price is $10, is there a shortage or a surplus of CDs? How much is the shortage or surplus? Will the price stay at $10? Explain.

4-2. Examine the following table, and then answer the questions.

	Price per Unit Last Year	Price per Unit Today
Heating oil	$1.00	$2.00
Natural gas	.80	3.20

What has happened to the absolute price of heating oil? Of natural gas? What has happened to the price of heating oil relative to the price of natural gas? What has happened to the relative price of natural gas? Will consumers, through time, change their relative purchases? If so, how?

4-3. Suppose that a survey for a later market period indicates that the quantities supplied in the table in Problem 4-1 are unchanged. The quantity demanded, however, has increased by 30 million at each price. Construct the resulting demand curve in the illustration you made for Problem 4-1. Is this an increase or a decrease in demand? What are the new equilibrium quantity and the new market price? Give two examples that might cause such a change.

4-4. Give an example of a complement and a substitute in consumption for each of the following items:

a. Bacon

b. Tennis racquets

c. Coffee

d. Automobiles

4-5. In the market for rock music CDs, explain whether the following events would cause an increase or a decrease in demand or an increase or decrease in the quantity demanded. Also explain what happens to the equilibrium quantity and the market price.

a. The price of CD packaging material declines.

b. The price of CD players declines.

c. The price of cassette tapes increases dramatically.

d. A booming economy increases the income of the typical CD buyer.

e. Many rock fans suddenly develop a fondness for country music.

4-6. Consider the market for laptop computers. Explain whether the following events would cause an increase or a decrease in supply or an increase or a decrease in the quantity supplied. Illustrate each, and show what would happen to the equilibrium market price, given a typical downward-sloping demand curve.

   a. The price of memory chips used in laptop computers declines.

   b. The price of memory chips used in desktop personal computers declines.

   c. The number of manufacturers of laptop computers increases.

   d. The price of computer peripherals, printers, fax-modems, and scanners decreases.

4-7. The following diagram describes the hypothetical monthly demand and supply conditions for eggs in a small provincial market.

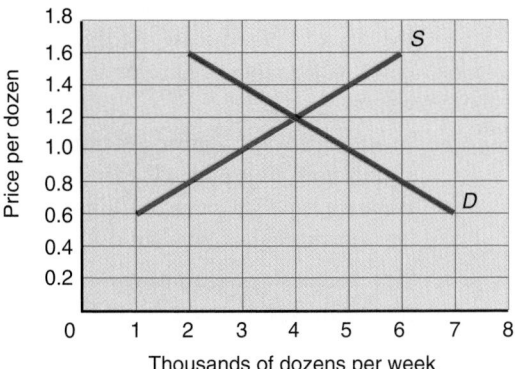

Thousands of dozens per week

   a. If the price in the egg market above was initially at $1.40 per dozen, there would be a (surplus or shortage) equal to ___ thousands of dozens of eggs per week. Will the price stay at $1.40?

   b. If the price in the egg market above was initially at $0.80 per dozen, there would be a (surplus or shortage) equal to ___ thousands of dozens of eggs per week. Will the price stay at $0.80?

   c. Determine the equilibrium price and equilibrium quantity in the egg market described above.

   d. In the egg market described above, explain whether each of the following events would cause an increase or a decrease in demand or supply. Also explain what happens to the equilibrium price and quantity.

   i. Studies show that daily use of eggs reduces the risk of getting serious diseases.

   ii. The cost of feeding chickens significantly increases.

   iii. Average consumer income increases, and eggs are an inferior good.

   iv. The government provides a subsidy to egg producers. A subsidy is a situation where the government pays the egg producers a set amount per dozen produced.

4-8. Airline routes are typically controlled by imposing a quota on the number of airline companies that may use the route and the number of flights on the route. Consequently, the government restricts the number of round-trip seats available on these flight routes. Suppose that the following table describes the daily demand and supply schedules for seats on round-trip flights between Toronto and Vancouver.

Price per seat ($)	Quantity Demanded (no. of seats)	Quantity Supplied (no. of seats)
200	2,000	1,200
300	1,800	1,400
400	1,600	1,600
500	1,400	1,800
600	1,200	2,000

   a. What is the equilibrium price and quantity for the Toronto to Vancouver airline seats? How much, in total dollars, do passengers spend on this route each day?

   b. Suppose the government limits the daily number of round-trip seats to ensure that only 1,200 seats can be available on the Toronto to Vancouver route. What will be the new price per round-trip seat on this route? With the quota policy, do passengers end up spending more or less each day on this same route, in total dollars? Can you think of how this quota policy might actually benefit the passengers (consumers) in the longer run?

4-9. The diagram on the top of the next page describes the hypothetical monthly demand and supply for one-bedroom apartments in a small college town.

   a. What is the equilibrium monthly rent (price) and equilibrium monthly quantity?

   b. Suppose that the mayor of this town decides to make housing more affordable for the local college students by imposing a rent control that holds the price of a one-bedroom apartment to $300 per month.

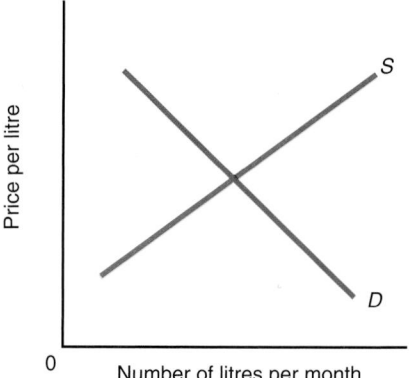

This rent control policy will result in a (shortage or surplus) of _____ units per month.

   c. What will this rent control policy do to the market for two-bedroom apartments which are not regulated by the government? What will happen to the equilibrium price and quantity for the unregulated two-bedroom apartments?

4-10. In May 2000, the Canadian government imposed a tax on bicycles imported from Taiwan and China. Show how this tax affects the market for Taiwanese and Chinese bicycles, shifting the appropriate curve and indicating a new market equilibrium quantity and price. In a separate graph, show the effect of the tax on Canadian-made bicycles, shifting the appropriate curve and indicating the new market equilibrium and price.

4-11. The following diagram describes the market for Canadian red wine. Explain how each of the following sets of events will affect the equilibrium price and equilibrium quantity of Canadian red wine. Note that, in some cases, your answer will be "indeterminate," meaning that, with the given information, you cannot predict the direction of change.

   a. Studies indicate that Canadian red wine reduces the risk of heart disease. At the same time, the cost of the grapes used to produce red wine decreases.

   b. Frost destroys a significant amount of the red grapes used to produce Canadian red wine. At the same time, the price of California red wine, a key substitute for Canadian red wine, increases.

   c. New technology significantly lowers the cost of producing wine. At the same time, the price of Canadian white wine decreases.

ECONOMICS ON THE NET

Canadian Taxes and Energy Markets

The federal government, like the governments of many countries, imposes taxes on some sources of energy and subsidizes other sources of energy. This application helps you apply the concepts you learned in this chapter to evaluate the effects of taxes and subsidies.

Internet URL: http://www.eia.doe.gov/emeu/env/canada.html

Title: Canada Environmental Review

Application: Read the first three sections of this article ("General Background," "Energy and Environmental Policy," and "Energy Taxes and Subsidies"). Then answer the following questions.

1. Draw a diagram of possible demand and supply curves for the market for gasoline. The tax described in the third section of the article is paid by sellers of gasoline. To induce each gasoline seller to supply the same quantity as it would have supplied before the tax, the price that the seller receives must be higher by the amount of the tax. Given this information, illustrate the effect of this tax on the market supply curve. Illustrate and explain how the tax reduces consumption of transportation gas.

2. Draw a diagram of the market for vehicles powered by natural gas. Illustrate the effect of a subsidy on the supply of natural-gas-powered vehicles, and explain how the subsidy encourages the use of these vehicles.

ELASTICITY

World oil prices reached 10-year highs of more than $37 per barrel on September 18, 2000. Those investing in oil and gas shares gleefully watched the Toronto Stock Exchange Oil and Gas Index rise 55 percent during the six-month period preceding September 2000.

Unfortunately, during this same period, European motorists desperate for relief at the pump were disrupting traffic, blockading refineries, and threatening strikes as gas prices soared on the backs of high fuel taxes. The level of frustration peaked in France, where nationwide protests had truckers blockading fuel depots, taxi drivers disrupting traffic, and farmers blocking freight access to the Channel Tunnel.

The theme of this chapter—elasticity—will enhance your understanding of these recent developments in the energy markets.

PREVIEW QUESTIONS

1. What are the different price elasticity of demand ranges?

2. How is total revenue related to the price elasticity of demand?

3. What are the determinants of the price elasticity of demand?

4. How does cross elasticity differ from income elasticity of demand?

5. What is the price elasticity of supply and how is it related to time?

DID YOU KNOW THAT... following the pro-baseball strike in the middle of the 1994-1995 baseball season, the Toronto Blue Jays group and season ticket sales fell by about 50 percent? In an effort to attract fans again, beer prices at the SkyDome were reduced by 20 percent. How could reducing beer prices affect baseball game attendance? The answer lies in understanding the relationship between the quantities that people demand at lower prices relative to the quantities of other goods that people demand at the same time. While attendance did not rise to the usual 51,000 capacity, it rose to about 42,000 and the ball club stayed solvent.

It is not only pro-sports clubs that have to know about how individuals respond to prices; it is important that all businesses take into account consumer response to changing prices. If McDonald's lowers its prices by 10 percent, will fast-food consumers respond by buying so many more Big Macs that the company's revenues will rise? At the other end of the spectrum, can Rolls Royce dealers "get away with" a 2 percent increase in prices? In other words, will Rolls Royce purchasers respond so little to the relatively small increase in price that the total revenues received for Rolls Royce sales will not fall and may actually rise? The only way to answer these questions is to know how responsive people in the real world will be to changes in prices. Economists have a special name for price responsiveness—*elasticity*, which is the subject of this chapter.

Price Elasticity

To begin to understand what elasticity is all about, just keep in mind that it means "responsiveness" or "stretchiness." Here we are concerned with the price elasticity of demand and the price elasticity of supply. We wish to know the extent to which a change in the price of, say, petroleum products will cause the quantity demanded and the quantity supplied to change, other things held constant. Let's restrict our discussion at first to the demand side.

Price Elasticity of Demand

Price elasticity of demand (E_p) The responsiveness of the quantity demanded of a commodity to changes in its price; defined as the percentage change in quantity demanded divided by the percentage change in price.

We will formally define the **price elasticity of demand,** which we will label E_p, as follows:

$$E_p = \frac{\text{percentage change in quantity demanded}}{\text{percentage change in price}}$$

What will price elasticity of demand tell us? It will tell us the relative amount by which the quantity demanded will change in response to a change in the price of a particular good.

Consider an example in which a 10 percent rise in the price of oil leads to a reduction in quantity demanded of only 1 percent. Putting these numbers into the formula, we find that the price elasticity of demand for oil in this case equals the percentage change in quantity demanded divided by the percentage change in price, or

$$E_p = \frac{-1\%}{+10\%} = -.1$$

An elasticity of $-.1$ means that a 1 percent *increase* in the price would lead to a mere 0.1 percent *decrease* in the quantity demanded. If you were now told, in contrast, that the price elasticity of demand for oil was -2, you would know that a 1 percent increase in the price of oil would lead to a 2 percent decrease in the quantity demanded.

Increasing Taxes on Cigarettes

Smoking is responsible for a variety of illnesses, including emphysema and lung cancer. In the 1980s, the federal government launched a two-pronged attack on smoking in an effort to reduce the costs to society. Virtually all smoking-related advertising was banned, even the printing of cigarette brandnames on T-shirts. Smoking was prohibited in all public areas and work sites under federal jurisdiction, and on all flights of domestic airlines. Part two involved a steep increase in the price of cigarettes via an increase in the sales tax, both at the federal level and at the provincial level. The price of cigarettes went up by over 30 percent in a three-year period. By the beginning of 1992, a package of cigarettes cost $5.50. This dramatic increase brought about a reduction in quantity demanded. As the price rose, per capita cigarette consumption dropped by 7 percent in 1989, an additional 6.5 percent in 1990, and a further 13 percent in 1991.

Data over a longer period of time confirm the responsiveness of cigarette consumers to price increases. From 1980 to 1993, the inflation-corrected price of cigarettes increased by 60 percent. Over the same time span, the estimated reduction in adult smoking was 43 percent. The approximate price elasticity of demand was therefore 43 percent ÷ 60 percent = 0.72. That means that in the long run, for every 10 percent increase in the relative price of cigarettes, the expected reduction in adult smoking will be about 7 percent.

For critical analysis: Does the rise of cigarette smuggling which followed the tax increases suggest that the price elasticity of demand for cigarettes is not 0.72? If so, would it be larger or smaller?

RELATIVE QUANTITIES ONLY. Notice that in our elasticity formula, we talk about *percentage* changes in quantity demanded divided by *percentage* changes in price. We are therefore not interested in the absolute changes, only in relative amounts. This means that it doesn't matter if we measure price changes in terms of cents, dollars, or hundreds of dollars. It also doesn't matter whether we measure quantity changes in bushels, grams, or litres. The percentage change will be independent of the units chosen. Refer to Policy Example 5-1 for an illustration.

ALWAYS NEGATIVE. The law of demand states that quantity demanded is *inversely* related to the relative price. An increase in the price of a good leads to a decrease in the quantity demanded. If a decrease in the relative price of a good should occur, the quantity demanded would increase by a certain percentage. The point is that price elasticity of demand will always be negative. By convention, *we will ignore the minus sign in our discussion from this point on.*

Basically, the greater the *absolute* price elasticity of demand (disregarding sign), the greater the demand responsiveness to relative price changes—a small change in price has a great impact on quantity demanded. The smaller the absolute price elasticity of demand, the smaller the demand responsiveness to relative price changes—a large change in price has little effect on quantity demanded. See the Thinking Critically About the Media box on the next page for further insight.

Thinking Critically About the Media 5-1   "If They Doubled the Price, We'd Still Drink Coffee"

Every time there is a frost in Brazil, the price of coffee beans rises, and everyone fears a big rise in the price of coffee. Members of the media interview coffee drinkers and ask how they will respond to the higher prices. Not surprisingly, even when coffee prices soared 150 percent a few years ago, some interviewees said they had to have their cup of coffee no matter what. But if that were true for all coffee drinkers, why don't coffee prices rise as much as bean prices? If what coffee drinkers tell us were really true, their price elasticity of demand would be zero, and the retail price of coffee could skyrocket. But it never does. The truth is, interviewing coffee drinkers (or other consumers) about intentions tells us little. We need to examine the change in total market quantity demanded after an increase in price. The data make it clear: At least some people drink less coffee when the relative price goes up.

CONCEPTS IN BRIEF

- Elasticity is a measure of the price responsiveness of the quantity demanded and quantity supplied.
- The price elasticity of demand is equal to the percentage change in quantity demanded divided by the percentage change in price.
- Price elasticity of demand is calculated in terms of percentage changes in quantity demanded and in price. Thus it is expressed as a unitless, dimensionless number.
- The law of demand states that quantity demanded and price are inversely related. Therefore, the price elasticity of demand is always negative, because an increase in price will lead to a decrease in quantity demanded, and a decrease in price will lead to an increase in quantity demanded. By convention, we ignore the negative sign in discussions of the price elasticity of demand.

Calculating Elasticity

To calculate the price elasticity of demand, we have to compute percentage changes in quantity demanded and in price. To obtain the percentage change in quantity demanded, we divide the change in the quantity demanded by the original quantity demanded:

$$\frac{\text{Change in quantity demanded}}{\text{Original quantity demanded}}$$

To find the percentage change in price, we divide the change in price by the original price:

$$\frac{\text{Change in price}}{\text{Original price}}$$

There is an arithmetic problem, though, when we calculate percentage changes in this manner. The percentage change, say, from 2 to 3—50 percent—is not the same as the percentage change from 3 to 2—$33\frac{1}{3}$ percent. In other words, it makes a difference where you start. One way out of this dilemma is simply to use average values.

To compute the price elasticity of demand, we need to deal with the average change in quantity demanded caused by the average change in price. That means that we take the average of the two prices and the two quantities over the range we are considering and compare the change with these averages. For relatively small changes in price, the formula for computing the price elasticity of demand then becomes

$$E_p = \frac{\text{change in quantity}}{\text{sum of quantities} / 2} \div \frac{\text{change in price}}{\text{sum of prices} / 2}$$

We can rewrite this more simply if we do two things: (1) We can let Q_1 and Q_2 equal the two different quantities demanded before and after the price change and let P_1 and P_2 equal the two different prices. (2) Because we will be dividing a percentage by a percentage, we simply use the ratio, or the decimal form, of the percentages. Therefore,

$$E_p = \frac{\Delta Q}{(Q_1 + Q_2) / 2} \div \frac{\Delta P}{(P_1 + P_2) / 2}$$

where the Greek letter Δ stands for "change in." International Example 5-1, below, provides a real-life example.

INTERNATIONAL EXAMPLE 5-1

The Price Elasticity of Demand for Newspapers

Newspaper owners are always seeking to increase their paper's circulation, not because they want the revenue generated from the sales of the paper, but because the larger the circulation, the more the newspaper can charge for its advertising space. The source of most of a paper's revenues—and profits—is its advertisers.

One newspaper owner, Rupert Murdoch, ran an experiment to see how high he could boost sales of a particular newspaper by lowering its price. For one day, he lowered the price of the British daily paper *Today* from 25 pence to 10 pence. According to London's *Financial Times*, the sales of *Today* almost doubled that day, increasing the circulation from 590,000 to 1.05 million copies. We can estimate the price elasticity of demand for *Today* by using the formula presented earlier (under the assumption, of course, that all other things were held constant):

$$E_p = \frac{\Delta Q}{(Q_1 + Q_2) / 2} \div \frac{\Delta P}{(P_1 + P_2) / 2}$$

$$= \frac{1,050,000 - 590,000}{(590,000 + 1,050,000) / 2} \div \frac{25 \text{ pence} - 10 \text{ pence}}{(10 \text{ pence} + 25 \text{ pence}) / 2}$$

$$= \frac{460,000}{820,000} \div \frac{15 \text{ pence}}{17.5 \text{ pence}} = 0.65$$

The price elasticity of demand of 0.65 means that a 1 percent decrease in price will lead to a 0.65 percent increase in quantity demanded.

For critical analysis: Would the estimated price elasticity of the *Today* newspaper have been different if we had not used the average-values formula? How?

Elastic demand A demand relationship in which a given percentage change in price will result in a larger percentage change in quantity demanded. Total expenditures and price changes are inversely related in the elastic region of the demand curve.

Unit elasticity of demand A demand relationship in which the quantity demanded changes exactly in proportion to the change in price. Total expenditures are invariant to price changes in the unit-elastic region of the demand curve.

Price Elasticity Ranges

We have names for the varying ranges of price elasticities, depending on whether a 1 percent change in price elicits more or less than a 1 percent change in the quantity demanded.

1. *Elastic demand.* We say that a good has an **elastic demand** whenever the price elasticity of demand is greater than 1. A 1 percent change in price causes a change of more than 1 percent in the quantity demanded.
2. *Unit elasticity of demand.* In a situation of **unit elasticity of demand,** a 1 percent change in price causes a response of exactly a 1 percent change in the quantity demanded.

Inelastic demand A demand relationship in which a given percentage change in price will result in a less than proportionate percentage change in the quantity demanded. Total expenditures and price are directly related in the inelastic region of the demand curve.

3. *Inelastic demand.* In a situation of **inelastic demand,** a 1 percent change in price causes a response of less than a 1 percent change in the quantity demanded. The most extreme inelastic demand is *perfectly inelastic;* no matter what the price, the quantity demanded remains the same, so the price elasticity of demand is zero.

When we say a commodity's demand is elastic, we are indicating that consumers are relatively responsive to changes in price. When we say that a commodity's demand is inelastic, we are indicating that its consumers are relatively unresponsive to price changes. When economists say that demand is inelastic, it does not mean that quantity demanded is totally unresponsive to price changes. Remember, the law of demand suggests that there will be some responsiveness in quantity demanded to a price change. The question is how much. That's what elasticity attempts to determine. See International Policy Example 5-1, below.

INTERNATIONAL POLICY EXAMPLE 5-1 — To Cut Drug Abuse, Make the Price of a "High" Higher

Recently, John Tauras of the University of Illinois at Chicago and Michael Grossman of the City University of New York conducted a study of teen use of cocaine. They found that, compared with adults, youthful drug abusers are three times more sensitive to price changes.

Whereas adult cocaine demand is inelastic, teen cocaine demand is nearly unit elastic over the range of market prices tabulated by the US Drug Enforcement Administration. In other words, a 33 percent increase in the market price of cocaine likely would reduce the teen purchases and consumption of cocaine by a third. Undoubtedly, some teens would substitute other drugs. Nonetheless, cocaine and a derivative drug, crack cocaine, are considered addictive substances. Inducing teens to reduce cocaine use might, therefore, take a significant bite out of the nation's longer-term problems with drug abuse.

A policy implication of this study is that legal crackdowns on cocaine dealers that restrict the supply of the drug and push up its price might be an appropriate strategy in the war against drugs.

For critical analysis: According to the elasticity of demand results cited in this example, will a legal crackdown policy on cocaine dealers be more effective in reducing adult or teen abuse of cocaine? Explain. Hint: You may wish to draw two separate demand and supply diagrams to think about this.

Perfectly inelastic demand A demand that exhibits zero responsiveness to price changes; no matter what the price is, the quantity demanded remains the same.

Perfectly elastic demand A demand that has the characteristic that even the slightest increase in price will lead to zero quantity demanded.

Extreme Elasticities

There are two extremes in price elasticities of demand. One extreme represents total unresponsiveness of quantity demanded to price changes, which is referred to as **perfectly inelastic demand,** or zero elasticity. The other represents total responsiveness, which is referred to as infinitely, or **perfectly elastic demand.**

We show perfect inelasticity in part (a) of Figure 5.1. Notice that the quantity demanded per year is 8 million units, no matter what the price. Hence for any percentage price change, the quantity demanded will remain the same, and thus the change in the quantity demanded will be zero. Look back at our formula for computing elasticity. If the change in the quantity demanded is zero, the numerator is also zero, and a nonzero number divided into zero results in an answer of zero too. Hence there is perfect inelasticity. At the opposite extreme is the situation depicted in part (b) of Figure 5.1. Here we show that at a price of 30 cents, an unlimited quantity will be demanded. At a price that is only slightly above 30 cents, no quantity will be demanded. There is complete, or infinite, responsiveness here, and hence we call the demand schedule in part (b) infinitely elastic.

FIGURE 5.1 Extreme Price Elasticities

In part (a), we show complete price unresponsiveness. The demand curve is vertical at the quantity of 8 million units per year. This means that the price elasticity of demand is zero. In part (b), we show complete price re-sponsiveness. At a price of 30 cents, in this example, consumers will de-mand an unlimited quantity of the par-ticular good in question. This is a case of infinite price elasticity of demand.

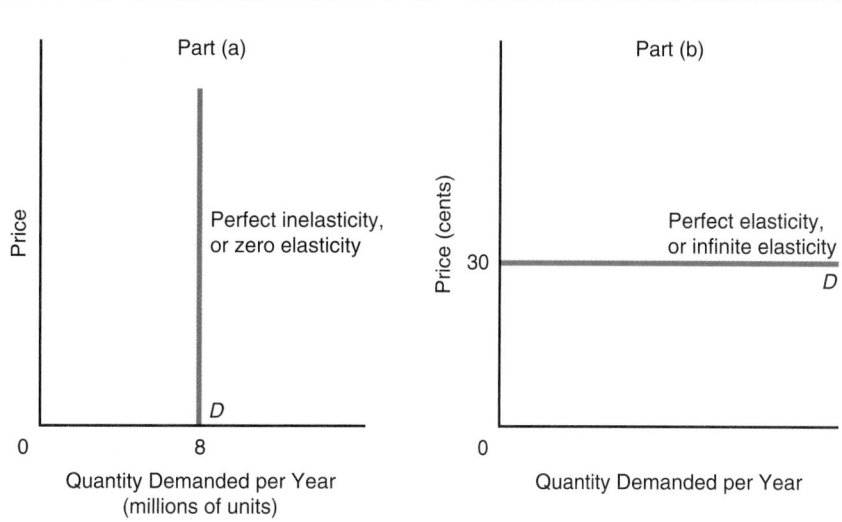

Try Preview Question 1:

What are the different price elasticity of demand ranges?

CONCEPTS IN BRIEF

● One extreme elasticity occurs when a demand curve is vertical. It has zero price elas-ticity of demand; it is completely inelastic.
● Another extreme elasticity occurs when a demand curve is horizontal. It has com-pletely elastic demand; its price elasticity of demand is infinite.

Elasticity and Total Revenues

Suppose that you are in charge of the pricing decision for a cellular telephone service company. How would you know when it is best to raise or not to raise prices? The answer depends in part on the effect of your pricing decision on total revenues, or the total receipts of your company. (The rest of the equation is, of course, your cost structure, a subject we examine in Chapter 10.) It is commonly thought that the way to increase total receipts is to increase price per unit. But is this always the case? Is it possible that a rise in price per unit could lead to a decrease in total revenues? The answers to these questions depend on the price elasticity of demand.

Let's look at Figure 5.2. In part (a), column 1 shows the price of cellular telephone serv-ice in dollars per minute, and column 2 represents billions of minutes per year. In column 3, we multiply column 1 by column 2 to derive total revenue because total revenue is always equal to the number of units (quantity) sold times the price per unit, and in col-umn 4, we calculate values of elasticity. Notice what happens to total revenues through-out the schedule. They rise steadily as the price rises from 10 cents to 50 cents per minute; but when the price rises further to 60 cents per minute, total revenues remain constant at $3 billion. At prices per minute higher than 60 cents, total revenues fall as price increases. Indeed, if prices are above 60 cents per minute, total revenues can be increased only by *cut-ting* prices, not by raising them.

Labelling Elasticity

The relationship between price and quantity on the demand schedule is given in columns 1 and 2 of part (a) in Figure 5.2. In part (b), the demand curve, D, representing that

Part (a)

(1) Price, P, per Minute of Cellular Phone Service	(2) Quantity Demanded, D (billions of minutes)	(3) Total Revenue ($ billions) = (1) × (2)	(4) Elasticity, $E_p = \dfrac{\text{Change in } Q}{(Q_1 + Q_2)/2} \div \dfrac{\text{Change in } P}{(P_1 + P_2)/2}$	
$1.10	0	0		
			21.000	
1.00	1	1.0		
			6.330	
.90	2	1.8		
			3.400	Elastic
.80	3	2.4		
			2.143	
.70	4	2.8		
			1.444	
.60	5	3.0		
			1.000	Unit-elastic
.50	6	3.0		
			.692	
.40	7	2.8		
			.467	
.30	8	2.4		Inelastic
			.294	
.20	9	1.8		
			.158	
.10	10	1.0		

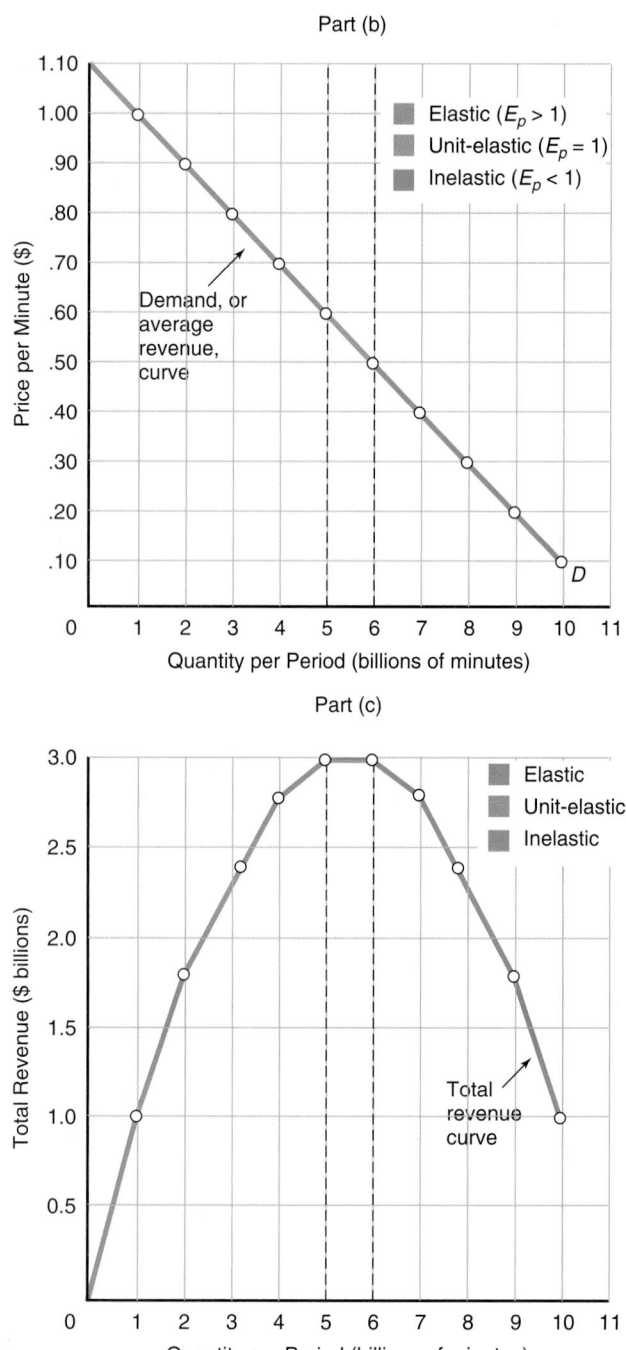

Part (b)

Part (c)

FIGURE 5.2   The Relationship Between Price Elasticity of Demand and Total Revenues for Cellular Phone Service

In part (a), we show the elastic, unit-elastic, and inelastic sections of the demand schedule according to whether a reduction in price increases total revenues, causes them to remain constant, or causes them to decrease, respectively. In part (b), we show these regions graphically on the demand curve. In part (c), we show them on the total revenue curve.

schedule is drawn. In part (c), the total revenue curve representing the data in column 3 is drawn. Notice first the level of these curves at small quantities. The demand curve is at a maximum height, but total revenue is zero, which makes sense according to this demand schedule—at a price of $1.10 and above, no units will be purchased, and therefore total revenue will be zero. As price is lowered, we travel down the demand curve, and total revenues increase until price is 60 cents per minute, remain constant from 60 cents to 50 cents per minute, and then fall at lower unit prices. Corresponding to those three sections, demand is elastic, unit-elastic, and inelastic. Hence we have three relationships among the three types of price elasticity and total revenues.

1. *Elastic demand.* A negative relationship exists between small changes in price and changes in total revenues. That is to say, if price is lowered, total revenues will rise when the firm faces demand that is elastic, and if it raises price, total revenues will fall. Consider another example. If the price of Diet Coke™ were raised by 25 percent and the price of all other soft drinks remained constant, the quantity demanded of Diet Coke™ would probably fall dramatically. The decrease in quantity demanded due to the increase in the price of Diet Coke™ would lead in this example to a reduction in the total revenues of the Coca-Cola Company. Therefore, if demand is elastic, price and total revenues will move in *opposite* directions.
2. *Unit-elastic demand.* Changes in price do not change total revenues. When the firm is facing demand that is unit-elastic, if it increases price, total revenues will not change; if it decreases price, total revenues will not change either.
3. *Inelastic demand.* A positive relationship exists between changes in price and total revenues. When the firm is facing demand that is inelastic, if it raises price, total revenues will go up; if it lowers price, total revenues will fall. Consider another example. You have just invented a cure for the common cold that has been approved by Health Canada for sale to the public. You are not sure what price you should charge, so you start out with a price of $1 per pill. You sell 20 million pills at that price a year. The next year, you decide to raise the price by 25 percent, to $1.25. The number of pills you sell drops to 18 million per year. The price increase of 25 percent has led to a 10 percent decrease in quantity demanded. Your total revenues, however, will rise to $22.5 million because of the price increase. We therefore conclude that if demand is inelastic, price and total revenues move in the *same* direction.

The elastic, unit-elastic, and inelastic areas of the demand curve are shown in Figure 5.2. For prices from $1.10 per minute of cellular phone time to 60 cents per minute, as price decreases, total revenues rise from zero to $3 billion. Demand is price-elastic. When price changes from 60 cents to 50 cents, however, total revenues remain constant at $3 billion; demand is unit-elastic. Finally, when price falls from 50 cents to 10 cents, total revenues decrease from $3 billion to $1 billion; demand is inelastic. In parts (b) and (c) of Figure 5.2, we have labelled the sections of the demand curve accordingly, and we have also shown how total revenues first rise, then remain constant, and finally fall.

The relationship between price elasticity of demand and total revenues brings together some important microeconomic concepts. Total revenues, as we have noted, are the product of price per unit times number of units sold. The law of demand states that along a given demand curve, price and quantity changes will move in opposite directions: One increases as the other decreases. Consequently, what happens to the product of price times quantity depends on which of the opposing changes exerts a greater force on total revenues. But this is just what price elasticity of demand is designed to measure—responsiveness of quantity demanded to a change in price. The relationship between price elasticity of demand and total revenues is summarized in Table 5.1 and illustrated in International Example 5-2.

Try Preview Question 2:
How is total revenue related to the price elasticity of demand?

TABLE 5.1

Relationship Between Price
Elasticity of Demand and Total
Revenues

Price Elasticity of Demand		Effect of Price Change on Total Revenues (TR)	
		Price Decrease	Price Increase
Inelastic	$(E_p < 1)$	TR ↓	TR ↑
Unit-elastic	$(E_p = 1)$	No change in TR	No change in TR
Elastic	$(E_p > 1)$	TR ↑	TR ↓

INTERNATIONAL EXAMPLE 5-2

A Pricing Decision at Disneyland Paris

Several years after it opened with great fanfare, the $4 billion US investment in Disneyland Paris (formerly called EuroDisney) was in trouble. In an attempt to improve profits (actually, to decrease losses), Disney management decided to lower prices starting in the summer of 1995. Entrance fees during peak periods (April 1 to October 1) dropped from 250 francs (about $60) to 195 francs (about $48). Was this 22 percent reduction in ticket prices a good management strategy for Disney officials? That depends in part on what happened to total revenues. As it turned out, park attendance increased by 700,000 visitors. Thus total revenues increased by more than 22 percent, indicating that the demand for Disneyland Paris is elastic in the price range between $48 to $60.

For critical analysis: What other factors may have affected attendance at Disneyland Paris?

CONCEPTS IN BRIEF

- Price elasticity of demand is related to total revenues (and total consumer expenditures).
- When demand is elastic, the change in price elicits a change in total revenues (and total consumer expenditures) in the direction opposite to that of the price change.
- When demand is unit-elastic, a change in price elicits no change in total revenues (or in total consumer expenditures).
- When demand is inelastic, a change in price elicits a change in total revenues (and in consumer expenditures) in the same direction as the price change.

Determinants of the Price Elasticity of Demand

We have learned how to calculate the price elasticity of demand. We know that, theoretically, it ranges numerically from zero, completely inelastic, to infinity, completely elastic. What we would like to do now is come up with a list of the determinants of the price elasticity of demand. The price elasticity of demand for a particular commodity at any price depends, at a minimum, on the following:

1. The existence, number, and quality of substitutes
2. The percentage of a consumer's total budget devoted to purchases of that commodity
3. The length of time allowed for adjustment to changes in the price of the commodity

Existence of Substitutes

The closer the substitutes for a particular commodity and the more substitutes there are, the greater will be its price elasticity of demand. At the limit, if there is a perfect substitute, the elasticity of demand for the commodity will be infinite. Thus even the slightest increase in the commodity's price will cause an enormous reduction in the quantity demanded: quantity demanded will fall to zero. We are really talking about two goods that the consumer believes are exactly alike and equally desirable, like five-dollar bills whose only difference is serial numbers. When we talk about less extreme examples, we can only speak in terms of the number and the similarity of substitutes that are available. Thus we will find that the more narrowly we define a good, the closer and greater will be the number of substitutes available. For example, the demand for a Diet Coke™ may be highly elastic because consumers can switch to Diet Pepsi™. The demand for diet drinks in general, however, is relatively less elastic because there are fewer substitutes.

Share of Budget

We know that the greater the percentage of a total budget spent on the commodity, the greater the person's price elasticity of demand for that commodity. The demand for pepper is thought to be very inelastic merely because individuals spend so little on it relative to their total budgets. In contrast, the demand for things such as transportation and housing is thought to be far more elastic because they occupy a large part of people's budgets—changes in their prices cannot be ignored so easily without sacrificing a lot of other alternative goods that could be purchased.

Consider a numerical example. A household earns $40,000 a year. It purchases $4 of pepper per year and $4,000 of transportation services. Now consider the spending power of this family when the price of pepper and the price of transportation both go up by 100 percent. If the household buys the same amount of pepper, it will now spend $8. It will thus have to reduce other expenditures by $4. This $4 represents only 0.01 percent of the entire household budget. By contrast, a doubling of transportation costs requires that the family spend $8,000—$4,000 more—on transportation, if it is to purchase the same quantity. That increased expenditure on transportation of $4,000 represents 10 percent of total expenditures that must be switched from other purchases. We would therefore predict that the household will react differently to the doubling of prices for pepper than it will for transportation. It will buy almost the same amount of pepper but will spend significantly less on transportation.

Time for Adjustment

When the price of a commodity changes and that price change persists, more people will learn about it. Further, consumers will be better able to revise their consumption patterns the longer the time period they have to do so. And in fact, the longer the time they do take, the less costly it will be for them to engage in this revision of consumption patterns. Consider a price decrease. The longer the price decrease persists, the greater will be the number of new uses that consumers will discover for the particular commodity, and the greater will be the number of new users of that particular commodity.

It is possible to make a very strong statement about the relationship between the price elasticity of demand and the time allowed for adjustment:

> The longer any price change persists, the greater the elasticity of demand, other things held constant. Elasticity of demand is greater in the long run than in the short run.

Let's take an example. Suppose that the price of electricity goes up 50 percent. How do you adjust in the short run? You can turn the lights off more often, you can stop using the stereo as much as you do, and so on. Otherwise it's very difficult to cut back on your consumption of electricity. In the long run, though, you can devise methods to reduce your consumption. Instead of using electric heaters, the next time you have a house built you will install gas heating. Instead of using an electric stove, the next time you move you will have a gas stove installed. You will purchase fluorescent bulbs because they use less electricity. The more time you have to think about it, the more ways you will find to cut your electricity consumption. We would expect, therefore, that the short-run demand curve for electricity would be relatively inelastic (in the price range around P_e), as demonstrated by D_1 in Figure 5.3. However, the long-run demand curve may exhibit much more elasticity (in the neighbourhood of P_e), as demonstrated by D_3. Indeed, we can think of an entire family of demand curves such as those depicted in that figure. The short-run demand curve is for the period when there is no time for adjustment. As more time is allowed, the demand curve goes first to D_2 and then all the way to D_3. Thus in the neighbourhood of P_e, elasticity differs for each of these curves. It is greater for the less steep curves (but, slope alone does not measure elasticity for the entire curve).

HOW TO DEFINE THE SHORT RUN AND THE LONG RUN. We've mentioned the short run and the long run. Is the short run one week, two weeks, one month, two months? Is the long run three years, four years, five years? The answer is that there is no single answer. What we mean by the long run is the period of time necessary for consumers to make a full adjustment to a given price change, all other things held constant. In the case of the demand for electricity, the long run will be however long it takes consumers to switch over to cheaper sources of heating, to buy houses that are more energy-efficient, to purchase appliances that are more energy-efficient, and so on. The long-run elasticity of demand for electricity therefore relates to a period of at least several years. The short run—by default—is any period less than the long run.

Try Preview Question 3:

What are the determinants of the price elasticity of demand?

FIGURE 5.3 Short-Run and Long-Run Price Elasticity of Demand

Consider an equilibrium situation in which the market price is P_e and the quantity demanded is Q_e. Then there is a price increase to P_1. In the short run, as evidenced by the demand curve D_1, we move from equilibrium quantity demanded, Q_e, to Q_1. After more time is allowed for adjustment, the demand curve rotates at original price P_e to D_2. Quantity demanded falls again, now to Q_2. After even more time is allowed for adjustment, the demand curve rotates at price P_e to D_3. At the higher price P_1, in the long run, the quantity demanded falls all the way to Q_3.

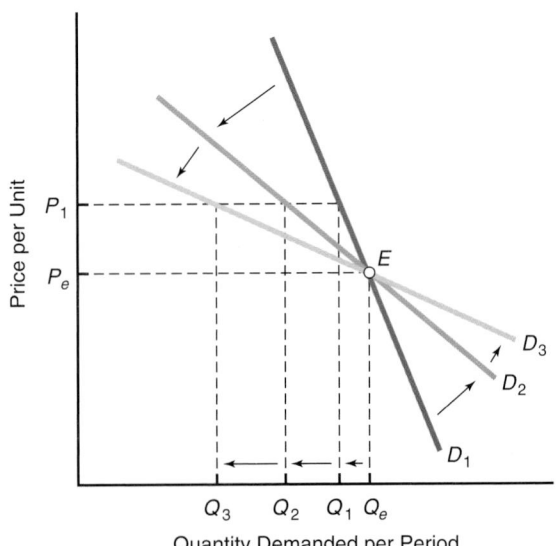

EXAMPLE 5-1   What Do Real-World Price Elasticities
of Demand Look Like?

In Table 5.2, we present price elasticity demand estimates for selected goods. Note that in all cases we are leaving off the negative sign. Remember that these elasticities represent averages over given price ranges. Choosing different price ranges, over a different period, would likely result in different elasticity estimates.

TABLE 5.2

Price Elasticity of Demand for
Selected Goods

Good or Service	Elasticity	Good or Service	Elasticity
Metals	1.52	Chemicals	0.89
Electrical engineering products	1.39	Beverages (all types)	0.78
Mechanical engineering products	1.30	Clothing	0.64
Furniture	1.26	Tobacco	0.61
Motor vehicles	1.14	Banking and insurance services	0.56
Instrument engineering products	1.10	Housing services	0.55
Professional services	1.09	Agricultural and fish products	0.42
Transportation services	1.03	Books, magazines, and newspapers	0.34
Gas, electricity, and water	0.92	Food	0.12
Oil	0.91		

Source: Reprinted from Henri Theil, Ching-Fan Chung, and James L. Seale Jr., *Advances in Econometrics,* Supplement I, 1989, International Evidence on Consumption Patterns (Greenwich, Conn.:JAI Press, 1989), with permission from Elsevier Science.

For critical analysis: What determinants of price elasticity of demand explain the difference in the price elasticity estimates for Food versus Motor vehicles?

Cross Elasticity of Demand

In Chapter 4, we discussed the effect of a change in the price of one good on the demand for a related good. We defined substitutes and complements in terms of whether a reduction in the price of one caused a decrease or an increase, respectively, in the demand for the other. If the price of compact discs is held constant, the amount of CDs demanded (at any price) will certainly be influenced by the price of a close substitute such as audiocassettes. If the price of stereo speakers is held constant, the amount of stereo speakers demanded (at any price) will certainly be affected by changes in the price of stereo amplifiers.

What we now need to do is come up with a numerical measure of the price responsiveness of demand to the prices of related goods. This is called the **cross elasticity of demand** (E_{xy}), which is defined as the percentage change in the quantity demanded of one good divided by the percentage change in the price of the related good. In equation form, the cross elasticity of demand for good X with respect to good Y is

Cross elasticity of demand (E_{xy}) The percentage change in the quantity demanded of one good (holding its price constant) divided by the percentage change in the price of a related good.

$$E_{xy} = \frac{\text{percentage change in quantity demanded of good X}}{\text{percentage change in price of good Y}}$$

When two goods are substitutes, the cross elasticity of demand will be positive. For example, when the price of margarine goes up, the demand for butter will rise too as consumers shift away from the now relatively more expensive margarine to butter. A producer of margarine could benefit from a numerical estimate of the cross elasticity of demand between butter and margarine. For example, if the price of butter went up by 10 percent and the margarine producer knew that the cross elasticity of demand was 1, the margarine producer could estimate that the demand for margarine would also go up by 10 percent at any given price. Plans for increasing margarine production could then be made.

When two related goods are complements, the cross elasticity of demand will be negative (and we will not disregard the minus sign). For example, when the price of stereo amplifiers goes up, the demand for stereo speakers will fall. This is because as prices of amplifiers increase, the quantity of amplifiers demanded will naturally decrease. Because amplifiers and stereo speakers are often used together, the demand for speakers is likely to fall. Any manufacturer of stereo speakers must take this into account in making production plans.

If goods are completely unrelated, their cross elasticity of demand will be zero. Read Policy Example 5-2 for further discussion on cross elasticity.

POLICY EXAMPLE 5-2 | **Should Public Libraries Be Shut Down?**

The public library has been an institution in Canada for years. Most public libraries are paid for out of property taxes. Some policymakers argue that there is no reason to subsidize public libraries anymore. Why? Because individuals are gradually shifting their demand from the use of *physical* public libraries to online information services, such as Netscape, and others available over the Internet. As the price of online information has fallen, the demand for traditional library services has dropped. Though no one has calculated the exact cross elasticity of demand for traditional library services, the decrease in usage of such libraries shows that it is significant.

For critical analysis: Compare your costs of using a library with those for using on-line information services.

Income Elasticity of Demand

In Chapter 4, we discussed the determinants of demand. One of those determinants was income. Briefly, we can apply our understanding of elasticity to the relationship between changes in income and changes in demand. We measure the responsiveness of quantity demanded to income changes by the **income elasticity of demand (E_i):**

Income elasticity of demand (E_i) The percentage change in the quantity demanded of any good holding its price constant, divided by the percentage change in income; the responsiveness of demand to changes in income, holding the goods relative price constant.

$$E_i = \frac{\text{percentage change in quantity demanded}}{\text{percentage change in income}}$$

holding relative price constant.

Income elasticity of demand refers to a *horizontal shift* in the demand curve in response to changes in income, whereas price elasticity of demand refers to a movement *along* the curve in response to price changes. Thus income elasticity of demand is calculated at a given price, and price elasticity of demand is calculated at a given income.

A simple example will demonstrate how income elasticity of demand can be computed. Table 5.3 gives the relevant data. The product in question is compact discs. We assume that the price of compact discs remains constant relative to other prices. In period 1, six

TABLE 5.3 How Income Affects Quantity of CDs Demanded		

Period	Number of CDs Demanded per Month	Income per Month
1	6	$400
2	8	600

CDs per month are purchased. Income per month is $400. In period 2, monthly income increases to $600, and the quantity of CDs demanded per month increases to eight. Using the same mid-point formula that we used in computing the price elasticity of demand, we get:

$$E_i = \frac{(8 - 6) / 7}{(600 - 400) / 500} = \frac{2/7}{2/5} = \frac{5}{7} = 0.714$$

Notice that the sign of the income elasticity of demand is positive. That is because as income rises, the quantity of CDs demanded also increases. In Chapter 4, we defined this kind of good as a "normal" good—one that we want more of as our income increases. An "inferior" good is one that we want less of as our income increases. The sign of the income elasticity of demand for an inferior good will therefore be negative, since quantity demanded will decrease as income increases. It is important to retain the negative sign on the income elasticity of demand for an inferior good, since the sign tells us whether the good is in fact normal or inferior.

You have just been introduced to three types of elasticities. Two of them—the price elasticity of demand (E_p), and income elasticity (E_i)—are the two most important factors in influencing the quantity demanded for most goods. Reasonably accurate estimates of these can go a long way towards making accurate forecasts of demand for goods or services. For an illustration of income elasticity, see Example 5-2, below.

Try Preview Question 4:

How does cross elasticity differ from income elasticity of demand?

EXAMPLE 5-2   Frequent Flyer Miles as Income

For the past 10 years, airlines have been discovering that consumers measure their incomes in more than one way. Most airlines now offer frequent flyer points for air travel, and many are affiliated with other carriers and businesses as well. For example, Air Canada gives frequent flyer points for travel on United Airlines and for renting cars from Budget Rent-a-Car. Travellers can also apply for a Visa card that gives them one frequent flyer mile for every dollar charged. The first of these programs began in 1981. Air Canada started its Aeroplan program in 1984 with 14,000 members; five months later it had 62,000. Now there are over 2 million members. Worldwide there are more than 42 million members of various plans, with over 2 trillion points outstanding.

At the same time, airlines have found the demand for their services increasing. Air Canada alone reported a 16 percent increase in passenger volumes between 1995 and 1996, with much of the increment attributed to "free flights" earned through frequent flyer programs. It appears that air travellers count their frequent flyer miles as part of their incomes, thus they demand more air travel as their incomes increase.

For critical analysis: The federal government has decided that the value of flights paid for with frequent flyer miles earned while travelling on business should be considered part of an individual's income—and thus be liable to income tax. What effect will this have on the income elasticity of demand for air travel?

CONCEPTS IN BRIEF

- Some determinants of price elasticity of demand are (1) the existence, number, and quality of substitutes, (2) the share of the total budget spent on the good in question, and (3) the length of time allowed for adjustment to a change in prices.
- Cross elasticity of demand measures one good's demand responsiveness to another's price changes. For substitutes, it is positive; for complements, it is negative.
- Income elasticity of demand tells you by what percentage demand will change for a particular percentage change in income.

Elasticity of Supply

Price elasticity of supply (E_s)
The responsiveness of the quantity supplied of a commodity to a change in its price; the percentage change in quantity supplied divided by the percentage change in price.

The **price elasticity of supply (E_s)** is defined similarly to the price elasticity of demand. Supply elasticities are generally positive; this is because at higher prices, larger quantities will generally be forthcoming from suppliers. The definition of the price elasticity of supply is as follows:

$$E_s = \frac{\text{percentage change in quantity supplied}}{\text{percentage change in price}}$$

Classifying Supply Elasticities

Just as with demand, there are different types of supply elasticities. They are similar in definition to the types of demand elasticities.

If a 1 percent increase in price elicits a greater than 1 percent increase in the quantity supplied, we say that at the particular price in question on the supply schedule, *supply is elastic.* The most extreme elastic supply is called **perfectly elastic supply**—the slightest reduction in price will cause quantity supplied to fall to zero.

Perfectly elastic supply A supply characterized by a reduction in quantity supplied to zero when there is the slightest decrease in price.

If, conversely, a 1 percent increase in price elicits a less than 1 percent increase in the quantity supplied, we refer to that as an *inelastic supply.* The most extreme inelastic supply is called **perfectly inelastic supply**—no matter what the price, the quantity supplied remains the same.

Perfectly inelastic supply A supply for which quantity supplied remains constant, no matter what happens to price.

If the percentage change in the quantity supplied is just equal to the percentage change in the price, we call this *unit-elastic supply.*

We show in Figure 5.4 two supply schedules, S and S'. You can tell at a glance, without reading the labels, which one is infinitely elastic and which one is perfectly inelastic. As you might expect, most supply schedules exhibit elasticities that are somewhere between zero and infinity.

Price Elasticity of Supply and Length of Time for Adjustment

We pointed out earlier that the longer the time period allowed for adjustment, the greater the price elasticity of demand. It turns out that the same proposition applies to supply. The longer the time for adjustment, the more elastic the supply curve. Consider why this is true:

1. The longer the time allowed for adjustment, the more firms are able to figure out ways to increase (or decrease) production in an industry.
2. The longer the time allowed for adjustment, the more resources can flow into (or out of) an industry through expansion (or contraction) of existing firms.

We therefore talk about short-run and long-run price elasticities of supply. The short run is defined as the time period during which full adjustment has not yet taken place. The long run is the time period during which firms have been able to adjust fully to the change in price.

FIGURE 5.4 The Extremes in Supply Curves

Here we have drawn two extremes of supply schedules: S is a perfectly elastic supply curve; S' is a perfectly inelastic one. In the former, an unlimited quantity will be supplied at price P_1. In the latter, no matter what the price, the quantity supplied will be Q_1. An example of S' might be the supply curve for fresh fish on the morning the boats come in.

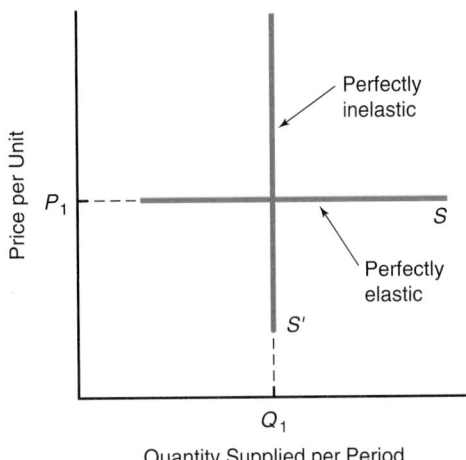

Consider an increase in the price of housing. In the very short run, when there is no time allowed for adjustment, the amount of housing offered for rent or for sale is relatively inelastic. However, as more time is allowed for adjustment, current owners of the housing stock can find ways to increase the amount of housing they will offer for rent from given buildings. The owner of a large house can decide, for example, to have two children move into one room so that a "new" extra bedroom can be rented out. This can also be done by the owner of a large house who decides to move into an apartment and rent each floor of the house to a separate family. Thus the quantity of housing supplied will increase. With more time, landlords will find it profitable to build new rental units.

We can show a whole set of supply curves similar to the ones we generated for demand. As Figure 5.5 shows, when nothing can be done in the short run, the supply curve is

FIGURE 5.5 Short-Run and Long-Run Price Elasticity of Supply

Consider a situation in which the price is P_e and the quantity supplied is Q_e. In the short run, we hypothesize a vertical supply curve, S_1. With the price increase to P_1, therefore, there will be no change in the short run in quantity supplied; it will remain at Q_e. Given some time for adjustment, the supply curve will rotate to S_2. The new amount supplied will increase to Q_1. The long-run supply curve is shown by S_3. The amount supplied again increases to Q_2.

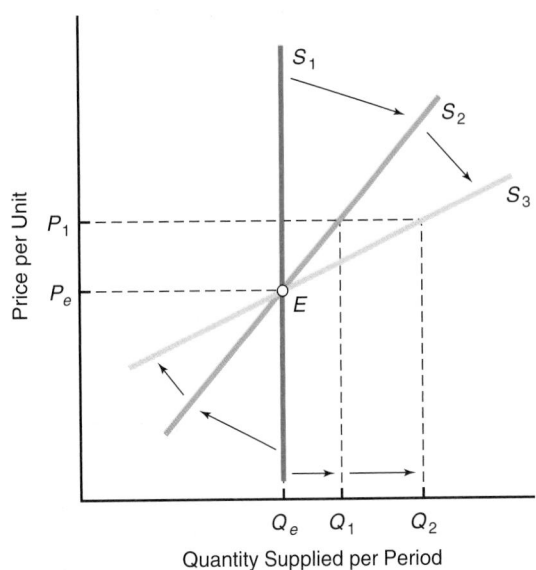

Try Preview Question 5:

What is the price elasticity of supply and
how is it related to time?

vertical, S_1. As more time is allowed for adjustment, the supply curve rotates to S_2 and then to S_3, becoming more elastic as it rotates.

CONCEPTS IN BRIEF

- Price elasticity of supply is calculated by dividing the percentage change in quantity supplied by the percentage change in price.
- Usually, price elasticities of supply are positive—higher prices yield larger quantities supplied.
- Long-run supply curves are more elastic than short-run supply curves because the longer the time allowed, the more resources can flow into or out of an industry when price changes.

NETNOMICS

How Clever Internet Companies Infer Their Customers' Price Elasticity of Demand

As you learned in this chapter, a company that wishes to increase its revenues should raise the price it charges customers with an inelastic demand for the goods it sells. By contrast, a firm can bring about an increase in its revenues by reducing the price it charges customers whose demand is elastic.

Increasingly, companies are using the Internet to try to have it both ways. One California software firm has developed a program that allows Internet sellers to track the shopping patterns of customers who visit their Web sites. The software studies a Web surfer's "clickstream"—the manner in which the customer navigates through the Web site. For example, if the customer quickly zeroes in on a specific item and makes little effort to shop around for substitutes or better prices, the software tags the customer as one whose demand for that item is likely to be relatively inelastic. The program then automatically quotes a relatively high price. If another Web surfer who visits the same site behaves like a price-sensitive shopper—perhaps by comparing many different products without jumping to buy—the program concludes that the customer's demand is more likely to be relatively elastic. It then automatically quotes a lower price for this price-sensitive customer.

ISSUES AND APPLICATIONS

The Y2K Energy Crisis

Concepts Applied: Supply and demand, price elasticity of demand, policy analysis

Truckers demonstrating in Toronto in 2000 asked the government for cuts to gasoline taxes.

Just after the Y2K bug fears subsided, economies around the globe were caught off guard by a problem which, ironically, had plagued the preceding millenium—an energy crisis brought on by the OPEC cartel.

Who is OPEC?

OPEC refers to the Organization of the Petroleum Exporting Countries which consists of 11 major nation suppliers of crude oil. It is estimated that OPEC members, in total, possess about 78 percent of the world's total proven crude oil reserves. Economists view OPEC as a cartel, that is, an association of producers that agrees to set production quotas (restricting oil supplies) in order to avoid competition. This strategy enhances the profits of these oil producers by keeping the crude oil prices higher than would be the case if these suppliers directly competed against each other.

World Oil Prices in the Late 1990s

Between 1997 and 1998, total OPEC crude oil production increased by a rate of 2.4 million barrels per day (mb/d). During this same period Japan and other Asia Pacific nations experienced a serious economic slowdown. As a result, with total OPEC crude oil production (excluding Iraq) at 25.65 mb/d, the price of oil fell to a low of $11.08 US per barrel of WTI (West Texas Intermediate Crude) in December 1998.

In a series of meetings held between 1998 and 1999, OPEC (excluding Iraq) agreed to cut back their members' total production rate to 23.77 mb/d by December 1999. As a result, the price of crude oil rose to $26.21 in December 1999.

In response to a renewed global concern over high energy prices, OPEC agreed to increase their total oil production rate to 25.4 mb/d in July 2000. On September 11 of the same year, OPEC agreed to increase production to 26.2 mb/d starting in October 2000. Despite the increases in OPEC oil production, oil prices reached 10-year highs of more than $37 per barrel on September 18, 2000.

In September 2000, a number of events and factors were affecting the world oil market. The OPEC nations, other than Saudi Arabia, were producing oil at close to full capacity. The world oil tanker fleet capacity had fallen by 13.1 m tonnes as a result of 171 tanker vessels recently being sent to demolition. In the Middle East, Iraq had revived accusations that Kuwait was stealing its oil and warned of unspecified measures against the neighbour it invaded in 1990. The global economy had been growing at a faster pace than in recent years. With the United States facing a situation of a 40 percent national shortfall in heating oil stocks, manufacturers of heating oil were desperately stepping up production plans for the cold winter months.

Should the Canadian Government Lower Excise Taxes on Gasoline?

Since 1998 gasoline fuel prices have increased in response to the upward trend in crude oil prices. In Canada, as displayed in Figure 5.6, in July 1998 the average price of regular unleaded gas (self-serve) was $0.53 per litre.

For the week ending September 22, 2000, the Canadian average price of regular unleaded gas was $0.75 per litre—an increase of 42 percent since 1998. The rapid increase in fuel prices has focused attention towards the size of the excise taxes that Canadian governments have imposed on a litre of gasoline in the fall of 2000. Since the federal government increased the gasoline excise tax by $0.015 per litre in 1995, the federal government had been imposing an overall excise tax of $0.10 per litre of gasoline sold. The Canadian provinces, on average, levied an additional $0.15 per-litre gasoline excise tax. In September 2000, the GST collected another $0.05 per litre of tax. In other words 40 percent of the retail gasoline price in Canada in September 2000 was due to government taxes.

In the fall of 2000 the Canadian parliament was in the midst of debating a motion by the opposition Canadian Alliance Party calling on the Liberal government to repeal the $0.015 increase in the federal oil excise tax which was supposed to have been a temporary tax hike aimed at reducing the federal deficit in 1995.

FIGURE 5.6 International Retail Gas Prices, July 1998

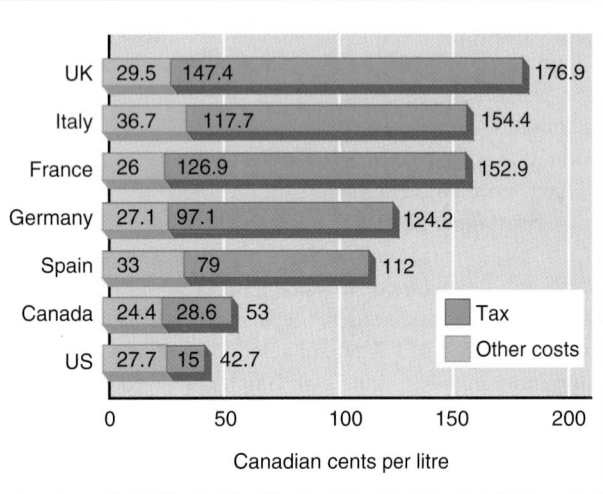

Canadian cents per litre

Sources: Adapted from "The OPEC Annual Report 1999." Publications. OPEC Online. 27 Sept. 2000. <http://www.opec.org/193.81.181.14/xxx1/publications.htm>; Announcements. OPEC Online. 27 Sept. 2000. <http://www.opec.org/193.81.181.14/xxx1/announcements.htm>; "Pressure builds to cut fuel taxes." Oil and Gas. 21 Sept. 2000. Canoe Money. 27 Sept. 2000. <http://www.canoe.ca/MoneyOilTemp/sept21_gastaxes-rtr.html>; "Canadian Retail Gas Prices, Week ending September 22." Weekly Gas Prices. 22 Sept. 2000. Petroleum Communication Foundation. <http://www.pcf.ab.ca/wk_gas_prices/default.asp>.

For Critical Analysis

1. With the aid of a supply and demand diagram, explain what happened to OPEC crude oil prices between 1997 and 1998.

2. Based on the information given above, compute the elasticity of demand for OPEC crude oil over the period December 1998 to December 1999. According to your elasticity calculation, is the demand for OPEC crude oil elastic or inelastic? Did the total oil revenue collected by the OPEC countries increase or decrease between December 1998 and December 1999? Is this consistent with the theory of elasticity? Explain.

3. What demand factors were responsible for the rapid increase in OPEC crude oil prices experienced in September, 2000? Similarly, what supply factors contributed to the increase in OPEC crude oil prices which occurred in September 2000?

4. In 1995, the liberal government increased the excise tax on gasoline in order to increase government revenue. Does this suggest that the liberal government believed that the demand for crude oil was elastic or inelastic? Explain.

5. With the aid of a supply and demand diagram, explain how a decrease in the gasoline excise tax would affect the equilibrium price and quantity of Canadian gasoline. In turn, how would this policy affect other markets such as taxi services, trucking services, and courier services?

6. From an environmental point of view, is it wise to decrease excise taxes on gasoline? Explain.

CHAPTER SUMMARY

1. Price elasticity of demand is a measure of the percentage change in quantity demanded relative to the percentage change in price, given income, the prices of other goods, and time. Because of the law of demand, price elasticity of demand is always negative.

2. We classify demand as *elastic* if a 1 percent change in price leads to a more than 1 percent change in quantity demanded, *unit-elastic* if it leads to exactly a 1 percent change in quantity demanded, and *inelastic* if it leads to less than a 1 percent change in quantity demanded.

3. When facing a perfectly elastic demand, the slightest increase in price leads to zero quantity demanded; when facing a perfectly inelastic demand, no matter what the price, the quantity demanded remains unchanged. Perfect inelasticity means absolutely no price responsiveness.

4. Price elasticity of demand falls as we move down a straight-line demand curve. It goes from infinity to zero. Elasticity and slope are not equivalent; for example, the slope of a straight-line curve is always constant, whereas elasticity changes as we move along a linear curve. A vertical demand curve is perfectly inelastic; a horizontal demand curve is perfectly elastic.

5. Price elasticity of demand depends on (a) the existence, number, and quality of substitutes, (b) the share of total budget accounted for by the commodity, and (c) the length of time allowed for adjustment to changes in price of the commodity.

6. Cross elasticity of demand measures the responsiveness of the demand for one product, either a substitute or a complement, to changes in the price of another product. When the cross elasticity of demand is negative, the two commodities under study are complements; when the cross elasticity of demand is positive, they are substitutes.

7. Income elasticity of demand is given by the percentage change in quantity demanded divided by the percentage change in income, given relative price. When the income elasticity of demand is positive, the good in question is a normal good; when the income elasticity of demand is negative, the good is an inferior good.

8. Price elasticity of supply is given by the percentage change in quantity supplied divided by the percentage change in price. The greater the time allowed for adjustment, the greater the price elasticity of supply.

DISCUSSION OF PREVIEW QUESTIONS

1. What are the different price elasticity of demand ranges?

A good has an elastic demand whenever the price elasticity of demand exceeds 1. This implies that a 1 percent change in price causes a change of more than 1 percent in the quantity demanded. In contrast, a good has an inelastic demand whenever the price elasticity of demand is less than 1. This means that a 1 percent change in price causes a change of less than 1 percent in the quantity demanded. In a situation of unit elasticity of demand, a 1 percent change in price causes a response of exactly a 1 percent change in the quantity demanded.

2. How is total revenue related to the price elasticity of demand?

Total revenue is defined as price times quantity demanded; because price changes lead to changes in quantity demanded, total revenue and elasticity are intimately related. If, over the price range in question, demand is inelastic, this means that buyers are relatively unrespon-sive to price changes. Intuitively, then, we know that if price rises and quantity demanded does not fall by much, total revenue will rise. Conversely, if price falls and quantity demanded rises only slightly, total revenue will fall. If, over the price range in question, demand is elastic, buyers will be quite responsive to price changes. We can tell intuitively that if price rises and quantity demanded falls greatly, total revenue will fall. Similarly, if price falls and quantity demanded rises greatly, total revenue will rise. Finally, if we are in the range of unit elasticity, given percentage changes in price will lead to equal percentage changes in quantity. Thus total revenue remains unaffected in the unit-elasticity range.

3. What are the determinants of the price elasticity of demand?

Three major determinants of price elasticity of demand are (a) the existence, number, and quality of substitutes, (b) the share of the total budget that the commodity represents, and (c) the length of time buyers have to react to price changes. Clearly, the more substitutes and the better they are, the greater will be the price elasticity of demand. Therefore, the price elasticity of demand rises as we consider the commodities "fruit," then "oranges," then "Mandarin oranges"; more and better substitutes exist for a specific brand of oranges than for the fruit group. Also, when a commodity takes up a small percentage of the consumer budget (other things being constant), we expect the price elasticity of demand to be lower, compared with items important to a budget. Presumably, buyers will have a greater incentive to shop around and seek substitutes for high-cost items than for low-cost items. Finally, for a given percentage change in price, quantity responsiveness (and therefore elasticity) will increase with the time period allowed for adjustment. With the passage of time, buyers are better able to find and use substitutes.

4. **How does cross elasticity of demand differ from income elasticity of demand?**

The cross elasticity of demand for a good measures the percentage change in the quantity demanded of one good divided by the percentage change in price of a related good. This measure can indicate how closely related a substitute or complement good is to the product being studied.

The income elasticity of demand for a good measures the percentage change in demand for a good divided by the percentage change in income. This measure can indicate whether the good being examined is either a normal or inferior good.

5. **What is the price elasticity of supply and how is it related to time?**

Price elasticity of supply refers to the responsiveness of sellers to changes in price. Technically, price elasticity of supply is defined as the percentage change in quantity supplied divided by the percentage change in price. The resulting measure can be greater than, equal to, or less than the number 1—referred to as elastic, unit-elastic, and inelastic supply, respectively. The longer the adjustment time, the greater the quantity responsiveness of sellers to given price changes (and hence the greater the price elasticity of supply).

PROBLEMS

(Answers to the odd-numbered problems appear at the back of the book.)

5-1. Use the following hypothetical demand schedule for tea to answer the questions.

Quantity Demanded per Week (kilograms)	Price per Kilogram	Elasticity
1,000	$ 5	
800	10	_____
600	15	_____
400	20	_____
200	25	

a. Using the mid-point formula, determine the elasticity of demand for each price change. (Example: When price changes from $5 to $10, quantity demanded changes from 1,000 to 800 kilograms, so the elasticity of demand, using average values, is $\frac{1}{3}$, or .33.)

b. The data given in the demand schedule would plot as a straight-line demand curve. Why is demand more elastic the higher the price?

5-2. Calculate the price elasticity of demand for the product in the table below using average values for the prices and quantities in your formula. Over the price range in question, is this demand schedule inelastic, unit-elastic, or elastic? Is total revenue greater at the lower price or the higher price?

Price per Unit	Quantity Demanded
$4	22
6	18

5-3. Calculate the income elasticity of demand for the product in the following table, using average values for incomes and quantities.

Quantity of VCRs per Year	Per Capita Annual Group Income
1,000	$15,000
2,000	20,000

a. Is the demand for this product income-elastic or income-inelastic?

b. Would you consider this commodity a luxury or a necessity?

5-4. Can any demand curve possibly be perfectly inelastic ($E_p = 0$) regardless of price? Explain.

5-5. A new mobile home park charges nothing whatsoever for water used by its inhabitants. Consumption is 100,000 litres per month. The decision is then made to charge according to how much each mobile home owner uses, at a rate of $10 per 1,000 litres. Consumption declines to 50,000 litres per month. What is the difficulty here in accurately estimating the price elasticity of the demand for water by these residents?

5-6. Which of the following cross elasticities of demand would you expect to be positive and which to be negative?

a. Tennis balls and tennis racquets

b. Tennis balls and golf balls

c. Dental services and toothpaste

d. Dental services and candy

e. Soft drinks and ice cubes

f. Soft drinks and fruit juices

5-7. Suppose that the price of salt rises from 15 cents to 17 cents a kilogram. The quantity demanded decreases from 525 kilograms to 475 kilograms per month, and the quantity supplied increases from 525 kilograms to 600 kilograms per month. (Use averages in calculating elasticities.)

a. Calculate the price elasticity of demand (E_p) for salt.

b. Is the demand for salt price-elastic or price-inelastic?

c. Calculate the elasticity of supply (E_s) for salt.

d. Is the supply for salt price-elastic or price-inelastic?

5-8. Suppose that an automobile dealer cuts his car prices by 15 percent. He then finds that his car sales revenues have increased by 10 percent.

a. What can you say about the price elasticity of demand for cars?

b. What will happen to the dealer's total revenue?

5-9. For any given relative price, would you think that the demand for canal transportation was more or less elastic in 1840 than in 1890? How about the demand for rail transportation before and after the Model T Ford? The demand for transatlantic cable-laying equipment before and after communications satellites? The demand for slide rules before and after introduction of the pocket-sized calculator? Why?

ECONOMICS ON THE NET

The Price Elasticity of Demand for Cigarettes

This activity will encourage you to review economic research which attempts to compare the price elasticity of demand for cigarettes for youth (and young adult) consumers with the price elasticity of demand for cigarettes for older adult consumers. This type of research can help governments decide if it is wise to significantly increase the price of cigarettes through higher excise taxes.

Internet URL:

http://www.scarcnet.org/hsap/tax.htm# youthestimates

Title: The Impact of Proposed Cigarette Price Increases by Frank K Chaloupka (Ph.D)

Application: After reviewing the contents of this site, answer the following questions.

a. Briefly explain two reasons why one might expect to find (in theory) that youth and young adults will be more responsive to changes in the price of cigarettes than older adults.

b. According to the recent studies concluded by Chaloupka and Wechsler (1997), does the price elasticity of demand evidence support a government policy of significantly increasing taxes on cigarettes as an effective way to achieve long-run reduction in smoking in all segments of the population?

THE PUBLIC SECTOR

In Canada, over the course of a year, thousands of tax lawyers and accountants labour alone or with clients to help those clients reduce their tax liabilities and fill out their tax returns. Canadian taxpayers are each estimated to spend approximately 20 hours a year preparing their taxes. The opportunity cost exceeds $4 billion a year. And that is not the end of the story—many individuals spend a lot of valuable time figuring out ways to change their behaviour so as to reduce the taxes they owe. Although there is never any way to avoid the cost of a tax system completely, there are ways to reduce compliance costs to society. One way is to switch to a more simplified tax system. To understand this issue, you need to know more about government and the public sector.

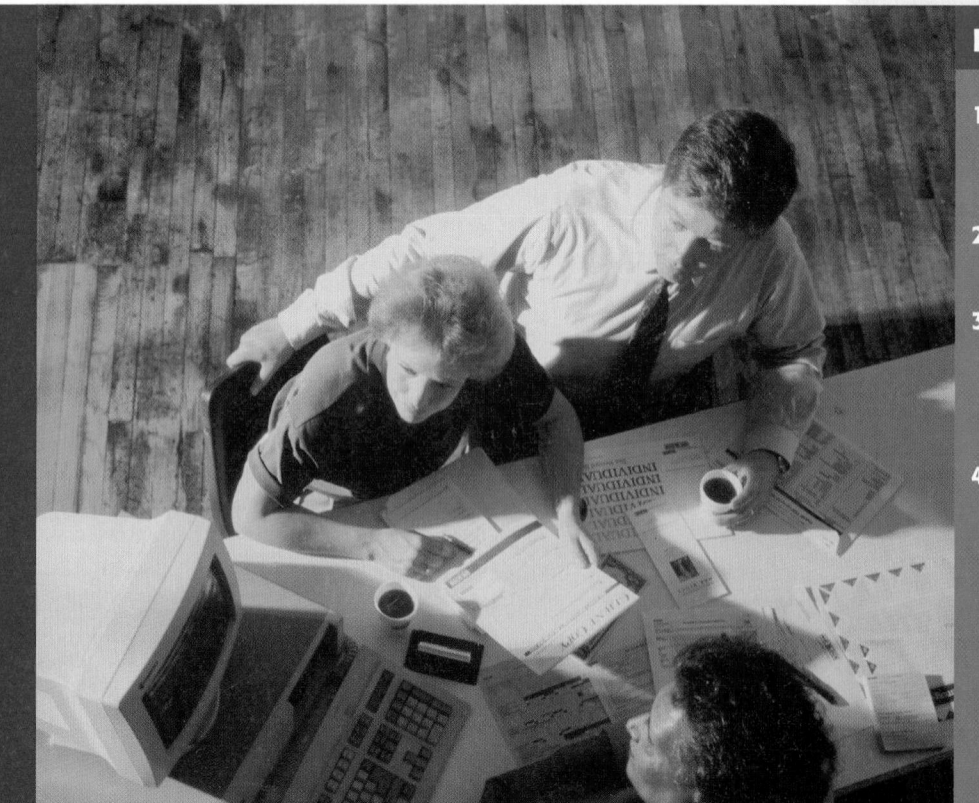

PREVIEW QUESTIONS

1. What are the economic and political functions of the public sector?

2. What is the foundation of public-choice theory?

3. In what ways do regressive, proportional, and progressive tax structures differ?

4. How do the federal government's spending habits differ from those of the provinces?

DID YOU KNOW THAT... the average Canadian works from January 1 through June 27 each year to pay for all municipal, provincial, and federal taxes? The average Vancouver resident works approximately two weeks longer to pay for all of the taxes owed each year when compared to the typical Ontario resident. Looked at another way, the average Canadian in a typical eight-hour day works about 3 hours and 54 minutes to pay for government at all levels. The average household with two or more people spends about $23,218 a year in taxes of all kinds. The total amount paid exceeds $270 billion. It would take more than 270,000 millionaires to have as much money as is spent each year by government. So we cannot ignore the presence of government in our society. Government exists, at a minimum, to take care of what the price system does not do well.

What a Price System Can and Cannot Do

Throughout the book so far, we have alluded to the benefits of a price system. High on that list of benefits is economic efficiency. In its most ideal form, a price system allows resources to move from lower-valued uses to higher-valued uses through voluntary exchange. The supreme point of economic efficiency occurs when all mutually advantageous trades have taken place. In a price system, consumers are sovereign; that is to say, they have the individual freedom to decide what they wish to purchase. Politicians and even business managers do not ultimately decide what is produced; consumers decide. Some supporters of the price system argue that this is its most important characteristic. A market organization of economic activity generally prevents one person from interfering with another in respect to most of that individual's activities. Competition among sellers protects consumers from coercion by one seller, and sellers are protected from coercion by one consumer because other consumers are available.

Sometimes the price system does not generate these results, with too few or too many resources going to specific economic activities. Such situations are called **market failures**. Market failures prevent the price system from attaining economic efficiency and individual freedom, as well as other social goals. Market failures offer one of the strongest arguments in favour of certain economic functions of government, which we now examine.

Market failure A situation in which an unrestrained market economy leads to too few or too many resources going to a specific economic activity.

Correcting for Externalities

In a pure market system, competition generates economic efficiency only when individuals know the true opportunity cost of their actions. In some circumstances, the price that someone actually pays for a resource, good, or service is higher or lower than the opportunity cost that all of society pays for that same resource, good, or service.

Consider a hypothetical world in which there is no government regulation against pollution. You are living in a town that until now has had clean air. A steel mill moves into town. It produces steel and has paid for the inputs—land, labour, capital, and entrepreneurship. The price it charges for the steel reflects, in this example, only the costs that the steel mill incurred. In the course of production, however, the mill gets one input—clean air—by simply taking it. This is indeed an input because in the making of steel, the furnaces emit smoke. The steel mill doesn't have to pay the cost of using the clean air; rather, it is the people in the community who pay that cost in the form of dirtier clothes, dirtier cars and houses, and more respiratory illnesses. The effect is similar to what would happen if the steel mill could take coal or oil or workers' services free. There has been an **externality**, an external cost. Some of the costs associated with the production of the steel have "spilled over" to affect **third parties**, parties other than the buyer and the seller of the steel.

Externality A consequence of an economic activity that spills over to affect third parties. Pollution is an externality.

Third parties Parties other than the buyer and seller of the product.

External Costs in Graphical Form

Look at part (a) in Figure 6.1. Here we show the demand curve for steel to be D. The supply curve is S_1. The supply curve includes only the costs that the firms have to pay. The equilibrium, or market clearing, situation will occur at quantity Q_1. Let us take into account the fact that there are externalities—the external costs that you and your neighbours pay in the form of dirtier clothes, cars, and houses, and increased respiratory disease due to the air pollution from the steel mill; we also assume that all other suppliers of steel use clean air without having to pay for it. Let's include these external costs in our graph to find out what the full cost of steel production really is. This is equivalent to saying that the price of an input used in steel production increased. Recall from Chapter 4 that an increase in input prices shifts the supply curve inward to the left. Thus in part (a) of the figure, the supply curve shifts from S_1 to S_2. If the external costs were somehow taken into account, the equilibrium quantity would fall to Q_2 and the price would rise to P_2. Otherwise, that price is implicitly being paid, but by two different groups of people. The lower price, P_1, is being explicitly paid for by the purchasers of steel and steel products. The difference between P_2 and P_1 represents the cost that third parties are bearing in the form of dirtier clothes, houses, and cars, and increased respiratory illnesses.

External Benefits in Graphical Form

Externalities can also be positive. To demonstrate external benefits in graphical form, we will use the example of vaccinations against influenza. In part (b) of Figure 6.1, we show the demand curve as D_1 (without taking account of any external benefits) and the supply curve as S. The equilibrium price is P_1, and the equilibrium quantity is Q_1. We assume,

FIGURE 6.1 External Costs and Benefits

In part (a), we show a situation in which the production of steel generates external costs. If the steel mills ignore pollution, at equilibrium the quantity of steel will be Q_1. If the mills had to pay for the additional cost borne by nearby residents that is caused by the steel mill's production, the supply curve would shift inward to the left to S_2. If consumers were forced to pay a price that reflected the spillover costs, the quantity demanded would fall to Q_2. In part (b), we show the situation in which vaccinations against influenza generate external benefits to those individuals who may not be vaccinated but who will benefit because epidemics will not occur. If each individual ignores the external benefit of the flu shot, the market clearing quantity will be Q_1. If external benefits are taken into account by purchasers of flu shots, however, the demand curve would shift rightward to D_2. The new equilibrium quantity would be Q_2 and the price would be higher, P_2.

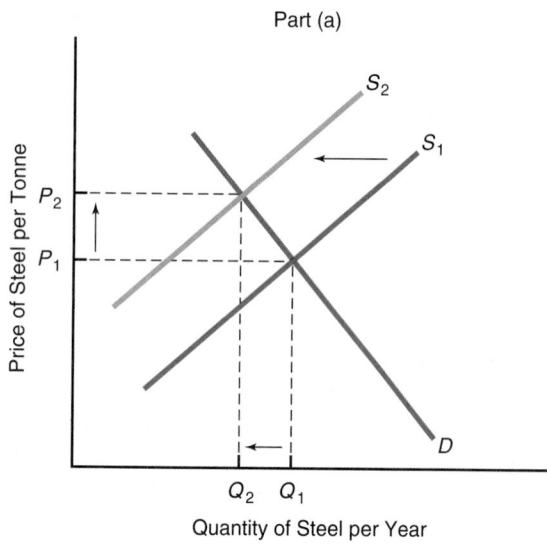

Part (a)

Price of Steel per Tonne

Quantity of Steel per Year

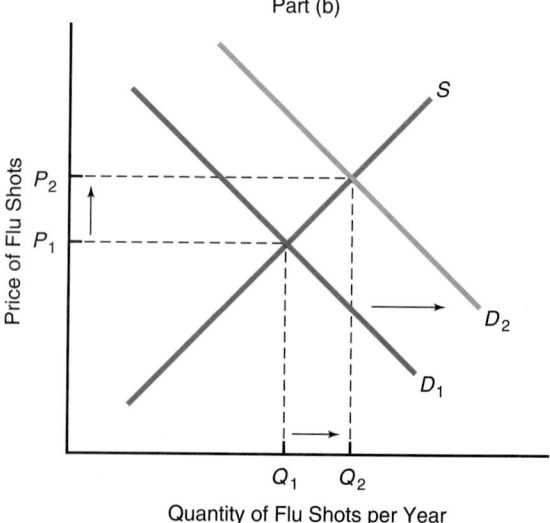

Part (b)

Price of Flu Shots

Quantity of Flu Shots per Year

however, that flu shots generate external benefits to individuals who may not be vaccinated but will benefit nevertheless because epidemics will not break out. If such external benefits were taken into account, the demand curve would shift outward from D_1 to D_2. The new equilibrium quantity would be Q_2, and the new equilibrium price would be P_2. With no corrective action, this society is not devoting enough resources to flu shots.

When there are external costs, the market will tend to overallocate resources to the production of the good or service in question, for those goods or services will be deceptively low-priced. With the example of steel, too much will be produced because the steel mill owners and managers are not required to take account of the external cost that steel production is imposing on the rest of society. In essence, the full cost of production is unknown to the owners and managers, so the price they charge the public for steel is lower than it would be otherwise. And of course, the lower price means that buyers are willing and able to buy more. More steel is produced and consumed than is socially optimal.

When there are external benefits, the market underallocates resources to the production of that good or service because the good or service is relatively too expensive (because the demand is relatively too low). In a market system, too many of the goods that generate external costs are produced and too few of the goods that generate external benefits are produced.

How the Government Corrects Negative Externalities

The government can in theory correct externality situations in a variety of ways in all cases that warrant such action. In the case of negative externalities, at least two avenues are open to the government: special taxes and legislative regulation or prohibition.

SPECIAL TAXES.   In our example of the steel mill, the externality problem originates from the fact that the air as a waste disposal place is costless to the firm but not to society. The government could make the steel mill pay a tax for dumping its pollutants into the air. The government could attempt to tax the steel mill commensurate with the cost to third parties from smoke in the air. This, in effect, would be a pollution tax, or an **effluent fee**. The ultimate effect would be to reduce the supply of steel and raise the price to consumers, ideally making the price equal to the full cost of production to society.

REGULATION. To correct a negative externality arising from steel production, the government could specify a maximum allowable rate of pollution. This action would require that the steel mill install pollution abatement equipment within its facilities, that it reduce its rate of output, or some combination of the two. Note that the government's job would not be that simple, for it still would have to determine the level of pollution and then actually measure its output from steel production in order to enforce such regulation.

How the Government Corrects Positive Externalities

What can the government do when the production of one good spills benefits over to third parties? It has several policy options: financing the production of the good or producing the good itself, subsidies (negative taxes), and regulation.

GOVERNMENT FINANCING AND PRODUCTION.   If the positive externalities seem extremely large, the government has the option of financing the desired additional production facilities so that the "right" amount of the good will be produced. Consider again vaccinations against communicable diseases. The government frequently finances campaigns to vaccinate the population. It even operates centres where such vaccinations are free.

Effluent fee A charge to a polluter that gives the right to discharge into the air or water a certain amount of pollution. Also called a pollution tax.

SUBSIDIES. A subsidy is a negative tax; it is a payment made either to a business or to a consumer when the business produces, or the consumer buys, a good or a service. In the case of vaccinations against influenza, the government could subsidize everyone who obtains a flu shot by directly reimbursing those vaccinated or by making payments to doctors who provide the shots. If you are attending a university or college, taxpayers are helping to pay the cost of providing your education; you are being subsidized by as much as 80 percent of the total cost. Subsidies reduce the net price to consumers, thereby causing a larger quantity to be demanded.

REGULATION. In some cases involving positive externalities, the government can require by law that a certain action be undertaken by individuals in the society. For example, regulations require that all school-aged children be vaccinated before entering public and private schools. Some people believe that a basic school education itself generates positive externalities. Perhaps as a result of this belief, we have regulations—laws—that require all school-aged children to be enrolled in a public or private school.

CONCEPTS IN BRIEF

- External costs lead to an overallocation of resources to the specific economic activity. Two possible ways of correcting these spillovers are taxation and regulation.
- External benefits result in an underallocation of resources to the specific activity. Three possible government corrections are financing the production of the activity, subsidizing private firms or consumers to engage in the activity, and regulation.

The Other Economic Functions of Government

Besides compensating for externalities, the government performs many other functions that affect the way in which exchange is carried out in the economy.

Let's look at four more economic functions of government.

Providing a Legal System

The courts and the police may not at first seem like economic functions of government (although judges and police personnel must be paid). Their activities nonetheless have important consequences on economic activities in any country. You and I enter into contracts constantly, whether they be oral or written, expressed, or implied. When we believe that we have been wronged, we seek redress of our grievances within our legal institutions. Moreover, consider the legal system that is necessary for the smooth functioning of our system. Our system has defined quite explicitly the legal status of businesses, the rights of private ownership, and a method for the enforcement of contracts. All relationships among consumers and businesses are governed by the legal rules of the game. We might consider the government in its judicial function, then, as the referee when there are disputes in the economic arena.

Property rights The rights of an owner to use and to exchange property.

Much of our legal system is involved with defining and protecting **property rights**. Property rights are the rights of an owner to use and to exchange that property. One might say that property rights are really the rules of our economic game. When property rights are well defined, owners of property have an incentive to use the property efficiently. Any mistakes in their decision about the use of property have negative consequences that the owners suffer. Furthermore, when property rights are well defined, owners of property have an incentive to maintain that property so that if those owners ever desire to sell it, it will fetch a better price.

Establishing and maintaining a well-functioning legal system is not a costless activity, as you can see in International Policy Example 6-1.

INTERNATIONAL POLICY EXAMPLE 6-1

Who Should Pay the High Cost of a Legal System?

When a huge multinational gets into a lengthy and expensive "shouting match" with its detractors, the public ends up footing part of the legal bill. McDonald's operates worldwide, with annual sales of about $50 billion. It has property rights in the goodwill associated with its name. When two unemployed British social activists published a pamphlet with such chapter headings as "McDollar, McGreedy, McCancer, McMurder, McRipoff, McTorture, and McGarbage," McDonald's was not pleased. The pamphlet accused the American company of torturing animals, corrupting children, and exploiting the Third World. So McDonald's went to court in London. When the case began, there were 26 preliminary hearings spread over a four-year time period, and when it went to trial, 180 witnesses were called. McDonald's itself will end up spending many millions of dollars, but British taxpayers will foot the entire bill for the use of the court system. According to the Lord Chancellor's Department, British taxpayers will pay at least £2.5 million (well over $5.5 million).

Should taxpayers continue to pay for all of the court system? No, according to policymakers in Britain. They have a plan to make litigants pay the full cost of court services, specifically judges' salaries. Such a system that forces litigants to pay for the full opportunity cost of the legal system has yet to be instituted in Canada or elsewhere.

For critical analysis: What other costs, besides judges' salaries, do citizens implicitly pay for in their legal system?

Promoting Competition

Anticombines legislation Laws that restrict the formation of monopolies and regulate certain anti-competitive business practices.

Monopoly A firm that has great control over the price of a good. In the extreme case, a monopoly is the only seller of a good or service.

Many people believe that the only way to attain economic efficiency is through competition. One of the roles of government is to serve as the protector of a competitive economic system. The federal and provincial governments have passed **anticombines legislation**. Such legislation makes illegal certain (but not all) economic activities that might, in legal terms, restrain trade—that is, prevent free competition among actual and potential rival firms in the marketplace. The avowed aim of anticombines legislation is to reduce the power of **monopolies**—firms that have great control over the price of the goods they sell. A number of laws have been passed that prohibit specific anti-competitive business behaviour. The Competition Bureau, which is part of Industry Canada, attempts to enforce these anticombines laws. Various provincial judicial agencies also expend efforts at maintaining competition.

Providing Public Goods

Private goods Goods that can be consumed by only one individual at a time. Private goods are subject to the principle of rival consumption.

Principle of rival consumption The recognition that individuals are rivals in consuming private goods because one person's consumption reduces the amount available for others to consume.

The goods used in our examples up to this point have been **private goods**. When I eat a cheeseburger, you cannot eat the same one. So you and I are rivals for that cheeseburger, just as much as rivals for the title of world champion are. When I use a CD player, you cannot use the same player. When I use the services of an auto mechanic, that person cannot work at the same time for you. That is the distinguishing feature of private goods—their use is exclusive to the people who purchase or rent them. The **principle of rival consumption** applies to all private goods by definition. Rival consumption is easy to understand. With private goods, either you use them or I use them.

Public goods Goods to which the principle of rival consumption does not apply; they can be jointly consumed by many individuals simultaneously at no additional cost and with no reduction in quality or quantity.

There is an entire class of goods that are not private goods. These are called **public goods**. The principle of rival consumption does not apply to them. That is, they can be consumed jointly by many individuals simultaneously. Military defence, police protection, and the legal system, for example, are public goods. If you partake of them, you do not necessarily take away from anyone else's share of those goods.

CHARACTERISTICS OF PUBLIC GOODS. Several distinguishing characteristics of public goods set them apart from all other goods.[1]

1. **Public goods are often indivisible.** You can't buy or sell $5 worth of the army's ability to protect you from foreign invasion. Public goods cannot usually be produced or sold very easily in small units.
2. **Public goods can be used by more and more people at no additional cost.** Once money has been spent on the armed forces, the defence protection you receive does not reduce the amount of protection bestowed on anyone else. The opportunity cost of your receiving military protection once it is in place is zero.
3. **Additional users of public goods do not deprive others of any of the services of the goods.** If you turn on your television set, your neighbours don't get weaker reception because of your action.
4. **It is difficult to design a collection system for a public good on the basis of how much individuals use it.** It is nearly impossible to determine how much any person uses or values defence. No one can be denied the benefits of military protection for failing to pay for that public good. This is often called the **exclusion principle**.

Exclusion principle The principle that no one can be excluded from the benefits of a public good, even if that person hasn't paid for it.

One of the problems of public goods is that the private sector has a difficult, if not impossible, time in providing them. There is little or no incentive for individuals in the private sector to offer public goods because it is so difficult to make a profit in so doing. Consequently, a true public good must necessarily be provided by government. Read International Example 6-1 on the next page for further discussion.

Free-rider problem A problem that arises when individuals presume that others will pay for public goods so that, individually, they can escape paying for their portion without causing a reduction in production.

FREE RIDERS. The nature of public goods leads to the **free-rider problem**, a situation in which some individuals take advantage of the fact that others will shoulder the burden of paying for public goods such as defence. Free riders will argue that they receive no value from such government services as defence and therefore really should not pay for it. Suppose that citizens were taxed directly in proportion to how much they tell an interviewer that they value military protection. Some people will probably say that they are unwilling to pay for it because they don't want any—it is of no value to them. Many of us may end up being free riders when we assume that others will pay for the desired public good. We may all want to be free riders if we believe that someone else will provide the commodity in question that we actually value.

The free-rider problem is a definite issue among nations with respect to the international burden of defence and how it should be shared. A country may choose to belong to a multilateral defence organization, such as the North Atlantic Treaty Organization (NATO), but then consistently attempt not to contribute funds to the organization. The nation knows it would be defended by others in NATO if it were attacked, but would rather not pay for such defence. In short, it seeks a "free ride."

---

[1] Sometimes the distinction is made between pure public goods, which have all the characteristics we have described here, and quasi- or near-public goods, which do not. The major feature of near-public goods is that they are jointly consumed, even though nonpaying customers can be, and often are, excluded—for example, movies, football games, and concerts.

INTERNATIONAL EXAMPLE 6-1 **Are Lighthouses a Public Good?**

One of the most common examples of a public good is a lighthouse. Arguably, it satisfies all the criteria listed in points 1 through 4. In one instance, however, a lighthouse was not a public good in that a collection system was devised and enforced on the basis of how much individuals used it. In the thirteenth century, the city of Aigues-Mortes, a port in southern France, erected a tower, called the King's Tower, designed to assert the will and power of Louis IX (Saint Louis). The 32-metre-high tower served as a lighthouse for ships. More importantly, it served as a lookout so that ships sailing on the open sea, but in its view, did not escape paying for use of the lighthouse. Those payments were then used for the construction of the city walls.

For critical analysis: Explain how a lighthouse satisfies the characteristics of public goods described in points 1, 2, and 3.

Ensuring Economy-wide Stability

The government attempts to stabilize the economy by smoothing out the ups and downs in overall business activity. Our economy sometimes faces the problems of unemployment and oscillating prices. The government, especially the federal government, has made an attempt to solve these problems by trying to stabilize the economy. The notion that the federal government should undertake actions to stabilize business activity is a relatively new idea in Canada, encouraged by high unemployment rates during the Great Depression of the 1930s and subsequent theories about possible ways by which government could reduce unemployment. In 1945, the government formally assumed responsibility for economic performance. It established three goals for government accountability: full employment, price stability, and economic growth. These goals have provided the justification for many government economic programs during the post-World War II period.

CONCEPTS IN BRIEF

- The economic activities of government include (1) correcting for externalities, (2) providing a judicial system, (3) promoting competition, (4) producing public goods, and (5) ensuring economywide stability.
- Public goods can be consumed jointly. The principle of rival consumption does not apply as it does with private goods.
- Public goods have the following characteristics: (1) They are indivisible; (2) once they are produced, there is no opportunity cost when additional consumers use them; (3) your use of a public good does not deprive others of its simultaneous use; and (4) consumers cannot conveniently be charged on the basis of use.

The Political Functions of Government

At least two areas of government are in the realm of political, or normative, functions rather than that of the economic ones discussed in the first part of this chapter. These two areas are (1) the regulation and/or provision of merit and demerit goods, and (2) income redistribution.

Merit and Demerit Goods

Merit good A good that has been deemed socially desirable through the political process. Museums are an example.

Certain goods are considered to have special merit. A **merit good** is defined as any good that the political process has deemed socially desirable. (Note that nothing inherent in any particular good makes it a merit good. It is a matter of who chooses.) Some examples of merit goods in our society are museums, ballets, sports stadiums (see International Policy Example 6-2), and concerts. In these areas, the government's role is the provision of merit goods to the people in society who would not otherwise purchase them at market clearing prices or who would not purchase an amount of them judged to be sufficient. This provision may take the form of government production and distribution of merit goods. It can also take the form of reimbursement for payment on merit goods or subsidies to producers or consumers for part of the cost of merit goods. Governments do indeed subsidize such merit goods as concerts, ballets, and museums. In most cases, such merit goods would rarely be so numerous without subsidization.

Demerit good A good that has been deemed socially undesirable through the political process. Cigarettes are an example.

Demerit goods are the opposite of merit goods. They are goods that, through the political process, are deemed socially undesirable. Cigarettes, gambling, and illegal drugs are examples. The government exercises its role in the area of demerit goods by taxing, regulating, or prohibiting their manufacture, sale, and use. Governments justify the relatively high taxes on alcohol and tobacco by declaring them demerit goods. The best-known example of governmental exercise of power in this area is the stance against certain psychoactive drugs. Most psychoactives (except nicotine, caffeine, and alcohol) are either expressly prohibited, as is the case for heroin, cocaine, and opium, or heavily regulated, as in the case of prescription psychoactives.

INTERNATIONAL POLICY EXAMPLE 6-2

Do Government-funded Sports Stadiums Have a Net Positive Effect on Local Economies?

Probably not, even though in recent years many cities have decided that new football and baseball stadiums are merit goods worthy of public funding. Their rationale is that there is no collective mechanism besides government to ensure the construction of the stadiums that will draw big crowds. A local government, goes the argument, can regard a stadium as an investment because the crowds it draws benefit the local economy. Spending by the crowds can also generate tax revenues that help the government recoup its expenses. According to economist Andrew Zimbalist, however, "There has not been an independent study by an economist over the last 30 years that suggests you can anticipate a positive economic impact" from government investments in sports facilities.

For critical analysis: In theory, explain how a sports stadium might result in positive externalities for the local economy.

Source: Noll, Roger G. & Andrew Zimbalist, Editors. *Sports, Jobs, and Taxes: The Economic Impact of Sports Teams and Stadiums.* Brookings Institution, 1997.

Income Redistribution

Transfer payments Money payments made by governments to individuals for which no services or goods are concurrently rendered in return. Examples are welfare, old age security payments, and Employment Insurance benefits.

Another relatively recent political function of government has been the explicit redistribution of income. This redistribution uses two systems: the progressive income tax (described later in this chapter) and **transfer payments**. Transfer payments are payments made to individuals for which no services or goods are concurrently rendered in return. The three key money transfer payments in our system are welfare, old age security payments, and employment insurance benefits. Income redistribution also includes a large amount of income **transfers in kind**, as opposed to money transfers. Two income transfers in kind are health care and low-cost public housing.

Transfers in kind Payments that are in the form of actual goods and services, such as public education, low-cost public housing, and health care, and for which no goods or services are rendered concurrently in return.

The government has also engaged in other activities as a form of redistribution of income. For example, the provision of public education is at least in part an attempt to redistribute income by making sure that the very poor have access to education (see Example 6-1).

EXAMPLE 6-1 Education Transfer Payments

The federal government has recently increased its transfers-in-kind to post-secondary students. The 1998 federal budget contained a number of incentives to encourage more Canadians to continue their education following secondary school. For example, the government is making available 25,000 Canada Study Grants of $3,000 each for needy students with dependants. In addition, the education credit and child-care expense deductions for income tax are extended to part-time as well as full-time students.

The federal government is also providing annual Canada Education Savings Grants of 20 percent of the first $2,000 in contributions to your registered education savings plan. You are also now able to make tax-free withdrawals from your RRSP of up to $10,000 per year to a maximum of $20,000 over four years. However, withdrawals must be paid back within 10 years.

Finally, the government has made a number of improvements to the Canada Student Loan program. For example, interest on student loans is now tax deductible. And for students who have problems repaying their student loans, the government provides up to 30 months of interest relief following graduation.

For critical analysis: Why might a tax deduction for post-secondary education expenses be more beneficial to society than an equivalent dollar tax deduction for home mortgage expenses?

Try Preview Question 1:

What are the economic and political functions of the public sector?

CONCEPTS IN BRIEF

- Political, or normative, activities of the government include the provision and regulation of merit and demerit goods and income redistribution.
- Merit and demerit goods do not have any inherent characteristics that qualify them as such; rather, collectively, through the political process, we make judgments about which goods and services are "good" for society and which are "bad."
- Income redistribution can be carried out by a system of progressive taxation, coupled with transfer payments, which can be made in money or in kind, such as health care and public education.

Collective Decision Making: The Theory of Public Choice

The public sector has a vast influence on the Canadian economy. Yet the economic model used until now has applied only to the behaviour of the private sector—firms and households. Such a model does not adequately explain the behaviour of the public sector. We shall attempt to do so now.

Governments consist of individuals. No government actually thinks and acts; rather, government actions are the result of decision making by individuals in their roles as elected representatives, appointed officials, and salaried bureaucrats. Therefore, to understand how government works, we must examine the incentives for the people in government as well as those who would like to be in government—avowed candidates or would-be candidates for elected or appointed positions—and special-interest lobbyists attempting to get government to do something. At issue is the analysis of **collective decision making**. Collective decision making involves the actions of voters, politicians, political parties, interest groups, and many other groups and individuals. The analysis of collective decision making is usually called the **theory of public choice**. It has been given

Collective decision making How voters, politicians, and other interested parties act and how these actions influence nonmarket decisions.

Theory of public choice The study of collective decision making.

this name because it involves hypotheses about how choices are made in the public sector, as opposed to the private sector. The foundation of public-choice theory is the assumption that individuals will act within the political process to maximize their individual (not collective) well-being. In that sense, the theory is similar to our analysis of the market economy, in which we also assume that individuals are motivated by self-interest.

To understand public-choice theory, it is necessary to point out other similarities between the private market sector and the public, or government, sector; then we will look at the differences.

Similarities in Market and Public-Sector Decision Making

In addition to the similar assumption of self-interest being the motivating force in both sectors, there are other similarities.

SCARCITY. At any given moment, the amount of resources is fixed. This means that for the private and the public sectors combined, there is a scarcity constraint. Everything that is spent by all levels of government, plus everything that is spent by the private sector, must add up to the total income available at any point in time. Hence every government action has an opportunity cost, just as in the market sector.

COMPETITION. Although we typically think of competition as a private market phenomenon, it is also present in collective action. Given the scarcity constraint government also faces, bureaucrats, appointed officials, and elected representatives will always be in competition for available government funds. Furthermore, the individuals within any government agency or institution will act as individuals do in the private sector: They will try to obtain higher wages, better working conditions, and higher job-level classifications. They will compete and act in their own, not society's, interest.

SIMILARITY OF INDIVIDUALS. Contrary to popular belief, there are not two types of individuals, those who work in the private sector and those who work in the public sector; rather, individuals working in similar positions can be considered similar. The difference, as we shall see, is that the individuals in government face a different **incentive structure** than those in the private sector. For example, the costs and benefits of being efficient or inefficient differ when one goes from the private to the public sector.

Incentive structure The system of rewards and punishments individuals face with respect to their own actions.

One approach to predicting government bureaucratic behaviour is to ask what incentives bureaucrats face. Take Canada Post as an example. The bureaucrats running that Crown Corporation are human beings with qualities similar to those possessed by workers in comparable positions at, say, Northern Telecom or Canadian Airlines. Yet the Post Office does not function like either of these companies. The difference can be explained, at least in part, in terms of the incentives provided for managers in the two types of institutions. When the bureaucratic managers and workers at Northern Telecom make incorrect decisions, work slowly, produce shoddy products, and are generally "inefficient," the profitability of the company declines. The owners—millions of shareholders—express their displeasure by selling some of their shares of company stock. The market value, as tracked on the stock exchange, falls. But what about Canada Post? If a manager, a worker, or a bureaucrat in the Post Office gives shoddy service, there is no straightforward mechanism by which the organization's owners—the taxpayers—can express their dissatisfaction. Despite the Post Office's status as a "government corporation," taxpayers as shareholders do not really own shares of stock in the organization that they can sell.

The key, then, to understanding purported inefficiency in the government bureaucracy is not found in an examination of people and personalities but rather in an examination of incentives and institutional arrangements.

Differences Between Market and Collective Decision Making

There are probably more dissimilarities between the market sector and the public sector than there are similarities.

Government, or political, goods Goods (and services) provided by the public sector; they can be either private or public goods.

GOVERNMENT GOODS AT ZERO PRICE. The majority of goods that governments produce are furnished to the ultimate consumers without direct money charge. **Government, or political, goods** can be either private goods or public goods. The fact that they are furnished to the ultimate consumer free of charge does not mean that the cost to society of those goods is zero, however; it only means that the price charged is zero. The full opportunity cost to society is the value of the resources used in the production of goods produced and provided by the government.

For example, none of us pays directly for each unit of consumption of most highways nor for police protection. Rather, we pay for all these things indirectly through the taxes that support our governments—federal, provincial, and municipal. This special feature of government can be looked at in a different way. There is no longer a one-to-one relationship between the consumption of a government-provided good and the payment for that good. Consumers who pay taxes collectively pay for every political good, but the individual consumer may not be able to see the relationship between the taxes paid and the consumption of the good. Indeed, most taxpayers will find that their tax bill is the same whether or not they consume, or even like, government-provided goods.

USE OF FORCE. All governments are able to engage in the legal use of force in their regulation of economic affairs. For example, governments can exercise the use of expropriation, which means that if you refuse to pay your taxes, your bank account and other assets may be seized by Revenue Canada. In fact, you have no choice in the matter of paying taxes to governments. Collectively, we decide the total size of government through the political process, but individually we cannot determine how much service we pay for just for ourselves during any one year.

Majority rule A collective decision-making system in which group decisions are made on the basis of 50.1 percent of the vote. In other words, whatever more than half of the electorate votes for, the entire electorate has to accept.

Proportional rule A decision-making system in which actions are based on the proportion of the "votes" cast and are in proportion to them. In a market system, if 10 percent of the "dollar votes" are cast for blue cars, 10 percent of the output will be blue cars.

VOTING VERSUS SPENDING. In the private market sector, a dollar voting system is in effect. This dollar voting system is not equivalent to the voting system in the public sector. There are, at minimum, three differences:

1. In a political system, one person gets one vote, whereas in the market system, the dollars one spends count as votes.
2. The political system is run by **majority rule**, whereas the market system is run by **proportional rule**.
3. The spending of dollars can indicate intensity of want, whereas because of the all-or-nothing nature of political voting, a vote cannot.

Ultimately, the main distinction between political votes and dollar votes here is that political outcomes may differ from economic outcomes. Remember that economic efficiency is a situation in which, given the prevailing distribution of income, consumers get the economic goods they want. There is no corresponding situation using political voting. Thus we can never assume that a political voting process will lead to the same decisions that a dollar voting process will lead to in the marketplace.

Indeed, consider the dilemma every voter faces. Usually a voter is not asked to decide on a single issue (although this happens); rather, a voter is asked to choose among candidates who present a large number of issues and state a position on each of them. Just consider the average Member of Parliament who has to vote on hundreds of different issues during a five-year term. When you vote for that representative, you are voting for a person who must make hundreds of decisions during the next five years.

The Role of Bureaucrats

Government programs require people to deliver them. This is manifested today in the form of well-established bureaucracies, in which **bureaucrats** (nonelected officials) work. **Bureaucracies** can exert great influence on matters concerning themselves—the amount of funding granted them and the activities in which they engage. In the political marketplace, well-organized bureaucracies can even influence the expression of public demand itself. In many cases, they organize the clientele (interest groups), coach that clientele on what is appropriate, and stick up for the "rights" of the clientele.

Bureaucrats Nonelected government officials who are responsible for the day-to-day operation of government and the observance of its regulations and laws.

Bureaucracy An administrative system run by a large staff following rules and procedures set down by government.

Gauging Bureaucratic Performance

It is tempting, but incorrect, to think of bureaucrats as mere "technocrats," executors of orders and channels of information, in this process. They have at least two incentives to make government programs larger and more resistant to attack than we might otherwise expect. First, society has decided that, in general, government should not be run on a profit-making basis. Measures of performance other than bottom-line profits must be devised. In the private market, successful firms typically expand to serve more customers; although this growth is often incidental to the underlying profitability, the two frequently go hand in hand. In parallel, performance in government is often measured by the number of clients served, and rewards are distributed accordingly. As a result, bureaucrats have an incentive to expand the size of their clientele—not because it is more profitable (beneficial) to society but because that is how bureaucrats' rewards are structured.

In general, performance measures that are not based on long-run profitability are less effective at gauging true performance. This makes it potentially easier for the government bureaucrat to appear to perform well, collect rewards for measured performance, and then leave for greener pastures. To avoid this, a much larger proportion of the rewards given bureaucrats are valuable only as long as they continue being bureaucrats—large staffs, expensive offices, generous pensions, and the like. Instead of getting large current salaries (which can be saved for a rainy day), they get rewards that disappear if their jobs disappear. Naturally, this increases the incentives of bureaucrats to make sure that their jobs don't disappear.

The federal government found recently that non-salary rewards were not sufficient to keep its top bureaucrats in the public service. More and more government executives were being lured away to the private sector with its promise of higher salaries. In 1996 alone, at least six deputy ministers and assistant deputy ministers left for private sector jobs. The government responded early in 1998 with salary increases that ranged from 4 to 19 percent, and implemented a bonus plan for performance that would take salaries even higher. The great majority of public servants were not impressed: they have had a single 3 percent raise between 1991 and 1998 and were not expecting great increases in the foreseeable future.

Rational Ignorance

At this point you may well be wondering why this system still goes on. The answer lies in rational ignorance on the part of voters, ignorance that is carefully cultivated by the members of special interest groups.

On most issues, there is little incentive for the individual voter to expend resources to determine how to vote. Moreover, the ordinary course of living provides most of us with enough knowledge to decide whether we should invest in learning more about a given issue. For example, suppose that Canadian voters were asked to decide if the sign marking the entrance to an obscure national park should be enlarged. Most voters would decide that the potential costs and benefits of this decision are negligible: The new sign is unlikely to be the size of Prince Edward Island, and anybody who has even heard of the national park in question probably already has a pretty good idea of its location. Thus most voters would choose to remain rationally ignorant about the exact costs and benefits of enlarging the sign, implying that (1) many will choose not to vote at all and (2) those who do vote will simply flip a coin or cast their ballot based on some other, perhaps ideological, grounds.

WHY BE RATIONALLY IGNORANT? For most political decisions, majority rule prevails. Only a coalition of voters representing slightly more than 50 percent of those who vote is needed. Whenever a vote is taken, the result is going to involve costs and benefits. Voters, then, must evaluate their share of the costs and benefits of any budgetary expenditure. Voters, however, are not perfectly informed. That is one of the crucial characteristics of the real world—information is a resource that is costly to obtain. Rational voters will, in fact, decide to remain at some level of ignorance about government programs because the benefits from obtaining more information may not be worth the cost, given each individual voter's extremely limited impact on the outcome of an election. For the same reason, voters will fail to inform themselves about taxes or other revenue sources to pay for proposed expenditures because they know that for any specific expenditure program, the cost to them individually will be small. At this point it might be useful to contrast this situation with what exists in the nonpolitical private market sector of the economy. In the private market sector, the individual chooses a mix of purchases and bears fully the direct and indirect consequences of this selection (ignoring for the moment the problem of externalities).

Try Preview Question 2:

What is the foundation of public-choice theory?

CONCEPTS IN BRIEF

- Collective decision making involves the actions of voters, politicians, political parties, bureaucrats, and interest groups.
- The similarities between market and public sector decision making include: assumption of self-interest as the motivating force, scarcity of resources, and competition for available funds and resources.
- The key differences between the market and public sector include: government goods at zero price, use of force, proportional rule vs. majority rule.
- The theory of public choice implies a situation called rational ignorance where on most issues there is little incentive for the individual voter to expend resources to determine how to vote. This allows bureaucrats and special interest groups to have a significant effect on choices in the public sector.

Paying for the Public Sector

Jean-Baptiste Colbert, the seventeenth-century French finance minister, said the art of taxation was in "plucking the goose so as to obtain the largest amount of feathers with the least possible amount of hissing." In Canada, governments have designed a variety of methods of plucking the private-sector goose. To analyze any tax system, we must first understand the distinction between marginal tax rates and average tax rates.

Marginal and Average Tax Rates

Marginal tax rate The change in the tax payment divided by the change in income, or the percentage of additional dollars that must be paid in taxes. The marginal tax rate is applied to the highest tax bracket of taxable income reached.

If somebody says, "I pay 28 percent in taxes," you cannot really tell what that person means unless you know whether the individual is referring to average taxes paid or the tax rate on the last dollars earned. The latter concept has to do with the **marginal tax rate**.[2]

---

[2] The word *marginal* means "incremental" (or "decremental") here.

The marginal tax rate is expressed as follows:

$$\text{Marginal tax rate} = \frac{\text{change in taxes due}}{\text{change in taxable income}}$$

It is important to understand that the marginal tax rate applies only to the income in the highest **tax bracket** reached, where a tax bracket is defined as a specified level of taxable income to which a specific and unique marginal tax rate is applied.

The **average tax rate** is not the same thing as the marginal tax rate, which is defined as follows:

$$\text{Average tax rate} = \frac{\text{total taxes due}}{\text{total taxable income}}$$

Taxation Systems

No matter how governments raise revenues—from income taxes, sales taxes, or other taxes—all of those taxes can fit into one of three types of taxation systems—proportional, progressive, and regressive, expressing a relationship between the percentage tax, or tax rate, paid and income. To determine whether a tax system is proportional, progressive, or regressive, we simply ask the question, What is the relationship between the average tax rate and the marginal tax rate?

PROPORTIONAL TAXATION. **Proportional taxation** means that regardless of an individual's income, the taxes comprise exactly the same proportion. In terms of marginal versus average tax rates, in a proportional taxation system, the marginal tax rate is always equal to the average tax rate. If every dollar is taxed at 20 percent, then the average tax rate is 20 percent, as is the marginal tax rate.

A proportional tax system is also called a flat-rate tax. Taxpayers at all income levels end up paying the same percentage of their income in taxes. If the proportional tax rate were 20 percent, an individual with an income of $10,000 would pay $2,000 in taxes, while an individual making $100,000 would pay $20,000, the identical 20 percent rate being levied on both.

PROGRESSIVE TAXATION. Under **progressive taxation**, as a person's taxable income increases, the percentage of income paid in taxes also increases. In terms of marginal versus average tax rates, in a progressive system, the marginal tax rate is above the average tax rate. If you are taxed 5 percent on the first $10,000 you make, 10 percent on the next $10,000 you make, and 30 percent on the last $10,000 you make, you face a progressive income tax system. Your marginal tax rate is always above your average tax rate.

REGRESSIVE TAXATION. With **regressive taxation**, a smaller percentage of taxable income is taken in taxes as taxable income increases. The marginal rate is below the average rate. As income increases, the marginal tax rate falls, and so does the average tax rate. The Goods and Services Tax (GST) is regressive. Someone earning $10,000 per year pays the same 7 percent sales tax on a tube of toothpaste as someone earning $100,000 per year. But the tube of toothpaste takes up a much larger proportion of the low income earner's budget, so the marginal tax rate for that person is higher. The federal government tries to address this inequity by giving GST rebates to low income earners who apply for them in their income tax returns each year.

Tax bracket A specified interval of income to which a specific and unique marginal tax rate is applied.

Average tax rate The total tax payment divided by total income. It is the proportion of total income paid in taxes.

Proportional taxation A tax system in which regardless of an individual's income, the tax bill comprises exactly the same proportion. Also called a flat-rate tax.

Progressive taxation A tax system in which as income increases, a higher percentage of the additional income is taxed. The marginal tax rate exceeds the average tax rate as income rises.

Regressive taxation A tax system in which as more dollars are earned, the percentage of tax paid on them falls. The marginal tax rate is less than the average tax rate as income rises.

Try Preview Question 3:

In what ways do regressive, proportional, and progressive tax structures differ?

INTERNATIONAL POLICY EXAMPLE 6-3

Average and Marginal Tax Rates Around the World

Canadians frequently complain that we pay too much income tax, especially when compared to the United States. However, the average tax rate for the average production worker is not as different as one would think, when social security and income tax deductions are combined.

The Organisation for Economic Co-operation and Development surveyed tax rates in the industrialized world. Table 6.1 shows average tax rates for an average production worker, and for workers in the highest income bracket. For a Canadian production worker making about $32,000 per year, the combined average tax rate—income taxes plus contributions to the Canada Pension Plan plus Employment Insurance premiums—is about 27 percent, just 1 percentage point above the US.

TABLE 6.1

Average and Marginal Tax Rates in the Industrialized World, 1998, 1999

	Combined Average Tax Rate (%) for an Average Production Worker (1998)	Marginal Tax Rate (%) for Highest Income Bracket (1999)
Australia	25	47
Canada	27	48.8
France	27	54
Germany	42	53
Italy	29	46
Japan	7	50
New Zealand	20	33
United Kingdom	25	40
United States	26	39.6

Source: Adapted from "Taxing Wages in OECD Countries 1998/1999." April 19, 2000. OECD. Sept. 22, 2000. <http://www.oecd.org/daf/fa/stats/wages.htm>

Canada's personal income tax structure is also less progressive than many other countries'. France, Germany, and Japan all have a higher marginal tax rate for the highest income bracket.

For critical analysis: Theoretically, do you think one's average tax rate or marginal tax rate plays a bigger role in affecting one's incentive to work harder to earn additional income?

CONCEPTS IN BRIEF

- Marginal tax rates are applied to marginal tax brackets, defined as spreads of income over which the tax rate is constant.
- Tax systems can be proportional, progressive, or regressive, depending on whether the marginal tax rate is the same as, greater than, or less than the average tax rate as income rises.

The Most Important Federal Taxes

The federal government imposes income taxes on both individuals and corporations, and collects sales taxes as well as a variety of other taxes.

The Federal Personal Income Tax

TABLE 6.2

Federal Marginal Income Tax Rates

These rates became effective in 1992. Taxpayers also pay a surcharge of 3 percent on taxes payable to $12,500 and an additional 5 percent on taxes payable above $12,500.

Marginal Tax Bracket	Marginal Tax Rate
$0–$29,590	17%
$29,590–$59,180	26%
$59,180 and up	29%

Source: Adapted from Revenue Canada

The most important tax in the Canadian economy is the federal personal income tax, which accounts for about 48 percent of all federal revenues. All Canadian citizens, resident aliens, and most others who earn income in Canada are required to pay federal income tax on all taxable income. The tax rates that are paid depend on the amount of taxable income earned, as can be seen in Table 6.2. Marginal income tax rates at the federal level have varied from as low as 4 percent after the passage of the Income Tax Act in 1917, to as high as 98 percent during World War II. In 1992, the government reduced the top marginal tax rate and cut the number of income tax brackets to three, but broadened the definition of taxable income. The effect of these changes was to make Canada's tax system less progressive.

Advocates of a more progressive income tax system in Canada argue that such a system redistributes income from the rich to the poor, taxes people according to their ability to pay, and taxes people according to the benefits they receive from government. Although there is much controversy over the "redistributional" nature of our progressive tax system, there is no strong evidence that in fact the tax system has ever done much income redistribution in this country. Currently, about 80 percent of all Canadians, rich or poor, pay roughly the same proportion of their income in federal income tax.

The Treatment of Capital Gains

Capital gain The positive difference between the purchase price and the sale price of an asset. If a share of stock is bought for $5 and then sold for $15, the capital gain is $10.

Capital loss The negative difference between the purchase price and the sale price of an asset.

The difference between the buying and selling price of an asset, such as a share of stock or a plot of land, is called a **capital gain** if it is a profit, and a **capital loss** if it is not. Capital gains are taxed at ordinary income marginal tax rates. The taxable part of a capital gain is 75 percent of the net amount of your capital gains minus your capital losses for the year.

Capital gains are not always real. If in one year you pay $100,000 for a house you plan to rent and sell it for 50 percent more 10 years later, your nominal capital gain is $50,000. But what if, during those 10 years, there had been inflation such that average prices had also gone up by 50 percent? Your real capital gain would be zero. But you still have to pay taxes on that $50,000. To counter this problem, many economists have argued that capital gains should be indexed to the rate of inflation.

The Corporate Income Tax

Corporate income taxes account for about 14 percent of all federal taxes collected, and 3.4 percent of all provincial taxes collected. Corporations are generally taxed at a flat rate of 28 percent on the difference between their total revenues (or receipts) and their expenses.

DOUBLE TAXATION. Because individual shareholders must pay taxes on the dividends they receive, paid out of after-tax profits by the corporation, corporate profits are taxed twice. If you receive $1,000 in dividends, you have to declare it as income, and you must pay taxes at your marginal tax rate. Before the corporation was able to pay you those dividends, it had to pay taxes on all its profits, including any that it put back into the company or did not distribute in the form of dividends. Eventually the new investment made possible by those **retained earnings**—profits not given out to shareholders—along with borrowed funds will be reflected in the increased value of the stock in that company. When you sell your shares in that company, you will have to pay taxes on the difference between what you paid for them and what you sold them for. In both cases, dividends and retained earnings (corporate profits) are taxed twice.

> **Retained earnings** Earnings that a corporation saves, or retains, for investment in other productive activities; earnings that are not distributed to stockholders.

WHO REALLY PAYS THE CORPORATE INCOME TAX? Corporations can exist only as long as consumers buy their products, employees make their goods, shareholders (owners) buy their shares, and bondholders buy their bonds. Corporations *per se* do not do anything. We must ask, then, who really pays the tax on corporate income. This is a question of **tax incidence**. (The question of tax incidence applies to all taxes, including sales and payroll taxes.) There remains considerable debate about the incidence of corporate taxation. Some economists say that corporations pass their tax burdens on to consumers by charging higher prices. Other economists believe that it is the shareholders who bear most of the tax. Still others believe that employees pay at least part of the tax by receiving lower wages than they would otherwise. Because the debate is not yet settled, we will not hazard a guess here as to what the correct conclusion should be. Suffice to say that you should be cautious when you advocate increasing corporation income taxes. You may be the one who ends up paying the increase, at least in part, if you own shares in a corporation, buy its products, or work for it.

> **Tax incidence** The distribution of tax burdens among various groups in society.

CONCEPTS IN BRIEF

- Because corporations must first pay an income tax on most earnings, the personal income tax shareholders pay on dividends received (or realized capital gains) constitutes double taxation.
- The corporate income tax is paid by one or more of the following groups: shareholder-owners, consumers of corporate-produced products, and employees in corporations.

Unemployment and Pension Taxes

An increasing percentage of federal revenues is accounted for each year by taxes (other than income taxes) levied on payroll. These payroll taxes are for Canada Pension Plan (CPP) benefits and Employment Insurance (EI).

Employment Insurance is a compulsory federal program which provides income assistance in the event of unemployment. EI premiums are paid by employees, and matched by employers. (The employer's contribution is really paid, at least in part, in the form of a reduced wage paid to employees, as explained in Thinking Critically About the Media 6-1). Self-employed people must pay both shares. The maximum personal contribution to EI in 1999 was $994.50. EI premiums become part of the government's general revenues; as of 1999, there was a large surplus in the EI account which helped the government balance the budget for the 1999-2000 fiscal year.

In 1999, the CPP premium payable on eligible earnings to $37,400 was 3 percent, with employers contributing an equal share on behalf of the employee. CPP premiums do not form part of the government's general revenue, but are managed separately from the government budget. The CPP is a system in which current

Thinking Critically About the Media 6-1   Employment Insurance

Countless articles have been written about the problem with the Employment Insurance (EI) system in Canada. They all make reference to the employer and employee "contributions" to the EI fund. One gets the impression that EI premiums paid by employees go into a special government account and that employees do not pay for their employers' "contribution" to this account. Both concepts are not merely flawed, but grossly misleading. EI premiums are mixed in with the rest of government taxes collected and spent every year. The "contributions" are not contributions at all; they are merely taxes paid to the federal government. The so-called employer contribution, which matches the employee payments, is not in fact paid for by employers but rather by employees because of the lower wages that they are paid. Anybody who quits a job and becomes self-employed finds this out when the time comes to pay one's self-employment taxes (Employment Insurance "contributions"), which effectively double the payments previously being made as an employee.

workers subsidize already retired workers. With the coming retirement of the post-war "baby boomers," the number of retired people will grow much more rapidly than the number of current workers. In anticipation of increased outlays in pension plan benefits, the combined (employer-employee) premium will rise to 9.9 percent of eligible earnings by the year 2003.

The GST

The Goods and Services Tax (GST) is a sales tax which makes up about 14 percent of federal government revenues. Consumers pay a 7 percent tax on virtually all goods and services they purchase in addition to any applicable provincial sales taxes. The GST is a regressive tax since it taxes consumption at the same rate for both the rich and the poor. The federal government tries to mitigate this, however, by giving a rebate of up to $76 four times a year to low-income earners. While consumers must pay GST on imports, Canadian exports are exempt. Visitors to Canada may apply for a rebate of the GST they paid on their Canadian purchases when they leave the country.

Some economists argue that in spite of the regressive nature of sales taxes, a tax like the GST is preferable to an income tax. Income taxes tax all income, whether it is spent or saved. Therefore, they argue, saving is discouraged. However, a sales tax taxes only income that is consumed, and so saving is encouraged. The Issues and Applications section at the end of this chapter revisits the pros and cons of this topic.

Spending, Government Size, and Tax Receipts

The size of the public sector can be measured in many different ways. One way is to count the number of public employees. Another is to look at government outlays. Government outlays include all of the government expenditures on goods and services, as well as all transfer payments. Transfer payments include Employment Insurance benefits, welfare, and old age security. In Figure 6.2 you see that, since 1961, total government outlays made by all levels of government in Canada peaked at 51 percent of the Canadian Gross Domestic Product (size of the Canadian economy) in 1992. As a percent of Canada's Gross Domestic Product, total government outlays has dropped from 51 percent in 1992 to 40 percent in 1999. In 1999, total US government outlays was 30 percent of US Gross Domestic Product and the corresponding G-7 country average was 37 percent.

FIGURE 6.2 Total Government Outlays Over Time

Here you see that total government outlays peaked in 1992 and has declined to 40 percent of the Canadian economy in 1999.

Source: G-7 Total Government Outlays, OECD Economic Outlook No. 67, Copyright OECD (June 2000).

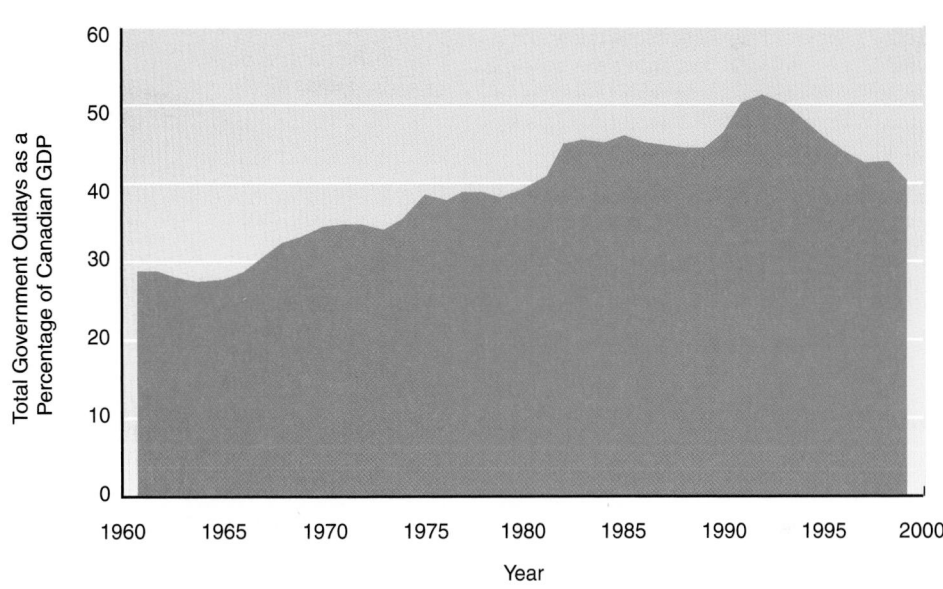

Government Receipts

The main revenue raiser for all levels of government is taxes. We show in the two pie diagrams in Figure 6.3 the percentage of receipts from various taxes obtained by the federal government and by provincial and municipal governments.

THE FEDERAL GOVERNMENT. The largest source of receipts for the federal government is the individual income tax. During the 1999-2000 fiscal year, it accounted for 47.8 percent of all federal revenues. After that come corporate income taxes which account for 14 percent of total revenues. Next come the GST revenues, Employment Insurance premiums, and a number of other items, such as taxes on imported goods and excise taxes on such things as gasoline and alcoholic beverages.

PROVINCIAL AND MUNICIPAL GOVERNMENTS. As can be seen in Figure 6.3, there is quite a bit of difference between the origin of receipts for provincial and municipal governments and for the federal government. Personal and corporate income taxes account for only 26.9 percent of total provincial and municipal revenues. The next largest source of receipts is from sales taxes (used by provincial governments), property taxes (used mainly by municipal governments), and transfers from the federal government.

COMPARING FEDERAL WITH PROVINCIAL AND MUNICIPAL SPENDING. A typical federal government budget is given in Figure 6.4. The largest three categories are interest on the debt, elderly benefits, and transfers to the provinces, which together constitute almost 60 percent of the total federal budget.

The makeup of provincial and municipal expenditures is quite different. Education and health are the biggest categories, accounting for over 40 percent of all expenditures.

FIGURE 6.3 Sources of Government Tax Receipts 1999-2000

About 77 percent of federal revenues come from income and Employment Insurance taxes, whereas provincial and municipal government revenues are spread more evenly across sources, with less emphasis on taxes based on individual income.

Source: Statistics Canada Website, <www.statcan.ca/english/Pgdb/state/Government/govt046.htm>, accessed on September 22, 2000.

Federal

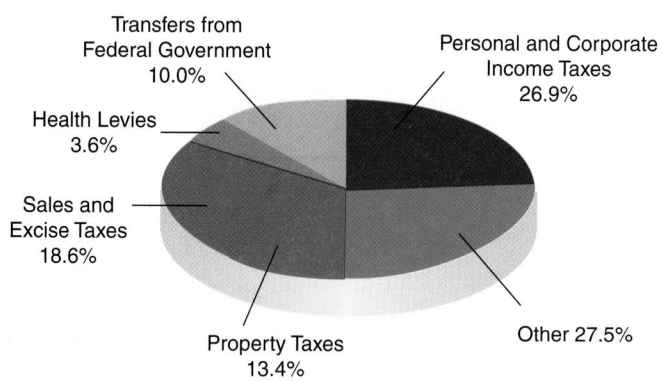

Provincial and Municipal

Try Preview Question 4:

How do the federal goverment's spending habits differ from those of the provinces?

CONCEPTS IN BRIEF

- In Canada, total government outlays as a percent of Canadian Gross Domestic Product peaked in 1992 at 51 percent, and has declined to 40 percent in 1999.
- Government spending at the federal level is different from that at the provincial and municipal levels. At the federal level, interest on the debt, elderly benefits, and transfers to the provinces account for almost 60 percent of the federal budget. At the provincial and municipal levels, education and health comprise over 40 percent of all expenditures.

FIGURE 6.4 Federal Government Spending Compared to Provincial and Municipal Spending

The federal government's spending habits are quite different from those of the provinces and municipalities. The categories of most importance in the federal budget are interest on the debt, elderly benefits, and transfers to the provinces, which make up almost 60 percent. The two most important categories at the provincial and municipal levels are education and health care, which make up over 40 percent.

Sources: Statistics Canada Website, <www.statcan.ca/english/Pgdb/Government/govt046.htm>, accessed on September 22, 2000.

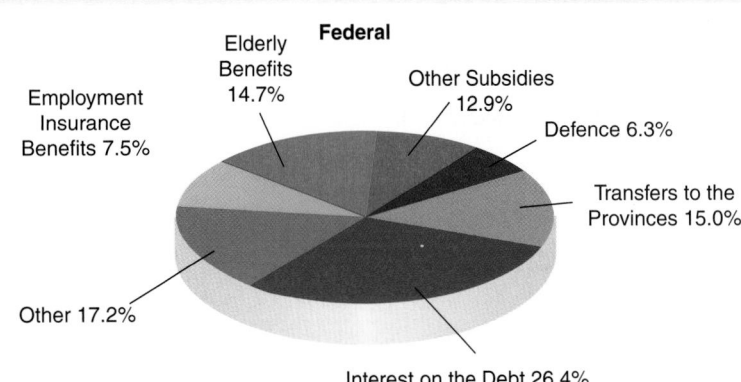

Federal

Elderly Benefits 14.7%
Employment Insurance Benefits 7.5%
Other Subsidies 12.9%
Defence 6.3%
Transfers to the Provinces 15.0%
Other 17.2%
Interest on the Debt 26.4%

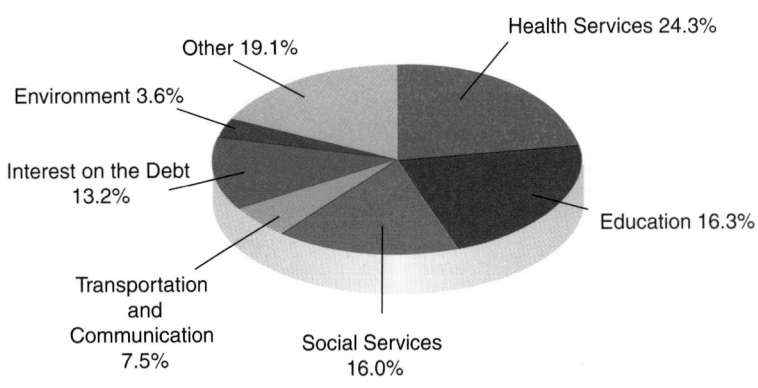

Provincial and Municipal

Other 19.1%
Health Services 24.3%
Environment 3.6%
Interest on the Debt 13.2%
Education 16.3%
Transportation and Communication 7.5%
Social Services 16.0%

NETNOMICS

Who Really Gains From Tax-Free Internet Purchases?

In 1998 the US Congress passed the Internet Tax Freedom Act, which placed a three-year moratorium on any new Internet-related taxes until the Internal Revenue Service is able to hash things out. From a practical point of view, this act provides a tax benefit to those who purchase items over the Internet. When you go to your local store and buy a CD or a book, you generally pay a sales tax on that purchase. You grumble, and you may even believe that a sales tax is a regressive and inefficient form of taxation.

Nevertheless, when you log on to CDNow.com or Amazon.com to make a purchase, the sales tax magically disappears. You are buying from outside the province, or even from outside the country, and hence do not pay local taxes. Your purchase arrives in the mail a few days later and you congratulate yourself on having beaten the system.

However, to the extent that a greater portion of upper-income households make Internet purchases than lower income households, the Internet provides a greater tax benefit to richer individuals. Put differently, the tax-free status of Internet purchases shifts the burden of supporting local services onto the backs of low-wage earners.

To the extent that the most popular Internet companies providing products and services are located outside of Canada, Canadian online purchasers are reducing the Canadian tax base. If these online purchases became significant, Canadian social programs could be eroded. Not to mention that these online purchases are supporting jobs outside of Canada!

ISSUES AND APPLICATIONS

Should We Switch to a Flat Tax?

Concepts Applied: Average versus marginal tax rates, opportunity cost, progressive income tax system

Each year, Canadian taxpayers spend numerous hours preparing their taxes or hire accountants to do so for them. Switching to a national sales tax, one alternative to our current system, would lead to the downsizing of Revenue Canada and all of the expenses associated with that organization.

Since the enactment of the federal income tax, Canadians have faced a progressive system. The top marginal tax rate soared to 98 percent in 1943, dropped to 80 percent in 1948, dropped again to 60 percent in 1968, and settled at 47 percent starting in 1971. The government reduced the top marginal tax rate to 34 percent in 1983; today it stands at 29 percent. The idea behind a progressive tax system is that the "rich" should pay more. In actuality, what happens is quite a different story. In Figure 6.5 you see that regardless of what the top tax rate is, the federal government obtains around 48 percent of its annual income as tax revenues.

Why? Because people respond to incentives. At high marginal tax rates, the following occurs: (1) rich people hire more tax lawyers and accountants to help them figure out loopholes in the tax system to avoid high marginal tax rates; (2) some people change their investments to take advantage of loopholes that allow them to pay lower marginal tax rates; (3) some people drop out of the labour force, particularly secondary income earners, such as lower-paid working women; and (4) more people engage in off-the-books "underground" activities for cash on which no income taxes are paid.

An Alternative: The Flat Tax

For decades, many economists have argued in favour of scrapping our progressive income tax system and replacing it with a so-called flat tax. The idea behind a flat tax is simple. To calculate what you owe, simply subtract the appropriate exemption from your income and multiply the rest by the flat tax rate, say, 20 percent. For example, a family of four might be able to earn as much as $25,000 or $35,000 a year before it paid any income tax. The major benefits of such a system, according to its advocates, would be the following: (1) fewer resources devoted to figuring out one's taxes; (2) fewer tax lawyers and accountants, who could then be engaged in more productive activities; (3) higher saving and investment; and (4) more economic growth. Opponents of a flat tax argue that (1) federal revenues will fall and a federal budget deficit will occur; and (2) the rich will pay few taxes.

Another Alternative: A National Sales Tax

Alternatively, we could apply some form of a value-added tax (VAT) in place of the current income tax. VATs are common throughout Europe. A value-added tax is assessed on the value added by a firm at each stage of production. It is a tax on the value of products that firms sell minus the value of the materials that it bought and used to produce the products. Such a tax is collected by all businesses and remitted directly to the federal government. One of the major benefits of a VAT is that it would significantly downsize Revenue Canada and the expenses associated with that government department. A VAT of, say, 15 to 20 percent in lieu of a federal income tax would be quite similar to a consumption tax.

FIGURE 6.5 Changing Maximum Marginal Income Tax Rates and Revenues Collected

At the top of the diagram, you can see listed the top marginal tax rates from 1960 to 1995. On the side is the percentage of total annual income collected by the federal government from the income tax system. No matter how high the marginal income tax rate has been, the government has collected about the same percentage of national income in taxes.

Source: W. Irwin Gillespie, *Tax, Borrow & Spend: Financing Federal Spending in Canada 1867-1990.*

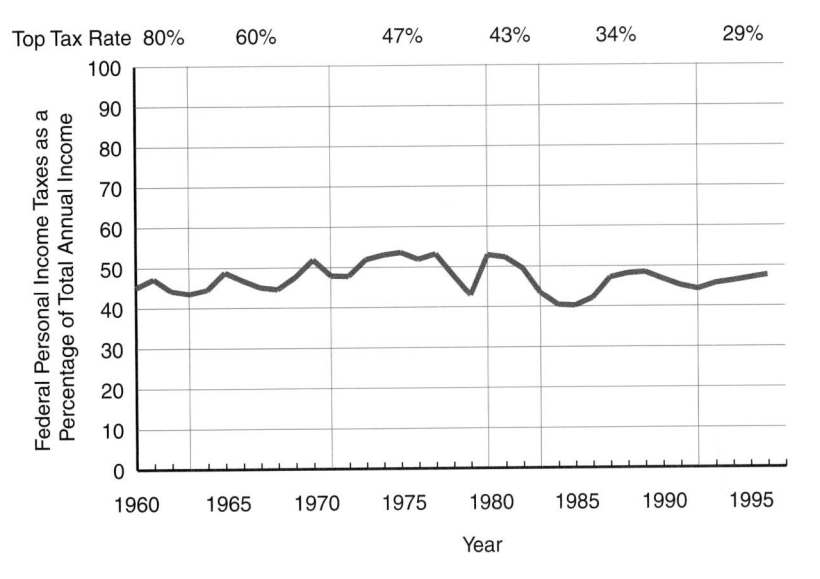

A Consumption Tax

With a consumption tax, taxpayers pay taxes only on what they consume (spend) out of income, not what they earn. One way to determine such consumption in any year is simply to subtract what is saved from what is earned. The difference is consumption, and that is the base to which a consumption tax would apply. (A consumption tax is actually equivalent to the GST on all goods and services purchased.) In essence, a consumption tax provides an unlimited deduction for saving. As such, it encourages more saving. As you learned in Chapter 2, the less people choose to consume today, the faster the production possibilities curve will shift outward to the right, leading to more economic growth.

What About Fairness?

Every time a new tax system is discussed, the issue of fairness arises. Is it fair, as with a flat federal income tax, that everybody pay the same marginal tax rate, no matter how much each individual earns? Stephen Entin of the Institute for Research on the Economics of Taxation thinks it is: "It is hard to find a definition of 'fairness' more compelling than the idea that every citizen is treated equally." What about a consumption tax, which might be regressive because the poor spend a larger portion of their income than the rich? Is that a "fair" system? For most economists, these are difficult questions, because they are in the realm of the normative, the value-laden. We can point out that an examination of the evidence shows what reality is. Simply stated, when marginal income tax rates are high, the rich do not, in fact, pay a higher average tax rate than when marginal tax rates are lower. It behooves the rich to find methods to reduce tax liabilities and to expend resources to influence politicians to insert an increasing number of loopholes in the Tax Act in order to reduce effective marginal tax rates on those who earn a lot.

For Critical Analysis

1. Do you think employees at Revenue Canada would be for or against the flat-tax system? Explain your choice.

2. Why is a flat-tax system more efficient than a progressive income tax system?

CHAPTER SUMMARY

1. Government can correct external costs through taxation, legislation, and prohibition. It can correct external benefits through financing or production of a good or service, subsidies, and regulation.

2. Government provides a legal system in which the rights of private ownership, the enforcement of contracts, and the legal status of businesses are provided. In other words, government sets the legal rules of the game and enforces them.

3. Public goods, once produced, can be consumed jointly by additional individuals at zero opportunity cost. If users of public goods know that they will be taxed on the basis of their expressed valuation of those public goods, their expressed valuation will be low. They expect to get a free ride.

4. Merit goods (chosen as such, collectively, through the political process) may not be purchased at all or not in sufficient quantities at market clearing prices. Therefore, government subsidizes or provides such merit goods at a subsidized or zero price to specified classes of consumers.

5. When it is collectively decided that something is a demerit good, government taxes, regulates, or prohibits the manufacture, sale, and use of that good.

6. The market sector and the public sector both face scarcity, feature competition, and contain similar individuals. They differ in that many government, or political, goods are provided at zero price, collective action may involve the use of force, and political voting can lead to different results than dollar voting.

7. Bureaucrats often exert great influence on the course of policy because they are in charge of the day-to-day operation of current policy and provide much of the information needed to formulate future policy. Bureaucracies often organize their clientele, coach clients on what is appropriate, and stick up for their rights.

8. Marginal tax rates are those paid on the last dollar of income, whereas average tax rates are determined by the proportion of income paid in income taxes.

9. With a proportional income tax system, marginal rates are constant. With a regressive system, they go down as income rises, and with a progressive system, they go up as income rises.

10. Government spending at the federal level is different from that at the provincial and municipal levels. Interest on the debt, elderly benefits, and transfers to the provinces account for almost 60 percent of the federal budget. Health care and education constitute over 40 percent of provincial government expenditures.

DISCUSSION OF PREVIEW QUESTIONS

1. **What are the economic and political functions of the public sector?**

   The economic functions which call for government intervention in the economy include: correcting market failures, providing a legal system, promoting competition, providing public goods, and ensuring economic stability. The two key political functions are: providing merit goods (and restricting demerit goods), and distributing income in a more equitable manner.

2. **What is the foundation of public-choice theory?**

   The foundation of public-choice theory is that politicians, bureaucrats, and voters will act so as to maximize their own self-interest (or economic well-being) rather than the community's. In other words, because such people are human, they are subject to the same motivations and drives as the rest of us. They will usually make decisions in terms of what benefits them, not society as a whole. Such an assumption permits economists to apply economic maximization principles to voters, candidates, elected officials, and policymakers.

3. **In what ways do regressive, proportional, and progressive tax structures differ?**

   Under a regressive tax structure, the average tax rate (the percentage of income paid in taxes) falls as income rises. The marginal tax rate is below the average tax rate. Proportional tax structures are those in which the average tax rate remains constant as income rises; the marginal tax rate equals the average tax rate. Under a progressive tax structure, the average tax rate rises as income rises; the marginal tax rate is above the average tax rate. Our federal personal income tax system is an example of a progressive system.

4. How do the federal government's spending habits differ from those of the provinces?

At the federal level, interest on the public debt, elderly benefits and transfers to the provinces account for almost 60 percent of the federal budget. Health care and education constitute over 40 percent of provincial government expenditures.

PROBLEMS

(Answers to the odd-numbered problems appear at the back of the book.)

6-1. Consider the following system of taxation, which has been labelled *degressive*. The first $5,000 of income is not taxed. After that, all income is assessed at 20 percent (a proportional system). What is the marginal tax rate on $3,000 of taxable income? $10,000? $100,000? What is the average tax rate on $3,000? $10,000? $100,000? What is the maximum average tax rate?

6-2. You are offered two possible bonds to buy as part of your investing program. One is a corporate bond yielding 9 percent. The other is a tax-exempt municipal bond yielding only 6 percent. Assuming that you are certain you will be paid your interest and principal on these two bonds, what marginal tax bracket must you be in to decide in favour of the tax-exempt bond?

6-3. Consider the following tax structure:

Income Bracket	Marginal Tax Rate
$0–$1,500	0%
$1,501–$2,000	14%
$2,001–$3,000	20%

Mr. Smith has an income of $2,500 per annum. Calculate his tax bill for the year. What is his average tax rate? His highest marginal tax rate?

6-4. In 1999, Canada Pension Plan premiums on wages were 3 percent of wages up to $37,400. No further CPP premiums are paid on earnings above this figure. Calculate the average CPP tax rate for annual wages of (a) $4,000, (b) $51,300, (c) $56,000, (d) $100,000. Is the CPP system a progressive, proportional, or regressive tax structure?

6-5. What is meant by the expression "market failure"?

6-6. TV signals have characteristics of public goods, yet TV stations and commercial networks are private businesses. Analyze this situation.

6-7. Assume that you live in a relatively small suburban neighbourhood called Parkwood. The Parkwood Homeowners' Association collects money from homeowners to pay for upkeep of the surrounding stone wall, lighting at the entrances to Parkwood, and mowing the lawn around the perimeter of the area. Each year you are asked to donate $50. No one forces you to do it. There are 100 homeowners in Parkwood.

   a. What percentage of the total yearly revenue of the homeowners' association will you account for?

   b. At what level of participation will the absence of your $50 contribution make a difference?

   c. If you do not contribute your $50, are you really receiving a totally free ride?

6-8. Assume that the only textile firm that exists has created a negative externality by polluting a nearby stream with the wastes associated with production. Assume further that the government can measure the external costs to the community with accuracy and charges the firm for its pollution, based on the social cost of pollution per unit of textile output. Show how such a charge will lead to a higher selling price for textiles and a reduction in the equilibrium quantity of textiles.

6-9. The existence of information and transactions costs has many implications in economics. What are some of these implications in the context of issues discussed in this chapter?

6-10. A favourite political campaign theme in recent years has been to reduce the size, complexity, and bureaucratic nature of the federal government. Nonetheless, the size of the federal government, however measured, continues to increase. Use the theory of public choice to explain why.

6-11. Figures 6.3 and 6.4 give revenues and expenditures for provincial and municipal governments combined. Visit Statistics Canada's Provincial and Territorial General Government Revenue and Expenditure Site at http://www.statcan.ca/english/Pgdb/State/Government/govt08a.htm and locate your province. Calculate what proportion of total revenues and expenditures each category forms. Compare your percentages to Figures 6.3 and 6.4.

a. Does your government receive relatively more or less of its revenues from any particular source? What characteristics of your provincial economy would account for this?

b. Does your government spend relatively more or less of its budget in any particular area? What characteristics of your provincial economy would account for this?

ECONOMICS ON THE NET

Reducing the Tax Burden for Middle-Class Canadians

In the 2000 Federal Budget Plan proposed by the current Liberal government, there are a number of planned personal income tax changes which are aimed at providing tax relief to middle-class Canadians. In this application we encourage you to use the Internet to view the proposed income tax changes of the federal Liberal government in their year 2000 budget.

Internet URL: http://www.fin.gc.ca/budget00/bpe/bpch4_2e.htm

Title: Five-Year Tax Reduction Plan

Application: Read through the first few Web pages at this site. Then answer the following questions:

1. Identify and explain three specific income tax changes proposed in the year 2000 budget which are designed to reduce the tax burden for middle-class Canadians.

2. Do you think that the income tax changes identified in 1. above were helpful to the re-election of the Liberal Party in the November 2000 federal election? Explain.

THE MACROECONOMY: UNEMPLOYMENT AND INFLATION

You know that you are affected by changes in the prices of the goods and services that you buy and by what happens to your wage rate or salary. To determine whether you are better off this year than you were last year, you have to compare the average percentage increase in all prices in Canada with the percentage increase in your income. For many decades, there have been increases, but no decreases, in the average price level in Canada. Thus, you have had to worry about inflation and how it affected your real standard of living. But, recently, the inflation rate has been dropping. So now some people are worried that the average of all prices may fall in the future. If this occurs, will you be better off or worse off? Before you can answer that question, you need to learn more about two important aspects of the macroeconomy.

PREVIEW QUESTIONS

1. What are the types of unemployment?

2. What is a price index?

3. Does it matter whether inflation is anticipated or not?

4. How do we describe the phases of national business fluctuations?

DID YOU KNOW THAT... although Canada is considered a highly advanced industrialized nation, less and less of its employment is involved in manufacturing? The same is true of the United States, Japan, Germany, France, Italy, and the United Kingdom, where the number of manufacturing workers has been dropping steadily since 1970, despite significant increases in total adult population. Yet the result has *not* been workers permanently out of jobs. Even so, work is a major policy issue facing many countries today. At the core of macroeconomics—the study of the performance and structure of the national economy—are the issues of employment and, more importantly, unemployment.

Unemployment

Unemployment The total number of adults aged 15 years or older who are willing and able to work, and who are actively looking for work but have not found a job.

Unemployment is the total number of adults 15 years or older who are willing and able to work, and who are actively looking for work, but have not found a job. Unemployment creates a cost to the entire economy in terms of loss of output. One researcher estimated that at the beginning of the 1990s when unemployment was about 10.5 percent and factories were running at 72 percent of their capacity, the amount of output that the economy lost due to idle resources was almost 6 percent of the total production throughout Canada. (In other words, we were somewhere inside the production possibilities curve that we talked about in Chapter 2.) That was the equivalent of almost $36 billion of schools, houses, restaurant meals, cars, and movies that *could have been* produced. It is no wonder that policymakers closely watch the unemployment figures published by Statistics Canada.

On a more personal level, being unemployed often results in hardship and failed opportunities as well as a lack of self-respect. Psychological researchers believe that being fired creates at least as much stress as the death of a close friend. The numbers that we present about unemployment can never fully convey its true cost to this or any other country.

Historical Unemployment Rates

Labour force Individuals aged 15 years or older who either have jobs or are looking and available for jobs; the number of employed plus the number of unemployed.

The unemployment rate, defined as a proportion of the measured **labour force** that is unemployed, dropped to a low of 2.4 percent of the Canadian labour force at the end of World War II, after having reached almost 20 percent during the Great Depression in the 1930s. You can see in Figure 7.1 what happened to unemployment in Canada over the past century. The highest level ever was reached in the Great Depression, but unemployment was also very high during the 1981–82 recession. Unemployment is currently as low as it has been in the past 25 years.

Employment, Unemployment, and the Labour Force

Figure 7.2 presents the population of individuals 15 years of age or older broken into three segments: (1) employed, (2) unemployed, and (3) not in the labour force (a category that includes homemakers, full-time students, and retired persons). Those who are employed and those who are unemployed, added together, make up the labour force. In 2000, the labour force amounted to 14.91 million + 1.09 million = 16.00 million Canadians. To calculate the unemployment rate, we simply divide the number of unemployed by the number of people in the labour force and multiply by 100:

$$\text{Unemployment rate} = \frac{\text{number of unemployed}}{\text{labour force}} \times 100$$

In 2000, the unemployment rate was $1.09 \div 16.00 \times 100 = 6.8$ percent.

FIGURE 7.1 **Eighty Years of Unemployment**

Unemployment reached a low of less than 2 percent during World War II, and a high of almost 20 percent during the Great Depression.

Source: Statistics Canada, *Historical Statistics of Canada,* Catalogue 11-516-X1E, Series D129, D132, D233; Statistics Canada, CANSIM Database, Series D31252, D31253, D984954.

Great Depression

1981-86 Recession

1991 Recession

World War II

Unemployment Rate (%)

Year

FIGURE 7.2 **Adult Population, 2000**

The population aged 15 and older can be broken down into three groups: people who are employed, those who are unemployed, and those not in the labour force.

Source: Adapted from Statistics Canada, CANSIM Database, Series D28597, D28598.

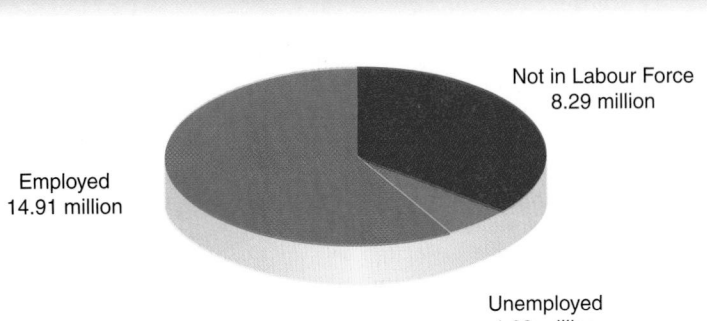

Not in Labour Force
8.29 million

Employed
14.91 million

Unemployed
1.09 million

While you may think that this definition of labour force is fairly obvious, there are important considerations to be made as to who should be counted, and who should not. Thinking Critically About the Media 7-1 illustrates how measuring unemployment in the United States is done quite differently than in Canada, and how comparing the two can be quite deceiving.

The Arithmetic Determination of Unemployment

Because there is a transition between employment and unemployment at any point in time—people are leaving jobs and others are finding jobs—there is a simple relationship between the employed and the unemployed, as can be seen in Figure 7.3. People departing jobs are shown at the top of the diagram, and people taking new jobs are shown at the bottom. If job leavers and job finders are equal, the unemployment rate stays the same. If departures exceed new hires, the unemployment rate rises.

The number of unemployed can be expressed as some number at any given point in time. It is a **stock** of individuals who do not have a job but are actively looking for one. The number of employed can be expressed the same way. The number of people departing jobs, whether voluntarily or involuntarily, is a **flow**, as is the number of people finding jobs. Picturing a bathtub, as illustrated in Figure 7.4, is a good way of remembering how stocks and flows work.

UNEMPLOYMENT CATEGORIES. According to Statistics Canada, an individual is considered unemployed if willing and able to work and in any of three categories:

1. Not working, but making specific efforts within the previous four weeks to find a job.
2. Laid off from a job within the previous 26 weeks and waiting for recall.
3. Waiting to begin a new job within the next four weeks.

If the unemployed person is not available for work, then that individual is not considered to be part of the labour force.

DURATION OF UNEMPLOYMENT. If you are out of a job for a week, your situation is typically much less serious than if you are out of a job for 14 weeks. An increase in the duration of unemployment can increase the unemployment rate because workers stay unemployed longer, thereby creating a greater number of them at any given time. The most recent information on duration of unemployment paints the following picture: 25.1 percent of those who become unemployed find a new job by the end of one month, 27.6

Stock The quantity of something, measured at a given point in time—for example, an inventory of goods or a bank account. Stocks are defined independently of time, although they are assessed at a point in time.

Flow A quantity measured per unit of time; something that occurs over time, such as the income you make per week or per year, or the number of individuals who are fired every month.

FIGURE 7.3 The Logic of the Unemployment Rate

Job leavers are individuals who are no longer employed and add to the unemployed (except for those who permanently leave the labour force, such as new retirees). When the unemployed find a job, they add to the employed. When both flows are equal, the unemployment rate is stable. If more people leave jobs than find them, the unemployment rate increases, and vice versa.

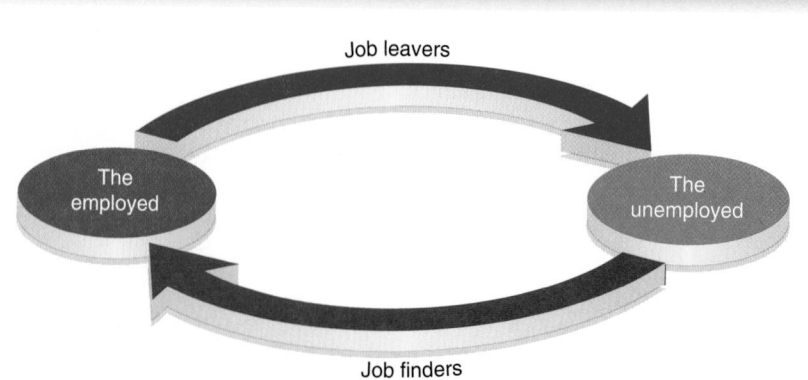

FIGURE 7.4 Visualizing Stocks and Flows

Unemployment at any point in time is some number that represents a stock, such as the amount of water in a bathtub. People who lose their job constitute a new flow into the bathtub. Those who find a job can be thought of as the water that flows out by the drain.

Stock of unemployment

Flow of people leaving jobs

Flow of people finding jobs

Thinking Critically About the Media 7-1   Is Unemployment Higher in Canada than in the United States?

Frequent reports in the media point out that Canada's 6.8 percent unemployment rate (in the year 2000) is almost 3 percentage points higher than that in the United States. The implication is that Canada is not as competitive, or perhaps as economically buoyant, as our neighbour to the south. However, Professor Craig Riddell, former president of the Canadian Economics Association, suggests that there are other reasons for this difference. In the US, the unemployed who only look at help wanted ads in their job search are not counted as unemployed because they haven't actively looked for work. In Canada they are. Furthermore, about 2 percent of unemployed men in the US are in prison, men who tra-ditionally have trouble finding jobs. Since they cannot be in prison and in the labour force both, the US unemployment rate is again biased downwards. Finally, the unemployed in the US are less likely to receive unemployment insurance benefits than the unemployed in Canada. Economists have long believed that the existence of these benefits lengthens a person's period of unemployment, thus raising the unemployment rate. Together, these differences may account for as much as 1.9 percentage points of the difference between our two rates. If the unemployed were counted in the same way in each country, we might find that our unemployment rate would be only one percent higher than in the US.

percent find a job within three months, and 27.5 percent are still unemployed after six months. Over the past decade the average duration of unemployment for all unemployed has been 21 weeks. When overall business activity goes into a downturn, the duration of unemployment tends to rise, thereby causing much of the increase in the estimated unemployment rate. In a sense, then, it is the increase in the duration of unemployment during a downturn in national economic activity which generates the bad news that concerns policymakers in Ottawa. Furthermore, the 27.5 percent who stay unemployed longer than six months are the ones who create the pressure on the federal government to "do something." What the government has typically done in the past is extend and supplement unemployment benefits. However, with the Employment Insurance plan implemented in mid-1996, employment insurance benefits are more difficult to get. The government hopes this will act as an incentive to the unemployed to look harder for work.

Discouraged workers Individuals who have dropped out of the labour force and are no longer looking for a job because they believe the job market has little to offer them. Typically, they become convinced of this after unsuccessfully searching for a job.

THE DISCOURAGED WORKER PHENOMENON. Critics of the published unemployment rate calculated by the federal government believe that there exist numerous **discouraged workers** and "hidden unemployed." Though there is no exact definition or way to measure discouraged workers, Statistics Canada defines them as people who have dropped out of the labour force and are no longer looking for a job because they believe that the job market has little to offer them. To what extent do we want to include in the measured labour force individuals who voluntarily choose not to look for work, or those who take only two minutes a day to scan the want ads and then decide that there are no jobs?

Some economists argue that people who work part time but are willing to work full time should be classified as "semi-hidden" unemployed. Estimates of this category of unemployment range as high as 2.5 million workers at any one time. Offsetting this factor, though, is *overemployment*. An individual working 50 or 60 hours a week, or a full-time *and* part-time job, is still counted as only one full-time worker.

Thinking Critically About the Media 7-2   Declining Job Security?

The decade of the 1990s has been labelled by the media as the one during which millions of workers lost job security. We have been told that corporate downsizing and global competition have resulted in Canadian workers having to accept changing jobs as a regular part of their lives. Between 1981 and 1985, 46 percent of new jobs created lasted 6 months or less. In 1996, that number had risen to 54 percent. Between 1981 and 1985, 34 percent of new jobs created lasted from six months to five years. Now only 27 percent last that long. Nevertheless, once a job has lasted for one year it is more likely to last longer than five years today (56 percent) than in 1991 (48 percent).

Labour force participation rate The percentage of working-age individuals who are employed or seeking employment.

LABOUR FORCE PARTICIPATION. The way in which we define unemployment and membership in the labour force will affect what is known as the **labour force participation rate.** It is defined as the proportion of working-age individuals who are employed or seeking employment. (If there are discouraged, or hidden, unemployed within any particular group, the labour force participation rate for that particular group will drop.)

Figure 7.5 illustrates the labour force participation rates since 1946. The major change has been the increase in female labour force participation. From a low of 23.2 percent in 1950, the female labour force participation rate climbed steadily to a high of 58.9 percent in 1999. The composition of the labour force seems to be changing, however, as is explained in Example 7.1.

FIGURE 7.5 Labour Force Participation Rates by Sex

The combined labour force participation rate has increased in recent years. However, over the same period, the male participation rate has fallen, and the female rate has risen markedly.

Source: Statistics Canada, *Historical Statistics of Canada,* Catalogue 11-516-X1E, Series D146, D147, D148, D149; Statistics Canada, CANSIM Database, Series D985016, D985032, D985048.

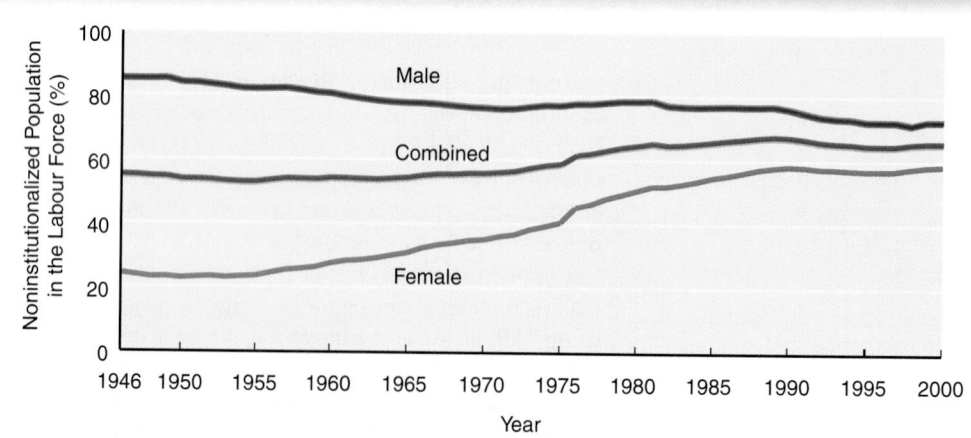

EXAMPLE 7-1   Does Increasing Employment Mean More People Are Hired?

It used to be that a rising employment rate indicated corporations were expanding, providing more jobs for the pool of unemployed. In Canada, however, that tide is changing with self-employment forming an ever-increasing share of paid employment.

During the 1980s, corporate expansion accounted for 47 percent of new full-time paid jobs, while in the 1990s it accounted for only 18 percent. Self-employment accounted for only 6 percent of new jobs in the 1980s, but increased to 58 percent in the 1990s.

It is too early to tell whether there has been a permanent shift in the way the labour market works in Canada. For example, self-employment may be on the increase because companies have changed the way they create work. They may be contracting out more work now, hiring independent consultants on term-specific contracts, rather than creating jobs for regular employees. Or the rise in self-employment may be a reaction to the high unemployment rates of the early 1990s: as discouraged workers gave up hope of finding traditional jobs, they found instead a way to create their own work.

For critical analysis: Over the 1990s, the labour force participation rate has fallen for men but grown slowly for women. What inferences can you make about the gender of the self-employed in the 1990s?

CONCEPTS IN BRIEF

- Unemployed persons are those 15 years of age and older who are willing and able to work and are actively looking for a job but have not found one.
- The unemployment rate is calculated by dividing the number of unemployed by the total labour force—those who are employed plus those who are unemployed—and multiplying the result by 100. The flow of people leaving jobs and people finding jobs determines the stock of unemployed as well as the stock of employed.
- The duration of unemployment affects the unemployment rate. The number of unemployed workers can remain the same, but if the duration of unemployment increases, the measured unemployment rate will go up.
- While overall labour force participation has risen only a bit since World War II, there has been a major increase in female labour force participation.

The Major Types of Unemployment

Unemployment has been categorized into four basic types: frictional, seasonal, structural, and cyclical.

Frictional unemployment
Unemployment due to the fact that workers must search for appropriate job offers. This takes time, and so they remain temporarily ("frictionally") unemployed.

FRICTIONAL UNEMPLOYMENT. Of the almost 16 million Canadians in the labour force, more than 1.3 million will have either changed jobs or taken new jobs during the year; every single month about 785,000 workers will have quit, been laid off (told that they will be rehired later), or been permanently fired; another 940,000 will have gone to new jobs or returned to old ones. In the process, more than 3 million persons will have reported themselves unemployed at one time or another. What we call **frictional unemployment** is the continuous flow of individuals from job to job and in and out of employment. There will always be some frictional unemployment as resources are redirected in the market because transaction costs are never zero. In the labour market, these costs involve time spent looking for a job, being interviewed, negotiating the pay, and so on.

To eliminate frictional unemployment, we would have to prevent workers from leaving their present jobs until they had already lined up other jobs at which they would start working immediately, and we would have to guarantee first-time job seekers a job *before* they started looking.

Seasonal unemployment
Unemployment resulting from the seasonal pattern of work in specific industries. It is usually due to seasonal fluctuations in demand or to changing weather conditions, rendering work difficult, if not impossible, as in the agriculture, construction, and tourist industries.

SEASONAL UNEMPLOYMENT. Seasonal unemployment comes and goes with seasons of the year in which the demand for particular jobs rises and falls. For example, construction workers can often work only during the warmer months; they are seasonally unemployed during the winter. Summer resort workers can usually get jobs in resorts only during the summer season. They, too, become seasonally unemployed during the winter; the opposite is true for ski resort workers.

Structural unemployment
Unemployment resulting from a mismatch of available jobs and skills. It occurs, for example, when the demand for a product falls drastically so that workers specializing in the production of that product find themselves out of work.

STRUCTURAL UNEMPLOYMENT. Structural changes in our economy cause some workers to become unemployed permanently or for very long periods of time because they cannot find jobs that use their particular skills. This is called **structural unemployment**. Structural unemployment is not caused by general business fluctuations, although business fluctuations may affect it. And unlike frictional unemployment, structural unemployment is not related to the movement of workers from low-paying to high-paying jobs. Structural unemployment occurs when there is a mismatch of available jobs and available skills. For example, a shipbuilding company in Nova Scotia may have job openings for qualified shipwrights, but all the qualified shipwrights live in British Columbia. Or a printing firm may update its technology, making the skills of its existing workforce obsolete. The firm hires new workers and lays off the old, who are now structurally unemployed. Sometimes, governments can create structural unemployment as evidenced in International Example 7-1.

INTERNATIONAL EXAMPLE 7-1   Structural Unemployment in Europe Never Seems to Go Away

From 1980 to 2000, about 3 million full-time jobs were created in Canada, mostly in the private sector. Yet in the European Union (EU) virtually no private-sector jobs were created during the same period. As Canadian unemployment dropped to a 25-year low of 6.7 percent, EU unemployment stayed well above 10 percent. Any modestly trained outside observer understands why the EU is in such trouble: high taxes paid by employers on all employees and rigid labour markets. Employers pay their governments an amount equal to 50 percent to 200 percent of employees' wages as "social charges." Moreover, government-mandated minimum wages often far exceed the value low-skilled workers might contribute to potential employers. Consequently, many low-skilled unemployed are unable to find jobs. Firing workers is legally difficult and always costly because obligatory severance pay is high. Even so, many fired European workers take their employers to court to try to regain their jobs or obtain even higher payments.

One result of this situation is that temporary employment is booming throughout Europe. One researcher estimated that about 30 percent of the world's temporary labour market resides in France alone. Almost 90 percent of new hires in France, for example, are on short-term contracts.

The hardest hit is the portion of the labour force under age 25. In the EU, the average unemployment rate for that group is about 20 percent and in France it exceeds 25 percent.

For critical analysis: If the reasons for the EU's high unemployment rate are so obvious, why aren't governments relaxing strict labour laws and reducing "social charges" levied on employers?

Cyclical unemployment Unemployment resulting from business recessions that occur when aggregate (total) demand is insufficient to create full employment.

CYCLICAL UNEMPLOYMENT. **Cyclical unemployment** is related to business fluctuations. It is defined as unemployment associated with changes in business conditions—primarily recessions and depressions. The way to lessen cyclical unemployment would be to reduce the intensity, duration, and frequency of ups and downs of business activity. Economic policymakers attempt, through their policies, to reduce cyclical unemployment by keeping business activity on an even keel.

Full Employment

Try Preview Question 1:
What are the types of unemployment?

Does full employment mean that everybody has a job? No, because not everyone is looking for a job—full-time students and full-time homemakers, for example, are not. Is it possible for everyone who is looking for a job always to find one? No, because transaction costs in the labour market are not zero.

We will always have some frictional unemployment as individuals move in and out of the labour force, seek higher-paying jobs, and move to different parts of the country. **Full employment** is therefore a vague concept implying some sort of balance or equilibrium in an ever-shifting labour market. In general, full employment exists if only frictional and structural unemployment exists. In this case, only workers who are between jobs, and those whose skills are not needed in the economy, are unemployed. In order to carry out appropriate policies to reduce unemployment, it is important to know when the economy has reached full employment. Economists estimate this through the **natural rate of unemployment**, which is the rate of unemployment that prevails when only frictional and structural unemployment exists. The natural rate of unemployment is then seasonally adjusted to reflect seasonal unemployment, and should therefore exclude cyclical unemployment. As an indication of how difficult it is to identify which type of unemployment is which, however, the Government of Canada and the Bank of Canada estimate that the natural rate of unemployment is somewhere between 7.4 and 9.5 percent. Given that the current rate of unemployment is near or even below the bottom of this range, it is not surprising to see reports of labour shortages in newspapers.

Full employment That level of unemployment when only frictional and structural unemployment exists.

Natural rate of unemployment The rate of unemployment that occurs when only frictional and structural unemployment exists.

CONCEPTS IN BRIEF

- Frictional unemployment occurs because of transaction costs in the labour market. For example, workers do not have all the information necessary about vacancies. Structural unemployment occurs when there is a mismatch for geographical or technological reasons of available jobs and available skills.
- Cyclical unemployment exists when the economy is in recession and firms have laid off employees.
- The level of frictional and structural unemployment is used to determine our (somewhat arbitrary) definition of full employment. The natural rate of unemployment is the rate of unemployment that occurs when only frictional and structural unemployment exists.

Inflation and Deflation

Inflation The situation in which the average of all prices of goods and services in an economy is rising.

Deflation The situation in which the average of all prices of goods and services in an economy is falling.

During World War II, you could buy bread for 10 to 15 cents a loaf and have milk delivered fresh to your door for about 25 cents a half gallon (2.25 litres). The average price of a new car was less than $1,000, and the average house cost less than $5,000. Today bread, milk, cars, and houses all cost more—a lot more. Prices are now 10 times what they were in 1940. Clearly, this country has experienced quite a bit of *inflation* since then. We define **inflation** as an upward movement in the average level of prices. The opposite of inflation is **deflation**, defined as a downward movement in the *average* level of prices. Notice that these definitions depend on the average level of prices. This means that even during a period of inflation, some prices can be falling if other prices are rising at a faster rate. The price of computers and computer-related equipment has dropped dramatically since the 1960s, even though there has been general inflation.

To discuss what has happened to inflation in this and other countries, we have to know how to measure it.

Inflation and the Purchasing Power of Money

A rose may be a rose may be a rose, but a dollar is not always a dollar. The value of a dollar does not stay constant when there is inflation. The value of money is usually talked about in terms of the **purchasing power** of money. A dollar's purchasing power is the amount of goods and services that it can buy. Consequently, another way of defining inflation is as a decline in the purchasing power of money. The higher the rate of inflation, the greater the drop in the purchasing power of money.

Thinking Critically About the Media 7-3 illustrates that the concept of purchasing power is also applied internationally. Relative prices across different countries, after accounting for exchange rates, show how purchasing power varies across countries as well as through time. When we get to Chapter 20 we will look at this in more detail.

One way to think about inflation and the purchasing power of money is to discuss dollar values in terms of nominal versus real values. The nominal value of anything is simply its price expressed in today's dollars. In contrast, the real value of anything is its value expressed in purchasing power, which varies with the rate of inflation. Let's say that you received a $100 bill as a gift for your birthday this year. One year from now, the nominal value of that bill will still be $100. The real value will depend on what the purchasing power of money is after one year's worth of inflation. Obviously, if there has been a lot of inflation in one year, the real value of that $100 bill will have dropped.

Measuring the Rate of Inflation

How do we come up with a measure of the rate of inflation? This is indeed a thorny problem for government statisticians. It is easy to determine how much the price of an individual commodity has risen: If last year a light bulb cost 50 cents and this year it costs 75 cents, there has been a 50 percent rise in the price of that light bulb over a one-year

Purchasing power The amount of goods and services a given amount of money can buy. If your money income stays the same but the price of one good that you are buying goes up, your effective purchasing power falls, and vice versa.

Thinking Critically About the Media 7-3   Gasoline Prices

We frequently read in the popular press about Canadian gasoline prices being so much higher than those in the United States because of the extra taxes we pay per litre. This cry grew in volume in mid-2000 when there was a temporary shortage of crude oil and gas prices rose sharply. However, before we feel too sorry for ourselves, we should look at gasoline prices elsewhere. The table at the right gives the price per litre for premium gasoline in Canadian currency for seven countries.

While the American price is about five-sixths the Canadian price, the Canadian price is low relative to those in Europe. Perhaps we are better off than the media would have us think!

Country	Price per Litre
United Kingdom (leaded)	$1.93
Netherlands (unleaded)	1.74
France (leaded)	1.63
Italy (leaded)	1.59
Germany (unleaded)	1.50
Canada (unleaded)	.85
United States (unleaded)	.71

period. We can express the change in the individual light bulb price in one of several ways: The price has gone up 25 cents; the price is one and a half (1.5) times as high; the price has risen by 50 percent. An *index number* of this price rise is simply the second way (1.5) multiplied by 100, meaning that the index number would be 150. We multiply by 100 to eliminate decimals because it is easier to think in terms of percentage changes using integers (whole numbers). This is the standard convention adopted for convenience in dealing with index numbers or price levels.

COMPUTING A PRICE INDEX. The measurement problem becomes more complicated when it involves a large number of goods, some of whose prices have risen faster than others and some with prices that have fallen. What we have to do is pick a representative bundle, a so-called market basket, of goods and services and compare the cost of that market basket of goods over time. When we do this, we obtain a **price index**, which is defined as the cost of a market basket of goods today, expressed as a percentage of the cost of that identical market basket of goods in some starting year, known as the **base year**.

Price index The cost of today's market basket of goods and services expressed as a percentage of the cost of the same market basket during a base year.

Base year The year that is chosen as the point of reference for comparison of prices in other years.

$$\text{Price index} = \frac{\text{cost of market basket today}}{\text{cost of market basket in base year}} \times 100$$

In the base year the price index will always be 100, because the year in the numerator and in the denominator is the same; therefore, the fraction equals 1, and when we multiply it by 100, we get 100. A simple numerical example is given in Table 7.1. In the table there are only two goods in the market basket—corn and microcomputers. The *quantities* in the basket remain the same between the base year, 1992, and the current year, 2000; only the *prices* change. Such a *fixed-quantity* price index is the easiest to compute because the statistician need only look at prices of goods and services sold every year rather than actually observing how much of these goods and services consumers actually purchase each year.

You can use a price index to calculate the annual rate of inflation. If the price index rose from 100 to 103 between 2000 and 2001, you could say that the annual rate of inflation was 3 percent. And you would be correct. Putting this into a formula, we have

$$\text{Annual rate of inflation} = \frac{\text{current price index} - \text{previous year's price index}}{\text{previous year's price index}} \times 100$$

Try Preview Question 2:
What is a price index?

Using our example from above, we could calculate the rate of inflation to be

$$\text{Rate of inflation} = \frac{103 - 100}{100} \times 100 = 3\%$$

TABLE 7.1

Calculating a Price Index for a Two-Good Market Basket

In this simplified example, there are only two goods—corn and microcomputers. The quantities and base-year prices are given in columns 2 and 3. The cost of the 1992 market basket, calculated in column 4, comes to $1,400. The 2000 prices are given in column 5. The cost of the market basket in 2000, calculated in column 6, is $1,700. The price index for 2000, compared with 1992 is 121.43.

(1) Commodity	(2) Market Basket Quantity	(3) 1992 Price per Unit	(4) Cost of Market Basket in 1992	(5) 2000 Price per Unit	(6) Cost of Market Basket at 2000 Prices
Corn	100 bushels	$ 4	$ 400	$ 8	$ 800
Microcomputers	2	500	1,000	450	900
Totals			$1,400		$1,700

$$\text{Price index} = \frac{\text{cost of market basket in 2000}}{\text{cost of market basket in base year 1992}} \times 100 = \frac{\$1,700}{\$1,400} \times 100 = 121.43$$

Consumer Price Index (CPI) A statistical measure of a weighted average of prices of a specified set of goods and services purchased by wage earners in urban areas.

Producer Price Index (PPI) A statistical measure of a weighted average of prices of commodities that firms purchase from other firms.

GDP deflator A price index measuring the changes in prices of all new goods and services produced in the economy.

REAL-WORLD PRICE INDEXES. Government statisticians calculate a number of price indexes. The most often quoted are the **Consumer Price Index (CPI)**, the **Producer Price Index (PPI)**, and the **GDP deflator**. The CPI attempts to measure changes only in the level of prices of goods and services purchased by wage earners. The PPI attempts to show what has happened to the price level for commodities that firms purchase from other firms. The GDP deflator attempts to show changes in the level of prices of all new goods and services produced in the economy. The most general indicator of inflation is the GDP deflator because it measures the changes in the prices of everything produced in the economy.

THE CPI. Statistics Canada has the task of identifying a market basket of goods and services of the typical consumer. Every so often (usually every 5 to 10 years), the prices of almost 500 goods and services are recorded and used to formulate the base year price level. The current base year is 1992.

Economists have known for years that the way Statistics Canada measures changes in the Consumer Price Index is flawed. Specifically, StatCan has been unable to account for the way consumers substitute less expensive items for higher-priced items. The reason is that the CPI is a fixed-quantity price index (like the index in Table 7-1), meaning that each month StatCan samples only prices, rather than relative quantities purchased by consumers. In addition, Statistics Canada has been unable to take account of quality changes as they occur. Even if it captures the dramatically falling price of personal computers, it has been unable to reflect the dramatic improvement in quality. Finally, the CPI ignores the introduction of new products.

THE PPI. There are a number of Producer Price Indexes, including one for food materials, another for intermediate goods (goods used in the production of other goods), and one for finished goods. Most of the producer prices included are in mining, manufacturing, and agriculture. The PPIs can be considered general-purpose indexes for nonretail markets.

Although in the long run the various PPIs and the CPI generally show the same rate of inflation, such is not the case in the short run. Most often the PPIs increase before the CPI because it takes time for producer price increases to show up in the prices that consumers pay for final products. Often changes in the PPIs are watched closely as a hint that inflation is going to increase or decrease.

THE GDP DEFLATOR. The broadest price index reported in Canada is the GDP deflator, where GDP stands for gross domestic product, or annual total national income. Unlike the CPI and the PPIs, the GDP deflator is not based on a fixed market basket of goods and services. The basket is allowed to change with people's consumption and investment patterns. In this sense, the changes in the GDP deflator reflect both price changes and the public's market responses to those price changes. Why? Because new expenditure patterns are allowed to show up in the GDP deflator as people respond to changing prices.

We calculate the GDP deflator by first choosing a base year, as with the other price indexes. Then we compare a subsequent year's GDP with the base year.

$$\text{GDP deflator} = \frac{\text{current year's GDP}}{\text{base year's GDP}} \times 100$$

In 1999, the GDP deflator was 108.8, which means the average level across the country has increased by 8.8 percent since 1992, the base year currently used by Statistics Canada.

HISTORICAL CHANGES IN THE CPI. The Consumer Price Index has shown a fairly dramatic trend upward since about World War II. Figure 7.6 shows the annual rate of change in the Consumer Price Index since 1867. Prior to World War II, there were numerous periods of deflation along with periods of inflation. Persistent year-in and year-out inflation seems to be a post-World War II phenomenon, at least in this country. As far back as before Confederation, prices used to rise during war periods but then would fall back to more normal levels afterward. This occurred during the War of 1812 and World War I. Consequently, the overall price level in 1940 wasn't much different from 150 years earlier. Other countries have not been so fortunate, however, as you will discover in International Example 7-2.

FIGURE 7.6 **Inflationary Periods in Canadian History**

Since Confederation, there have been numerous periods of inflation in Canada. Here we show them as reflected by changes in the Consumer Price Index. Since World War II, the periods of inflation have not been followed by periods of deflation; that is, even during peacetime, the price index has continued to rise. The yellow areas represent wartime.

Source: Statistics Canada, *Historical Statistics of Canada,* CANSIM Database, Series P200000; Data from A. Green and A. Urquhart, "New Estimates of Output Growth in Canada," *Perspectives on Canadian Economic History,* 1994. Reprinted with permission of Pearson Education Canada.

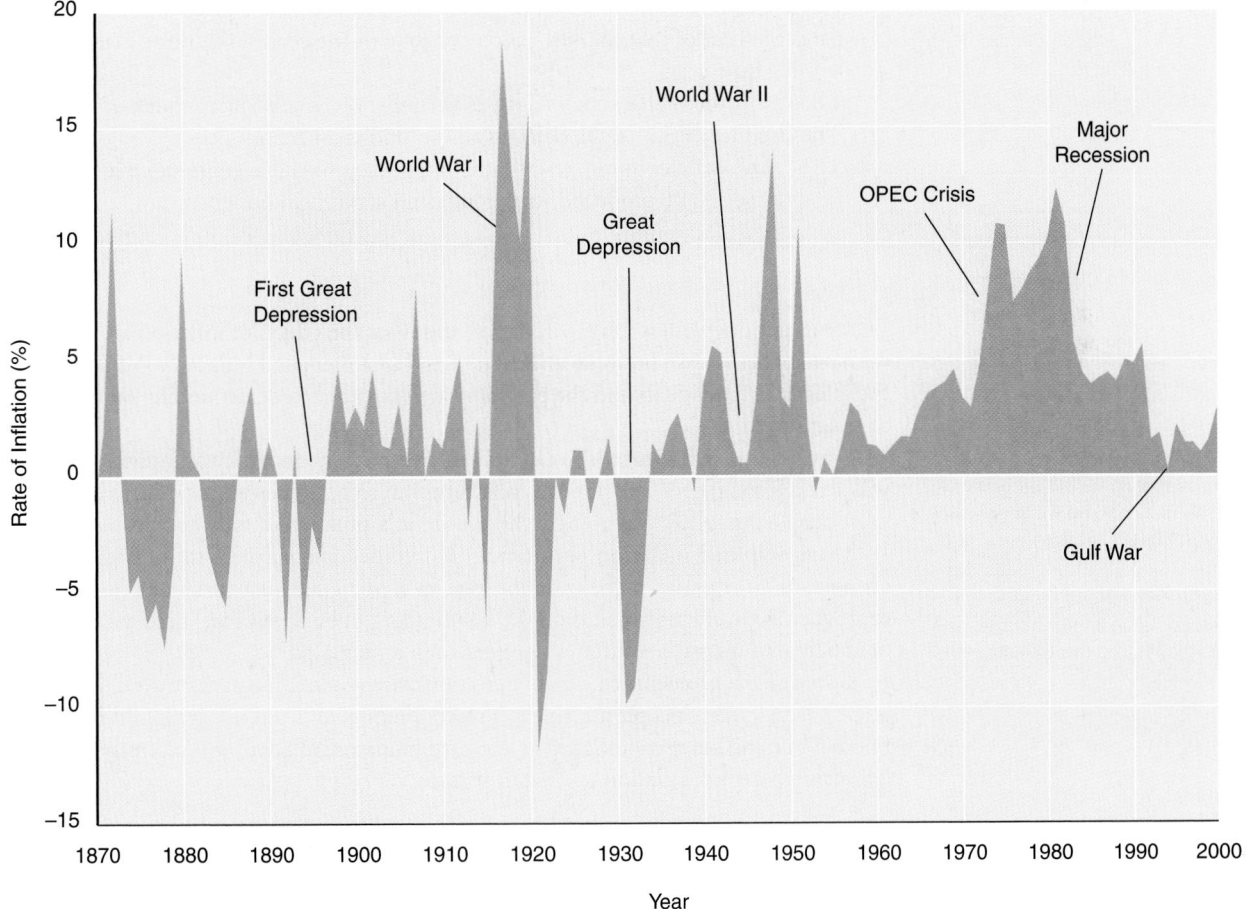

INTERNATIONAL EXAMPLE 7-2

Hyperinflation

Hyperinflation Extremely rapid rise of the average of all prices in an economy.

Referring to Figure 7.6, look at the highest rates of inflation that Canada has experienced. At the start of the 1981 recession, the estimated inflation rate was over 10 percent. Rarely have we experienced such high inflation rates. Consider, in contrast, the rest of the world. Many countries have experienced and continue to experience **hyperinflation**, an extreme form of inflation during which average prices rise very rapidly. In 1989, Argentina had an inflation rate of 4,923 percent; the following year, in Peru, the rate was 7,481 percent. Russia's 1995 inflation of 340 percent seems almost modest in comparison. The most extreme hyperinflation ever to occur was in Germany in 1923, when prices increased by *700 billion* percent.

For critical analysis: As a consumer, how would your behaviour change during a period of hyperinflation?

CONCEPTS IN BRIEF

- Once we pick a market basket of goods, we can construct a price index that compares the cost of that market basket today with the cost of the same market basket in a base year.
- The Consumer Price Index (CPI) is the most often used price index in Canada. The Producer Price Index (PPI) is the second most mentioned.
- The GDP deflator measures what is happening to the average price level of *all* new, domestically produced final goods and services in our economy.

Anticipated Versus Unanticipated Inflation

Before examining who is hurt by inflation and what the effects of inflation are in general, we have to distinguish between anticipated and unanticipated inflation. We will see that the effects on individuals and the economy are vastly different, depending on which type of inflation exists.

Anticipated inflation The inflation rate that the majority of individuals believe will occur; when it does, we are in a situation of fully anticipated inflation.

Anticipated inflation is the rate of inflation that the majority of individuals believe will occur. If the rate of inflation this year turns out to be 10 percent, and that's about what most people thought it was going to be, we are in a situation of fully anticipated inflation.

Unanticipated inflation Inflation at a rate that comes as a surprise, either higher or lower than the rate anticipated.

Unanticipated inflation is inflation that comes as a surprise to individuals in the economy. For example, if the inflation rate in a particular year turns out to be 10 percent when on average people thought it was going to be 5 percent, there will have been unanticipated inflation—inflation greater than anticipated.

Some of the problems caused by inflation arise when it is unanticipated, for when it is anticipated, many people are able to protect themselves from its ravages. With the distinction in mind between anticipated and unanticipated inflation, we can easily see the relationship between inflation and interest rates.

Inflation and Interest Rates

Nominal rate of interest The market rate of interest expressed in today's dollars.

Let's start in a hypothetical world in which there is no inflation and anticipated inflation is zero. In that world, you may be able to borrow money—to buy a computer or a car, for example—at a **nominal rate of interest** of, say, 10 percent. If you borrow the money to purchase a computer or a car and your anticipation of inflation turns out to be accurate, neither you nor the lender will have been fooled. The dollars you pay back in the years to come will be just as valuable in terms of purchasing power as the dollars that you borrowed.

Real rate of interest The nominal rate of interest minus the anticipated rate of inflation.

What you ordinarily need to know when you borrow money is the *real rate of interest* that you will have to pay. The **real rate of interest** is defined as the nominal rate of interest minus the anticipated rate of inflation. If you are able to borrow money at 10 percent and you anticipated an inflation rate of 10 percent, your real rate of interest would be zero—lucky you, particularly if the actual rate of inflation turned out to be 10 percent. In effect, we can say that the nominal rate of interest is equal to the real rate of interest plus an *inflationary premium* to take account of anticipated inflation. That inflationary premium covers depreciation in the purchasing power of the dollars repaid by borrowers.[1] Consider the purchase of a home. In 1982, mortgage rates for the purchase of new homes were around 18 percent. By 1999, they had fallen to around 7 percent. Why would anyone have paid 18 percent in 1982 to borrow money to buy a home? Well, home prices in some parts of the country had been rising for several years at 25 percent per year, so at 18 percent, mortgage rates seemed like a good deal. By the late 1990s, home prices in most places were holding steady.

There is fairly strong evidence that inflation rates and nominal interest rates move in parallel fashion. Periods of rapid inflation create periods of high interest rates. In the early 1970s, when the inflation rate was between 4 and 5 percent, average interest rates were around 9 percent. At the beginning of the 1980s, when the inflation rate was near 10 percent, interest rates had risen to between 14 and 16 percent. By the late 1990s, when the inflation rate was about 2 percent, nominal interest rates had again fallen to between 5 and 8 percent. International Example 7-3 describes what happens when inflation rates are negative.

Does Inflation Necessarily Hurt Everyone?

Most people think that inflation is bad. After all, inflation means higher prices, and when we have to pay higher prices, are we not necessarily worse off? The truth is that inflation affects different people in different ways. Its effects also depend on whether it is anticipated or unanticipated.

INTERNATIONAL EXAMPLE 7-3

Deflation and Real Interest Rates in Japan

Wholesale prices in Japan have been falling for several years. In the past few years, consumer prices also have been falling, which means that Japan has been experiencing *deflation*. What does this have to do with real interest rates in Japan? Real interest rates are roughly equivalent to nominal, or market, rates minus the expected rate of inflation. Market interest rates are rarely negative. If the nominal interest rate a Japanese person has to pay for a mortgage is 4 percent and the expected rate of *deflation* is 3 percent, then the expected real rate of interest is 7 percent, which is extremely high by historical standards. (In Canada, for example, real interest rates have hovered around 4 percent for most of its history.) The point is that in Canada, where we have learned to expect some inflation, we subtract that anticipated inflation from nominal interest rates to obtain real interest rates. In Japan, with expectations of deflation, the Japanese end up adding the expected deflationary rate to the nominal rate of interest to get real rates of interest.

For critical analysis: Why can't nominal interest rates be negative?

---

[1] Whenever there are relatively high rates of anticipated inflation, we must add an additional factor to the inflationary premium—the product of the real rate of interest times the anticipated rate of inflation. Usually this last term is omitted because the anticipated rate of inflation is not high enough to make much of a difference.

UNANTICIPATED POSITIVE INFLATION: CREDITOR LOSES, DEBTOR GAINS. Creditors lose and debtors gain with unanticipated positive inflation. In most situations, unanticipated inflation benefits borrowers because they are not charged a nominal interest rate that fully covers the rate of inflation that actually occurred. Why? Because the lender did not anticipate inflation correctly. The past several decades have known periods of considerable unanticipated (higher than anticipated) inflation—the late 1960s, the early 1970s, and the late 1970s. During those years, creditors lost and debtors gained.

PROTECTING AGAINST ANTICIPATED INFLATION. Banks attempt to protect themselves against inflation by raising nominal interest rates to reflect anticipated inflation. Adjustable-rate mortgages in fact do just that: The interest rate varies according to what happens to interest rates in the economy. Workers can protect themselves by **cost-of-living adjustments (COLAs)**, which are automatic increases in wage rates to take account of increases in the price level.

> **Cost-of-living adjustments (COLAs)** Clauses in contracts that allow for increases in wage rates to take account of increases in the cost of living.

You can tell if you have been hurt by inflation by calculating the change in your **real income**. Your real income measures how much you can purchase with a given amount of money. If you could purchase two loaves of bread with money earned during one hour of work last year, and you can still purchase that bread with the same number of hours of work this year, then your purchasing power, or your real income, has not changed. If you cannot purchase two loaves of bread with one hour of work, but can only afford one and one-half loaves, then your real income has declined. Conversely, if you can purchase more than two loaves of bread, your real income has increased. To determine the effect of inflation on your real income, calculate the percentage increase (or decrease) in your income in dollars and subtract the annual rate of inflation. Returning to our earlier example, assume that the change in the CPI is 3 percent. Assume also that your money income has risen from $75 per week to $78 per week, giving you an increase in your money income of 4 percent. What effect have these two changes had on your real income?

> **Real income** The purchasing power of money after the effects of inflation have been taken into account.

$$\text{\% change in real income} = 4\% - 3\% = 1\%$$

In other words, inflation has not hurt you because your money income has risen faster than the rate of inflation. Example 7-2 illustrates what has happened to Canadian workers' incomes over the second half of the 1990s.

To the extent that you hold non-interest-bearing cash, you will lose because of inflation. If you have hidden $100 under your mattress and the inflation rate is 10 percent for the year, you will have lost 10 percent of the purchasing power of that $100. If you have your funds in a non-interest-bearing chequing account, you will suffer the same fate. Individuals attempt to reduce the cost of holding cash by putting it into interest-bearing accounts, a wide variety of which often pay nominal rates of interest that reflect anticipated inflation.

EXAMPLE 7-2 **Do Rising Nominal Wages Mean Rising Real Wages Too?**

The last half of the 1990s have been good for Canada. Unemployment has been falling, and wages have been rising. Or have they?

Figure 7-7 shows the course of average nominal and real industrial wages over the last half of the 1990s. Average nominal wages have risen from $568.19 per week in 1994 to $624.82 in the year 2000, an increase of 9.97 percent. But over the same period, the Consumer Price Index (1992 = 100) has risen from 102 to 113.7, an increase of 11.5 percent. On average, then, workers have experienced a *decrease* in their real wages of 1.53 percent, the opposite from what the increase in nominal wages would suggest.

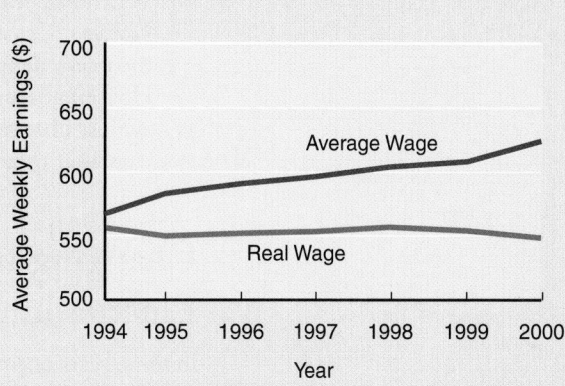

FIGURE 7.7 Average Nominal and Real Earnings

Average nominal earnings have been on the rise in the last half of the 1990s, but the rise in the cost of living has kept real earnings from rising as well.

Source: Statistics Canada, CANSIM Database, Series L57711 and P200000.

For critical analysis: What has happened to the average worker's purchasing power over the last half of the 1990s?

THE RESOURCE COST OF INFLATION. Some economists believe that the main cost of unanticipated inflation is the opportunity cost of resources used to protect against inflation and the distortions introduced as firms attempt to plan for the long run. Individuals have to spend time and resources to figure out ways to cover themselves in case inflation is different from what it has been in the past. That may mean spending a longer time working out more complicated contracts for employment, for purchases of goods in the future, and for purchases of raw materials.

Repricing, or menu, cost of inflation
The cost associated with recalculating prices and printing new price lists when there is inflation.

Inflation requires that price lists be changed. This is called the **repricing**, or **menu, cost of inflation**. The higher the rate of inflation, the higher the repricing cost of inflation. Imagine the repricing cost of Argentina's rapid inflation in 1989 compared to that in Canada, where the average inflation rate rarely reaches double digits.

Another major problem with inflation is that usually it does not proceed perfectly evenly. Consequently, the rate of inflation is not exactly what people anticipate. When this is so, the purchasing power of money changes in unanticipated ways. Because money is what we use as the measuring rod of the value of transactions we undertake, we have a more difficult time figuring out what we have really paid for things. As a result, resources tend to be misallocated in such situations because people have not really valued them accurately.

Think of any period during which you have to pay a higher price for something that was cheaper before. You are annoyed. But every time you pay a higher price, that represents the receipt of higher income for someone else. Therefore, it is impossible for all of us to be worse off because of rising prices. There are numerous costs to inflation, but they aren't the ones commonly associated with inflation. One way to think of inflation is that it is simply a *change in the accounting system*. One year the price of fast-food hamburgers averages $1; 10 years later the price of fast-food hamburgers averages $2. Clearly, $1 doesn't mean the same thing 10 years later. If we changed the name of our unit of account each year so that one year we paid $1 for fast-food hamburgers and 10 years later we paid, say, 1 peso, this lesson would be driven home.

Try Preview Question 3:

Does it matter whether inflation is anticipated or not?

CONCEPTS IN BRIEF

● Whenever inflation is greater than anticipated, creditors lose and debtors gain.
● Holders of cash lose during periods of inflation because the purchasing power of their cash depreciates at the rate of inflation.
● Households and businesses spend resources in attempting to protect themselves against unanticipated inflation, thus imposing a resource cost on the economy whenever there is unanticipated inflation.

Changing Inflation and Unemployment: Business Fluctuations

Business fluctuations The ups and downs in overall economic activity, as evidenced by changes in national income, employment, and the price level.

Expansion A business fluctuation in which overall economic activity is rising at a more rapid rate than previously, or at a more rapid rate than the overall historical trend for the nation.

Contraction A business fluctuation during which the pace of overall economic activity is slowing down.

Recession A period of time during which the rate of growth of economic activity is consistently less than its long-term trend, or is negative.

Depression An extremely severe recession.

Try Preview Question 4:
How do we describe the phases of national business fluctuations?

In some years unemployment goes up, in others it goes down. In some years there is a lot of inflation, in other years there isn't. We have fluctuations in all aspects of our macro-economy. The ups and downs in overall economic activity are sometimes called **business fluctuations**. When business fluctuations are positive, they are called **expansions**—speedups in the pace of national economic activity. The opposite of an expansion is a **contraction**, which is a slowdown in the pace of national economic activity. The top of an expansion is usually called its *peak*, and the bottom of a contraction is usually called its *trough*. Business fluctuations used to be called *business cycles*, but that term no longer seems appropriate because *cycle* implies predetermined or automatic recurrence, and we certainly haven't had automatic recurrent fluctuations in general economic activity. What we have had are contractions and expansions that vary greatly in length.

If the contractionary phase of business fluctuations becomes severe enough, we call it a **recession**. An extremely severe recession is called a **depression**. Typically, at the beginning of a recession, interest rates rise, and as the recession gets worse, they fall. At the same time, people's income starts to fall and the duration of unemployment increases, so that the unemployment rate increases. In times of expansion, the opposite occurs. During a peak period, unemployment will reach low levels and shortages of labour will appear. Inflation will begin to rise as many markets experience shortages simultaneously.

In Figure 7.8, you see that typical business fluctuations occur around a growth trend in overall national business activity shown as a straight upward-sloping line. Starting out at a peak, the economy goes into a contraction (recession). Then an expansion starts that moves up to its peak, higher than the last one, and the sequence starts over again.

A Brief History of Canadian Business Fluctuations

Figure 7-9 traces changes in real national output and unemployment from 1926 to the present. Notice that when real GDP is decreasing, unemployment is usually increasing and vice versa. While it is difficult to pinpoint the exact time a recession or expansion begins or ends, the economy has experienced in the range of six cycles of expansion and recession over that period.

During the 1920s, the economy was extremely buoyant, but a relatively sudden drop in consumption and investment, coupled with the crash of the American stock market, plunged the economy into the Great Depression of the 1930s. World War II pulled the economy out of the Depression as the government commandeered factories for the production of munitions and put most of the young unemployed males to work in the armed services.

Following the war, the government stopped its war-related expenditures, and military personnel were demobilized, thereby forcing the economy into a short recession. However, the economy soon recovered and shortly received another wartime boost from Canadian

FIGURE 7.8 The Typical Course of Business Fluctuations

An idealized business cycle would go from peak to trough and back again in a regular cycle.

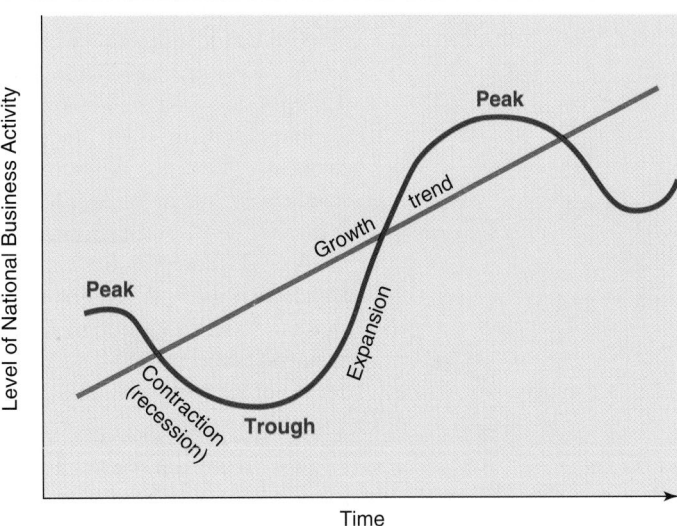

FIGURE 7-9 Business Fluctuations Peak-to-Peak, 1926–1999

The blue line shows changes in real national output from year to year, while the shaded area shows the unemployment rate in each year. The vertical lines show when the peak of each cycle was reached. Notice that on average, when output is falling during a contraction, unemployment is rising, and when output is rising during an expansion, unemployment is falling.

Source: Statistics Canada, *Historical Statistics of Canada,* Catalogue 11-516-X1E, Series D233; Statistics Canada, CANSIM Database, Series D14442, D14872, D31252, D31253, D984954.

involvement in the Korean War. The end of the Korean War brought another, shorter recession fuelled by a sudden decrease in government expenditure.

The Canadian economy prospered throughout the last half of the 1950s and all of the 1960s. However, in 1973 and again in 1976, the Oil Producing and Exporting Countries (OPEC) surprised the Western world by drastically cutting oil production. The price of oil soared, raising costs for virtually all firms. Many firms went bankrupt, and while prices rose due to the oil price decrease, real national output fell and employment fell. The economy entered over a decade of stagflation—the economy was stagnant while prices were rising. The 1982 recession was deeper than any since the Great Depression of the 1930s.

A brief recovery in the late 1980s was followed by the 1991-92 recession. Some economists attribute this decline to the Canada-US Free Trade Agreement: the inflow of cheaper American goods to the Canadian economy was putting Canadian firms out of business. Since the 1991-92 recession, however, the economy has experienced almost a decade of recovery and growth, currently approaching its end.

Explaining Business Fluctuations: External Shocks

As you might imagine, because changes in national business activity affect everyone, economists for decades have attempted to understand and explain business fluctuations. For years, one of the most obvious explanations has been external events that tend to disrupt the economy. As noted above, wars are critical points in a country's economic history. A war is certainly an *external shock*—something that originates outside our economy.

Other examples of external shocks, particularly for an agrarian nation, have to do with abrupt changes in the weather. Long-term drought tended to create downturns in national business activity when the majority of Canadians worked on farms. Today, major droughts or floods usually affect specific regions of the Canadian economy. Even if a drought dramatically affected one area, it would rarely cause a national economic downturn. The actions of the OPEC countries in the 1970s gave Canada an "oil shock."

It is not enough for us to say simply that business downturns are caused by external shocks. In the first place, if that were the only determinant of recessions, there would be little reason to study macroeconomics. Second, we know that historically we have had business recessions in the absence of any external shocks. For example, domestic technological change can start an expansion in an economy, as is shown in International Example 7-4.

We therefore need a theory of why national economic activity changes. This book develops a series of models that will help you understand the ups and downs of our business fluctuations.

INTERNATIONAL EXAMPLE 7-4 | Technology and Long Cycles

During the 1920s, a Russian economist named Nikolai Kondratieff studied business fluctuations. He thought that capitalist economies regularly went through cycles of 50 years or so, from bust to boom and back to bust, driven by technological change. It all starts when scientists make a technological breakthrough. Businesses then expand to produce and incorporate the new technology into industry, creating an upswing in the economy. However, markets eventually become saturated with the new products, and output starts to decline. The economy then enters the contractionary phase of the cycle. What puts an end to the contraction? Yet another new scientific discovery.

More recent economists have built on Kondratieff's work, and offer the following as evidence to support his theory. In 1709, Englishman Abraham Darby discovered a way to make good-quality iron in a coke-fired furnace. This discovery led to all kinds of new industrial uses for iron, including steam engines. Steam power then helped drive the Industrial Revolution in England which began in the mid-1700s and peaked around 1815. The English economy fell into a depression shortly thereafter.

The next discovery was an economical way to make steel, thus advancing railway technology. The world's first railway opened in England in 1825 and its subsequent proliferation led to a 30-year boom which began in the 1840s. The inevitable recession followed, when scientists began work on chemicals, electricity and automobiles. These new discoveries fuelled economic expansion from the late 1890s until the Great Depression.

During the Great Depression, new discoveries were made in airplane technology and in consumer goods such as refrigerators and televisions. Production of these products drove the expansion of the 1950s and 1960s. The economic decline of the 1970s saw scientists working on microprocessors and biotechnology, which drive our current expansion. If Kondratieff's theory holds, the good times we are now experiencing should last until the 2020s.

For critical analysis: How can the theory of shorter business fluctuations be reconciled with Kondratieff's long-cycle theory?

CONCEPTS IN BRIEF

- The ups and downs in economywide business activity are called business fluctuations, which consist of expansions and contractions in overall economic activity.
- The lowest point of a contraction is called the trough; the highest point of an expansion is called the peak.
- A recession is a downturn in business activity that lasts for some length of time.
- One possible explanation for business fluctuations relates to external shocks, such as wars, dramatic increases in the price of oil, floods, and droughts.

NETNOMICS

Is Frictional Unemployment on Its Way Out?

Even in tight labour markets, frictional unemployment still exists because of the transaction costs incurred in changing jobs. The advent of the Internet, however, may be reducing frictional unemployment more than anticipated by reducing search time. Of course, some frictional unemployment will always exist, but perhaps less than prior to the Internet.

The standard way of looking for another job is some combination of asking friends for contacts, looking at the "help wanted" ads, submitting résumés, using an employment agency, and even knocking on doors.

Now there's an Internet job market that is growing at lightning speed. Newspaper employment ads have started to instruct job seekers to send their résumés to a particular e-mail address. One reason is convenience, but an even more important reason is that electronic résumés allow prospective employers to scan for keywords and in that way rapidly locate qualified candidates for unfilled jobs. A big company like Nortel Networks, the world's largest maker of fibre-optic cable, receives thousands of résumés electronically each year via the Internet. The company can then search electronically for key candidate qualifications.

Employment agencies on the Net are taking off. Monster.ca is the best known Canadian Internet employment agency with almost 400,000 job postings at any given time. Another agency, Workopolis.com, was set up in January of 2000 by *The Globe and Mail* and the *Toronto Star*. By mid-2000, Workopolis.com enabled searchers to both search for and apply for jobs online 24 hours a day, and will send them e-mails regarding new postings that might match their qualifications. Even big-time "power" executives can go to Workopolis.com to find job openings suited to their experience.

Jobshark.com, founded in 1997, initially recruited for the information technology industry. It now serves as a clearinghouse for recruiters and job-searchers in many Canadian industries. And if job-searchers are interested in overseas work, Jobshark.com also has job listings for the United Kingdom, Ireland, and five South American countries. ●

ISSUES AND APPLICATIONS Do We Need to Worry About Deflation?

Concepts Applied: Inflation, deflation, real income

When prices fall, the effects can be just as difficult for people as rising prices.

Just when you thought everything was getting better—the inflation rate has been relatively low for almost a decade—a sudden spate of articles is telling you to be worried. Why? Because there is the prospect of the opposite of inflation—*deflation*. Deflation is defined as a consistent decline in average prices in the economy over time. The last time deflation occurred in Canada was during the Great Depression, when prices fell by up to 10 percent annually between 1929 and 1933. That was a period when the economy suffered from high unemployment and falling standards of living.

A current example of deflation can be found in Japan. Its price level has been falling every year since 1994. Its economy has been in a depressed state during that time period. The conclusion, of course, is that deflation can be accompanied by recessions and depressions.

Who Would Benefit from Deflation?

Obviously, if you hold cash, you are better off during a period of deflation. If prices drop by 5 percent during the next year, the dollar that you hold for a year would buy 5 percent more goods and services. Retired individuals on fixed incomes would find themselves richer each year during a deflation. Moreover, if the deflation were unanticipated, creditors would benefit. They would be paid back the same amount of dollars as before, but those dollars would have greater purchasing power. Therein lies the main problem with *unanticipated* deflation.

Debtors and Businesses Lose Out

If deflation is unanticipated, creditors gain, but debtors lose out. They pay back their debts in dollars that are worth more and more. Certain companies in particular are highly susceptible to unanticipated deflation. They are companies that are "leveraged"—that have borrowed heavily to purchase other companies or to expand rapidly. And any business that sells a product that takes a long time to produce loses out. That business must purchase its inputs long before it can sell its output—at a falling price. An unanticipated deflation would trigger a wave of business and personal bankruptcies. Investment and economic growth might collapse.

Don't Confuse Deflation with Falling Relative Prices

Even during a period of low or nonexistent inflation, some prices rise and some prices fall. Some of the popular press has focused on price decreases in the goods sector, particularly in computers, telecommunications, and imported items. But at the same time, in the services sector, many prices have been rising—this is simple arithmetic, for if the Consumer Price Index is still going up, albeit at a relatively slow rate, some prices have to be rising. Remember that deflation is defined as a *consistent* decline in the average of all prices. In Canada,

prices on average have been rising, but at a decreasing rate. This is called *disinflation*, not deflation. And even if there were deflation, the key to understanding deflation's impact is to determine whether or not it is anticipated. Anticipated deflation would be reflected in lower nominal interest rates, reduced labour requests for salary increases, and other market phenomena.

For Critical Analysis

1. How could you protect yourself against deflation?
2. Why is deflation usually accompanied by rising unemployment?

CHAPTER SUMMARY

1. The labour force consists of all persons who are employed plus those who are unemployed. Those over age 15 who are not in the labour force are full-time students, homemakers, and retired persons. The rate of unemployment is obtained by dividing the number of unemployed by the size of the labour force. If the duration of unemployment increases, the rate of unemployment also increases. Labour force participation rates have increased dramatically for women since World War II.

2. There are four types of unemployment in Canada: frictional, seasonal, structural, and cyclical. The economy has reached full employment when only frictional and structural unemployment exist. The natural rate of unemployment is the rate that occurs when only frictional and structural unemployment exist, that is, when there is no cyclical unemployment in the economy.

3. Frictional unemployment is caused by the temporary inability of workers to find jobs.

4. Structural unemployment occurs when there is a long-term mismatch, due to technological or geographical reasons, of available jobs and available skills.

5. Inflation occurs when the average of all prices of goods and services is rising; deflation occurs when the average of all prices is falling. During periods of inflation, the purchasing power of money falls (by definition).

6. The most commonly used measures of changes in general prices are the Consumer Price Index (CPI), the Producer Price Index (PPI), and the GDP deflator.

7. The nominal rate of interest includes the anticipated rate of inflation. Therefore, when the anticipated inflation increases, nominal rates of interest will rise.

8. Whenever the actual rate of inflation turns out to exceed the anticipated rate of inflation, creditors lose and debtors gain because the latter are able to repay debts in cheaper dollars. Of course, if everybody anticipates rising prices, nominal interest rates will rise to take account of this future expected reduction in the purchasing power of the dollar.

9. Workers can protect themselves against inflation by having cost-of-living adjustment (COLA) clauses in their employment contracts.

10. Business fluctuations consist of expansions and contractions. Long contractions are called recessions, and a severe recession is called a depression. One explanation for changes in national economic activity relates to external shocks, such as earthquakes, droughts, floods, wars, and dramatic increases in the price of oil.

DISCUSSION OF PREVIEW QUESTIONS

1. What are the types of unemployment?

Unemployment exists when people who are willing and able to work and actively looking for jobs, are not able to find jobs. People may be *frictionally* unemployed: they have just entered the job market, or are between jobs, but have not yet found employment. This kind of unemployment is temporary. People may also be *structurally* unemployed: there is a mismatch of the skills of the unemployed and the jobs that are available. Structural unemployment may be due to geographical or technological reasons. People may be *seasonally* unemployed: their jobs exist during certain seasons, and between those seasons they do not have work. Finally, people may be *cyclically* unemployed: they have been released from their jobs because the economy is recessionary and their employers do not need their services.

2. What is a price index?

A price index measures the change in prices of specific goods and services, or of all new goods and services in the economy. The Consumer Price Index (CPI) measures the change in prices of over 500 consumer goods and services. The CPI holds quantities and qualities fixed—that is, it does not allow for changes in the quantities that consumers purchase or changes in the quality of the goods and services. The Producer Price Index (PPI) is the same as the CPI, except it tracks prices of goods and services purchased by producers rather than by consumers. The GDP deflator is the broadest measure of price changes in our economy. It measures the change in value of all the new production in the economy from year to year. Thus, the GDP deflator measures changes in quantities, qualities, and prices—changes in the overall cost of what we produce from year to year.

3. Does it matter whether inflation is anticipated or not?

Whether inflation is anticipated or not is important to households and firms. When everyone fully and correctly anticipates the rate of future inflation, all contracts will take account of the declining purchasing power of the dollar. Debtors will not be able to gain at the expense of creditors, and employers will not be able to fool employees into agreeing to accept wage increases that do not have an inflationary factor built in. Only when inflation is not anticipated can it have unexpected negative effects on households and firms.

4. How do we describe the phases of national business fluctuations?

When business fluctuations are positive, they are called expansions, and when they are negative, they are called contractions. The top of the expansion is the peak, and the bottom is the trough. A long-lasting trough is called a recession. If a recession gets very serious, it is called a depression.

PROBLEMS

(Answers to the odd-numbered problems appear at the back of the book.)

7-1. An economic slump occurs and two things happen:

a. Many people stop looking for work because they know that the probability of finding a job is low.

b. Many people who become laid off start doing such work at home as growing food and painting and repairing their houses and cars.

Which of these events implies that the official unemployment rate overstates unemployment, and which implies the opposite?

7-2. A country's frictional unemployment rate is one percent. There is no seasonal unemployment. Its cyclical unemployment rate is 3 percent, and its structural unemployment rate is 4 percent.

a. What is the country's unemployment rate?

b. What is the country's unemployment rate when it has full employment?

c. What is the country's natural rate of unemployment?

7-3. Assume that the labour force consists of 100 people, and that every month five individuals become unemployed while five others who were unemployed find jobs.

a. What is the frictional unemployment rate?

b. What is the average duration of unemployment?

Now assume that the only type of unemployment in this economy is frictional.

c. What is the unemployment rate?

Suppose that a system of unemployment compensation is instituted, and the average duration of unemployment rises to two months.

d. What will the unemployment rate for this economy be now?

e. Does a higher unemployment rate necessarily mean that the economy is weaker or that labourers are worse off?

7-4. Suppose that a country has a labour force of 100 people. In January, Miller, Pulsinelli, and Hooper are unemployed; in February, those three find jobs but Stevenson, Conn, and Lee become unemployed. Suppose further that every month the previous three that were unemployed find jobs and three different people become unemployed. Throughout the year,

however, the same three people—Ito, Jack, and Kelley—continually remain unemployed because they lack sufficient skills to obtain the available jobs.

a. What is this country's unemployment rate?

b. What is its frictional unemployment rate?

c. What is its structural unemployment rate?

7-5. The data in the table below gives unit prices and quantities sold for three consumption goods in an economy.

	Prices per Unit		Quantities Sold	
	1999	2001	1999	2001
Pop	$1	$1	10	15
Chocolate Bars	$2	$4	30	35
Indigestion Pills	$5	$6	20	20

a. Calculate the consumer price index (CPI) for 2001, assuming that the base year is 1999.

b. What is the inflation rate between 1999 and 2001?

c. Now assume that these three goods make up the economy's entire production. Using 1999 as a base year, what is the GDP deflator in 2001?

7-6. Suppose that you receive two offers to begin employment after you complete your studies one year from now. You wish to take one of the two positions. You are indifferent between the jobs and their locations, however, and both job offers include the same benefits package. Job A will pay an annual salary of $24,000 beginning a year from now, and Job B will pay $25,000. Neither salary will be adjusted until you complete one full year of employment. After you study the economies of the provinces where the firms are located, you determine that there is likely to be no inflation over the two years where employer A is located. But employer B is in a province where the annual inflation rate over the next two years is likely to be 5 percent. Which job should you accept?

7-7. a. Suppose that the nominal interest rate is currently 12 percent. If the anticipated inflation rate is zero, what is the real interest rate?

b. The anticipated inflation rate rises to 13 percent, while the nominal interest rate remains at 12 percent. Does it make sense to lend money under these circumstances?

7-8. Suppose that in 2003 there is a sudden, unanticipated burst of inflation. Consider the situations faced by the following individuals. Who gains and who loses?

    a. A homeowner whose wages will keep pace with inflation in 2003 but whose monthly mortgage payments to a credit union remain fixed.

    b. An apartment landlord who has promised his tenants that their monthly rent payments during 2003 will be the same as they were during 2002.

    c. A banker who made a loan to an automobile buyer who will repay at a fixed rate of interest during 2003.

    d. A retired individual who earns a pension with fixed monthly payments in 2003 from her past employer.

7-9. Columns 1 and 3 in the table show employment and the price level in the economy.

    a. Assume that the labour force in the economy is 10 million. Compute and enter in column 2 the unemployment rate at each level of employment.

    b. For each row (except the first), compute and enter in column 4 the annual rate of inflation.

(1) Employment (millions of workers)	(2) Unemployment Rate (%)	(3) Price Level	(4) Rate of Inflation (%)
9.0		1.00	N.A.
9.1		1.08	
9.2		1.17	
9.3		1.28	
9.4		1.42	
9.5		1.59	
9.6		1.81	
9.7		2.10	

7-10. In January 2000, a country's economic activity reaches a peak, and a trough occurs in July 2000. The next peak occurs in August 2001, and another trough occurs in November 2002. Finally, there is another peak in October 2003. How many months long was each contraction and each expansion?

ECONOMICS ON THE NET

Looking at Unemployment and Inflation Data

This chapter reviewed key concepts relating to unemployment and inflation. In this exercise, you get a chance to examine Canadian unemployment and inflation data on your own.

Internet URL: www.statcan.ca

Title: Economic Conditions and Inflation (price indexes)

Navigation: Begin at homepage of Statistics Canada (http://www.statcan.ca). Then click on English, followed by Canadian Statistics, and then Economic Conditions.

Application: Perform the indicated operations, and answer the following questions:

a. Click on Labour Market, then on Labour Force, Employment and Unemployment. What has been happening to the labour force, employment, unemployment rate in the last 5 years? Would you say that the economy has been in an expansion or a contraction during that time? Explain.

b. Click on Prices, then on Consumer Price Index, 1996 classification, annual average indexes, the provinces. Using the All Items CPI, calculate the inflation rate for the last 4 years. Compare the inflation rate in each year with the unemployment rate. Is there a relationship between changes in the two rates?

MEASURING THE ECONOMY'S PERFORMANCE

If you watch the evening news, read newspapers, or listen to the radio, you cannot miss hearing about the economy. If you have ever bought a cheap umbrella or a wristwatch from a street vendor, both you and the vendor may have been partaking in the underground economy. How big is the underground economy? How distorted are official statistics that measure our nation's performance? Much is at stake here. Federal government policy is aimed at stabilizing the economy as a whole. A whole industry has developed to predict what will happen to the overall economy—and what the next policy change will be. How successful are these economic soothsayers? To understand all of these things, you need to know about how the government officially measures the economy's performance each year.

PREVIEW QUESTIONS

1. What is gross domestic product (GDP), and what does it measure?

2. Why are only *final* goods and services evaluated in deriving GDP?

3. Why must depreciation and indirect business taxes less subsidies be added to national income at factor cost in order to derive GDP via the income approach?

4. How does correcting GDP for changes in the price level and population improve the usefulness of GDP estimates?

DID YOU KNOW THAT... whenever a single person who is currently paying a housekeeper marries that housekeeper, government statistics show that the economy's performance has declined? The reason for this seeming anomaly is that government statisticians do not yet consider unpaid housework as contributing to the total annual national income of the country (even though the same services would have to be purchased if not provided free of charge). In spite of such measurement problems, the statistics about the nation's economic performance are watched closely throughout the year by investors, bankers, businesspeople, and macroeconomic policy makers. After all, most people like to know where they stand financially at the end of each month or year. Why shouldn't we have similar information about the economy as a whole? The way we do this is by using what has become known as **national income accounting,** the main focus of this chapter.

But first we need to revisit the flow of income within an economy, for it is the flow of goods and services from businesses to consumers and payments from consumers to businesses that constitute economic activity.

The Simple Circular Flow

The concept of a circular flow of income (ignoring taxes) involves two principles:

1. In every economic exchange, the seller receives exactly the same amount that the buyer spends.
2. Goods and services flow in one direction and money payments flow in the other.

In the simple economy shown in Figure 8.1, there are only businesses and households. It is assumed that businesses sell their *entire* output *immediately* to households, and that households spend their *entire* income *immediately* on consumer products. Households receive their income by selling the use of whatever factors of production they own, such as labour services.

Profits Explained

We have indicated in Figure 8.1 that profit is a cost of production. You might be under the impression that profits are not part of the cost of producing goods and services; but profits are indeed a part of this cost because businesspeople and entrepreneurs must be rewarded for providing their services or they won't provide them. Their reward, if any, is profit. The reward—the profit—is included in the cost of the factors of production. If there were no expectations of profit, entrepreneurs would not incur the risk associated with the organization of productive activities. That is why we consider profits as a cost of doing business.

Total Income or Total Output

At the bottom of Figure 8.1 is an arrow that goes from businesses to households, labelled "Total income." What would be a good definition of **total income?** If you answered "the total of all individuals' income," you would be right. But all income is actually a payment for something, whether it be wages paid for labour services, rent paid for the use of land, interest paid for the use of capital, or profits paid to entrepreneurs. It is the amount paid to the resource suppliers. Therefore, total income can also be defined as the annual *cost* of producing the entire output of **final goods and services.**

The arrow at the top of Figure 8.1, going from households to businesses, represents the dollar value of output in the economy. It represents total monetary businesses and goods and services consumed by households. Business receipts are the opposite side of household expenditures. When households purchase goods and services with money,

National income accounting A measurement system used to estimate national income and its components; one approach to measuring an economy's aggregate performance.

Total income The yearly amount earned by the nation's resources (factors of production). Total income therefore includes wages, rents, interest and profits that are received, respectively, by workers, land-owners, capital owners, and entrepreneurs.

Final goods and services Goods and services that are at their final stage of production and will not be transformed into yet other goods or services. For example, wheat is normally not a final good because usually it is used to make bread, which *is* a final good.

FIGURE 8.1 The Circular Flow of Income and Product

Businesses provide final goods and services to households (upper clockwise loop), who in turn pay for them with money (upper counterclockwise loop). Money flows in a counterclockwise direction and can be thought of as a circular flow. The dollar value of output is identical to total income because profits are defined as being equal to total business receipts minus business outlays for wages, rents, and interest.

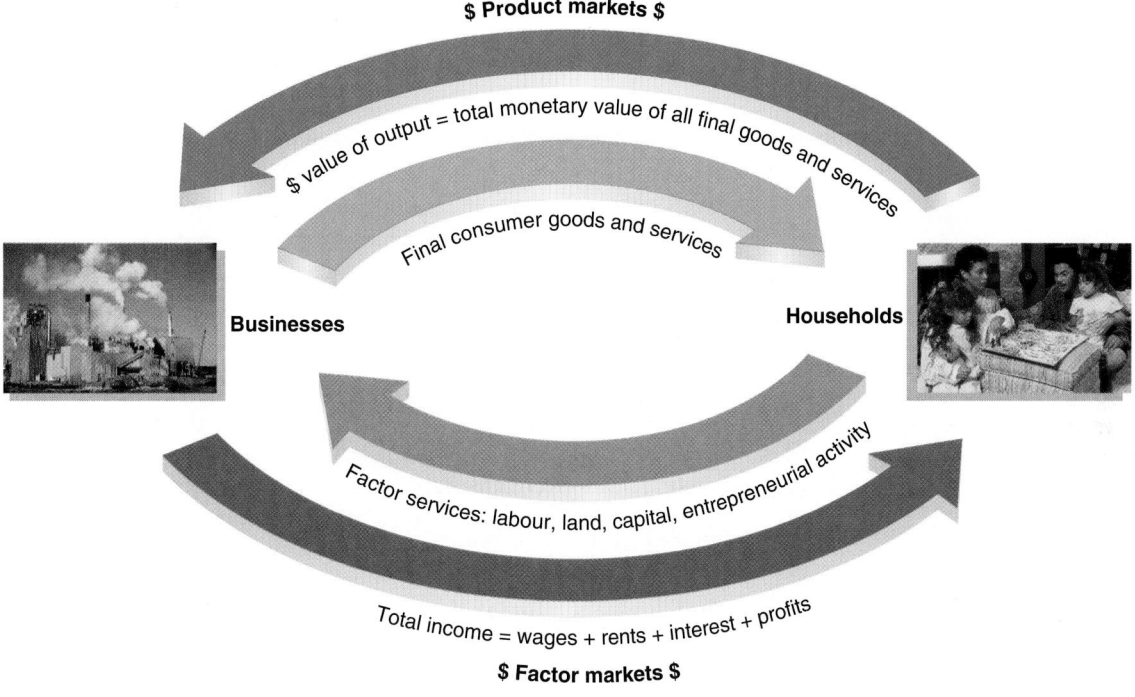

$ Product markets $

$ value of output = total monetary value of all final goods and services

Final consumer goods and services

Businesses

Households

Factor services: labour, land, capital, entrepreneurial activity

Total income = wages + rents + interest + profits

$ Factor markets $

that money becomes a *business receipt*. Every transaction, therefore, simultaneously involves an expenditure as well as a receipt.

PRODUCT MARKETS. Transactions in which households buy goods and services take place in the product markets—that's where households are the buyers and businesses are the sellers of consumer goods. *Product market* transactions are represented in the upper loops in Figure 8.1. Note that consumer goods and services flow to household demanders, while money flows in the opposite direction to business suppliers.

FACTOR MARKETS. *Factor market* transactions are represented by the lower loops in Figure 8.1. In the factor market, households are the sellers; they sell resources such as labour, land, capital, and entrepreneurial ability. Businesses are the buyers in factor markets; business expenditures represent receipts or, more simply, income for households. Also, in the lower loops of Figure 8.1, factor services flow from households to businesses, while the money paid for these services flows in the opposite direction from businesses to households. Observe also the circular flow of money (counterclockwise) from households to businesses and back again from businesses to households; it is an endless circular flow.

Why the Dollar Value of Total Output Must Equal Total Income

Total income represents the income received by households in payment for the production of goods and services. Why must total income be identical to the dollar value of total output? First, as Figure 8.1 shows, spending by one group is income to another. Second, it is a matter of simple accounting and the economic definition of profit as a cost of production. Profit is defined as what is *left over* from total business receipts after all other costs—wages, rents, interest—have been paid. If the dollar value of total output is $1,000 and the total of wages, rent, and interest for producing that output is $900, profit is $100. Profit is always the *residual* item that makes total income equal to the dollar value of total output.

CONCEPTS IN BRIEF

- In the circular flow model of income and output, households sell factor services to businesses that pay for those factor services. The receipt of payments is total income. Businesses sell goods and services to households that pay for them.
- The dollar value of total output is equal to the total monetary value of all final goods and services produced.
- The dollar value of final output must always equal total income.

National Income Accounting

We have already mentioned that policy makers need information about the state of the national economy. Historical statistical records on the performance of the national economy aid economists in testing their theories about how the economy really works. We keep tabs on the health of the economy through national income accounting. Policy gurus use national income accounting for formulating policies that will enhance the nation's economy. National income accounting is measured through GDP.

Gross Domestic Product

Gross domestic product (GDP) The total market value of all final goods and services produced in the economy during the year.

Gross domestic product (GDP) represents the total market value of the country's annual final product, or output, produced per year by factors of production located within national borders. We therefore formally define GDP as the total market value of all final goods and services produced in the economy during a year. We are referring here to a *flow of production*. A country produces at a certain rate, just as you receive income at a certain rate. Your income flow might be at a rate of $5,000 per year or $50,000 per year. Suppose you are told that someone earns $500. Would you consider this a good salary? There is no way to answer that question unless you know whether the person is earning $500 per month or per week or per day. Thus you have to specify a time period for all flows. Income received is a flow. You must contrast this with, for example, your total accumulated savings, which is a stock measured at a point in time, not across time. Implicit in just about everything we deal with in this chapter is a time period—usually one year. All the measures of domestic product and income are specified as rates measured in dollars per year.

Try Preview Question 1:

What is gross domestic product (GDP), and what does it measure?

Avoid Double Counting

Intermediate goods Goods used up entirely in the production of final goods.

GDP does not count **intermediate goods** (goods used up entirely in the production of final goods) because to do so would be to count them twice. For example, even though grain that a farmer produces may be that farmer's final product, it is not the final product for the nation. It is sold to make bread. Bread is the final product.

We can use a numerical example to clarify this point further. Our example will involve determining the **value added** at each stage of production. Value added is the amount of dollar value contributed to a product at each stage of its production. In Table 8.1 we see the difference between total value of all sales and value added in the production of a

Value added The dollar value of an industry's sales minus the value of intermediate goods (for example, raw materials and parts) used in production.

TABLE 8.1

Sales Value and Value Added at Each Stage of Donut Production

(1) Stage of Production	(2) Dollar Value of Sales		(3) Value Added
Stage 1: Fertilizer and seed	$0.03	_____	$0.03
Stage 2: Growing	0.06	_____	0.03
Stage 3: Milling	0.12	_____	0.06
Stage 4: Baking	0.30	_____	0.18
Stage 5: Retailing	0.45	_____	0.15
Total dollar value of all sales	$0.96	Total value added	$0.45

Stage 1: A farmer purchases 3 cents' worth of fertilizer and seed, which are used as factors of production in growing wheat.

Stage 2: The farmer grows the wheat, harvests it, and sells it to a miller for 6 cents. Thus we see that the farmer has added 3 cent's worth of value. Those 3 cents represent income paid to the farmer.

Stage 3: The miller purchases the wheat for 6 cents and adds 6 cents as the value added; that is, there is 6 cents for the miller as income. The miller sells the ground wheat flour to a donut-baking company.

Stage 4: The donut-baking company buys the flour for 12 cents and adds 18 cents as the value added. It then sells the donut to the final retailer.

Stage 5: The donut retailer sells fresh hot donuts at 45 cents apiece, thus creating an additional value of 15 cents.

We see that the total value of sales resulting from the production of one donut was 96 cents, but the total value added was 45 cents, which is exactly equal to the retail price. The total value added is equal to the sum of all income payments or to the final retail sale price of the good.

Try Preview Question 2:

Why are only *final* goods and services evaluated in deriving GDP?

donut. We also see that the sum of the values added is equal to the sale price to the final consumer. It is the 45 cents that is used to measure GDP, not the 96 cents. If we used the 96 cents, we would be double-counting from stages 2 through 5, for each intermediate good would be counted at least twice—once when it was produced and again when the good it was used in making was sold. Such double-counting would grossly exaggerate GDP.

Exclusion of Financial Transactions, Transfer Payments, and Secondhand Goods

Remember that GDP is the measure of the value of all final goods and services *produced* in one year. Many transactions occur that have nothing to do with final goods and services produced. There are financial transactions, transfers of the ownership of pre-existing goods, and other transactions that should not and do not get included in our measure of GDP.

FINANCIAL TRANSACTIONS. There are three general categories of purely financial transactions: (1) the buying and selling of securities, (2) government transfer payments, and (3) private transfer payments.

1. **Securities.** When you purchase a share of existing stock in the Bank of Nova Scotia, someone else has sold it to you. In essence, there was merely a *transfer* of ownership rights. You paid $100 to obtain the share certificate. Someone else received the $100

and gave up the share certificate. No producing activity took place at that time. Hence the $100 transaction is not included when we measure gross domestic product.

2. **Government transfer payments.** Transfer payments are payments for which no productive services are provided in exchange at the same time. The most obvious government transfer payments are old age security benefits, veterans' payments, welfare payments, and unemployment compensation. The recipients make no contribution to current production in return for such transfer payments (although they may have made contributions in the past to receive them). Government transfer payments are not included in GDP.

3. **Private transfer payments.** Are you receiving money from your parents in order to attend school? Has a wealthy relative ever given you a gift of money? If so, you have been the recipient of a private transfer payment. This is simply a transfer of funds from one individual to another. As such, it does not constitute productive activity and is not included in gross domestic product.

TRANSFER OF SECONDHAND GOODS. If I sell you my two-year-old minivan, no current production is involved. I transfer to you the ownership of a vehicle that was produced two years ago; in exchange, you transfer to me $20,000. The original purchase price of the minivan was included in GDP in the year it was produced. To include it again when I sell it to you would be counting the value of the van a second time.

OTHER EXCLUDED TRANSACTIONS. Many other transactions are not included in GDP for practical reasons:

1. Household production—home cleaning, child care, and other tasks performed by people within their own households and for which they are not paid through the marketplace
2. Otherwise legal underground transactions—those that are legal but not reported and hence not taxed, such as paying housekeepers in cash that is not declared as income
3. Illegal underground activities—these include prostitution, illegal gambling, and the sale of illicit drugs

You will learn more about the size of the underground economy in this and other countries in the Issues and Applications section at the end of this chapter. Right now, let's consider some suggestions for measuring unpaid household production in Policy Example 8-1.

CONCEPTS IN BRIEF

- GDP is the total market value of final goods and services produced in the economy during a one-year period by factors of production within the country's borders. It represents the flow of production over that one-year period.
- To avoid double-counting, we look only at final goods and services produced or, alternatively, at value added.
- In measuring GDP, we must exclude (1) purely financial transactions, such as the buying and selling of securities; (2) government transfer payments; (3) private transfer payments; and (4) the transfer of secondhand goods.
- Many other transactions are excluded from GDP, among them household services rendered by homemakers, underground economy transactions, and illegal economic activities.

POLICY EXAMPLE 8-1

Measuring Household Production

In the 1980s, the Decade for Women World Conference passed a resolution calling for all nations to include the unpaid contributions of women in GDP calculations. At least two countries, France and Norway, have started to release "satellite" GDP figures that incorporate estimates of unpaid household production. Australia and Germany are studying a similar procedure, as is Canada.

Of course, any estimate of unremunerated household work has serious problems. For instance, parents do housework, raise children, and cook meals while others volunteer to look after seniors and help the disadvantaged. All of these tasks could be accomplished through market forces, which would then make them part of GDP. But the puzzle has been—how can this work be valued? Is housework a minimum wage job, in which case we could just count up the number of hours spent doing housework and multiply them by the minimum wage? Or should we look at the opportunity cost of housework? If someone who would make $20 per hour working at an "outside" job does housework instead, should that housework be valued at the $20 per hour rate, or at the minimum wage rate?

Another problem concerns the quality of household work. Some homemakers serve fabulous gourmet meals while others warm up canned and frozen foods. Should they be valued equally? Yet another difficulty lies in knowing where to stop counting: A person can hire a valet to help him or her get dressed in the morning. Should we therefore count the time spent getting dressed as part of unpaid household work? Both men and women perform services around the house every day of the year. Should all of these unpaid services be included in a new measurement of GDP?

In 1995, Statistics Canada published a study called *Households' Unpaid Work: Measurement and Valuation*, in which it estimated that Canadians of working age performed up to 25 billion hours of unpaid work in 1992. This figure is 23 percent more than the number of paid hours worked that same year. Convert this figure to 40 hours-per-week, 49 weeks-per-year jobs, and you'll find that Canadians are collectively doing the unpaid work of 730,000 people!

The dollar estimates of the value of this unpaid work vary greatly, largely because of the measuring problems we discuss above. The lowest estimate of its value in 1992 was $235 billion; the highest was $374 billion. If this amount were added to GDP, nominal GDP would be 34 to 54 percent larger.

The Canadian government is not yet ready to include a measure of unpaid work in GDP. But it did include questions in the 1996 Census about the amount of non-market work done by women. This may be a first step towards putting a dollar value on this recognized but uncounted source of labour in the Canadian economy.

For critical analysis: In general, which countries would have the smallest amount of unpaid household production? (Hint: Think about labour force participation rates.)

Two Main Methods of Measuring GDP

If the definition of GDP is the total value of all final goods and services produced during a year, then to measure GDP we could add up the prices times the quantities of every individual commodity produced. But this would involve a monumental, if not impossible, task for government statisticians.

Expenditure approach A way of computing national income by adding up the dollar value at current market prices of all final goods and services.

Income approach A way of measuring national income by adding up all components of national income, including wages, interest, rent, and profits.

Durable consumer goods Consumer goods that have a life span of more than three years.

Nondurable consumer goods Consumer goods that are used up within three years.

Services Mental or physical labour or help purchased by consumers. Examples are the assistance of doctors, lawyers, dentists, repair personnel, housecleaners, educators, retailers, and wholesalers; things purchased or used by consumers that do not have physical characteristics.

Gross private domestic investment The creation of capital goods, such as factories and machines, that can yield production and hence consumption in the future. Also included in this definition are changes in business inventories and repairs made to machines or buildings.

Investment Any use of today's resources to expand tomorrow's production or consumption.

Producer durables, or capital goods Durable goods having an expected service life of more than three years that are used by businesses to produce other goods and services.

Fixed investment Purchases by businesses of newly produced producer durables, or capital goods, such as production machinery and office equipment.

Inventory investment Changes in the stocks of finished goods and goods in process, as well as changes in the raw materials that businesses keep on hand. Whenever inventories are decreasing, inventory investment is negative; whenever they are increasing, inventory investment is positive.

The circular flow diagram presented in Figure 8.1 gives us a shortcut method for calculating GDP. We can look at the *flow of expenditures*, which consists of consumption, investment, government purchases of goods and services, and net expenditures in the foreign sector (net exports). This is called the **expenditure approach** to measuring GDP, in which we add the dollar value of all final goods and services. Alternatively, we could also use the *flow of income*, looking at the income received by everybody producing goods and services. This is called the **income approach**, in which we add the income received by all factors of production, including wages, interest, rent, and profits.

Deriving GDP by the Expenditure Approach

To derive GDP using the expenditure approach, we must look at each of the separate components of expenditures and then add them together. These components are: consumption expenditures, investment, government expenditures, and net exports.

CONSUMPTION EXPENDITURES. How do we spend our income? As households or as individuals, we spend our income through consumption expenditure *(C)*, which falls into three categories: **durable consumer goods, nondurable consumer goods**, and **services**. Durable goods are *arbitrarily* defined as items that last more than three years; they include automobiles, furniture, and household appliances. Nondurable goods are all the rest, such as food and gasoline. Services are intangible commodities: medical care, education, and so on.

Housing expenditures constitute a major proportion of anybody's annual expenditures. Rental payments on apartments are automatically included in consumption expenditure estimates. People who own their homes, however, do not make rental payments. Consequently, government statisticians estimate what is called the *implicit rental value* of owner-occupied homes. It is equal to the amount of rent you would have to pay if you did not own the home but were renting it from someone else.

GROSS PRIVATE DOMESTIC INVESTMENT. We now turn our attention to **gross private domestic investment** *(I)* undertaken by businesses. When economists refer to investment, they are referring to additions to productive capacity. **Investment** may be thought of as an activity that uses resources today in such a way that they allow for greater production in the future and hence greater consumption in the future. When a business buys new equipment or puts up a new factory, it is investing; it is increasing its capacity to produce in the future.

The layperson's notion of investment often relates to the purchase of stocks and bonds. For our purposes, such transactions simply represent the *transfer of ownership* of assets called stocks and bonds. Thus you must keep in mind the fact that in economics, investment refers *only* to additions to productive capacity, not to transfers of assets.

In our analysis, we will consider the basic components of investment. We have already mentioned the first one, which involves a firm buying equipment or putting up a new factory. These are called **producer durables**, or **capital goods**. A producer durable, or a capital good, is simply a good that is purchased not to be consumed in its current form but to be used to make other goods and services. The purchase of equipment and factories—capital goods—is called **fixed investment**.

The other type of investment has to do with the change in inventories of raw materials and finished goods. Firms do not immediately sell off all their products to consumers. Some of this final product is usually held in inventory waiting to be sold. Firms hold inventories to meet future expected orders for their products. When a firm increases its inventories of finished products, it is engaging in **inventory investment**. Inventories consist of all finished goods on hand, goods in process, and raw materials.

The reason that we can think of a change in inventories as being a type of investment is that an increase in such inventories provides for future increased consumption possibilities. When inventory investment is zero, the firm is neither adding to nor subtracting from the total stock of goods or raw materials on hand. Thus if the firm keeps the same amount of inventories throughout the year, inventory *investment* has been zero.

In estimating gross private domestic investment, government statisticians also add consumer expenditures on *new* residential structures because new housing represents an addition to our future productive capacity in the sense that a new house can generate housing services in the future.

GOVERNMENT EXPENDITURES. In addition to personal consumption expenditures, there are government purchases of goods and services *(G)*. The government buys goods and services from private firms and pays wages and salaries to government employees. Generally, we value goods and services at the prices at which they are sold. But many government goods and services are not sold in the market. Therefore, we cannot use their market value when computing GDP. The value of these goods is considered equal to their cost. For example, the value of a newly built road is considered equal to its construction cost and is included in the GDP for the year it was built.

NET EXPORTS (FOREIGN EXPENDITURES). To get an accurate representation of gross domestic product, we must include the foreign sector. As Canadians, we purchase foreign goods called *imports*. The goods that foreigners purchase from us are our *exports*. To get an idea of the *net* expenditures from the foreign sector, we subtract the value of imports from the value of exports to get net exports (X) for a year:

$$\text{Net exports } (X) = \text{total exports} - \text{total imports}$$

To understand why we subtract imports rather than ignoring them altogether, consider that we are using the expenditures approach. If we want to estimate *domestic* output, we have to subtract Canadian expenditures on the goods of other nations.

Thinking Critically About the Media 8-1   Avoiding GDP Mania

Every quarter, the federal government publishes its estimates of the rate of growth of real GDP for the previous quarter on an annualized basis. If, for example, GDP corrected for inflation was estimated to increase by one-half of 1 percent, the government would announce a first-quarter growth rate of 2 percent per year. Once these statistics are announced, journalists have a field day analyzing whether the economy is growing, not growing, slowing down, heading for a soft landing, overheating, and so on. The problem with these initial quarterly statistics is that they are often wrong. On occasion, quarterly annualized GDP growth rates have been corrected a month later by as much as 75 percent! Consequently, it is a good idea to wait a few months and to examine only revised GDP statistics from Statistics Canada.

Mathematical Representation Using the Expenditure Approach

We have just defined the components of GDP using the expenditure approach. When we add them all together, we get a definition for GDP, which is as follows:

$$\text{GDP} = C + I + G + X$$

where

$$C = \text{consumption expenditures}$$
$$I = \text{investment expenditures}$$
$$G = \text{government expenditures}$$
$$X = \text{net exports}$$

THE HISTORICAL PICTURE. To get an idea of the relationship among *C, I, G,* and *X,* look at Figure 8.2, which shows gross domestic product, personal consumption expenditures, government purchases, and gross private domestic investment plus net exports from 1926 to 1999. When we add up the expenditures of the household, business, government, and foreign sectors, we get GDP.

DEPRECIATION AND NET DOMESTIC PRODUCT. We have used the terms *gross domestic product* and *gross private domestic investment* without really indicating what *gross* means. The dictionary defines it as "without deductions," as opposed to *net*. Deductions for what, you might ask. The deductions are for something we call **depreciation**. In the course of a year, machines and structures wear out or are used up in the production of domestic product. For example, houses deteriorate as they are occupied, and machines need repairs or they will fall apart and stop working. Most capital, or durable, goods depreciate. An estimate of this is subtracted from gross domestic product to arrive at a figure called **net domestic product (NDP)**, which we define as follows:

Depreciation Reduction in the value of capital goods over a one-year period due to physical wear and tear and also to obsolescence; also called capital consumption allowance.

Net domestic product (NDP) GDP minus depreciation.

$$\text{NDP} = \text{GDP} - \text{depreciation}$$

FIGURE 8.2 Seventy Years of GDP and Its Components

Here we see a display of gross domestic product, personal consumption expenditures, government purchases, gross private domestic investment and net exports for the years 1926–1999. Actually, during the Great Depression of the 1930s, gross private domestic investment decreased dramatically, pulling down GDP with it. Because of the scale of the figure the huge drop in investment spending is not immediately obvious.

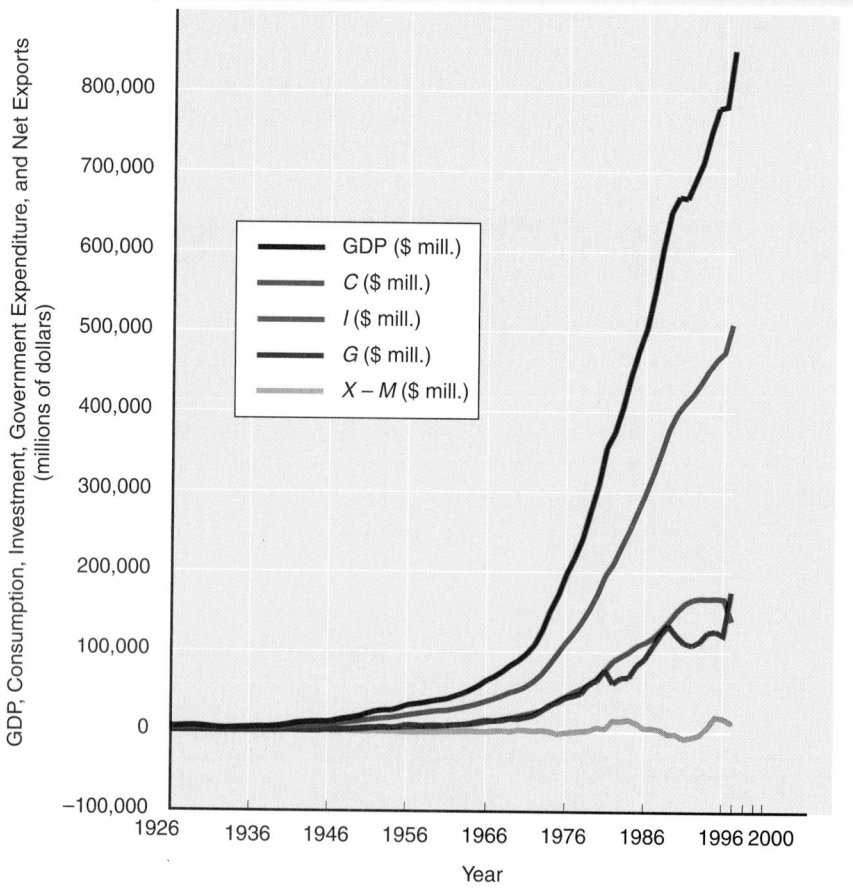

Capital consumption allowance
Another name for depreciation, the amount that businesses would have to save in order to take care of the deterioration of machines and other equipment.

Depreciation is also called **capital consumption allowance** because it is the amount of the capital stock that has been consumed over a one-year period. In essence, it equals the amount a business would have to put aside to repair and replace deteriorating machines. Because we know that

$$GDP = C + I + G + X$$

we know that the formula for NDP is

$$NDP = C + I + G + X - \text{depreciation}$$

Alternatively, because net $I = I - \text{depreciation}$,

$$NDP = C + \text{net } I + G + X$$

Net investment Gross private domestic investment minus an estimate of the wear and tear on the existing capital stock (depreciation). Net investment therefore measures the change in capital stock over a one-year period.

Net investment measures *changes* in our capital stock over time and is positive nearly every year. This is consistent with an expanding economy and means that the economy is making net additions to its capital stock. Because depreciation does not vary greatly from year to year as a percentage of GDP, we get a similar picture of what is happening to our national economy by looking at either NDP or GDP data.

CONCEPTS IN BRIEF

- The expenditure approach to measuring GDP requires that we add up consumption expenditures, gross private investment, government purchases, and net exports. Consumption expenditures include consumer durables, consumer nondurables, and services.
- Gross private domestic investment *excludes* transfers of asset ownership. It includes only additions to the productive capacity of a nation, repairs on existing capital goods, and changes in business inventories.
- We value government expenditures at their cost because we do not usually have market prices at which to value government goods and services.
- To obtain net domestic product (NDP), we subtract from GDP the year's depreciation of the existing capital stock.

Deriving GDP by the Income Approach

If you go back to the circular flow diagram in Figure 8.1, you see that product markets are at the top of the diagram and factor markets are at the bottom. We can calculate the value of the circular flow of income and product by looking at expenditures—which we just did—or by looking at total factor payments. Factor payments are called income. We calculate **gross domestic income (GDI)**, which we will see is identical to gross domestic product (GDP). Using the income approach, we calculate five categories of payments to individuals: wages, corporate profits before taxes, interest and investment income, farm and non-incorporated nonfarm business income, and an inventory valuation adjustment.

Gross domestic income (GDI) The sum of all income—wages, corporate profits before taxes, interest, farm and non-incorporated nonfarm income, and inventory valuation adjustment—paid to the four factors of production.

1. *Wages.* The most important category is, of course, wages, including salaries and other forms of labour income, such as income in kind, and incentive payments. We also count payroll deductions for Employment Insurance and pension plans (both the employees' and the employers' contributions), and other fringe benefits.
2. *Corporate Profits Before Taxes.* Businesses either pay out their profits before taxes to their shareholders, the households, or reinvest them in the business. Regardless of the distribution, these corporate profits are counted as income.

3. *Interest and Investment Income.* Here, interest payments do not equal the sum of all payments for the use of funds in a year. Instead, interest is expressed in net rather than in gross terms. Net interest received by households is the difference between the interest they receive (from savings accounts, certificates of deposit, and the like) and the interest they pay (to banks for mortgages, credit cards, and other loans).

4. *Farm and Non-incorporated Nonfarm Business Income.* This category includes income earned by owners of businesses who supply their own labour and capital to their businesses. It could also be referred to as "proprietors' income." Rent and imputed rents are also included here.

5. *Inventory Valuation Adjustment.* Our final category allows for an adjustment to corporate profits to account for price changes. If a business is holding inventory and inflation increases the market price of the business's output, the value of that output will not reflect its value when it was produced. This category is subtracted (in the case of inflation) from corporate profits to get a more accurate measure of new production.

All of the payments listed are *actual* factor payments made to owners of the factors of production. When we add them together, though, we do not yet have gross domestic income. We have to take account of two other components: **indirect business taxes less subsidies**, such as sales and business property taxes, and depreciation, which we have already discussed.

Indirect business taxes less subsidies
All business taxes except the tax on corporate profits. Indirect business taxes include sales and business property taxes. Subsidies to business from government are subtracted because they represent a flow of taxes back to business.

INDIRECT BUSINESS TAXES LESS SUBSIDIES. Indirect taxes are the (nonincome) taxes paid by consumers when they buy goods and services. When you buy a book, you pay the price of the book plus GST (or HST in the Atlantic provinces). The business is actually acting as the government's agent in collecting the sales tax, which it in turn passes on to the government. Such taxes therefore represent a business expense and are included in gross domestic income.

The government sometimes subsidizes a business by giving it money to help reduce its production costs. Since a subsidy returns to the business some of the taxes paid, we need to subtract the value of subsidies from indirect business taxes.

Try Preview Question 3:

Why must depreciation and indirect business taxes less subsidies be added to national income at factor cost in order to derive GDP via the income approach?

DEPRECIATION. Just as we had to deduct depreciation to get from GDP to NDP, so we must *add* depreciation to go from net domestic income to gross domestic income. Depreciation can be thought of as the portion of the current year's GDP that is used to replace physical capital consumed in the process of production. Because somebody has paid for the replacement, depreciation must be added as a component of gross domestic income.

The last two components of GDP—indirect business taxes less subsidies and depreciation—are called **nonincome expense items**.

Nonincome expense items The total of indirect business taxes less subsidies and depreciation.

Figure 8.3 shows a comparison between gross domestic product and gross domestic income for 2000. Whether you decide to use the expenditure approach or the income approach, you will come out with the same number. There are usually statistical discrepancies, but they are normally relatively small.

CONCEPTS IN BRIEF

- To derive GDP using the income approach, we add up all factor payments, including wages, corporate profits, interest and investment income, farm and nonincorporated nonfarm business income, and inventory valuation adjustment.
- To get an accurate estimate of GDP with this method, we must also add indirect business taxes less subsidies and depreciation to those total factor payments.

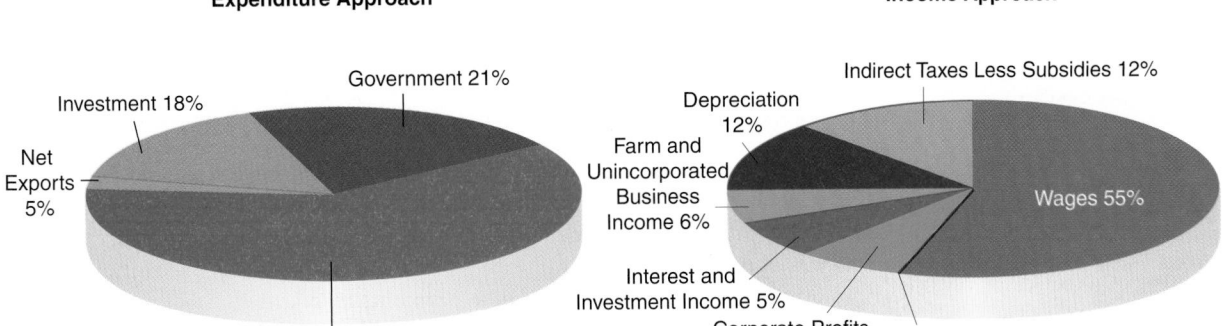

FIGURE 8.3 Gross Domestic Product and Gross Domestic Income, 2000 (in millions of 2000 dollars per year)

By using the two different methods of computing the output of the economy, we come up with gross domestic product and gross domestic income, which are by definition equal. One approach focuses on expenditures, or the flow of product; the other approach concentrates on income, or the flow of costs.

Source: Based on information from Statistics Canada Web sites, <www.statcan.ca/english/Pgdb/Economy/Economic/econ03.htm> and <www.statcan.ca/english/Pgdb/Economy/Economic/econ04.htm>, accessed on March 11, 2001.

Expenditure Point of View—Product Flow		Income Point of View—Cost Flow	
Expenditures by Different Sectors:		Domestic Income (at Factor Cost):	
Household sector		*Wages*	
Personal consumption expenses	$591,051	All wages, salaries, and supplemental employee compensation	$534,601
Government sector		*Corporate profits before taxes*	
Purchase of goods and services	213,823	All business profits earned prior to payment of taxes	137,102
Business sector		*Interest and investment income*	
Gross private domestic investment (including depreciation)	184,931	Payments on deposits and on loans	52,050
Foreign sector		*Farm and non-incorporated nonfarm business income*	
Net exports of goods and services	48,460	Income earned by small business owners and farmers	64,179
Statistical discrepancy	529	*Inventory valuation adjustment*	
		Change in value of inventory due to inflation during the year	−2,310
		Nonincome expense items	
		Indirect business taxes less subsidies	128,536
		Capital consumption allowance	125,165
		Statistical discrepancy	−529
Gross domestic product	$1,038,794	Gross domestic income	$1,038,794

Other Components of National Income Accounting

Gross domestic income or product does not really tell how much income people have access to for spending purposes. To get to those kinds of data, we must make some adjustments, which we now do.

National Income at Factor Cost (NI)

We know that net domestic product (NDP) represents the total market value of goods and services available for both consumption, used in a broader sense here to mean "resource exhaustion," and net additions to the economy's stock of capital. NDP does not, however, represent the income available to individuals within that economy because it includes indirect business taxes, such as sales taxes. We therefore deduct these indirect business taxes less subsidies from NDP to arrive at the figure for all factor income of resource owners. The result is what we define as **national income at factor cost (NI)**—income *earned* by the factors of production.

National income (NI) The total of all factor payments to resource owners. It can be obtained by subtracting indirect business taxes less subsidies from NDP.

Personal Income (PI)

National income does not actually represent what is available to individuals to spend—because some people obtain income for which they have provided no concurrent good or service, and others earn income but do not receive it. In the former category are mainly recipients of transfer payments from the government, such as old age security, welfare, and Employment Insurance benefits. These payments represent shifts of funds within the economy by way of the government, where no good or service is concurrently rendered in exchange. The other category, income earned but not received, consists primarily of corporate retained earnings. When transfer payments are added and when income earned but not received is subtracted, we end up with **personal income (PI)**—income *received* by the factors of production prior to the payment of personal income taxes.

Personal income (PI) The amount of income that households actually receive before they pay personal income taxes.

Disposable Personal Income (DPI)

Everybody knows that you do not get to take home all your salary. To get **disposable personal income (DPI),** we subtract all personal income taxes from personal income. This is the income that individuals have left for consumption and saving.

Disposable personal income (DPI) Personal income after personal income taxes have been paid.

Personal Saving (S)

This is the amount that is left over from disposable personal income after consumption.

Personal saving (S) The amount that is left over from disposable personal income after consumption.

Deriving the Components of GDP

Table 8.2 takes you through the steps necessary to derive the various components of GDP. It shows how you go from gross domestic product to net domestic product, to national income at factor cost, to personal income, to disposable personal income, and then to personal savings.

TABLE 8.2

Going from GDP to Disposable Income, 2000

	Millions of Dollars
Gross domestic product (GDP)	$1,038,794
Minus depreciation	−125,165
Net domestic product (NDP)	913,629
Minus indirect business taxes less subsidies	−128,536
National income at factor cost (NI)	785,093
Minus corporate retained earnings	−49,866
Minus other earnings not paid to persons	−26,501
Plus government and other transfer payments	+114,386
Personal income (PI)	823,112
Minus personal income tax and nontax payments	−199,392
Disposable personal income (DPI)	623,720
Minus personal consumption expenses	−591,051
Personal Saving (S)	$ 32,669

Source: Statistics Canada.

We have completed our rundown of the different ways that GDP can be computed and of the different variants of national income and product. What we have not yet touched on is the difference between national income measured in this year's dollars, and national income representing real goods and services.

CONCEPTS IN BRIEF

- To obtain national income, we subtract indirect business taxes less subsidies from net domestic product. National income gives us a measure of all factor payments to resource owners.
- To obtain personal income, we must add government transfer payments, such as old age security benefits and veterans' allowances. We must subtract income earned but not received by factor owners, such as corporate retained earnings, Employment Insurance premiums, and corporate income taxes.
- To obtain disposable personal income, we subtract all personal income taxes from personal income. Disposable personal income is income that individuals actually have for consumption or saving.

Distinguishing Between Nominal and Real Values

Nominal values The values of variables such as GDP and investment expressed in current dollars, also called *money values;* measurement in terms of the actual market prices at which goods are sold.

Real values Measurement of economic values after adjustments have been made for changes in the average of prices between years.

So far we have shown how to measure nominal income and product. When we say "nominal," we are referring to income and product expressed in the current "face value" of today's dollar. Given the existence of inflation or deflation in the economy, we must also be able to distinguish between the **nominal values** that we will be looking at and the **real values** underlying them. Nominal values are expressed in current dollars. Real income involves our command over goods and services—purchasing power—and therefore depends on money income and a set of prices. Thus real income refers to nominal income corrected for changes in the weighted average of all prices or inflation. In other words, we must make an adjustment for changes in the price level. Consider an example. Nominal income per person in 1960 was only about $1,675 per year. In 2000, nominal income per person was just over $27,125. Were people really that badly off in 1960? No, for nominal income in 1960 is expressed in 1960 prices, not in the prices of today. In today's dollars, the per-person income of 1960 would be closer to $10,275, or almost 38 percent of today's income per person. This is a meaningful comparison between income in 1960 and income today. (The uncorrected 1960 data show per-person income to be only 6 percent of today's income.) Next we will show how we can translate nominal measures of income into real measures by using an appropriate price index, such as the CPI or the GDP deflator discussed in Chapter 7.

Correcting GDP for Price Changes

Constant dollars Dollars expressed in terms of real purchasing power, using a particular year as the base or standard of comparison, in contrast to current dollars.

If a compact disc (CD) costs $15 this year, 10 CDs have a market value of $150. If next year a CD costs $20, the same 10 CDs will have a market value of $200. In this case, there is no increase in the total quantity of CDs, but the market value will have increased by one-third. Apply this to every single good and service produced and sold in Canada and you realize that changes in GDP, measured in *current* dollars, may not be a very useful indication of economic activity. If we are really interested in variations in the *real* output of the economy, we must correct GDP (and just about everything else we look at) for changes in the average of overall prices from year to year. Basically, we first need to generate an index that approximates the changes in average prices. We then must divide that estimate into the value of output in current dollars to adjust the value of output to what is called **constant dollars,** or dollars corrected for general price level changes. This price-corrected GDP is called *real GDP.* Refer to Example 8-1 on the next page.

EXAMPLE 8-1   Correcting GDP for Price Level Changes, 1990–2000

Let's take a numerical example to see how we can adjust GDP for changes in prices. We must pick an appropriate price index in order to adjust for these price level changes. We mentioned the Consumer Price Index, the Producer Price Index, and the GDP deflator in Chapter 7. Let's use the GDP deflator to adjust our figures. Table 8.3 gives 10 years of GDP figures. Nominal GDP figures are shown in column 2. The price level index (GDP deflator) is in column 3, with base year of 1992 when the GDP deflator equals 100. Column 4 shows real (inflation-adjusted) GDP in 1992 dollars.

The formula for real GDP is

$$\text{Real GDP} = \frac{\text{nominal GDP}}{\text{price level}} \times 100$$

TABLE 8.3

Correcting GDP for Price Changes

To correct GDP for price changes, we first have to pick a price level index (the GDP deflator) with a specific year as its base. In our example, the base year is 1992; the price level index for that year is 100% = 100. To obtain 1992 constant-dollar GDP, we divide the price level index into nominal GDP. In other words, we divide column 3 into column 2 (and multiply by 100). This gives us column 4, which is a measure of real GDP expressed in 1992 purchasing power.

(1) Year	(2) Nominal GDP (billions of dollars per year)	(3) Price Level Index (base year 1992 = 100)	(4) = [(2)÷(3)] × 100 (billions of dollars per year in constant 1992 dollars)	(5) Real GDP Percentage Change
1990	668.0	95.0	703.2	0.3
1991	690.8	100.1	690.1	−1.9
1992	696.4	100.0	696.4	0.9
1993	714.9	100.3	712.5	2.3
1994	743.2	99.4	747.6	4.7
1995	789.8	102.7	769.2	2.8
1996	833.1	106.7	780.2	1.5
1997	877.9	107.7	815.0	4.4
1998	901.8	107.1	842.0	3.3
1999	957.9	108.8	880.3	4.5
2000	1038.8	112.7	921.5	4.7

Source: Adapted from Statistics Canada website, www.statcn.ca/english/Pgdb/Economy/Economic/economics.htm; and Bank of Canada, *Bank of Canada Review,* Winter 2000-2001, p. 78.

The step-by-step derivation of real (constant-dollar) GDP is as follows: The base year is 1992, so the price index must equal 100. In 1992, nominal GDP was $696.4 billion, and so too was real GDP expressed in 1992 dollars. In 1993, the price level increased to 100.3. Thus to correct 1993's nominal GDP for inflation, we divide the price index, 100.3, into the nominal GDP figure of $714.9 billion and then multiply it by 100. The result is $712.5 billion, which is 1993 GDP expressed in terms of the purchasing power of dollars in 1992. What about a situation when the price level is lower than in 1992? Look at 1990. Here the price index shown in column 3 is 95.0. That means that in 1991, the average of all prices was about 95 percent of prices in 1992. To obtain 1990 GDP expressed in terms of 1992 purchasing power, we divide nominal GDP, $668.0 billion, by 95.0 and then multiply by 100. The result is a larger number –$703.2 billion. Column 4 in Table 8.3 is a better measure of how the economy has performed than column 2, which shows nominal GDP changes.

For critical analysis: A few years ago, the base year for the GDP deflator was 1986. What does a change in the base year for the price level index affect?

Plotting Nominal and Real GDP

Nominal GDP and real GDP from 1970 to 2000 are plotted in Figure 8.4. Notice that there is quite a big gap between the two GDP figures, reflecting the amount of inflation that has occurred. Note further that the choice of a base year is arbitrary. We have chosen 1992 as the base year in our example. This happens to be the base year recently used by the government.

Per Capita GDP

Looking at changes in real gross domestic product may be deceiving, particularly if the population size has changed significantly. If real GDP over a 10-year period went up 100 percent, you might jump to the conclusion that the material well-being of the economy had increased by that amount. But what if during the same period population increased by 200 percent? Then what would you say? Certainly, the amount of real GDP per person, or *per capita real GDP*, would have fallen, even though total GDP had risen. What we must do to account not only for price changes but also for population changes is first deflate GDP and then divide by the total population, doing this for each year. If we were to look at certain less-developed countries, we would find that in many cases, even though real GDP has risen over the past several decades, per capita real GDP has remained constant or fallen because the population has grown just as rapidly or more quickly.

GDP and Economic Welfare

GDP measures aggregate domestic economic activity reasonably accurately. It does not measure social and economic well-being (see the United Nations' attempt to construct a more genuine indicator on page 194). Numerous other factors not measured by GDP affect economic and social welfare as shown in the following examples.

FIGURE 8.4 Nominal and Real GDP

Here we plot both nominal and real GDP. Real GDP is expressed in the purchasing power of 1992 dollars. The gap between the two represents price level changes.

Source: Adapted from Statistics Canada website, www.statcn.ca/ english/Pgdb/Economy/ Economic/economics.htm; and Bank of Canada, *Bank of Canada Review,* Winter 2000-2001, p. 78.

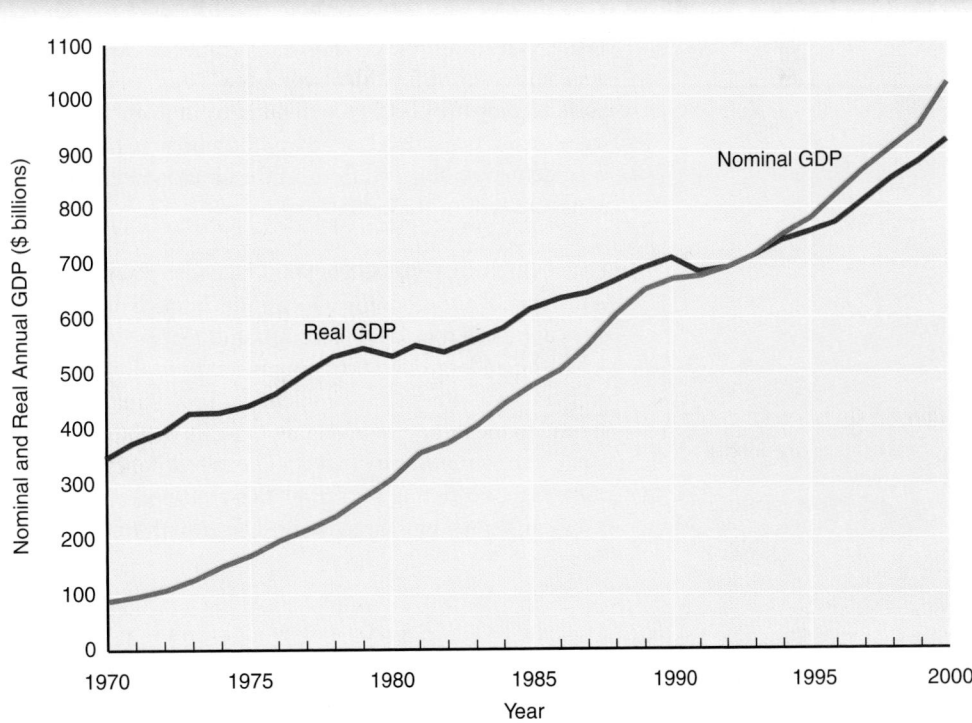

QUALITY IMPROVEMENTS. Improvements in quality, not just increases in quantity, contribute to economic well-being. The computer that you could buy today for $3,000 is clearly superior to one you could have purchased 3 years ago for much more. Cars today last longer, are safer, more comfortable, and more fuel-efficient. Failure to account for quality improvements means that GDP understates increases in our real economic well-being. GDP is only a quantitative measure.

Furthermore, when we calculate GDP, we use price indexes that take into account only price changes and not changes in quality. Therefore, this creates a downward bias to the real GDP calculations.

NONMARKET AND HOUSEHOLD TRANSACTIONS. The production transactions of home-makers, handymen, or volunteers do not appear in GDP. GDP measures only market transactions, that is, only where money exchanges hands for goods or services (see Policy Example 8-1). Because this production is not counted, GDP understates productive activity in the economy.

LEISURE. Leisure time contributes to our economic welfare. If our income stays the same, then the more leisure we have, the better off we feel. In the twentieth century our income went up and our hours of work declined from over 50 hours per week to under 40 and included expanded paid vacations and holidays. These benefits are not reflected in GDP and the improvement in economic welfare is understated.

COMPOSITION AND DISTRIBUTION OF OUTPUT. GDP does not distinguish between those things that are a benefit to society and those which are not. For example, a $25 switchblade used for crime and a music CD are weighed equally in the composition of GDP.

Further, GDP measures do not tell us anything about the distribution of income among individuals in the society. It does not distinguish between most of the output going to a small elite versus output that it more evenly distributed.

THE ENVIRONMENT. GDP growth comes at the expense of the environment but GDP does not account for this. Economic "bads" such as pollution, congestion, waste, and noise accompany GDP growth but are not deducted from the GDP calculations. In fact, when an oil spill, a flood, or an ice storm occurs, the clean-up effort adds to GDP but there is no deduction for the effect on the environment. GDP will overstate the value of economic growth in these cases.

THE UNDERGROUND ECONOMY. The underground economy (see Issues and Applications) is the part of the economy which is deliberately hidden from the government. This activity is unreported in GDP accounts and means that GDP is understated.

If the underground economy is stable as a proportion of the economy over time, its omission will not pose a problem for policy makers. However, shifts from the underground to the rest of the economy, or shifts the other way can cause distortions in assessing overall economic activity that could mislead policy makers. For example, the introduction of the GST tax during the early 1990s probably resulted in a shift towards the underground economy and showed as slower GDP growth than was real in the economy.

Try Preview Question 4:

How does correcting GDP for changes in the price level and population improve the usefulness of GDP estimates?

CONCEPTS IN BRIEF

- To correct nominal GDP for price changes, we first use a base year for our price index and assign it the number 100 percent (or 1.00). Then we construct an index based on how a weighted average of the price level has changed relative to that base year. For example, if in the next year a weighted average of the price level indicates that prices have increased by 10 percent, we would assign it the number 110 (or 1.10). We then divide each year's price index, so constructed, into its respective nominal GDP figure (and multiply by 100).
- We can divide the population into real GDP to obtain per capita real GDP.
- GDP and related measures of national income accounting must be interpreted with their limitations in mind. Real GDP undervalues quality improvements, omits some production, and ignores indicators of economic welfare such as leisure time, the environment, and the composition and distribution of income.

Comparing Living Standards Throughout the World

It is relatively easy to compare the standard of living of a family in Montreal with that of one living in Saskatoon. Both families get paid in dollars, and can buy the same goods and services at Canadian Tire, McDonald's, and Safeway. It is not so easy, however, to make a similar comparison between a family living in Canada and one in, say, India. The first problem concerns money. Indians get paid in rupees, their national currency, and buy goods and services with those rupees. That means that just as we can compare families in Montreal and Saskatoon, we can compare the living standards of a family in Delhi with one in Bombay. But how do we compare the average standard of living in India with that in Canada?

Foreign Exchange Rates

Foreign exchange rate The price of one currency in terms of another.

In earlier chapters, you have encountered international examples that involved local currencies, but the dollar equivalent always has been given. The dollar equivalent is calculated by looking up the **foreign exchange rate** that is published daily in major newspapers throughout the world. If you know that you can exchange $1 for 6 francs, the exchange rate is 6 to 1 (in other words, a franc is worth about 17 cents). So if French incomes per capita are, say, 100,000 francs, that translates to $17,000 at an exchange rate of 6 francs to $1. For years, statisticians calculated relative GDP by simply adding up each country's GDP in its local currency and dividing by each respective dollar exchange rate.

True Purchasing Power

The problem with simply using foreign exchange rates to convert other countries' GDP and per capita GDP into dollars is that not all goods and services are bought and sold in a world market. Restaurant food, housecleaning services, and home repairs do not get exchanged across countries. In countries that have very low wages, those kinds of services are much cheaper than foreign exchange rate computations would imply. Government statistics claiming that per capita income in some poor country is only $300 a year seems shocking. But such a statistic does not tell you the true standard of living of people in that country. Only by looking at what is called **purchasing power parity** can you determine other countries' true standards of living compared to ours.

Purchasing power parity Adjustment in exchange rate conversions that takes into account differences in the true cost of living across countries.

But even purchasing power does not tell the whole story of the relative well-being of countries. We need to look beyond incomes to other factors such as life expectancy and literacy levels to get a truer picture of living standards. In International Example 8-1 you'll see that the United Nations has done just that.

Comparing Standards of Living

In 1990, the United Nations Development Programme (UNDP) declared that comparing per capita incomes across nations did not provide a balanced picture of relative standards of living. Therefore, the UNDP created a Human Development Index (HDI) which takes into account both the real GDP of each country, and the life expectancy at birth, as well as educational attainment of its citizens. By combining these factors, the UNDP hoped to illustrate that the size of an economy measured by its GDP does not necessarily indicate the state of human well-being.

The 1995 HDI declared Canada amongst 174 countries studied as the best place in the world to live, although our per capita income ranked third behind the United States and Hong Kong. Second overall was the United States, and third was Japan. The Netherlands and Norway placed fourth and fifth. The top five developing nations on the HDI were Cyprus, Barbados, Bahamas, Korea, and Argentina.

To illustrate the difficulty of using real GDP as a measure of human well-being, the UNDP pointed out that while New Zealand and Switzerland ranked 14th and 15th on the HDI, New Zealand's real per capita income was US$12,600 compared to Switzerland's US$35,760. Both Ecuador and Morocco had per capita incomes of about US$1,000, but Ecuador placed 64th while Morocco placed 123rd.

After the release of the 1995 HDI, Informetrica, a Canadian think tank, applied the same criteria to the Canadian provinces. The result? Saskatchewan is the best province in the best country in which to live.

For critical analysis: Which country's citizens enjoy a greater well-being? New Zealand's or Switzerland's? Ecuador's or Morocco's?

CONCEPTS IN BRIEF

- The foreign exchange rate is the price of one currency in terms of another.
- Statisticians often calculate relative GDP by adding up each country's GDP in its local currency and dividing by the dollar exchange rate.
- Because not all goods and services are bought and sold in the world market, we must correct exchange rate conversions of other countries' GDP figures in order to take into account differences in the true cost of living across countries.

INTERNATIONAL EXAMPLE 8-2

Purchasing Power Parity Comparisons of World Incomes

A few years ago, the International Monetary Fund accepted the purchasing power parity approach as the correct one. It started presenting international statistics on each country's GDP relative to every other's based on purchasing power parity. The results were surprising. As you can see from Table 8-4, India has a higher per capital GDP compared to what was measured at market foreign exchange rates.

TABLE 8-4

Comparing GDP Internationally

Country	Annual GDP Based on Purchasing Power Parity (billions of US dollars)	Per Capita GDP Based on Purchasing Power Parity (US dollars)	Per Capita GDP Based on Foreign Exchange Rates (US dollars)
United States	6,897.2	26,528	26,528
Japan	2,493.8	19,399	26,424
China	2,490.1	1,692	375
Germany	2,007.4	19,870	24,421
France	1,421.6	18,450	23,489
Russia	1,101.8	6,903	2,640
India	1,100.4	1,155	379
Italy	1,099.0	17,050	17,990
United Kingdom	1,088.0	16,352	16,804
Brazil	980.4	5,251	2,794
Canada	715.3	23,617	19,845

Sources: International Monetary Fund; World Bank; Organization for Economic Cooperation and Development.

For critical analysis: What percentage increase is there in per capita GDP in India when one switches from foreign exchange rates to purchasing power parity?

NETNOMICS

Has Real GDP Measurement Kept Pace with the Internet?

A key ingredient in the measurement of real GDP is, of course, the price index. Changes in the prices of things you buy eventually show up as changes in the measured price index. The price you pay for many items, however, consists really of two prices: the nominal price you pay in dollars plus the price of your time involved in the transaction, measured by its opportunity cost. If a good was sold at an artificially low price, thereby creating lines of people waiting to buy it, the measured price of the good would not reflect its true price.

Slowly but surely, the Internet is reducing the time spent engaging in many transactions. For example, people who trade stocks and bonds online do not have to spend any time dealing with securities brokers. Individuals who use the Internet for online banking spend considerably less time per transaction than they did only a few years ago. Online purchasing of airline tickets also often saves time for each transaction.

There is a time saving on the seller's side also. But this time saving translates into lower costs for the sellers. These lower costs are generally picked up by government statisticians. In contrast, the other half of the equation—the consumer's reduced time spent per each transaction—is apparently not picked up by official government statistics.

The point is that in a world of increasing Internet use and consequent reductions in time spent per transaction, the level and rate of growth of real GDP may be greater than measured. Why? Because the price level may not be accurately reflecting the changes in true prices by including the opportunity cost of time.

ISSUES AND APPLICATIONS

The Worldwide Underground Economy

Concepts Applied: GDP, unemployment rate, incentives, marginal tax rate

GDP statistics do not include "informal" market activities that occur in countries because it is impossible to track these activities. While Canada has a large underground economy, it is much larger in Spain and other European countries. Here in Spain, street vendors entice shoppers with their goods.

Beyond the difficulties of obtaining accurate measurements of GDP and NDP and the like, government statisticians have to face the reality that a certain amount of economic activity can never be captured by official statistics. Why? Because each year, a variety of economic transactions take place completely outside the system. Ordinarily, when one thinks about unofficial or underground activities, one's thoughts immediately turn to drug trafficking, illegal gambling, and prostitution. To be sure, these underground activities are significant. But tens of millions of otherwise law-abiding citizens participate frequently in the "informal" economy. Anybody who buys, sells, or works for cash or an equivalent payment for which no record is kept and on which no taxes are paid is participating in the underground economy.

Incentives Lead the Way

At the heart of the underground economy are the incentives for individuals and businesses. With respect to criminal activity, the incentives are clear: Fines and jail time are enough of an incentive to cause criminals to make sure that none of their activities are reported. For people engaged in noncriminal off-the-books activities, there is one major incentive: to reduce or avoid income and sales taxes. The greater the marginal income tax rate, the greater the incentive to be paid in cash without declaring it. Hence the underground economy was presumably much smaller in Canada prior to 1917, when Canada started collecting federal income taxes. With respect to sales taxes, one would surmise that the amount of unreported retail sales is lower in Alberta, which has no provincial sales taxes, than in provinces such as Nova Scotia and Newfoundland, which have relatively high combined GST and provincial sales taxes.

Unemployment and Welfare Benefits Count Too

An additional incentive for some individuals to work in the underground economy is to avoid losing unemployment benefits or welfare benefits. Consequently, measured unemployment rates are typically biased upward because a certain percentage of the people receiving unemployment benefits are actually working "off-the-books." In some countries, such as Spain, at least 35 percent of the recipients of unemployment benefits now have jobs.

How Big Is the Underground Economy?

By definition, the underground economy is not measured. Therefore, its size is even harder to assess than the size of the "aboveground" economy. Nonetheless, we do have estimates. At an international conference in 1994, estimates of the size of Canada's underground economy ranged from 3 percent to 21 percent of GDP. In dollar terms this would translate into $37.5 billion to $158 billion of underground transactions each year.

The Global Underground Economy

Professor Avi Shama of the University of Mexico believes 90 percent of all private-sector production, sales, and profits are never reported to the tax authorities in Russia. But look at Figure 8-5. There you see the size of the underground economy in Europe, Canada, Australia, Japan, and the United States.

FIGURE 8.5 The Underground Economy in Selected Countries

Source: Organisation for Economic Cooperation and Development.

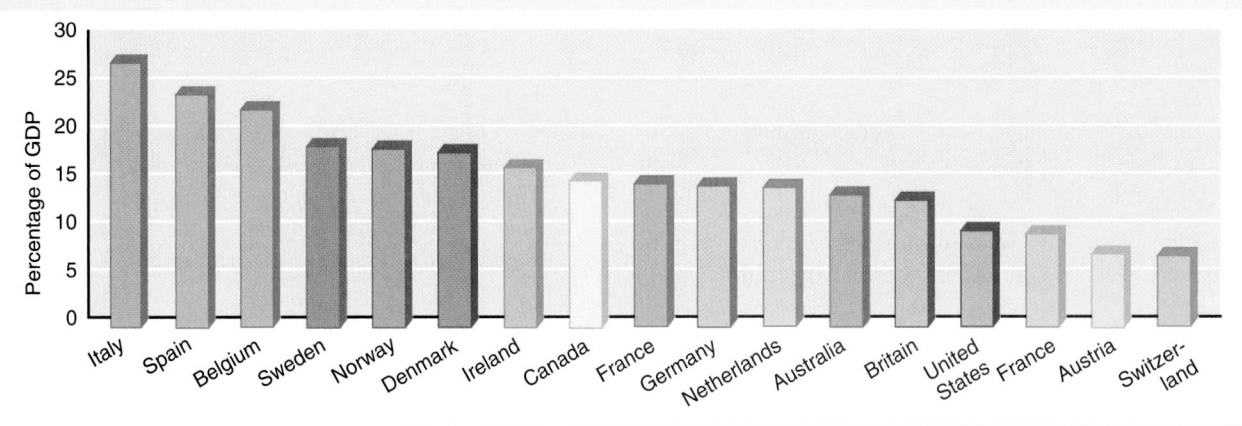

For Critical Analysis

1. Revenue Canada periodically makes estimates of tax revenues lost because of the underground economy. It simply multiplies current tax rates by estimated "off-the-books" income to come up with the figures. Why is Revenue Canada overestimating tax revenues lost due to the underground economy?

2. What change in government policy would reduce the size of the underground economy in Canada?

CHAPTER SUMMARY

1. Households provide labour services, land, capital, and entrepreneurship, for which they are paid wages, rent, interest, and profits. Profits are considered a factor cost— they are the reward for entrepreneurship or risk taking. Profits are a residual payment.

2. In the simplest representation of our economy, there are only households and businesses. The circular flow goes from households to factor markets to businesses and from businesses to product markets to households.

3. National income accounting is the method by which economists attempt to measure statistically the variables with which they are concerned in their study of macroeconomics.

4. One of the concepts most often used in national income accounting is gross domestic product (GDP), which is defined as the total market value of all *final* goods and services produced in the economy during the year by domestic factors of production. The stress on *final* is important to avoid the double-counting of intermediate goods used in the production of other goods.

5. We can compute GDP using the expenditure approach or the income approach. In the former, we merely add up the dollar value of all final goods and services; in the latter, we add up the payments generated in producing all those goods and services, or wages, corporate profits before taxes, interest, farm and non-incorporated nonfarm

income, and inventory valuation adjustment, plus indirect business taxes less subsidies and depreciation.

6. It is difficult to measure the market value of government expenditures because generally government-provided goods are not sold at a market clearing price. We therefore value government expenditures at their cost for inclusion in our measure of GDP.

7. Investment does not occur when there is merely a transfer of assets among individuals; rather, it occurs only when new productive capacity, such as a machine tool, is built.

8. Part of our capital stock is worn out or becomes obsolete every year. To take account of the expenditures made

merely to replace such capital equipment, we subtract depreciation from GDP to yield net domestic product (NDP).

9. To correct for price changes, we deflate GDP with a price index to come up with real GDP. To take account of rising population, we divide by population to arrive at per capita real GDP.

10. To compare GDP across countries, we must first apply the foreign exchange rate to GDP expressed in the local currency and then adjust the exchange rate to take account of the purchasing power of that income. This is called the purchasing power parity approach.

DISCUSSION OF PREVIEW QUESTIONS

1. What is gross domestic product (GDP), and what does it measure?

Gross domestic product is defined as the market value of all final goods and services produced during one year by domestic factors of production. Because GDP is measured per unit of time, it is a flow concept. Economists try to estimate GDP in order to evaluate the productive performance of an economy during the year; economists also use GDP estimates to aid them in judging overall economic well-being.

2. Why are only *final* goods and services evaluated in deriving GDP?

Because GDP estimates are an attempt to evaluate an economy's performance and to generalize about group well-being, we must be careful to evaluate only final goods and services; otherwise GDP would be exaggerated. For example, because an automobile uses plastic, steel, coke, rubber, coal, and other products in its manufacture, to count each of these and the value of the automobile would be double counting. Thus to count steel *and* the automobile when it is sold is to count steel twice and hence to exaggerate the economy's performance and the group's economic well-being. Steel in this instance would not be a final good; it would be an intermediate good.

3. Why must depreciation and indirect business taxes less subsidies be added to national income at factor cost in order to derive GDP via the income approach?

The expenditure approach to GDP counts expenditures on *all* final goods and services; in particular, expenditures on all investment goods amount to gross investment. The income approach to GDP estimation, by contrast, sums the wages, profits, interest, and other receipts of income earners. Because depreciation is not a wage, profit, interest, or other income, the expenditure approach would yield a higher number. In order to compare correctly, we must add depreciation to national income at factor cost to calculate GDP via the income approach. Similarly, indirect business taxes (excise, sales, and property taxes) less subsidies are automatically reflected in the expenditure approach, whereas this category is not included in wages, profit, interest, or other receipts to factors of production.

4. How does correcting GDP for changes in the price level and population improve the usefulness of GDP estimates?

When the price level is rising (during periods of inflation), GDP estimates would overstate true productive activity and group economic well-being. Similarly, when the general price level is falling (during periods of deflation), GDP estimates would understate productive activity and group economic well-being. If population is rising more rapidly than real output, real GDP estimates would rise, but living standards might well fall. Dividing by population corrects for such cases. Per capita real GDP is a better clue to productive activity and overall economic well-being than nominal GDP.

PROBLEMS

(Answers to the odd-numbered problems appear at the back of the book.)

8-1. The following are a year's data for a hypothetical economy.

	Billions of Dollars
Consumption	400
Government spending	350
Gross private domestic investment	150
Exports	150
Imports	100
Depreciation	50
Indirect business taxes less subsidies	25

a. Based on the data, what is the value of GDP? NDP? NI?

b. Suppose that in the next year exports increase to $175 billion, imports increase to $200 billion, and consumption falls to $350 billion. What will GDP be in that year?

c. If the value of depreciation (capital consumption allowance) should ever exceed that of gross private domestic investment, how would this affect the future productivity of the nation?

8-2. Look back at Table 8.3, which explains how to correct GDP for price level changes. Column 4 of that table gives real GDP in terms of 1992 constant dollars. Change the base year to 1994. Recalculate the price level index and then recalculate real GDP—that is, express column 4 in terms of 1994 dollars instead of 1992 dollars.

8-3. Study the following table; then answer the questions.

Stage of Production	Sales Receipts	Intermediate Costs	Value Added
Coal	$2	$0	$2
Steel	5	2	3
Manufactured autos	8	5	3
Sold autos	9	8	1

a. What is the intermediate good for steel production? How much did it cost?

b. What is the value added resulting from auto manufacturing?

c. If automobiles are the only final goods produced in this economy, what would be the GDP via the expenditures approach?

d. If automobiles are the only final goods produced in this economy, what would be the GDP via the income approach?

8-4. At the top of a piece of paper, write the headings "Production Activity" and "Nonproduction Activity." List each of the following under one of these headings by determining which would go into our measure of GDP.

a. Mr. X sells his used car to Mr. Y.

b. Joe's used car lot sells a car to Mr. Z and receives a $50 profit for doing so.

c. Merrill Lynch receives a brokerage commission for selling stocks.

d. Ms. Arianas buys 100 shares of Dofasco stock.

e. Mrs. LeMaistre cooks and keeps house for her family.

f. Mr. Singh mows his own lawn.

g. Mr. Singh mows lawns for a living.

h. Mr. Smith receives a welfare payment.

i. Mrs. Johnson sends her daughter $500 for a semester of studies at College U.

8-5. What happens to the official measure of GDP in each of the following situations?

a. A man marries his housekeeper, who then quits working for wages.

b. A drug addict marries her supplier.

c. Homemakers perform the same jobs but switch houses and charge each other for their services.

8-6. Construct a value-added table for various stages in the production and sale of bread.

8-7. Consider the following table for an economy that produces only four goods.

Good	1992 Price	1992 Quantity	2000 Price	2000 Quantity
Pizza	$ 4	10	$ 8	12
Cola	12	20	36	15
T-shirts	6	5	10	15
Business Equipment	25	10	30	12

Assuming a 1992 base year:

a. What is nominal GDP for 1992 and 2000?

b. What is real GDP for 1992? For 2000?

8-8. Examine the following figures for a hypothetical year; then calculate GDP, NDP, NI, PI, and DPI.

	Billions of Dollars
Consumption	400
Net exports	−20
Transfer payments	20
Gross investment	100
E.I. and C.P.P. contributions	10
Government purchases	120
Net investment	50
Dividends	20
Indirect business taxes less subsidies	10
Corporate income taxes	30
Personal income taxes	60
Undistributed corporate profits	20

ECONOMICS ON THE NET

Tracking Gross Domestic Product and Its Components

You can track GDP and its components using the Statistics Canada Web site.

Internet URL: http://www.statcan.ca

Title: Economic Indicators — Canada

Navigation: Begin at the homepage of Statistics Canada (http://www.statcan.ca). Then click on English, followed by Canadian Statistics.

Application:

Perform the operations indicated above and answer the following questions:

a. Under The Economy, click on Latest indicators, then on Summary table, Canada and the provinces. How has nominal GDP grown in the latest quarter? In the past year? How has real GDP grown in the latest quarter? In the past year? What have been the changes in the Personal savings rate? What has been the change in prices as measured by CPI during the last year? Now go to the top of the page and submit a province in the appropriate box, and compare changes in prices in this province to the Canadian CPI.

b. Under The Economy, click on Economic conditions, then National accounts, then on Gross domestic product at 1992 prices (expenditure-based). Calculate and compare the rate of growth of GDP to Personal expenditure on consumer goods and services. How do consumers fare in this economy? Calculate and compare the rate of growth of Personal expenditure on consumer goods and services to its sub-component, Durable goods. What do the different rates of growth suggest about the state of the economy?

c. Under The Economy, click on Economic conditions, then National accounts, then Gross domestic product at 1992 prices, the provinces and territories. Take two provinces and compare their rates of growth.

ECONOMIC GROWTH: TECHNOLOGY, RESEARCH AND DEVELOPMENT, AND KNOWLEDGE

In June of 2000, the United Nations reported that, for the seventh successive year, Canada topped the Human Development Index (HDI), which ranks 174 countries in terms of life expectancy, education, and income. Norway and the United States were second and third. At the other end of the Index, Sierra Leone and Niger were again the bottom two.

Canadians enjoy one of the highest standards of living in the world. Compared to most people in the world and to our grandparents and great-grandparents, we have far more of everything than they did. We live longer, have better education, enjoy better health, and have many more material possessions and access to many services.

Economists have focused their attention on economic growth as the means for achieving this increased standard of living. In this chapter, you will look at economic growth, how it is measured and, just as importantly, what it doesn't measure.

PREVIEW QUESTIONS

1. What is economic growth?

2. What does economic growth measure?

3. What are some of the ways in which you can experience economic growth for yourself or for your family?

4. What are the determinants of economic growth?

5. Is economic growth good for us?

DID YOU KNOW THAT... at the beginning of the twentieth century, Argentina had the sixth highest per capita income in the world, but now at the beginning of the twenty-first century it is around fortieth, somewhat below Iran? Consider also that 100 years ago, Hong Kong was basically a barren rock, but today its per capita income exceeds that of France and the United Kingdom. How can we explain such dramatic changes in relative living standards? From an arithmetic point of view, the answer is simple: Argentina experienced little, and in some cases negative, economic growth over the past century, whereas Hong Kong had significant economic growth. That answer, though, does not tell us *why* economic growth rates differed in these two countries. That is the task of this chapter. Should you care about the rate of economic growth in Canada? The answer is yes, if you care about your future standard of living and that of your children and grandchildren. You have already demonstrated that you care about your future standard of living; otherwise, you would not be bothering to obtain a higher education. Obviously, you want to make sure that you experience economic growth as an individual. Now it is time to consider the country as a whole.

What Is Economic Growth?

Remember from Chapter 2 that we can show economic growth graphically as an outward shift of a production possibilities curve, as is seen in Figure 9.1. If there is economic growth between 2000 and 2025, the production possibilities curve will shift outward. The distance that it shifts represents the amount of economic growth, defined as the increase in the productive capacity of a nation. Although it is possible to come up with a measure of a nation's increased productive capacity, it is not easy. Therefore, we turn to a more readily obtainable definition of economic growth.

Most people have a general idea of what economic growth means. When a nation grows economically, its citizens must be better off in some ways, usually in terms of their material well-being. Typically, though, we do not measure the well-being of any country solely in terms of its total output of real goods and services, or in terms of real GDP without making some adjustments. After all, India has a GDP about three times as large as that of Switzerland. The population of India, though, is about 125 times greater than that of Switzerland. Consequently, we view India as a relatively poor country and Switzerland as a relatively rich one. Thus to measure how much a country is growing in terms of annual increases in real GDP, we have to adjust for population growth. Our formal definition becomes this: **Economic growth** occurs when there are increases in

Economic growth Increases in per capita real GDP measured by its rate of change per year.

FIGURE 9.1 Economic Growth

If there is growth between 2000 and 2025, the production possibilities curve for the entire economy will shift outward from the line labelled 2000 to the line labelled 2025. The distance that it shifts represents an increase in the productive capacity of the nation.

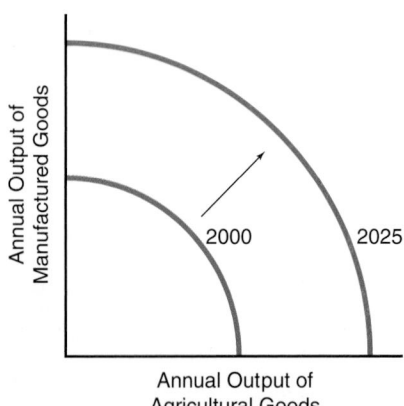

Try Preview Question 1:
What is economic growth?

per capita real GDP; it is measured by the rate of change in per capita real GDP per year. Figure 9.2 presents the historical record of real GDP per person in Canada. Read International Example 9-1 to see how Canada stacks up against the world.

INTERNATIONAL EXAMPLE 9-1

Growth Rates Around the World

TABLE 9.1

Per Capita Growth Rates in Various Countries

Table 9.1 shows the annual average rate of growth of income per person in selected countries. Notice that Canada during the time period under study is positioned about midway in the pack. In other words, even though we are one of the world's richest countries, our recent rate of economic growth is not particularly high.

Sources: World Bank; International Monetary Fund.

Country	Average Annual Rate of Growth of Income per Capita, 1970–1997 (%)
Sweden	1.8
Switzerland	1.8
Germany	2.2
Netherlands	2.3
France	2.4
United Kingdom	2.4
Canada	**2.7**
Italy	2.9
Spain	2.9
United States	2.9
Japan	4.4
Turkey	5.5
China	6.2

For critical analysis: "The largest change is from zero to one." Does this statement have anything to do with relative growth rates in poorer versus richer countries?

FIGURE 9.2 The Historical Record of Canadian Economic Growth

The graph traces per capita real GDP in Canada since 1870. Data are given in 1986 dollars.

Source: Statistics Canada.

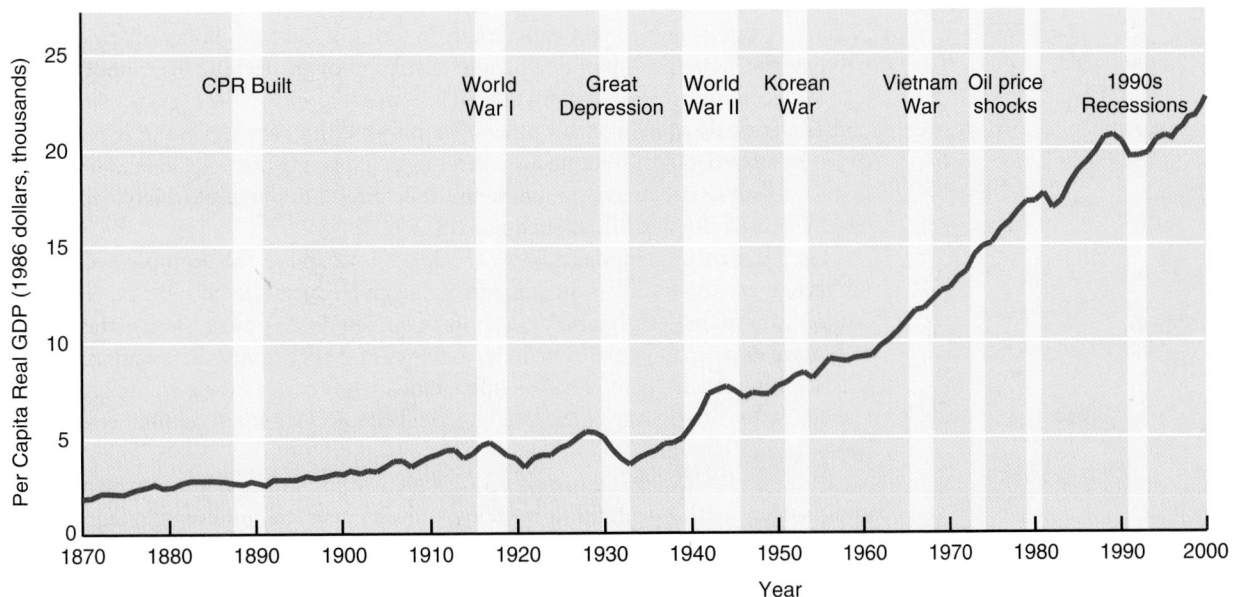

One of the fundamental reasons that Canada has stayed near the top of the world in living standards and improves so much from the time of Confederation is that is has sustained economic growth for many years. While the percentage differences in Table 9-1 are small, the effect of those differences over many years accumulates to very big differences. Canadian per capita real GDP has grown by a factor of thirteen times since 1870, even though the average yearly increase has been about 2 percent. Example 9-1 shows how a small difference in growth rates can make a big difference in standards of living over many years.

EXAMPLE 9-1   What if Canada Had Grown a Little Bit Less or More Each Year?

In 1870, the per person real GDP expressed in 2000 dollars was $2,448. That figure had grown to $33,600 by the middle of 2000. The average economic growth rate was, therefore, about 2 percent per year. What if the Canadian growth rate over the same century and a third had been simply 1 percent less—only 1 percent per year? Per capita real GDP in 2000 would have been only about 25 percent of what it actually was! Canada would now rank somewhere around thirty-eighth on the scale of per capita income throughout the world. We would be poorer than Greece or Portugal.

Consider a rosier scenario: What if the Canadian economic rate of growth had been one point higher, or 3 percent per year? Today's per capita real GDP would be more than three times its actual value, or about $110,000! This would have about doubled the highest per capita income in the world today!

For critical analysis: Can you relate this example to anything in your life? (Hint: How is your standard of living higher than your parents and grandparents?)

Problems in Definition

Our definition of economic growth says nothing about the *distribution* of output and income. A nation might grow very rapidly in terms of increases in per capita real output, while at the same time its poor people remain poor or become even poorer. Within Canada, economic development has been very uneven, with some regions enjoying much higher standards of living than others. Thinking Critically About the Media 9-1 discusses in more detail the reasons why this might happen. Therefore, in assessing the economic growth record of any nation, we must be careful to pinpoint which income groups have benefited the most from such growth.

The Human Development Index (HDI), mentioned at the beginning of this chapter, recognizes this problem by measuring income, education, and life expectancy. The index measures these three basic indicators of human development because the UN wants to capture more than just income in its assessment. For the publishers of this index, how a nation's income is spent is just as important as how much they earn. So, even though Canada is not first in any of these three categories, we come out on top because of how we spend our income.

Real standards of living can go up without any positive economic growth. This second problem with our definition occurs if individuals are, on average, enjoying more leisure by working fewer hours but producing as much as they did before. For example, if per capita real GDP in Canada remained at $20,000 a year for a decade, we could not automatically jump to the conclusion that Canadians were, on average, no better off. What if, during that same 10-year period, average hours worked fell from 37 per week to

33 per week? That would mean that during the 10 years under study, individuals in the labour force were "earning" four hours more leisure a week. Actually, nothing so extreme has occurred in this country, but something similar has. Average hours worked per week fell steadily until the 1960s, at which time they levelled off. That means that during much of the history of this country, the increase in per capita real GDP *understated* the actual economic growth that we were experiencing because we were enjoying more and more leisure time as things progressed.

Try Preview Question 2:
What does economic growth measure?

Thinking Critically About the Media 9-1   How Does Productivity Affect Our Standard of Living in Canada?

One of the major recurring themes of Canadian life is the difference in living standards that occurs between different regions of the country. This difference is called regional disparity, and provinces are sometimes divided between "have" and "have not," Programs such as equalization payments and the controversial Human Resource Development Commission (HRDC) are used to try to reduce these differences in living standards. While some commentators have suggested that the difference in standard of living can be traced to an ethic in some areas of people who are unwilling to work, it is clear to economists that much of the difference is better explained by differences in productivity between provinces. Alberta and Ontario have the highest living standards because they have a different industrial mix than the other regions of the country. A recent study by WEFA Inc. suggests that Alberta and Ontario have the highest level of productivity with GDP per worker being $65,000 per year, while PEI has the lowest productivity, with GDP per worker of only $46,000!

CONCEPTS IN BRIEF

- Economic growth can be defined as the increase in real per capita output measured by its rate of change per year.
- The definition of economic growth does not reflect how a nation distributes its goods and services. It does not reflect how this distribution affects its population in terms of literacy or longevity and it does not capture increases in leisure that can also be "bought" with economic growth.
- Small percentage-point differences in growth rates lead to large differences in real GDP over time.

Productivity Increases: The Heart of Economic Growth

Let's say that you are required to type 10 term papers and homework assignments a year. You have a word processor to do so, but you do not know how to touch-type. You end up spending an average of two hours per typing job. The next summer, you buy a touch-typing tutorial to use on your word processor and spend a few minutes a day improving your typing speed. The following term, you spend only one hour per typing assignment, thereby saving 10 hours a semester. You have become more productive. This concept of productivity relates to your ability (and everyone else's) to produce the same output with fewer labour hours. Thus **labour productivity** is normally measured by dividing the total real domestic output (real GDP) by the number of workers or the number of labour hours. Labour productivity increases whenever average output produced per worker during a specified time period increases. Clearly, there is a relationship between economic

Labour productivity Total real domestic output (real GDP) divided by the number of workers (output per worker).

growth and increases in labour productivity. If you divide all resources into just capital and labour, economic growth can be defined simply as follows:

Economic growth = rate of growth of capital + rate of growth of labour + rate of growth in the productivity of capital and of labour

If everything else remains constant, improvements in labour productivity ultimately lead to economic growth and higher living standards.

In the same way, increases in real GDP are closely linked to the productivity of all underlying inputs in production, capital, labour, and technology. An increase in the amount of resources available or productivity of any of these input resources contributes to overall growth. For example, there is a very strong relationship between the average level of education and the standard of living for both individuals and for countries. In the western economies, new technologies have been a source of much economic growth in the past 100 years.

Although productivity growth seemed to lag in Canada from the mid-1970s through the mid-1980s, there is quite a bit of evidence that it has been on the rise since then. Figure 9.3 traces productivity growth in the manufacturing and service sectors of the economy.

While Canadian productivity has generally been high when compared to the rest of the world (as shown in International Example 9-1), it has not been evenly spread across the country. There are large differences in standards of living and productivity between provinces in Canada. Thinking Critically About the Media 9-1 gives a brief introduction to this issue.

FIGURE 9.3 Nonfarm Canadian Productivity Growth

Whereas productivity growth in the services sector was relatively robust until the early 1980s, productivity in the manufacturing sector has been increasing almost consistently since the 1960s. The recessions of the 1980s and 1990s slowed productivity growth in both sectors.

Source: Statistics Canada, CANSIM Database, Series I60008, I60009.

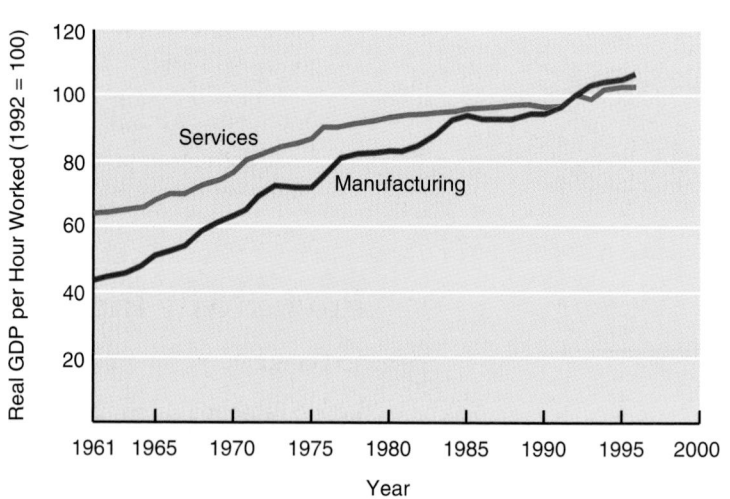

| INTERNATIONAL EXAMPLE 9-2 | How Does Canadian Productivity Compare to the Rest of the World? |

One way economists use productivity is as a rough measure of competitiveness: the more productive the resources, all else held constant, the lower the cost of the product. However, in measures of productivity and competitiveness, all else is not held constant. For example, some countries have governments which encourage high productivity by making access to education or new technology easy. Other countries have governments which discourage growth of productivity by enforcing regulations which make labour market changes in response to technology changes difficult.

The World Economic Forum is one body which tries to measure relative productivity among 49 countries. It ranks countries in order of their ability "to achieve sustained high rates of growth in GDP per capita." In Table 9.2, you will note that Canada is ranked 8th out of the top 25 countries. Notice that some countries which we usually point to as being very productive are indeed ahead of Canada: Singapore, Hong Kong, the United States. But notice too that some countries we do not usually think of as being less productive than Canada have a lower rank: Taiwan, Japan, South Korea.

The World Economic Forum cannot guarantee that Canada will grow faster than the lower ranked countries in the years to come. Perhaps the better measure of improvement would be to see Canada move up in the list.

TABLE 9.2
Relative Competitiveness of Countries

Source: "The C-word Strikes Back," *The Economist,* June 1, 1996, p. 76.

Country	Rank	Country	Rank
Singapore	1	Thailand	14
Hong Kong	2	Britain	15
New Zealand	3	Finland	16
United States	4	Netherlands	17
Luxembourg	5	Chile	18
Switzerland	6	Austria	19
Norway	7	South Korea	20
Canada	8	Sweden	21
Taiwan	9	Germany	22
Malaysia	10	France	23
Denmark	11	Israel	24
Australia	12	Belgium	25
Japan	13		

For critical analysis: Could Canada move up in the list because of events in other countries? Would that mark an improvement in Canada's competitiveness?

Saving and Investment: A Fundamental Determinant of Economic Growth

Economic growth does not occur in a vacuum. It is not some predetermined fate of a nation. Rather, economic growth depends on certain fundamental factors. One of the most important factors that affect the rate of economic growth and hence long-term living standards is the rate of saving.

A basic proposition in economics is that if you want more tomorrow, you have to take less today.

To have more consumption in the future, you have to consume less today and save the difference between your consumption and your income.

This reduction in consumption frees up resources to be used for economic investment in physical and human capital, fundamental resources needed for growth.

On a national basis, this implies that higher saving rates eventually mean higher living standards in the long run, all other things held constant. Concern has been growing in Canada that we are not saving enough, which means that our rate of saving may be too low. Saving is important for economic growth because without saving, we cannot have investment. If all income is consumed each year, there is nothing left over for saving, which could be used by business for investment. If there is no investment in our capital stock, there could be little hope of much economic growth.

The relationship between the rate of savings and per capita real GDP is shown in Figure 9.4. A nation with one of the highest rates of saving is Japan. Why? (See International Example 9-3 for a partial explanation.)

Other Determinants of Economic Growth

There are a number of other factors that influence the growth of an economy. A number of political and economic institutions have been identified as important to encouraging growth. Supply-side economists often focus on these factors, since they are particularly interested in stimulating growth.

Private property is one of those institutions underpinning economic growth. Unless people can accrue some of the gains from growth for themselves, then there may be little incentive to work harder. In the same way, *copyright* and *patent* laws protect the creative processes. Without the protection of these laws, there would be little incentive to create new products and to spend money on research and development.

Try Preview Question 3:

What are some of the ways in which you can experience economic growth for yourself or for your family?

FIGURE 9.4 Relationship Between Rate of Saving and per Capita Real GDP

This diagram shows the combination of per capita real GDP and the rate of saving expressed as the average percentage of annual real GDP for many nations since 1960. Centrally planned economies and major oil-producing countries are not shown.

Source: After Robert Summers and Alan Heston, "A New Set of International Comparisons of Real Product and Price Level," *Review of Income and Wealth,* March 1988.

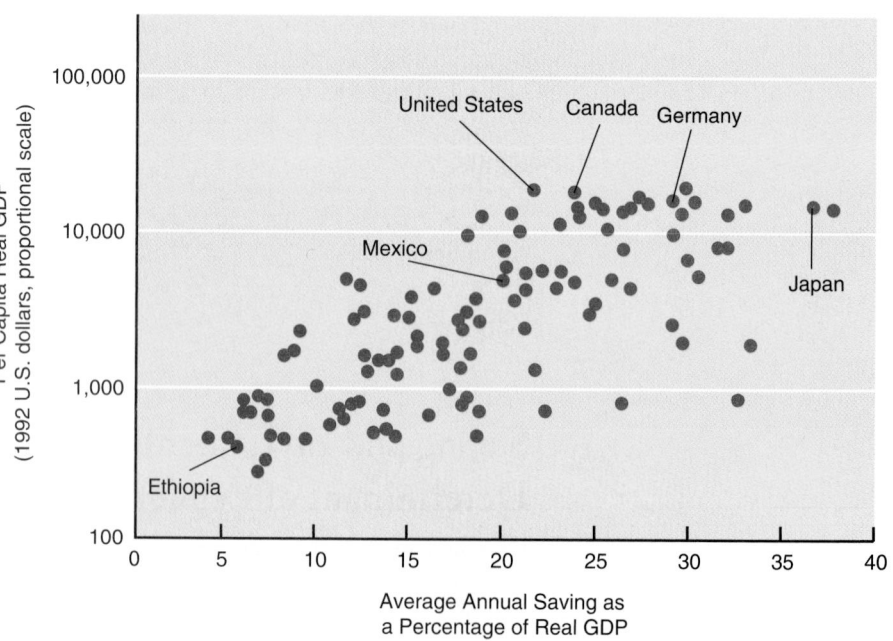

| | |

INTERNATIONAL EXAMPLE 9-3   Why Do the Japanese Save So Much?

The rate of saving in Japan is roughly one-third more than what it has been in Canada, expressed as a percentage of income. One possible reason is that the Japanese have been unable to borrow as freely as their Canadian counterparts. The typical down payment for a Japanese family wishing to buy a house is 40 percent, compared with only 15 percent in Canada. The average house price in Japan is more than twice what it is in Canada. Consequently, to purchase a home, a typical Japanese family has to save more than a typical Canadian family. In addition, the Japanese have for many years been rewarded more for saving than in Canada because their tax system has taxed the rate of return to saving relatively less than in Canada.

For critical analysis: Explain why you might consider paying off a mortgage on your home as a form of saving.

Market-driven economies generally seem better at growth than non-market economies. The economies with the highest standard of living all have capitalist markets as a basic institution. Within those systems almost all have some methods for redistributing income to the poorest in society. Governments usually play an important role in regulation, protecting the market system from monopolies and other side effects of production, such as pollution. Countries that have corrupt government bureaucracies do not do as well either.

Political stability is an important prerequisite for economic growth. If you were in a country where bank accounts and businesses were periodically seized by the government, how willing would you be to leave your money in a savings account or to invest in a business? In general, the more certain private property rights are, the more capital accumulation there will be. We need only to look at how all the gains from many years of economic growth in Yugoslavia were lost when the country flew apart in civil war in the 1990s. New investment in war-torn countries is often difficult to find, even though that investment can be critical for starting over.

Population growth and immigration can affect economic growth in several ways. Population growth means an increase in the amount of labour, which, as we have previously learned, is one component of economic growth. Immigration also helps economic growth. Most studies indicate immigrants have high labour force participation rate and lower unemployment rate than other Canadians. This should, in the long run, boost potential output. In addition, on average, immigrants have more education than other Canadians, and call upon our social programs less frequently. These theories are not agreed to by all researchers, however, and are still the focus of much research.

CONCEPTS IN BRIEF

- Economic growth is numerically equal to the rate of growth of capital plus the rate of growth of labour plus the rate of growth in the productivity of capital and of labour. Improvements in labour productivity, all other things being equal, lead to greater economic growth and higher living standards.
- One fundamental determinant of the rate of growth is the rate of saving and investment. To have more consumption in the future, we have to save and invest rather than consume. In general, countries that have had higher rates of saving have had higher rates of growth in real GDP.

- Protection of private property, market economies, and political stability are important underpinnings to encouraging economic growth. Population growth and immigration also affect economic growth by influencing the mix of human capital in a country.

New Growth Theory and What Determines Growth

A simple arithmetic definition of economic growth has already been given. Growth rates of capital and labour plus the growth rate in their productivity are simply defined as the components of economic growth. Economists have had good data on the growth of the labour force as well as the growth of the physical capital stock in Canada. But when you add those two growth rates together, you still do not get the total economic growth rate in Canada. The difference has to be due to improvements in productivity. Economists typically labelled this "improvements in technology," and that was that. More recently, proponents of what is now called the **new growth theory** argue that technology cannot simply be looked at as an outside factor without explanation. Technology must be examined from the point of view of what drives it. What are the forces that make productivity grow in Canada and elsewhere?

New growth theory A relatively modern theory of economic growth which examines the factors that determine why technology, research, innovation, and the like are undertaken and how they interact.

Growth in Technology

Consider some startling statistics about the growth in technology. Microprocessor speeds may increase from 1,000 megahertz to 10,000 megahertz by the year 2011. By that same year, the size of the thinnest circuit line within a transistor will decrease by 77 percent. The typical memory capacity of computers will jump from 64 megabytes, or about the equivalent text in the *Encyclopaedia Britannica*, to 64 gigabytes—a thousandfold increase.

By 2005, new microchip plants will produce 1,000 transistors a week for every person on earth. Predictions are that computers may become as powerful as the human brain by 2020.

Thinking Critically About the Media 9-2   Do New Technologies Signal the End of Work?

Throughout the world, the media as well as numerous "experts" have painted a gloomy picture for the average working person. They point out that the newest technologies have led to a reduction in the percentage of workers who devote their time to manufacturing. Efficient production lines certainly do require fewer workers, and sophisticated telecommunications have reduced the need for physical offices. During one recent talk show in England, the commentator stated that "the rich no longer need the poor. More and more goods can be produced with fewer and fewer workers. Therefore, permanent unemployment will grow." Such commentaries have been popular since the weaving machine and its single operator replaced the work that 10 people did before. The idea is that the other 9 workers were unemployed forever. Both theory and data render such media analyses basically meaningless.

In Canada, in spite of dramatic increases in technology, the population increased over 7 million between 1975 and 1998, while the number of unemployed has increased by only 800,000. And theoretically, there is no limit to employment. Labour employment is a function of the supply and demand for labour. Demand is not a fixed constant somehow based on a mechanical relationship between the number of widgets produced and the number of workers needed to produce them. Workers released from industries that are more productive because of new technologies must—and do—find employment elsewhere, often in other industries that are expanding. (After all, wants *are* unlimited.)

Technology: A Separate Factor of Production

We now recognize that technology must be viewed as a separate factor of production that is sensitive to rewards. In other words, one of the major foundations of new growth theory is this:

The greater the rewards, the more technological advances we will get.

Let's first consider several aspects of technology here, starting with research and development.

Research and Development

A certain amount of technological advance results from research and development (R&D) activities that have as their goal the development of specific new materials, new products, and new machines. How much spending a nation devotes to R&D can have an impact on its long-term economic growth. Part of how much a nation spends depends on what businesses decide is worth spending. That, in turn, depends on their expected rewards from successful R&D. If your company develops a new way to produce computer memory chips, how much will it be rewarded? The answer depends on whether others can freely copy the new technique.

Patent A government protection that gives an inventor the exclusive right to make, use, or sell an invention for a limited period of time (typically, 20 years in Canada).

PATENTS. To protect new techniques developed through R&D, we have a system of **patents**, protections whereby the federal government gives the patent holder the exclusive right to make, use, and sell an invention for a period of 20 years. One can argue that this special position given to owners of patents increases expenditures on R&D and therefore adds to long-term economic growth.

POSITIVE EXTERNALITIES AND R&D. Positive externalities are benefits from an activity that do not spill over to the instigator of the activity. In the case of R&D spending, a certain amount of the benefits go to other companies that do not have to pay for them. In particular, according to economists David Coe and Elhanan Helpman, about a quarter of the global benefits of R&D investment in the top seven industrialized countries goes to foreigners. For every 1 percent rise in the stock of research and development in North America alone, for example, productivity in the rest of the world increases by about 0.04 percent. One country's R&D expenditures benefit foreigners because foreigners are able to import goods from technologically advanced countries and then use them as inputs in making their own industries more efficient. In addition, countries that import high-tech goods are able to imitate the technology.

The Open Economy and Economic Growth

People who study economic growth today tend to emphasize the importance of the openness of the economy. Free trade encourages a more rapid spread of technology and industrial ideas. Moreover, open economies may experience higher rates of economic growth because their own industries have access to a bigger market. When trade barriers are erected in the form of tariffs and the like, domestic industries become isolated from global technological progress. This occurred for many years in former communist countries and in many developing countries in Latin America and elsewhere. Figure 9.5 shows the relationship between economic growth and the openness as measured by the level of protectionism of a given economy.

FIGURE 9.5 The Relationship Between Protectionism and Economic Growth

Closed economies are ones in which the government prevents imports from entering the country and, sometimes, exports from leaving the country. Such protectionism closes off the economy to new technologies. Here you see the relationship between the level of protectionism and economic growth rates measured on a per capita basis. The data seem to indicate that the more closed an economy, the lower its rate of growth, all other things held constant.

Source: Economic Review, Fourth Quarter 1993, p. 3.

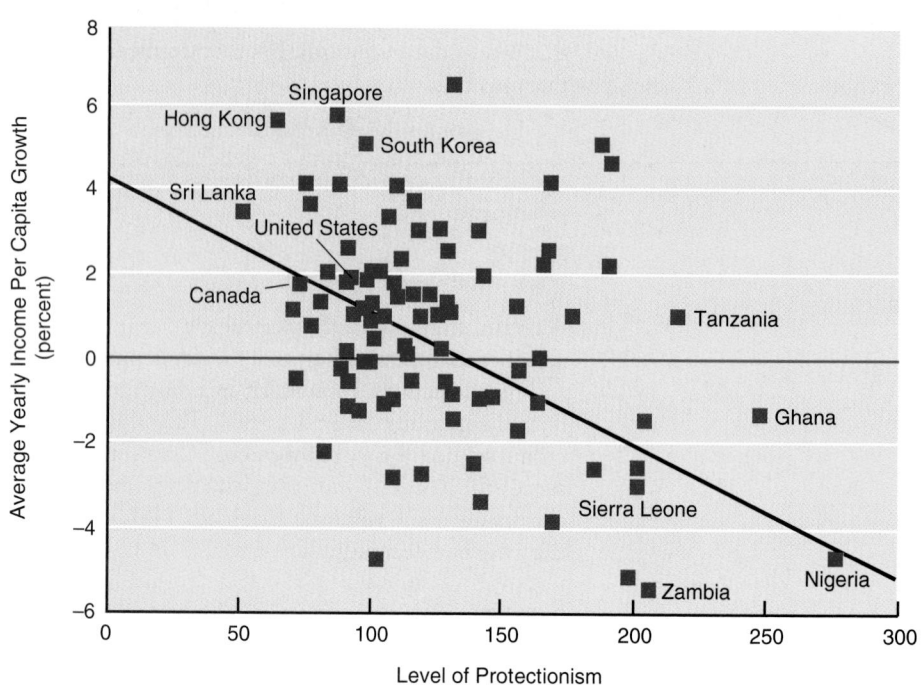

Innovation and Knowledge

We tend to think of technological progress as, say, the invention of the transistor. But invention means nothing by itself; **innovation** is required. Innovation involves the transformation of something new, such as an invention, into something that benefits the economy either by lowering production costs or providing new goods and services. Indeed, the new growth theorists believe that real wealth creation comes from innovation and that invention is but one aspect of innovation.

Historically, technologies have moved relatively slowly from invention to innovation to widespread use, and the dispersion of new technology remains for the most part slow and uncertain. The inventor of the transistor thought it might be used to make better hearing aids. At the time it was invented, the only reference to it in the *New York Times* was in a small weekly column called "News of Radio." When the laser was invented, no one really knew what it could be used for. It was initially used to help in navigation, measurement, and chemical research. Today, it is used in the reproduction of music, printing, surgery, and telecommunications. Tomorrow, who knows?

Much innovation involves small improvements in the use of an existing technology. Such improvements develop from experimentation and discovery, which have been fostered in the Japanese automobile market, for example, as seen in International Example 9-4.

Innovation Transforming an invention into something that is useful to humans.

The Importance of Ideas and Knowledge

Economist Paul Romer has added at least one important factor that determines the rate of economic growth. He contends that production and manufacturing knowledge is just as important as the other determinants and perhaps even more so. He considers knowledge a factor of production that, like capital, has to be paid for by forgoing current consumption. Economies must therefore invest in knowledge just as they invest in machines. Because past investment in capital may make it more profitable to acquire more knowledge, there ex-

INTERNATIONAL EXAMPLE 9-4 ## Innovation in the Japanese Auto Industry

The automobile has been around for a century. By the 1950s, American automobile manufacturers were fairly well convinced that they had developed the best and most efficient assembly-line operation in the world. They did so through what were called time-and-motion studies. A "final" set of directions was given to each worker on the assembly line, and that worker adhered to those directions. The Japanese decided to improve on this through a process of experimentation and discovery. In Japanese automobile plants, workers were encouraged to experiment with small changes in how they assembled a car—should the door moulding go on before or after the door is put on the car? Gradually, Japanese automobile workers became more efficient than their American counterparts. The process came about through small innovative changes, not one great invention.

For critical analysis: How many ways are there to put together a car?

ists the possibility of an investment-knowledge cycle in which investment spurs knowledge and knowledge spurs investment. A once-and-for-all increase in a country's rate of investment may permanently raise that country's growth rate. (According to traditional theory, a once-and-for-all increase in the rate of saving and therefore in the rate of investment simply leads to a new steady-state standard of living but not one that continues to increase.)

Another way of looking at knowledge is that it is a store of ideas. According to Romer, ideas are what drive economic growth. We have become, in fact, an idea economy. Consider Seattle's Microsoft Corporation. A relatively small percentage of that company's labour force is involved in actually producing diskettes. Rather, a majority of Microsoft workers are attempting to discover new ideas that can be translated to computer code that can then be placed on diskettes. The major conclusion that Romer and other new growth theorists draw is this:

Economic growth can continue as long as we keep coming up with new ideas.

The Importance of Human Capital

Knowledge, ideas, and productivity are all tied together. One of the threads is the quality of the labour force. Increases in the productivity of the labour force are a function of increases in human capital, the fourth factor of production discussed in Chapter 2. Recall that human capital is the knowledge and skills that people in the workforce acquire through education, on-the-job training, and self-teaching. To increase your own human capital, you have to invest by forgoing income-earning activities while you attend school. Society also has to invest in the form of libraries and teachers. According to the new growth theorists, human capital is at least as important as physical capital, particularly when trying to explain international differences in living standards.

As you will see in Chapter 21, one of the most effective ways that developing countries can become developed is by investing in secondary schooling.

One can argue that policy changes that increase human capital will lead to more technological improvements. One of the reasons concerned citizens, policymakers, and politicians are looking for a change in Canada's schooling system is that our educational system seems to be falling behind that of other countries. This lag is greatest in science and mathematics—precisely the areas that are required for developing better technology.

Try Preview Question 4:

What are the determinants of economic growth?

The Role of the Government in Encouraging Growth

Governments have an important role to play in economic growth, and governments can help or hinder the process through their policies. Governments play a large role in the factors listed on pages 208 and 209, by supporting competitive markets and private property, encouraging political stability, and controlling immigration. While many of these actions are political in nature, they have important impacts on the economy of a country as well and, without them, the opportunity for growth is likely to be very limited.

At the same time, governments have chosen to take direct action in encouraging economic development. Governments encourage investment in human capital by subsidizing both primary and post-secondary education. Many studies have shown investment in education to be very worthwhile both for the individuals and for the government itself which receives higher taxes in the future from the better paid citizens. Governments also have encouraged growth through investment in infrastructure, such as roads or electricity. These and similar policies have been used in most countries around the world as the basis for economic growth and development for many years.

Another form of government action is through reduction in taxes on activities that encourage growth. The Canadian government encourages savings through Registered Retirement Savings Plans, which defer taxes until people retire. The government has also encouraged the development of new technology through its Scientific Tax Research Credits, which gives tax breaks for companies engaging in scientific research. We'll look at this topic in a broader way in Chapter 18.

Finally, the government may choose to give or lend money directly to businesses. These kinds of policies are often controversial, as they conflict with the natural forces of the market place. Why should one failing business be subsidized, and not one that is surviving? While many such loans and subsidies do help businesses during an important startup phase, some are used to achieve political ends, not economic ones.

CONCEPTS IN BRIEF

- New growth theory argues that the greater the rewards, the more rapid the pace of technology. And greater rewards spur research and development.
- The openness of an economy seems to correlate with its economic rate of growth.
- Invention and innovation are not the same thing. Inventions are useless until innovation transforms them into things that people find valuable.
- According to the new growth economists, economic growth can continue as long as we keep coming up with new ideas.
- Increases in human capital can lead to greater rates of economic growth. These come about by increased education, on-the-job training, and self-teaching.
- Government actions can make a substantial difference in supporting economic growth through subsidization of some basic investments, such as education and infrastructure, and by giving tax breaks to activities that encourage growth.

The Benefits and Costs of Economic Growth

The growth that western economies have experienced is controversial. Many people believe that economic growth is generally good. Many others have looked at the cost of that growth and wonder if it is worth the cost. Let's look at how these two groups differ in their ideas about growth.

Limits to Growth

Humanity is very aware of the limited resources that the world holds. Since the Second World War, the population of the world has increased from 2.5 billion to 6 billion people. At the current rates of population growth, the world population will reach 10 billion within our lifetimes. With the strong economic growth that has occurred, each person in the many nations of the world consumes much more of the world's resources now than they did 50 years ago. When all these factors are combined, the strain on the earth is tremendous, and has clearly had some detrimental effects.

ENVIRONMENTAL DISASTERS.   The partial destruction of the ozone layer, global warming due to the emission of greenhouse gases, the collapse of the east coast fishery, acid rain and the destruction of rain forests are all signs that the earth is approaching its limit. Without a radical change in the way that pollution and other resources are managed, there is little doubt that there will be disastrous consequences for the earth. Already weather watchers have noted the increase in hurricane activity in the Atlantic Ocean. They suggest that the destruction of property and loss of lives that results is caused by global warming.

UNEVEN CONSUMPTION AROUND THE WORLD.   Others suggest that the problem of pollution worsens with high levels of consumption that occur in developed nations. They argue that the high use of resources by western countries is a poor example for the rest of the world. The destruction of the rain forest in Brazil by ranchers, for example, is linked to the consumption of beef. If we consumed less beef, they argue, then there would be less incentive for the clearing of the tropical rain forests. If all countries were to consume oil at the rate that Canada does, there would need to be a tenfold increase in oil production, with all of the extra greenhouse gas emissions that would create and the effect on global warming.

POVERTY FOR SOME PEOPLE CAUSES MORE ENVIRONMENTAL PRESSURE.   In much of the world poverty results in environmental stress through overharvesting of fuel wood, fish, and endangered species, poor waste disposal, and wasteful agricultural practices. In 1972, at the first United Nations Conference on the Environment in Stockholm, the developing countries took the position that environmental concerns were not their main problem. They would not support any environmental restrictions that would deprive them of the prospect of prosperity enjoyed by the industrial countries of the developed countries. On the other hand, most of the population growth in the next 50 years will occur in these nations, so it becomes more important to find better ways to deal with the environmental costs of growth.

Sustainable Development Economic development that meets the needs of the present without compromising the ability of future generations to meet their own needs.

THE BRUNDTLAND COMMISSION.   In response to these issues, the United States created the World Commission on Environment and Development. The Brundtland Commission's report, *Our Common Future*, published in 1987, described environmental degradation, poverty, a rapidly growing human population, the military arms race, and war as interlocking crises demanding action on all fronts. It defined a new term—**sustainable development**—with the following sentence: "Humanity has the ability to make development sustainable—to ensure that it meets the needs of the present without compromising the ability of future generations to meet their own needs."

The Commission called for the development of new institutions, tools, and strategies that would address the goals of peace, economic and social development, and environmental quality simultaneously, instead of piecemeal. Its main goal is to turn around the idea that development usually occurs at the expense of the environment. In its place would be a principle that accepts development at little or no environmental cost.

Benefits of Economic Growth

The main benefit of economic growth is the higher standard of living that usually comes with it. There can be little doubt that people are better off now than they were at the turn of the century. They are healthier, live longer, are better educated, and enjoy many more material goods than they did then.

A HIGHER STANDARD OF LIVING. Economic growth can also allow society to buy many goods and services that it could not previously afford. The higher economic growth allows for greater spending on education, health and income redistribution programs. It also allows for society to clean up the environment without lowering existing living standards.

HIGHER INCOME RESULTS IN LESS POPULATION GROWTH. In third world countries and in our own history, higher incomes have generally resulted in a reduction in birth rates. Almost paradoxically, the growth of incomes, and in particular the education of women, reduce the population growth in society and the resulting stress on the environment. Healthy people with reasonably high incomes tend to have fewer children.

NEW TECHNOLOGIES TO SOLVE THESE PROBLEMS. Growth advocates also point out that new technologies that accompany economic growth have come along through history to deal with the issues of the day. For example, as oil has begun to be used up, new "enhanced recovery" methods allowed for greater use of existing oil fields. Recycling technology has made it worthwhile to recycle old paper just as forests began to be in short supply. In the future, as oil disappears, firms will have a greater incentive to develop solar and fusion power as replacements. Both of these technologies will also be less polluting, and provide more power than existing technology.

Try Preview Question 5:

Is economic growth good for us?

EXAMPLE 9-2 Sustainable Development in Canada?

In its election promises of the election of 1993, the Liberal party of Canada promised in its "red book":

"Managing economic development and human growth without destroying the life-support systems of our planet demands of Canadians a fundamental shift in values and public policy. We must aspire to be less wasteful of our natural and human resources, to place greater worth on the welfare of future generations, and to take pride in maintaining a healthy, productive Earth."

For critical analysis:

1. What kinds of taxes and incentives could the government use to reduce pollution? What effect would this have on business and economic growth? If a new industry were to locate in your neighbourhood, how much pollution would you be willing to accept?
2. Are you "pro" or "anti" growth? Is small beautiful?

CONCEPTS IN BRIEF

- Economic growth results in environmental disasters, such as the destruction of the ozone layer. Sustainable development, a concept first suggested by the Brundtland Commission, is suggested as an alternative economic model for the future.
- Economic growth benefits people through a higher standard of living. People can consume more goods and services, such as education, health, and income redistribution. Income growth in poor nations usually results in a slower population growth. As well, new technologies can be used to clean up environmental problems.

NETNOMICS

Evidence Supports New Growth Theory

Economists have been looking for the last few years to explain how the North American economy has kept growing without a serious inflation threat. Their forecasts have been far off the mark, and they have been hard pressed to understand the sources of growth and productivity and to measure the impact of the technology revolution.

A recent report from two economists, Dale Jorgensen of Harvard University and Kevin Stiroh of the New York Federal Reserve Bank, argues that the stunning success of the past decade has allowed the economy to sustain a high rate of productivity growth, and led to a "virtuous circle of an investment-led expansion." Their analysis suggests that the biggest gains in the last five years have come from technological progress, and less from the other two main sources for productivity growth, capital investment and labour quality. The "tech" sector has become so much more productive that it has lifted productivity across the economy. They also note that "non-information technology" industries have contributed more to gains in technological progress than the computer industries.

Source: The Globe and Mail, August 1, 2000, Page B10.

ISSUES AND APPLICATIONS
Setting Goals for a Nation: What Do We Aim For?

Concepts Applied: Economic Growth, GDP National Income Accounting

Progress or villainy?

While many economists have focused on growth in real GDP as a measure of economic success for a country, others suggest that different measures of a nation's growth are needed. One such measure is the **Genuine Progress Indicator,** which takes into account many of the issues that we have noted that are not dealt with in GDP measures.

Some 32 years ago the US economic research think tank, Redefining Progress, devised an alternative measurement for growth called the Genuine Progress Indicator—the GPI—to begin addressing the problems caused by using only GDP as the yardstick for progress. The researchers at this think tank want to reverse much of the unhealthy focus on GDP as the only measure of progress, noting that the architects of the GDP—John Maynard Keynes (UK) and Simon Kuznets (US)—did caution against using GDP as a measure of the welfare of a nation. In 1962 Kuznets lamented that "the welfare of a nation can scarcely be inferred from a measurement of national income as defined by the GDP... goals for 'more' growth should specify of what and for what."

The researchers note that the ideal economic or GDP hero is a chain-smoking terminal cancer patient going through an expensive divorce whose car is totalled in a 20-car pileup, while munching on fast-take-out-food and chatting on a cell-phone. All add to GDP growth. The GDP villain is non-smoking, eats home-cooked wholesome meals, and cycles to work. The litany of crimes against genuine progress that GDP accounting sustains includes:

- GDP adds up all money transactions without accounting for costs.
- GDP takes no account of the inequality of income, wealth, and spending power.
- GDP treats crime, imprisonment, divorce, and other forms of family and social breakdown as economic gain, yet the value of housework, parenting, and volunteering count for nothing.
- GDP increases with each environmental calamity, each polluting activity, and then again in repairing the damage.
- GDP does not account for the depletion or degradation of natural resources and the environment.
- GDP treats war expenditures as economic gain both during the destruction and the rebuilding phases.
- GDP ignores the liabilities of living on debt and foreign borrowing.

In contrast to the GDP, the GPI attempts to measure the costs and benefits of human, social, natural and human-made capital, by adjusting national income figures for these various factors. While US GDP per capita has shown relentless real (adjusted for inflation) positive growth since 1950, the US GPI per capita has been sinking ever since the mid-1970s. In fact, the 1990s have seen the largest erosion of the real GPI, which declined at an average annual rate of 2.7 percent, compared with per capita GDP growth of 1.4 percent. The main factors driving the decline in the US GPI include:

- income inequality (the gap between the rich and everyone else) has risen 18 percent, reaching its highest level in 50 years: by 1997 the top 20 percent of households were getting almost 48 percent of the national income while the lowest 20 percent of households got only 4 percent;
- negative costs from the depletion of non-renewable resources (oil, gas, coal);
- negative costs of lost leisure time and family breakdown; and
- increasing foreign indebtedness.

While similar GPI accounting work in Canada has only just begun, the results are similar. Professor Ron Colman, director of the GPI Atlantic Project, has estimated the value of unpaid housework/parenting, volunteerism, and the cost of crime. Colman has estimated that modern two-parent working Canadian families, despite numerous household innovations, are actually spending more time working for pay and at unpaid housework and childcare than 100 years ago. He suggests that Canadian and US households appear to be caught in a cycle of earning less, spending more, going deeper into debt, and working harder to pay for their increased expenses.

For these researchers, the GPI gives concrete expression to something many Canadians and Americans sense about the economy; that we are living off natural, human, and social capital. They argue that we are cannibalizing both the social structure and the natural habitat to keep the GDP growing at the rate the experts and money markets deem necessary. Yet the nation's economic reportage and debate proceed as though this erosion of real wealth does not exist. The indicators that should alert us to such tendencies serve to hide them instead.

New national and provincial accounting systems like the GPI might not necessarily lead to smarter economic policies. However, retiring the laments of Kuznets and economic ghosts of Keynes will go a long way toward ensuring governments begin to account for genuine well-being and the true state of our natural, social and human capital. This journey must be taken with hopeful expectations to reclaim, as per T.S. Eliot, "the wisdom we have lost in knowledge and the knowledge we have lost in information."

For Critical Analysis

1. Much of the growth in Newfoundland's economy in the last few years can be attributed to the development of offshore oil projects. Why would the GPI give a smaller measure of progress to this development when compared to GDP measures?

2. Which of the "crimes against genuine progress that GDP accounting sustains" do you agree should be deducted from GDP measures? Why?

3. Many activities that are now bought and sold were, in previous generations, done at home, with the biggest changes occurring for women. Does this change in lifestyle mean we have "progressed?" Why or why not?

Condensed from:
The Genuine Progress Indicator—A Principled Approach to Economics
by Mark Anielski.
Source: *Encompass Magazine*, Oct-Nov, 1999, Volume 4 No. 1.

CHAPTER SUMMARY

1. Economic growth is defined as the rate of increase in per capita real GDP per year. It can be shown graphically as an outward shift in the production possibilities curve. Small changes in rates of growth lead to large differences in GDP over time because of compounding.

2. Economic growth can be defined as being numerically equal to the rate of growth of capital plus the rate of growth of labour plus the rate of growth in the productivity of capital and of labour.

3. To consume more in the future, you have to save —not consume—today. The rate of saving is a key determinant of a nation's rate of economic growth.

4. The new growth theorists argue that advances in technology are a function of the rewards to those advances. In particular, research and development will increase the more it is rewarded. Government policy can make a substantial difference in encouraging economic growth.

5. The more open an economy, the faster its rate of economic growth.

6. Although inventions are important, they have no value until they are made useful by innovation. Innovations may be slow to occur and may involve small improvements in the use of existing technologies. Economic growth can continue as long as we keep coming up with new ideas.

7. Increases in human capital can occur because of schooling and on-the-job training. Schooling requires a personal investment by the student—giving up consumption that would otherwise be available through paid work— as well as investment by society in teachers and libraries. Differences in standards of living across countries can, to some extent, be explained by differences in the level of human capital investment.

8. Economic growth has costs as well as benefits. A big cost of economic growth is its impact on the environment. Our current economic patterns may not be sustainable in the long run. Economic growth also brings with it some benefits besides a higher standard of living, including a reduction in population growth and new technologies to help clean up the environment.

DISCUSSION OF PREVIEW QUESTIONS

1. What is economic growth?

By economic growth, economists are referring to the rate of increase in an economy's real level of output over time. It is generally agreed that the rate of changes in per capita (corrected for population change) real (corrected for price level changes) GDP is a good measure of an economy's economic growth. The very long-run economic growth rate for Canada is approximately 2 percent per year— with much deviation around this trend line, of course.

2. What does economic growth measure?

Many people try to make inferences about changes in economic well-being from a nation's economic growth rate; presumably, higher growth rates imply more rapid increases in living standards. Others have argued that increased income inequality may accompany rapid economic growth, as a relatively small percentage of the population may benefit from economic growth while the majority experiences little economic improvement. Critics also point out that rapid economic growth is not necessarily consistent with increases in the spiritual, cultural,

or environmental quality of life. However, because per capita increases in real GDP do not measure the increased leisure that usually accompanies economic growth, this measure may *understate* economic well-being. Economic growth is therefore a rather crude measure of changes in a nation's well-being and is perhaps a better indicator of its productive activity.

3. What are some of the ways in which you can experience economic growth for yourself or for your family?

You can experience economic growth only if you are willing to sacrifice something. When you continue to go to school, you are sacrificing your current ability to earn and consume income. But in exchange for that sacrifice, you are developing skills and talents that will allow you to have a higher income in the future. You are investing in yourself (human capital) by sacrificing current consumption now.

If you wish to accumulate much wealth during your lifetime, you must be willing to sacrifice current consumption. You do this by not consuming all of your income—that is, by saving part of it. The more you save, the more you can accumulate. In particular, if you invest your accumulated savings in wise savings outlets, you will be rewarded by a compounded rate of growth so that in the future you will have accumulated larger amounts of wealth.

4. What are the determinants of economic growth?

One obvious determinant of economic growth is the quantity and quality of a nation's natural resources—although this determinant can easily be exaggerated. Hence many slowly developing nations have bountiful natural resources, and some rapidly developing areas have very few. The quality and quantity of labour and capital are also important determinants of economic growth, as is a nation's rate of technological progress. A decidedly underrated determinant of economic growth is the indus-triousness and willingness of people to be productive—which is surely related to personal incentives related to property rights. The certainty of property rights may also affect a nation's growth rate.

5. Is economic growth good for us?

Economic growth has many benefits, but some costs as well. We have a higher standard of living when compared to previous generations. We have more material goods, better education, a longer life, and less poverty. At the same time, there is a significant and growing impact upon the environment that detracts from those benefits. The ability of the environment to absorb the ever-increasing amount of pollution created by our economic activity is being questioned by many economists and environmentalists.

PROBLEMS

(Answers to the odd-numbered problems appear at the back of the book.)

9-1. The graph shows the production possibilities frontier for an economy. Which of the labelled points would be associated with the highest feasible growth rate for this economy?

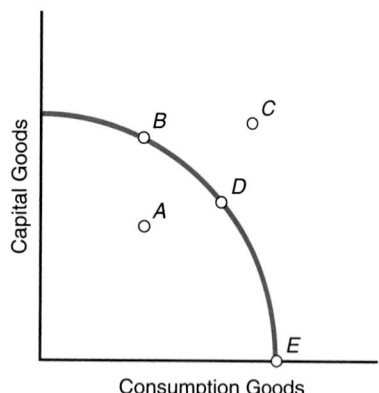

9-2. Why might an economy be operating inside its production possibilities curve?

9-3. Consider the following table, which describes growth-rate data for four countries between 1991 and 2000.

Country	Annual Growth Rate (%)			
	J	K	L	M
Nominal GDP	20	15	10	5
Price level	5	3	6	2
Population	5	8	2	1

a. Which country has the largest rate of output growth per capita?

b. Which country has the smallest rate of output growth per capita?

9-4. In 2001, a nation's population was 10 million. Its nominal GDP was $40 billion and its price index was 100. In 2002, its population had increased to 12 million. Its nominal GDP had risen to $57.6 billion and its price index had increased to 120. What was the nation's real economic growth rate during the year? What was its growth rate on a per capita basis?

9-5. Read Thinking Critically About the Media 9-1. What industries exist in your region of Canada? What level of pay do the workers receive? How has technology affected that industry in recent years?

ECONOMICS ON THE NET

Economic Development

How well we are doing against the rest of the world is one of the important comparisons that we make when we ask about development and growth. This application gives you the opportunity to make those comparisons on a number of different measures.

Internet URL: http://www.cia.gov/cia/publications/factbook/

Title: *CIA Factbook*

Navigation: Begin at the homepage for the factbook. Then click on the Country Listings.

Application. Click on Canada in the country listing, and then on the Economy.

a. What major statistics are tracked by the CIA? Note the ones that relate to GDP.

b. Back up to the Country Listings, and pick two other countries that are of interest to you. Many Canadians have themselves come from other countries, or their parents or grandparents were immigrants, so you might want to choose that country if you have such a connection. Note the same GDP statistics that you noted for Canada. Do a quick analysis of the differences and similarities.

c. Now do a similar comparison, but looking at the structure of industries, as noted in the labour force statistics. Find some countries that are poor, such as Burundi, and note the statistics for that country. How is our industrial structure different from theirs?

MODELLING THE ECONOMY: AGGREGATE DEMAND AND AGGREGATE SUPPLY

We have a vital interest in the performance of our economy. Naturally, we would like low unemployment, low inflation, and a rising standard of living. Unfortunately, we know that economies do experience difficult times.

In order to make sensible choices today, we have to make reasonable guesses about what will happen depending on the choices we make. Using a model helps us do this. A model lets us try out different "what if" scenarios before we have to choose. In this chapter we will discuss a basic model of our economy. We've already looked at one simple model of the economy in Chapter 2, but it did not deal effectively with prices, and said nothing about the demand side of the economy. The model we will look at in this chapter is the Aggregate Demand/Aggregate Supply model. Like Quebecers who have seriously considered whether to separate from Canada, we need to look at what might happen with alternative choices, and then decide what we want to do to.

PREVIEW QUESTIONS

1. Why does the aggregate demand curve slope downward?

2. Why is the long-run aggregate supply curve vertical?

3. Why does the short-run aggregate supply curve slope upward?

4. How can we show improvements in technology using aggregate demand and aggregate supply analysis?

DID YOU KNOW THAT... when economic analysts forecast how quickly the Canadian economy will grow in future years, they have to estimate how much consumers will spend *and* how much businesses will produce in response *and* how these two events will interact to change the price level across the economy. No wonder it's so difficult to come up with reliable estimates! To make matters worse, unforeseen events—called "shocks" to the economy—occur and often make existing forecasts look way off the mark. In this chapter you will learn about one method economists use to explain changes in output, unemployment, and the price level in our economy.

Spending and Production

As explained in Chapter 8, GDP is the dollar value of total expenditures on domestically produced final goods and services. Because all expenditures are made by individuals, firms, or governments, the total value of these expenditures must be what each of these market participants decides it will be. The decisions of individuals, managers of firms, and government officials determine the annual dollar value of total expenditures. You can certainly see this in your role as an individual. You decide what the total value of your expenditures will be in a year. You decide how much you want to spend and how much you want to save. Thus if we want to know what determines the total value of GDP, the answer would be clear: the spending decisions of individuals like you; firms; and municipal, provincial, and federal governments. In an open economy, we must also include foreign individuals, firms, and governments (foreigners, for short) that decide to spend their money income in Canada.

In the same way, simply measuring the amount that is spent by firms for resources (as we also did in Chapter 8) doesn't tell us about how firms meet demand. They often have to find new workers and machines, borrow money and other resources, and have to pay for them. What if those resources are in limited supply? What difference does it make if firms have to pay more for those resources? How do these decisions affect the long-run growth of the economy?

Simply stating that the dollar value of total expenditures and total production in this country depends on what individuals, firms, governments, and foreigners decide to do really doesn't tell us much, though. Two important issues remain:

1. What determines the total amount that individuals, firms, governments, and foreigners want to spend?
2. What determines whether this spending will result in a higher output of goods and services (quantities) or higher prices (inflation)?

The way we will answer these questions in this chapter is by developing the concepts of *aggregate demand* and *aggregate supply*. **Aggregate demand** is the total of all planned expenditures in the economy. **Aggregate supply** is the total of all planned production in the economy. Given these definitions, we can now proceed to construct an aggregate demand curve and an aggregate supply curve.

Aggregate demand The total of all planned expenditures for the entire economy.

Aggregate supply The total of all planned production for the entire economy.

Modelling Spending in the Economy: The Aggregate Demand Curve

The Aggregate demand curve plots on a graph the total of all planned real expenditures in the economy, at various price levels, all other things held constant. Recall the components of GDP that you studied in Chapter 8: consumption spending, investment

The aggregate demand curve is a curve showing the total of all planned real expenditures in the economy, at various price levels, all other things held constant.

expenditures, government purchases, and net foreign demand for domestic production. They are all components of aggregate demand. Since the price level has a very important influence on aggregate demand, it is plotted against the price level.

However, in Chapter 8, we simply were measuring the amount that was spent in the economy, after that spending had taken place. Throughout this chapter and the next, whenever you see aggregate demand curve, realize that it is a shorthand way of talking about the components of GDP that are modelled by economists. We are looking at what influences and affects spending and production, not just how much took place.

Aggregate Demand Curve

The aggregate demand curve models the total amount of *real* domestic income that will be purchased at each price level in a graphical form. Real domestic income consists of the output of final goods and services in the economy—everything produced for final use by either businesses or households. This includes computer software, socks, shoes, medical and legal services, sailboats, and millions of other goods and services that people buy each year. A graphic representation of an aggregate demand curve is seen in Figure 10.1. The horizontal axis measures real gross domestic output, or real GDP. For our measure of the price level, we use the GDP price deflator on the vertical axis. The aggregate demand curve is labelled *AD*. If the GDP deflator is 100, aggregate quantity demanded is $800 billion per year (point *A*). At price level 120 it is $700 billion per year (point *B*). At price level 140 it is $600 billion per year (point *C*). The higher the price level, the lower will be the total real output demanded by the economy, everything else remaining constant, as shown by the arrow along *AD* in Figure 10.1. Conversely, the lower the price level, the higher will be the total real output demanded by the economy, everything else staying constant. We'll see in a moment why aggregate demand is shown with a negative slope in Figure 10.1.

Let's take the year 2000. Looking at Statistics Canada data reveals the following information:

- nominal GDP was $1033 billion
- The price level as measured by the GDP deflator was 111.1 (base year 1992, when the index equalled 100).
- Real GDP (output) was $930 billion in 1992 dollars.

FIGURE 10.1 The Aggregate Demand Curve

Because of the real-balance, interest rate, and open economy effects, the aggregate demand curve, *AD*, slopes downward. If the price level is 100, we will be at point *A* with $800 billion of real GDP demanded per year. As the price level increases to 120 and 140, we will move up the aggregate demand curve to points *B* and *C*.

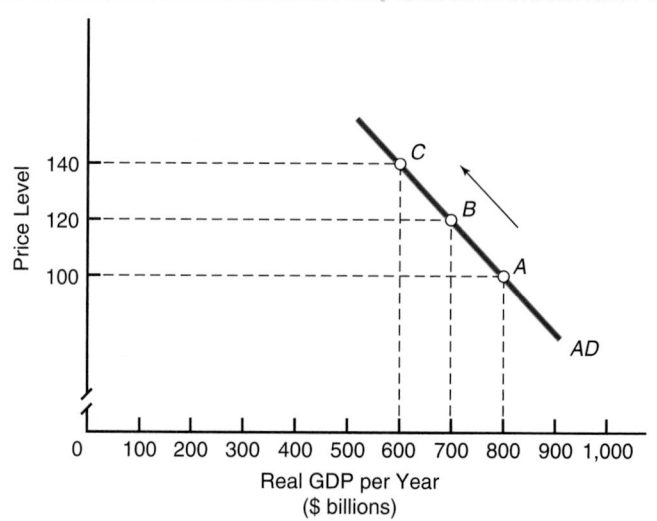

What can we say about 2000? Given the dollar cost of buying goods and services, and all of the other factors that go into spending decisions by individuals, firms, governments and foreigners, the total amount of real output demanded by firms, individuals, governments, and foreigners was $930 billion in 2000 (in terms of 1992 dollars).

What Happens When the Price Level Rises?

What if the price level in the economy rose to 120 tomorrow? What would happen to the amount of real goods and services that individuals, firms, governments, and foreigners wish to purchase in Canada? When we asked that question about individual commodities in Chapter 4, the answer was obvious: The quantity demanded would fall if the price went up. Now we are talking about the *price level*—the average price of *all* goods and services in the economy. The answer is still that the total quantities of real goods and services demanded would fall, but the reasons are different. Remember that in Chapter 4, when the price of one good or service went up, the consumer would substitute other goods and services. For the entire economy, when the price level goes up, the consumer doesn't simply substitute one good for another, for now we are dealing with the demand for all goods and services in the entire country. There are *economywide* reasons that cause the aggregate demand curve to slope downward. They involve at least three distinct forces: the *real-balance effect*, the *interest rate effect*, and the *open economy effect*.

THE REAL-BALANCE EFFECT. A rise in the price level will have a direct effect on spending. Individuals, firms, governments, and foreigners carry out transactions using money. Money in this context only consists of currency and coins that you have in your pocket (or stashed away) right now. Because people use money to purchase goods and services, the amount of money that people have influences the amount of goods and services they want to buy. For example, if you found a $10 bill on the sidewalk, the amount of money you had would rise. Given your greater level of money balances—currency in this case— you would almost surely increase your spending on goods and services. Similarly, if while on a trip downtown you had your pocket picked, there would be an effect on your desired spending—probably to reduce it.

While increases in the price level don't take money out of your wallet, they do reduce your *purchasing power*. A 5 percent increase in prices means that all of the money you have in your wallet will buy 5 percent less goods and services. Suppose on your shopping trip downtown instead of having your pocket picked, it turned out that the sale that you thought was on today actually ended yesterday. You have the same amount of money, but it will buy less than you expected. As a result of the price increases, you would ultimately buy fewer goods and services.

> **Real-balance effect** Higher price levels reduce the real value of cash balances which, in turn, reduces desired expenditures, all other things held constant. Also called the *wealth effect*.

This response is called the **real-balance effect** (or sometimes the *wealth effect*) because it relates to the real value of your cash balances. While your nominal cash balances may remain the same, any change in the price level will cause a change in the real value of those cash balances—hence the real-balance effect on the quantity of aggregate goods and services demanded.

When you think of the real-balance effect, just think of what happens to your real wealth if you have, say, a $100 bill hidden under your mattress. If the price level increases by 10 percent, the purchasing power of that $100 bill drops by 10 percent, so not only may you feel less wealthy, you actually are. This will reduce your spending on all goods and services by some small amount.

THE INTEREST RATE EFFECT. There is a second more subtle, but equally important, *indirect* effect on your desire to spend. As the price level rises interest rates will rise (assuming the amount of money in circulation remains constant). This raises borrowing costs for consumers and businesses. They will borrow less and consequently spend less. The

Interest rate effect Higher price levels increase the interest rate, which, in turn, causes businesses and consumers to reduce desired expenditures due to the higher cost of borrowing.

fact that a higher price level pushes up interest rates and thereby reduces borrowing and spending is known as the **interest rate effect**.

Because most people and businesses use cash in their everyday transactions, a certain amount of cash is needed for the smooth running of business. Suppose, for example, that the place where you buy lunch raises its prices from $5 to $7 for the daily special. While you would normally carry $5 in your wallet for purchasing the special, now you will have to have $7. You are therefore carrying less of your money in the bank, and more in your wallet. In the same way, the restaurant where you buy your lunches will be carrying more cash in its till every day. When this happens across the economy, the net effect of everyone trying to get more money out of the bank means that there is less money for banks to lend out, and so interest rates (the price of borrowing money) rise.

Higher interest rates make it less attractive for people to buy houses and cars. Higher interest rates also make it less profitable for firms to install new equipment and to erect new office buildings. Whether we are talking about individuals or firms, the indirect effect of a rise in the price level will cause a higher level of interest rates, which in turn reduces the amount of goods and services that people are willing to purchase when the price level rises. Therefore, an increase in the price level will tend to reduce the quantity of aggregate goods and services demanded. (The opposite occurs if the price level declines.)

THE OPEN ECONOMY EFFECT.   Remember from Chapter 8 that GDP includes net exports—the difference between exports and imports. In an open economy, we buy imports from other countries and ultimately pay for them through the foreign exchange market. The same is true for foreigners who purchase our goods (exports). Given any set of exchange rates between the Canadian dollar and other currencies, an increase in the price level in Canada makes Canadian goods more expensive relative to foreign goods. Foreigners have downward-sloping demand curves for Canadian goods. When the relative price of Canadian goods goes up, foreigners buy fewer Canadian goods and more of their own. In Canada, the cheaper-priced foreign goods now result in Canadians wanting to buy more foreign goods rather than Canadian goods. The result is a fall in exports and a rise in imports when the domestic price level rises. That means that a price level increase tends to reduce net exports, thereby reducing the amount of real goods and services purchased in Canada. This is known as the **open economy effect** or sometimes called the *substitution effect*.

Open economy effect Higher price levels result in foreigners desiring to buy fewer Canadian-made goods while Canadians now desire more foreign-made goods, thereby reducing net exports, which is equivalent to a reduction in the amount of real goods and services purchased in Canada. Also called the *substitution effect*.

What Happens When the Price Level Falls?

What about the reverse? Suppose now that the GDP deflator falls to 100 from an initial level of 120. You should be able to trace the three effects on desired purchases of goods and services. Specifically, how do the real-balance, interest rate, and open economy effects cause people to want to buy more? You should come to the conclusion that the lower the price level, the greater the quantity of output of goods and services demanded.

The aggregate demand curve, *AD*, shows the quantity of aggregate output that will be demanded at alternative price levels. It is downward-sloping, as is the demand curve for individual goods. The higher the price level, the lower the quantity of aggregate output demanded, and vice versa.

Aggregate Demand Versus *Individual* Demand

Even though the aggregate demand curve, *AD*, in Figure 10.1 looks quite similar to the individual demand curve, *D*, to which you were introduced in Chapter 4, it is not the same. When we derive the aggregate demand curve, we are looking at the entire economic system. The aggregate demand curve, *AD*, differs from an individual demand curve, *D*, because we are looking at the *entire* circular flow of income and product when we construct *AD*.

Try Preview Question 1:

Why does the aggregate demand curve slope downward?

Shifts in the Aggregate Demand Curve

In Chapter 4 you learned that any time a nonprice determinant of demand changed, the demand curve shifted inward to the left or outward to the right. The same analysis holds for the aggregate demand curve, except we are now talking about the non-price-level determinants of aggregate demand. So when we ask the question, "What determines the position of the aggregate demand curve?" the fundamental proposition is as follows:

> Any non-price-level change that increases aggregate spending (on domestic goods) shifts *AD* to the right. Any non-price-level change that decreases aggregate spending (on domestic goods) shifts *AD* to the left.

The list of potential determinants of the position of the aggregate demand curve is virtually without limit. Some of the most important "curve shifters" with respect to aggregate demand are presented in Table 10.1. An example of this is drawn in Figure 10.2.

TABLE 10.1

Determinants of
Aggregate Demand

Aggregate demand consists of the demand for domestically produced consumption goods, investment goods, government purchases, and net exports. Consequently, any change in the demand for any one of these components of real GDP will cause a change in aggregate demand. Here are some possibilities.

Changes That Cause an Increase in Aggregate Demand	Changes That Cause a Decrease in Aggregate Demand
A drop in the foreign exchange value of the dollar	A rise in the foreign exchange value of the dollar
Increased security about jobs and future income	Decreased security about jobs and future income
Improvements in economic conditions in other countries	Declines in economic conditions in other countries
A reduction in real interest rates (nominal interest rates corrected for inflation) not due to price level changes	A rise in real interest rates (nominal interest rates corrected for inflation) not due to price level changes
Tax decreases	Tax increases
An increase in the amount of money in circulation	A decrease in the amount of money in circulation

FIGURE 10.2 Aggregate Demand Curve Shift

Any non-price-level determinant that causes a decrease in total planned expenditure will shift the aggregate demand curve left from AD_1 to AD_2. For example, a rise in interest rates will reduce investment expenditure, and thus reduce planned expenditure.

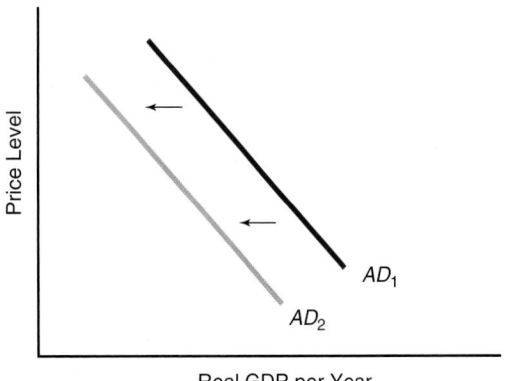

CONCEPTS IN BRIEF

- Aggregate demand is the total of all planned expenditures in the economy, and aggregate supply is the total of all planned production in the economy. The aggregate demand curve shows the various quantities of all commodities demanded at various price levels; it is downward-sloping.
- There are three reasons the aggregate demand curve is downward-sloping: the direct effect, the indirect effect, and the open economy effect.
- The real-balance effect occurs because price level changes alter the real value of cash balances, thereby causing people to desire to spend more or less, depending on whether the price level decreases or increases.
- The interest rate effect is caused via interest rate changes that mimic price level changes. At higher interest rates, people desire to buy fewer houses and cars, and vice versa.
- The open economy effect occurs because of the substitution of foreign goods for domestic goods when the domestic price level increases and a shift away from foreign goods when the domestic price level decreases.

Modelling Production in the Economy: The Aggregate Supply Curve

The aggregate demand curve tells us how much output will be demanded given the price level. It also indicates the point towards which the price level will gravitate for any *given* total output. Knowing the position and shape of the aggregate demand curve does not tell us anything about how the *total* dollar value of spending will ultimately be divided between output—real goods and services—and prices. To determine this and thus the equilibrium level of real GDP, we must introduce supply conditions.

When we talk about aggregate supply, we have to distinguish between the long run, when all adjustments to changes in the price level can be made, and the short run, when all adjustments to changes in the price level cannot be made. Therefore, we must derive two different aggregate supply curves and deal with the different issues arising in modelling production with these two curves.

Long-Run Aggregate Supply Curve

In Chapter 2 we showed the derivation of the production possibilities curve. At any point in time, the economy can be inside or on the production possibilities curve, but never outside it. The only way we can have more of everything is through economic growth—the production possibilities curve moves outward as shown in part (a) of Figure 10.3. The idea behind the production possibilities curve can be translated into what we call the **long-run aggregate supply curve** (*LRAS*). Using the long-run aggregate supply curve, we can model the economic growth of the economy, as we discussed in Chapter 9.

Put yourself in a world in which nothing has been changing, year in and year out. The price level has not changed. Technology has not changed. The prices of inputs that firms must purchase have not changed. Labour productivity has not changed. This is a world that is fully adjusted and in which people have all the information they are ever going to get about that world. The long-run aggregate supply curve in this world is some amount of output of real goods and services, say, $700 billion of real GDP. We can show long-run aggregate supply simply by a vertical line at $700 billion of real GDP. This is what you see in part (b) of Figure 10.3. That curve, labelled *LRAS*, is a vertical line determined by tastes, technology, and the **endowments** of resources that exist in our economy.

Long-run aggregate supply curve A vertical line representing real output of goods and services based on full information and after full adjustment has occurred. Can also be viewed as representing the real output of the economy under conditions of full employment—the full-employment level of real GDP.

Endowments The various resources in an economy, including both physical resources and such human resources as ingenuity and management skills.

FIGURE 10.3 The Long-Run Aggregate Supply Curve and Shifts in It

In part (a), we repeat a diagram that we used in Chapter 2 to show the meaning of economic growth. Over time, the production possibilities curve shifts outward. In part (b), we demonstrate the same principle by showing the long-run aggregate supply curve as initially a vertical line at *LRAS* at $700 billion of real GDP per year. As our endowments increase, the *LRAS* moves outward to *LRAS*$_{2004}$.

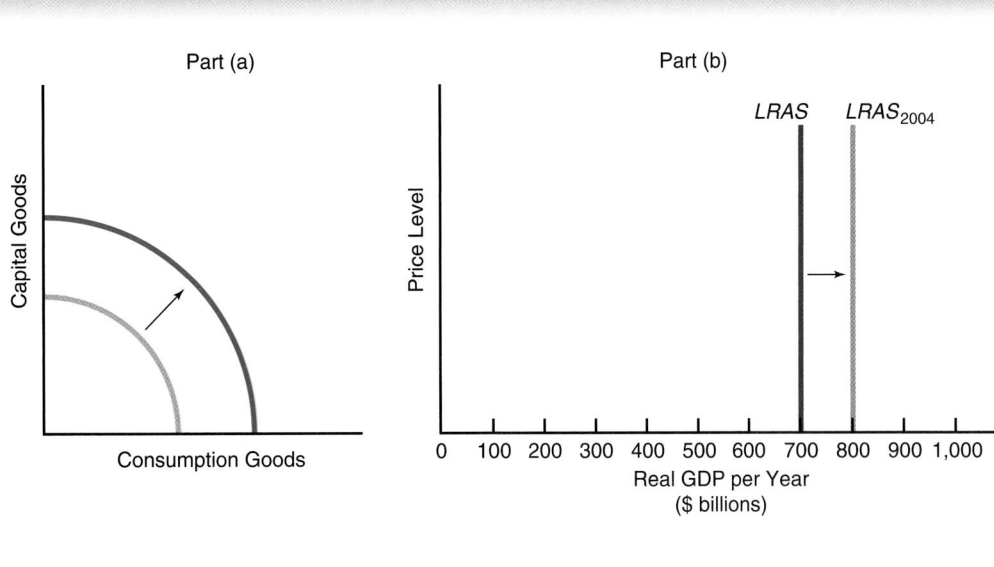

The assumptions of full information and full adjustment can be difficult to understand, so let's take a simple example. Imagine that you work in a unionized environment, where the employment contracts are regularly signed for three years. The contract fixes the price of labour when signed so that both sides know what their wages will be. On the other hand, there is no similar restriction on the price being charged by the business for the output that is being produced. Suppose that shortly after a contract is signed, inflation in the economy rises unexpectedly from 2 percent to 5 percent. In the *short run* (when adjustments to input prices cannot be made), the business is free to raise its prices in line with the inflation rate, but for the remainder of the union contract, wages are fixed for the employees. At the end of the three years, the employees are able to renegotiate their contract to bring their wages back into line with the higher inflation rate, and to compensate for the lost purchasing power they encountered from the unexpected inflation. This ability to adjust input prices is assumed to happen for *all markets* (not just the labour market) in the *long run*.

Full information is a similar sort of assumption. We assume that all of the economic players are able to find and incorporate into their decision making any information that affects them. From our previous example, the unionized workers know what their true value is to the company they are negotiating with, and the company would know what the productivity of the workers is. Similarly, unemployed workers know where they can find jobs and what wage they can expect to receive for their labour. There would be no involuntary unemployment, then, because workers would immediately fill vacant jobs, and adjust their wage expectations accordingly. In reality, of course, much information like this is not available to everyone. It is the level of real output that will continue being produced year after year, forever, if nothing changes.

Another way of viewing the *LRAS* is to think of it as the full-employment level of real GDP. When the economy reaches full employment, no further adjustments will occur unless a fundamental change occurs.

To understand why the long-run aggregate supply curve is vertical, think about the long run. The price level has no effect on real output (real GDP per year) because higher output prices will be accompanied by comparable changes in input prices, and suppliers will

Try Preview Question 2:

Why is the long-run aggregate supply curve vertical?

therefore have no incentive to increase or decrease output. Remember that in the long run, everybody has full information and there is full adjustment to price level changes.

WHAT IF NON-PRICE-LEVEL VARIABLES CHANGE? Clearly, as the years go by, things do change. Population increases, we discover more resources, and we improve technology. That means that over time, at least in a growing economy such as ours, *LRAS* will shift outward to the right, as in Figure 10.3. We have drawn *LRAS* for the year 2004 to the right of our original *LRAS* of $700 billion of real GDP. The number we attached to $LRAS_{2004}$ is $800 billion of real GDP, but that is only a guess; the point is that it is to the right of today's *LRAS*.

AGGREGATE DEMAND AND LONG-RUN OUTPUT. Because *LRAS* depends on technology and endowments, aggregate demand in the long run has no direct bearing on the level of output of real goods and services. Draw any *AD* curve on $LRAS_{2004}$ in part (b) of Figure 10.3, and you will see that the only thing that changes will be the price level. In the long run, the output of real goods and services is supply-side determined. Only shifts in *LRAS* will change long-run levels of output of real goods and services.

Short-Run Aggregate Supply Curve

Short-run aggregate supply curve The relationship between aggregate supply and the price level in the short run, all other things held constant; the curve is normally positively sloped.

The **short-run aggregate supply curve,** *SRAS,* represents the relationship between the price level and the real output of goods and services in the economy *without* full adjustment and full information. Just as we drew the supply curve for an individual good or service in Chapter 4 holding everything constant except the price of the good or service, we will do the same here. The short-run aggregate supply curve is drawn under the assumption that all determinants of aggregate supply other than the price level will be held constant. Most notably, we hold constant the prices of the inputs used in the production of real goods and services. Now, what does this mean? It means that when we hold the prices of the factors of production constant in the short run, as the price level rises, it becomes profitable for all firms to expand production. Otherwise stated, changes in the price level in the short run can affect real output because some production costs might be relatively fixed in nominal terms. Therefore, an increase in the price level increases expected profits.

WHY CAN OUTPUT BE EXPANDED IN THE SHORT RUN? In the short run, if the price level rises, output can be expanded (even beyond the economist's notion of the normal capacity of a firm). That is to say, the overall economy can temporarily produce beyond its normal limits or capacity, for a variety of reasons:

1. In the short run, most labour contracts implicitly or explicitly call for flexibility in hours of work at the given wage rate. Therefore, firms can use existing workers more intensively in a variety of ways: They can get them to work harder. They can get them to work more hours per day. And they can get them to work more days per week. Workers can also be switched from *uncounted* production, such as maintenance, to *counted* production, which generates counted output. The distinction between counted and uncounted is simply what is measured in the marketplace, particularly by government statisticians and accountants. If a worker cleans a machine, there is no measured output. But if that worker is put on the production line and helps increase the number of units produced each day, measured output will go up. That worker's production has then been counted.
2. Existing capital equipment can be used more intensively. Machines can be worked more hours per day. Some can be made to work at a faster speed. Maintenance can be delayed.
3. Finally, and just as important, if wage rates are held constant, a higher price level means that profits go up, which induces firms to hire more workers. The duration

of unemployment falls, and thus the unemployment rate falls. And people who were previously not in the labour force (homemakers and younger or older workers) can be induced to enter.

All these adjustments cause national output to rise as the price level increases.

THE SHAPE OF THE SHORT-RUN SUPPLY CURVE. Even if firms want to continue increasing production because the price level has risen, they cannot do this forever. Which means that when we hold input prices constant, the extra output that will be forthcoming for the three reasons just listed must eventually come to an end. Individual workers get tired. Workers are more willing to work one extra weekend than they are eight extra weekends in a row. Machines cannot go forever without maintenance. Finally, as all firms are hiring more workers from the pool of unemployed, it gets harder (more costly) to find workers at the existing level of wages.

What does all this mean? Simply that the short-run aggregate supply curve at some point must get steeper and steeper.

GRAPHING THE SHORT-RUN AGGREGATE SUPPLY CURVE. Look at Figure 10.4. There you see the short-run aggregate supply curve, *SRAS*. As we have drawn it, after a real GDP of $700 billion, it starts to become steeper and steeper, and by the time it gets close to $800 billion, it is very steep indeed.[1] If the price index, as represented by the GDP deflator, is 100, the economy will supply $600 billion per year of real GDP in Figure 10.4. If the GDP deflator increases to 120, the economy will move up the *SRAS* to $700 billion of real GDP per year.

Try Preview Question 3:

Why does the short-run aggregate supply curve slope upward?

FIGURE 10.4 The Short-Run Aggregate Supply Curve

The short-run aggregate supply curve, *SRAS*, slopes upward because with fixed input prices, at a higher price level firms make more profits and desire more output. They use workers and capital more intensively. At price level 100, $600 billion of real GDP per year is supplied. If the price level rises to 120, $700 billion of real GDP per year will be supplied.

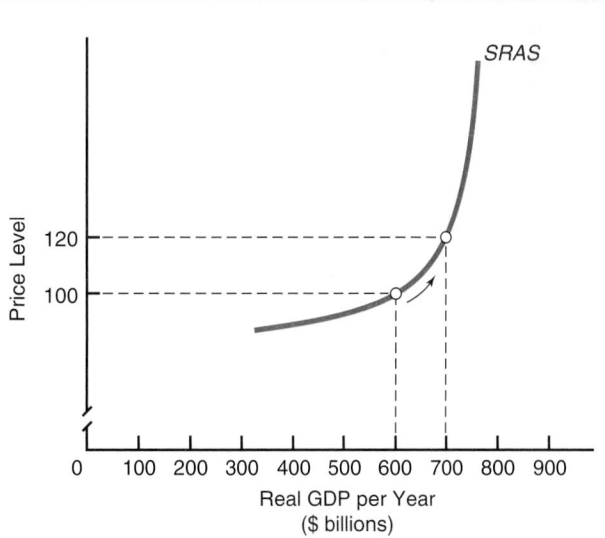

---

[1] If there is a maximum short-run amount of output, at some point the *SRAS* becomes vertical. However, there is always some way to squeeze a little bit more out of an economic system, so the *SRAS* does not necessarily have to become vertical, just extremely steep.

Aggregate Supply versus *Individual* Supply

Although the aggregate supply curve tends to look like the supply curve for an individual commodity, the two curves are not exactly the same. A commodity supply curve reflects a change in the price of an individual commodity *relative* to the prices of other goods, whereas the aggregate supply curve shows the effects of changes in the price *level* for the entire economy.

Shifts in the Aggregate Supply Curve

Just as there were non-price-level factors that could cause a shift in the aggregate demand curve, there are non-price-level factors that can cause a shift in the aggregate supply curve. The analysis here is not quite so simple as the analysis for the non-price-level determinants for aggregate demand, for here we are dealing with both the short run and the long run—*SRAS* and *LRAS*. Still, anything other than the price level that affects supply will shift aggregate supply curves.

Shifts in Both Short- and Long-Run Aggregate Supply

There is a core class of events that causes a shift in both the short-run aggregate supply curve and the long-run aggregate supply curve. These include any change in our endowments of the factors of production.[2] Any change in land, labour, or capital will shift *SRAS* and *LRAS*. Furthermore, any change in the level of our technology or knowledge will also shift *SRAS* and *LRAS*. Look at Figure 10.5. Initially, the two curves are $SRAS_1$ and $LRAS_1$. Now consider a big oil discovery in Manitoba in an area where no one thought oil existed. This shifts $LRAS_1$ to $LRAS_2$ at \$750 billion of real GDP. $SRAS_1$ also shifts outward horizontally to $SRAS_2$. This shift in the *LRAS* curve will also reduce the natural rate of unemployment.

Try Preview Question 4:

How can we show improvements in technology using aggregate demand and aggregate supply analysis?

FIGURE 10.5 Shifts in Both Short- and Long-Run Aggregate Supply

Initially, the two supply curves are $SRAS_1$ and $LRAS_1$. Now consider a big oil find in Manitoba in an area where no one thought oil existed. This shifts $LRAS_1$ to $LRAS_2$ at \$750 billion of real GDP. $SRAS_1$ also shifts outward horizontally to $SRAS_2$.

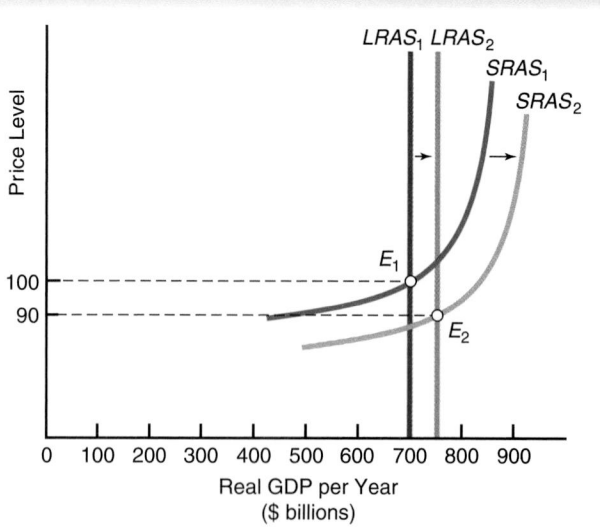

---

[2] There is a complication here. A big enough increase in natural resources not only shifts aggregate supply outward but also affects aggregate demand. Aggregate demand is a function of people's wealth, among other things. A big oil discovery in Canada will make enough people richer that desired total spending will increase. For the sake of simplicity, we ignore this complication.

Shifts in *SRAS* Only

Some events, particularly those that are short-lived, will temporarily shift *SRAS* but not *LRAS*. One of the most obvious is a temporary shift in input prices, particularly those caused by external events that are not expected to last forever. Consider the possibility of an announced 90-day embargo of oil from the Middle East to Canada. Oil is an important input in many production activities. The 90-day oil embargo will cause at least a temporary increase in the price of this input. You can see what happens in Figure 10.6. *LRAS* remains fixed, but $SRAS_1$ shifts to $SRAS_2$ reflecting the increase in input prices—the higher price of oil. This is because the rise in costs at each level of real GDP per year requires a higher price level to cover those costs.

We summarize the possible determinants of aggregate supply in Table 10.2. These determinants will cause a shift in either the short-run or the long-run aggregate supply curve, or both, depending on whether they are temporary or permanent.

TABLE 10.2

Determinants of Aggregate Supply

The determinants listed here can affect short-run or long-run aggregate supply (or both), depending on whether they are temporary or permanent.

Changes That Cause an Increase in Aggregate Supply	Changes That Cause a Decrease in Aggregate Supply
Discoveries of new raw materials	Depletion of raw materials
Increased competition	Decreased competition
A reduction in international trade barriers	An increase in international trade barriers
Fewer regulatory impediments to business	More regulatory impediments to business
An increase in labour supplied	A decrease in labour supplied
Increased training and education	Decreased training and education
A decrease in marginal tax rates	An increase in marginal tax rates
A reduction in input prices	An increase in input prices

FIGURE 10.6 Shifts in *SRAS* Only

A temporary increase in an input price will shift the short-run aggregate supply curve from $SRAS_1$ to $SRAS_2$.

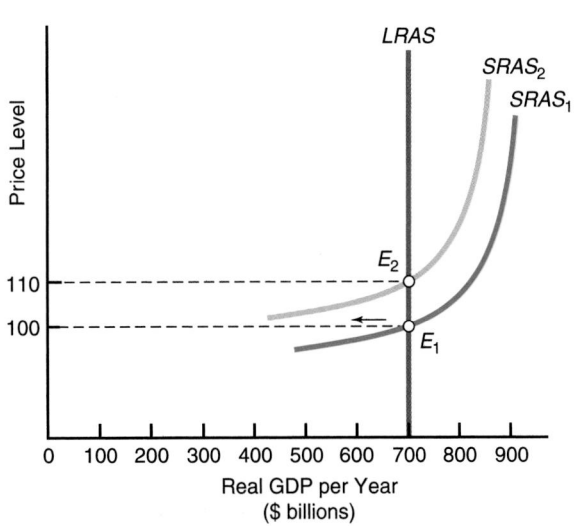

Concepts in Brief

- The long-run aggregate supply curve, *LRAS*, is a vertical line determined by technology and endowments of natural resources in an economy. It is the full-information and full-adjustment level of real output of goods and services.
- If population increases, more resources are discovered, or technology improves, *LRAS* will shift outward to the right.
- The short-run aggregate supply curve, *SRAS*, shows the relationship between the price level and the real output of goods and services in the economy without full adjustment or full information. It is upward-sloping.
- Output can be expanded in the short run because firms can use existing workers and capital equipment more intensively. Also, in the short run, when input prices are fixed, a higher price level means higher profits, which induces firms to hire more workers.
- Any change in land, labour, or capital will shift both *SRAS* and *LRAS*. A temporary shift in input prices, however, will shift only *SRAS*.

Equilibrium

As you discovered in Chapter 4, equilibrium occurs where demand and supply curves intersect. It is a little more complicated here because we have two types of aggregate supply curves, long-run and short-run. Let's look first at short-run equilibrium. It occurs at the intersection of aggregate demand, *AD,* and short-run aggregate supply, *SRAS,* as shown in Figure 10.7. The equilibrium price level is 120, and the equilibrium annual level of real GDP is $700 billion. If the price level increased to 140, there would be an excess quantity of real goods and services supplied in the entire economy, and the price level would tend to fall. If the price level were 100, aggregate quantity demanded would be greater than aggregate quantity supplied, and buyers would bid up prices so that the price level would move towards 120.

FIGURE 10.7 Equilibrium

Equilibrium will occur where the aggregate demand curve intersects the short-run aggregate supply curve and the long-run aggregate supply curve. In this diagram it is at price level 120 and a real GDP of $700 billion per year.

In Figure 10.7 you see that we have drawn the long-run aggregate supply curve, *LRAS,* so that there is full equilibrium in both the short run and the long run at price level 120. At price level 120 this economy can operate forever at $700 billion without the price level changing.

In the short run, it is possible for us to be on *SRAS* to the right and above the intersection with *AD* and *LRAS.* Why? Because more can be squeezed out of the economy in the short run than would occur in the long-run, full-information, full-adjustment situation. Although in this economy a real GDP greater than $700 billion per year is possible, it is not consistent with long-run aggregate supply. Firms would be operating beyond long-run desired capacity, and inputs would be working too long and too hard for too little money. Input prices would begin to rise. When this happens, we can no longer stay with the same *SRAS,* because it was drawn with input prices held constant. *SRAS* will then shift left.

If the economy finds itself on *SRAS* below and to the left of the intersection of *AD* and *LRAS,* the opposite will occur. Firms are operating well below long-run capacity, and there are too many unemployed inputs. Input prices will begin to fall. We can no longer stay with the same *SRAS,* because it was drawn with constant input prices. *SRAS* will shift right.

Consequences of Changes in Aggregate Supply and Demand

We now have a basic model of the entire economy. We can trace the movement of the equilibrium price level and the equilibrium real GDP when there are shocks to the economy. Whenever there is a shift in our economy's curves, the equilibrium price level or real GDP level (or both) may change. These shifts are called **aggregate demand shocks** on the demand side and **aggregate supply shocks** on the supply side.

In Chapter 3 you learned what happened to the equilibrium price and quantity when there was a shift in demand, then a shift in supply, and then shifts in both curves. In the analysis that follows, we will be using the same basic analysis, but you should remember that we are now talking about changes in the overall price level and changes in the equilibrium level of real GDP per year.

Aggregate demand shock Any shock that causes the aggregate demand curve to shift inward or outward.

Aggregate supply shock Any shock that causes the aggregate supply curve to shift inward or outward.

Aggregate Demand Shifts While Aggregate Supply Is Stable

Now we can show what happens when aggregate supply remains stable but aggregate demand falls. The outcome may be the possible cause of a recession and can, under certain circumstances, explain a rise in the unemployment rate. In Figure 10.8 you see that with AD_1, both long-run and short-run equilibrium are at $700 billion of real GDP per year (because *SRAS* and *LRAS* also intersect AD_1 at that level of real GDP). The long-run equilibrium price level is 120. A reduction in aggregate demand shifts the aggregate demand curve to AD_2. The new intersection with *SRAS* is at $680 billion per year, which is below the economy's long-run aggregate supply. The difference between $700 billion and $680 billion is called the **contractionary gap,** which is defined as the difference between the short-run equilibrium level of real GDP and how much the economy could be producing if it were operating at full employment on its *LRAS.* This is also known as a recessional gap.

Contractionary gap The gap that exists whenever the equilibrium level of real national income per year is less than the full-employment level as shown by the position of the long-run aggregate supply curve. Also known as a recessionary gap.

Effect on the Economy of an Increase in Aggregate Demand

We can reverse the situation and have aggregate demand increase to AD_2, as is shown in Figure 10.9. The initial equilibrium conditions are exactly the same as in Figure 10.8. The move to AD_2 increases the short-run equilibrium from E_1 to E_2 such that the

FIGURE 10.8 The Effects of Stable Aggregate Supply and a Decrease in Aggregate Demand: The Contractionary Gap

If the economy is at equilibrium at E_1, with price level 120 and real GDP per year of $700 billion, a shift inward and to the left of the aggregate demand curve to AD_2 will lead to a new short-run equilibrium at E_2. The equilibrium price level will fall to 115, and the short-run equilibrium level of real GDP per year will fall to $680 billion. There will be a contractionary gap.

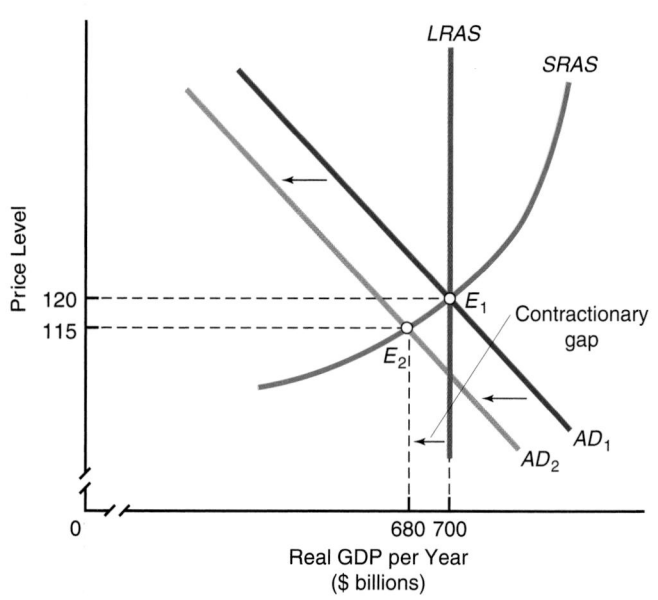

FIGURE 10.9 The Effects of Stable Aggregate Supply with an Increase in Aggregate Demand: The Expansionary Gap

The economy is at equilibrium at E_1. An increase in aggregate demand to AD_2 leads to a new short-run equilibrium at E_2 with the price level rising from 120 to 125 and the equilibrium level of real GDP per year rising from $700 billion to $720 billion. The difference is called the expansionary gap.

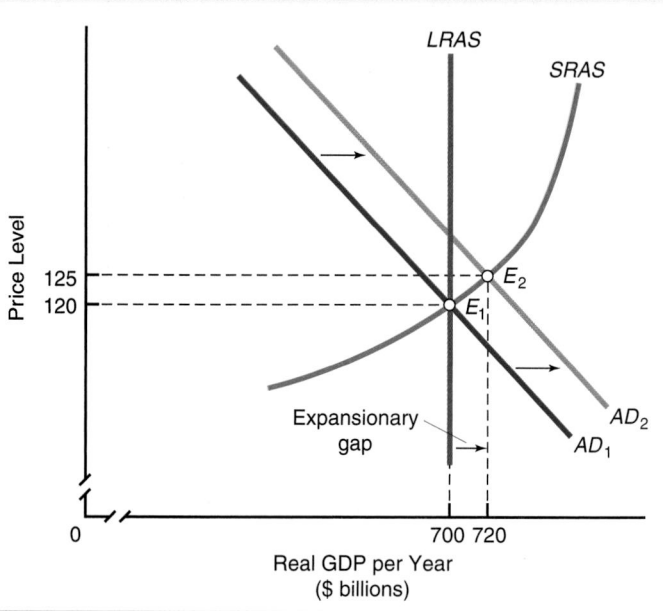

Expansionary gap The gap that exists whenever the equilibrium level of real national income per year is greater than the full-employment level as shown by the position of the long-run aggregate supply curve. Also known as an inflationary gap.

economy is operating at $720 billion of real GDP per year, which exceeds *LRAS*. This is a condition of an overheated economy, typically called an **expansionary gap.** This is also called an *inflationary gap.*

EXAMPLE 10-1   The Effect of World War I

One way we can show what happens to the equilibrium price level and the equilibrium real GDP level with an aggregate demand shock is to consider the effect on Canada's economy of fighting World War I (1914–18) in Europe. In Figure 10.10 you see the equilibrium price level of 133 (1900=100) and the equilibrium real GDP level of $1.8 billion at the long-run aggregate supply curve. The war effort shifts aggregate demand from AD_{prewar} to $AD_{World War I}$. Equilibrium moves from E_1 to E_2, and the price level moves from 133 to 176. The short-run equilibrium real GDP increases to $2.3 billion per year by 1917. The government's spending for the war caused AD to shift outward to the right. Also notice that the war effort temporarily pushed the economy above its long-run aggregate supply curve.

FIGURE 10.10 The Effects of War on Equilibrium

World War I shifted aggregate demand to $AD_{World War I}$. Equilibrium moved from E_1 to E_2 temporarily.

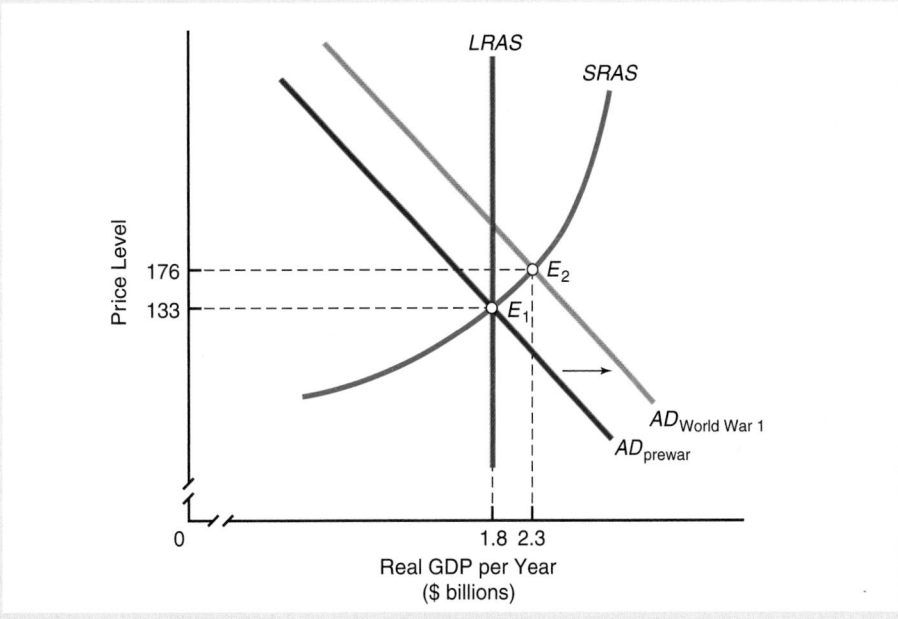

For critical analysis: What would have happened if World War I had lasted for 10 years instead of 4? How would you show it on Figure 10.10?

Explaining Inflation: Demand-Pull or Cost-Push?

When you first examined inflation in Chapter 7, no theory was given for why the general level of prices might rise. You can use the *AD-AS* framework to explain inflation. Indeed, Figure 10.9 is what is known as a theory of demand-side inflation, sometimes called *demand-pull inflation*. Whenever the general level of prices rises because of continual increases in aggregate demand, we say that the economy is experiencing **demand-pull inflation**—inflation caused by increases in aggregate demand. (Some economists argue

Demand-pull inflation Inflation caused by increases in aggregate demand not matched by increases in aggregate supply.

that economywide increases in demand—increased aggregate demand—often occur when the amount of money in circulation increases faster than the growth in the economy. You will read more about this subject in Chapter 17.)

An alternative explanation comes from the supply side. Look at Figure 10.11. The initial equilibrium conditions are the same as in Figure 10.9 and Figure 10.10. Now, however, there is a decrease in the aggregate supply curve, from $SRAS_1$ to $SRAS_2$. Equilibrium shifts from E_1 to E_2. The price level has increased from 120 to 125, too, while the equilibrium level of real GDP per year decreased from $700 billion to $680 billion. If there are continual decreases in aggregate supply, the situation is called **cost-push inflation.**

Cost-push inflation Inflation caused by a continually decreasing short-run aggregate supply curve.

As the example of cost-push inflation shows, if the economy is initially in equilibrium on its *LRAS*, a decrease in *SRAS* will lead to a rise in the price level. Thus any abrupt change in one of the factors that determine aggregate supply will shift the equilibrium level of real GDP and the equilibrium price level. If the economy for some reason is operating to the left of its *LRAS*, an increase in *SRAS* will lead to a simultaneous *increase* in the equilibrium level of real GDP per year and a *decrease* in the price level. You should be able to show this in a graph similar to Figure 10.11.

FIGURE 10.11 The Effects of Stable Aggregate Demand and a Decrease in Aggregate Supply: Supply-Side Inflation

If aggregate demand remains stable but $SRAS_1$ shifts to $SRAS_2$, equilibrium changes from E_1 to E_2. The price level rises from 120 to 125. If there are continual decreases in aggregate supply of this nature, the situation is called cost-push inflation.

EXAMPLE 10-2   The Oil Price Shock of the 1970s

One of the best examples of an aggregate supply shock occurred in the 1970s. During several periods, the supply of crude oil to Canada was restricted. These restrictions were the result of actions taken by the Organization of Petroleum Exporting Countries (OPEC). The oil embargo had an almost immediate impact on the price of oil and petroleum products, mainly gasoline and heating oil. Higher oil prices raised the cost of production in many Canadian industries that relied on petroleum. The result was a shift in the aggregate supply curve as shown in Figure 10.12. The equilibrium shifted from E_1—$300 billion of real GDP per year and a price level of 115—to E_2—equilibrium real GDP of $280 billion and a price level of 120.

FIGURE 10.12 The Effects of Oil Price Shocks on the Economy

In the 1970s, the supply of crude oil to Canada was restricted. Higher oil prices raised the cost of production. $SRAS_1$ shifted to $SRAS_2$, and equilibrium went from E_1 to E_2 with a higher price level and a lower equilibrium real GDP per year.

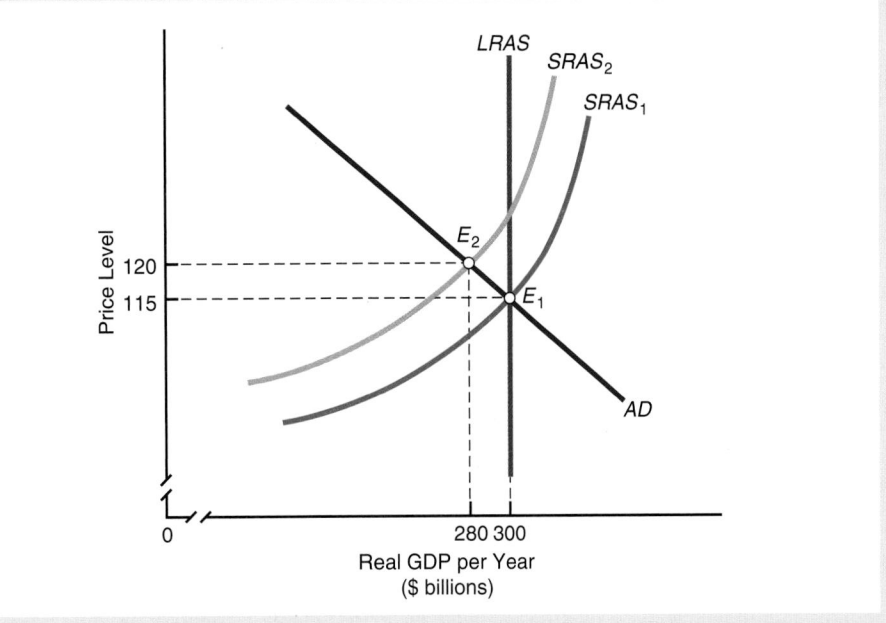

For critical analysis: If the price of oil had remained permanently high, what would have happened to LRAS in Figure 10.12?

CONCEPTS IN BRIEF

- Short-run equilibrium occurs at the intersection of the aggregate demand curve, AD, and the short-run aggregate supply curve, $SRAS$. Long-run equilibrium occurs at the intersection of AD and the long-run aggregate supply curve, $LRAS$. Any unanticipated shifts in aggregate demand or supply are called aggregate demand shocks or aggregate supply shocks.
- When aggregate demand shifts while aggregate supply is stable, a contractionary gap can occur, defined as the difference between the equilibrium level of real GDP and how much the economy could be producing if it were operating on its $LRAS$. The reverse situation leads to an expansionary gap.
- With stable aggregate supply, an abrupt shift in AD may lead to what is called demand-pull inflation. With a stable aggregate demand, an abrupt shift inward in $SRAS$ may lead to what is called cost-push inflation.

Aggregate Demand and Supply in an Open Economy

In many of the international examples in the preceding chapters, we had to translate foreign currencies into dollars when the open economy was discussed. We used the exchange rate, or the price of the dollar relative to other currencies. Earlier in this chapter you also discovered that the open economy effect was one of the reasons the aggregate demand curve slopes downward. When the domestic price level rises, Canadians want to buy cheaper-priced foreign goods. The opposite occurs when the Canadian domestic price level falls. Currently, the foreign sector of the Canadian economy constitutes about 33 percent of all economic activities.

How a Stronger Dollar Affects Aggregate Supply

Assume that the dollar becomes stronger in international foreign exchange markets. If last week the dollar could buy 4 euros but this week it now buys 5 euros, it has become stronger. To the extent that Canadian companies import raw and partially processed goods from abroad, a stronger dollar can lead to lower input prices. This will lead to a shift outward to the right in the short-run aggregate supply curve as shown in part (a) of Figure 10.13. In that simplified model, equilibrium GDP would rise and the price level would fall. The result might involve increased employment and lower inflation.

How a Stronger Dollar Affects Aggregate Demand

There is another effect of a stronger dollar that we must consider. Foreigners will find that Canadian goods are now more expensive, expressed in their own currency. After all,

FIGURE 10.13 The Effects of a Stronger Dollar

When the dollar increases in value in the international currency market, lower prices for imported inputs result, causing a shift outward to the right in the short-run aggregate supply schedule from $SRAS_1$ to $SRAS_2$ in part (a). If nothing else changes, equilibrium shifts from E_1 to E_2 at a lower price level and a higher equilibrium real GDP per year. A stronger dollar can also affect the aggregate demand curve because it will lead to fewer net exports and cause AD_1 to fall to AD_2 in part (b). Equilibrium would move from E_1 to E_2, a lower price level, and a lower equilibrium real GDP per year.

Part (a)

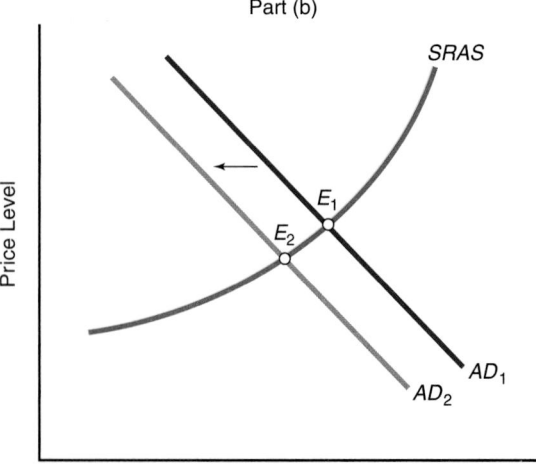

Part (b)

a $15 Nova Scotia lobster before the stronger dollar cost a French person 60 euros when the exchange rate was 4 to 1. After the dollar became stronger and the exchange rate increased to 5 to 1, that same $15 lobster would cost 75 euros. Conversely, Canadians will find that the stronger dollar makes imported goods cheaper. The result for Canadians is fewer exports and more imports, or lower net exports (exports minus imports). If net exports fall, employment in export industries will fall: This is represented in part (b) of Figure 10.13. After the dollar becomes stronger, the aggregate demand curve shifts inward from AD_1 to AD_2. The result is a tendency for equilibrium real GDP and the price level to fall, and unemployment to rise.

The Net Effect

We have learned, then, that a stronger dollar *simultaneously* leads to an increase in *SRAS* and a decrease in *AD*. Remember from Chapter 3 that in such situations, the result depends on which curve shifts more. If the aggregate demand curve shifts more than the short-run aggregate supply curve, equilibrium real GDP will fall. Conversely, if the aggregate supply curve shifts more than the aggregate demand curve, equilibrium real GDP will rise.

You should be able to redo this entire analysis for a weaker dollar.

Economic Growth in an Aggregate Demand and Supply Framework

Much (not all) of the Keynesian macroeconomic analysis to which you have been introduced in this chapter, and which you will examine in the next chapter, relates to short-run fluctuations in unemployment, inflation, and other macroeconomic variables. Whether one uses some variant of classical macroeconomic analysis or the Keynesian analysis, over time, short-term business fluctuations tend to iron out. We are left with economic growth, which can occur with or without inflation.

Economic Growth Without Inflation

Look at Figure 10.14 on the next page. We start in equilibrium with AD_1 and $SRAS_1$ intersecting at the long-run aggregate supply curve, $LRAS_1$, at a price level of 100. Real GDP per year is $700 billion. Economic growth occurs due to labour force expansion, capital investments, and other occurrences. The result is a rightward shift in the long-run aggregate supply curve to $LRAS_2$. As the long-run productive capacity of the nation grows, the economy doesn't stay on its short-run aggregate supply curve, *SRAS*. Rather, *SRAS* shifts along with shifts in aggregate demand due to population increases and rising per capita income. It is thus possible for us to achieve real GDP of $800 billion without any increase in the price level. The short-run aggregate supply curve moves outward to $SRAS_2$ and intersects AD_2 at E_2 where the new long-run aggregate supply curve, $LRAS_2$, has moved.

In the world just hypothesized, aggregate demand shifts outward so that at the same price level, 100, it intersects the new short-run aggregate supply curve, $SRAS_2$ at the rate of real GDP that is consistent with more or less full employment (on $LRAS_2$). Firms sell all the output produced at the new level without changing prices. In some situations, however, inflation may accompany growth.

FIGURE 10.14 Economic Growth, Aggregate Demand, and Aggregate Supply

Economic growth can be shown using short-run and long-run aggregate demand and supply curves. Aggregate demand, AD_1, intersects short-run aggregate supply, $SRAS_1$, at E_1, yielding $700 billion of real GDP per year at a price level of 100. This yearly real GDP is consistent with full employment. The long-run aggregate supply curve is vertical at $700 billion and is labelled $LRAS_1$. With economic growth, $LRAS_1$ moves outward to $800 billion per year. Short-run aggregate supply shifts to $SRAS_2$, and aggregate demand increases to AD_2. New equilibrium is at E_2, still at a price level of 100. There is no inflation.

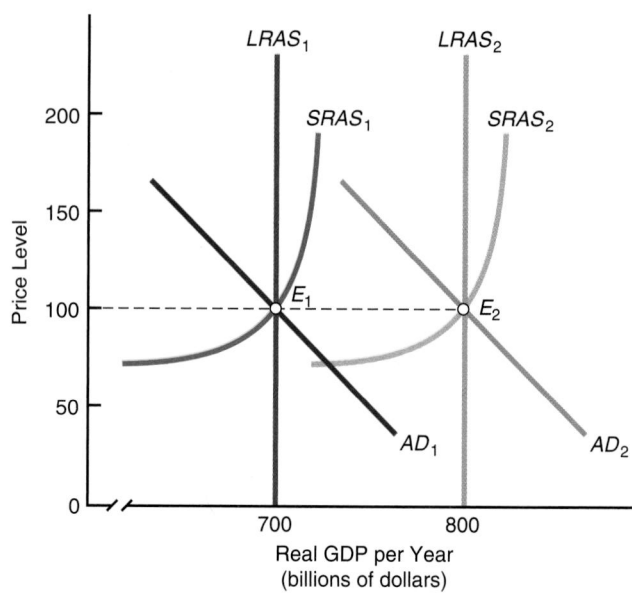

CONCEPTS IN BRIEF

- A change in the international value of the dollar can affect both the SRAS and aggregate demand.
- A stronger dollar will reduce the cost of imported inputs, thereby causing the SRAS to shift outward to the right, leading to a lower price level and a higher equilibrium real GDP per year, given no change in aggregate demand.
- In contrast, a stronger dollar will lead to lower net exports, causing the aggregate demand curve to shift inward, leading to a lower price level and a lower equilibrium real GDP per year. The net effect depends on which shift is more important. The opposite analysis applies to a weakening dollar in international currency markets.
- It is possible to have economic growth with and without inflation. If the aggregate demand curve shifts outward to the right at the same speed as the aggregate supply curve, there will be no inflation accompanying economic growth. See Example 10-3 on the next page for a discussion of Canada's economic growth in relation to inflation.

EXAMPLE 10-3   The Canadian Record over the Past Few Decades

What has been Canada's experience regarding economic growth and the rate of inflation over the past few decades? Has it resembled Figure 10.14? The answer can be seen in Figure 10.15, which reflects the Canadian experience from 1962 to 2000. In essence, each of the points represents the intersection of aggregate supply and aggregate demand for that year. Since 1962, the price level has clearly risen. So, too, has real GDP. Apparently, the Canadian economy has been unable to experience economic growth without inflation.

FIGURE 10.15 Economic Growth and Inflation in Canada

This figure shows the points where aggregate demand and aggregate supply have intersected each year from 1962 to the present. Canada has experienced economic growth over this period, but not without inflation.

Source: Statistics Canada, *Historical Statistics of Canada,* Catalogue No. 11-516-X1E, Series D18, D34; Statistics Canada, CANSIM Database, Series D474760, D474810, D11000.

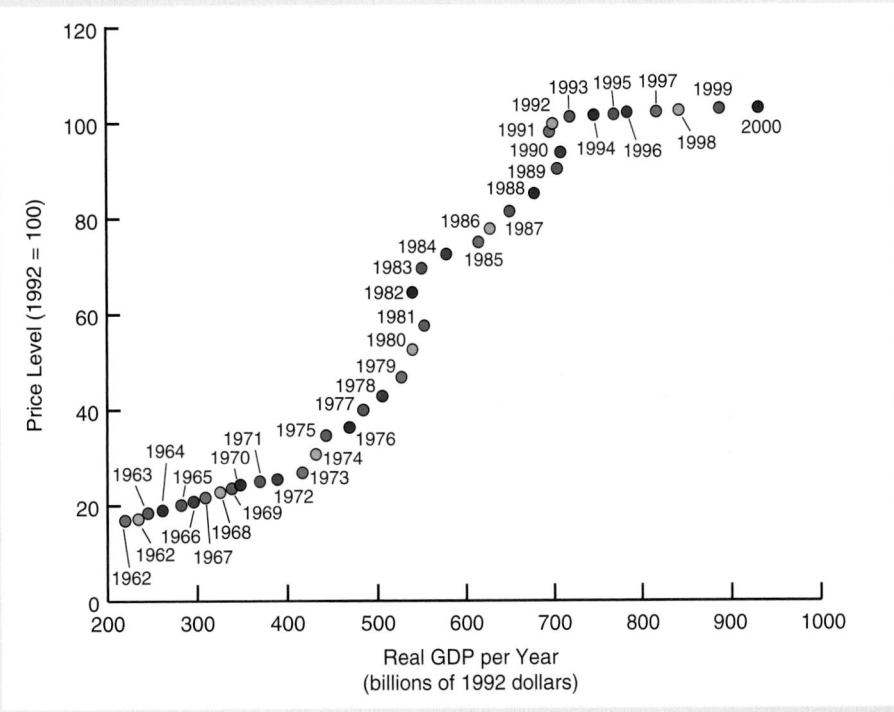

For critical analysis: As an individual, should you care whether Canada has economic growth with or without inflation? Explain your answer.

NETNOMICS

The "New" Economy, the Long-Run Aggregate Supply Curve, and Inflation

Call it what you may: the Internet economy, the new economy, the network economy, or even the information economy, the most promising technologies today are chiefly due to communications among computers—connections rather than computations. We are currently enhancing and extending the relationships between all businesses and all people around the world.

Sometimes it may seem that economists do not agree about much. Nevertheless, one thing they do agree about is a likely high rate of growth in the portion of GDP marketed and sold on the Internet. The value of electronic-commerce transactions, including those among businesses, grew from almost zero in 1996 to $43 billion (US) in 1998. Current forecasts call

for commerce over the Internet to more than double every year and reach as much as $1.3 trillion by 2003, which would likely be more than the entire GDP of Canada.

Furthermore, the growth of the Internet has allowed for the creation of more entrepreneurial talent among people whose creative lives have become enmeshed in the Web. Recall from Chapter 2 that entrepreneurship is an important factor of production. If, in fact, the new economy creates more entrepreneurship, then the long-run aggregate supply curve (*LRAS*) may be moving out to the right faster than previously thought possible. This could well help temper rises in the long-run equilibrium price level and help keep a lid on the inflation rate.

ISSUES AND APPLICATIONS
What If ...?

Concepts Applied: Models, forecasting, economic growth

When making choices, such as Quebecers had to make in the referendum of 1995, a model is a good way to help us choose one way over another.

In this speech delivered in January 1996, Matthew Barrett, the chairman of the Bank of Montreal, predicted that separation by Quebec from Canada would lead to lower growth, a devalued Canadian dollar, higher interest rates and a bigger government deficit. Quebecers heard this warning, and had to make a choice: independence and some economic problems, or stay in Canada with some political problems. The issue is an ongoing one that Canadians will continue to struggle with in the future.

"At Bank of Montreal we were analyzing the probable results of separation even before the referendum was called. Such analysis is routine in our business. Confident of a decisive vote for Canadian unity, we thought the exercise interesting but somewhat academic.

Our confidence was misplaced. Our analysis, in retrospect, would prove more relevant than we ever imagined. Let me tell you about the bullet we dodged by a hair's breadth. If break-up occurs, expect at a minimum:

- First, a sharp rise in interest rates of as much as 3 to 4 percent. We could see mortgages at 12 or 13 percent. The cost of paying interest on our public debts would swell so much we could wave goodbye to any thought of eliminating our government deficits.

- A fall in the dollar to as low as 68.5 US cents. We would pay more for everything we import, and spend much more of our incomes on servicing our huge foreign debts.
- Economic growth would falter across Canada. It is possible that the more vulnerable parts of the country would be pushed into recession. In the special case of Quebec, there is the prospect of a fall in GDP of as much as 7 percent in the first year of independence alone.
- Worst of all, for at least the following five years, high interest rates, population movements, capital outflows, and reduced capital inflows would bring economic growth for all of Canada well below the average rate of growth if the country stays together. In that regard, we estimated the total growth forgone for all of Canada at between $150 billion and $200 billion. That equals at least $20,000 for every family of four. And that would be a permanent loss.

These are sobering numbers. Quebec particularly hard hit, and a serious hit for the whole of Canada.

I am not advancing these figures to bully Canadians into doing something they don't want to do, still less in order to defend the status quo. Far from it. For me, these potential outcomes are a compelling argument for all of us to overcome fatigue, set aside politician-bashing, and work together for bold and innovative change.

Let's come out of this post-referendum denial. We can no longer afford to be disengaged or tuned out. We have to accept the true seriousness of the risks we are running. Only then will we call on our political leaders to act before it is too late. And I know our leaders will respond if we do. As good politicians they have an ear to the ground for public opinion. We have already seen them respond to public opinion on debts and deficits. I am convinced they are seized of the seriousness of our governance problems."

(The full text of the speech can be found at http:www.bmo.com/company_info/index_speeches.html. The speeches are sorted by speaker).

For Critical Analysis

1. How would you analyze the effect of separation using the aggregate demand and aggregate supply model? Explain how each curve could be affected.

2. Why would the Bank of Montreal, and other large businesses, routinely forecast economic events in Canada?

CHAPTER SUMMARY

1. Aggregate demand is the total of all planned expenditures on final goods and services, and aggregate supply is the total of all planned production.

2. The aggregate demand curve gives the various quantities of all commodities demanded at various price levels. It slopes downward due to the real-balance effect, the interest rate effect, and the open economy effect.

3. Aggregate demand is not the same thing as individual demand, because individual demand curves are drawn holding income, among other things, constant. The aggregate demand curve reflects the entire circular flow of income and product.

4. Any non-price-level change that increases aggregate spending on domestic goods shifts the aggregate demand curve to the right. Any non-price-level change

that decreases aggregate spending on domestic goods shifts the aggregate demand curve to the left.

5. There are two aggregate supply curves. The long-run aggregate supply curve is a vertical line, the location of which depends on tastes, technology, and endowments of natural resources; it assumes full information and full adjustment. The short-run aggregate supply curve is drawn without full information and full adjustment and slopes upward, but it is not vertical.

6. Output can be expanded in the short run because firms can work both capital and labour more intensively and because firms with fixed input prices experience higher profits as the price level increases and therefore desire to hire more workers. The closer to capacity the economy is running, the steeper the short-run aggregate supply curve becomes.

7. There are events that shift both the long-run and short-run aggregate curves simultaneously. These include any change in the endowments of factors of production (land, labour, or capital). A temporary change in an input price, by contrast, shifts only the short-run aggregate supply curve.

8. Equilibrium occurs at the intersection of aggregate demand, short-run aggregate supply, and long-run aggregate supply.

9. The economy may experience shifts in aggregate demand and supply, called aggregate demand shocks and aggregate supply shocks. The impacts of such shocks on the equilibrium level of real output depend on the time period under study and other factors.

10. A stronger dollar will reduce the cost of imported inputs, thereby causing the *SRAS* to shift outward to the right, leading to a lower price level and a higher equilibrium real GDP per year, given no change in aggregate demand.

11. In contrast, a stronger dollar will lead to lower net exports, causing the aggregate demand curve to shift left, leading to a lower price level and a lower equilibrium real GDP per year. The net effect depends on which shift is more important. The opposite analysis applies to a weakening dollar in international currency markets.

12. It is possible to have economic growth with or without inflation. If the aggregate demand curve shifts outward to the right at the same speed as the aggregate supply curve, there will be no inflation accompanying economic growth.

DISCUSSION OF PREVIEW QUESTIONS

1. Why does the aggregate demand curve slope downward?

There are three reasons for believing that the quantity demanded for real output rises as the price level falls, and vice versa. A decrease in the price level leads to higher real money balances, all other things held constant. This increased real wealth causes a direct effect on consumers' spending decisions. There is an indirect effect via interest rates, which move with price level changes. As the price level falls, the interest rate will fall, and consumers will want to spend more on houses and cars. Finally, in an open economy, if the price level falls, people will want domestic goods rather than imports, and foreigners will want to buy more of our goods.

2. Why is the long-run aggregate supply curve vertical?

The definition of the long-run aggregate supply curve is the amount of real output of goods and services that will be produced in the long run with full information and full adjustment. With full information and full adjustment, changes in the price level do not affect real output. Real output in the long run is solely a function of tastes, technology, and endowments of land, labour, and capital. Hence the long-run aggregate supply curve is a vertical line.

3. Why does the short-run aggregate supply curve slope upward?

As the price level increases, firms face fixed input prices in the short run. Their profits go up, and will rise even more if they increase production. They do so by working their labour force and their capital equipment more intensively, thereby generating more output.

4. How can we show improvements in technology using aggregate demand and aggregate supply analysis?

Improvements in technology shift both the long-run aggregate supply curve and the short-run aggregate supply curve outward. Essentially, you can show this using aggregate supply and aggregate demand analysis by drawing the curves that are shown in Figure 10.5.

PROBLEMS

(Answers to the odd-numbered problems appear at the back of the book.)

10-1. Given the curves in the accompanying graph, discuss why the equilibrium price level will be at P_e and not at P_1 or P_2.

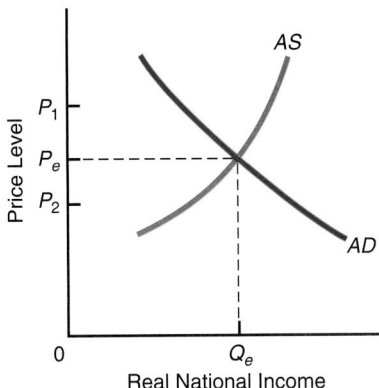

10-2. In the discussion of why the *AD* curve slopes downward from left to right, notice that nothing was said about what happens to the quantity of real output demanded when the price level rises and causes wealth to fall for people in businesses who own mortgages on houses and buildings. Why not? (Hint: What is the *net* effect to the whole economy when the price level rises and causes a wealth loss to lenders who get paid back in fixed nominal dollars?)

10-3. Distinguish between short-run and long-run supply curves.

10-4. How is aggregate demand affected when the price level in *other* economies decreases? What happens to aggregate demand when the price level in *this* economy falls?

10-5. Suppose that aggregate supply decreases while aggregate demand is held constant.

   a. What happens to the price level?

   b. What happens to national output?

10-6. List four other determinants of aggregate demand or aggregate supply, in the same way as those listed in Table 10.1 and Table 10.2. Explain how these determinants affect aggregate demand and aggregate supply, and the effect on the price level and real GDP.

10-7. What effect will an economic recession in the European Community have on the economy of Canada? Show how this would be modelled using the aggregate demand and aggregate supply curves.

10-8. Natural disasters such as an ice storm or a flood occur frequently in Canada. They often destroy many buildings and, occasionally, such as in earthquakes, kill many people. Model this disaster using the aggregate demand and aggregate supply curves. Be sure to distinguish the effects on the short-run and long-run aggregate supply curve.

10-9. Explain the effect of each of the following factors on the economy's price level and real GDP. Illustrate your explanations with appropriate diagrams.

   a. A rise in the value of the domestic currency relative to other world currencies.

   b. An increase in the real interest rate.

   c. A decrease in taxes.

   d. A rise in incomes of Americans.

   e. An increase in the investment in technology.

ECONOMICS ON THE NET

Finding Forecasts on the Net

In this application, you'll explore one of the sites where you can find regular use of economic modelling, by the Bank of Montreal. Banks in Canada routinely forecast for the state of the economy, and for a number of key economic variables.

Internet URL:

http://www.bmo.com/economic/econ.htm

Title: Bank of Montreal Economics Home Page

Navigation: Begin at the home page and look at the various reports that are given. Because this site changes regularly, you will need to check out the various current reports offered to complete the following application exercise.

Application:

a. Read through the reports to find out what outlook for your region/province is being forecast. What are the primary reasons for the prediction regarding the economy? How do they relate to the four main types of expenditure?

b. Find out what is happening with the US economy. Why is the US economy such a significant factor for most of our economy?

CLASSICAL AND KEYNESIAN MACRO ANALYSES

The Great Depression left a deep scar on the Canadian psyche, which resonates with today's problems of high unemployment, government debts, and globalization. Out of the experience of the Depression, a new era of government intervention and activism in the economy was born. Many of today's government programs and international trading agreements have their origin in the new economic thinking that emerged from that era.

The magnitude of the problems of the 1930s created an urgent need to throw out the previous economic models and to replace them with models that could explain what was happening. In response to that need, John Maynard Keynes, a British economist, introduced a new model for economic analysis. That new model helped economists and politicians out of their dilemma, and paved the way for the prosperous times that followed. Although that model has its weaknesses and has been surpassed by newer models, its impact was so profound that some economists still call themselves "Keynesians."

PREVIEW QUESTIONS

1. What are the assumptions of the classical macro model?

2. What determines the rate of interest in the classical model?

3. Why do Keynesian economists believe that the short-run aggregate supply curve is horizontal?

4. Why is real GDP said to be demand-determined when the short-run aggregate supply curve is horizontal?

DID YOU KNOW THAT... in spite of continuing general inflation, magazine publishers tend to keep the same magazine prices for more than a year? According to one study by economist Stephen G. Cecchetti, the typical magazine publisher lets inflation eat away at a quarter of the magazine's price before a new price is printed on the magazine. This common example of "sticky" prices gives just a hint that our economy may not instantaneously adapt itself to changes in macroeconomic variables such as an increase in the rate of inflation. Economists want to know what causes fluctuations in employment, output, and the price level. The fact that magazine prices are sticky is just one empirical observation that would lead researchers to develop macroeconomic models that somehow reflect the less flexible nature of certain prices. Such was not the case with the classical economists, who had a different view of how the macroeconomy operated. We will start this chapter with a look at the classical model of the economy and then examine a model developed in the twentieth century.

The Classical Model

The classical model, which traces its origins to the 1770s, was the first systematic attempt to explain the determinants of the price level and the national levels of output, income, employment, consumption, saving, and investment. The term *classical model* was coined by John Maynard Keynes, a Cambridge University economist, who used it to refer to the way in which earlier economists had analysed economic aggregates. Classical economists—Adam Smith, J. B. Say, David Ricardo, John Stuart Mill, Thomas Malthus, and others—wrote from the 1770s to the 1870s. They assumed, among other things, that all wages and prices were flexible and that competitive markets existed throughout the economy. Starting in the 1870s, so-called neoclassical economists, including Alfred Marshall, introduced a mathematical approach that allowed them to refine earlier economists' models.

Say's Law

Every time you produce something for which you receive income, you generate the income necessary to make expenditures on other goods and services. That means that an economy producing $700 billion of GDP (final goods and services) simultaneously produces the income with which these goods and services can be supplied. As an accounting identity, *actual* aggregate income always equals *actual* aggregate expenditures. Classical economists took this accounting identity one step further by arguing that total national supply creates its own demand. They asserted what has become known as **Say's law:**

> Supply creates its own demand; hence it follows that *desired* expenditures will equal *actual* expenditures.

Say's law A dictum of economist J. B. Say that supply creates its own demand; producing goods and services generates the means and the willingness to purchase other goods and services.

What does Say's law really mean? It states that the very process of producing specific goods (supply) is proof that other goods are desired (demand). People produce more goods than they want for their own use only if they seek to trade them for other goods. Someone offers to supply something only because that person also has a demand for something else. The implication of this, according to Say, is that no general glut, or overproduction, is possible in a market economy. From this reasoning, it seems to follow that full employment of labour and other resources would be the normal state of affairs in such an economy.

Say acknowledged that an oversupply of some goods might occur in particular markets. He argued that such surpluses would simply cause prices to fall, thereby decreasing production in the long run. The opposite would occur in markets in which shortages temporarily appeared.

FIGURE 11.1 Say's Law and the Circular Flow

Here we show the circular flow of income and output. The very act of supplying a certain level of goods and services necessarily equals the level of goods and services demanded, in Say's simplified world.

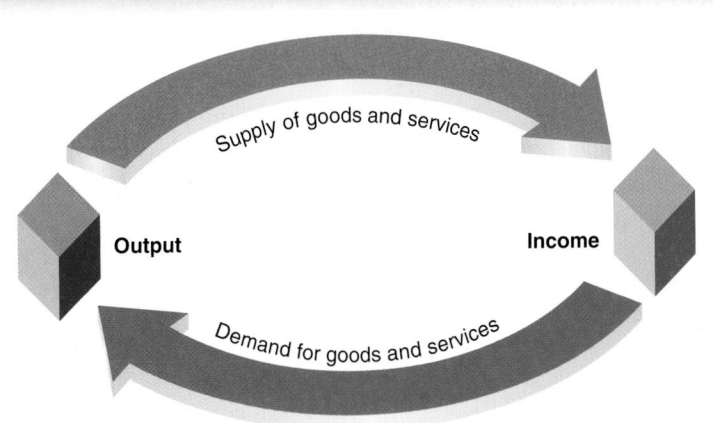

Output

Supply of goods and services

Income

Demand for goods and services

All this seems reasonable enough in a simple barter economy in which households produce most of the goods they need and trade for the rest. This is shown in Figure 11.1, where there is a simple circular flow. But what about a more sophisticated economy in which people work for others and there is no barter but rather the use of money? Can these complications create the possibility of unemployment? And does the fact that labourers receive money income, some of which can be saved, lead to unemployment? No, said the classical economists to these last two questions. They based their reasoning on a number of key assumptions.

Assumptions of the Classical Model

The classical model makes four major assumptions:

1. *Pure competition exists.* No single buyer or seller of a commodity or an input can affect its price.
2. *Wages and prices are flexible.* The assumption of pure competition leads to the notion that prices, wages, interest rates, and the like are free to move to whatever level supply and demand dictate (in the long run). Although no *individual* buyer can set a price, the community of buyers or sellers can cause prices to rise or to fall to an equilibrium level.
3. *People are motivated by self-interest.* Businesses want to maximize their profits, and households want to maximize their economic well-being.
4. *People cannot be fooled by money illusion.* Buyers and sellers react to changes in relative prices. That is to say, they do not suffer from **money illusion.** For example, workers will not be fooled into thinking they are better off by a doubling of wages if the price level has also doubled during the same time period.

The classical economists concluded, after taking account of the four major assumptions, that the role of government in the economy should be minimal. If all prices, wages, and markets are flexible, any problems in the macroeconomy will be temporary. The market will come to the rescue and correct itself.

Money illusion Reacting to changes in money prices rather than relative prices. If workers whose wages double when the price level also doubles think they are better off, the workers are suffering from money illusion.

Try Preview Question 1:

What are the assumptions of the classical macro model?

Equilibrium in Financial Markets

When income is saved, it is not reflected in product demand. It is a type of *leakage* in the circular flow of income and output because saving withdraws funds from the income

Thinking Critically About the Media 11-1 What Will Interest Rates Be Tomorrow?

Interest rates are more than just the prices that cause equilibrium to occur in the saving and investment markets. Changes in the interest rate can determine the profitability of banks and other institutions. They can also determine whether an investment was a smart move or a foolish one. Not surprisingly, the media frequently quote economic forecasters to inform readers and viewers whether interest rates will be high or low in the future. Virtually all such predictions should be taken with a grain of salt. One study of interest rate forecasts at the beginning of the 1990s showed that all major interest rate moves were missed by forecasters. Long-term studies demonstrate that forecasters do no better than someone guessing interest rate changes by flipping a coin.

stream. Consumption expenditures can fall short of total output now. In such a situation, it does not appear that supply necessarily creates its own demand.

The classical economists did not believe that the complicating factor of saving in the circular flow model of income and output was a problem. They contended that each dollar saved would be invested by businesses so that the leakage of saving would be matched by the injection of business investment. *Investment* here refers only to additions to the nation's capital stock. The classical economists believed that businesses as a group would intend to invest as much as households wanted to save. Equilibrium between the saving plans of consumers and the investment plans of businesses comes about, in the classical economists' world, through the working of the credit market. In the financial markets, the *price* of credit is the interest rate. At equilibrium, the price of credit—the interest rate—is such that the quantity of credit demanded equals the quantity of credit supplied. Planned investment just equals planned saving, for saving represents the supply of credit and investment represents the demand for credit.

THE INTEREST RATE: EQUATING DESIRED SAVING AND INVESTMENT. In Figure 11.2, the vertical axis measures the rate of interest in percentage terms; on the horizontal axis are the quantities of desired saving and desired investment per unit time period. The de-

FIGURE 11.2 Equating Desired Saving and Investment in the Classical Model

The demand curve for investment is labelled "Desired investment." The supply of resources used for investment occurs when individuals do not consume but save instead. The desired saving curve is shown as an upward-sloping supply curve of saving. The equilibrating force here is, of course, the interest rate. At higher interest rates, people desire to save more. But at higher interest rates, businesses demand less investment because it is more expensive to invest. In this model, at an interest rate of 5 percent, the quantity of investment desired just equals the quantity of saving desired (supply), which is $70 billion per year.

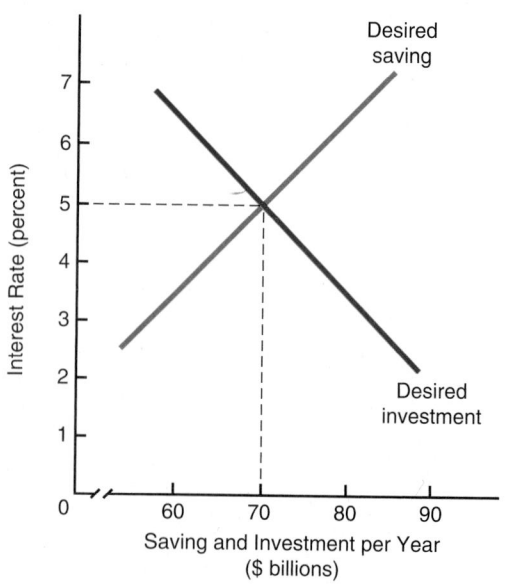

sired saving curve is really a supply curve of saving. It shows how much individuals and businesses wish to save at various interest rates. People want to save more at higher interest rates than at lower interest rates. Refer to Example 11-1 for a discussion of Registered Retirement Savings Plans.

Investment, primarily desired by businesses, responds in a predictable way. The higher the rate of interest, the more expensive it is to invest and the lower the level of desired investment. The desired investment curve slopes downward. In this simplified model, the equilibrium rate of interest is 5 percent, and the equilibrium quantity of saving and investment is $70 billion per year.

Try Preview Question 2:

What determines the rate of interest in the classical model?

EXAMPLE 11-1   Registered Retirement Savings Plans

Registered Retirement Savings Plans (RRSP) encourage Canadians to save for retirement. The plan works by allowing people to defer paying income taxes on their income for many years, and to hopefully pay less taxes overall. Since most people earn less money during their retirement years than their working years, the money taken out of their RRSP will be taxed less heavily than when they are working, because tax rates are lower on smaller income earnings. The money saved in these plans is directed back into the financial markets, and allows for businesses and individuals to borrow for investment. RRSPs therefore are an important foundation for financial planning for individual Canadians, and a source of capital for businesses.

For critical analysis: Canadians must invest most of their money in RRSP in Canadian stocks or bonds. How might the removal of this restriction change interest rates in Canada?

Equilibrium in the Labour Market

Now consider the labour market. If an excess quantity of labour is supplied at a particular wage level, the wage level is above equilibrium. By accepting lower wages, unemployed workers will quickly be put back to work. We show equilibrium in the labour market in Figure 11.3.

Equilibrium of $12 per hour and 13.5 million workers employed represents full-employment equilibrium. If the wage rate were $14 an hour, there would be unemployment—14.5 million workers would want to work, but businesses would want to hire only 12.5 million. In the classical model, this unemployment is eliminated rather rapidly by wage rates dropping back to $12 per hour. As you will see in the Issues and Applications section at the end of this chapter, there are forces that may prevent workers from offering to work at the lower wage rates that would lead to full employment.

THE RELATIONSHIP BETWEEN EMPLOYMENT AND REAL GDP. Employment is not simply some isolated figure that government statisticians estimate. Rather, the level of employment in an economy determines its real GDP (output), other things held constant. A hypothetical relationship between input (number of employees) and output (rate of real GDP per year) is shown in Table 11.1. We have highlighted the row that has 13.5 million workers per year as the labour input. That might be considered a hypothetical level of full employment, and it is related to a rate of real GDP of $700 billion per year.

FIGURE 11.3 Equilibrium in the Labour Market

The demand for labour is downward-sloping; at higher wage rates, firms will employ fewer workers. The supply of labour is upward-sloping; at higher wage rates, more workers will work longer and more people will be willing to work. The equilibrium wage rate is $12, with an equilibrium employment per year of 13.5 million workers.

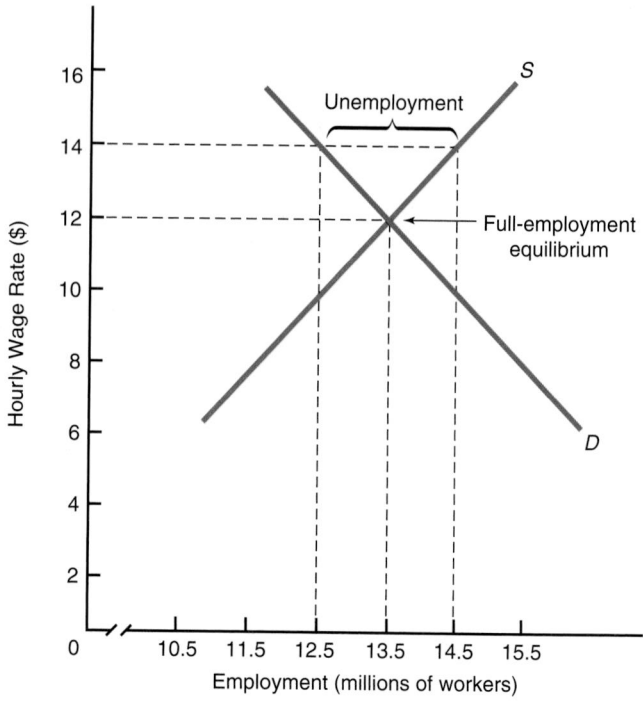

TABLE 11.1

The Relationship Between Employment and Real GDP

Labour Input per Year (millions of workers)	Real GDP per Year ($ billions)
9.8	400
10.4	500
12.0	600
13.5	700
14.5	800
16.0	900

Classical Theory, Vertical Aggregate Supply, and the Price Level

In the classical model, long-term unemployment is impossible. Say's law, coupled with flexible interest rates, prices, and wages, would always tend to keep workers fully employed so that the aggregate supply curve, as shown in Figure 11.4, is vertical at Q_0. We have labelled the supply curve *LRAS*, consistent with the long-run aggregate supply curve introduced in Chapter 10. It was defined there as the quantity of output that would be produced in an economy with full information and full adjustment of wages and prices year in and year out. In the classical model, this happens to be the *only* aggregate supply curve that exists in equilibrium. Everything adjusts so fast that we are essentially always on or quickly moving towards *LRAS*. Furthermore, because the labour market is working well, Q_0 is always at, or soon to be at, full employment. Full employment is defined as the amount of employment that would exist year in and year out if all parties in the labour market fully anticipated any inflation or deflation that was occurring. Full employment does

FIGURE 11.4 **Classical Theory and Increases in Aggregate Demand**

The classical theorists believed that Say's law and flexible interest rates, prices, and wages would always lead to full employment at Q_0 along the vertical aggregate supply curve, *LRAS*. With aggregate demand, AD_1, the price level is 100. An increase in aggregate demand shifts AD_1 to AD_2. At price level 100, the quantity of real GDP per year demanded is A on AD_2, or Q_1. But this is greater than at full employment. Prices rise, and the economy quickly moves from E_1 to E_2 at the higher price level of 110.

not mean zero unemployment because there is always some frictional unemployment (discussed in Chapter 7), even in the classical world.

EFFECT OF AN INCREASE IN AGGREGATE DEMAND IN THE CLASSICAL MODEL. In this model, any change in aggregate demand will soon cause a change in the price level. Consider starting at E_1, at price level 100. If the aggregate demand shifts to AD_2, at price level 100, output would increase to Q_1. But that is greater than the full-employment level of output of real GDP, Q_0. The economy will attempt to get to point A, but because this is beyond full employment, prices will rise, and the economy will find itself back on the vertical *LRAS* at point E_2 at a higher price level, 110. The price level will increase at output rates in excess of the full-employment level of output because employers will end up bidding up wages for now more relatively scarce workers. In addition, factories will be bidding up the price of other inputs at this greater-than-full-employment rate of output.

The level of real GDP per year clearly does not depend on any changes in aggregate demand. Hence we say that in the classical model, the equilibrium level of real GDP per year is completely *supply-determined.* Changes in aggregate demand affect only the price level, not the output of real goods and services.

EFFECT OF A DECREASE IN AGGREGATE DEMAND IN THE CLASSICAL MODEL. The effect of a decrease in aggregate demand in the classical model is the converse of the analysis just presented for an increase in aggregate demand. You can simply reverse AD_2 and AD_1 in Figure 11.4. To help you see how this analysis works, consider the flowchart in Figure 11.5.

FIGURE 11.5 Effect of a Decrease in Aggregate Demand in the Classical Model

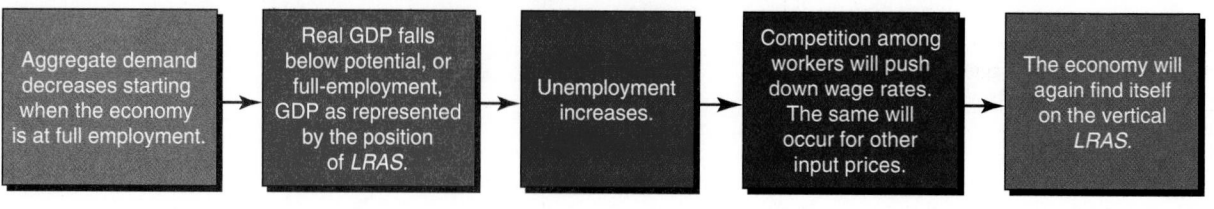

Concepts in Brief

- Say's law states that supply creates its own demand and therefore desired expenditures will equal actual expenditures.
- The classical model assumes that (1) pure competition exists, (2) wages and prices are completely flexible, (3) individuals are motivated by self-interest, and (4) they cannot be fooled by money illusion.
- When saving is introduced into the model, equilibrium occurs in that market through changes in the interest rate such that desired saving equals desired investment at the equilibrium rate of interest.
- In the labour market, full employment occurs at a wage rate at which quantity demanded equals quantity supplied. That particular level of employment is associated with a certain value of real GDP per year.
- In the classical model, because the *LRAS* is vertical, the equilibrium level of real GDP is supply-determined. Any changes in aggregate demand simply change the price level.

Keynesian Economics and the Keynesian Short-Run Aggregate Supply Curve

The classical economists' world was one of fully utilized resources. There would be no unused capacity and no unemployment. However, post–World War I Europe entered a period of long-term economic decline that could not be explained by the classical model. John Maynard Keynes developed an explanation that has since become known as the Keynesian model, which presented an explanation of the Great Depression in the 1930s. Keynes argued that if we are in a world in which there are large amounts of excess capacity and unemployment, a positive aggregate demand shock will not raise prices and a negative aggregate demand shock will not cause firms to lower prices. This situation is depicted in Figure 11.6. The short-run aggregate supply curve is labelled as the horizontal line *SRAS*. If we start out in equilibrium with aggregate demand at AD_1, the equilibrium level of real GDP per year will be Q_1 and the equilibrium price level will be P_0. If there is an aggregate demand shock such that the aggregate demand curve shifts outward to the right to AD_2, the equilibrium price level will not change; only the equilibrium level of real GDP per year will increase, to Q_2. Conversely, if there is an aggregate demand shock that shifts the aggregate demand curve to AD_3, the equilibrium price level will again remain at P_0, but the equilibrium level of real GDP per year will fall to Q_3.

Under such circumstances, the equilibrium level of real GDP per year is completely *demand-determined*.

FIGURE 11.6 Demand-Determined Income Equilibrium

If we assume that prices will not fall when aggregate demand falls and that there is excess capacity so that prices will not rise when aggregate demand increases, the short-run aggregate supply curve is simply a horizontal line at the given price level, P_0, represented by SRAS. An aggregate demand shock that increases aggregate demand to AD_2 will increase the equilibrium level of real national income per year to Q_2. An aggregate demand shock that decreases aggregate demand to AD_3 will decrease the equilibrium level of real national income to Q_3. The equilibrium price level will not change.

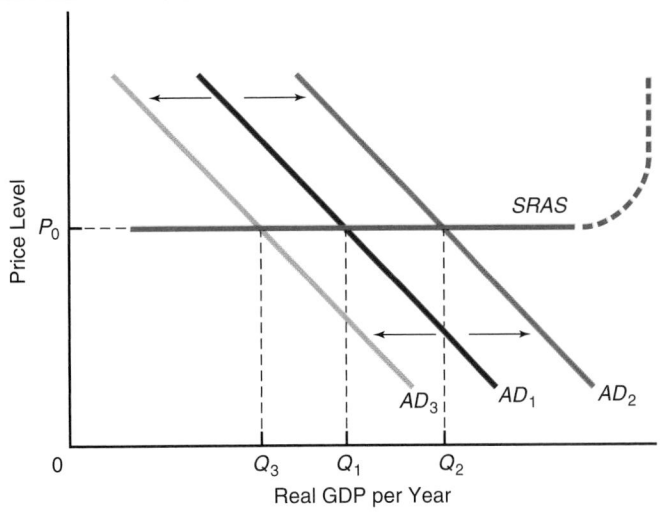

Keynesian short-run aggregate supply curve The horizontal portion of the aggregate supply curve in which there is unemployment and unused capacity in the economy.

The horizontal short-run aggregate supply curve represented in Figure 11.6 is often called the **Keynesian short-run aggregate supply curve.** It is so named because Keynes hypothesized that many prices, especially the price of labour (wages), are "sticky downward." According to Keynes, the existence of unions and of long-term contracts between workers are real-world factors that can explain the downward inflexibility of *nominal* wage rates. Such "stickiness" of wages makes *involuntary* unemployment of labour a distinct possibility. The classical assumption of everlasting full employment no longer holds.

Further, even in situations of excess capacity and large amounts of unemployment, we will not necessarily see the price level falling; rather, all we will see is continuing unemployment and a reduction in the equilibrium level of real GDP per year. Thus general economywide equilibrium can occur and endure even if there is excess capacity. Keynes and his followers argued that capitalism was therefore not necessarily a self-regulating system sustaining full employment. At the time, Keynes was attacking the classical view of the world, which argued that markets would all eventually be in equilibrium—prices and wages would adjust—so that full employment would never be far away.

Try Preview Question 3:

Why do Keynesian economists believe that the short-run aggregate supply curve is horizontal?

Keynesian Analysis of the Great Depression

At the beginning of 1929, the Canadian economy was doing quite well, with the unemployment rate hovering around 3 percent. A year later, it was over 9 percent, and by 1933 it had climbed to almost 20 percent. The real GDP of 1929 was not reached again until 1937, when another business downturn hit the economy. We use the Keynesian analysis shown in Figure 11.7 to illustrate what happened.

Aggregate demand to start with in 1929 is AD_{1929}. According to Keynesian theory, the economy experienced a dramatic reduction in aggregate demand, represented by a shift to AD_{1933}. To prevent massive unemployment, wages and prices would have to have fallen such that a new equilibrium would have been at point A on LRAS. Even though many wages and prices did fall, they didn't fall sufficiently to reach such a point. Consequently, a new equilibrium was established at E_2. Real GDP fell from about $52 billion to $37 billion (expressed in 1986 dollars). By 1933, the economy was operating about 20 percent below its potential output (represented by LRAS).

FIGURE 11.7 Keynesian Analysis of the Great Depression

Aggregate demand dropped from AD_{1929} to AD_{1933}. The price level would have had to drop to point A on LRAS in order to avoid unemployment. In reality, it did not, so that the new equilibrium shifted from E_1 to E_2. By 1933, the economy was operating at about 20 percent below its potential output.

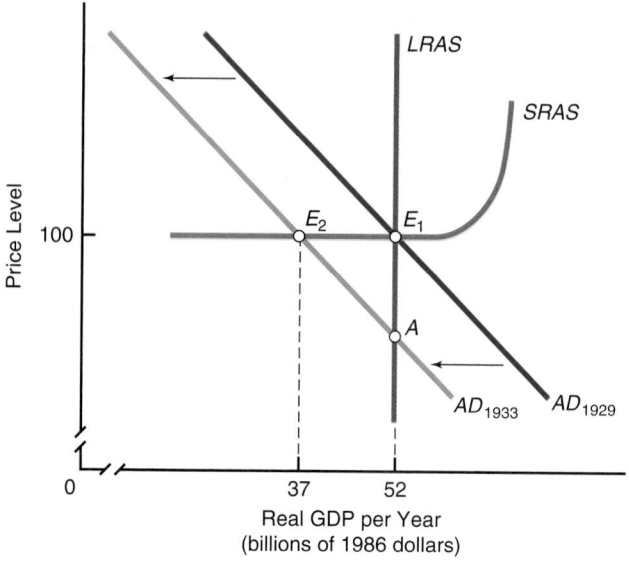

Income Determination Using Aggregate Demand and Aggregate Supply: Fixed Versus Changing Price Levels

The underlying assumption of the simplified Keynesian model is that the relevant range of the short-run aggregate supply schedule (*SRAS*) is horizontal, as shown in part (a) of Figure 11.8. There you see that short-run aggregate supply is fixed at price level 120. If aggregate demand is AD_1, the equilibrium level of real GDP is at $700 billion per year. If aggregate demand increases to AD_2, the equilibrium level of real GDP increases to

FIGURE 11.8 Income Determination with Fixed vs. Flexible Prices

In part (a), the price level index is fixed at 120. An increase in aggregate demand from AD_1 to AD_2 moves the equilibrium level of real GDP from $700 billion per year to $800 billion per year. In part (b), SRAS is upward-sloping. The same shift in aggregate demand yields an equilibrium level of real GDP of only $750 billion per year and a higher price level index at 130.

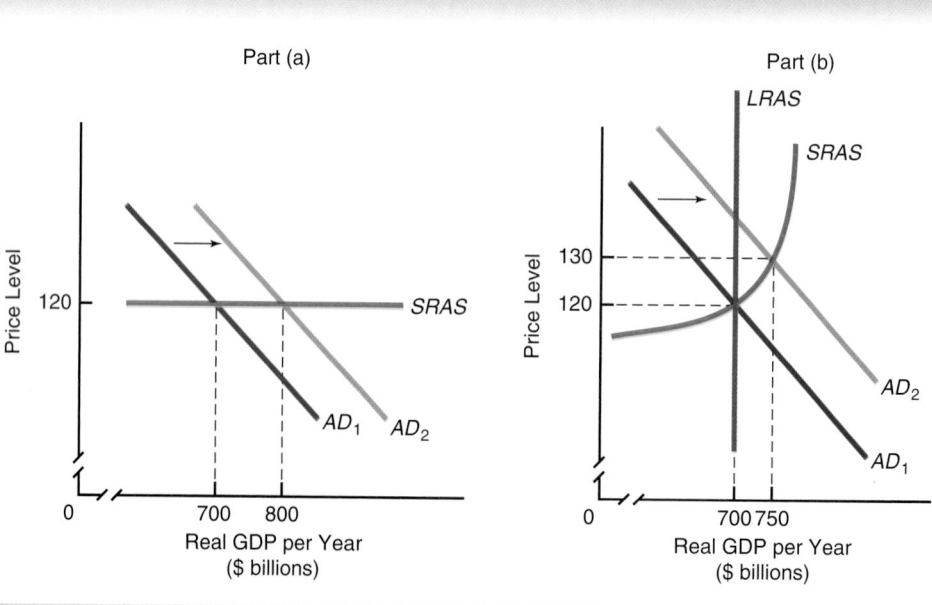

$800 billion per year. Compare this situation with the standard upward-sloping short-run aggregate supply curve presented in Chapter 10. In part (b) of Figure 11.8, *SRAS* is upward-sloping, with its slope becoming steeper and steeper after it crosses long-run aggregate supply, *LRAS*. Recall that *LRAS* is the level of real GDP that the economy would produce year in and year out with full information and full adjustment. It is sometimes called the full-employment level of real GDP because, presumably, full employment occurs when there is full information and full adjustment possible in the economy. If aggregate demand is AD_1, the equilibrium level of real GDP in part (b) is also $700 billion per year, also at a price level of 120. A similar increase in aggregate demand to AD_2 as occurred in part (a) produces a different equilibrium, however. Equilibrium real GDP increases to $750 billion per year, which is less than in part (a) because part of the increase in *nominal* GDP has occurred through an increase in the price level to 130.

In modern Keynesian theory, when the price level rises gradually, output can be expanded beyond the level consistent with its long-run growth path for a variety of reasons:

1. In the short run, most labour contracts implicitly or explicitly call for flexibility in hours of work at the given wage rate. Therefore, firms can use existing workers more intensively in a variety of ways: they can get them to work harder; they can get them to work more hours per day; and they can get them to work more days per week. Also, workers can be switched from *uncounted* production, such as maintenance, to counted production, which generates *counted* output. The distinction between counted and uncounted is simply what is measured in the marketplace, particularly by government statisticians and accountants. If a worker cleans a machine, there is no measured output. But if that worker is put on the production line and helps increase the number of units produced each day, measured output will go up. That worker's production has then been counted.

2. Existing capital equipment can be used more intensively. Machines can be worked more hours per day. Some can be made to work at a faster speed. Maintenance can be delayed.

3. Finally, and just as importantly, if wage rates are held constant, a higher price level means that profits go up, which induces firms to hire more workers. The duration of unemployment falls, and thus the unemployment rate falls. And people who were previously not in the labour force (homemakers and younger or older workers) can be induced to enter.

All these adjustments cause national output to rise as the price level increases, giving the *SRAS* curve an upward slope.

Try Preview Question 4:

Why is real GDP said to be demand-determined when the short-run aggregate supply curve is horizontal?

INTERNATIONAL EXAMPLE 11-1

Why Have Unemployment Rates Fallen in North America Without Increasing Inflation?

The United States economy has been hovering around 4 percent unemployment rates through the latter part of the 1990s. With such a low rate of unemployment, many economists have been wondering if the natural rate of unemployment (and the associated *LRAS*) has changed to a lower rate. Some economists are now suggesting that businesses have altered their methods of doing business so much that the shortages of labour have forced businesses to improve their productivity. In doing so, the *LRAS* curve is also shifting, and this is showing up as improved productivity in the United States and in Canada as well. Coming at the end of a long period of slow productivity growth, these improvements in productivity have been very welcome.

For critical analysis: What might happen to wages and inflation if productivity growth does not continue into the future, but the unemployment rate continues to be low?

CONCEPTS IN BRIEF

- If we assume that we are operating on a horizontal short-run aggregate supply curve, the equilibrium level of real GDP per year is completely demand-determined.
- The horizontal short-run aggregate supply curve has been called the Keynesian short-run aggregate supply curve because Keynes believed that many prices, especially wages, would not be reduced even when aggregate demand decreased.
- Modern Keynesian theory suggests that the *SRAS* curve is upward sloping, and that output can be temporarily pushed beyond its long-run path through a variety of adjustments in the economy.

NETNOMICS

Are New Information Technologies Making the Short-Run Aggregate Supply Schedule Less Steeply Sloped?

Evidence has been increasing that the short-run aggregate supply curve (*SRAS*) has become less steeply sloped since the early 1990s. Some economists credit widespread deregulation in the 1970s and 1980s with laying the foundation for a more shallowly sloped *SRAS* curve. The increase in domestic and international rivalry among sellers of goods and services, they argue, has made consumers much more sensitive to price differences across products. In equilibrium, therefore, the general level of prices exhibits less change, relative to years past, in response to a given change in output—hence a less steeply sloped *SRAS* curve.

Now, continuing developments in information technologies promise to take this trend a step further. For the first time ever, information technologies are the biggest job creators. Depending on whose statistics you look at, such industries are producing between 25 and 40 percent of all new jobs. An information economy is fundamentally different from an industrial economy. Software and databases, for example, can be scaled up to gigantic capacity at little cost. Indeed, because of the ease of communicating data over the Internet, they have unlimited capacity at the very beginning. In other words, capacity as previously defined may be an outdated concept.

Hence, beyond the point at which the *SRAS* curve crosses the *LRAS* curve, there will likely be less of a tendency for the *SRAS* curve to bend upward as Canada becomes more of an information economy. Perhaps today's and especially tomorrow's *SRAS* will have to be represented by a curve that is more nearly horizontal.

The Impact of the Great Depression

Concepts Applied: Unemployment, Keynesian analysis, inflation

The Depression era laid down a new belief that governments could never allow this kind of thing to happen again.

The Great Depression

Nobody could tell exactly when it began and nobody could predict when it would end. At the outset, they didn't even call it a depression. At worst it was a recession, a brief slump, a "correction" in the market, a glitch in the rising curve of prosperity. Only when the full import of those heartbreaking years sank in did it become the Great Depression—Great, because there had been no other remotely like it and (please God!) there would never be another like it again.

In retrospect, we see it as a whole—as a neat decade tucked in between the Roaring Twenties and the Second World War, perhaps the most significant ten years in our history, a watershed era that scarred and transformed the nation. But it hasn't been easy for later generations to comprehend its devastating impact.... There are not very many left who can remember what it was like to live on water for an entire day, as the Templeton family did in the Parkdale district of Toronto in 1932, or how it felt to own only a single dress—made of flour sacks—as Etha Munro did in the family farmhouse on the drought-ravaged Saskatchewan prairie in 1934.

This army of the deprived was treated shabbily by a government that used words like "fiscal responsibility" and "a sound dollar" as excuses to ignore human despair. Balancing the budget was more important than feeding the hungry. The bogey of the deficit was enlisted to tighten the purse strings.

Both the Liberal and Conservative governments stumbled from crisis to crisis, adopting band-aid solutions that often became part of the problem. At every level of government the authorities attacked the symptoms and not the cause, trying vainly to hold down the lid on the bubbling kettle of protest. If single transients clog the streets of the big cities—get them out of sight. If radicals demand a better deal for the jobless—jail them. If "foreigners" ask for relief—deport them. If farmers stage hunger strikes—disperse them with policies billies.

Every level of government tried to evade its responsibilities for the unemployed. Ottawa washed its hands of the problem, as Ottawa often does, and tried to lay it on the provinces. The provinces tried to lay it on the municipalities. The municipalities tried to lay it on the local taxpayers, who couldn't cope with it because so many were themselves out of work.

Canadians have always been a cautious people. The Depression made them more cautious than ever. The longing for security that brought family allowances, medicare, and unemployment insurance is still deep in the subconscious of the Depression generation. The children of those years cling to their jobs as a shipwrecked sailor clings to a raft. Three decades later, the adult world raised in the Thirties would be baffled by what it saw as the irresponsibility of a new generation that thought nothing of quitting work, having a good time, and then casually seeking other employment.

The Depression also played havoc with *laissez-faire*. For the first time, Canadians began to realize that government must interfere in the private affairs of the nation. The Canadian Wheat Board, the Bank of Canada, the Canadian Broadcasting Corporation, and Trans-Canada Airlines were among the public corporations born of those hungry years. Anyone who advocated today's social services in the pre-Depression era would have been considered a social radical.

FIGURE 11.9 Real GDP and the Price Level, 1931–1939

In a depressed economy, increased aggregate spending can increase output without raising prices. This is what John Maynard Keynes believed, and the data for Canada's recovery from the Great Depression seem to bear this out. In such circumstances, the level of real output is demand-determined.

Source: Adapted from Statistics Canada, CANSIM Database, Series D14442, D11000.

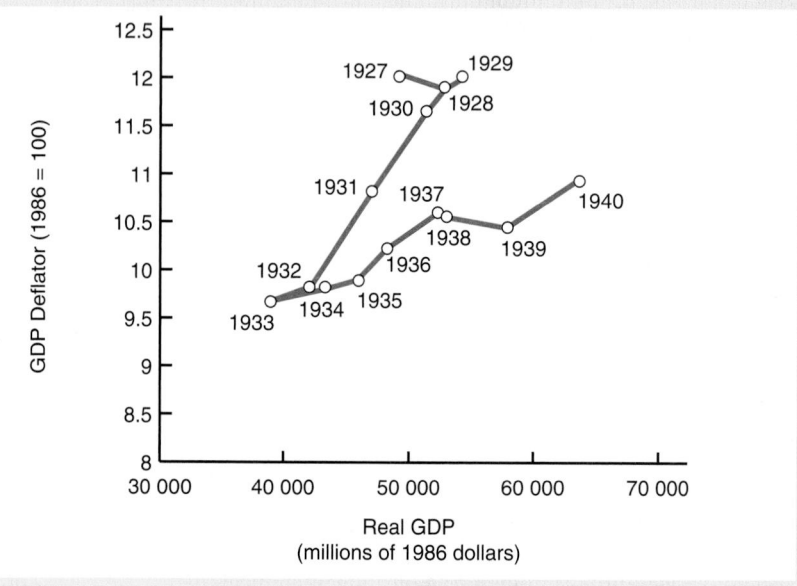

New Thinking About the Role of Governments

As a result of the economic downturn of the 1930s, the need for governments to help steer capitalist economies rather than just let them drift aimlessly became the new thinking for economists and politicians alike. Many new income-support programs and the knowledge that governments can soften the blow of recessions have became a reality today because of the experiences people had in that difficult decade in Canadian and world history.

The programs for income support that we have today reduce the problems that individuals face, so we haven't had a crisis similar to what we had then. Unemployment has never again reached the 25 per cent level that it reached in the 1930s, and we have a social net that captures people when they are destitute. The economic growth in Canada over the years has always been enough to create many jobs, although not always enough to reach full employment.

Similarities to The 1990s

The similarities to the 1990s economic climate, however, are striking. In the 1930s there were work camps for the unemployed. In the 1990s, we had "workfare." Instead of transients travelling on the railroads, we have government-subsidized bus tickets for welfare recipients. The Regina Riot of 1935 was matched by demonstrations on the lawn of the Ontario legislature. Governments trying to balance their books used the same jargon as they did in the 1930s.

In Figure 11.9, you can see why this decade is referred to as "ten lost years." The level of real GDP achieved in 1929 was not achieved again until 1939, and that doesn't account for the increase in population during that time! Many billions of dollars of GDP were lost, and many people suffered enormously during that period. It is no wonder that, with such hardship, the existing economic theories proved inadequate for solving the problems of the Depression.

Look at Figure 11.9, where you see real GDP in millions of 1971 dollars on the horizontal axis and the price level index on the vertical axis. From the early days of recovery from the Great Depression through the outbreak of World War II, real GDP increased without much rise in the price level. During this period the economy experienced neither supply constraints nor any dramatic changes in the price level. The most simplified Keynesian model in which prices do not change is essentially an immediate post-Depression model that fits the data very well during this period.

Source: Excerpts from Pierre Berton, *The Great Depression: 1929-1939*. Toronto: McClelland & Stewart, 1990.

For Critical Analysis

1. What income-replacement programs in Canada exist to reduce lost income during periods of unemployment for individuals? Why do these programs tend to reduce the effect of recessions? (Hint: Think back to the circular flow in Chapter 8.)

2. Why did the Second World War bring Canada out of recession?

CHAPTER SUMMARY

1. The classical model was developed in the 1770s by such economists as Adam Smith, David Ricardo, John Stuart Mill, and Thomas Malthus. It attempted to explain the determinants of the price level and national income and employment.

2. Say's law holds that supply creates its own demand. A more complete classical model assumes (a) pure competition, (b) wage and price flexibility, (c) self-interest motivation throughout the population, and (d) no money illusion. With the introduction of saving, the classical economists believed, the market economy would still reach full employment of resources because planned saving would be met by planned investment. Saving is the supply of credit, and investment is the demand for credit. The interest rate in the credit market was assumed to be flexible, like all other prices, so equilibrium would always prevail, and therefore planned saving would always equal planned investment.

3. Because the classical model posits a vertical long-run aggregate supply curve, any changes in aggregate demand simply change the equilibrium price level. The equilibrium level of real GDP per year is completely supply-determined.

4. Whenever we are operating on a horizontal short-run aggregate supply curve, the equilibrium level of real GDP is completely demand-determined by the position of the aggregate demand curve. The Keynesian short-run aggregate supply curve is typically given as horizontal because Keynes assumed that wages and prices would not be reduced even if aggregate demand decreased substantially.

5. If we relax the assumption of a fixed price level, we are then operating on the upward-sloping portion of the short-run aggregate supply curve. Hence an increase in aggregate demand will lead to some increase in the price level. This increase in the price level will have an offsetting effect on equilibrium total planned expenditures because of wealth, interest rate, and foreign goods substitution effects. Under such circumstances, any increase in aggregate demand will lead to both an increase in the price level and an increase in output.

DISCUSSION OF PREVIEW QUESTIONS

1. What are the assumptions of the classical macro model?

In the classical model, the following four assumptions are made: (a) the existence of pure competition, (b) complete wage and price flexibility, (c) individuals motivated by self-interest, and (d) individuals not fooled by money illusion.

2. What determines the rate of interest in the classical model?

In the classical model, the interaction between desired investment and desired saving determines the equilibrium rate of interest in the economy. Otherwise stated, the equilibrium rate of interest is determined at the intersection of the desired investment curve and the desired saving curve.

3. Why do Keynesian economists believe that the short-run aggregate supply curve is horizontal?

In the horizontal range of the SRAS curve, changes in real GDP (output) occur without changes in the price level. This pure quantity response (no price response) to changes in AD reflects Keynes' assumption that during a depression or a very deep recession, businesses have so much excess capacity that *increases* in AD will elicit only an increase in output; businesses that try to increase prices in such a situation discover that they lose sales to competitors. Similarly, a *reduction* in AD will lead only to a reduction in output; businesses won't reduce prices. Keynes assumed that in modern economies the existence of unions and contracts to support the unemployed imply that wages are sticky downward—wages aren't likely to fall even during periods of significant unemployment. Businesses have a certain control over prices and, confronting wages that are sticky, prefer to reduce output instead of price.

4. Why is real GDP said to be demand-determined when the short-run aggregate supply curve is horizontal?

When the SRAS curve is horizontal, real GDP will change only in response to a change in AD. If AD increases, real GDP rises; if AD decreases, real GDP falls. Therefore, real GDP merely responds to changes in AD, which is therefore the primary mover in the economy.

According to Keynes, businesses are prepared to produce *any* output level; the output level that they do produce is the most profitable one, and that depends on *AD*. This theory says that if you want to predict what real GDP and national employment will be in the future, discover what is happening to *AD* now.

PROBLEMS

(Answers to the odd-numbered problems appear at the back of the book.)

11-1. The desired investment curve intersects the desired saving curve in the economy at an interest rate of 8 percent. The current market rate of interest is 9 percent. Outline what will now take place in the economy so that the saving and investment market is in equilibrium.

11-2. Look at Figure 11.3 again. At a wage rate of $12 per hour, 13.5 million workers are employed. This is called full-employment equilibrium. Does that mean there is no unemployment?

11-3. Show the effects of a decrease in aggregate demand in the classical model, using Figure 11.4.

11-4. At a point along the short-run aggregate supply curve that is to the right of the point where it crosses the long-run aggregate supply curve, what must be true of the *actual* unemployment rate relative to the *natural* rate of unemployment? Why?

11-5. Suppose that there is a stock market crash in an economy with an upward-sloping short-run aggregate supply curve, and consumer and business confidence plummets. What are the short-run effects on equilibrium real GDP and the equilibrium price level?

ECONOMICS ON THE NET

Examining The Great Depression in More Detail

In this exercise, we'll look more closely at some of the economic data that illustrate the historical experience of the Depression.

Internet URL:

http://www.statcan.ca/english/freepub/11-516-XIE/sectiona/toc.htm

Navigation:
Scroll down to the section on the Economy Section F and click on the series number

F1-F152 National Income and Expenditure.
Now download the file on Gross National Expenditure for the period 1926-1976, which is given in two parts.

You will need to display this data with a program that can read **comma separated values** tables, such as Microsoft Excel.
http://www.statcan.ca/english/freepub/11-516-XIE/sectionf/F33_55a.csv
and
http://www.statcan.ca/english/freepub/11-516-XIE/sectionf/F33_55b.csv

Application:
Look at the four major components of GNE, government spending, investment, consumption expenditure, and net exports. Plot the years from 1929 to 1939 on a graph. How did each of these sectors perform during those years?

CONSUMPTION, INCOME, AND THE MULTIPLIER

On October 25, 2000, the Toronto Stock Exchange dropped by 840 points, or 8.1 percent of its value. This percentage drop in a given day was the second worst single day in the TSE, and the largest decline in points. Most of the decline was attributed to the drop in a single share, Nortel Networks, which fell about 25 percent that day.

    In the past, such declines have often (but not always) heralded the beginning of a recession. To understand why such events are important to an economy, we need to have a better understanding of the relationship between consumption, investment, and the multiplier, the subject of this chapter.

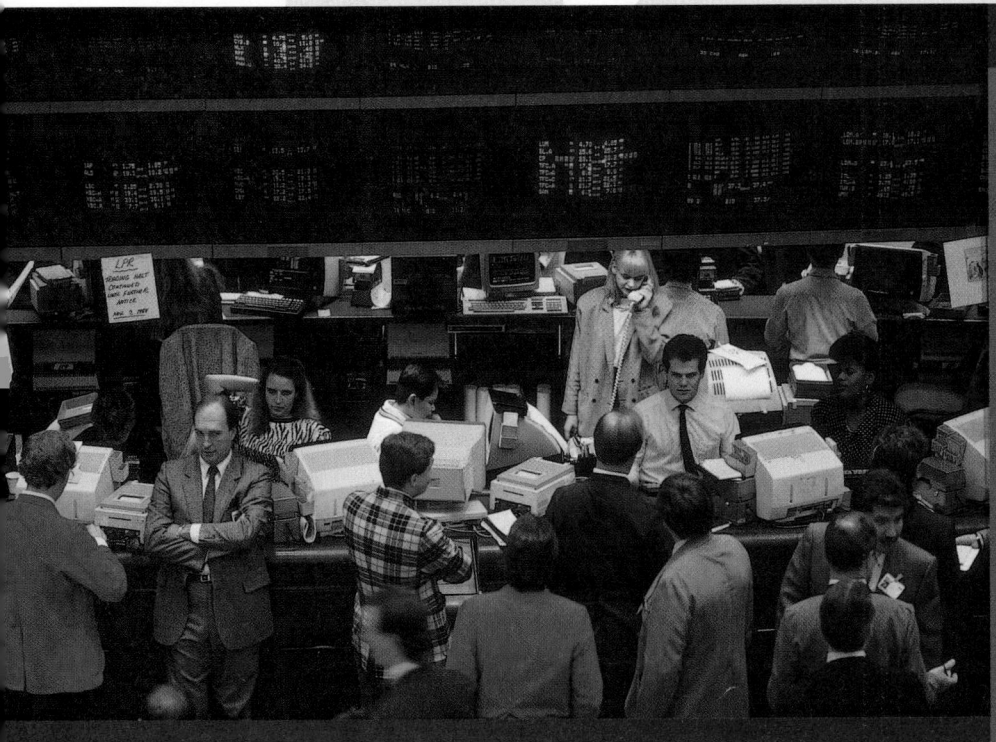

PREVIEW QUESTIONS

1. How do we interpret the 45-degree reference line?

2. What does the total planned expenditures curve indicate?

3. What is the concept of the multiplier, how does it work, and what is its main determinant?

4. What might cause shifts in the total planned expenditures curve?

DID YOU KNOW THAT... personal consumption expenditures in Canada have averaged about 60 percent of gross domestic product for decades? Each year, Canadians purchase millions of television sets, millions of pairs of shoes, millions of compact discs, and billions of stress-reducing pills, among other products and services. We are a nation of spenders, and our personal consumption expenditures help to keep the Canadian economic machine moving day in and day out. As it turns out, John Maynard Keynes focused much of his research on what determines how much you and I decide to spend each year. Remember that aggregate demand consists of consumption expenditures, plus expenditures for investment purposes, what the government spends, and what foreigners spend on domestically produced output. As you will learn in this chapter, Keynes focused on the relationship between how much people earn and their willingness to engage in personal consumption expenditures. In this chapter you will learn about that relationship as well as the influence of investment, government, and the foreign sector on the economy's equilibrium level of real output per year.

Some Simplifying Assumptions in a Keynesian Model

Continuing in the Keynesian tradition, we will assume that the short-run aggregate supply curve within the relevant range is horizontal. That is to say, we assume that it is similar to Figure 11.6, meaning that the equilibrium level of real GDP is demand-determined. That is why Keynes wished to examine the elements of desired aggregate expenditures.

Also, for the time being we will not be concerned with the problem of inflation, because by definition, along the Keynesian short-run aggregate supply curve, inflation is impossible. Finally, given that the price level is assumed to be unchanging, all of the variables with which we will be dealing will be expressed in real terms. After all, with no change in the price level, any change in the magnitude of an economic variable, such as income, will be equivalent to a real change in terms of purchasing power. Hence we will be examining Keynes' income-expenditure model of real GDP determination in a world of inflexible prices.

To simplify the income determination model that follows, a number of assumptions are made:

1. Businesses pay no indirect taxes (for example, sales taxes).
2. Businesses distribute all of their profits to shareholders.
3. There is no depreciation (capital consumption allowance), so gross private domestic investment equals net investment.
4. The economy is closed—that is, there is no foreign trade.

Given all these simplifying assumptions, real disposable income will be equal to real national income minus taxes.[1] This relationship can be algebraically written as:

$$Y_d \equiv Y - T$$

Definitions and Relationships Revisited

You can do only two things with a dollar of income (in the absence of taxes): consume it or save it. If you consume it, it is gone forever. If you save the entire dollar, however, you

---

[1] Strictly speaking, we are referring here to net taxes—that is, the difference between taxes paid and transfer payments received. If taxes are $100 billion but individuals receive transfer payments—Old Age Security benefits, unemployment benefits, and so forth—of $30 billion, net taxes are equal to $70 billion.

Consumption Spending on new goods and services out of a household's current income. Whatever is not consumed is saved. Consumption includes such things as buying food and going to a concert.

Saving The act of not consuming all of one's current income. Whatever is not consumed out of spendable income is, by definition, saved. *Saving* is an action measured over time (a flow), whereas *savings* are a stock, an accumulation resulting from the act of saving in the past.

Consumption goods Goods bought by households to use up, such as food, clothing, and movies.

will be able to consume it (and perhaps more if it earns interest) at some future time. That is the distinction between **consumption** and **saving.** Consumption is the act of using income for the purchase of consumption goods. **Consumption goods** are goods purchased by households for immediate satisfaction. Consumption goods are such things as food, clothing, and movies. By definition, whatever you do not consume you save and can consume at some time in the future.

STOCKS AND FLOWS: THE DIFFERENCE BETWEEN SAVING AND SAVINGS. It is important to distinguish between *saving* and *savings*. *Saving* is an action that occurs at a particular rate—for example, $10 a week or $520 a year. This rate is a flow. It is expressed per unit of time, usually a year. Implicitly, then, when we talk about saving, we talk about a *flow* or rate of saving. *Savings*, by contrast, is a *stock* concept, measured at a certain point or instant in time. Your current *savings* are the result of past *saving*. You may presently have *savings* of $2,000 that are the result of four years' *saving* at a rate of $500 per year. Consumption, being related to saving, is also a flow concept. You consume from after-tax income at a certain rate per week, per month, or per year.

RELATING INCOME TO SAVING AND CONSUMPTION. Obviously, a dollar of take-home income can be either consumed or not consumed. Realizing this, we can see the relationship among saving, consumption, and disposable income:

$$\text{Consumption} + \text{saving} \equiv \text{disposable income}$$

Written algebraically, this is written as:

$$C + S \equiv Y_d$$

This is called an *accounting identity*. It has to hold true at every moment in time. From it we can derive the definition of saving:

$$\text{Saving} \equiv \text{disposable income} - \text{consumption}$$

or algebraically:

$$S \equiv Y_d - C$$

Recall that disposable income is what you actually have left to spend after you pay taxes.

Investment

Investment The spending by businesses on things such as machines and buildings, which can be used to produce goods and services in the future. The investment part of total income is the portion that will be used in the process of producing goods in the future.

Capital goods Producer durables; nonconsumable goods that firms use to make other goods.

Investment is also a flow concept. *Investment* as used in economics differs from the common use of the term, as we have already pointed out. In everyday speech, it is often used to describe putting money into the stock market or real estate. In economic analysis, investment is defined as expenditures by firms on new machines and buildings—**capital goods**—that are expected to yield a future stream of income. This we have already called *fixed investment*. We also included changes in business inventories in our definition. This we have already called *inventory investment*.

- If we assume that we are operating on a horizontal short-run aggregate supply curve, the equilibrium level of real GDP per year is completely demand-determined.
- Consumption is a flow which occurs repeatedly over time. It represents the purchase of consumer goods and services such as food, clothing, and restaurant meals.
- *Saving* is also a flow, something that occurs over time. It equals disposable income minus consumption. *Savings* are a stock. They are the accumulated results of saving.
- Investment too is a flow. It includes expenditures on new machines, buildings, and equipment, as well as changes in business inventories.

Determinants of Planned Consumption and Planned Saving

In the classical model, the supply of saving was determined by the rate of interest: The higher the rate of interest, the more people wanted to save and therefore the less people wanted to consume. According to Keynes, the interest rate is not the primary determinant of an individual's saving and consumption decisions.

Keynes argued that saving and consumption decisions depend primarily on an individual's real current income.

Consumption function The relationship between amount consumed and disposable income. A consumption function tells us how much people plan to consume at various levels of disposable income.

The relationship between planned consumption expenditures of households and their current level of real income has been called the **consumption function.** It shows how much all households plan to consume per year at each level of real disposable income per year. Using for the moment only columns 1, 2, and 3 of Table 12.1, we will present a consumption function for a hypothetical household.

We see from Table 12.1 that as real disposable income rises, planned consumption also rises, but by a smaller amount, as Keynes suggested. Planned saving also increases with disposable income. Notice, however, that below an income of $10,000, the planned saving of this hypothetical family is actually negative. The further that income drops below that level, the more the family engages in **dissaving,** either by going into debt or by using up some of its existing wealth.

Dissaving Negative saving; a situation in which spending exceeds income. Dissaving can occur when a household is able to borrow or use up existing owned assets.

Graphing the Numbers

When we constructed demand and supply curves in Chapter 4, we merely plotted the points from a table showing price-quantity pairs onto a diagram whose axes were labelled "Price" and "Quantity." We will graph the consumption and saving relationships presented in Table 12.1 in the same manner. In the upper part of Figure 12.1, the vertical axis measures the level of planned real consumption per year, and the horizontal axis measures the level of real disposable income per year. In the lower part of the figure, the horizontal axis is again real disposable income per year, but now the vertical axis is planned real saving per year. All of these are on a dollars-per-year basis, which emphasizes the point that we are measuring flows, not stocks.

As you can see, we have taken income-consumption and income-saving combinations *A* through *K* and plotted them. In the upper part of Figure 12.1, the result is called the *consumption function.* In the lower part, the result is called the *saving function.* Mathematically, the saving function is the *complement* of the consumption function because consumption plus saving always equals disposable income. What is not consumed is, by definition, saved. The difference between actual disposable income and the planned level of consumption per year *must* be the planned level of saving per year.

TABLE 12.1

Real Consumption and Saving Schedules: A Hypothetical Case

Column 1 presents real disposable income from zero up to $20,000 per year; column 2 indicates planned consumption per year; column 3 presents planned saving per year. At levels of disposable income below $10,000, planned saving is negative. In column 4, we see the average propensity to consume, which is merely planned consumption divided by disposable income. Column 5 lists average propensity to save, which is planned saving divided by disposable income. Column 6 is the marginal propensity to consume, which shows the proportion of additional income that will be consumed. Finally, column 7 shows the proportion of additional income that will be saved, or the marginal propensity to save.

Combination	(1) Real Disposable Income per Year (Y_d)	(2) Planned Real Consumption per Year (C)	(3) Planned Real Saving per Year $(S \equiv Y_d - C)$ (1) − (2)	(4) Average Propensity to Consume $(APC \equiv C/Y_d)$ (2) ÷ (1)	(5) Average Propensity to Save $(APS \equiv S/Y_d)$ (3) ÷ (1)	(6) Marginal Propensity to Consume $(MPC \equiv \Delta C/\Delta Y_d)$	(7) Marginal Propensity to Save $(MPS \equiv \Delta S/\Delta Y_d)$
A	$ 0	$ 2,000	$ −2,000	—	—	—	—
B	2,000	3,600	−1,600	1.8	−0.8	0.8	0.2
C	4,000	5,200	−1,200	1.3	−0.3	0.8	0.2
D	6,000	6,800	− 800	1.133	−0.133	0.8	0.2
E	8,000	8,400	− 400	1.05	−0.05	0.8	0.2
F	10,000	10,000	0	1.0	0.0	0.8	0.2
G	12,000	11,600	400	0.967	0.033	0.8	0.2
H	14,000	13,200	800	0.943	0.057	0.8	0.2
I	16,000	14,800	1,200	0.925	0.075	0.8	0.2
J	18,000	16,400	1,600	0.911	0.089	0.8	0.2
K	20,000	18,000	2,000	0.9	0.1	0.8	0.2

45-degree reference line The line along which planned real expenditures equal real national income per year.

How can we find the rate of saving or dissaving in the upper part of Figure 12.1? We draw a line that is equidistant from both the horizontal and the vertical axes. This line is 45 degrees from either axis and is often called the **45-degree reference line.** At every point on the 45-degree reference line, a vertical line drawn to the income axis is the same distance from the origin as a horizontal line drawn to the consumption axis. Thus at point *F*, where the consumption function intersects the 45-degree line, real disposable income equals planned consumption. Point *F* is sometimes called the *break-even income point* because there is neither positive nor negative saving. This can be seen in the lower part of Figure 12.1 as well. The planned annual rate of saving at a real disposable income level of $10,000 is indeed zero.

Dissaving and Autonomous Consumption

To the left of point *F* in either part of Figure 12.1, this hypothetical family engages in dissaving, either by going into debt or by consuming existing assets, including savings. The amount of saving or dissaving in the upper part of the figure can be found by measuring the vertical distance between the 45-degree line and the consumption function. This simply tells us that if our hypothetical family starts above $10,000 of real disposable income per year and then temporarily finds its real disposable income below $10,000, it will not cut back its consumption by the full amount of the reduction. It will instead go into debt or consume existing assets in some way to compensate for part of the loss.

FIGURE 12.1 The Consumption and Saving Functions

If we plot the combinations of real disposable income and planned real consumption from columns 1 and 2 in Table 12.1, we get the consumption function. At every point on the 45-degree line, a vertical line drawn to the income axis is the same distance from the origin as a horizontal line drawn to the consumption axis. Where the consumption function crosses the 45-degree line at *F*, we know that consumption equals real disposable income and there is zero saving. The vertical distance between the 45-degree line and the consumption function measures the rate of saving or dissaving at any given income level. If we plot the relationship between column 1, real disposable income, and column 3, planned real saving, from Table 12.1, we arrive at the saving function shown in the lower part of this diagram. It is the complement of the consumption function presented above it.

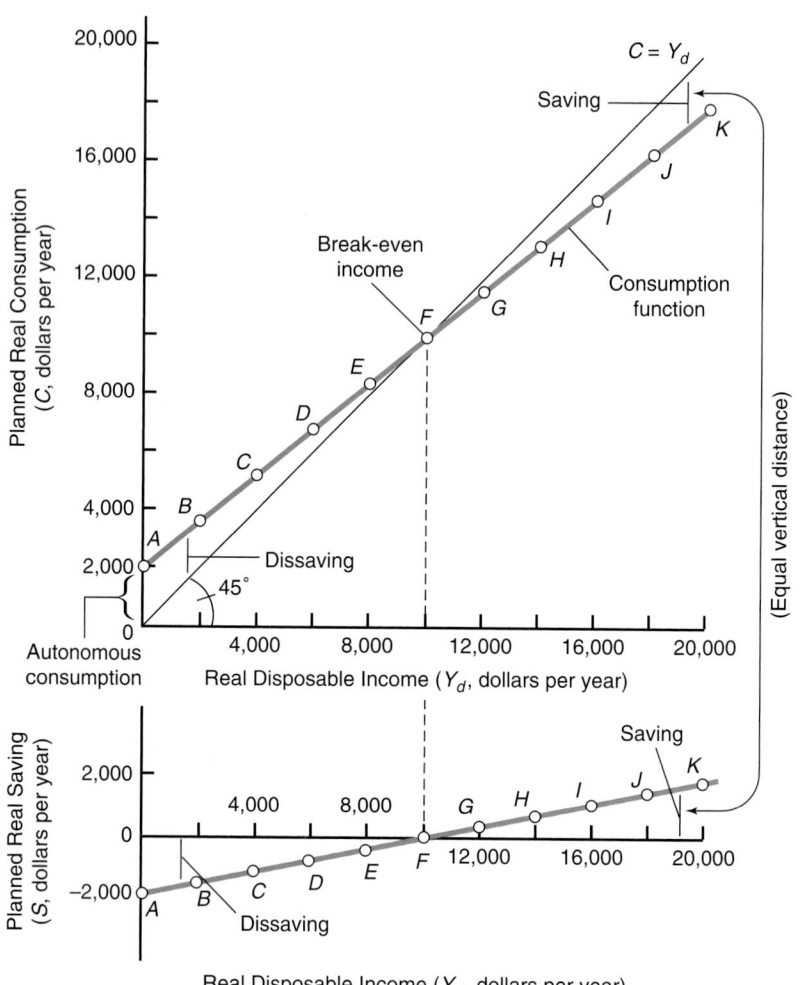

Autonomous consumption The part of consumption that is independent of (does not depend on) the level of disposable income. Changes in autonomous consumption shift the consumption function.

Now look at the point on the diagram where real disposable income is zero but planned consumption per year is $2,000. This amount of planned consumption, which does not depend at all on actual disposable income, is called **autonomous consumption.** The autonomous consumption of $2,000 is *independent* of the level of disposable income. That means that no matter how low the level of income of our hypothetical family falls, the family will always attempt to consume at least $2,000 per year. (We are, of course, assuming here that the family's real disposable income does not equal zero year in and year out. There is certainly a limit to how long our hypothetical family could finance autonomous consumption without any income.) That $2,000 of yearly consumption is determined by things other than the level of income. We don't need to specify what determines autonomous consumption; we merely state that it exists and that in our example it is $2,000 per year. Just remember that the word *autonomous* means "existing independently." In our model, autonomous consumption exists independently of the hypothetical family's level of real disposable income. (Later we will review some of the non-real-disposable-income determinants of consumption.) There are many possible types of autonomous expenditures. Hypothetically, we can consider that investment is autonomous—independent of income. We can assume that government expenditures are autonomous. We will do just that at various times in our discussions to simplify our analysis of income determination.

Average Propensity to Consume and to Save

Average propensity to consume (APC) Consumption divided by real disposable income; for any given level of income, the proportion of total disposable income that is consumed.

Let's now go back to Table 12.1, and this time look at columns 4 and 5: **average propensity to consume (APC)** and **average propensity to save (APS).** They are defined as follows:

$$APC \equiv \frac{consumption}{real\ disposable\ income}$$

$$APS \equiv \frac{saving}{real\ disposable\ income}$$

Average propensity to save (APS) Saving divided by real disposable income; for any given level of income, the proportion of total disposable income that is saved.

Notice from column 4 in Table 12.1 that for this hypothetical family, the average propensity to consume decreases as real disposable income increases. This decrease simply means that the fraction of the family's real disposable income going to saving rises as income rises. The same fact can be found in column 5. The average propensity to save (APS), which at first is negative, finally hits zero at an income level of $10,000 and then becomes positive. In this example, the APS reaches a value of 0.1 at income level $20,000. This means that the household saves 10 percent of a $20,000 income.

It's quite easy for you to figure out your own average propensity to consume or to save. Just divide your total real disposable income for the year into what you consumed and what you saved. The result will be your personal APC and APS, respectively, at your current level of income. This gives the proportions of total income that are consumed and saved.

Marginal Propensity to Consume and to Save

Marginal propensity to consume (MPC) The ratio of the change in consumption to the change in real disposable income. A marginal propensity to consume of 0.8 tells us that an additional $100 in take-home pay will lead to an additional $80 consumed.

Now we go to the last two columns in Table 12.1: **marginal propensity to consume (MPC)** and **marginal propensity to save (MPS).** We have used the term *marginal* before. It refers to a small incremental or decremental change (represented by Δ in Table 12.1). The marginal propensity to consume, then, is defined as:

$$MPC \equiv \frac{change\ in\ consumption}{change\ in\ real\ disposable\ income}$$

marginal propensity to save is defined similarly as:

$$MPS \equiv \frac{change\ in\ saving}{change\ in\ real\ disposable\ income}$$

Marginal propensity to save (MPS) The ratio of the change in saving to the change in real disposable income. A marginal propensity to save of 0.2 indicates that out of an additional $100 in take-home pay, $20 will be saved. Whatever is not saved is consumed. The marginal propensity to save plus the marginal propensity to consume must always equal 1, by definition.

What do MPC and MPS tell you? They tell you what percentage of a given increase or decrease in income will go towards consumption and saving, respectively. The emphasis here is on the word *change.* The marginal propensity to consume indicates how much you will change your planned rate of consumption if there is a change in your real disposable income. If your marginal propensity to consume is 0.8, that does not mean that you consume 80 percent of *all* disposable income. The percentage of your real disposable income that you consume is given by the average propensity to consume, or APC, which is not, in Table 12.1, equal to 0.8. In contrast, an MPC of 0.8 means that you will consume 80 percent of any *increase* in your disposable income. In general, we assume that the marginal propensity to consume is between zero and 1. We assume that individuals increase their planned consumption by more than zero and less than 100 percent of any increase in real disposable income that they receive.

Consider a simple example in which we show the difference between the average propensity to consume and the marginal propensity to consume. Assume that your consumption behaviour is exactly the same as our hypothetical family's behaviour depicted in Table 12.1. You have an annual real disposable income of $18,000. Your planned consumption rate, then, from column 2 of Table 12.1 is $16,400. So your average propensity to consume is $16,400 ÷ $18,000 = 0.911. Now suppose that at the end of the year your boss gives you an after-tax bonus of $2,000. What would you do with that additional $2,000 in real disposable income? According to the table, you would consume $1,600 of it and save $400. In that case, your *marginal* propensity to consume would be $1,600 ÷ $2,000 = 0.8, and your marginal propensity to save would be $400 ÷ $2,000 = 0.2. What would happen to your *average* propensity to consume? To find out, we add $1,600 to $16,400 of planned consumption, which gives us a new consumption rate of $18,000. The average propensity to consume is then $18,000 divided by the new higher salary of $20,000. Your APC drops from 0.911 to 0.9. By contrast, your MPC remains in our simplified example 0.8 all the time. Look at column 6 in Table 12.1. The MPC is 0.8 at every level of income. (Therefore, the MPS is always equal to 0.2 at every level of income.) Underlying the constancy of MPC is the assumption that the amount that you are willing to consume out of additional income will remain the same in percentage terms no matter what level of real disposable income is your starting point.

Some Relationships

Consumption plus saving must equal income. Both your total real disposable income and the change in total real disposable income are either consumed or saved. The proportions of either measure must equal 1, or 100 percent. This allows us to make the following statements:

$$APC + APS = 1 \; (= 100 \text{ percent of total income})$$

$$MPC + MPS = 1 \; (= 100 \text{ percent of the } \textit{change} \text{ in income})$$

The average propensities as well as the marginal propensities to consume and save must total 1, or 100 percent. Check the two statements by adding the figures in columns 4 and 5 for each level of real disposable income in Table 12.1. Do the same for columns 6 and 7.

Causes of Shifts in the Consumption Function

A change in any other relevant economic variable besides real disposable income will cause the consumption function to shift. There is a virtually unlimited number of such non-income determinants of the position of the consumption function. When population increases or decreases, for example, the consumption function will shift up or down, respectively. Changes in expectations can also shift the consumption function. If the average household believes that the rate of inflation is going to fall dramatically in the years to come, the current consumption function will probably shift down: Planned consumption would be less at every level of real disposable income than before this change in expectations. Real household **wealth** is also a determinant of the position of the consumption function. An increase in real wealth of the average household will cause the consumption function to shift upward. A decrease in real wealth will cause it to shift downward.

Wealth The stock of assets owned by a person, household, firm, or country. For a household, wealth can consist of a house, cars, personal belongings, bank accounts, and cash.

CONCEPTS IN BRIEF

- The consumption function shows the relationship between planned rates of consumption and real disposable income per year. The saving function is the complement of the consumption function because saving plus consumption must equal real disposable income.
- The average propensity to consume (APC) is equal to consumption divided by real disposable income. The average propensity to save (APS) is equal to saving divided by real disposable income.
- The marginal propensity to consume (MPC) is equal to the change in planned consumption divided by the change in real disposable income. The marginal propensity to save (MPS) is equal to the change in planned saving divided by the change in real disposable income.
- Any change in real disposable income will cause the planned rate of consumption to change; this is represented by a movement along the consumption function. Any change in a nonincome determinant of consumption will shift the consumption function.

Determinants of Investment

Investment, you will remember, is defined as expenditures on new buildings and equipment and changes in business inventories. Real gross private domestic investment in Canada has been extremely volatile over the years relative to real consumption. If we were to look at net private domestic investment (investment after depreciation has been deducted), we would see that in the depths of the Great Depression and at the peak of the World War II effort, the figure was negative. In other words, we were eating away at our capital stock—we weren't even maintaining it by completely replacing depreciated equipment.

If we compare real investment expenditures historically with real consumption expenditures, we find that the latter are relatively less variable over time than the former. Why is this so? The answer is that the real investment decisions of businesspeople are based on highly variable, subjective estimates of how the economic future looks. We just discussed the role of expectations in determining the position of the consumption function. Expectations play an even greater role in determining the position of the investment function. This could account for much of the instability of investment over time. We'll examine the role of expectations at the end of the chapter in the Issues and Applications section.

Expectations Estimates of future economic conditions.

The Planned Investment Function

Consider that at all times, businesses perceive an array of investment opportunities. These investment opportunities have rates of return ranging from zero to very high, with the number (or dollar value) of all such projects inversely related to the rate of return. Because a project is profitable only if its rate of return exceeds the opportunity cost of the investment—the rate of interest—it follows that as the interest rate falls, planned investment spending increases, and vice versa. Even if firms use retained earnings (internal financing) to fund an investment, the higher the market rate of interest, the greater the *opportunity cost* of using those retained earnings. Thus it does not matter in our analysis whether the firm must seek financing from external sources or can obtain such financing by using retained earnings. Just consider that as the interest rate falls, more investment opportunities will be profitable, and planned investment will be higher.

It should be no surprise, therefore, that the investment function is represented as an inverse relationship between the rate of interest and the value of planned investment. A hypothetical investment schedule is given in part (a) of Figure 12.2, and plotted in

FIGURE 12.2 Planned Investment

In the hypothetical planned investment schedule in part (a), the rate of planned investment is asserted to be inversely related to the rate of interest. If we plot the data pairs from part (a), we obtain the investment function, *I*, in part (b). It is negatively sloped.

Part (a)

Rate of Interest (percent per year)	Planned Investment per Year ($ billions)
7.5	20
7	30
6.5	40
6	50
5.5	60
5	70
4.5	80
4	90
3.5	100
3	110

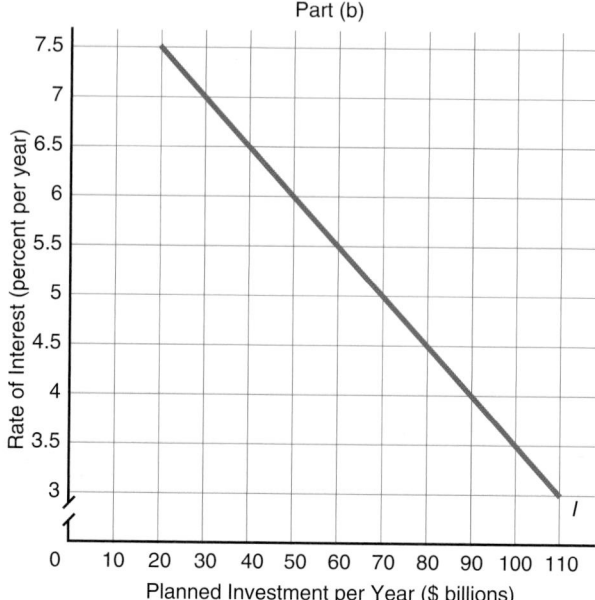

Part (b)

part (b). We see from this schedule that if, for example, the rate of interest is 5.5 percent, the dollar value of planned investment will be $60 billion per year. Notice, by the way, that planned investment is also given on a per-year basis, showing that it represents a flow, not a stock. (The stock counterpart of investment is the stock of capital in the economy measured in dollars at a point in time.)

What Causes the Investment Function to Shift?

Because planned investment is assumed to be a function of the rate of interest, any non-interest-rate variable that changes can have the potential of shifting the investment function. Expectations of businesspeople is one of those variables. If higher future sales are expected, more machines and bigger plants will be planned for the future. More investment will be undertaken because of the expectation of higher future profits. In this case the investment schedule, *I*, would shift outward to the right, meaning that more investment would be desired at all rates of interest. Any change in productive technology can potentially shift the investment function. A positive change in productive technology would stimulate demand for additional capital goods and shift the investment schedule, *I*, outward to the right. Changes in business taxes can also shift the investment schedule. If they increase, we predict a leftward shift in the planned investment function.

Consumption as a Function of Real National Income

We are interested in determining the equilibrium level of real national income per year. But when we examined the consumption function earlier in this chapter, it related planned consumption expenditures to the level of real disposable income per year. We have already shown where adjustments must be made to GDP in order to get real disposable income (see Table 8.2 in Chapter 8). Real disposable income turns out to be less than real national income because net taxes (taxes minus government transfer payments) are usually about 16 to 24 percent of national income. A representative average in the 1990s is about 20 percent, so disposable income, on average, has in recent years been around 80 percent of national income.

If we are willing to assume that real disposable income, Y_d, differs from real national income by an amount T every year, we can relatively easily substitute real national income for real disposable income in the consumption function.

We can now plot any consumption function on a diagram in which the horizontal axis is no longer real disposable income but rather real national income, as in Figure 12.3. Notice that there is an autonomous part of consumption that is so labelled. The difference between this graph and the graphs presented earlier in this chapter is the change in the horizontal axis from real disposable income to real national income per year. For the rest of this chapter, assume that this calculation has been made, and the result is that the

FIGURE 12.3 Consumption as a Function of Real National Income

This consumption function shows the rate of planned expenditures for each level of real national income per year. There is an autonomous component in consumption equal to $30 billion. Along the 45-degree reference line, planned consumption expenditures per year, C, are identical to real national income per year, Y. The consumption curve intersects the 45-degree reference line at a value of $150 billion per year.

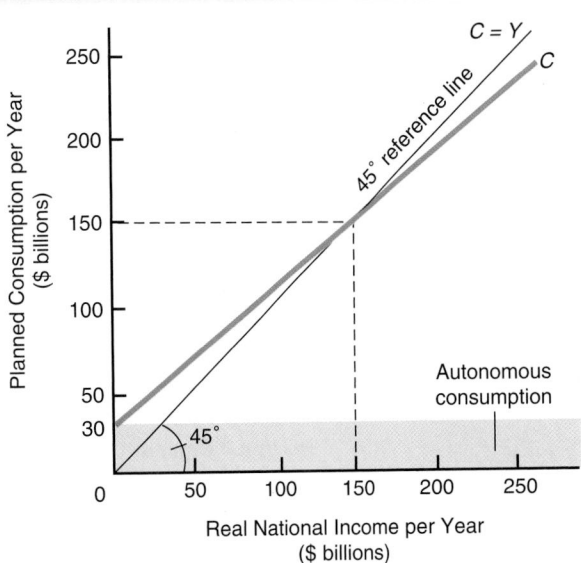

MPC out of real national income equals 0.8, suggesting that 20 percent of changes in real national income are either saved or paid in taxes: In other words, of an additional $100 earned, an additional $80 will be consumed.

The 45-Degree Reference Line

Like the earlier graphs, Figure 12.3 shows a 45-degree reference line. The 45-degree line bisects the quadrant into two equal spaces. Thus along the 45-degree reference line, planned consumption expenditures, C, equal real national income per year, Y. One can see, then, that at any point where the consumption function intersects the 45-degree reference line, planned consumption expenditures will be exactly equal to real national income per year, or $C = Y$. Note that in this graph, because we are looking only at planned consumption on the vertical axis, the 45-degree reference line is where planned consumption, C, is always equal to real national income per year, Y. Later, when we add investment, government spending, and net exports to the graph, the 45-degree reference line with respect to *all* planned expenditures will be labelled as such on the vertical axis. In any event, consumption and real national income are equal at $150 billion per year. That is where the consumption curve, C, intersects the 45-degree reference line. At that income level, all income is consumed.

Adding the Investment Function

Another component of private aggregate demand is, of course, investment spending, I. We have already looked at the planned investment function, which related investment to the rate of interest. You see that as the downward-sloping curve in part (a) of Figure 12.4. Recall from Figure 12.2 that the equilibrium rate of interest is determined at the intersection of the desired savings schedule, which is labelled S and is upward-sloping. The equilibrium rate of interest is 5 percent, and the equilibrium rate of investment is $70 billion per year. The $70 billion of real investment per year is *autonomous* with respect to real national income—that is, it is independent of real national income. In other words, given that we have a determinant investment level of $70 billion at a 5 percent rate of interest, we can treat this level of investment as constant, regardless of the level of national income. This is shown in part (b) of Figure 12.4. The vertical distance of investment spending is $70 billion. Businesses plan on investing a particular amount—$70 billion per year—and will do so no matter what the level of real national income.

How do we add this amount of investment spending to our consumption function? We simply add a line above the C line that we drew in Figure 12.3 that is higher by the vertical distance equal to $70 billion of autonomous investment spending. This is shown by the arrow in part (c) of Figure 12.4. Our new line, now labelled $C + I$, is called the *total planned expenditures curve*. In our simple economy without government expenditures and net exports, the $C + I$ curve represents total planned expenditures as they relate to different levels of real national income per year.

The final step in completing this very simplified model of the economy is to plot the 45-degree reference line. This line shows where planned expenditures ($C + I$ in this simplified model) equals national income. Since national income equals the value of national production at the point where the total planned expenditures curve crosses the 45-degree line, we will match the desires of those purchasing goods and services and the plans of producers to make goods and services. In short, equilibrium occurs where total planned expenditures equals total planned production. In the example shown in Figure 12.4, this equilibrium occurs at $500 billion per year.

This equilibrium between production and planned expenditures doesn't just happen by itself. In the next sections we'll look more closely at how this equilibrium comes about.

Try Preview Question 1:

How do we interpret the 45-degree reference line?

Try Preview Question 2:

What does the total planned expenditures curve indicate?

FIGURE 12.4 Combining Consumption and Investment

In part (a), we show the determination of real investment in billions of dollars per year. It occurs where the investment schedule intersects the saving schedule at an interest rate of 5 percent and is equal to $70 billion per year. In part (b), investment is a constant $70 billion per year. When we add this amount to the consumption line, we obtain in part (c) the $C + I$ line, which is vertically higher than the C line by exactly $70 billion. Real national income is equal to $C + I$ at $500 billion per year where total planned expenditure, $C + I$, is equal to actual real national income, for this is where the $C + I$ line intersects the 45-degree reference line, on which $C + I$ is equal to Y at every point.

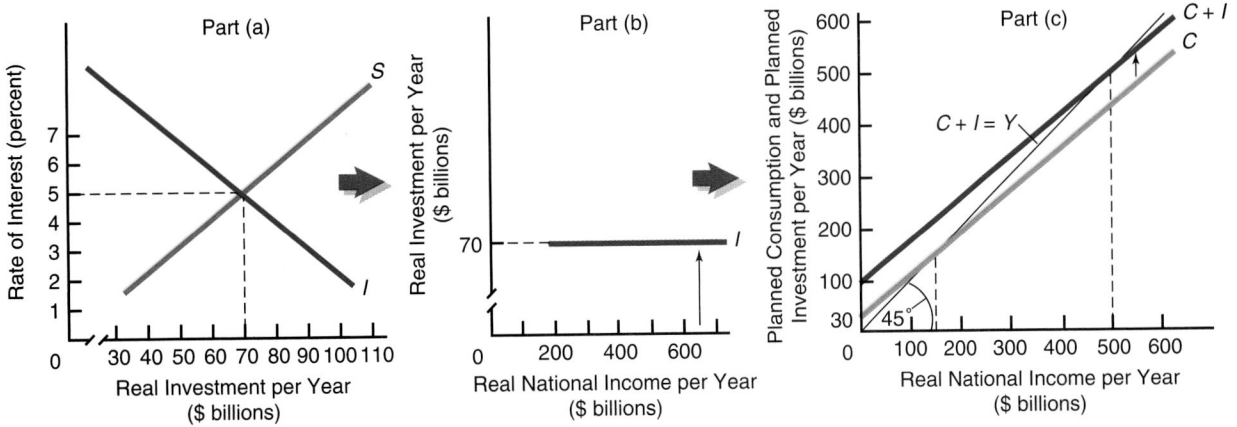

EXAMPLE 12-1   The Cost of Separation

In the referendum of October 30, 1995, 50.6 percent of Quebeckers voted "No" to separation from the rest of Canada. There was much economic and political uncertainty leading up to the referendum, and this was seen in the form of higher interest rates. As we know, when interest rates are relatively high, both consumption and investment fall. What might happen to the Canadian economy if Quebec does vote in the future to separate? While predictions vary from optimistic low-cost to pessimistic high-cost , a middle-of-the-road estimate was given by the Chair of the Bank of Montreal, Matthew Barrett, at the Bank's 1996 annual general meeting. He suggested that the political uncertainty that would follow a "Yes" vote would cause interest rates to rise, possibly to 13 percent. In response, consumption and investment would fall, eventually costing the rest of Canada $150 billion to $200 billion in forgone GDP over the following 5 years. This translates to about $20,000 for every family of four in Canada.

How could we portray this information in terms of Figure 12.4? The rise in interest rates would shift the C curve down (the interest rate effect), thus also shifting the $C + I$ curve down. But the higher interest rates would also lead to reduced investment, shifting the $C + I$ curve down closer to the C curve. This double effect would reduce real national GDP by a significant amount.

For critical analysis: What would happen to consumption and investment in the new independent Quebec?

CONCEPTS IN BRIEF

• We assume that the consumption function has an autonomous part that is independent of the level of real national income per year. It is labelled "autonomous consumption."
• For simplicity, we assume that investment is autonomous with respect to real national income and therefore unrelated to the level of real national income per year.

Keynesian Equilibrium with Government and the Foreign Sector Added

Government

We have to add government spending, G, to our macroeconomic model. We assume that the level of resource-using government purchases of goods and services (federal, provincial, and municipal), *not* including transfer payments, is determined by the political process. In other words, G will be considered autonomous, just like investment (and a certain component of consumption). In Canada, resource-using government expenditures are around 20 percent of real national income. The other side of the coin, of course, is that there are taxes, which are used to pay for much of government spending. We will simplify our model greatly by assuming that there is a constant **lump-sum tax** of $100 billion a year to finance $100 billion of government spending. This lump-sum tax will reduce disposable income and consumption by the same amount. We show this in Table 12.2 (column 2), where we give the numbers for a complete model.

Lump-sum tax A tax that does not depend on income or the circumstances of the taxpayer. An example is a $1,000 tax that every family must pay, irrespective of its economic situation.

TABLE 12.2 The Determination of Equilibrium Real National Income with Net Exports
Figures are billions of dollars.

(1) Real National Income	(2) Taxes	(3) Real Disposable Income	(4) Planned Consumption	(5) Planned Saving	(6) Planned Investment	(7) Government Spending	(8) Net Exports (exports − imports)	(9) Total Planned Expenditures (4)+(6)+(7)+(8)	(10) Unplanned Inventory Changes	(11) Direction of Change in Real National Income
200	100	100	110	−10	70	100	10	290	−90	Increase
250	100	150	150	0	70	100	10	330	−80	Increase
300	100	200	190	10	70	100	10	370	−70	Increase
400	100	300	270	30	70	100	10	450	−50	Increase
500	100	400	350	50	70	100	10	530	−30	Increase
600	100	500	430	70	70	100	10	610	−10	Increase
650	100	550	470	80	70	100	10	650	0	Neither (equilibrium)
700	100	600	510	90	70	100	10	690	+10	Decrease
800	100	700	590	110	70	100	10	770	+30	Decrease

The Foreign Sector

Not a week goes by without a commentary in the media about the size of our foreign trade balance. In some years, our trade balance is positive (the value of exports exceeds the value of imports) while in others it is negative (the value of imports exceeds the value of exports). The difference between exports and imports is *net exports*, which we label X in our graphs. For simplicity, let us assume that exports exceed imports (net exports, X, is positive) and furthermore that the level of net exports is autonomous—independent of national income. Assume a level of X of $10 billion per year. In Table 12.2, net exports is shown in column 8 as $10 billion per year.

In fact, the level of exports depends on international economic conditions, especially in the countries that buy our products. If there is a decline in the foreign exchange value of the Canadian dollar or if our trading partners experience economic growth, they will want to purchase more of our products. If the converse holds true, our exports will fall. We have seen this recently with the economic crisis in Asia. The economies of Japan, South Korea, and several other Asian countries faltered severely, leaving consumers and businesses in those countries less willing to purchase our goods and services. As a result, we saw our own net exports fall. This would be portrayed as a downward shift of our $C + I + G + X$ curve.

The level of imports depends on economic conditions here in Canada. If the foreign exchange value of the Canadian dollar falls, we will purchase fewer of the now more expensive goods and services from other countries. If the federal government raises import taxes or tariffs on imported goods, those goods become more expensive for us to import and we will purchase fewer of them. Since the value of imports is subtracted from the value of exports to find net exports, a *decrease* in the value of imports will *increase* the value of net exports, and vice versa.

Determining the Equilibrium Level of Real National Income per Year

We are now in a position to determine the equilibrium level of real national income per year under the continuing assumptions that the short-run aggregate supply curve is horizontal; that investment, government, and the foreign sector are autonomous; and that planned consumption expenditures are determined by the level of real national income. As can be seen in Table 12.2, total planned expenditures of $650 billion per year equal real national income of $650 billion per year, and this is where we reach equilibrium.

Remember that equilibrium *always* occurs when total planned expenditures equal total production (given that any amount of production in this model in the short run can occur without a change in the price level).

Now look at Figure 12.5, which shows the equilibrium level of real national income. There are two curves, one showing the consumption function, which is the exact duplicate of the one shown in Figure 12.3, and the other being the $C + I + G + X$ curve, which intersects the 45-degree reference line (representing equilibrium) at $650 billion per year.

Whenever total planned expenditures differ from real national income, there are unplanned inventory changes. When total planned expenditures are greater than real national income, inventory levels drop in an unplanned manner. To get them back up, firms seek to expand their production, which increases real national income. Real national income rises towards its equilibrium level. Whenever total planned expenditures are less than real national income, the opposite occurs. There are unplanned inventory increases, causing firms to cut back on their production. The result is a drop in real national income towards the equilibrium level.

FIGURE 12.5 The Equilibrium Level of Real National Income

The consumption function, with no government and thus no taxes, is shown as C. When we add autonomous investment, government, taxes, and net exports, we obtain $C + I + G + X$. We move from E_1 to E_2. The equilibrium level of real national income is $650 billion per year.

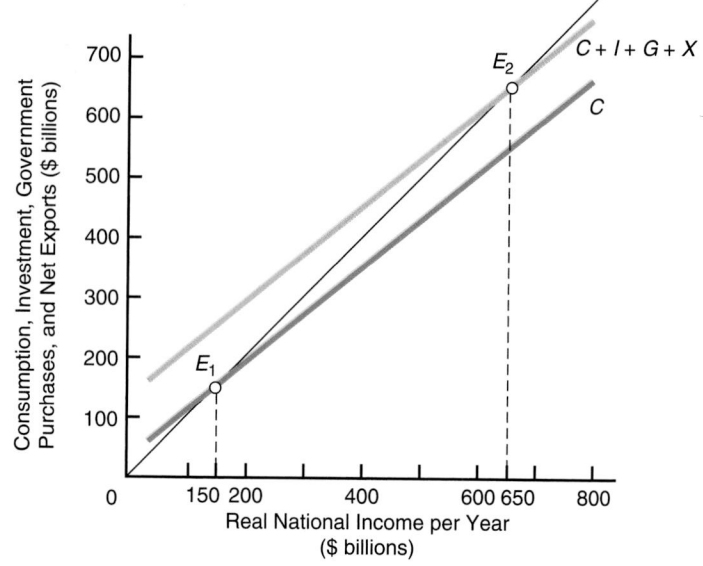

CONCEPTS IN BRIEF

- When we add autonomous investment, I, and autonomous government spending, G, to the consumption function, we obtain the $C + I + G$ curve, which represents total planned expenditures for a closed economy. In an open economy, we add the foreign sector, which consists of exports minus imports, or net exports, X. Total planned expenditures are thus represented by the $C + I + G + X$ curve.
- The equilibrium level of real national income can be found by locating the intersection of the total planned expenditures curve with the 45-degree reference line. At that level of real national income per year, planned consumption plus planned investment plus government expenditures plus net exports will equal real national income.
- Whenever total planned expenditures exceed real national income, there will be unplanned decreases in inventories; the size of the circular flow of income will increase, and a higher level of equilibrium real national income will prevail. Whenever planned expenditures are less than real national income, there will be unplanned increases in inventories; the size of the circular flow will shrink, and a lower equilibrium level of real national income will prevail.

The Multiplier

Look again at part (c) of Figure 12.4. Assume for the moment that the only expenditures included in real national income are consumption expenditures. Where would the equilibrium level of income be in this case? It would be where the consumption function *(C)* intersects the 45-degree reference line, which is at $150 billion per year. Now we add the autonomous amount of planned investment, or $70 billion, and then determine what the new equilibrium level of income will be. It turns out to be $500 billion per year. Adding $70 billion per year of investment spending increased the equilibrium level of income by *five* times that amount, or by $350 billion per year.

Multiplier The ratio of the change in the equilibrium level of real national income to the change in autonomous expenditures; the number by which a change in autonomous investment or autonomous consumption, for example, is multiplied to get the change in the equilibrium level of real national income.

What is operating here is the multiplier effect of changes in autonomous spending. The **multiplier** is the number by which a permanent change in autonomous investment or autonomous consumption is multiplied to get the change in the equilibrium level of real national income. Any permanent increases in autonomous investment or in any autonomous component of consumption will cause an even larger increase in real national income. Any permanent decreases in autonomous spending will cause even larger decreases in the equilibrium level of real national income per year. As a formula, we use the multiplier in the following way:

$$\text{Multiplier} \times \text{change in autonomous spending} =$$
$$\text{change in equilibrium level of real national income}$$

Knowing the multiplier for an economy does two things for us. First, it is a quick method for calculating how changes in autonomous spending will affect the equilibrium in the economy without having to go through the entire procedure of recalculating the equations or tables as we just did. Secondly, it tells us about the *stability* of the economy. A low multiplier implies that the economy will be relatively stable, a high multiplier tells us that we will likely have a much greater degree of variability in the economy. Of course, an economy like Canada's that trades with other countries will reflect the stability of the economy of its major trading partners. In Canada's case, this is the United States.

To understand why this multiple expansion (or contraction) in the equilibrium level of real national income occurs, let's look at a simple numerical example.

We'll use the same figures we used for the marginal propensity to consume and to save. MPC will equal 0.8, or $\frac{4}{5}$, and MPS will equal 0.2, or $\frac{1}{5}$. Now let's run an experiment and say that businesses decide to increase planned investment permanently by $10 billion a year. We see in Table 12.3 that during what we'll call the first round in column 1, investment is increased by $10 billion; this also means an increase in real national income of $10 billion, because the spending by one group represents income for another, shown in column 2. Column 3 gives the resultant increase in consumption by households that received this additional $10 billion in real income. This is found by multiplying the MPC

TABLE 12.3

The Multiplier Process

We trace the effects of a permanent $10 billion increase in autonomous investment spending on the equilibrium level of real national income. If we assume a marginal propensity to consume of 0.8, such an increase will eventually elicit a $50 billion increase in the equilibrium level of real national income per year.

(1) Round	(2) Annual Increase in Real National Income ($ billions per year)	(3) Annual Increase in Planned Consumption ($ billions per year)	(4) Annual Increase in Planned Saving ($ billions per year)
Assumption: MPC = 0.8, or $\frac{4}{5}$			
1 ($10 billion per year increase in *I*)	10.00	8.000	2.000
2	8.00	6.400	1.600
3	6.40	5.120	1.280
4	5.12	4.096	1.024
5	4.09	3.277	0.819
.	.	.	.
.	.	.	.
.	.	.	.
All later rounds	16.38	13.107	3.277
Totals (*C + I + G*)	50.00	40.000	10.000

by the increase in real income. Because the MPC equals 0.8, consumption expenditures during the first round will increase by $8 billion.

But that's not the end of the story. This additional household consumption is also spending, and it will provide $8 billion of additional real income for other individuals. Thus during the second round, we see an increase in real income of $8 billion. Now, out of this increased real income, what will be the resultant increase in consumption expenditures? It will be 0.8 times $8 billion, or $6.4 billion. We continue these induced expenditure rounds *ad infinitum* and find that because of an initial increase in autonomous investment expenditures of $10 billion, the equilibrium level of real national income has increased by $50 billion. A permanent $10 billion increase in autonomous investment spending has induced an additional $40 billion increase in consumption spending, for a total increase in real national income of $50 billion. In other words, the equilibrium level of real national income has changed by an amount equal to five times the change in investment.

The Multiplier Formula

So where does the multiplier number come from? The multiplier effect depends on income received by one group being spent on goods and services produced by another group, in the way we just described. In that example, for each dollar received, 80¢ was passed on in a new round of spending, reflecting the circular nature of the economy that we studied in Chapter 8. Suppose now, instead of 80¢, that only 50¢ of each additional dollar had been passed on. In that case, the value of each round would be substantially smaller because more money would "leak" out from the circular flow as saving, and we would end up with a much smaller multiplier.

In addition to saving, there are two other such "leakages" from an economy, imports and taxes. When money is paid to purchase foreign-made goods, obviously that does not pass on income to Canadian producers, but instead to foreign producers. In the same way, taxes remove money from the economy. The higher the proportion of such leakages of each additional dollar in each round of spending, the smaller is the multiplier.

In general, the multiplier can be calculated as the *reciprocal of the proportion of leakages*, or:

$$\text{Multiplier} = \frac{1}{\text{proportion of leakages}}$$

In our first simple model, the MPC was $\frac{4}{5}$; therefore, because MPC + MPS = 1, the MPS was equal to $\frac{1}{5}$. The reciprocal is 5. That was our multiplier. A $10 billion increase in planned investment led to a $50 billion increase in the equilibrium level of real income. Our multiplier in such simple models would be:

$$\text{Multiplier} \equiv \frac{1}{1 - \text{MPC}} \equiv \frac{1}{\text{MPS}}$$

Let's examine some more cases. If MPS = $\frac{1}{4}$,

$$\text{Multiplier} = \frac{1}{\frac{1}{4}} = 4$$

Now let's add imports as another leakage into our models. Look back at Table 12.2 and, instead of a constant net export level of $10 billion, assume that exports are constant at $140 billion, and imports are equal to 20 percent of real GDP. This means that we

Marginal propensity to import The ratio of the change in imports to the change in real national income.

are spending 20 percent of our additional income on imports. This ratio of the change in imports to the change in national income is called the **marginal propensity to import**.

The equilibrium value for the economy in this example will still remain at $650 billion. However, if you work through this example, you will see that since the multiplier is the reciprocal of the proportion of leakages, it will be much smaller. In this case:

$$\text{Multiplier} = \frac{1}{\text{proportion of leakages}} = \frac{1}{\text{MPS} + \text{MPM}} = \frac{1}{0.2 + 0.2} = \frac{1}{0.4} = 2.5$$

Since we have doubled our leakages from the economy, our multiplier has been halved. In the same way, adding taxes that depend on national income (such as income or sales taxes) will also reduce the multiplier.

By taking a few numerical examples, you can demonstrate to yourself an important property of the multiplier:

The smaller the marginal propensity to save, the larger the multiplier.

The smaller the marginal propensity to import, the larger the multiplier.

The lower the marginal income tax rate, the larger the multiplier.

Try Preview Question 3:

What is the concept of the multiplier, how does it work, and what is its main determinant?

The multiplier, as we have mentioned, works for a permanent increase or permanent decrease in autonomous spending. In our earlier example, if the autonomous component of consumption had fallen by $10 billion, the reduction in the equilibrium level of real national income per year would have been $50 billion per year with our simple model. With a marginal propensity to import of 0.2 added in, the multiplier will only be 2.5, so a $10 billion decline in autonomous consumption will only reduce real national income per year by $25 billion. See Example 12-2, below, for a discussion of Canada's multiplier.

EXAMPLE 12-2   Estimating Actual Multipliers

Multipliers are very much a reflection of the kind of economy that a country has. In Canada, we have a relatively small multiplier. Estimates of the multiplier range from 1.0 to 1.9. The value of the multiplier changes with time as the proportion of leakages changes. Because of the rising proportion of imports to Canada (approaching 40 percent of GDP), the value of the multiplier in Canada has fallen in recent years. In the United States, the multiplier is estimated at a value around 2.0, primarily because the United States imports a much smaller proportion of goods (about 10 percent of GDP) than Canada and has generally lower savings and marginal tax rates.

For critical analysis: Which country would you expect to have a higher multiplier—Germany or Holland? Explain.

Significance of the Multiplier

Depending on the size of the multiplier, it is possible that a relatively small change in planned investment or autonomous consumption can trigger a much larger change in the equilibrium level of real national income per year. In essence, the multiplier magnifies the fluctuations in the equilibrium level of real national income initiated by changes in autonomous spending.

As was just stated, the larger the marginal propensity to consume, the larger the multiplier. If the marginal propensity to consume is $\frac{1}{2}$, the multiplier is 2. In that case, a $1 billion decrease in (autonomous) investment will elicit a $2 billion decrease in the equilibrium level of real national income per year. Conversely, if the marginal propensity to consume is $\frac{9}{10}$, the multiplier will be 10. That same $1 billion decrease in planned investment expenditures with a multiplier of 10 will lead to a $10 billion decrease in the equilibrium level of real national income per year.

EXAMPLE 12-3   Changes in Investment and The Great Depression

Changes in autonomous spending lead to shifts in the total expenditures $(C + I + G + X)$ curve and, as you have seen, cause a multiplier effect on the equilibrium level of real GDP per year. A classic example apparently occurred during the Great Depression. Indeed, some economists believe that it was an autonomous downward shift (collapse) in the investment function that provoked the Great Depression. Look at part (a) of Figure 12.6. There you see the net investment in Canada from 1929 to 1941 (expressed in 1986 dollars). Clearly, during business contractions, decision makers in the business world can and do decide to postpone long-range investment plans for buildings and equipment. This causes the business recovery to be weak unless those business plans are revised. If you examine real GDP in part (b) of Figure 12.6, you see

FIGURE 12.6 Net Private Domestic Investment and Real GDP During the Great Depression

In part (a), you see how net private investment expressed in billions of 1986 dollars declined starting in 1930 and continued to decline for several years. It started to increase in 1934, although it declined again in 1936. Look at part (b). There you see how changes in GDP seem to mirror changes in net private domestic investment.

Source: Adapted from Statistics Canada, CANSIM Database Series.

Part (a)

Year	Net Private Domestic Investment (billions of 1986 dollars)
1929	10.08
1930	8.33
1931	4.43
1932	1.71
1933	1.04
1934	2.82
1935	3.79
1936	3.53
1937	5.93
1938	6.13
1939	7.97
1940	9.40
1941	10.31

Part (b)

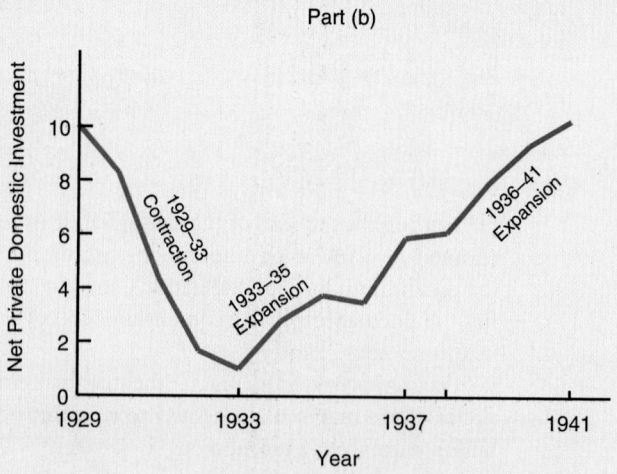

that the contraction that started in 1929 reached its trough in 1933. The expansion was relatively strong for the following five years, but then strengthened dramatically as the economy geared up to fight World War II. Some researchers argue that had World War II not occurred when it did, the Canadian economy would have remained weak, since business would have had no reason to revise their investment plans upward.

For critical analysis: Relatively speaking, how healthy was the national economy in 1941? (Hint: Look at part (b) of Figure 12.6.)

The Multiplier Effect When the Price Level Can Change

Clearly, the multiplier effect on the equilibrium overall level of *real* national income will not be as great if part of the increase in *nominal* national income occurs because of increases in the price level. We show this in Figure 12.7. The intersection of AD_1 and *SRAS* is at a price level of 120 with equilibrium real national income of $500 billion per year. An increase in autonomous spending shifts the aggregate demand curve outward to the right to AD_2. If price level remained at 120, the short-run equilibrium level of real GDP would increase to $550 billion per year because, for the $10 billion increase in autonomous spending, the multiplier would be 5, as it was in Table 12.3. But the price level does not stay fixed because ordinarily *SRAS* is positively sloped. In this diagram, the new short-run equilibrium level of real national income is hypothetically $530 billion of real national income per year. Instead of the multiplier being 5, the multiplier with respect to the equilibrium changes in the output of real goods and services—real national income—is only 3. The multiplier is smaller because part of the additional income is used to pay higher prices; not all is spent on increased output, as is the case when the price level is fixed.

If the economy is at an equilibrium level of real national income that is greater than *LRAS*, the implications for the multiplier are even more severe. Look again at Figure 12.7.

FIGURE 12.7 Multiplier Effect on Equilibrium of Real National Income

A $10 billion increase in autonomous spending (investment, government, or net exports), which moves AD_1 to AD_2, will yield a full multiplier effect only if prices are constant. If the price index increases from 120 to 125, the multiplier effect is less, and the equilibrium level of real national income goes up only to, say, $530 billion per year instead of $550 billion per year.

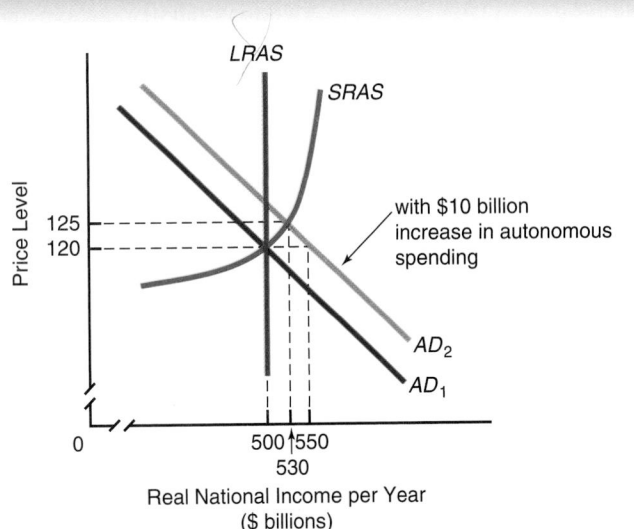

The *SRAS* curve starts to slope upward more dramatically after $500 billion of real national income per year. Therefore, any increase in aggregate demand will lead to a proportionally greater increase in the price level and a smaller increase in the equilibrium level of real national income per year. The multiplier effect of any increase in autonomous spending will be relatively small because most of the changes will be in the price level. Moreover, any increase in the short-run equilibrium level of real national income will tend to be temporary because the economy is temporarily above *LRAS*—the strain on its productive capacity will raise prices.

The Relationship Between Aggregate Demand and the Total Planned Expenditures Curve

There is clearly a relationship between the aggregate demand curves that you studied in Chapters 10 and 11 and the total planned expenditures curve developed in this chapter. After all, aggregate demand consists of consumption, investment, and government purchases, plus the foreign sector of our economy. There is a major difference, however, between the aggregate demand curve, *AD,* and the total planned expenditures curve: The latter is drawn with the price level held constant, whereas the former is drawn, by definition, with the price level changing. In other words, the total planned expenditures curve shown in Figure 12.5 is drawn with the price level fixed. To derive the aggregate demand curve, we must now allow the price level to change. Look at the upper part of Figure 12.8. Here we show the total planned expenditures curve at a price level equal to 100 and equilibrium at $800 billion of income per year. This gives us point *A* in the lower graph, for it shows what real income would be at a price level of 100.

Now let's assume that in the upper graph, the price level doubles to 200. What are the effects?

1. A higher price level can decrease the purchasing power of any cash that people hold (the real-balance effect). This is a decrease in real wealth, and it causes consumption expenditures, *C,* to fall, thereby putting downward pressure on the total planned expenditures curve.
2. Because individuals attempt to borrow more to replenish their real cash balances, interest rates will rise, which will make it more costly for people to buy houses and cars (the interest rate effect). Higher interest rates make it more costly, for example, to install new equipment and to erect new buildings. Therefore, the rise in the price level indirectly causes a reduction in the quantity of aggregate goods and services demanded.
3. In an open economy, our higher price level causes the foreign demand for our goods to fall (the open economy effect). Simultaneously, it increases our demand for others' goods. If the foreign exchange price of the dollar stays constant for a while, there will be an increase in imports and a decrease in exports, thereby reducing the size of *X,* again putting downward pressure on the total planned expenditures curve. The result is that a new total planned expenditures curve at a price level equal to 200 generates an equilibrium at E_2 at $600 billion of real income per year. This gives us point *B* in the lower part of Figure 12.8. When we connect points *A* and *B*, we obtain the aggregate demand curve, *AD.*

Table 12.4 sets out some of the non-price factors that will change total planned expenditure and therefore affect aggregate demand.

Try Preview Question 4:

What might cause shifts in the total planned expenditures curve?

FIGURE 12.8 The Relationship Between _AD_ and the Total Planned Expenditures Curve

In the upper graph, the total planned expenditures curve at a price level equal to 100 intersects the 45-degree reference line at E_1, or $800 billion of real income per year. That gives us point _A_ (price level = 100; real income = $800 billion) in the lower graph. When the price level increases to 200, the total planned expenditures curve shifts downward, and the new equilibrium level of real income is at E_2 at $600 billion per year. This gives us point _B_ in the lower graph. Connecting points _A_ and _B_, we obtain the aggregate demand curve.

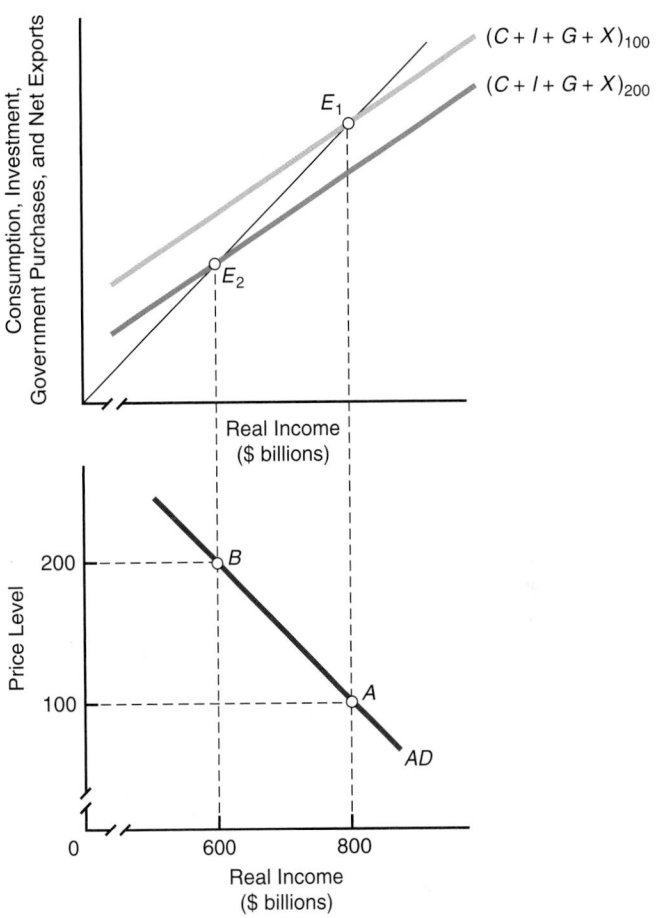

TABLE 12.4

Non-Price Factors That Affect Aggregate Demand

Changes in consumption, investment, government expenditure, and net exports can increase or decrease aggregate demand.

Increases Aggregate Demand	Decreases Aggregate Demand
Consumption	
• rise in level of personal wealth	• fall in level of personal wealth
• fall in personal taxes	• rise in personal taxes
• fall in personal level of debt	• rise in personal level of debt
• more optimistic expectations about the economy	• less optimistic expectations about the economy
Investment	
• fall in real interest rates	• rise in real interest rates
• decrease in business taxes	• increase in business taxes
• more optimistic expectations of profitability	• less optimistic expectations of profitability
Government	
• more spending in the economy	• less spending in the economy
Net Exports	
• decrease in value of the Canadian dollar	• increase in value of the Canadian dollar
• increase in value of our trading partners' currency	• decrease in value of our trading partners' currency
• increase in our trading partners' GDP	• decrease in our trading partners' GDP
• decrease in Canadian import taxes	• increase in Canadian import taxes

Concepts in Brief

- Any change in autonomous spending shifts the expenditure curve and causes a multiplier effect on the equilibrium level of real national income per year.
- The multiplier is equal to the reciprocal of the proportion of leakages.
- The larger the marginal propensity to save, the marginal propensity to import, or the marginal income tax rates, the smaller the multiplier.
- The total planned expenditures curve is drawn with the price level held constant, whereas the *AD* curve allows the price level to change. Each different price level generates a new total planned expenditures curve.

NETNOMICS

The Internet is Making Investment a Fuzzier Concept

Internet software, like all computer software, can last for a long time. This is why the government now counts business software expenditures as investment spending, classifying these expenditures as equivalent to spending on the computers and high-speed communications equipment that are the nuts and bolts of the Internet.

Some economists are now having second thoughts about this classification of software. Currently, most businesses purchase new or updated software for on-site installation on the hard drives of office computers. Sun Microsystems and other companies, however, are championing a new approach to computer software distribution that would fundamentally change how businesses use software. In this proposed model for computer operations, businesses would no longer store software on hard drives. Instead, companies would pay monthly or annual fees to software providers in exchange for real-time access to computer operating systems, word processing software, and computer spreadsheet programs directly from the Internet. The Internet-based providers of these new "software services" would automatically update the software as often as new versions became available.

Currently, fees that companies pay for services rendered are costs of doing business and are not counted as investment. Even though there is no *functional* distinction between software stored on a hard drive for months or years and software accessed in real time on the Internet for a while, the new approach to measuring investment makes a distinction: Spending on software that businesses purchase and store on hard drives is investment, but fees paid for real-time computer operations using software downloaded from the Internet are a short-term cost of doing business. It remains to be seen how government statisticians will deal with this new wrinkle.

ISSUES AND APPLICATIONS | Can Stock Market Crashes Affect the Economy?

Concepts Applied: Expectations, multiplier, investment

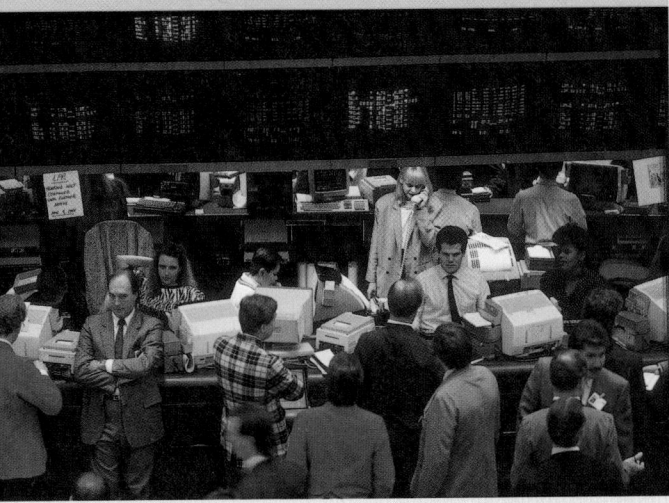

Business and consumer confidence is very important in determining national income.

Stock market crashes of the kind that occurred in October 2000 are rare, and cause considerable consternation in the business world. A similar crash occurred in 1987, and the most famous crash occurred in October 1929. Yet, such crashes do not always result in recession or depressions. The 1987 stock market declines were not followed by a recession. As one forecaster put it, "stock market crashes have predicted 7 of the last 4 recessions." So what is the link between the stock market and the economy?

Linking Stock Markets and Economic Investment

The linkage between the financial investment that occurs and the real investment that economists talk about is fairly straightforward. Businesses use the financial instruments that are sold on the stock markets (such as bonds and shares) to raise money for their operations. These instruments are all different forms of borrowing. Typically, the money raised from the sale of these instruments is used to buy capital equipment or to invest in new products and is especially important for new businesses. When financial investors are con-

fident about the growth of the economy and the ability of the firms to repay their loans, they are much more likely to lend their money. In some cases, lending this money to these firms will reap very high returns, as the companies can often quickly grow and prosper. The value that the financial investors put on these stocks and bonds is a reflection of the expectations that they have for the companies.

The Importance of Business Expectations

A stock market crash is a sign that expectations about the future have dramatically changed, sometimes because of a single event. In the October 2000 crash, the major change in expectations occurred when Nortel Networks announced that it did not meet all of the growth in sales and profitability that the market had expected. Because of this change in expectations in a company that was experiencing a very high growth rate, many investors changed their minds about the value of its shares, and sold them. Because this change was experienced in only one company and, in general, limited largely to one sector, expectations for other firms were not much affected. While information technology firms experienced greater difficulty in raising new money for their operations, the expectations for the rest of the economy did not change much.

Consumers Expectations Matter as Well

Consumers experience two different "hits" to their pocketbooks when stock markets decline. They experience a tremendous loss of wealth because of the decline in the stock market, and so may stop spending as much in the economy. If a recession does follow, then many will become unemployed. Unemployed people have much less money for purchasing housing, and so residential construction is usually affected. These declines in investment and in consumption expenditure (and net exports if the phenomenon is worldwide), are all magnified because of the multiplier effect.

The Crash of 1929

Let's briefly review what happened in 1929 to illustrate how a stock market crash can be part of a bigger picture of decline in the economy. Following the famous stock market crash of October 1929 and the subsequent failure of 1/3 of the banks in the United States (although none went bankrupt in Canada) investment expenditure dropped nearly 75 percent of its total from the peak in 1929. (This is shown in Figure 12-6.) This was the largest percentage drop in any category of expenditure in the economy during that period, and a reflection of the deep decline in confidence about the economy. Indeed, the economy did not recover to its 1929 levels until a decade later.

This loss of confidence in the future created a dramatic drop in investment in all categories of investment, residential construction, non-residential construction and equipment and machinery. Businesses who couldn't use their existing equipment saw no need to buy more. With a shattered business confidence, and the subsequent decline in consumer spending, the country had to live through a very difficult period.

For Critical Analysis

1. How would a decline in business confidence affect the planned investment schedule in Figure 12.2? Explain your answer and draw a graph to illustrate.

2. How would a decline in confidence affect the consumption function as drawn in Figure 12.3? Explain how it might affect both autonomous expenditure and the MPC. What effect might this have on the multiplier?

CHAPTER SUMMARY

1. If we assume that there are large amounts of excess capacity and labour unemployment, we can use the horizontal portion of the short-run aggregate supply curve. Therefore, prices are assumed to be constant, and nominal values are equivalent to real values.

2. A consumption function, in its simplest form, shows that current real consumption is directly related to current real disposable income. The complement of a consumption function is a saving function. A saving function shows the relationship between current real saving and current real disposable income.

3. The marginal propensity to consume shows how much additional income is devoted to consumption. The marginal propensity to save is the difference between 1 and the marginal propensity to consume. Otherwise stated, the marginal propensity to save plus the marginal propensity to consume must equal 1.

4. We must be careful to distinguish between average and marginal propensities. The average propensity to consume is the amount of total real consumption divided by total real disposable income. The average propensity to save is the total amount of real saving divided by total real disposable income. The marginal propensities relate to changes in consumption and saving resulting from changes in income.

5. Some nonincome determinants of planned consumption are wealth, expectations, and population.

6. Investment is made by the business sector of the economy. Investment is the spending by businesses on such things as new machines and buildings that can be used later in the production of goods and services. Investment is the use of resources to provide for future production. There are numerous determinants of investment, including the rate of interest, changes in expectations, innovation and technology, and business taxes.

7. When we add the consumption function, autonomous investment, autonomous government spending, and the autonomous net exports function, we obtain the total planned expenditures curve, which gives us total planned expenditures per year. The equilibrium level of real national income occurs where the total planned expenditures curve intersects the 45-degree reference line, or where total planned expenditures exactly equal real national income (total production).

8. When total planned expenditures exceed real national income, inventories will be drawn down more rapidly than planned. As a result, firms will expand production and, in the process, hire more workers, thus leading to an increase in output and employment. The opposite occurs when total planned expenditures are less than real national income.

9. Because of the circular flow that occurs in the economy, changes in autonomous spending are magnified into larger changes in equilibrium national income. This multiplier effect is positively related to the proportion of income that is passed on to domestic producers, and therefore negatively related to the proportion of money that "leaks out" in each round. The three types of leakages that occur are savings, imports, and taxes. The multiplier can be calculated for any Keynesian equilibrium model as the reciprocal of the proportion of leakages in the circular flow. If 30 percent of income leaks out, and only 70 percent is respent in the economy, then the multiplier is 1/0.3 = 3.33.

The multiplier effect is less in an aggregate demand model because part of the increase in spending will result in higher prices instead of higher real output.

10. The total planned expenditures function is related to the *AD* function through price level changes. A shift up in the total planned expenditures function due to a price level decrease represents a movement down along the *AD* curve. Conversely, a shift down of the total planned expenditures function due to a price level increase represents a movement up along the *AD* curve.

DISCUSSION OF PREVIEW QUESTIONS

1. How do we interpret the 45-degree reference line?

Because the 45-degree reference line bisects the total planned expenditures/real national income quadrant, total planned expenditures *exactly* equal real national income at all points on this line. Hence equilibrium is possible at any point on the 45-degree reference line.

2. What does the total planned expenditures curve indicate?

The total planned expenditures curve indicates what the community intends to spend at every level of real national income. In a closed (omitting international transactions), private (omitting government transactions) economy, the total planned expenditures curve equals the value of consumption expenditures plus the value of investment expenditures at every level of real national income.

3. What is the concept of the multiplier, how does it work, and what is its main determinant?

The multiplier concept says, simply, that a $1 shift in the total planned expenditures curve will cause the equilibrium level of national income to change by more than $1. In particular, a $1 increase (shift upward) in the total planned expenditures curve will cause the equilibrium level of national income to rise by more than $1; a $1 decrease (shift downward) in the total planned expenditures curve will cause the equilibrium level of national income to fall by more than $1. In a closed, private economy, changes (shifts) in the total planned expenditures curve are caused by changes (shifts) in autonomous consumption and autonomous investment.

Let's take an example. Suppose that we start from an equilibrium position and then autonomous net investment rises by $1 due to an increase in the output and sale of one machine priced at $1. The people who produced this machine receive an extra $1 in income (above last year's income). Thus income already rises by $1 in the first round. The people who produced the machine will spend some of the increase in their income and save some of it. Because one person's expenditure is another's income, income will rise again. Thus, if 75 cents of every dollar is spent on domestic goods, and 25 cents is saved, taxed, or spent on foreign imports, the group that received the $1 increase in income will in turn create 75 cents of income for a subsequent group. Note that after two rounds, national income has already increased by $1.75 ($1 + $0.75); we already have a multiplier effect. Moreover, there is no reason this process should stop here; the people who just received an increase in income of 75 cents will spend some and save some. The amount they spend becomes income for others. Thus the multiplier effect exists because increases in income lead to increases in expenditures, which in turn lead to further income increases. Because one person's expenditure is another's income, it follows that the less that leaks out of the circular flow, the more the equilibrium level of income will change for given changes in autonomous expenditures.

4. What might cause shifts in the total planned expenditures curve?

In our model, total planned expenditures equal consumption *(C)*, investment *(I)*, government purchases of goods and services *(G)*, and net exports *(X)*. For simplicity, we have made the last three components of total planned expenditures autonomous—that is, independent of the level of real disposable income. Consumption also has an autonomous component. Therefore, any change in the nonincome determinants of consumption—for example, changes in expectations—will shift the total planned expenditures curve. Furthermore, because *I*, *G*, and *X* are all considered autonomous, any change in those functions will also shift the total planned expenditures curve.

PROBLEMS

(Answers to the odd-numbered problems appear at the back of the book.)

12-1. Complete the accompanying table.

  a. Plot the consumption and saving schedules on graph paper.

  b. Determine the marginal propensity to consume and the marginal propensity to save.

  c. Determine the average propensity to consume and the average propensity to save for each level of income.

Disposable Income	Consumption	Saving
$ 500	$510	$_____
600	600	_____
700	690	_____
800	780	_____
900	870	_____
1,000	960	_____

12-2. Make a list of determinants, other than income, that might affect your personal MPC.

12-3. List each of the following under the heading "Stock" or "Flow."

  a. The Chens have $100 of savings in the bank.

  b. Smith earns $200 per week.

  c. Labatt's Breweries owns 2,000 trucks.

  d. Inventories rise at 400 units per year.

  e. Brochu consumes $80 per week out of income.

  f. The equilibrium quantity is 1,000 per day.

  g. The corporation spends $1 billion per year on investments.

12-4. The rate of return on an investment on new machinery is 9 percent.

  a. If the market interest rate is 9.5 percent, will the investment be carried out?

  b. If the interest rate is 8 percent, will the machinery be purchased?

  c. If the interest rate is 9 percent, will the machinery be purchased?

12-5. The data in the table below apply to a hypothetical economy. Assume that the marginal propensity to consume is constant at all levels of income. Further assume that investment is autonomous.

Real National Income	Consumption Expenditures	Saving	Investment	APC	APS	MPC	MPS
$1,000	$1,100	$_____	$100	_____	_____	_____	_____
2,000	2,000	_____		_____	_____	_____	_____
3,000		_____		_____	_____	_____	_____
4,000		_____		_____	_____	_____	_____
5,000		_____		_____	_____	_____	_____
6,000		_____		_____	_____	_____	_____

a. Draw a graph of the consumption function. Then add the investment function, giving you $C + I$.

b. Right under the first graph, draw in the saving and investment curves. Does the $C + I$ curve intersect the 45-degree line in the upper graph at the same level of real national income as where saving equals investment in the lower graph? (If not, redraw your graphs.)

c. What is the multiplier effect from the inclusion of investment?

d. What is the numerical value of the multiplier?

e. What is the equilibrium level of real national income and output without investment? With investment?

f. What will happen to income if autonomous investment increases by $100?

g. What will the equilibrium level of real national income be if autonomous consumption increases by $100?

12-6. Assume a closed, private economy.

a. If the MPC = 0, what is the multiplier?

b. What is the multiplier if the MPC = $\frac{1}{2}$? If the MPC = $\frac{3}{4}$? If the MPC = $\frac{9}{10}$? If the MPC = 1?

c. What happens to the multiplier as the MPC rises?

d. In what range does the multiplier fall?

12-7. Calculate the multiplier for the following cases:

a. MPC = 0.9, MPM = 0.2, Income tax rate = 0.1

b. MPS = 0.2, MPM = 0.0, Income tax rate = 0.3

c. MPS = 0.1, MPM = 0.4, Income tax rate = 0.2

12-8. What component of the Canadian total planned expenditures curve will the following events affect, and will these events lead to an increase or a decrease in our aggregate demand?

a. Japan recovers from its economic crisis and consumers start to spend again.

b. The federal government pays out $3 million in scholarships to post-secondary students.

c. Because of the low value of the Canadian dollar, Canadians take their summer holidays in Canada instead of in other countries.

d. Low inflation during the last quarter causes the Bank of Canada to reduce its interest rates.

12-9. Suppose that the European Union decides to place a ban on many Canadian products. What effect will this have on net exports? How will this shift the total planned expenditures curve? What will happen to real GDP? Draw this situation in a diagram.

12-10. (More advanced) Suppose that we have a consumption function given as:

$$C = 50 + 0.6 (Y - T)$$

where T = taxes, set at 100 billion, and the remaining expenditures are given by $I + G + X = 350$. Everything is measured in billions of dollars.

a. Find the equilibrium value for real GDP.

b. Suppose T is increased to 110. What happens to real GDP?

c. Now decrease T to 80. What happens to real GDP?

d. How would you forecast real GDP and its relationship to taxes, knowing these outcomes?

ECONOMICS ON THE NET

Business Leading Indicators

Internet URL: http://www.statcan.ca/english/

Navigation: Start by navigating to the Statistics Canada page. Call up the Business Leading Indicators matrix 193, and download the data for the TSE 300 index series D100040.

Application: Plot the information on a graph, and note the peaks and valleys of the TSE. Now compare this to the data in Figure 7.9. How do the movements of the stock market relate to the movements of the economy through the business cycle?

PPENDIX B

THE KEYNESIAN CROSS AND THE MULTIPLIER

We can see the multiplier effect more clearly if we look at Figure B-1, in which we see only a small section of the graphs that we used in Chapter 12. We start with an equilibrium level of real national income of $650 billion per year. This equilibrium occurs with total planned expenditures represented by $C + I + G + X$. The $C + I + G + X$ curve intersects the 45-degree reference line at $650 billion per year. Now we increase investment, I, by $10 billion. This increase in investment shifts the entire $C + I + G + X$ curve vertically to $C + I + G + X$. The vertical shift represents that $10 billion increase in autonomous investment. With the higher level of planned expenditures per year, we are no longer in equilibrium at E. Inventories are falling. Production will increase. Eventually, planned production will catch up with total planned expenditures. The new equilibrium level of real national income is established at E at the intersection of the new $C + I + G + X$ curve and the 45-degree reference line, along which $C + I + G + X = Y$ (total planned expenditures equal real national income). The new equilibrium level of real national income is $700 billion per year. Thus the increase in equilibrium real national income is equal to five times the permanent increase in planned investment spending.

FIGURE B-1 Graphing the Multiplier

We can translate Table 12.3 into graphic form by looking at each successive round of additional spending induced by an autonomous increase in planned investment of $10 billion. The total planned expenditures curve shifts from $C + I + G + X$, with its associated equilibrium level of real national income of $650 billion, to a new curve labelled $C + I' + G + X$. The new equilibrium level of real national income is $700 billion. Equilibrium is again established.

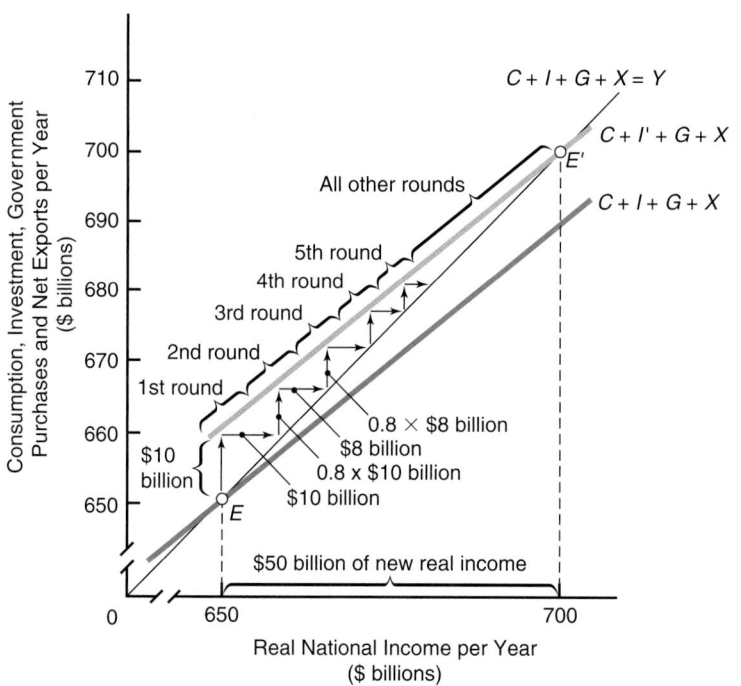

FISCAL POLICY

Since the creation of Canada, there has been a system of government, the purpose of which is "to make laws for the Peace, Order, and good Government of Canada." However, the role of that government has grown immensely since Confederation, and today the government's role in the economy is much greater than it was in 1867. In fact, the economic role of the government is much greater now than it was before the Second World War. Combined government spending and transfers account for about 40 percent of GDP, and that is substantially more than Canadians spent even 25 years ago. The effect of the government's role in the economy through its fiscal policies is the topic of this chapter.

PREVIEW QUESTIONS

1. What is fiscal policy?

2. How does the crowding-out effect tend to offset expansionary fiscal policy?

3. What types of time lags exist between the need for fiscal stimulus and the time when such stimulus actually affects the national economy?

4. What is automatic fiscal policy, and how does it lend stability to an economy?

Fiscal policy The discretionary changing of government expenditures and/or taxes in order to achieve national economic goals, such as high employment with price stability.

DID YOU KNOW THAT... the first type of income tax was probably established in the 1200s and 1300s during times of war in the Italian city-states? Canada's first income tax, introduced in 1917 to help pay for World War I, ranged from 1 percent on incomes over $2,000 a year to 6.6 percent on incomes over $20,000 per year. Two years later it was raised so that the bottom rate was 1.3 percent on incomes over $1,500, and the top rate was 10.7 percent on incomes over $20,000. At first the government promised the tax would be temporary; hence its name—"Dominion Income War Tax." Today, federal income taxes are taken for granted. More important for this chapter, the federal tax system is now viewed as being capable of affecting the equilibrium level of real GDP. On the spending side of the budget, changes in the federal government's expenditures are also viewed as potentially capable of changing the equilibrium level of real GDP.

Fiscal Policy

Deliberate, discretionary changes in government expenditures and/or taxes in order to achieve certain national economic goals is the realm of **fiscal policy**. Some national goals are high employment (low unemployment), price stability, economic growth, and improvement in the nation's international payments balance. Fiscal policy can be thought of as a deliberate attempt to cause the economy to move to full employment and price stability more quickly than it otherwise might.

Fiscal policy has typically been associated with the economic theories of John Maynard Keynes and what is now called *traditional* Keynesian analysis. Recall from Chapter 11 that Keynes' explanation of the Great Depression was that there was insufficient aggregate demand. Because he believed that wages and prices were "sticky downward," he argued that the classical economists' view of the economy automatically moving towards full employment was inaccurate. To Keynes and his followers, government had to step in to increase aggregate demand. In other words, expansionary fiscal policy initiated by the federal government was the way to ward off recessions and depressions.

Traditional Keynesian economics dominated academic and government policymaking debates (and often actions) in the 1960s and 1970s. The federal budget of 1973, for example, was expressly focused on halting rising unemployment. In true Keynesian fashion, taxes were cut and government expenditures increased in the hope of "kickstarting" the economy.

Changes in Government Spending

Recall that in Chapter 10 (Figures 10.8 and 10.9), we looked at the contractionary gap and the expansionary gap. The former was defined as the amount by which the current level of real GDP fell short of how much the economy could be producing if it were operating on its *LRAS*. The latter was defined as the amount by which the equilibrium level of real GDP exceeds the long-run equilibrium level as given by *LRAS*. In this section we examine fiscal policy in the context of a contractionary gap.

WHEN THERE IS A CONTRACTIONARY GAP. The government, along with firms, individuals, and foreigners, is one of the spending agents in the economy. When the government decides to spend more, all other things held constant, the dollar value of total spending must rise. Look at part (a) of Figure 13.1. We start at short-run equilibrium with AD_1 intersecting *SRAS* at $650 billion of real GDP per year. There is a contractionary gap of $50 billion of real GDP per year—the difference between *LRAS* (the economy's long-run potential) and the short-run equilibrium level of real GDP per year. When the government decides to spend more, the aggregate demand curve shifts to the right to AD_2. Here we assume that the government knows exactly how much more to spend so that AD_2

FIGURE 13.1 Expansionary Fiscal Policy: Two Scenarios

If there is a contractionary gap and equilibrium is at E_1 in part (a), fiscal policy can increase aggregate demand to AD_2. The new equilibrium is at E_2 at higher real GDP per year and a higher price level. If, though, we are already on LRAS as in part (b), expansionary fiscal policy will simply lead to a temporary equilibrium at E_2 and a final equilibrium at E_3, again at LRAS of $700 billion of real GDP per year but at a higher price level of 135.

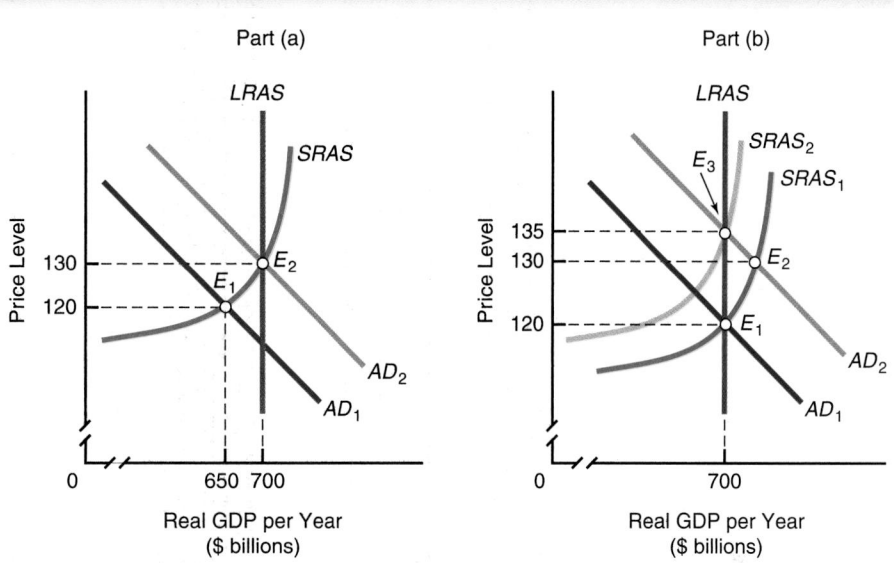

intersects *SRAS* at $700 billion, or at *LRAS*. Because of the upward-sloping *SRAS*, the price level has risen from 120 to 130. Real GDP has gone to $700 billion per year. (Nominal GDP has gone up by even more because it consists of the price level index times real GDP. Here the GDP deflator has gone up by 10 ÷ 120 = 8.33 percent.)[1]

WHEN THE ECONOMY IS OPERATING ON ITS LRAS. Suppose that the economy is operating on *LRAS*, as in part (b) of Figure 13.1. An increase in government spending shifts the aggregate demand curve from AD_1 to AD_2. Both prices and real output of goods and services begin to rise towards the intersection of E_2. But this rate of real GDP per year is untenable in the long run because it exceeds *LRAS*. In the long run, expectations of input owners—workers, owners of capital and raw materials, and so on—are revised. The short-run aggregate supply curve shifts from $SRAS_1$ to $SRAS_2$ because of higher prices and higher resource costs. Real GDP returns to the *LRAS* level of $700 billion per year. The full impact of the increased government expenditures is on the price level only, which increases to 135. Therefore, an attempt to increase real GDP above its long-run equilibrium can be accomplished only in the short run.

REDUCTIONS IN GOVERNMENT SPENDING. The entire process shown in Figure 13.1 can be reversed. Government can reduce spending, thereby shifting the aggregate demand curve inward. You should be able to show how this affects the equilibrium level of the price index and the real output of goods and services (real GDP) on similar diagrams.

Changes in Taxes

The spending decisions of firms, individuals, and foreigners depend on the taxes levied on them. Individuals in their roles as consumers look to their disposable (after-tax) income when determining their desired rate of consumption. Firms look at their after-tax

---

[1] Percent change in price index = change in price index/price index = (130 − 120)/120 = 8.33 percent

profits when deciding on the level of investment to undertake. Foreigners look at the tax-inclusive cost of goods when deciding whether to buy in Canada or elsewhere. Therefore, holding all other things constant, a rise in taxes causes a reduction in aggregate demand for three reasons: (1) It reduces consumption, (2) it reduces investment, and (3) it reduces net exports. What actually happens depends, of course, on whom the taxes are levied.

WHEN THE CURRENT SHORT-RUN EQUILIBRIUM IS GREATER THAN *LRAS*. Assume that aggregate demand is AD_1 in part (a) of Figure 13.2. It intersects *SRAS* at E_1, which is at a level greater than *LRAS*. In this situation, an increase in taxes shifts the aggregate demand curve inward to the left. For argument's sake, assume that it intersects *SRAS* at E_2, or exactly where *LRAS* intersects AD_2. In this situation, the equilibrium level of real GDP falls from $750 billion per year to $700 billion per year. The price level index falls from 120 to 100.

IF THE ECONOMY IS IN LONG-RUN EQUILIBRIUM. Assume that the economy is already at short-run and long-run equilibrium as shown in part (b) of Figure 13.2. The aggregate demand curve, AD_1, intersects both *LRAS* and *SRAS* at $700 billion of real GDP per year. If aggregate demand decreases to AD_2, a new temporary equilibrium will occur at E_2 with the price level at 110 and real equilibrium GDP at $650 billion per year. That means that in the short run, prices and the real output of goods and services fall. Input suppliers revise their expectations downward. The short-run aggregate supply curve shifts to $SRAS_2$. The real level of equilibrium GDP returns to the *LRAS* level of $700 billion per year. The full long-run impact of fiscal policy in this situation is solely on the price level, which falls to 100.

Try Preview Question 1:
What is fiscal policy?

EFFECTS OF A REDUCTION IN TAXES. The effects of a reduction in taxes are exactly the reverse of the effects of an increase in taxes. Figure 13.1 and the accompanying discussion of the effects of an increase in government expenditures provide the full analysis.

FIGURE 13.2
Contractionary Fiscal Policy: Two Scenarios

In part (a), the economy is initially at E_1, which exceeds *LRAS*. Contractionary fiscal policy can move aggregate demand to AD_2 so the new equilibrium is at E_2 at a lower price level and now at *LRAS*. In part (b), similar contractionary fiscal policy initially moves equilibrium from E_1 to E_2, but then it goes to E_3 at *LRAS*. The only long-run effect is to lower the price level to 100.

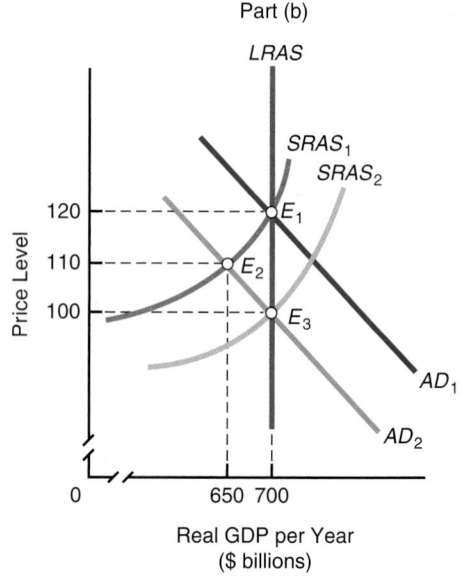

Thinking Critically About the Media 13-1 Tax Rates and Tax Revenues

Every time the federal government—or provincial and municipal governments, for that matter—announces a change in tax rates, the media are quick to pick up on projected increases or decreases in tax revenues. The arithmetic is simple: If Revenue Canada obtains $10 billion from the highest-earning individuals, it will garner $12 billion if their tax rates are increased by 20 percent. But tax revenues received after the tax rate increase are nowhere near those projected. Why? Because individuals and businesses are not static—they respond to higher marginal tax rates by retiring earlier, entering the job market later, engaging in the off-the-books underground economy, quitting second jobs, and compensating in other ways. The rule must be this: Never assume a static economy.

INTERNATIONAL EXAMPLE 13-1   Did Roosevelt's New Deal Really Provide a Stimulus?

During the Great Depression, US President Franklin Roosevelt implemented his "New Deal," which was influenced by Keynes' view that government had to increase "effective" aggregate demand to get an economy going again. To be sure, Roosevelt's New Deal included what appeared on the surface to be large federal government expenditures and numerous government jobs programs. We have to look at the total picture of the American economy, however. During the Great Depression, taxes were raised repeatedly. The Revenue Act of 1932, for example, passed during the depths of the Depression, brought the largest percentage increase in federal taxes in the history of the United States in peacetime—it almost doubled total federal tax revenues. Federal government deficits during the Depression years were small. In fact, in 1937 the total government budget—including federal, state, and local levels—was in surplus by $300 million. That means that at the same time that the federal government was increasing expenditures, local and state governments were decreasing them. If we measure the total of federal, state, and local fiscal policies, we find that they were truly expansive only in 1931 and 1936, compared to what the government was doing prior to the Great Depression. No wonder the New Deal failed to kickstart the American economy!

For critical analysis: Did the New Deal have any effect on the Canadian economy?

CONCEPTS IN BRIEF

- Fiscal policy is defined as the discretionary change in government expenditures and/or taxes in order to achieve such national goals as high employment or reduced inflation.
- If there is a contractionary gap and the economy is operating at less than long-run aggregate supply (*LRAS*), an increase in government spending can shift the aggregate demand curve to the right and perhaps lead to a higher equilibrium level of real GDP per year. If the economy is already operating on *LRAS*, in contrast, expansionary fiscal policy in the long run simply leads to a higher price level.
- Changes in taxes can have similar effects on the equilibrium rate of real GDP and the price level. A decrease in taxes can lead to an increase in real GDP, but if the economy is already operating on its *LRAS*, eventually such decreases in taxes will lead only to increases in the price level.

Possible Offsets to Fiscal Policy

Fiscal policy does not operate in a vacuum. Important questions have to be answered: If government expenditures increase, how are those expenditures financed, and by whom? If taxes are increased, what does the government do with the taxes? What will happen if individuals worry about increases in *future* taxes because there is more government spending today with no increased taxes? What will happen when provinces and municipalities also exercise their fiscal powers? All of these questions involve *offsets* to the effects of fiscal policy. We will look at the following reasons why fiscal policy may not work as effectively as we might hope:

1. Crowding Out
2. Direct Expenditure Offsets
3. The Open Economy Effect
4. Combined Government Spending Effect
5. The Supply-Side Effects of Changes in Taxes
6. The Ricardian Equivalence Theorem

Crowding Out

Consider an increase in government expenditures. If government expenditures rise and taxes are held constant, something has to give. Our government does not simply take goods and services when it wants them. It has to pay for them. When it pays for them and does not simultaneously collect the same amount in taxes, it must borrow. This means that an increase in government spending without raising taxes creates additional government borrowing from the private sector (or from foreigners).

THE CROWDING-OUT EFFECT. Holding everything else constant, if the government attempts to borrow more from the private sector to pay for its increased budget deficit, it is not going to have an easy time selling its bonds. If the bond market is in equilibrium, when the government tries to sell more bonds, it is going to have to offer a better deal in order to get rid of them. A better deal means offering a higher interest rate. This is the interest rate effect of expansionary fiscal policy financed by borrowing from the public. In this sense, when the federal government finances increased spending by additional borrowing, it may push interest rates up. When interest rates go up, it is more expensive for firms to finance new construction, equipment, and inventories. It is also more expensive for individuals to finance their cars and homes. Thus a rise in government spending, holding taxes constant (in short, deficit spending), tends to crowd out private spending, dampening the positive effect of increased government spending on aggregate demand. This is called the **crowding-out effect**. In the extreme case, the crowding out may be complete, with the increased government spending having no net effect on aggregate demand. The final result is simply more government spending and less private investment and consumption. Figure 13.3 shows how the crowding-out effect occurs.

Further, as you'll discover in the next chapter, as the government borrows more and more money, its overall debt climbs. As the debt grows large relative to GDP, investors may question the government's ability to use fiscal policy to manage the economy. They perceive an increased risk in buying more bonds. Thus the government has to offer even higher interest rates to continue to finance its spending.

THE FIRM'S INVESTMENT DECISION. To understand the crowding-out effect better, consider a firm that is contemplating borrowing $100,000 to expand its business. Suppose that the interest rate is 6 percent. The interest payments on the debt will be 6 percent times $100,000, or $6,000 per year ($500 per month). A rise in the interest rate to 9 percent will push the payments to 9 percent of $100,000, or $9,000 per year ($750 per month). The

Crowding-out effect The tendency of expansionary fiscal policy to cause a decrease in planned investment or planned consumption in the private sector; this decrease normally results from the rise in interest rates.

FIGURE 13.3 The Crowding-out Effect in Words

Government spending exceeds taxes → Government deficit increases → Government sells more bonds → To sell more bonds, government must offer higher interest yields → Fewer private bonds are offered for sale because of higher interest cost → Fewer private investment projects are undertaken and fewer purchases of homes and cars; government spending crowds out private spending

extra $250 per month in interest expenses will discourage some firms from making the investment. Consumers face similar decisions when they purchase houses and cars. An increase in the interest rate causes their monthly payments to go up, thereby discouraging some of them from purchasing cars and houses.

GRAPHICAL ANALYSIS. You see in Figure 13.4 that the initial equilibrium, E_1, is below *LRAS*. But suppose that government expansionary fiscal policy in the form of increased government spending (without increasing taxes) shifts aggregate demand from AD_1 to AD_2. In the absence of the crowding-out effect, the real output of goods and services would increase to $700 billion per year, and the price level would rise to 120 (point E_2). With the (partial) crowding-out effect, however, as investment and consumption decline, partly offsetting the rise in government spending, the aggregate demand curve shifts inward to the left to AD_3. The new equilibrium is now at E_3, with real GDP of $675 billion per year at a price level of 115.

Direct Expenditure Offsets

Government has a distinct comparative advantage over the private sector in certain activities such as diplomacy and national defence. In other words, certain resource-using activities

FIGURE 13.4 The Crowding-out Effect

Expansionary fiscal policy that causes deficit financing initially shifts AD_1 to AD_2. Equilibrium initially moves towards E_2. But because of crowding out, the aggregate demand curve shifts inward to AD_3, and the new short-run equilibrium is at E_3.

Direct expenditure offsets Actions on the part of the private sector in spending money that offset government fiscal policy actions. Any increase in government spending in an area that competes with the private sector will have some direct expenditure offset.

in which the government engages do not compete with the private sector. In contrast, some of what government does—such as education—competes directly with the private sector. When government competes with the private sector, **direct expenditure offsets** to fiscal policy may occur. For example, if the government starts providing milk at no charge to students who are already purchasing milk, there is a direct expenditure offset. Households spend less directly on milk, but government spends more.

The normal way to analyze the impact of an increase in government spending on aggregate demand is implicitly to assume that government spending is not a substitute for private spending. This is clearly the case for defence spending. Whenever government spending is a substitute for private spending, however, a rise in government spending causes a direct reduction in private spending to offset it.

Much government spending has a private-sector substitute. When government expenditures increase, there is a tendency for private spending to decline somewhat (but not in proportion), thereby mitigating the upward impact on total aggregate demand. To the extent that there are some direct expenditure offsets to expansionary fiscal policy, predicted changes in aggregate demand will be reduced. Consequently, real output and the price level will be less affected.

Try Preview Question 2:

How does the crowding-out effect tend to offset expansionary fiscal policy?

INTERNATIONAL POLICY EXAMPLE 13-1

French Policymakers Ignore Crowding-out Effects

In the past few years, persistent high unemployment rates have been a major campaign topic in virtually every national election in the European Union. It came as no surprise, therefore, that the latest president of France, Jacques Chirac, chose a "pro-employment" prime minister, Alain Juppé. Juppé quickly put into effect the French government's plan to increase jobs. At the heart of the plan was a sum of 50 billion francs (about $14 billion) to create jobs at small and medium-sized companies. This was done by reducing some of the employer taxes owed on low-salaried employees. In addition, the government offered subsidies to companies that hired long-term unemployed persons. The French government projected that 700,000 jobs would be created from mid-1995 through the beginning of 1997. Clearly, French government policymakers do not believe that much, if any, crowding out will occur.

At the same time, though, the French government increased marginal tax rates on corporations, increased the value-added tax on virtually everything sold in France from 18.6 percent to 20.6 percent, and imposed a "temporary" 10 percent tax surcharge on "large fortunes."

For critical analysis: Soon after the new French policy was announced, the head of the forecasting unit of the Paris Chamber of Commerce argued that the government would need to spend as much as 80 billion francs (about $22 billion) if it were "really serious" about fighting unemployment. What does this criticism ignore?

The Open Economy Effect

While the crowding-out effect reduces the effectiveness of fiscal policy by reducing investment expenditure, the open economy effect reduces the effectiveness of fiscal policy by reducing net exports. If government spending is increased without a rise in taxes, or if taxes are decreased without a reduction in government spending, the federal government must borrow more. As we pointed out, the government has to offer more attractive interest rates, so overall interest rates go up. When interest rates go up in Canada, foreigners demand more securities such as Canadian government bonds. When they do this, they have to pay for the bonds with dollars. After all, the typical Japanese stock and bond firm cannot buy more Canadian government bonds without getting its hands on more Canadian dollars. This increases the demand for dollars at the same time that it increases the supply of yen. The value of the yen falls relative to the value of the dollar in international transactions. When this occurs, Japanese-made goods become cheaper in Canada, and Canadian-made goods become more expensive in Japan. Canadians want to buy more Japanese goods, and the Japanese want to buy fewer Canadian goods. This causes a reduction in net exports (X) and cuts into any increase in aggregate demand. In sum, to the extent that federal deficit spending reduces net exports, the effect of expansionary fiscal policy will be less.

Combined Government Spending Effect

The federal government is not the only government with the power to tax and spend. We saw in Chapter 5 that provinces collect taxes to spend on highway maintenance, environmental protection, education, and welfare for example. Cities and towns collect taxes to spend on local streets, police, and property development. Because provinces and municipalities have less access to financing through the bond market, they are typically more reluctant to finance their expenditures through debt.

This greater reluctance to deficit finance means that provinces and municipalities usually cut their expenditure during recessions as tax revenues fall, and increase spending as the economy and tax revenues improve. This pro-cyclical behaviour can offset federal government attempts to bolster a foundering economy with deficit spending.

The Supply-Side Effects of Changes in Taxes

We have talked about changing taxes and changing government spending, the traditional tools of fiscal policy. We have not really talked about the possibility of changing marginal tax rates. In our federal tax system, higher incomes are taxed at higher rates. In that sense, Canada has a progressive federal individual income tax system. Expansionary fiscal policy might involve reducing marginal tax rates. Advocates of such changes argue that (1) lower tax rates will lead to an increase in productivity because individuals will work harder and longer, save more, and invest more; and (2) increased productivity will lead to more economic growth, which will lead to higher real GDP. The government, by applying lower marginal tax rates, will not necessarily lose tax revenues, for the lower marginal tax rates will be applied to a growing tax base because of economic growth—after all, tax revenues are the product of a tax rate times a tax base. People who support this notion are called supply-side economists. **Supply-side economics** involves changing the tax structure to create incentives to increase productivity. Due to a shift outward to the right in the aggregate supply curve, there can be greater output without upward pressure on the price level. We'll look more closely at supply-side economics in Chapter 18.

Supply-side economics The notion that creating incentives for individuals and firms to increase productivity will cause the aggregate supply curve to shift outward.

The Ricardian Equivalence Theorem

Economists have implicitly assumed that people look at changes in taxes or changes in government spending only in the present. What if people actually think about the size of *future* tax payments? Does this have an effect on how they react to an increase in government spending with no tax increases? Some economists believe that the answer is yes. What if people's horizons extend beyond this year? Don't we then have to take into account the effects of today's government policies on the future?

Consider an example. If the government wants to spend $1 today, it can raise tax revenues by $1 and the public's responsibility to the government for that particular dollar has now been met and will never return. Alternatively, the government can borrow $1 today and the public will owe $1 plus interest later. Realizing that $1 today is mathematically equivalent to $1 plus interest next year, people may save the $1 to meet the future tax liabilities. Therefore, whether the $1 spending is financed by taxation or by borrowing, the two methods of finance are equivalent.

Increased government spending without an increase in taxes, according to the new classical economists, will not necessarily have a large impact on aggregate demand. In terms of Figure 13-4, the aggregate demand curve will shift inward from AD_1 to AD_3. In the extreme case, if consumers fully compensate for a higher future tax liability by saving more, the aggregate demand curve shifts all the way back to AD_1 in Figure 13-4. This is the case of individuals fully discounting their increased tax liabilities. The result is that an increased budget deficit created entirely by a current tax cut has literally no effect on the economy. This is known as the **Ricardian equivalence theorem**, after the nineteenth-century economist, David Ricardo, who first developed the argument publicly.

Ricardian equivalence theorem The proposition that an increase in the government budget deficit has no effect on aggregate demand.

For economists who believe in the Ricardian equivalence theorem, it does not matter how government expenditures are financed—by taxes or by issuing debt. Is the Ricardian equivalence theorem correct? The evidence is not clear. Between 1983 and 1997, government spending exceeded taxes by over $20 billion per year. Private savings rates declined by about one-half over the same period, to the lowest they have ever been.

CONCEPTS IN BRIEF

- Crowding out occurs because of an interest effect in which the government's efforts to finance its deficit spending cause interest rates to rise, thereby crowding out private investment and spending, particularly on cars and houses. This is called the crowding-out effect.
- Direct expenditure offset occurs when government spending competes with the private sector. If public spending simply replaces private spending, fiscal policy is reduced in effectiveness.
- Direct crowding out occurs when government spending competes with the private sector and is increased. Direct expenditure offsets to fiscal policy may occur.
- There is an open economy effect that offsets fiscal policy. Like the crowding-out effect, it occurs because the government's increased deficit causes interest rates to rise. This encourages foreigners to invest more in Canadian securities. When they do so, they demand more dollars, thereby increasing the international value of the dollar. As a result, Canadian-made goods become more expensive abroad and foreign goods cheaper here, so Canada exports fewer goods and imports more.
- Changes in marginal tax rates may cause supply-side effects if a reduction in marginal tax rates induces enough additional work, saving, and investing. Government tax receipts can actually increase. This is called supply-side economics.
- Some economists believe in the Ricardian equivalence theorem, which argues that an increase in the government budget deficit has no effect on aggregate demand because individuals correctly perceive their increased future taxes and therefore save more today to pay for them.

Discretionary Fiscal Policy in Practice

We can discuss fiscal policy in a relatively precise way. We draw graphs with aggregate demand and supply curves to show what we are doing. We could even in principle estimate the offsets that were just discussed. However, even if we were able to measure all of these offsets exactly, would-be fiscal policymakers still face problems: which fiscal policy mix to choose, and the various time lags involved in conducting fiscal policy.

Fiscal Policy Mix

What is the proper mix of taxes and government expenditures? Let's say that policy-makers decide that a change in taxes is desirable. At least seven options are available:

1. Permanent change in personal income taxes
2. Permanent change in corporate income taxes
3. Temporary change in personal income taxes
4. Temporary change in corporate income taxes
5. Change payroll taxes such as EI and CPP contributions
6. Change depreciation allowance on investment expenditures
7. Change specific consumption taxes, such as on oil

Note that all of these are tax changes, but their effects on individual groups will be different, and special-interest groups will be lobbying politicians to protect specific interests.

Alternatively, assume policymakers decide that a change in government expenditures is desirable. There are disadvantages to these changes. Political wrangling will arise over the amount, type, and geographic location of the expenditure change ("spend more in my city or province, less in someone else's"). Furthermore, if the expenditure is to be made on a capital goods project, such as a highway, a dam, or a public transportation system, the problem of timing arises. If started during a recession, should or could such a project be abandoned or delayed if inflation emerges before the project is finished? Are delays or reversals politically feasible, even if they are economically sensible?

Time Lags

Policymakers must be concerned with various time lags. Quite apart from the fact that it is difficult to measure economic variables, it takes time to collect and assimilate such data. Thus policymakers must be concerned with the **recognition time lag**, the period of months that may elapse before economic problems can be identified.[2]

After an economic problem is recognized, a solution must be formulated; thus there will be an **action time lag**, the period between the recognition of a problem and the implementation of policy to solve it. For fiscal policy, the action time lag is particularly long. It must be approved by Parliament, and much political wrangling and infighting accompany legislative fiscal policy decision making. It is not at all unusual for the action time lag to last a year or two. Then it takes time to put the policy into effect. After Parliament enacts a fiscal policy as legislation, it takes time to decide, for example, who gets the new federal construction contract, and so on.

When we add the recognition time lag to the action time lag, we get what is known as the *inside lag*. That is how long it takes to get a policy from inside the institutional structure of our federal government.

Finally, there is the **effect time lag:** After fiscal policy is enacted, it takes time for it to affect the economy. Multiplier effects take more time to work through the economy than it takes an economist to shift a curve on a chalkboard.

Because the various fiscal policy time lags are long, a policy designed to combat a recession might not produce results until the economy is experiencing inflation, in which case the fiscal policy would worsen the situation. Or a fiscal policy designed to eliminate inflation might not produce effects until the economy is in a recession; in that case, too, fiscal policy would make the economic problem worse rather than better.

Recognition time lag The time required to gather information about the current state of the economy.

Action time lag The time required between recognizing an economic problem and putting policy into effect. The action time lag is short for monetary policy but quite long for fiscal policy, which requires legislative approval.

Effect time lag The time that elapses between the onset of policy and the results of that policy.

---

[2] Final annual data for GDP, after various revisions, are not forthcoming for three to six months after the year's end.

Try Preview Question 3:
What types of time lags exist between the need for fiscal stimulus and the time when such stimulus actually affects the national economy?

Furthermore, because fiscal policy time lags tend to be *variable* (anywhere from one to three years), policymakers have a difficult time fine-tuning the economy. Clearly, fiscal policy is more an art than a science.

Government Budgets and Politics

One of the important realities to remember in this discussion is that government budgets are as much about politics and chance as they are about economics. Government budgets are often driven by ideology, luck, and a desire to be re-elected, as well as by the need to steer the economy. Keynes' idea of using government spending to offset the business cycle, as we discussed in the first part of this chapter, has a very checkered history. Some observers would suggest that the governments that adopted Keynesian theory in the 1930s did so not so much because it was a good economic theory, but because it suited their basic ideology for a larger government.

In the mid 1980s, for example, Brian Mulroney was elected on a platform of fiscal restraint and the need to get the large government deficits of the day under control. Even though the economy grew from 1984 until 1990, the deficits experienced under the Conservative government did not drop significantly. Instead, much of the new taxes generated by the growth was spent on new projects, and tax increases proposed to deal with the issue of a growing deficit were quietly dropped.

In the early 1990s, the Liberal government was elected, again on a platform of fiscal restraint. The deficit incurred by the Liberal government in 1994 (over 40 billion) has been turned around into a surplus of about $15 billion per year by the fiscal year 2000-2001. The Liberal government had transformed the annual deficit through a number of tax increases and through growth in the economy. The growth in the Canadian economy in the 1990s was largely due to an expansion of exports to the United States, which has boomed through the 1990s.

At the end of the year 2000, the Liberals are now proposing a series of tax reductions and spending increases. A similar proposal of tax reduction amounting to $1.3 trillion is proposed by the new President of the United States in the 2000 American election. These stimulatory policies come at a time when the North American economy has arguably eliminated any contractionary gap in the economy. The effect of such a stimulus may be such that we overshoot our targets, and create an expansionary gap.

All of these examples, and many others, suggest that it is difficult to evaluate the true effect of fiscal policy on the economy, and that the use of discretionary fiscal policy in fighting contractionary or expansionary GDP gaps is quite limited.

Automatic Stabilizers

Not all changes in taxes (or in tax rates) or in government spending (including government transfers) constitute discretionary fiscal policy. There are several types of automatic (or nondiscretionary) fiscal policies. Such policies do not require new legislation. Specific automatic fiscal policies—called **automatic**, or **built-in, stabilizers**—include the progressive federal income tax system itself and the government transfer system; the latter includes Employment Insurance (EI) and Old Age Security benefits (OAS).

Automatic, or built-in, stabilizers
Special provisions of the tax law that cause changes in the economy without the direct action of the government. Examples are the progressive income tax system and Employment Insurance.

The Federal Progressive Income Tax

We have in Canada a progressive income tax (in the year 2001) that ranges from 16 percent for taxable incomes below $30,000 to 26 percent on incomes above $61,000. (Provincial and municipal taxes are extra.) For an individual, as taxable income rises, the marginal tax rate rises, and as taxable income falls, so does the marginal tax rate. Think

Keynesian Fiscal Policy Loses its Luster

Some analysts argue that John Maynard Keynes was the most influential economist of the twentieth century, for he supposedly armed policymakers with fiscal weapons that allowed them to fight recession. Yet, at the beginning of the twenty-first century, influential policymakers throughout the world are ignoring the concept of government spending as a way out of recessions.

Even though European governments have long favoured welfare spending, the 11 that joined together to use the common currency called the euro also agreed to some specific anti-governmental spending stipulations. These countries, including France and Germany, are committed to keeping public deficits at 3 percent or less of gross domestic product. Whenever a country's public deficit exceeds this figure, the offending government can be fined up to 0.5 percent of its GDP. Deficit spending—a favourite Keynesian fiscal policy action—is tightly constrained in these countries.

In 1999 Brazil's president, Fernando Enrique Cardoso, stated that in the face of the then-current recession, "we will need to put in place as rapidly as possible a fiscal austerity plan so that interest rates can fall and Brazil can begin to grow again." He publicly announced that the country's government sector should shrink by 3 percent the following year even when his government economists predicted a probable 4 percent decrease in real GDP.

The International Monetary Fund did a study on fiscal policy a few years ago. It examined attempts by governments to reduce public spending and public debt. It looked at 62 attempts over two and a half decades. Its conclusion was that in the 14 cases for which the governments had aggressively reduced government spending, as in Denmark and Ireland, those economies had the fastest growth rates. The IMF contended that there may have been a "virtuous circle between economic growth and debt-reduction programs."

For critical analysis: How might Keynes have responded to this increase in anti-Keynesianism?

about this now in terms of the entire economy. If the nation is at full employment, personal income taxes may yield the government, say, $60 billion per year. Now suppose that, for whatever reason, business activity suddenly starts to slow down. Workers are not allowed to put in as much overtime as before. Some workers are laid off, and some must change to jobs that pay less. Some workers and executives might take voluntary pay cuts. What happens to federal income taxes when wages and salaries go down? Across the economy taxes are still paid, but at a lower marginal rate than before, because the tax schedule is progressive. As a result of these decreased taxes, disposable income—the amount remaining after taxes—doesn't fall by the same percentage as before-tax income. In other words, the individual doesn't feel the pinch of recession as much as we might think if we ignored the progressive nature of our tax schedule. The *average* tax rate falls when less is earned.

Conversely, when the economy suddenly comes into a boom period, people's incomes tend to rise. They can work more overtime and can change to higher-paying jobs. Their *disposable* income does not, however, go up as rapidly as their total income because their average tax rates are rising at the same time. Revenue Canada ends up taking a bigger bite. In this situation, the progressive income tax system tends to stabilize any abrupt changes in economic activity. (Actually, the progressive tax structure simply magnifies any stabilization effect that might exist.)

Employment Insurance

Like the progressive income tax, Employment Insurance stabilizes aggregate demand. Throughout the business cycle, it reduces changes in people's disposable income. When business activity drops, most laid-off workers automatically become eligible for Employment Insurance benefits. Their disposable income therefore remains positive, although certainly it is less than when they were employed. During boom periods there is less unemployment, and consequently fewer Employment Insurance payments are made to the labour force. Less purchasing power is being added to the economy because fewer benefits are paid out. Historically, the relationship between the unemployment rate and unemployment insurance schemes has been strongly positive. We'll look more closely at the EI program in the Issues and Application section at the end of the chapter.

Stabilizing Impact

The key stabilizing impact of the progressive income tax and Employment Insurance is their ability to mitigate changes in disposable income, consumption, and the equilibrium level of national income. If disposable income is prevented from falling as much as it would during a recession, the downturn will be moderated. In contrast, if disposable income is prevented from rising as rapidly as it would during a boom, the boom will not get out of hand. The progressive income tax and unemployment benefits thus provide automatic stabilization to the economy. We present the argument graphically in Figure 13.5.

Old Age Security Benefits

Every Canadian is eligible to receive Old Age Security (OAS) benefits on turning 65 years of age. This non-contributory program is aimed at reducing the amount a person's income falls on retirement from the workforce. Because everyone at every economic level receives this benefit, the government "claws back" through increased taxes the OAS paid to wealthier Canadians. This way, those pensioners whose consumption would otherwise drop drastically are able to continue consuming, thus supporting *AD* across the economy.

Try Preview Question 4:

What is automatic fiscal policy, and how does it lend stability to an economy?

FIGURE 13.5 Automatic Stabilizers

Here we assume that as real national income rises, tax revenues rise and government transfers fall, other things remaining constant. Thus as the economy expands from Y_f to Y_1, a budget surplus automatically arises; as the economy contracts from Y_f to Y_2, a budget deficit automatically arises. Such automatic changes tend to drive the economy back towards its full-employment output level.

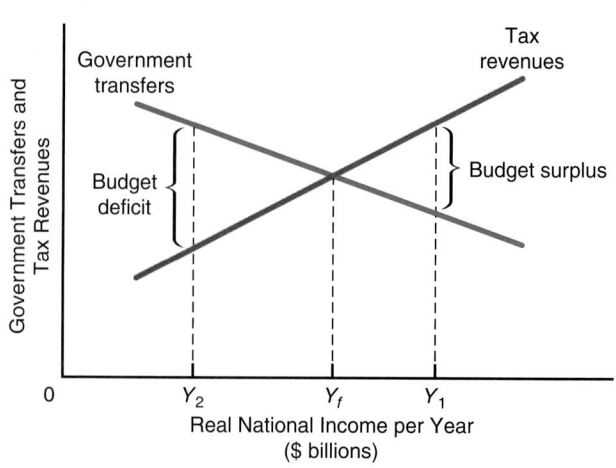

What Do We Really Know About Fiscal Policy?

There are two ways of looking at fiscal policy, one that prevails during normal times and the other during abnormal times.

Fiscal Policy During Normal Times

During normal times (without "excessive" unemployment, inflation, or problems in the national economy), we know that given the time lag between the recognition of the need to increase aggregate demand and the impact of any expansionary fiscal policy, and given the very modest size of any fiscal policy action that the government actually will take, discretionary fiscal policy is probably not very effective. The government ends up doing too little too late to help in a minor recession. Moreover, fiscal policy that generates repeated tax changes (as it has done) creates uncertainty, which may do more harm than good. To the extent that fiscal policy has any effect during normal times, it probably achieves this by way of automatic stabilizers rather than by way of discretionary policy.

Fiscal Policy During Abnormal Times

During abnormal times, fiscal policy can be effective. Consider some classic examples: the Great Depression and times of war.

THE GREAT DEPRESSION. When there is a substantial catastrophic drop in real GDP, as there was during the Great Depression, fiscal policy probably can do something to stimulate aggregate demand. Because so many people are cash-constrained, government spending is a good way during such periods to get cash into their hands.

WARTIME. Wars are in fact reserved for governments. War expenditures are not good substitutes for private expenditures—they have little or no direct expenditure offsets. Consequently, war spending as part of expansionary fiscal policy usually has noteworthy effects, such as during World War II, when real GDP increased dramatically, bringing an end to the Great Depression.

The "Soothing" Effect of Keynesian Fiscal Policy

One view of traditional Keynesian fiscal policy does not relate to its being used on a regular basis. As you have learned in this chapter, there are many problems associated with attempting to use fiscal policy. But if we should encounter a severe downturn, fiscal policy is available. Knowing this may reassure consumers and investors. After all, the ability of the federal government to prevent another Great Depression—given what we know about how to use fiscal policy today—may take some of the large risk out of consumers' and particularly investors' calculations. This may induce more buoyant and stable expectations of the future, thereby smoothing investment spending.

CONCEPTS IN BRIEF

- Time lags of various sorts reduce the effectiveness of fiscal policy. These include the recognition time lag, the action time lag, and the effect time lag.
- Government budgets are driven as much by politics and luck as by their effect on the economy. This makes it difficult to use fiscal policy in steering the economy.
- Two automatic, or built-in, stabilizers are the progressive income tax and Employment Insurance.
- Built-in stabilizers tend automatically to moderate changes in disposable income resulting from changes in overall business activity.
- Though discretionary fiscal policy may not necessarily be a useful tool in normal times because of time lags and the government debt, it may work well during abnormal times, such as depressions and wartime. In addition, the existence of fiscal policy may have a soothing effect on consumers and investors.

NETNOMICS

Government Plays a Role in Creating the Internet

Government spending, in trying to achieve one objective, often has consequences that are not foreseen by the policymakers. Many new technologies have been unintentionally created through government spending. Freeze-dried food was an offshoot of US government spending on space programs, while the jet engine and nuclear power were created through government spending during the Second World War.

The Internet is one such technology. In the early 1960s the US government was trying to set up a computer-controlled system that would be relatively impervious to nuclear attack. RAND Corporation, working on behalf of the government, came up with the idea that the computer system would, from its outset, be assumed to be in "tatters." It would have no central authority, so no single attack would be able to take the system out by itself. Each node in the network of computers would be equal to every other node, and it didn't matter what route the information would take to reach its final destination, only the outcome mattered. Thus was born the first computer network, called ARPANET.

ARPANET proved to be a good way for scientists to share computing power, but an even better way to share news and e-mail. Much of the early traffic on the ARPANET was a forerunner of what was to come, consisting more of e-mail than anything else. Besides establishing that the basic concept of linked computers was a useful and viable way of doing things, ARPANET established the TCP/IP protocol which is still used on the Internet today.

ARPANET eventually became only a small part of a growing host of linked computer networks working on the same principles. The nodes in this growing network-of-networks were broken into various categories. Computers hosted in foreign countries, and a few American ones, chose to be denoted by their geographical locations. The remainder were grouped into six basic Internet domains: gov, mil, edu, com,org and net. Gov, mil, and edu denoted governmental, military, and educational institutions, which were the pioneers of the Internet. Com stood for "commercial" institutions, which began to take advantage of the Internet in the 1990s, along with a number of nonprofit "orgs." "Net" computers served as gateways between networks.

With various upgrades and changes, and the exponential growth of the Internet, today's Internet and standards bear only a small resemblance to the original linkage of four computers in 1972. The role that the US government played in creating the Internet and many other technologies has been very significant.

ISSUES AND APPLICATIONS | Employment Insurance and the Deficit

Concepts Applied: Automatic stabilizers, the multiplier, payroll taxes

Changes to the EI program have made it harder to collect, thus reducing its value as a stabilizer.

From 1970 to 1994, the federal government's deficit increased nearly every year. In 1994, the Chrétien government made severe policy changes in a number of areas in order to bring the deficit under control. It used both tax increases and expenditure reductions to achieve this goal.

Employment Insurance, unlike the Canada Pension Plan, is paid for directly by the government out of its general revenues, and is not independent of the overall government's budget. Because of the desire to reduce the deficit that the government was incurring, changes were brought about to the EI plan that made it harder to qualify, such as increasing the amount of working time required to qualify. Benefit levels, as a percentage of regular pay were also reduced. Because of these changes, the government quickly found that the amount collected in EI premiums outstripped the payments to beneficiaries and this at a time when unemployment was quite high.

Less Effective Automatic Stabilizer

Employment Insurance (and its predecessor Unemployment Insurance) was designed to keep Canada from again falling into a depression like that of the 1930s. When the economy contracts, workers who are laid off claim Employment Insurance, and are provided with an income. That income allows them to continue consuming, although at reduced levels, and continued consumption acts as an incentive for firms to keep investing and producing. Eventually, the economy will recover and these workers will go back to work.

Under the stricter rules laid down by the government in the mid 1990s, the lower benefit payments detract from the plan's force as a stabilizer. Once the economy stalls, the workers who lose their jobs will be able to consume even less, and the multiplier effect will work to magnify those changes into larger ones in the economy. This means that the cushioning effect that EI was supposed to have is smaller than it was.

Enlarging the Tax Base

At the same time, a higher premium rate also has a disincentive effect on employers who might otherwise hire employees. Employers must pay about $2.95 for each $100 of payroll. These taxes along with Canada Pension Plan payments are called payroll taxes.

A recent University of Toronto study claims that if the EI payroll tax were to be reduced from $2.95 to $2.10 per $100 of payroll, the private sector would be able to create about 200,000 jobs over two years. Since business costs for labour would be lower, prices would likely fall, quantity demanded for their products would rise, and employers would be able to hire more workers. These new jobs, which would result in less claims against EI and, likely, payment of new income taxes to the government, would at least partially offset the lost EI revenue.

Trade-offs

As with all government policies, there is opportunity cost involved in this decision. The government had an overriding goal of setting the fiscal house "in order," and the deficit has been eliminated. However, there are adverse effects on other parts of the economy. Employers have less incentive to create new jobs with these higher payroll taxes, so the policy has slowed the economic recovery that occurred during the 1990s. Without this policy, however, there would have been other problems with maintaining the high level of deficit previously incurred. We'll look more closely at those problems in the next chapter.

For Critical Analysis

1. Employees and employers both pay payroll taxes. If the employees' EI payroll tax were reduced as well, what effect would that reduction have on consumers and the deficit?

2. Suppose, instead of using payroll taxes, the government had raised the GST to a higher rate. What effect would that have had on the economy? In general, what trade-offs does the government have in trying to deal with a large deficit in a period of high unemployment?

CHAPTER SUMMARY

1. Fiscal policy involves deliberate discretionary changes in government expenditures and personal income taxes. Typically, policymakers argue in favour of fiscal policy during a contractionary gap.

2. Increased government spending when there is a contractionary gap can lead to a shift outward in the aggregate demand curve such that the equilibrium level of real GDP per year increases. If, however, the economy is already operating on its long-run aggregate supply curve (*LRAS*), the increase in aggregate demand will simply lead in the long run to a rise in the price level, all other things held constant.

3. Individuals respond to changes in after-tax profits, after-tax (disposable) income, and the tax-inclusive cost of foreign goods. Consequently, changes in taxes will change aggregate demand by changing consumption, investment, and net exports.

4. A decrease in taxes can lead to an increase in aggregate demand and in the equilibrium level of real GDP per year, provided that the economy is not already on its long-run aggregate supply curve. If it is, such tax decreases will simply lead to a higher price level.

5. There are numerous possible offsets to any fiscal policy. Crowding out occurs when increased deficit spending requires the government to borrow more and drives interest rates up. Increased interest rates cause private firms to undertake fewer investments. This is called the crowding-out effect.

6. The new classical economists believe in the Ricardian equivalence theorem, a proposition stating that an increase in the government budget deficit has no effect on aggregate demand because individuals properly discount increased future tax liabilities and therefore increase saving when the government engages in new deficit spending.

7. Direct expenditure offsets occurs when the government competes with the private sector and then increases spending in those areas of competition. This occurs, for example, when the government increases direct payments for school lunches that students' parents have been paying for anyway.

8. There is a possible open-economy effect offsetting fiscal policy. Deficit spending that leads to increased interest rates causes foreigners to invest more in Canada. To do so, they demand more dollars, thereby increasing the international price of our currency. Our goods become more expensive to foreigners, they buy less, and the result is a reduction in net exports that offsets the fiscal policy stimulus.

9. If marginal tax rates are lowered, individuals and firms may react by increasing work, saving, and investing. People who believe this favour supply-side economics, which involves changing the tax structure to create incentives to increase productivity.

10. Time lags, including the recognition time lag, the action time lag, and the effect time lag, tend to reduce the

effectiveness of fiscal policy. When we add the recognition time lag to the action time lag, we get what is known as the inside lag, because this is how long it takes to get a policy from inside the institutional structure of our federal government.

11. Politics and luck play an important role in determining the fiscal policies of government. These political and ex-

ternal constraints limit the role of fiscal policy in trying to reduce unemployment and inflation.

12. Automatic stabilizers include personal income taxes and Employment Insurance. Automatic stabilizers counter ups and downs in fiscal activity without the necessity for legislative action.

DISCUSSION OF PREVIEW QUESTIONS

1. What is fiscal policy?

Fiscal policy refers to the changing of governmental expenditures and/or taxes in order to eliminate expansionary and contractionary gaps. Proponents of fiscal policy make the value judgment that price stability and full employment are worthwhile goals. Proponents also assume that our knowledge of positive economics is sufficient to achieve these normative goals.

2. How does the crowding-out effect tend to offset expansionary fiscal policy?

When the government spends more without increasing taxes or taxes less without reducing spending, it increases the government budget deficit. When the government attempts to sell more bonds to finance the increased deficit, it may end up increasing interest rates. Higher interest rates induce private businesses to reduce investment projects and also cause consumers to reduce their purchases of houses and cars. Therefore, expansionary fiscal policy tends to crowd out private investment and spending.

3. What types of time lags exist between the need for fiscal stimulus and the time when such stimulus actually affects the national economy?

There is a lag between the start of a recession and the availability of relevant data—the recognition time lag. There is a lag between the recognition of a need for a fiscal policy and putting one in motion—the action time

lag. And there is a lag between policy implementation and tangible results—the effect time lag.

4. What is automatic fiscal policy, and how does it lend stability to an economy?

With discretionary fiscal policy, government spending and taxing policies are consciously applied to stabilize an economy. Automatic fiscal policy, by contrast, does not require conscious policy or government legislation; automatic fiscal policy results from institutional characteristics in the economy. Thus a progressive tax structure and an unemployment insurance system (which are already in force) automatically change taxes and government outlays as national income changes. In particular, as national income falls in a recession, government outlays for unemployed workers automatically increase, and tax revenues fall as lower incomes push people into lower marginal tax brackets. These automatic stabilizers counteract declining national income. Similarly, in an expansionary period, tax revenues automatically rise (as people are forced into higher marginal tax brackets), and Employment Insurance benefits fall. Thus aggregate demand is automatically counteracted by higher tax revenues and decreased government outlays. Because income increases or decreases are automatically countered to a certain extent by a progressive tax system and an unemployment insurance program, we say that automatic fiscal policy lends stability to the Canadian economy.

PROBLEMS

(Answers to the odd-numbered problems appear at the back of the book.)

13-1. What is discretionary fiscal policy? What are automatic stabilizers? Give examples of each.

13-2. Assume that you are a new Member of Parliament. You believe that expansionary government fiscal policy will pull the country rapidly out of its recession. What are some of the possible tax and spending changes you could recommend? What are the possible mixes?

13-3. Given the existence of automatic stabilizers, a recession is expected to generate a budget deficit, and an expansion is expected to generate a budget surplus. If the generation of such budget deficits or surpluses is to be countercyclical, what assumptions must be made about how consumers react to such budget deficits or surpluses?

13-4. How do economists distinguish between budget deficits or surpluses that occur automatically and those that are the result of discretionary policy?

13-5. Visit Canada's Finance Department at http://www.fin.gc.ca/fedprove/mfte.html. This site sets out the major transfers from the federal to the provincial governments. Scroll through this document until you find your province. You will find a table setting out the amount the federal government has transferred for each of the last three fiscal years. Do you think that these transfers have allowed your province to pursue expansionary or contractionary policy? Explain your answer.

13-6. Suppose that Parliament enacts a significant tax cut with the expectation that this action will stimulate aggregate demand and push up real GDP in the short run. In fact, however, neither real national income nor the price level changes significantly following the tax cut. What might account for this outcome?

13-7. Suppose there is an inflationary gap. Discuss one discretionary fiscal policy action that might eliminate it. Illustrate your answers using the *AD-AS* model.

13-8. Suppose there is a contractionary gap. Discuss one discretionary fiscal policy action that might eliminate it. Illustrate your answers using the *AD-AS* model.

ECONOMICS ON THE NET

Government Budgets

Internet URL: http://www.fin.gc.ca
http://www.statcan.ca/

Navigation: The federal government budgets for recent years can be found at the first URL listed above. For detailed federal and provincial information, navigate to the Statistics Canada page. Call up the matrices 8181-8193 which shows detailed information on different areas of revenue spending for the federal and provincial/local governments.

Application: Check out the fiscal stance of the province/territory you reside in. Why would provincial/local governments not engage in deficit financing and counter-cyclical fiscal policy as much as the federal government does? (Hint: What is the size of the multiplier for a small region?)

PPENDIX C

FISCAL POLICY: A KEYNESIAN PERSPECTIVE

The traditional Keynesian approach to fiscal policy differs in three ways from that presented in Chapter 13. First, it emphasizes the underpinnings of the components of aggregate demand. Second, it assumes that government expenditures are not substitutes for private expenditures and that current taxes are the only taxes taken into account by consumers and firms. Third, the traditional Keynesian approach focuses on the short run and so assumes that as a first approximation, the price level is constant.

Changes in Government Spending

Figure C-1 measures real national income along the horizontal axis and total planned expenditures (aggregate demand) along the vertical axis. The components of aggregate demand are consumption *(C)*, investment *(I)*, government spending *(G)*, and net exports *(X)*. The height of the schedule labelled $C + I + G + X$ shows total planned expenditures (aggregate demand) as a function of income. This schedule slopes upward because consumption depends positively on income. Everywhere along the 45-degree reference line, planned spending equals income. At the point Y^*, where the $C + I + G + X$ line intersects the 45-degree line, planned spending is consistent with real national income. At any income less than Y^*, spending exceeds income, and so income and thus spending will tend to rise. At any level of income greater than Y^*, planned spending is less than income, and so income and thus spending will tend to decline. Given the determinants of *C, I, G,* and *X*, total spending (aggregate demand) will be Y^*.

The Keynesian approach assumes that changes in government spending cause no direct offsets in either consumption or investment spending because *G* is not a substitute for *C, I,* or *X*. Hence a rise in government spending from *G* to *G'* causes the $C + I + G + X$ line to shift upward by the full amount of the rise in government spending, yielding the line

FIGURE C-1 The Impact of Higher Government Spending on Aggregate Demand

Government spending increases, causing $C + I + G + X$ to move to $C + I + G' + X$. Equilibrium increases to Y^{**}.

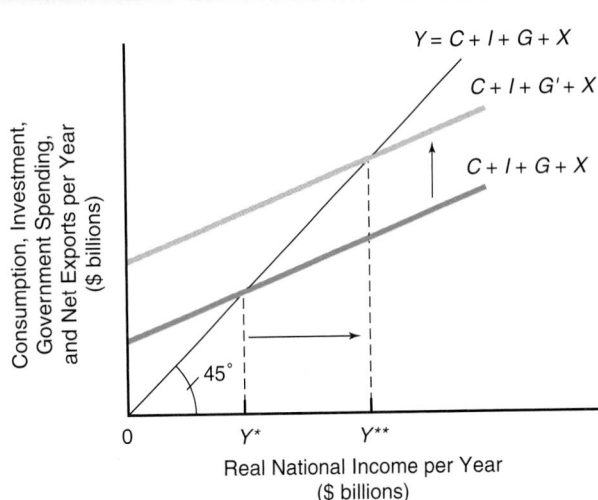

FIGURE C-2 The Impact of Higher Taxes on Aggregate Demand

Higher taxes cause consumption to fall to C'. Equilibrium decreases to Y^{**}.

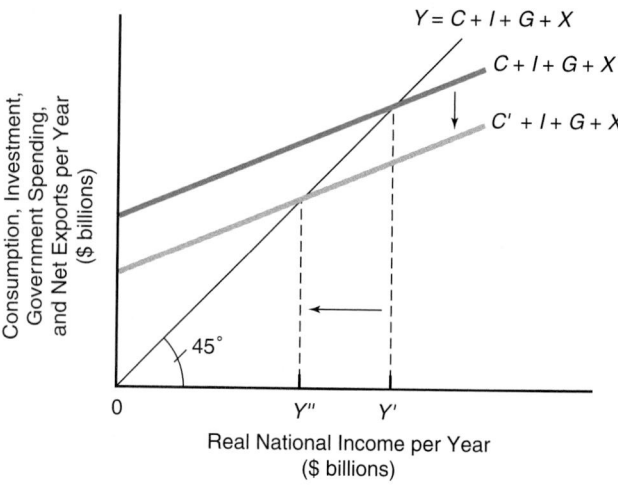

$C + I + G' + X$. The rise in government spending causes income to rise, which in turn causes consumption spending to rise, which further increases income. Ultimately, aggregate demand rises to Y^{**}, where spending again equals income. A key conclusion of the Keynesian analysis is that total spending rises by *more* than the original rise in government spending because consumption spending depends positively on income.

Changes in Taxes

According to the Keynesian approach, changes in current taxes affect aggregate demand by changing the amount of disposable (after-tax) income available to consumers. A rise in taxes reduces disposable income and thus reduces consumption; conversely, a tax cut raises disposable income and thus causes a rise in consumption spending. The effects of a tax increase are shown in Figure C-2. Higher taxes cause consumption spending to decline from C to C', causing total spending to shift downward to $C' + I + G + X$. In general, the decline in consumption will be less than the increase in taxes because people will also reduce their saving to help pay the higher taxes. Thus although aggregate demand declines to Y'', the decline is *smaller* than the tax increase.

The Balanced-Budget Multiplier

One interesting implication of the Keynesian approach concerns the impact of a balanced-budget change in government spending. Suppose that the government increases spending by $100 million and pays for it by raising current taxes by $100 million. Such a policy is called a *balanced-budget increase in spending*. Because the higher spending tends to push aggregate demand *up* by *more* than $100 million while the higher taxes tend to push aggregate demand *down* by *less* than $100 million, a most remarkable thing happens: A balanced-budget increase in G causes total spending to rise by *exactly* the amount of the rise in G—in this case, $100 million. We say that the *balanced-budget multiplier* is equal to 1. Similarly, a balanced-budget reduction in spending will cause total spending to fall by exactly the amount of the spending cut.

The Fixed-Price Level Assumption

The final key feature of the Keynesian approach is that it typically assumes that as a first approximation, the price level is fixed. Recall that nominal income equals the price level multiplied by real output. If the price level is fixed, an increase in government spending that causes nominal income to rise will show up exclusively as a rise in *real* output. This will in turn be accompanied by a decline in the unemployment rate because the additional output can be produced only if additional factors of production, such as labour, are utilized.

PROBLEMS

C-1. In this problem, equilibrium income is $500 billion and full-employment equilibrium is $640 billion. The marginal propensity to save is $\frac{1}{7}$. Answer the questions using the data in the following graph.

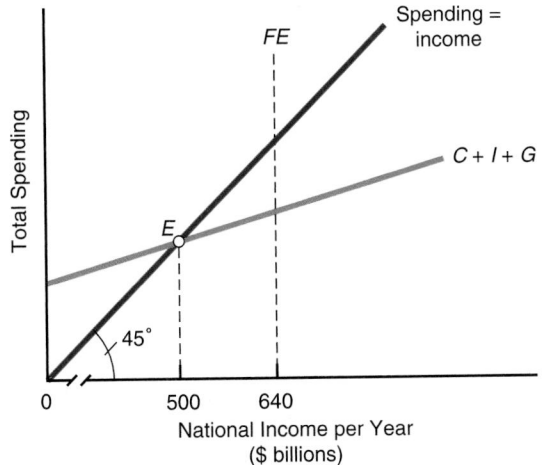

a. What is the marginal propensity to consume?

b. By how much must new investment or government spending increase to bring the economy up to full employment?

c. By how much must government cut personal taxes to stimulate the economy to the full-employment equilibrium?

C-2. Consider the following model; then answer the questions.

If $C = 30 + \frac{3}{4}Y$ and $I_n = 25$, equilibrium $Y = \$220$.

a. If government expenditures equal $5, what will be the new equilibrium level of national income? (Hint: Aggregate spending $\equiv C + I + G$.)

b. What was the government spending multiplier in this example?

C-3. Assume that MPC $= \frac{9}{10}$; then answer the following questions.

a. If government expenditures fall by $500, by how much will the aggregate expenditure curve shift downward? By how much will equilibrium income change?

b. If taxes fall by $500, by how much will the aggregate expenditure curve shift upward? By how much will equilibrium income change?

C-4. Assume that MPC $= \frac{3}{4}$; then answer the following questions.

a. If government expenditures rise by $100 million, by how much will the aggregate expenditure curve shift upward?

b. If taxes rise by $100 million, by how much will the aggregate expenditure curve shift downward?

c. If both taxes and government expenditures rise by $100 million, by how much will the aggregate expenditure curve shift? What will happen to the equilibrium level of income?

d. How does our conclusion in the second part of (c) change if MPC $= \frac{9}{10}$? If MPC $= \frac{1}{2}$?

DEFICIT SPENDING AND THE PUBLIC DEBT

In January 1995, the *Wall Street Journal*, an influential newspaper in the financial markets of the United States, proclaimed that Canada had "now become an honorary member of the Third World in the unmanageability of its debt problem." Yet, by the year 2000, the federal election was fought between parties who all promised substantial tax cuts and restoration of program funding to historical levels.

The story of how Canada has been dealing with its debt problems, which took many years to accumulate, is a remarkable one. The decisions and trade-offs made were not easy ones. This chapter will look at the debt issue and how we have been able to turn around this problem.

PREVIEW QUESTIONS

1. By what methods can the federal government obtain purchasing power?

2. What is the difference between the gross public debt and the net public debt?

3. What is the burden of the public debt?

4. How have governments succeeded in turning around the debt problem?

Budget balance The difference between government revenue and spending.

Budget deficit When government spending exceeds its revenue.

Budget surplus When government revenue exceeds its spending.

Debt The cumulative total amount of borrowing that the government has undertaken to cover all past deficits.

Money financing The government pays its bills by creating new money.

DID YOU KNOW THAT... until 1998 your federal government so consistently spent more than it received that by the time you read this, the total accumulated net public debt will be around $600 billion? Here is what $600 billion could buy: about 1.2 trillion pieces of sushi, or 400 billion cheeseburgers, or 400 textbooks for every man, woman, and child in Canada. Your individual share of what the federal government owes is around $20,000. Should you be worried? The answer is both yes and no, as you will see in this chapter. First, let's examine what the government actually does when it spends more than it receives.

Government Budgets and Finances

A deficit occurs when the government's **budget balance** (government revenue minus spending) is negative. This occurs when the government's total revenue (mostly taxes) is less than it spends in one year. The budget balance is usually calculated on an annual fiscal year ending March 31. A **surplus** occurs when the budget balance is positive or, in other words, the tax revenue is greater than what the government spends. A **balanced budget** is one in which the revenue and spending are equal.

The **debt** is the cumulative total amount of borrowing that the government has undertaken to cover all past deficits. (There have been occasional small surpluses.) It owes this money to households, firms, and foreigners. If you own a Canada Savings Bond, for example, you have lent the government some money to cover part of this debt. This debt will be added to in any year that the government has a deficit, and reduced in any year that the government has a surplus. When governments have a deficit, there are several ways that it can handle the problem. It can alter its budget by raising taxes or reduce spending, borrow the money or, in the case of a national government, it can use money creation to pay its bills.

We've already discussed in the last chapter some of the problems associated with the first two methods for dealing with the deficit, such as the contractionary effect of raising taxes or the crowding-out effects of borrowing, so governments may be tempted to pay their bills by **money financing**. Money financing means that the government pays its bills by creating new money.

How is this money created? It is created when the government sells its bonds to the Bank of Canada rather than to the public at large. The Bank of Canada pays for its purchases of the treasury bills by creating new money. Effectively, the Bank of Canada "prints" up the money for the government to pay its bills, thus creating no new debt. We'll look at this process in greater detail in Chapters 15-17.

However, the amount of new money that can be created to pay its bills, without other kinds of problems occurring, is very limited—at most, a few billion dollars each year. The various governments over the years have had much larger deficits than could reasonably be financed through money creation, so the preferred choice has been to borrow money.

The Historical Record of Deficit Financing

The federal government's record has not been good over the past 30 years, although it has been much improved recently. In part (a) of Figure 14.1, you can see that while federal government tax revenues have remained less than 20 percent of GDP, from 1981 to 1996 federal government expenditures have consistently been greater than 20 percent. The difference in the two curves in part (a) represents the federal budget deficit expressed as a percentage of GDP. Notice that in 1998 the government recorded a budget surplus—its revenues exceeded its expenditures for the first time since 1977—and has maintained a small surplus each year since then. In part (b), you see the absolute growth in federal

Try Preview Question 1:

By what methods can the federal government obtain purchasing power?

FIGURE 14.1 Two Ways of Viewing the Historical Record of Federal Deficit Financing

In part (a), federal expenditures and revenues are expressed as a percentage of GDP. The difference is the federal deficit, also expressed as a percentage of GDP. Since the mid-1990s expenditures as a percentage of GDP have fallen, and in 1998 they were less than revenues. In part (b), we express federal expenditures and federal revenues in nominal dollar terms. The difference is, of course, the nominal dollar deficit or surplus.

Source: Statistics Canada, *Historical Statistics of Canada,* Catalogue No. 11-576-XIE, Series D18, D34; Statistics Canada, CANSIM Database, Series D474760, D474810, D11000

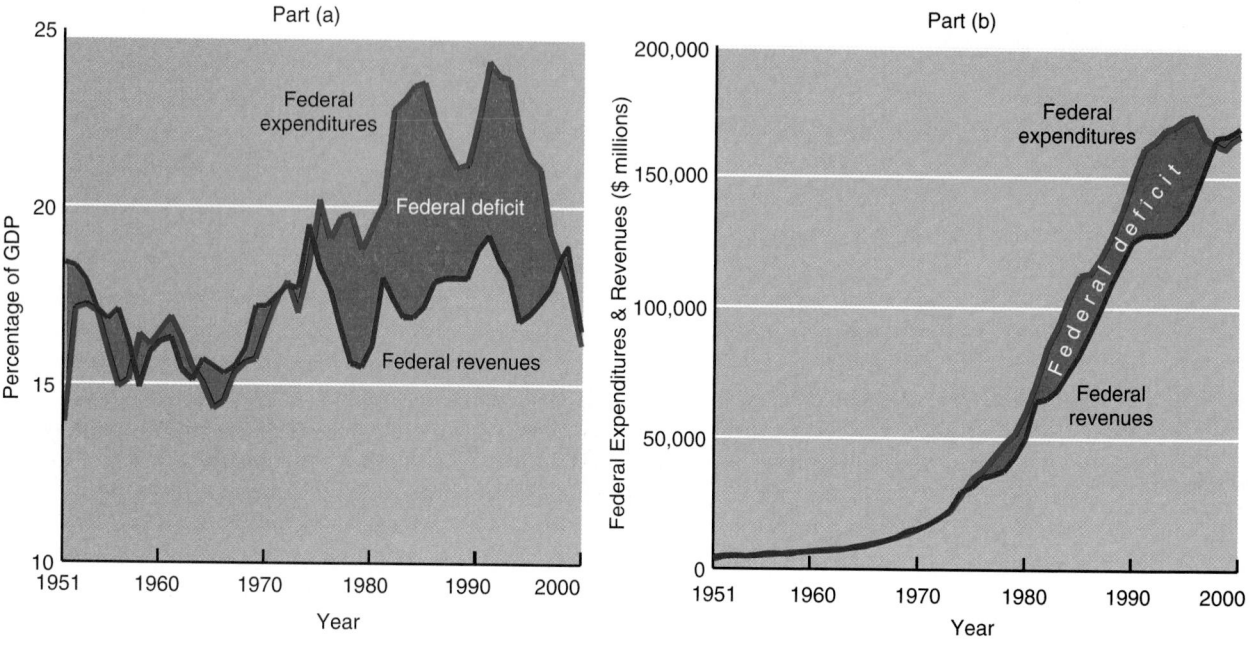

government tax revenues and expenditures. The shaded red area represents the actual dollar size of the deficit since World War II.

Deficits Versus Debt: The Distinction Between Stocks and Flows

Public debt The total value of all outstanding federal government securities.

You have already learned the distinction between stocks and flows. The same analysis can be applied to the difference between the federal budget deficit and the total accumulated **public debt.** The public debt is a stock. At any point in time, it is some number, such as $500 billion. The federal budget deficit, in contrast, is a flow. If it is $20 billion, that means that the federal government is spending at a rate of $20 billion per year more than it is receiving in taxes and other revenues. Hence if this year the public debt is $500 billion and each year the federal government has a deficit of $20 billion, then next year the public debt will be $520 billion, the year after that it will be $540 billion, and so on.

The Relative Size of the Federal Deficit

The problem with looking at part (b) of Figure 14.1 is that the annual deficit is expressed as a current dollar figure. In a growing economy (both through real output increases and inflation), what is perhaps more important is the relative size of the federal budget deficit expressed as a percentage of GDP. This is shown in Figure 14.2. You can see that the federal budget deficit expressed as a percentage of GDP reached its peak during the late 1980s before falling back, again rose until 1993, and has been falling ever since. In 1998, the deficit was negative—that is, the government recorded a budget surplus.

FIGURE 14.2 The Federal Budget Deficit Expressed as a Percentage of GDP

The budget deficit reached its peak during the late 1980s and hit another peak during early 1994, but has fallen ever since.

Source: Statistics Canada, *Historical Statistics of Canada,* Catalogue No. 11-576-XIE, Series D18, D34; Statistics Canada, CANSIM Database, Series D4592, D93712, D14442, D14872, D474760, D474810, D11000.

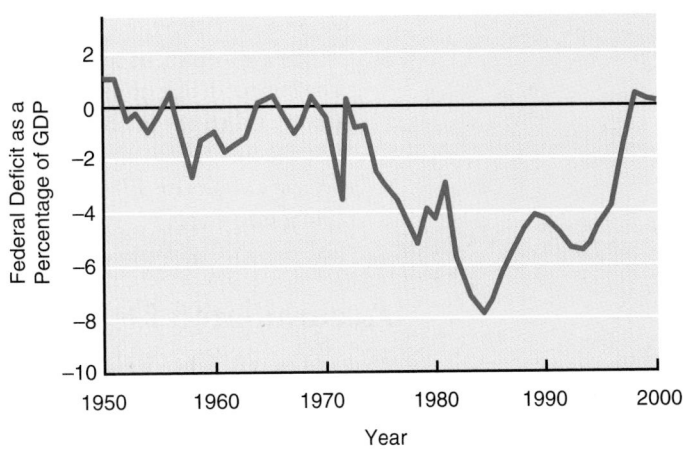

INTERNATIONAL POLICY EXAMPLE 14-1

Government Budget Balances in the European Union

The European Union has outlined a policy strategy that required all of its 15 members to limit any government deficits to 3 percent of GDP or less. Each country had to reach this goal by the year 1999 in order for all EU countries to adopt a common currency. As shown in Figure 14.3, by 1996, only 7 of the 15 EU countries had met that goal.

FIGURE 14.3 European Union Budget Deficits

Only 7 of the 15 EU countries have deficits that fall below 3 percent of GDP.

Source: European Commission.

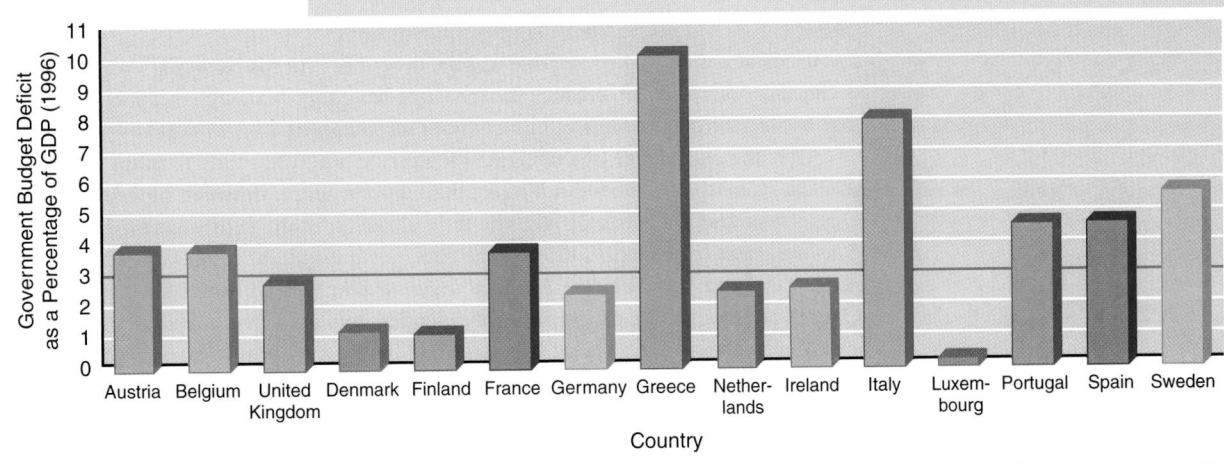

For critical analysis: If Canada were part of the European Union, how would its annual government budget balance stack up against the deficits of other members?

> ### CONCEPTS IN BRIEF
> - Whenever a government spends more than it receives, it runs a budget deficit. When a government spends less than it receives, it runs a budget surplus.
> - The budget deficit or surplus is a flow, whereas the accumulated budget deficits are a stock, called the public debt.
> - The federal deficit expressed as a percentage of GDP hit a peak of around 6.5 percent in the late 1980s, fell back, rose to another peak in 1994, and has been falling ever since.

Accumulated Deficits: The Public Debt and Interest Payments On It

As you have already learned, every time the federal government runs a deficit, it must borrow from the private sector and foreigners, thereby increasing its debt.

The Public Debt

Gross public debt All federal government debt irrespective of who owns it.

Net public debt Gross public debt minus the value of financial assets held by government agencies.

Try Preview Question 2:

What is the difference between the gross public debt and the net public debt?

All federal public debt, taken together, is called the **gross public debt.** When we subtract from the gross public debt the financial assets held by government agencies, we arrive at the **net public debt.** The net public debt normally increases whenever the federal government runs a budget deficit—that is, whenever total government outlays are greater than total government revenues. Look at column 3 in Table 14.1. The total net public debt grew steadily from 1970 to 1997. In 1998, the federal government began to run small surpluses, and used some of that to reduce the public debt. Taking into account inflation and population growth, the per capita debt has grown less quickly than the total numbers suggest. A better way to look at the Canadian national debt is to examine it as a percentage of GDP, which we do in Figure 14.4. We see that after World War II, this ratio fell steadily until the mid-1970s. Then it rose sharply through the mid-1990s, and has recently fallen back to just under 60% of GDP. The provinces have followed a similar pattern with debt of about 27% of GDP, as seen in Figure 14-6.

How Did Our Debt Get So Big?

If you look at Figure 14.4 you will see that the net public debt soared during World War II, then declined steadily until 1974. Since then the debt has grown, although recent budget surpluses may be used for debt reduction. How did this second growth get its start?

After the experience of the Great Depression when so many families were poverty-stricken, Canadians decided not to let that happen again. Between the end of the Great Depression and the early 1970s, the federal government legislated programs like the *Unemployment Insurance Act* (1941), the *Family Allowance Act* (1944), the *Old Age Security Act* (1951), and the *National Hospital Insurance Act* (1957) better known as medicare. Over the decades these programs were amended, making them universal (i.e., available to everyone) and indexing them to inflation. The long economic expansion of the 1950s and 1960s made the government believe these programs would always be affordable.

In 1973 the Organization of Petroleum Exporting Countries (OPEC) cut back on oil production to raise the price and increase their revenues. The price of oil, an input to virtually everything produced in the West, quadrupled. Prices soared, Canadian firms went bankrupt, thousands of employees lost their jobs, and consumers cut back spending. With universal unemployment insurance indexed to inflation, benefits paid to the unemployed mushroomed, while premiums paid in, as well as personal and corporate taxes, declined. Further, the federal government, to help out struggling firms, reduced oil taxes and provided subsidies to keep firms producing.

TABLE 14.1

The Federal Deficit, Our Public Debt, and the Interest We Pay on It

Net public debt in column 3 is defined as total federal debt minus total federal financial assets. Per capita net public debt is obtained by dividing population into the net public debt.

(1) Year	(2) Budget Balance (millions of current dollars)	(3) Net Public Debt (millions of current dollars)	(4) Net Public Debt per Capita (current dollars)	(5) Net Interest Costs (millions of current dollars)	(6) Net Interest as a Percentage of GDP
1940	−378	3,271	290	146	2.1
1945	−2,123	11,298	936	438	3.6
1950	212	11,645	846	439	2.3
1955	−71	11,263	720	514	1.8
1960	−330	12,089	677	798	2.0
1965	203	15,529	791	1,111	1.9
1970	−372	17,788	836	1,818	2.0
1975	−4,023	23,958	1,037	3,561	2.0
1980	−13,171	72,555	2,965	9,794	3.1
1981	−10,787	86,280	3,481	13,584	3.8
1982	−22,051	99,600	3,971	17,627	4.6
1983	−29,260	128,302	5,064	17,360	4.2
1984	−35,646	164,532	6,433	21,230	4.7
1985	−36,011	209,891	8,131	25,322	5.2
1986	−31,363	245,151	9,404	25,417	5.0
1987	−30,910	276,735	10,481	26,742	4.8
1988	−27,692	305,438	11,414	27,622	4.5
1989	−26,667	333,519	12,251	33,190	5.1
1990	−28,023	362,920	13,129	38,771	5.7
1991	−32,369	395,075	14,115	42,484	6.2
1992	−38,617	428,682	15,132	41,139	5.9
1993	−40,601	471,061	16,430	39,292	5.4
1994	−40,432	513,219	17,700	37,899	4.9
1995	−36,735	550,685	18,785	41,927	5.2
1996	−33,212	578,718	19,530	46,692	5.6
1997	−13,500	588,402	19,650	44,916	5.1
1998	4,507	581,931	19,261	43,443	4.8
1999	2,591	578,323	18,988	43,898	4.6
2000	2,566	564,793	18,388	41,565	4.0

Sources: Statistics Canada, *Historical Statistics of Canada,* Catalogue No. 11-576-XIE, Series D18, D29, D34; Statistics Canada, CANSIM Database series D1, D5131, D14816, D469384, D474760, D474810, D474887, D93711, and D11000.

FIGURE 14.4 Net Canadian Public Debt as a Percentage of GDP

During World War II, the net public debt grew dramatically. It fell until the mid-1970s, then started rising again. After reaching a peak in 1995, it has started to decline again.

Source: Statistics Canada, CANSIM Database series D469384, D14816, D11000; Public Sector Finance, Catalogue No. 68-212-XPB, 1994-95, Table 1.9, pp 1–12..

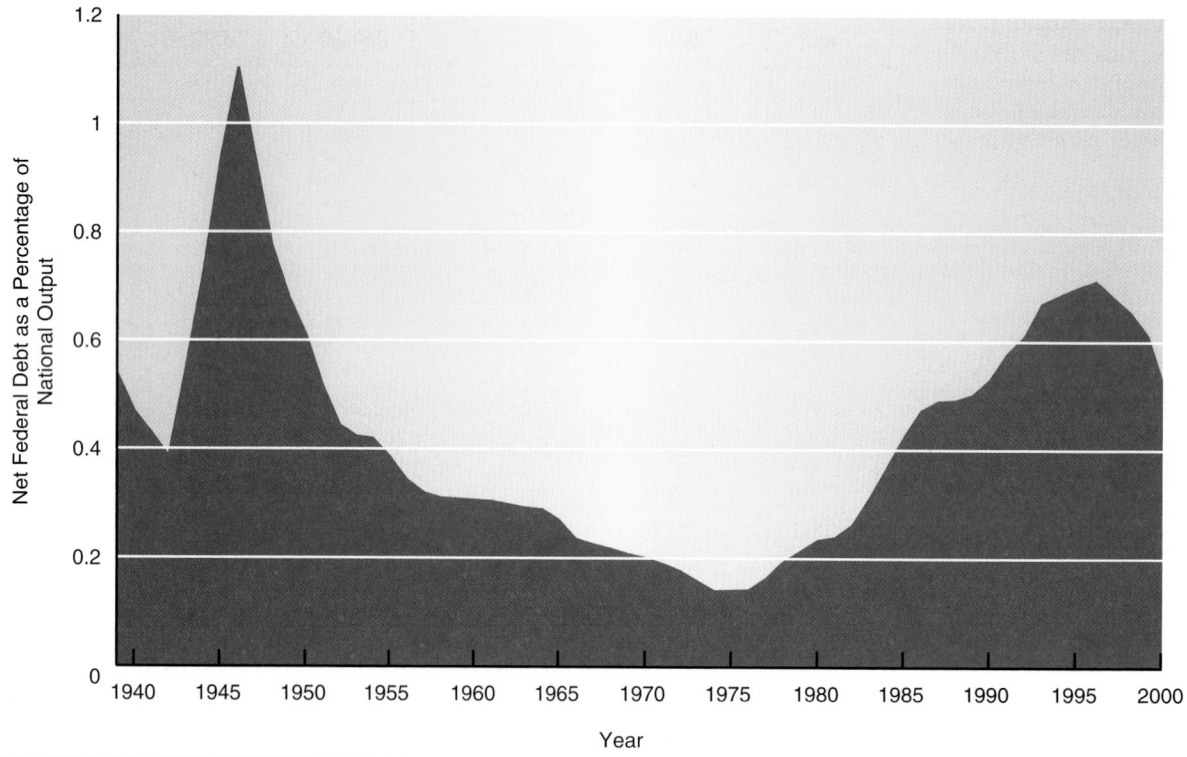

As the Canadian economy started to recover from this shock, the entire Western world slipped into the 1981–83 recession. Once again, payments out in social programs rose relative to revenues, and the debt climbed again. As well, interest payments on the (now much larger) debt were higher as well, because interest rates rose to over 20 percent in 1980. Although economic growth in the 1980s was substantial, the Conservative government of the day did allow spending to grow and debt to continue to accumulate. By the time the 1990 recession occurred, it was even more difficult to make the adjustments needed to bring the budget balance back to appropriate levels. Interest rate payments on the gross public debt accounted for almost $50 billion of a budget of about $160 billion in total by the 1995 fiscal year. These interest payments were about double what the government was spending on health, post-secondary education, and social assistance.

In 1995, the federal government made a substantial change in policy direction to bring down the annual deficit. We'll look at how the government was able to bring about this change.

Provincial Government Debt

While each individual province is small relative to the federal government, the provinces, territories, and local governments when combined spend more than the federal government. The problem of the federal debt has been compounded by the provincial debts that have been added in the last 20 years. Figure 14.5 shows the history of both governments in adding to the debt.

FIGURE 14.5 Recent Federal and Provincial-territorial Surplus/deficit(-)

Public Accounts basis

Source: The Fiscal Balance in Canada, Department of Finance Publication. August 2000.

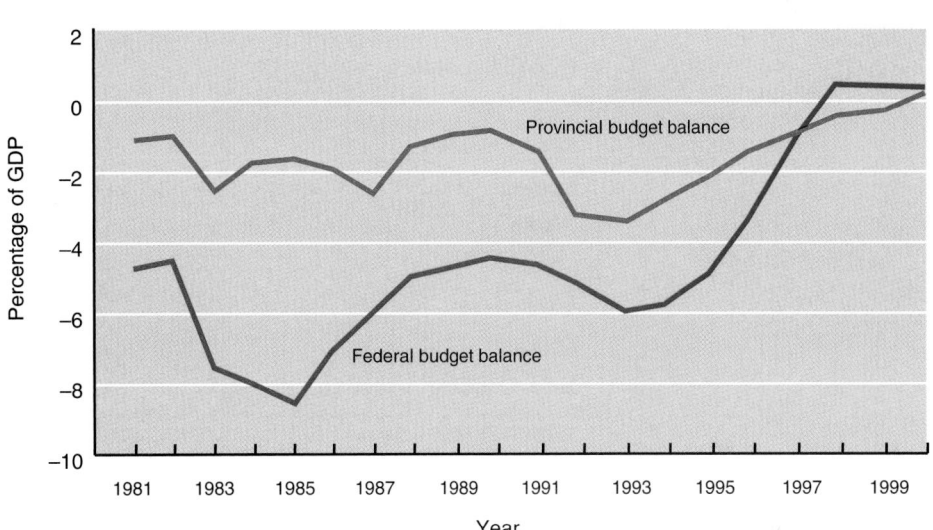

Before 1982, the provincial governments' combined financial assets were more or less balanced. Starting in 1983, the provinces began adding significantly to the debt. All 10 were running deficits in 1986, a time of economic expansion. Since government financing of post-secondary education, health care, and the Canada Assistance Plan (welfare) is shared between provincial and federal governments, part of the problem arose because of the federal government. The federal government made the decision in the late 1980s to begin reducing the funding for those programs to the provinces, and that decision has been continued up until the latest federal government budgets. Thus, the provincial governments were facing reduced help from the federal government in the face of rising expenditures.

It is understandable that provinces would run deficits during a recession, such as the one in 1982, but the provinces were not following basic Keynesian counter cyclical policy and were running surpluses in the expansion period from 1984-1989. Alberta, an oil-rich province which had been experiencing large surpluses until this time because of the oil revenues, was experiencing a prolonged depression in the energy and agriculture sectors. Ontario, the largest province, was also experiencing deficits throughout the 1980s, even though there had been an economic expansion since 1983. Other provinces, like Newfoundland and Saskatchewan, have a chronic deficit because of regional economic problems. When the next recession came in 1990, the provinces were unable to deal with the fiscal deficit problem except by further borrowing.

More recently, most provinces have reversed their borrowing trend. Several achieved balanced positions in the 1995 fiscal year through changes in fiscal policy and, by the year 2000, have achieved a combined surplus. Alberta has once again run large surpluses largely because of high energy prices, while Ontario, Quebec, and British Columbia have gone from running large deficits to balanced budgets. Table 14.2 shows the budget balances for the year 2000 for the provinces. As a result of these changes in fiscal policy and the growth in the economy, the net debt to GDP ratio for all levels of government has fallen significantly since the mid-1990s. Figure 14-6 shows how this trend has affected our debt.

TABLE 14.2

Province	Year 2000 Budget Balance (millions of dollars)
Newfoundland	24
Prince Edward Island	1
Nova Scotia	45
New Brunswick	−777
Quebec	−436
Ontario	1391
Manitoba	−131
Saskatchewan	406
Alberta	2375
British Columbia	−1582

Source: Adapted from Statistics Canada, CANSIM Database, Matrices 3777-3786.

The provincial and federal pattern of debt accumulation is very similar to that of other countries (although not as dramatic) over this same time period. Figure 14.7 gives a brief summary of the international picture.

Annual Interest Payments on the Public Debt

Consider the size of interest payments on the public debt as shown in column 5 of Table 14.1. Those interest payments started rising dramatically around 1975. Expressed as a percentage of GDP in column 6, today they are more than twice what they were a half century ago. As long as the government borrows from Canadians, the interest payments will be made to Canadians. In other words, we owe the debt to ourselves; some people are taxed so that the government can pay interest to others (or themselves). But we have seen a rising share of the public debt owned by foreigners, reaching its peak in 1993 at 26.6 percent. Foreigners still own around 24 percent of our public debt. So we don't just owe it to ourselves.

FIGURE 14.6 Recent Federal and Provincial-territorial Net Debt

Public Accounts basis

Source: Statistics Canada, *Historical Statistics of Canada,* Catalogue No. 11-576-XIE, Series D18, D34; Statistics Canada, CANSIM Database, Series D58032, D474892, D4592, D93712.

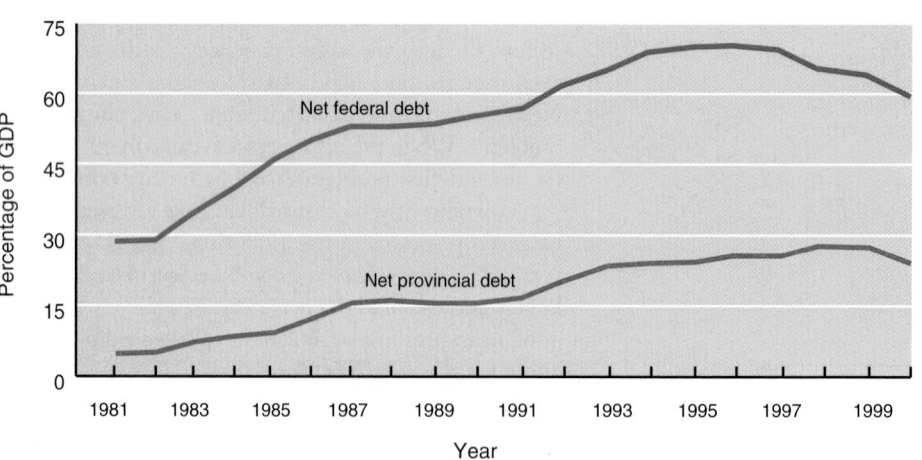

INTERNATIONAL POLICY EXAMPLE 14-2

Public Debt Around the World

Our debt problem reached its peak in 1995 at about 70 percent of GDP. Figure 14.7 shows public debt to GDP ratios for several of Canada's most important trading partners. It is clear that while some countries have been able to get their problems under control, some have not.

FIGURE 14.7 Rising Debt in Canada's Trading Partners

Over the next few years, the public debt of Canada's trading partners is expected to rise.

- ■ 1991
- ■ 1995
- ■ 1999

Source: Adapted from Federal Budget 2000, Department of Finance.

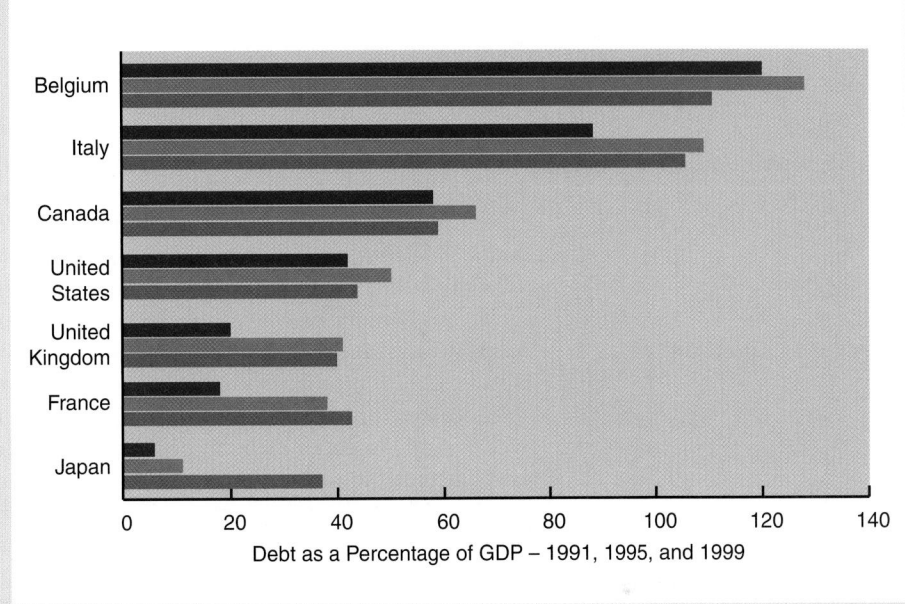

Debt as a Percentage of GDP – 1991, 1995, and 1999

For critical analysis: Has Japan done a better or a worse job than Canada in controlling its growing debt, relatively speaking?

INTERNATIONAL POLICY EXAMPLE 14-3

Belgium's Diminishing Policy Options

Belgium's public debt is approaching 110 percent of GDP. This figure has little meaning until one examines its effect on the Belgian government's policy options. The interest costs of its public debt have risen to over 40 percent of its government's budget. This increasing net interest cost of the public debt in Belgium is steadily crowding out everything else the government wants to do. Recently, it stopped maintaining its national road system. If Belgium continues to add to its public debt through annual budget deficits the way it has done in the past, the net interest payment on that public debt will eventually crowd out every other government expenditure!

For critical analysis: The government of Canada now pays out about 23 percent of its revenues in interest costs. What actions is our government taking to stall the rise in interest payments?

Thinking Critically About the Media 14-1   Canada Pension Plan

During 1996 when the Canada Pension Plan was under review, the media frequently warned that the Plan would go broke in the next 10 to 15 years unless premiums were doubled at once. The media decried the possibility of this hike, claiming Canadians and businesses would not be willing to pay it. But Canada's premiums, then at 4.6 percent of insured earnings, are actually low relative to other countries'. A World Bank study shows the rate of pension premiums in the United States is 12.4 percent, 20 percent in France, 23 percent in Austria, and 26 percent in Italy. Only Iceland, at 2 percent, was lower than Canada of all the OECD countries!

The Burden of the Public Debt

From 1984 to 1997, the net public debt of Canada more than tripled, to about $600 billion. The public debt is the total of all the outstanding debt owed by the federal government to its individual and institutional lenders. Whenever the federal government is in deficit, the public debt rises; for example, in fiscal 1996, the federal government deficit was about $33 billion, so the public debt increased by that amount in that fiscal year. Because of the large deficits incurred by the federal government in the 1980s and 1990s, the public debt rose dramatically—at least in nominal values. We shall now analyze whether federal deficits, and the accompanying increase in the public debt that they generate, impose a burden on future generations or are irrelevant.

As you read the remainder of this chapter, try to keep two things in mind. First, given the level of government expenditures, the main alternative to the deficit is higher taxes; therefore, the costs of a deficit should be compared to the costs of higher taxes, not to zero. Second, it is important to distinguish between the effects of deficits when full employment exists and when substantial unemployment exists.

Federal Budget Deficits: A Burden on Future Generations?

Assume that the federal government decides to increase government expenditures on final goods and services by $10 billion, and that it can finance such expenditures either by raising taxes by $10 billion or by selling $10 billion of bonds. Many economists maintain that the second option, deficit spending, would lead to a higher level of national consumption and a lower level of national private saving than the first option.

The reason this is so, say these economists, is that if people are taxed, they will have to forgo private consumption now as they substitute government goods for private goods. Suppose that taxes are not raised, but instead the public buys bonds to finance the $10 billion in government expenditures. The community's disposable income is the same, and it has increased its assets by $10 billion in the form of bonds. The community will either (1) fail to realize that its liabilities (in the form of future taxes due to an increased public debt that must eventually be paid) have *also* increased by $10 billion or (2) believe that it can consume the governmentally provided goods and simultaneously purchase the same quantity of privately provided consumer goods because the bill for the currently governmentally provided goods will be paid by *future* taxpayers.

If full employment exists, then as people raise their present consumption (the same quantity of private consumption goods, but more public consumption goods), something must be crowded out. In a closed economy, investment (spending on capital goods) is crowded out. The mechanism by which this crowding out occurs is an increase in the interest rate: Deficit spending increases the total demand for credit but leaves the total supply of credit unaltered. The rise in interest rates that causes a reduction in the growth of investment and capital formation in turn slows the growth of productivity and improvement in the community's living standard.

The foregoing analysis suggests that deficit spending can impose a burden on future generations in two ways. First, unless income grows dramatically, future generations will have to be taxed at a higher rate to retire the higher public debt resulting from the present generation's increased consumption of governmentally provided goods. Second, the increased level of consumption by the present generation crowds out investment and reduces the growth of capital goods; this leaves future generations with a smaller capital stock and thereby reduces their wealth.

PAYING OFF THE PUBLIC DEBT IN THE FUTURE.   Suppose that after 50 years of running deficits, the public debt becomes so large that each adult person's tax liability is $50,000. Suppose further that the government chooses (or is forced) to pay off the debt at that time. Will that generation be burdened with our generation's overspending? The debt is, after all, owed (mostly) to ourselves. It's true that every adult will have to come up with $50,000 in taxes to pay off the debt; but then the government will use that money to pay off bondholders, who are (mostly) the same people. Thus *some* people will be burdened because they owe $50,000 and own less than $50,000 in government bonds. But others will receive more than $50,000 for the bonds they own. As a generation or a community, they will pay and receive about the same amount of money.

Of course, there could be a burden on some low-income adults who will find it difficult or impossible to obtain $50,000 to pay the tax liability. Still, nothing says that taxes to pay off the debt must be assessed equally; it seems likely that a special tax would be levied, based on the ability to pay.

OUR DEBT TO FOREIGNERS.   We have been assuming that most of the debt is owed to ourselves. What about the 24 percent of our public debt that is owned by foreigners?

It is true that if foreigners buy Canadian government bonds, we do not owe that debt to ourselves, and a potential burden on future generations may result. But not necessarily. Foreigners will buy our government's debt if the inflation-adjusted, risk-adjusted, after-tax rate of return on such bonds exceeds what the investors can earn in their own country or some other country. If they buy Canadian bonds voluntarily, they perceive a benefit in doing so.

It is important to realize that not all government expenditures can be viewed as consumption; government expenditures on such things as highways, bridges, dams, research and development, and education might properly be perceived as investments. If the rate of return on such investments exceeds the interest rate paid to foreign investors, both foreigners and future Canadians will be economically better off. What really matters is on what the government spends its money. If government expenditures financed by foreigners are made on wasteful projects, a burden may well be placed on future generations.

We can use the same reasoning to examine the problem of current investment and capital creation being crowded out by current deficits. If deficits lead to slower growth rates, future generations will be poorer. But if the government expenditures are really investments, and if the rate of return on such public investments exceeds the interest rate paid on the bonds, both present and future generations will be economically richer.

THE EFFECT OF UNEMPLOYMENT.   If the economy is operating at a level substantially below full-employment real GDP, crowding out need not take place. In such a situation, an expansionary fiscal policy via deficit spending can increase current consumption (of governmentally provided goods) without crowding out investment. Indeed, if some government spending is in the form of high-yielding public investments, both present and future generations can be economically richer; such public investments will provide positive benefits in the future.

NOT ALL BORROWING IS BAD.   Don't get the impression that the government should never borrow. After all, borrowing is not always bad. Consider an example of a student who has a choice of borrowing money for one of two purposes: the purchase of a home entertainment centre or tuition payments to attend college. Borrowing for the first purpose may prove to be burdensome; borrowing for the second purpose—building human capital—may allow the student to reap greater returns in the form of higher income later. The same analysis can be applied to government borrowing. There is a difference between government borrowing to purchase Canada Day fireworks shows, and government borrowing to invest in the Trans-Canada Highway system. One can conclude, therefore, that increased public debt is not necessarily bad if it creates a net investment for the future.

Try Preview Question 3:

What is the burden of the public debt?

Are Deficits Relevant?

Much of the analysis to this point has assumed that deficit spending increases the demand for credit, while the supply of credit remains constant. Hence the interest rate rises and investment is crowded out. But what if the community realizes that an increase in the public debt also represents an increase in its future tax liabilities—the Ricardian equivalence theorem? Further, what if people wish not to burden their own children with an increased public debt? Because the deficit has increased, they would increase their current saving in order to enable their children to meet future debt obligations. In fact, because their taxes do not rise, their disposable income is higher, and they can save by purchasing the new government bonds. In the process, interest rates will not rise. Deficit spending may not lead to crowding out.

Many people plan to (and do) bestow wealth on others. The latest research shows that from 25 to 50 percent of all saving is undertaken in order to transfer wealth to relatives (usually children) during an individual's lifetime. And most people also bestow wealth on their heirs at death. To illustrate the point, assume that parents intend to leave $200,000 to their descendants and that they have saved sufficiently to achieve that goal. Then suppose that the government engages in deficit spending so that their heirs' future tax liabilities rise by $20,000. Realizing that they no longer have achieved their goal, the parents might increase the amount they save now so as to cover their heirs' additional future $20,000 tax liability.

If both the supply of credit (saving) and the demand for credit rise, there is no theoretical reason for believing that the interest rate will rise. If that is so, crowding out won't occur; the growth of investment and capital production won't be retarded, and future generations need not have lower living standards.

Solving the Debt Problem

It may seem simple, but the most obvious ways to reduce the debt and deficit problem are:

- Reduce spending
- Increase taxes
- Have GDP grow.

EXAMPLE 14-1   Balancing Budgets

Several provinces have enacted what is called "balanced budget" legislation. Essentially, they restrict the government's ability to run a deficit. If it appears that a deficit is going to happen in a particular year, then the legislation requires the government to take some action to correct the problem.

The problem with such legislation is that it restricts the ability of the government to make sensible economic choices. If the government is running a large surplus, would it be required to spend that amount of money? What if the economy is already running at capacity? Won't a tax break equal to the surplus overheat the economy?

Governments borrow money for capital spending in the same way that businesses borrow. Yet the government cannot write off depreciation the way that private businesses can, as there is no agreed way to measure how fast many of the assets of government depreciate. How do you depreciate a national park?

Of course, there is always the ability of any government to repeal or amend the legislation. What one government put into place, another can take out. So in the end, the legislation is probably not much more than a stated intention to make sure that governments don't get into the problems that they've encountered in the past. Trying to balance budgets each and every year is probably no more sensible than for individuals to try to balance their income and expenses every year.

For critical analysis: What effect would balanced budget legislation that required governments to balance their budgets every year have on discretionary fiscal policy?

Reduce Spending

A reduction of spending by government is the first way that many would advocate to eliminate the problem. This is not without problems, however.

First, it must be remembered that cutting back on spending by government has a contractionary effect on the economy. The people who are laid off from the bureaucracy see a sharp reduction in income, and will reduce their spending in turn, and so the spending cuts are multiplied through our expenditure multiplier process. This has the effect of reducing aggregate demand and GDP. In a time of recession, this may be quite difficult to accept. Politically, the unions may be able to mount an effective political strategy to stop this, since the employees of government are also voters. If these cuts are made in popular programs like education or medicare, then the government suffers the possibility that they will lose out across the population.

Second, cutting back on transfer payments may be seen by the public as mean spirited, and may be politically very difficult to achieve. The groups that are cut back will probably raise their objection to those cuts in a vocal way. This kind of event happened with Brian Mulroney in 1984, when he attempted to deindex old age security payments. Since transfer payments are primarily received by the poorest sectors of the population, any government that cuts back on transfer payments is subject to the criticism that it is achieving the goal on the backs of those least able to afford it.

Third, politicians near elections must pay some attention to the voters they are trying to woo, and it is often the case that announcements about new projects creating jobs in important ridings have the effect of winning over key voters. Other political parties vying for power may make extravagant promises to win those voters. The message that the "cupboard is bare" and local concerns cannot be addressed is not usually popular.

Increase Taxes

A second way to reduce the deficit and debt is to increase taxes. Again, this method for reducing the size of the problem has its own political and economic dangers.

As we learned before, increasing taxes takes money out of the hands of the consumers, and so lessens their consumption demand. This has the effect of reducing aggregate demand, reducing GDP, and increasing unemployment.

Corporations argue that higher taxes tend to drive businesses out of the country. Since taxes are generally lower in the United States, it is possible for some of them to move their operations to other countries. This could happen more if their operations were taxed more heavily in Canada.

Many individual Canadians feel that they are overtaxed already. They do not want to pay more taxes. The rise in taxes over the last 10 years has already reduced the after-tax income of many Canadians significantly. The rise of the Reform Party in Canada can be attributed in part to this feeling.

GDP Growth

The best way to cure the deficit and debt problem is to have the economy grow. Earlier in the chapter we noted that we were measuring the debt against GDP, because this provides a consistent measure across time. It also provides a measure of the ability to repay the debt. *As the economy grows, our ability to repay also improves.* A larger nominal GDP means greater tax revenue for the government. A larger real GDP typically means fewer people collecting welfare and other income support from the government.

Many successful corporations have much higher levels of debt today than they had in the past, but no one is concerned about their level of debt. Many are more profitable than they were part in the past. Their ability to repay has also grown with the debt, because they have more revenue with which to repay this debt more easily as the economy grows.

Part of that growth in nominal GDP comes through rising prices, and part comes through growing output. The size of the debt relative to GDP will fall, and the government will benefit any time that prices rise faster than expected. This kind of redistribution between lenders and borrowers is the same as that which we discussed earlier in Chapter 8.

As well, a larger real economy will mean that the government also collects more revenue from the new business and employment that is created. It's a lot easier politically to collect taxes from profitable businesses and formerly unemployed people, than to cut entitlements to the unemployed!

The problem with this solution is that it requires the economy to grow. If the economy is in recession, and if policymakers are committed to a low inflation rate, then the government gets little help from this method. Government programs can have an indirect effect on productivity such as have occurred elsewhere (in Japan, for example).

We've Been There Before

It is important to remember that this situation is not entirely new to Canada. A similar situation occurred during the Second World War. Canada borrowed heavily to finance its war effort and had run up its debt to a level higher than today's debt, relative to GDP. This borrowing came on the heels of the Great Depression in which the economy faced 10 years of declining and stagnant economic growth.

Debt levels after the War were brought down to manageable levels over 15 years. This happened at a time when the Canadian economy went through considerable restructuring and several small recessions. What ultimately reduced the debt problem was the growth of Canadian GDP in the post-war years. Nominal GDP grew at about 8 percent annually, and real GDP grew at about 4.5 percent annually. Having a bigger income helps tremendously in terms of paying off debt!

Managing the Current Debt Problem

The current debt problem has been brought under control, both at the federal and provincial levels, by combinations of all three methods of deficit reduction. The 1995 budget was particularly pivotal for the federal government and, in that budget, quite a number of changes were introduced to both spending and taxation policy. Let's look at the federal government's policies, which are representative of what has happened in the provinces.

Paul Martin, as Finance Minister, released the federal government budget in February 1995 and gave as his target two years to reduce the deficit to 3.0 percent of GDP. Within that guideline, he has used fairly pessimistic forecasts for GDP growth and interest rates. He also has set aside a contingency fund to help ensure that those goals are met. He proposes cutting program expenditures by about $12 billion from current levels (reducing benefits under Employment Insurance and other programs, as well as reducing civil servant employment by 15 percent). Further, he has increased some taxes by a small amount, although personal income taxes remain unchanged. Payroll taxes were also increased. Old Age Security and the Guaranteed Income Supplement are now "taxed back" from higher-income earners. Tax brackets had been previously "deindexed" from inflation rates, so there was additional help from that source as inflation raised peoples' incomes.

The budget deficits were further reduced by the expansion of the economy. The Canadian economy grew very substantially in the 1990s primarily because of the booming US economy. This brought in more tax revenue and reduced employment insurance claims further as people went back to work.

As a result of these measures, the debt problem has clearly turned the corner. It is clear, too, that the governments of Canada have been fortunate that the North American economy has had the longest post-war expansion period in the 1990s. Attempting to do what they did during a recession would have been very difficult.

These measures have not come without substantial costs to the public. The increases in taxes and reduction in expenditures have acted as a "drag" on the economy as it recovered in the 1990s and have delayed the recovery longer in Canada than in the United States. Canadians continue to be very concerned about the ability of the health care system to cope with a reduced level of funding and the Chrétien government has promised to return some of the money cut in earlier federal budgets. Post-secondary education has been affected and classrooms typically have many more students than they did twenty years ago. Many social assistance programs, such as low-income housing, have been completely eliminated and our assistance to developing nations, whose problems are much worse than ours, has been substantially reduced. There continues to be a shortage of skilled people willing to work for the government because wages have been held back or even cut during these years. The rate of taxation is still quite high compared to historical averages.

Try Preview Question 4:

How have governments succeeded in turning around the debt problem?

CONCEPTS IN BRIEF

- When we subtract the value of financial assets held by government agencies from the gross public debt, we obtain the net public debt.
- There may be a burden of the public debt on future generations if they have to be taxed at higher rates to pay for the current generation's increased consumption of governmentally provided goods; also there may be a burden if there is crowding out of current investment, resulting in less capital formation and hence a lower economic growth rate.
- If a significant part of our public debt is bought by foreigners, then we no longer "owe it to ourselves." If the rate of return on the borrowed funds is higher than the interest to be paid, future generations can be made better off by government borrowing, but will be worse off if the opposite is true.

Federal Budget Deficits In An Open Economy

Many economists believe that the Canadian current account deficit is just as serious a problem as the government budget deficit. The current account balance is the sum of the values of exports minus imports, plus interest payments we receive from other countries minus payments out to other countries, plus net gifts. (We'll spend more time looking at the balance of payments in Chapter 20.) Since our net gifts balance tends to be around zero and our exports usually exceed our imports, this means that a deficit on the current account arises because we are paying out to other countries more interest and dividends on their investments in Canada than we are receiving from the rest of the world. The

FIGURE 14.8 **Canada's Twin Deficits**

Canada's current account balance hovered around zero until 1986. Then we started running large deficits, as shown in this diagram. The federal budget has been in deficit for many years, starting in earnest in 1978. The question is, has the federal budget deficit created the current account deficit?

Source: Based on Statistics Canada, Canadian Economic Observer and Canadian Economic Observer Historical Supplement.

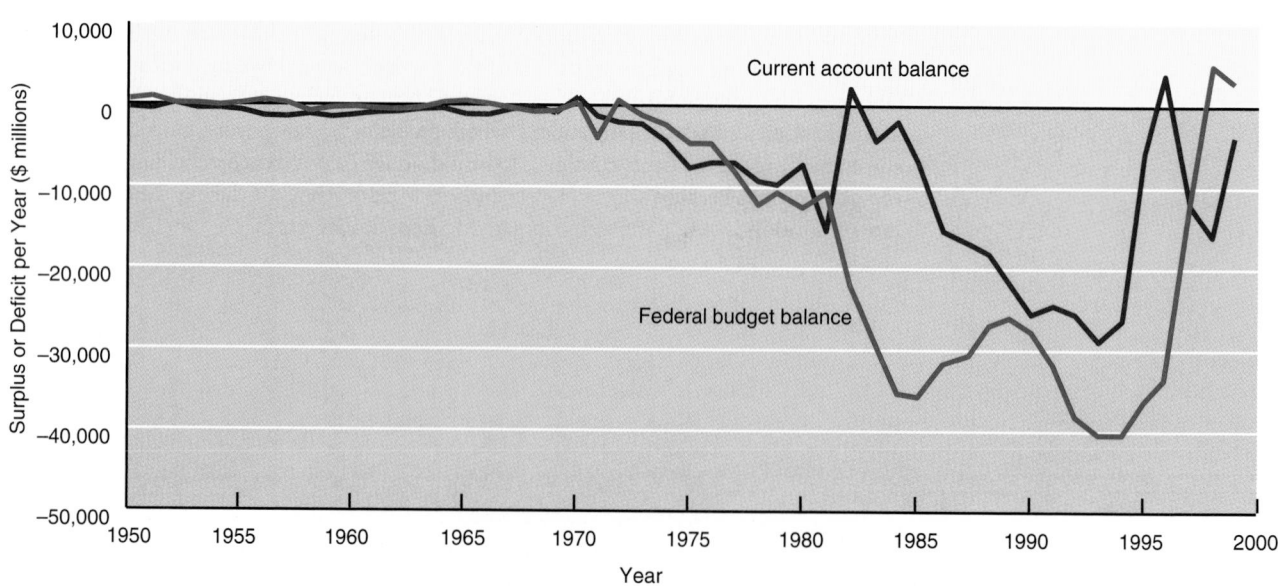

current account went from a surplus of $2.6 billion in 1984 to a deficit of over $28 billion in 1993, and back down to a small deficit of $3 billion in 1999.

By virtue of this current account deficit, foreigners have accumulated Canadian dollars and have purchased Canadian assets (real estate, corporate stocks, bonds, and so on). If this country continues to incur these deficits, foreigners will continue to purchase assets here. This could eventually present problems. For one, what if foreign investors suddenly decide to sell such assets or take their money out of the country? Another concern is with foreigners gaining political power along with their accumulation of Canadian assets. Here we concentrate on the linkage between federal budget deficits and current account deficits.

What the Evidence Says

Figure 14.8 shows the Canadian current account deficits and surpluses compared to federal budget deficits and surpluses. The year 1986 appears to be a watershed year, for that is when the current account took a marked turn for the worse. Concurrently, the federal budget deficit grew progressively larger.

On the basis of the evidence presented in Figure 14.8, it appears that there is a close relationship between the current account and fiscal deficits: Larger current account deficits follow shortly after larger fiscal deficits.

Why the Two Deficits Are Related

Intuitively, there is a reason we would expect federal budget deficits to lead to current account deficits. You might call this the unpleasant arithmetic of current account and federal budget deficits.

Assume that the federal government runs a budget deficit. Assume further that Canadians use their savings to buy government-issued bonds to finance the deficit. Where, then, does the money come from to finance business investment? The answer is that part of it must come from abroad. That is to say, dollar holders abroad invest in Canadian businesses by buying their stocks, or by investing directly in business operations. In this case, the dividends earned on their stocks, or the interest earned on their investments, flow out of the country. The current account goes into deficit because this outflow of capital exceeds to a large measure the capital flowing into Canada from similar Canadian investment abroad. In other words, the outflow is large enough to offset the surplus on the trade account.

The reason that foreigners are induced to invest in Canadian business is that domestic Canadian interest rates will normally rise, all other things held constant, whenever there is an increase in government deficits financed by increased borrowing.

Has the Deficit Been Measured Correctly?

Part of the problem, according to some economists, is that we are measuring the deficit incorrectly, and that we need to change the government accounting system to come up with a better measure of the deficit.

Capital Budgeting Theory

The federal government has only one budget to guide its spending and taxing each fiscal year. It does not distinguish between current spending for upkeep on the Prime Minister's residence, for example, and spending for a new park that's going to last for many years to come. By contrast, businesses have two budgets. One, called the *operating budget*, includes expenditures for current operations, such as salaries and interest payments. The other is called a *capital budget*, which includes expenditures on investment items, such as machines and buildings.

Some economists recommend that the government should set up a capital budget, thereby removing investment outlays from its operating budget. Opponents of such a change in the accounting rules for the federal government point out that such an action would allow the government to grow even faster than currently because many new expenditures could be placed in the capital budget, thereby reducing the operating budget deficit and reducing the pressure to cut the growth in federal government spending.

Thinking Critically About the Media 14-2   The Flat Tax

The idea of replacing our progressive income tax system with a flat tax is gaining support in the media. A flat tax would tax incomes at one rate—say 20 percent—after allowing only substantial personal exemptions—say $40,000 for a family of four. One of the attractive aspects of the flat tax is that it is simple: there are no loopholes, and the tax return would probably be one page long. Tax evasion would decline, and the $60 billion per year which now goes to the accountants and tax lawyers of the wealthy could be put to more productive use. However, if the poor don't pay tax because their incomes are less than the allowable personal deductions, and if the wealthy pay less tax on investment and other income, then where will the tax revenues come from? The media seldom dwell on the travails of the middle class, who would pay more under this system than they do under the current one.

Pick a Deficit, Any Deficit

Even using standard accounting techniques, the federal budget deficit can vary dramatically depending on what is, or is not, included. Three sets of accounts are published each year, each with a different calculation of the federal government deficit. The *public accounts* calculation is the narrowest measure of the federal deficit. It includes only budgets of government departments, and excludes those of government agencies, boards, or business enterprises. The *Financial Management System (FMS)* and the *System of National Accounts (SNA)* include both the budgets of government departments and of government

NETNOMICS

Deficit Financing: A Thing of the Past?

Governments throughout the world have often resorted to deficit financing when they have expanded government spending faster than tax collections. Most governments in Europe, for example, since World War II have gradually added more welfare programs. In addition, European governments have frequently argued that they can "create jobs" by expanding public-sector employment. Recently, for example, the French prime minister said that he would create 350,000 new jobs by hiring young people to engage in worthwhile public jobs. Such "job creation" requires funding nonetheless. The French government, like virtually all European governments, has been unable to match government spending with government revenues. It has consistently issued government securities to pay for increased government spending—debt financing.

Enter the Internet, and over goes the apple cart. Today, information about all aspects of governmental activities—spending, revenues, and the like—is available to everyone in the world on a second's notice via the Internet. Even more important, dealers in government securities can obtain this information at the speed of light. Because capital flows worldwide depend on perceived real rates of return—that is, rates of return corrected for inflation in whatever currency the securities are denominated—the owners of government securities anywhere in the world (pension plans, mutual funds, speculators, and the like) can instantaneously pull their capital out of a country when they get a sense that things aren't right. If the French government announces a new jobs program that must be financed by the sale of additional French government securities, the French government could be punished. How? By a quick net outflow of capital from France, thereby increasing its domestic interest rates.

The Internet helps spread information about government actions, the possibility of their positive or negative effects, and the economic growth outlook as a result. It also allows capital to be moved in and out of countries with the click of a mouse. Consequently, no government has the ability to engage in serious deficit financing anymore without being instantly punished.

ISSUES AND APPLICATIONS
The Baby Boom Generation Moves into Retirement Years

Concepts Applied: Demographic change, opportunity cost

As Canada's population ages, governments must decide how to provide the necessary services that the elderly need without creating another debt problem.

Facing the Future

While the current problems of debt management have been brought under control, governments in Canada are already facing a new problem, that of an aging population. Figure 14-9 shows that the proportion of seniors in the population will rise dramatically by the year 2030, while the number of young people (and the number of working-age people) will decline. This change is due to the aging of the "baby-boom" population—the generation of people born between 1945 and 1965.

Obviously, there will be massive changes in the kinds of programs that governments will be funding in the future. Health care (now a provincial responsibility with some funding from the federal government) will experience even more pressure than currently exists. The federal government will be pressured to find more money for old age security programs. As was mentioned earlier in the chapter, the Canada Pension Plan, the most basic pension that almost everyone will receive, has had to double its contribution rates to account for the fact that the population demographics are changing.

Because of the decline in the proportion of population that is young, there will be some relief for governments. There will be less spent on child tax credits, for example.

Another proposed source of funding is to move money out of post-secondary education, as there is thought to be fewer students enrolled. While on the surface it might appear that there will be fewer students coming into the system at a young age, there are two reasons for an increasing demand for post-secondary education. First, the participation by people in the 18-24 year age group is growing. Second, the number of students enrolling and re-enrolling at older ages is also increasing. In today's world, the need for post-secondary training and lifelong learning and upgrading is more important than ever.

Finally, with the projected reduction in debt over the next 30 years, the government will likely be able to reallocate the interest payments it must pay now to other programs. Given that up to one-third of the budget was allocated for this purpose alone, this will represent a substantial improvement from where we are today.

For Critical Analysis

1. Why would the increase in life expectancy, if not anticipated, create problems for the Canada Pension Plan?

2. What can the government do today with RRSP programs to reduce the cost of future income-support programs for the elderly?

**FIGURE 14.9
Canadian
Demographic
Trends**

Both levels of government will face increased future spending pressures as a result of population aging.

Source: The Fiscal Balance in Canada, Department of Finance Publication. August 2000.

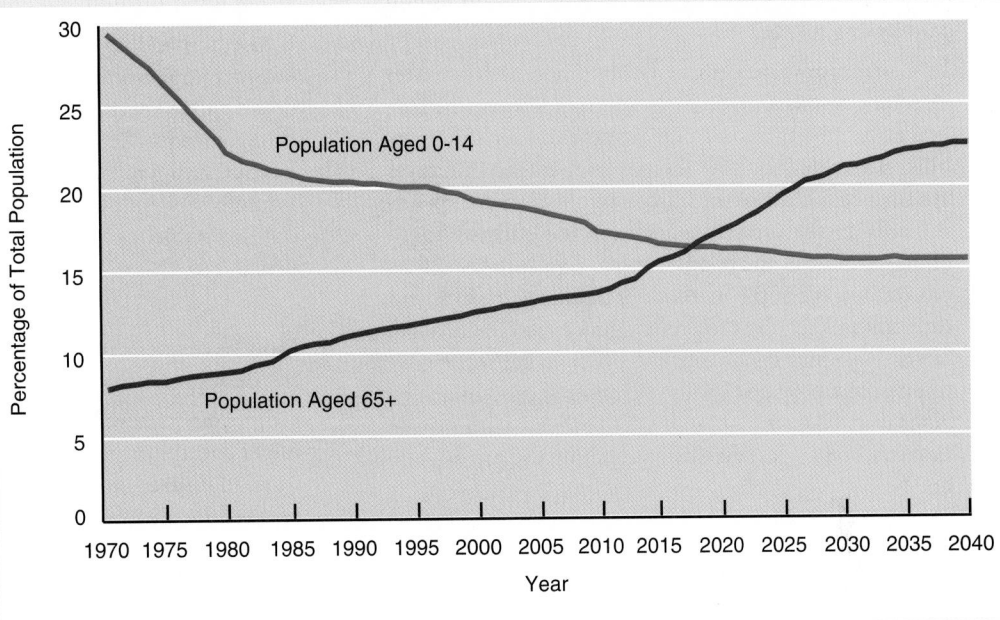

CHAPTER SUMMARY

1. The budget balance is the difference between government revenue and spending. A deficit occurs when the government spends more than it receives in revenue, and a surplus occurs when the government spends less than it receives in revenue. Federal budgets were in deficit from 1974 until 1998, when they were brought back into a balanced position.

2. Governments can cover their deficits by either borrowing the money or printing new money. Because of the negative effects of printing too much money, governments have chosen instead to borrow the money. The public debt is the cumulative total amount of borrowing that the government has undertaken to cover its previous deficits. Some of that debt is held by other government agencies, such as the Bank of Canada, so the net debt is smaller than the total amount of debt issued by the government itself.

3. Government debt does impose a burden on future generations because of the effect it has on crowding out investments and because some of the debt is owed to foreigners. Debt owed to other Canadians, however, is less of a burden. If debt is incurred to finance investment by the government, then there is the possibility that future generations will be richer because of the debt.

4. If all taxpayers perfectly anticipate increased future tax liabilities due to higher deficits, saving will increase to cover those tax liabilities. Future productivity will therefore not be affected, nor will interest rates rise; there will be no crowding-out effect.

5. Some people argue that the federal budget deficit is measured incorrectly because it lumps together spending on capital and spending on consumption. It is therefore argued that there should be an operating budget and a capital budget.

6. Three basic ways exist to bring debt problems under control: increasing taxes, reducing spending, or having GDP grow.

DISCUSSION OF PREVIEW QUESTIONS

1. **By what methods can the federal government obtain purchasing power?**

   In Canada, governments can obtain purchasing power by selling bonds and levying taxes. In addition, the federal government can also create new money to pay its bills. Regardless of how the government expenditures are financed, most of the burden of government spending falls on the present generation; the effects of government creation and bonds sales are similar to the effects of taxation. All of the methods of financing government expenditures require the present generation to consume fewer consumer goods today in order to get more governmentally provided goods. Taxation does so in an obvious way; government bond sales compete with private industry bond sales, thereby contracting the private sector.

2. **What is the difference between the gross public debt and the net public debt?**

   The gross public debt is all federal government debt irrespective of the owner of the debt. The net public debt is the gross public debt minus federally owned financial assets.

3. **What is the burden of the public debt?**

   If federal spending that increases the public debt crowds out private investment, future generations will be burdened with a lower capital stock and lower incomes. If the Ricardian equivalence theorem holds—if people, in fact, increase saving today to pay for higher tax liabilities in the future when there is deficit spending—crowding out is not inevitable, and this burden may not be as great as presumed.

4. **How have governments succeeded in turning around the debt problem?**

   Governments have been able to bring the debt problem under control through reductions in spending, increases in various taxes, and growth in the economy. This has resulted in the government being able to restore some of the cut funding and to reduce taxes in some areas where they had been increased in the early 1990s. These policies have come at the cost of considerable strain on the public sector, and have acted as a drag on economic recovery in the 1990s.

PROBLEMS

(Answers to the odd-numbered problems appear at the back of the book.)

14-1. In 1999, government spending is $800 billion and taxes collected are $770 billion. What is the federal budget balance in 1999?

Year	Federal Budget Receipts ($ billions)	Federal Budget Spending ($ billions)	GDP ($ billions)
1988	109.3	127.8	605.9
1989	117.4	137.7	650.7
1990	125.6	150.8	669.5
1991	130.9	161.1	667.5

14-2. Look at the accompanying table showing federal budget spending and federal budget receipts. Calculate the federal budget deficit as a percentage of GDP for each year.

14-3. It may be argued that the effects of a higher public debt are the same as the effects of higher taxes. Why?

14-4. To reduce the size of the deficit (and reduce the growth in the net public debt), a politician suggests that "we should tax the rich." The politician makes a simple arithmetic calculation in which he applies the increased tax rate to the total income reported by "the rich" in a previous year. He says that this is how much the government could receive from the increased taxes on "the rich." What is the major fallacy in such calculations?

14-5. Proponents of capital budgeting theory argue that whenever the government invests in capital expenditures, such as roads and dams, such government spending should be put in a separate budget called the capital budget. In doing so, the federal government's budget deficit would thereby be reduced by the amount of government capital spending. Would such a change in measuring the government deficit change anything? Explain.

14-6. What is the relationship between the annual federal government budget deficit and the net public debt?

14-7. The Statistics Canada Web site http://www. statcan.ca/english/Pgdb/ contains information which will help you fill out a table similar to Table 14.1 for your province.

a. Choose "The State" and then "Government." Calculate your province's deficit for the year listed.

b. How much were the interest charges on your provincial public debt?

c. From the main page, choose "The Economy in Detail" and "Economic Conditions." Calculate the interest charges as a percentage of your province's GDP.

d. Compare your answers to Table 14.1. Is your province or Canada as a whole in better fiscal shape (i.e., which has less interest costs as a percentage of GDP)?

ECONOMICS ON THE NET

Government debt

Internet URL:

http://www.statcan.ca/english/pgdb/state/government/govt03.htm

Navigation: A breakdown of the federal government's debt into its various components can be found at the above site.

Application: Check out the proportion of debt held in the various categories. How much is held in Canada Savings Bonds as a proportion of the total? Does it make any difference to our debt whether the bond is denominated in Canadian or foreign exchange?

MONEY AND THE BANKING SYSTEM

A couple of years ago, Argentina's government made a startling announcement. It was, it said, thinking about scrapping the nation's currency, the peso. Furthermore, it might not even replace the peso with a new national money. Instead, the government might declare US dollars to be the legal money of Argentina. Since then, a few other Latin American nations have contemplated the same plan. In Canada, some economists have floated a plan for dropping the Canadian dollar in favour of the US dollar. Why would a country think about giving up its own national currency and using US dollars instead? Before you can consider this question, you must learn about the functions of money. You must also understand how economists measure the total quantity of money in circulation. These are key topics in this chapter.

PREVIEW QUESTIONS

1. What is money?

2. What "backs" the Canadian dollar?

3. Who is involved in the process of transferring funds from savers to investors?

Money Any medium that is universally accepted in an economy both by sellers of goods and services as payment for those goods and services and by creditors as payment for debts.

DID YOU KNOW THAT... The typical dollar coin changes hands 50 times a year? Cash, of course, is not the only thing we use as money. As you will see in this chapter, our definition of money is much broader. Money has been important to society for thousands of years. In 300 BC Aristotle claimed that everything had to "be accessed in money, for this enables men always to exchange their services, and so makes society possible." Money is indeed a part of our everyday existence. We have to be careful, though, when we talk about money because it means two different things. Most of the time when people say "I wish I had more money," they mean that they want more income. Thus the normal use of the term *money* implies the ability to purchase goods and services. In this chapter, in contrast, you will use the term **money** to mean anything that people generally accept in exchange for goods and services. Most people think of money as the paper bills and coins they carry. But the concept of money is normally more inclusive. Table 15.1 provides a list of some items that various civilizations have used as money. The best way to understand how those items served this purpose is to examine the functions of money.

TABLE 15.1

Types of Money

This is a partial list of items that have been used as money. Native Canadians used wampum, beads made from shells. Fijians used whale teeth. The early colonists in North America used tobacco. And cigarettes were used in prisoner-of-war camps during World War II and in post–World War II Germany.

Iron	Boar tusk	Playing cards
Copper	Red woodpecker scalps	Leather
Brass	Feathers	Gold
Wine	Glass	Silver
Corn	Polished beads (wampum)	Knives
Salt	Rum	Pots
Horses	Molasses	Boats
Sheep	Tobacco	Pitch
Goats	Agricultural implements	Rice
Tortoise shells	Round stones with centres removed	Cows
Porpoise teeth	Crystal salt bars	Paper
Whale teeth	Snail shells	Cigarettes

Source: Roger LeRoy Miller and David D. VanHoose, *Modern Money and Banking,* 3d ed. (New York: McGraw-Hill, 1993), p. 13.

The Functions of Money

Money is what money does. Money traditionally serves three functions. The one that most people are familiar with is money's function as a *medium of exchange*. Money also serves as a *unit of account*, and a *store of value* or *purchasing power*. Anything that serves these three functions is money. Anything that could serve these three functions could be considered money.

Money as a Medium of Exchange

Medium of exchange Any asset that sellers will accept as payment.

Barter The direct exchange of goods and services for other goods and services without the use of money.

When we say that money serves as a **medium of exchange,** what we mean is that sellers will accept it as payment in market transactions. Without some generally accepted medium of exchange, we would have to resort to barter. In fact, before money was used, transactions took place by means of barter. **Barter** is simply a direct exchange—no intermediary good called money is used. In a barter economy, the shoemaker who wants to obtain a dozen water glasses must seek out a glassmaker who at exactly the same time is interested in obtaining a pair of shoes. For this to occur, there has to be a *double coincidence of wants.*

If there isn't, the shoemaker must go through several trades in order to obtain the desired dozen glasses—perhaps first trading shoes for jewellery, then jewellery for some pots and pans, and then the pots and pans for the desired glasses. See Thinking Critically About the Media 15-1 for more discussion.

Money facilitates exchange by reducing the transaction costs associated with means-of-payment uncertainty—that is, with regard to goods that the partners in any exchange are willing to accept. The existence of money means that individuals no longer have to hold a diverse collection of goods as an exchange inventory. As a medium of exchange, money allows individuals to specialize in any area in which they have a comparative advantage and to receive money payments for their labour. Money payments can then be exchanged for the fruits of other people's labour. The use of money as a medium of exchange permits more specialization and the inherent economic efficiencies that come with it (and hence greater economic growth). Money is even more important when used for large amounts of trade.

Thinking Critically About the Media 15-1   A Return to Barter

Every few years you read stories about Canadians (or Americans) deciding to "return to bartering." An electrician agrees to rewire a dentist's house in exchange for major dental work; a lawyer agrees to prepare a will in exchange for an annual physical checkup by a doctor. Such actions are not really designed to avoid the use of money and return to the "simple life." Rather, such exchanges without the use of money are typically undertaken to avoid the payment of income taxes. Barter is not back.

Money as a Unit of Account

Unit of account A measure by which prices are expressed; the common denominator of the price system; a way to compare the relative value of goods and services; a central property of money.

A **unit of account** is a way of placing a specific price on economic goods and services. Thus as a unit of account, the monetary unit is used to measure the value of goods and services *relative* to other goods and services. It is the common denominator, or measure, the commonly recognized unit of value measurement. The dollar is the monetary unit in Canada. It is the yardstick that allows individuals easily to compare the relative value of goods and services. Accountants at Statistics Canada use dollar prices to measure national income and domestic product, a business uses dollar prices to calculate profits and losses, and a typical household budgets regularly anticipated expenses using dollar prices as its unit of account.

Another way of describing money as a unit of account is to say that it serves as a *standard of value* that allows economic actors to compare the relative worth of various goods and services. It allows for comparison shopping, for example.

A related function of money is that it can be used as a *standard of deferred payment*. Debts that are to be settled in the future are calculated in money. Money's ability to function as a *unit of account over time* can be seriously diminished by inflation.

Money as a Store of Value

Store of value The ability to hold value over time; a necessary property of money.

One of the most important functions of money is that it serves as a **store of value** or purchasing power. The money you have today can be set aside to purchase things later on. In the meantime, money retains its nominal value, which you can apply to those future purchases. If you have $1,000 in your chequing account, you can either spend it today on goods and services, spend it tomorrow, or spend it a month from now. In this way, money provides a way to transfer value (wealth) into the future.

Liquidity

Money is an asset—something of value—that accounts for part of personal wealth. Wealth in the form of money can be exchanged later for some other asset. Although it is

Liquidity The degree to which an asset can be acquired or disposed of without much danger of any intervening loss in *nominal* value and with small transaction costs. Money is the most liquid asset.

not the only form of wealth that can be exchanged for goods and services, it is the one most widely and readily accepted. This attribute of money is called **liquidity**. We say that an asset is liquid when it can easily be acquired or disposed of without high transaction costs and with relative certainty as to its value. Money is by definition the most liquid asset there is. Just compare it, for example, with a share of stock listed on the Toronto Stock Exchange. To buy or sell that share, you usually call a stockbroker, who will place the buy or sell order for you. This generally must be done during normal business hours. You have to pay a commission to the broker. Moreover, there is a distinct probability that you will get more or less for the stock than you originally paid for it. This is not the case with money. Money can be easily converted to other asset forms. Therefore, most individuals hold at least a part of their wealth in the form of the most liquid of assets, money. You can see how assets rank in liquidity relative to one another in Figure 15.1.

When we hold money, however, we pay a price for this advantage of liquidity. That price is the interest yield that could have been obtained had the asset been held in another form—for example, in the form of stocks and bonds.

Try Preview Question 1:
What is money?

The cost of holding money (its opportunity cost) is measured by the alternative interest yield obtainable by holding some other asset.

FIGURE 15.1 Degrees of Liquidity

The most liquid asset is, of course, cash. Liquidity decreases as you move from right to left.

Low Liquidity   **High Liquidity**

Monetary Standards, or What Backs Money

Today in Canada, all of us accept coins, paper currency, and cheques in exchange for items sold, including labour services. The question remains, why are we willing to accept as payment something that has no intrinsic value? After all, you could not sell cheques to anybody for use as a raw material in manufacturing. The reason is that in this country the payments arise from a **fiduciary monetary system**. This means that the value of the payments rests on the public's confidence that such payments can be exchanged for goods and services. *Fiduciary* comes from the Latin *fiducia*, which means "trust" or "confidence." In our fiduciary monetary system, money, in the form of currency or chequing accounts, is not convertible to a fixed quantity of gold, silver, or some other precious commodity. This **fiat money** is widely accepted because it is declared by government to be *legal tender*, which means that it must be accepted in the payment of a debt. In other words, fiat money is money because the government says it is. In addition, currency and deposit accounts perform the functions of money because of their acceptability and predictability of value.

Fiduciary monetary system A system in which currency is issued by the government and its value is based uniquely on the public's faith that the currency represents command over goods and services.

Fiat money Fiat money is money because the government says it is.

Acceptability

Demand deposits and currency are money because they are accepted in exchange for goods and services. They are accepted because people have confidence that they can later be exchanged for other goods and services. This confidence is based on the knowledge that such exchanges have occurred in the past without problems. Even during a period of relatively rapid inflation, we would still be inclined to accept money in exchange for goods

INTERNATIONAL EXAMPLE 15-1

Is Gold Worth Its Weight?

For centuries, gold has been precious because it has been scarce. Today, however, this glittering metal may be overabundant, especially for international agencies, governments, and central banks. Gold accounts for more than a third of the official international reserves of a number of developed nations. Combined gold holdings of the International Monetary Fund (IMF) and the world's central banks exceed 30,000 tons, or the equivalent of about a dozen years of global mining output. All this gold is very expensive to move around. For this reason, it typically just sits unused, in sturdy vaults surrounded by armed guards. This is an expensive use for a metal. Moreover, over the past 25 years, gold has turned out to be a poor store of value. Returns on relatively low-risk bonds have been much higher than the rate of return from holding gold. Switzerland, for instance, determined that the cost of interest foregone by holding gold rather than US Treasury bonds is about $400 a year per Swiss household.

Recently, the Swiss government began selling off half its 2,600 tons of gold reserves, third-largest in the world behind the United States and the European Monetary Union. More recently, the IMF has auctioned off some of its gold holdings to finance debt relief for poor countries. The European System of Central Banks, which began the new century with 30 percent of its reserves in the form of gold, decided to reduce this fraction to 15 percent.

Official gold sales until late 1999 contributed to a decline in the world price of gold, thereby worsening the return to holding gold. This led companies operating gold mines in the United States to lobby their representatives and senators, who successfully pushed through a law threatening a reduction of US funding of the IMF unless it agreed to scale back gold sales it had planned for the early 2000s. It did so, and central banks also agreed to stop selling gold.

For critical analysis: It appears that today central banks' portfolios are weighted too heavily in favour of gold. Under what circumstances might central banks again determine that huge stocks of gold are worth holding?

and services because it is so useful. Barter is a costly and time-consuming alternative.

Realize always that money is socially defined. Acceptability is not something that you can necessarily predict. For example, you will probably have trouble spending Canadian currency in most businesses in the United States. Unless they are close to the Canadian border and deal frequently with Canadians, Americans do not have faith in Canadian money and therefore will not accept it in payment for goods and services.

Predictability of Value

The purchasing power of the dollar (its value) varies inversely with the price level. The more rapid the rate of increase of some price level index, such as the Consumer Price Index, the more rapid the decrease in the value, or purchasing power, of a dollar. Money still retains its usefulness even if its value—its purchasing power—is declining year in and year out, as in periods of inflation, because it still retains the characteristic of predictability of value. If you believe that the inflation rate is going to be around 10 percent next year, you know that any dollar you receive a year from now will have a purchasing power equal to 10 percent less than that same dollar this year. Thus you will not necessarily refuse to use money or accept it in exchange simply because you know that its value will decline by the rate of inflation next year.

Try Preview Question 2:

What "backs" the Canadian dollar?

Concepts in Brief

● Money is defined by its functions, which are as a medium of exchange, a unit of account or standard of value, and a store of value or purchasing power.
● Because money is a highly liquid asset, it can be disposed of without high transaction costs and with relative certainty as to its value.
● Canada has a fiduciary monetary system—our money is not convertible into a fixed quantity of a commodity such as gold or silver. It is fiat money.
● Money is accepted in exchange for goods and services because people have confidence that it can later be exchanged for other goods and services. Another reason for this is that it has a predictable value.

Defining the Canadian Money Supply

Money supply The amount of money in circulation.

Money is important. Changes in the total **money supply**—the amount of money in circulation—and changes in the rate at which the money supply increases or decreases affect important economic variables, such as the rate of inflation, interest rates, employment, and the equilibrium level of real national income. Although there is widespread agreement among economists that money is indeed important, they have never agreed on how to define or measure it. Therefore we have several measures of the money supply.

The Narrowest Measure: M1

One measure of the money supply consists of the following:

1. Currency outside banks
2. Demand deposits

M1 The money supply, taken as the total value of currency plus demand deposits in chartered banks.

The narrowest official designation of the money supply, including currency outside banks and demand deposits, is **M1**. The two elements of M1 for a typical year are presented in part (a) of Figure 15.2.

FIGURE 15.2 **Composition of the M1 and M2 Money Supply, 2000**

Part (a) shows the M1 money supply, the larger component of which is demand deposits (about 69 percent). M2 consists of M1 plus personal savings deposits and non-personal notice deposits at chartered banks (about 78 percent).

Source: Bank of Canada Review. Data are for 2000.

Part (a)

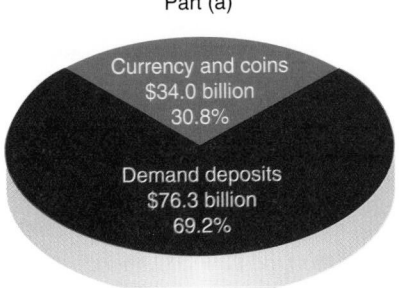

M1 = $110.3 billion

Part (b)

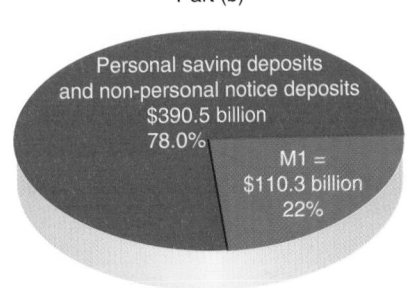

M2 = $500.8 billion

TABLE 15.2

Money in Canada,
December, 2000

	Millions of Dollars	Percent of M1	Percent of M2	Percent of M2+
Currency outside banks	$34.0	30.8	6.8	4.8
+ Demand deposits (current and personal chequing accounts)	76.3	69.2	15.2	10.8
= **M1**	110.3	100.0	22.0	15.6
+ Personal savings deposits and nonpersonal notice deposits	390.5		78.0	55.6
= **M2**	500.8		100.0	71.2
+ Deposits at trust and mortgage companies, credit unions, and *caisses populaires*	202.6			28.8
+ Money market mutual funds and deposits at other institutions				
= **M2+**	$703.4			100.0

Seasonally adjusted average monthly data

Source: Bank of Canada, *Weekly Financial Statistics,* March 2001, pp. 11–12.

CURRENCY.   Currency includes Canadian coins and paper currency, usually in the form of bank notes, issued by the Bank of Canada (see Policy Example, below, for a discussion of increased Canadian coin use). Although not nearly as important as chequable deposits as a percentage of the money supply, currency has increased in significance in Canada. One of the major reasons for the increased use of currency in the Canadian economy is the growing number of illegal transactions, including under-the-table work agreements and the drug trade.

POLICY EXAMPLE 15-1   Eliminating the $1 and $2 Bills

Since 1990, the federal government has replaced our $1 and $2 bills with coins—the "loonie" and the "toonie." What drove the government to weigh down our pockets and purses with heavy money? There are three reasons, all related to government revenue: coins last longer than bills, coins are quite inexpensive to produce, and the government makes a tidy profit on the replacement of bills with coins.

Coins Are Durable.   You've probably been given in change a $5 bill which looks like it is about to fall apart. This is due to the wear and tear on paper currency as it is circulated in the economy. As paper currency wears out, banks and other financial institutions return to the Bank of Canada those bills that are on their last legs. The Bank then arranges for new replacement bills. A coin like the toonie, however, does not wear out quickly and has to be replaced much less frequently. A loonie or a toonie has a 20-year life span, while a paper note will last for just one year. The government saves about $12.5 million per year just on production costs of the $1 and $2 coins.

Coins Are Cheap to Produce.   The government buys its coins from the Royal Canadian Mint, located in Winnipeg, at a price which includes the cost of production and a margin of profit for the Mint. While the government doesn't make money purchasing pennies at 1.4¢ each and nickels at 5¢

each, it makes a profit on the other coins. For example, it costs 4¢ to produce a dime, 8¢ to produce a quarter, 13¢ to produce a $1 coin, and only 16¢ to turn out a $2 coin.

Coins Earn a Profit for the Government. In 1996, the Mint turned out about 14 new coins per second, 24 hours per day, to meet the government's target of putting about 300 million $2 coins into circulation by 1997. Each time the Bank of Canada returned a $2 coin to a chartered bank in exchange for a used $2 bill, the Bank earned $1.84 in profit—after all, the chartered bank paid $2 for the coin which cost 16¢ to make. This profit amounted to about $500 million during the first two years of toonie production.

Will we see the replacement of our $5 and $10 bills with coins in the near future? Probably not, as those bills don't circulate as quickly and therefore do not wear out as fast.

For critical analysis: If the government decided to replace the $20 bill with a coin, what would happen to the amount of seigniorage—the profit it makes from producing our currency—it would earn?

DEMAND DEPOSITS. Most major transactions today are done with cheques. The convenience and safety of using cheques has made chequing accounts the most important component of the money supply. For example, it is estimated that in 1997 currency transactions accounted for only about 0.5 percent of the *dollar* amount of all transactions. The rest (excluding barter) involved cheques. Cheques are a way of transferring the ownership of deposits in financial institutions. They are normally acceptable as a medium of exchange. The financial institutions that offer **chequable deposits** are numerous and include virtually all **near banks**—trust companies, and credit unions and *caisses populaires*. However, only chequing accounts held in chartered banks are included in the measure of M1.

Chequable deposits Any deposits in a chartered bank or a near bank on which a cheque may be written.

Near bank Financial institutions such as trust companies, credit unions and *caisses populaires* that offer most of the same services as chartered banks.

What About Credit Cards?

Even though a large percentage of transactions are accomplished by using a plastic credit card, we do not consider the credit card itself money. Remember the functions of money. A credit card is not a unit of account or a store of value. The use of your credit card is really a loan to you by the issuer of the card, be it a bank, a retail store, or a gas company. The proceeds of the loan are paid to the business that sold you something. You must pay back the loan to the issuer of the credit card, either when you get your statement or with interest throughout the year if you don't pay off your balance. (We ignore those with credit card debt which they cannot repay.) It is not a store of value. Credit cards *defer*, rather than complete, transactions that ultimately involve the use of money. Refer to Example 15-1 for insight into the use of credit cards in Canada.

A relative newcomer, the *debit card* automatically withdraws money from your bank account. When you use your debit card to purchase something, you are giving an instruction to your bank to transfer money directly from your bank account to the store's bank account. If the store in which you are shopping has a direct electronic link to the bank, that transfer may be made instantaneously. Use of a debit card does not create a loan. A debit card is therefore not a new type of "money."

A Broader Measure of Money: M2

A broader measure of the money supply involves taking into account not only the most liquid assets that people use as money, which are already included in the definition of M1, but also other assets that are highly liquid—that is, that can be converted into money

EXAMPLE 15-1 Credit Cards and Canadians

Canadians hold more than 58.5 million credit cards of all types: gasoline cards, retail store cards, and all-purpose cards like Visa, MasterCard, and American Express. Canadians use these cards for about 15 percent of their purchases, the rest being made with cash and cheques.

Since 1992, credit card use has grown by almost 60 percent in spite of slow average real income growth of about 1 percent over the same time period. Outstanding balances on Visa and MasterCard alone totalled $17.4 billion in 1995, boosting total consumer bank loans in the economy. These are expensive loans, however, for the average credit card interest rate is 10.5 percent above bank rates.

At these high rates, what induces consumers to buy on credit? First, the convenience of purchasing now without waiting for payday is a big attraction. Second, consumers are attracted by competition between bank card companies. Some cards award credit, based on the amount of purchases each month, towards purchase of an automobile. Other cards award frequent flyer miles based on card use. Recently, Visa has offered 25 percent discounts on selected products as an inducement to buy on credit. Consumers have shown they find these offers hard to resist.

For critical analysis: What effect will these non-money transactions have on aggregate demand in the economy?

M2 M1 plus (1) personal savings and (2) non-personal notice deposits.

quickly without loss of nominal dollar value and without much cost. These assets are personal savings accounts (many of which have chequing privileges) and non-personal notice deposits. Table 15-2 shows the components of **M2**—money as a temporary store of value. We examine each of these components in turn.

Savings deposits Interest-earning funds at chartered banks that can be withdrawn at any time without payment of a penalty.

SAVINGS DEPOSITS. **Savings deposits** in chartered banks are part of the M2 money supply. A savings deposit is distinguishable from a time deposit because savings funds may be withdrawn without payment of a penalty. Funds are fully protected against loss in their nominal value.

Non-personal notice deposits Interest-earning funds deposited by firms at chartered banks which can in practice be withdrawn at any time without payment of a penalty.

NON-PERSONAL NOTICE DEPOSITS. **Non-personal notice deposits** are similar to savings deposits, but are funds deposited by firms. Although legally the firms are required to give the bank "notice" of withdrawal, this requirement is rarely observed.

OTHER MONEY SUPPLY DEFINITIONS. When all of these assets are added together, the result is M2. The composition of M2 is given in Table 15-2.

A still broader measure, M2+, includes M2 plus the deposits held at the financial institutions that are *not* banks, the near banks such as trust companies, credit unions, and *caisse populaires*. The composition of M2+ is shown in Table 15-2 .

The narrowest measure money supply, called M1, stresses the role of the chartered banks and money as a medium of exchange. Other measures, M2, M3, and M2+ stress the role of money as a temporary store of value and other financial institutions.

Just remember that there is no one best definition of the money supply. For different purposes, different definitions are appropriate. If we want to use a definition that seems to correlate best with economic activity on an economy-wide basis, M2 is probably best.

The Canadian Banking Structure

Canada's banking system consists of a large number of commercial banks (also called chartered banks), which are privately owned, profit-seeking institutions, and near banks.

Financial Intermediaries: Sources and Uses of Funds

Financial intermediation The process by which financial institutions accept savings from businesses, households, and governments and lend the savings to other businesses, households, and governments.

Financial intermediaries Institutions that transfer funds between ultimate lenders (savers) and ultimate borrowers.

Liabilities Amounts owed; the legal claims against a business or household by nonowners.

Assets Amounts owned; all items to which a business or household holds legal claim.

The financial institutions in our banking system are all in the same business—transferring funds from savers to investors. This process has become known as **financial intermediation**, and its participants are called **financial intermediaries**. Savers lend funds through financial intermediaries (banks, credit unions, etc.) to borrowers such as businesses, governments, and home buyers. The process of financial intermediation is illustrated in Figure 15.3.

Each financial intermediary has its own primary source of funds, which are called **liabilities**. When you deposit $100 in your chequing account in the bank, the bank creates a liability—it owes you $100—in exchange for the funds deposited. A commercial bank gets its funds from chequing and savings accounts; an insurance company gets its funds from insurance policy premiums.

Each financial intermediary normally has a different primary use of its **assets**. For example, a credit union usually makes small consumer loans, whereas a mortgage loan company makes mainly home mortgage loans. Table 15.3 lists the assets and liabilities of financial intermediaries. Be aware, though, that the distinction between different financial institutions is becoming more and more blurred. As the laws and regulations change, there will be less need to make any distinction. All may ultimately be treated simply as financial intermediaries.

Try Preview Question 3:

Who is involved in the process of transferring funds from savers to investors?

FIGURE 15.3 The Process of Financial Intermediation

The process of financial intermediation is depicted here. Note that ultimate lenders and ultimate borrowers are the same economic units—households, businesses, and governments—but not necessarily the same individuals. Whereas individual households can be net lenders or borrowers, households as an economic unit are net lenders. Specific businesses or governments similarly can be net lenders or borrowers; as economic units, both are net borrowers.

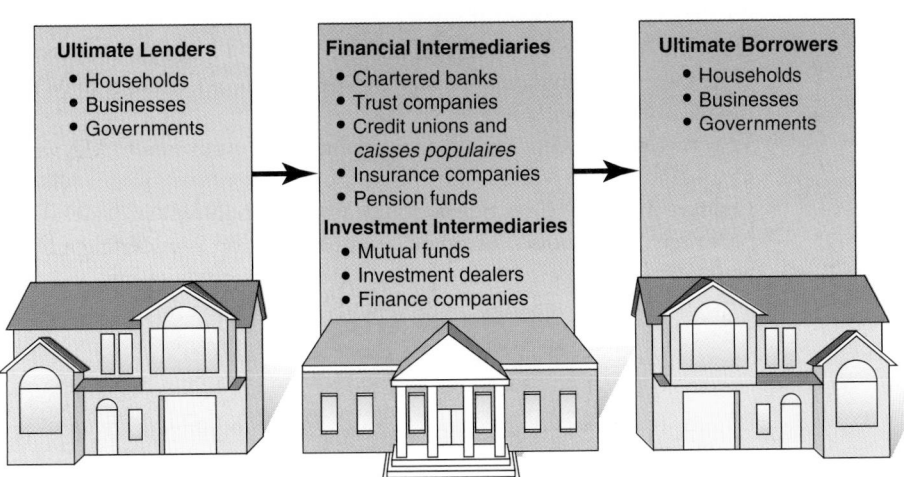

TABLE 15.3

Financial Intermediaries and
Their Assets and Liabilities

	Percent of Total Financial Assets	Primary Assets (Uses of Funds)	Primary Liabilities (Sources of Funds)
Financial Intermediaries			
Chartered Banks	39.3%	Bank loans, mortgages, and consumer credit	Currency and bank deposits
Trust companies, Credit unions and *Caisses populaires*	6.4	Mortgages, consumer credit	Deposits
Insurance companies and Pension funds	34.7	Mortgages, bonds, short-term paper, and shares	Life insurance, pensions, shares
Investment Intermediaries			
Mutual funds	15.8	Short-term paper, shares, and foreign investment	Shares
Investment dealers	0.7	Short-term paper	Loans
Finance companies	3.1	Consumer credit, loans	Short-term paper, bonds

Source: Statistics Canada, CANSIM Database, Series SDDS 1804 STC (13-214).

CONCEPTS IN BRIEF

- The money supply can be defined in a variety of ways. M1, which consists of currency and demand deposits in chartered banks, is the most narrowly defined.
- Demand deposits (chequing accounts) are any deposits in financial institutions on which the deposit owner can write cheques.
- Credit cards are not part of the money supply, for they simply defer transactions that ultimately involve the use of money.
- When we add savings deposits and non-personal notice deposits to M1, we obtain the measure known as M2.
- When we add the deposits of non-bank financial institutions to M2, we obtain the measure known as M2+.
- Financial intermediaries transfer funds from ultimate lenders (savers) to ultimate borrowers. This process of financial intermediation is undertaken by chartered banks, trust companies, mortgage loan companies, credit unions and *caisses populaires*, insurance companies, mutual funds, and pension funds.

The Transformation of Smart Cards

The Holy Grail of smart technology applications is the smart card. Smart cards have unlimited uses. They can store unlimited data, replace cash and credit cards for online and in-store purchases, and verify your identity. So, why don't all of us carry smart cards instead of wallets? Well, that's the most interesting part of this story.

There is a general agreement that smart cards have an infinite number of applications, and that many people would benefit from widespread use of the technology, but there is no agreement on how to make that happen. Industry players, including credit card companies, retailers, e-tailers, and others, have yet to adopt a standard of "inter-operability."

Consequently, one smart card can't talk to multiple smart-card readers. What we've ended up with are a handful of single-purpose smart cards—and that isn't really all that smart. The multifunction cards that do exist are limited to a specific venue, such as a college campus.

To date, the most ambitious smart-card project was launched in Southampton, England, in conjunction with the European Union and Paris, France-based Schlumberger, the largest maker of smart cards. The project is testing the possibilities of using smart cards to meet every transactional need in the entire city.

Regardless of how successful the experiment is, it is still a limited-use card. You couldn't use the card in London or Paris, or anywhere else for that matter—just Southampton. A representative of Schlumberger pointed out that the very fact the smart cards have such widespread application is contributing to the delay in widespread use.

For lots of reasons, few companies produce smart cards on their own, or as a stand-alone product. Most are part of a joint venture or co-marketing initiative. The prospect of commercial success leads to arguments over which company logo goes on the front, which on the back, and which gets left off all together.

What exists now are 20 or more different platforms and no agreement for future development. That will change. Consumers will begin to demand smart cards. The increasingly global economy will find that functioning without them slows growth. Also, smart cards will become lifelines for the increasingly nomadic global workforce. ●

Source: Reprinted with permission from *Trend Letter,* published by Briefings Publishing Group.

ISSUES AND APPLICATIONS

The Dollarization Movement: Is the US Fed Destined to be a Multinational Central Bank?

Concepts Applied: Federal Reserve system, money, currency

This advertising billboard in Buenos Aires, Argentina, may someday be displaying prices in US dollars instead of the local currency. If Argentina used US dollars instead of pesos, would Argentinians be better off?

In 1998, Brazil faced an economic crisis, and Brazilian interest rates shot up considerably. So did interest rates in Argentina, Brazil's main international trading partner. This spillover from Brazil's crisis induced Argentina to contemplate a radical change in its monetary arrangements.

The Prospect of Latin American Dollarization

The change that Argentina's leaders considered was *dollarization*. This would entail abandoning Argentina's peso in favour of the US dollar as a medium of exchange, unit of account, and store of value. To implement dollarization, Argentina would have to import sufficient US currency for people to use in hand-to-hand transactions. It also would have to convert all Argentine financial accounts and contracts to dollars at the prevailing fixed rate of exchange. Such a conversion would not be too difficult for Argentina, however, because it already has a *currency board* system, in which Argentina issues pesos on a one-to-one basis with the number of US dollars it has on reserve. Thus Argentina's monetary system is already closely linked to that of the United States.

Nevertheless, Federal Reserve and US Treasury officials have expressed concerns about dollarization. Fed policy actions consistent with stabilizing the US economy could have negative consequences outside the United States, fostering resentment and encouraging policymakers in dollarized countries to deflect blame onto US policymakers. This could give governments of dollarized countries political cover for dodging tough decisions regarding appropriate economic policies.

A North American Monetary Union?

So far, Latin American nations, except for Ecuador, have not pursued the dollarization idea any further. Recently, a Toronto-based think tank released a study proposing "North American currency integration" by establishing the US dollar as the single circulating currency in Canada. The authors of the Canadian proposal were not quite as willing as Latin Americans to contemplate unilateral dollarization, however. Their proposal called for the Federal Reserve's Board of Governors to have one Canadian member.

So far the United States has expressed little interest in sharing control of its central bank, but many Canadians seem to be coming around to the idea. After watching the value of the Canadian dollar fall from about 0.90 Canadian dollar per US dollar in 1991 to about 0.65 Canadian dollar per US dollar today, more than a third of Canadians surveyed in public opinion poles indicated support for abolishing the Canadian currency altogether. Three-fourths of Canadians polled said they expected to see a common dollar for the United States and Canada by 2020.

For Critical Analysis

1. Why would Argentina and Canada choose to dollarize their economies?

2. Do you see any merit to the arguments by critics of dollarization proposals, who argue that unilateral dollarization in Latin America and Canada would lead to "taxation without representation"?

CHAPTER SUMMARY

1. The functions of money are a medium of exchange, a unit of account (standard of value), and a store of value or purchasing power.

2. We have a fiduciary monetary system in Canada—our money, whether in the form of currency or chequing accounts, is not convertible into a fixed quantity of a commodity, such as gold or silver.

3. Our money is exchangeable for goods and services because it has acceptability: People have confidence that whatever money they receive can be exchanged for other goods and services later. Our money also has a predictable value.

4. There are numerous ways to define the money supply. The narrowest measure, called M1, stresses the role of the chartered banks and money as a medium of exchange. Other methods, M2, M3, and M2+ stress the role of money as a temporary store of value and other financial institutions.

DISCUSSION OF PREVIEW QUESTIONS

1. What is money?

Money is defined by its functions. Thus money is whatever is generally accepted for use as a medium of exchange, a unit of account, and a store of value or purchasing power. In various places in the world throughout history, different items have performed these functions: wampum, gold, silver, cows, stones, paper, diamonds, salt, cigarettes, and many others.

2. What "backs" the Canadian dollar?

Some students think that the Canadian dollar is "backed" by gold, but alas (some experts say fortunately), this is not the case. Canada is presently on a fiduciary monetary standard, and as such the Canadian dollar is backed only by faith—the public's confidence that it can be exchanged for goods and services. This confidence comes from the fact that other people will accept the dollar in transactions because our government has declared it legal tender and because, despite inflation, it still retains the characteristic of predictability of value.

3. Who is involved in the process of transferring funds from savers to investors?

Financial intermediation involves the transfer of funds from savers to investors. The ultimate lenders are the savers—households, businesses, and governments, including the federal government and provincial and municipal governments. The ultimate borrowers are also households, businesses, and governments—the same economic units but not necessarily the same individuals. Between ultimate lenders and ultimate borrowers are financial intermediaries, including commercial banks, trust companies, mortgage loan companies, credit unions and *caisses populaires*, insurance companies, mutual funds and pension funds.

PROBLEMS

(Answers to the odd-numbered problems appear at the back of the book.)

15-1. Consider each type of asset in terms of its potential use as a medium of exchange, a unit of account, and a store of value or purchasing power. Indicate which use is most appropriately associated with each asset.

a. A painting by Renoir

b. A 90-day Canadian Treasury bill

c. A notice deposit account with a trust company in St. John's, Newfoundland

d. One share of IBM stock

e. A $50 Bank of Canada note

f. A MasterCard credit card

g. A chequing account in a credit union in Manitoba

h. A lifetime pass to the Montreal Expos' home baseball games

15-2. The value of a dollar is the reciprocal of the price index. In 1986 the CPI had a value of 1; hence the value of a dollar in 1986 equalled $1. If the price index now is 2, what is the value of the dollar in 1986 prices? If the price index is 2.5?

15-3. What are the components of M2?

15-4. How have technological changes altered the form of money?

15-5. Elsa Lee can make several uses of her money. Indicate for each case whether her money is being used as a medium of exchange (E), a unit of account (A), or a store of value (V).

   a. Lee has accumulated $600 in her chequing account at a chartered bank.

   b. Lee decides to use this $600 to purchase a new washing machine and goes shopping to compare the prices being charged by different dealers for the machine she wishes to buy.

   c. Lee finds that the lowest price at which she can purchase the machine she wants is $498.50. She has the dealer deliver the machine and agrees to pay the dealer in 30 days.

   d. Thirty days later, Lee sends the dealer a cheque drawn on her chequing account to pay for the washer.

15-6. Explain why a debit card is not a new form of money.

15-7. Consider a barter economy in which 10 goods and services are produced and exchanged. How many exchange rates exist in that economy, which does not use money?

15-8. Cash and cheques account for nearly 75 percent of the total number of all payments in Canada, and wire transfers account for over 60 percent of the dollar value of all payments in Canada. How can both situations be true simultaneously?

ECONOMICS ON THE NET

What is Canadian Money?

Internet URL: http://www.bankofcanada.ca

Title: Currency

Navigation: Begin at the homepage of the Bank of Canada (http://www.bankofcanada.ca). Click on English, followed by Currency, then on Currency Converter and, finally, Nominal Rate.

Application:

Perform the operations indicated above and answer the following questions:

   a. When did dollars and cents vs. pounds, shillings, and pence first come into use in Canada? When was the first Currency Act proclaimed, allowing dollars and cents to be used in provincial accounts?

   b. At the time of Confederation (July 1, 1867), under the BNA Act, which level of government was given jurisdiction over currency and banking?

   c. Begin at the homepage of Statistics Canada (http://www.statcan.ca). Click on English, followed by Canadian Statistics. Under The Economy, click on Latest Indicators, then on Summary Table, Canada and the Provinces. How have M1, M2, and M3 changed over the past year?

MONEY CREATION AND DEPOSIT INSURANCE

Life used to be simple for someone who wished to finance the purchase of a house, acquire stocks and bonds, take out insurance, or obtain a credit card. Each of those decisions involved going to any of a well-defined set of separate institutions. Insurance was always bought from an insurance company, for example; stocks and bonds were sold only by stock brokers; and money for a house was borrowed from a bank or credit union. Today, the choices are much more complicated and the distinctions between banks and "nonbanks" are becoming ever more blurred. All of this comes about in an era of deregulation of depository institutions. To understand the effects of deregulation, you need to learn about the regulation of such institutions and, before that, how money is created in our economy.

PREVIEW QUESTIONS

1. What is a fractional reserve banking system?
2. What happens to the money supply when a person deposits currency in a single depository institution?
3. What happens to the money supply when a bank makes a loan?
4. What happens to the overall money supply when a person deposits currency in a single depository institution which is part of a banking system?
5. How does the existence of deposit insurance affect a financial institution's choice of risky versus nonrisky assets?

DID YOU KNOW THAT... seemingly overnight, Nick Leeson, a 27-year-old manager in the Singapore branch of Barings Bank, was able to inflict losses of several billion dollars on the institution? Barings was founded in 1762. In 1803, it helped the United States purchase the Louisiana Territory from France. It provided credit to the British government during the Napoleonic Wars (1803–1815). During the 1850s, it financed the construction of Canada's Grand Trunk Railway. When Barings collapsed in 1995, it was bought by former competitors, thereby ending the life of one of the longest-running financial institutions in the world. Could the collapse of such an important bank lead to serious problems in the world's banking sector? A lot depends on whether the losses suffered by Barings' depositors would cause other depositors to lose confidence in other banks too. That, in turn, depends on the relationship between deposits at different banks.

If you were to attend a luncheon of bankers and ask the question, "Do you as bankers create money?" you would get a uniformly negative response. Bankers may not believe they create money. But along with the Bank of Canada, depository institutions do create money; they determine the total deposits outstanding. In this chapter we will examine the **money multiplier process,** which explains how an injection of new money into the banking system leads to an eventual multiple expansion in the total money supply. We will also take a look at deposit insurance and its role in investment decisions made by financial institutions.

Money multiplier process The process by which an injection of new money into the banking system leads to a multiple expansion in the total money supply.

Links Between Changes in the Money Supply and Other Economic Variables

How fast the money supply grows or does not grow is important because no matter what model of the economy is used, theories link the money supply growth rate to economic growth or to business fluctuations. There is in fact a long-standing relationship between changes in the money supply and changes in GDP. Some economists use this historical evidence to argue that money is an important determinant of the level of economic activity in the economy.

Another key economic variable in our economy is the price level. At least one theory attributes changes in the rate of inflation to changes in the growth rate of money in circulation. Figure 16.1 shows the relationship between the rate of growth of the money supply and the inflation rate. There seems to be a loose, albeit consistent, direct relationship between changes in the money supply and changes in the rate of inflation. Increases in the money supply growth rate seem to lead to increases in the inflation rate, after a time lag.

The Origins of Fractional Reserve Banking

As early as 1000 BC, uncoined gold and silver were being used as money in Mesopotamia. Goldsmiths weighed and assessed the purity of those metals; later they started issuing paper notes indicating that the bearers held gold or silver of given weights and purity on deposit with the goldsmith. These notes could be transferred in exchange for goods and became the first paper currency. The gold and silver on deposit with the goldsmiths were the first bank deposits. Eventually, goldsmiths realized that the amount of gold and silver on deposit always exceeded the amount of gold and silver withdrawn—often by a predictable ratio. These goldsmiths started issuing to borrowers paper notes that exceeded in value the amount of gold and silver they actually kept on hand. They charged interest on these loans. This constituted the earliest form of what is now called **fractional reserve banking.** We know that goldsmiths operated this way in Delphi, Didyma, and Olympia

Fractional reserve banking A system in which depository institutions hold reserves that are less than the amount of total deposits.

FIGURE 16.1 Money Supply Growth Versus the Inflation Rate

These time-series curves indicate a loose correspondence between money supply growth and the inflation rate. Actually, closer inspection reveals a direct relationship between changes in the growth rate of money and changes in the inflation rate *in a later period*. Increases in the rate of growth of money seem to lead to subsequent increases

in the inflation rate; decreases in the rate of money growth seem to lead to subsequent reductions in the inflation rate.

Sources: Statistics Canada, CANSIM Database, Series P200000; *Bank of Canada Review,* Winter 2000-2001, pp. 78-79.

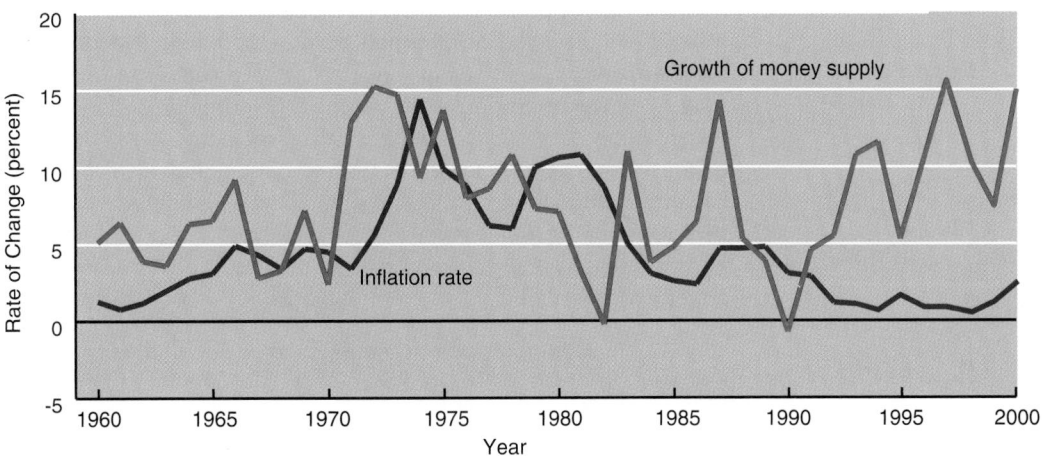

in Greece as early as the seventh century BC. In Athens, fractional reserve banking was well developed by the sixth century BC.

In a fractional reserve banking system, banks do not keep sufficient reserves on hand to cover 100 percent of their depositors' accounts. And the reserves that are held by depository institutions in Canada are not kept in gold and silver, as they were with the early goldsmiths, but rather in vault cash, and in the case of the chartered banks, in the form of deposits on reserve with the Bank of Canada.

Try Preview Question 1:

What is a fractional reserve banking system?

Reserves

Reserves In the Canadian banking system, deposits held by the chartered banks at the Bank of Canada, and vault cash.

Depository institutions maintain some percentage of their customer deposits as **reserves.** Different types of depository institutions hold different percentages of reserves. Normally, the larger the institution, the larger the desired reserves. On chequing accounts, most depository institutions will keep typically one to 10 percent as reserves.

Take a hypothetical example. If the desired level of reserves is 10 percent and the bank[1] has $1 billion in customer chequing deposits, it will hold at least $100 million as reserves. These can be either deposits with the Bank of Canada or vault cash. Credit unions and trust companies, because they cannot hold reserves in the Bank of Canada, usually maintain accounts with the chartered banks that can act as reserves. The following discussion will focus on the chartered banks, but could be broadened to include the near banks as well. There are two distinguishable types of reserves: desired and excess.

---

[1] The term *bank* is used interchangeably with the term *depository institution* in this chapter because distinctions among financial institutions are becoming less and less meaningful. However, only the chartered banks keep reserves at the Bank of Canada, so the Bank of Canada only directly affects money creation at chartered banks.

Desired reserves The value of reserves that a depository institution wishes to hold in the form of vault cash or other deposits, or, in the case of the chartered banks, in the form of deposits with the Bank of Canada.

Excess reserves The difference between actual reserves and desired reserves.

1. *Desired reserves.* **Desired reserves** are the *minimum* amount of reserves—vault cash plus deposits with the Bank of Canada—that a depository institution wishes to hold to back its chequable deposits. They are expressed as a ratio of desired reserves to total chequable deposits (banks do not necessarily hold reserves on nonchequable deposits).

2. *Excess reserves.* Banks often hold reserves in excess of what they wish to hold. This difference between actual reserves and desired reserves is called **excess reserves.** Excess reserves can be negative, but they rarely are. (Negative excess reserves indicate that banks do not have sufficient reserves to meet their desired level. When this happens, they borrow from the Bank of Canada, sell assets such as securities, or call in loans.) Excess reserves are an important potential determinant of the rate of growth of the money supply, for as we shall see, it is only to the extent that banks have excess reserves that they can make new loans. Because reserves produce no income, profit-seeking financial institutions have an incentive to minimize excess reserves. They use them either to purchase income-producing securities or to make loans with which they earn income through interest payments received. In equation form, we can define excess reserves in this way:

$$\text{Excess reserves} = \text{actual reserves} - \text{desired reserves}$$

In the analysis that follows, we examine the relationship between the level of reserves and the size of the money supply. This analysis implies that factors influencing the level of the reserves of the banking system as a whole will ultimately affect the level of the money supply, other things held constant. We show first what happens when someone deposits currency in one depository institution. Next we show how excess reserves can lead to an individual bank making loans that expand the money supply or create money. Then we show how the banking system can create a multiple expansion of the money supply.

CONCEPTS IN BRIEF
- Ours is a fractional reserve banking system in which depository institutions hold only a percentage of their deposits as reserves, either as vault cash or, in the case of the chartered banks, on deposit with the Bank of Canada.
- Desired reserves are usually expressed as a ratio, in percentage terms, of desired reserves to total deposits.

The Relationship Between Reserves and Total Deposits

To show the relationship between reserves and depository institution deposits, we first analyze a single bank (existing alongside many others). A single bank is able to make new loans to its customers only to the extent that it has reserves above the desired level for covering the new deposits. When an individual bank has no excess reserves, it cannot make loans.

How a Single Bank Reacts to an Increase in Reserves

Balance sheet A statement of the assets and liabilities of any business entity, including financial institutions and the Bank of Canada. Assets are what is owned; liabilities are what is owed.

To examine the **balance sheet** of a single bank after its reserves are increased, the following assumptions are made:

1. The desired reserve ratio is 10 percent for all chequable deposits; that is, the bank holds an amount equal to 10 percent of all chequable deposits in reserve at the Bank of Canada or in vault cash.

2. Chequable deposits are the bank's only liabilities; reserves at the Bank of Canada and loans are the bank's only assets. Loans are promises made by customers to repay some amount in the future; that is, they are IOUs and as such are assets of the bank.
3. An individual bank can lend all it wants at current market interest rates.
4. Every time a loan is made to an individual (consumer or business), all the proceeds from the loan are put into a chequing account; no cash (currency or coins) is withdrawn.
5. Chartered banks seek to keep their excess reserves at a zero level because reserves at the Bank of Canada do not earn interest. (Chartered banks and near banks are run to make profits; we assume that all depository institutions wish to convert excess reserves that do not pay interest into interest-bearing loans.)

Look at the simplified initial position of the bank in Balance Sheet 16.1. Liabilities consist of $1 million in chequable deposits. Assets consist of $100,000 in reserves, which you can see are the desired reserves in the form of vault cash or deposits in the institution's reserve account at the Bank of Canada, and $900,000 in loans to customers. Total assets of $1 million equal total liabilities of $1 million. With a 10 percent reserve and $1 million in chequable deposits, the bank has the actual desired level of reserves of $100,000 and no excess reserves. The simplifying assumption here is that the bank has a zero net worth. A depository institution rarely has a **net worth** of more than a small percentage of its total assets.

Net worth The difference between assets and liabilities.

BALANCE SHEET 16.1

Bank 1

Assets			Liabilities	
Total reserves		$100,000	Chequable deposits	$1,000,000
Desired reserves	$100,000			
Excess reserves	0			
Loans		900,000		
Total		$1,000,000	Total	$1,000,000

Assume that a *new* depositor takes $10,000 in currency out of a safety deposit box and deposits it in Bank 1. Chequing deposits in Bank 1 immediately increase by $10,000, bringing the total to $1,010,000. Total reserves of Bank 1 increase to $110,000. A $1,010,000 total in chequing deposits means that desired reserves will have to be 10 percent of $1,010,000, or $101,000. Bank 1 now has excess reserves equal to $110,000 minus $101,000, or $9,000. This is shown in Balance Sheet 16-2.

BALANCE SHEET 16.2

Bank 1

Assets			Liabilities	
Total reserves		$110,000	Chequable deposits	$1,010,000
Desired reserves	$101,000			
Excess reserves	9,000			
Loans		900,000		
Total		$1,010,000	Total	$1,010,000

Try Preview Question 2:

What happens to the money supply when a person deposits currency in a single depository institution?

EFFECT ON THE MONEY SUPPLY. Has the currency deposit at Bank 1 changed the economy's money supply? No. There has been a change in the composition of the money supply—chequable deposits have *increased* by $10,000 but currency in circulation has *decreased* by $10,000. Currency held by a bank is not part of the money supply.

Look at excess reserves in Balance Sheet 16-2. Excess reserves were zero before the $10,000 deposit, and now they are $9,000—that's $9,000 worth of assets not earning any income. By assumption, Bank 1 will now lend out this entire $9,000 in excess reserves in order to earn interest income. Loans will increase to $909,000. This is shown in Balance Sheet 16-3.

BALANCE SHEET 16.3

Bank 1
(money created before cheque-clearing)

Assets		Liabilities	
Total reserves	$110,000	Chequable deposits	$1,019,000
Desired reserves			
Excess reserves			
Loans	909,000		
Total	$1,019,000	Total	$1,019,000

Try Preview Question 3:

What happens to the money supply when a bank makes a loan?

When banks lend, they create chequable deposits that are money. Bank 1 has monetized a loan or IOU. Cheques drawn against a chequable deposit are acceptable as a medium of exchange. Bank 1 has created money. It is through extension of loans by the chartered banks that the major portion of money used in our economy is created.

Borrowers borrow for a purpose. The borrower writes a $9,000 cheque to buy a second-hand car. If that cheque was deposited in another bank, actual reserves at Bank 1 will fall to $101,000 (as planned) after cheque-clearing, and deposits will fall to $1,010,000. Excess reserves will again become zero, as indicated in Balance Sheet 16-4.

BALANCE SHEET 16.4

Bank 1
(after cheque-clearing)

Assets			Liabilities	
Total reserves		$101,000	Chequable deposits	$1,010,000
Desired reserves	$101,000			
Excess reserves	0			
Loans		909,000		
Total		$1,010,000	Total	$1,010,000

In this example, a person deposited an additional $10,000. That $10,000 became part of the reserves of Bank 1. Because that deposit immediately created excess reserves in Bank 1, further loans were possible for Bank 1. The excess reserves were loaned out to earn interest. A bank will not lend more that its excess reserves because prudent banking practice dictates that it hold a certain amount of reserves at all times.

The maximum amount of new deposits that any single bank can create is equal to its excess reserves.

Money Expansion by the Banking System

Consider now the entire banking system. For practical purposes, we can look at all depository institutions taken as a whole.

NOT THE END OF THE PROCESS. When Bank 1 made a loan for $9,000 it created money or expanded the money supply. The process of money creation does not stop here.

The borrower spent the loan made by Bank 1 by writing a cheque which was deposited at Bank 2. For the sake of simplicity, ignore the previous assets and liabilities in Bank 2 and concentrate only on the balance sheet *changes* resulting from this new deposit, as shown in Balance Sheet 16-5. A plus sign indicates that the entry has increased, and a minus sign indicates that the entry has decreased. For the depository institution, Bank 2, the $9,000 deposit becomes an increase in reserves (assets) as well as an increase in chequing deposits (liabilities). Because the desired reserve ratio is 10 percent, or $900, Bank 2 will have excess reserves of $8,100. But, of course, excess reserves are not income producing, so Bank 2 will reduce them to zero by making loans of $8,100 (which will earn interest income) by creating deposits for borrowers equal to $8,100. The money supply has increased by $8,100. This is shown in Balance Sheet 16-6.

BALANCE SHEET 16.5

Bank 2 (changes only)

Assets			Liabilities	
Total reserves		$9,000	New chequable deposits	+$9,000
Desired reserves	$900			
Excess reserves	+8,100			
Total		+$9,000	Total	+$9,000

BALANCE SHEET 16.6

Bank 2
(money created before
cheque-clearing)

Assets			Liabilities	
Total reserves		$9,000	Chequable deposits	+$17,100
Desired reserves				
Excess reserves				
Loans		+$8,100		
Total		+$17,100	Total	+$17,100

Assume that a borrower that has received the $8,100 loan from Bank 2 writes a cheque that is deposited in an account at Bank 3. After cheque-clearing has occurred, Bank 2's excess reserves will again be zero, as shown in Balance Sheet 16-7.

BALANCE SHEET 16.7

Bank 2
(after cheque-clearing)

Assets			Liabilities	
Total reserves		$900	Chequable deposits	+$9,000
Desired reserves	$900			
Excess reserves	0			
Loans		+8,100		
Total		+$9,000	Total	+$9,000

CONTINUATION OF THE DEPOSIT CREATION PROCESS. At Bank 3, chequable deposits and total reserves have increased by $8,100. Look at Bank 3's simplified account in Balance Sheet 16-8, where, again, only changes in the assets and liabilities are shown.

Because the desired reserve ratio is 10 percent, or $810, Bank 3's excess reserves are therefore $7,290. Bank 3 will want to lend those non-interest-earning assets (excess reserves). When it does, loans (in the form of created chequing deposits) will increase by $7,290 and the money supply will have increased by $7,290. Bank 3's total reserves will fall to $810, and excess reserves become zero as the $7,290 loan is spent and deposited at another bank.

BALANCE SHEET 16.8

Bank 3 (changes only)

Assets			Liabilities	
Total reserves		$8,100	New chequable deposits	+$8,100
Desired reserves	$810			
Excess reserves	+7,290			
Total		+$8,100	Total	+$8,100

PROGRESSION TO OTHER BANKS. This process continues to Banks 4,5,6, and so on. Each bank obtains smaller and smaller increases in deposits because 10 percent of each deposit is held in reserves; therefore, each succeeding depository institution makes correspondingly smaller loans. Table 16-1 shows the new deposits, possible loans, and desired reserves for the remaining depository institutions in the system.

EFFECT ON TOTAL MONEY SUPPLY. In this simple example, the money supply initially increases by $9,000 at Bank 1. It was further increased by $8,100 at Bank 2, and it was again increased by $7,290 at Bank 3. Eventually, the money supply will increase by $90,000, as shown in Table 16-1. The money multiplier process is portrayed graphically in Figure 16-2.

TABLE 16.1

Maximum Money Creation with 10 Percent Desired Reserves

This table shows the maximum new loans plus investments that banks can make, given a currency deposit of $10,000 in Bank 1. The desired reserve ratio is 10 percent. We assume that all excess reserves in each bank are used for new loans or investments.

Bank	New Deposits	New Desired Reserves	Maximum New Loans Equal Maximum New Money (excess reserves)
1	$10,000	$1,000	$9,000
2	9,000	900	8,100
3	8,100	810	7,290
4	7,290	729	6,561
.	.	.	.
.	.	.	.
.	.	.	.
All other banks	65,610	6,561	59,049
	Totals $100,000	$10,000	$90,000

Increase in Overall Reserves

When excess reserves are created , the money supply can increase. In our example, the depository institutions use their excess reserves to make loans. It is not important how they put the money back into the system. If they bought certificates of deposit or any other security, the analysis would be the same because the party they bought those securities from would receive a cheque from the purchasing depository institution. The recipient of the cheque would then deposit it into its own depository institution. The deposit expansion process would be the same as we have already outlined.

This process can work in reverse if there is a decrease in reserves, for example, when loans are repaid. The result is a multiple contraction of deposits and therefore of the total money supply in circulation.

Try Preview Question 4:

What happens to the overall money supply when a person deposits currency in a single depository institution which is part of a banking system?

FIGURE 16.2 The Multiple Expansion in the Money Supply Due to a Currency Deposit of $10,000 When the Desired Reserve Ratio Is 10 Percent

The banks are all aligned in decreasing order of new deposits created. Bank 1 receives the $10,000 in new currency creating new excess of $9,000 reserves and lends out $9,000. Bank 2 receives the $9,000 and lends out $8,100. The process continues through Banks 3 to 19 and then the rest of the banking system. Ultimately, assuming no leakages, the $9,000 of new excess reserves results in an increase in the money supply of $90,000, or 10 times the initial excess reserves, because the desired reserve ratio is 10 percent.

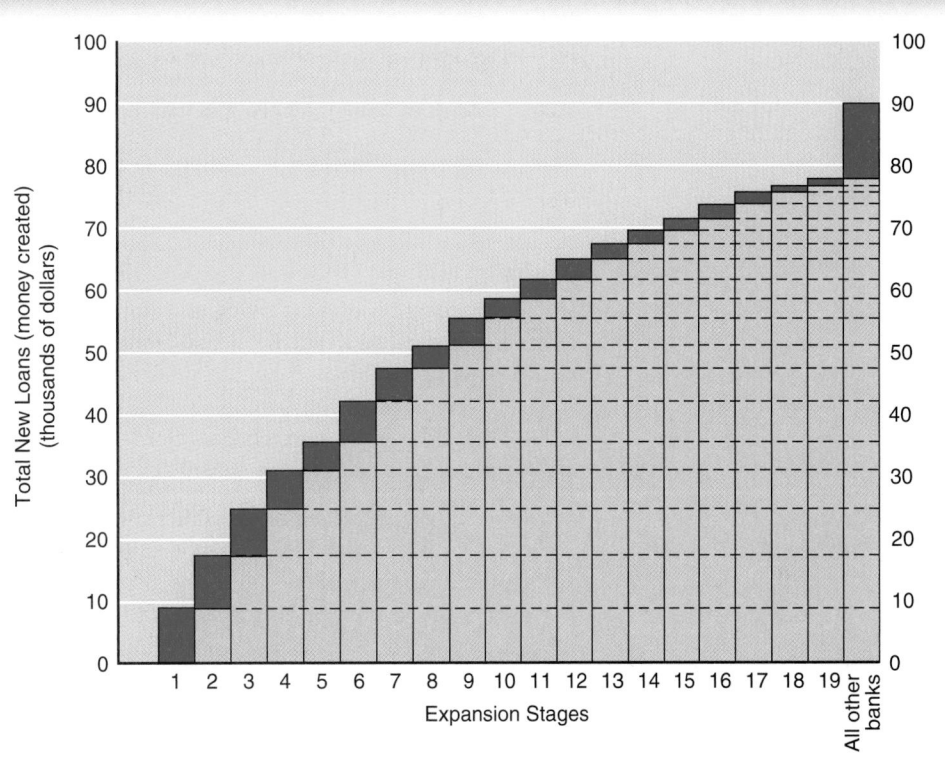

Concepts in Brief

- When reserves increase at a single bank in the banking system, the result is a multiple expansion of loans and therefore of the money supply.
- If there is a reduction in the reserves of a bank in the banking system, the result is a multiple contraction of loans and therefore of the money supply.

The Money Multiplier

In the example just given, with a desired reserve ratio of 10 percent, a new $10,000 currency deposit increased excess reserves at Bank 1 by $9,000 and yielded a $90,000 increase in total new loans in the banking system, an increase of $90,000 in the money supply. Loans increased by a multiple of 10 times the initial $9,000 increase in overall reserves. Conversely, a $9,000 decrease in excess reserves will yield a $90,000 decrease in total loans in the banking system—a decrease in the money supply; loans will decrease by a multiple of 10 times.

We can now make a generalization about the extent to which the money supply will change when the banking system's reserves are increased or decreased. The **money multiplier** gives the change in the money supply due to a change in reserves. If we assume that no excess reserves are kept and that all loan proceeds are deposited in depository institutions in the system, the following equation applies:

Money multiplier The reciprocal of the required reserve ratio, assuming no leakages into currency and no excess reserves. It is equal to 1 divided by the required reserve ratio.

$$\text{Potential money multiplier} = \frac{1}{\text{desired reserve ratio}}$$

That is, the maximum possible value of the money multiplier is equal to 1 divided by the desired reserve ratio for chequable deposits. The *actual* change in the money supply—currency plus chequable account balances—will be equal to the following:

Actual change in money supply = actual money multiplier × change in excess reserves

Now we examine why there is a difference between the potential money multiplier—1 divided by the required reserve ratio—and the actual multiplier.

Forces That Reduce the Money Multiplier

We made a number of simplifying assumptions to come up with the potential money multiplier. In the real world, the actual money multiplier is considerably smaller. Several factors account for this.

LEAKAGES. The entire loan (cheque) from one bank is not always deposited in another bank. At least two leakages can occur:

- *Currency drains.* When deposits increase, the public may want to hold more currency. Currency that is kept in a person's wallet remains outside the banking system and cannot be held by banks as reserves from which to make loans. The greater the amount of cash leakage, the smaller the actual money multiplier.
- *Excess reserves.* Depository institutions may wish to maintain excess reserves. Depository institutions do not, in fact, always keep excess reserves at zero. To the extent that they want to keep positive excess reserves, the money multiplier will be smaller. A bank receiving $1 million in new deposits might, in our example with the 10 percent desired reserve ratio, keep more than $100,000 as reserves. The greater the excess reserves, the smaller the actual money multiplier.

Empirically, the currency drain is more significant than the effect of excess reserves.

REAL-WORLD MONEY MULTIPLIERS. The desired reserve ratio determines the maximum potential money multiplier because the reciprocal of the desired reserve ratio tells us what that is. The maximum is never attained for the money supply as a whole because of currency drains and excess reserves. Also, each definition of the money supply, M1 or M2, will yield different results for money multipliers. For several decades, the M1 multiplier has varied between 1.5 and 2.5. The M2 multiplier, however, has shown a trend upward, ranging from 2.25 at the beginning of the 1960s, to over 12.5 in the 1990s.

CONCEPTS IN BRIEF

- The maximum money multiplier is equal to the reciprocal of the desired reserve ratio.
- The actual multiplier is much less than the maximum money multiplier because of currency drains and excess reserves voluntarily held by banks.

Deposit Insurance and Flawed Bank Regulation

When businesses fail, they create hardships for creditors, owners, workers, and customers. But when a depository institution fails, an even greater hardship results because many individuals and businesses depend on the safety and security of banks. While Canada has a history of relatively few bank failures, we are not immune to them. Between 1967 and 1989 there were 23 failures, and there have been a further 22 failures since then. However, when compared to the American experience of 1,065 failures between 1985 and 1993, the Canadian record looks quite good.

Canadian Deposit Insurance Corporation (CDIC) A government agency that insures the deposits held in federally incorporated financial institutions.

Nevertheless, in 1967 the federal government set up the **Canadian Deposit Insurance Corporation (CDIC)** to protect small investors who do not have the resources to accurately assess the soundness of federally incorporated financial institutions. Credit unions now have similar deposit insurance through their own institutions.

The Need for Deposit Insurance

Bank runs Attempts by many of a bank's depositors to convert chequing and time deposits into currency out of fear for the bank's solvency.

The CDIC was established to mitigate the primary cause of bank failures, **bank runs**—the simultaneous rush of depositors to convert their demand deposits or time deposits into currency.

Consider the following scenario. A bank begins to look shaky; its assets may not seem sufficient to cover its liabilities. If the bank has no deposit insurance, depositors in this bank (and any banks associated with it) will all want to withdraw their money from the bank at the same time. Their concern is that this shaky bank will not have enough money to return their deposits to them in the form of currency. Indeed, this is what happens in a bank failure when insurance doesn't exist. Just as with the failure of a regular business, the creditors of the bank may not all get paid, or if they do, they will get paid less than 100 percent of what they are owed. Depositors are creditors of a bank because their funds are on loan to the bank. In a fractional reserve banking system, banks do not hold 100 percent of their depositors' money in the form of reserves. Consequently, all depositors cannot withdraw all their money at the same time. It would be desirable to assure depositors that they can have their deposits converted into cash when they wish, no matter how serious the financial situation of the bank.

The CDIC provides this assurance. By insuring deposits, the CDIC bolsters trust in the banking system and provides depositors with the incentive to leave their deposits with the bank, even in the face of rumours of bank failures. In 1967, it was sufficient for the CDIC to cover each account up to $20,000. The current maximum is $60,000.

All financial institutions insured by the CDIC pay the same premium—one-sixth of one percent of insured deposits. The Canadian Bankers' Association opposes this method of determining premiums as it claims that the large chartered banks are at much less risk of failing than smaller financial institutions. If, for example, economic conditions led to widespread loan defaults in British Columbia, the chartered banks could rely on their more profitable operations in the rest of the country to keep them solvent. Smaller trust and mortgage loan companies do not have that option and consequently are at greater risk of failing. The CBA believes that those smaller companies should pay higher premiums to match their higher risk.

A Flaw in the Deposit Insurance Scheme

Because deposit insurance premiums are not based on the degree of risk of the depository institution's investments, there is no reward for investing in relatively non-risky assets. The result is that bankers have an incentive to invest in more high-yield assets, which carry more risk, than they would if there were no deposit insurance. Thus the premium rate is artificially low, permitting institution managers to obtain deposits at less than market price (because depositors will accept a lower interest payment on insured deposits); and even if the institution's portfolio becomes riskier, its deposit insurance premium does not rise. Consequently, depository institution managers can increase their net interest margin by using lower-cost insured deposits to purchase higher-yield, higher-risk assets. The gains to risk taking accrue to the managers and stockholders of the depository institutions; the losses go to the deposit insurer (and, as we will see, ultimately to taxpayers).

To combat the inherent flaws in the financial institution industry and in the deposit insurance system, a vast regulatory apparatus was installed. The CDIC was given regulatory powers to offset the risk-taking temptations to depository institution managers; those powers included the ability to require sound business practices by the insured institutions.

Deposit Insurance, Adverse Selection, and Moral Hazard

Asymmetric information Information possessed by one side of a transaction but not the other. The side with more information will be at an advantage.

When financial transactions take place, one party often does not have all the knowledge needed about the other party to make correct decisions. This is known as the problem of **asymmetric information**. For example, borrowers generally know more than lenders about the returns and risks associated with the investment projects they intend to undertake.

Adverse selection A problem created by asymmetric information prior to a transaction. Individuals who are the most undesirable from the other party's point of view end up being the ones who are most likely to want to engage in a particular financial transaction, such as borrowing.

ADVERSE SELECTION. **Adverse selection** arises when there is asymmetric information before a transaction takes place. In financial markets, it often occurs because individuals and firms that are worse credit risks than they appear to be are the ones most willing to borrow at any given interest rate. This willingness makes them likely to be selected by lenders, yet their inferior ability to repay (relative to the interest rate being charged) means that loans to them more often yield adverse outcomes for lenders (default). The potential risks of adverse selection make lenders less likely to lend to anyone, and more inclined to charge higher interest rates when they do lend.

Adverse selection is often a problem when insurance is involved because people or firms that are relatively poor risks are sometimes able to disguise that fact from insurers. It is instructive to examine the way this works with the deposit insurance provided by the CDIC. Deposit insurance shields depositors from the potential adverse effects of risky decisions and so makes depositors willing to accept riskier investment strategies by their banks. Clearly, this encourages more high-flying, risk-loving entrepreneurs to become managers of banks. The consequences for the CDIC—and often for the taxpayer—are larger losses.

Moral hazard A situation in which, after a transaction has taken place, one of the parties to the transaction has an incentive to engage in behaviour that will be undesirable from the other party's point of view.

MORAL HAZARD. **Moral hazard** arises as the result of information asymmetry after a transaction has occurred. In financial markets, lenders face the hazard that borrowers may engage in activities that are contrary to the lender's interest and thus might be said to be immoral from the lender's perspective. For example, because lenders do not share in the profits of business ventures, they generally want borrowers to agree to invest prudently. Yet once the loan has been made, borrower-investors have an incentive to invest in high-risk, high-return projects because they are able to keep all of the extra profits if the projects succeed. Such behaviour subjects the lender to greater hazards than are being compensated for under the terms of the loan agreement.

Thinking Critically About the Media 16-1   Bailouts That Cost Taxpayers Millions

When the Canadian Commercial Bank failed in 1985, the media alarmed us with inflated figures of how much the Canadian taxpayer was paying to bail out this bank. The same sorts of numbers are being bandied about for the potential bailout of banks in Japan. Although technically not inaccurate, such stories fail to point out that such bailouts always occur *after the fact*. The billion or so dollars lost by the Canadian Commercial Bank had already been lost by the time of the bailout. That is to say, the economy had already

seen a $1 billion reduction in its wealth because of bad investments by the Canadian Commercial Bank. The same is now true for the Japanese economy. The investments made by Japanese banks that turned sour will not magically increase in value if the Japanese government decides to use taxpayers' money to bail out the banks. Banking rescue plans as such are simply a determination of who will bear losses that have already occurred.

Moral hazard is also an important phenomenon in the presence of insurance contracts, such as the deposit insurance provided by the CDIC. Insured depositors know that they will not suffer losses if their bank fails. Hence they have little incentive to monitor their bank's investment activities or to punish their bank by withdrawing their funds if the bank assumes too much risk. Thus insured banks have incentives to take on more risks than they otherwise would—and with those risks come higher losses for the CDIC and for taxpayers.

Try Preview Question 5:

How does the existence of deposit insurance affect a financial institution's choice of risky versus nonrisky assets?

INTERNATIONAL POLICY EXAMPLE 16-1 — Will the Japanese Bail Out Their Banks?

Japan is facing a banking crisis that makes recent bank failures in Canada look like child's play. The policy question is how the Japanese government is going to bail out the banking system there. The Japanese banks in the mid-1990s held problem loans equal to about $1 trillion, or a quarter of Japan's GDP. Japanese authorities continued to allow banks to lend problem debtors enough money to cover unpaid interest. If the Japanese government chooses to bail out its banking system, the estimated cost will be close to $400 billion. Alternatively, the Japanese government could simply let the weakest banks go bankrupt. Some observers believe that a third solution will eventually come about: The Japanese government will pour in enough reserves to shore up the banking system in exchange for the nation's banks' agreeing to use all of their profits for the foreseeable future to write off bad debts. In the fall of 1995, the largest credit union in Japan, Cosmo Credit Corporation, failed. The Bank of Japan (Japan's central bank) stepped in and prevented a panic. By the time you read this, many more such interventions by the Bank of Japan will almost certainly have occurred.

For critical analysis: Who pays for the Japanese banking bailout if the "third way" is chosen?

CONCEPTS IN BRIEF

- Federal deposit insurance was created in 1967 when the Canadian Deposit Insurance Corporation (CDIC) was founded to insure deposits in federally incorporated depository institutions.
- Credit unions and *caisses populaires* have their own deposit insurance schemes.
- Deposit insurance was designed to prevent bank runs in which individual demand deposit and savings deposit holders attempt to turn their deposits into currency.
- Because of the way deposit insurance is set up in Canada, it encourages bank managers to invest in riskier assets to make higher rates of returns.

NETNOMICS

What Will Digital Cash Replace?

If people start to use smart cards, personal computers, and cellular phones to store and transmit digital cash, presumably they will have less desire to use other forms of money. To understand why, consider Table 16-2, which lists the key characteristics of cheques, government-issued currency, and digital cash.

In comparing currency with cheques, it is clear that people must trade off features that each offers. Cheques promise greater security, because if a thief steals a woman's handbag containing cash and cheques, she can contact her depository institution to halt payment on all cheques in the handbag. Currency payments are final, however, so the thief can spend all the cash he has taken from her. She can send cheques through the mail, but using currency requires face-to-face contact. In addition, currency transactions are anonymous, which may be desirable under some circumstances. Nevertheless, not everyone will accept a cheque in payment for a transaction, and a cheque payment is not final until the cheque clears. Cheque transactions are also more expensive. After evaluating these features of currency and cheques, people typically choose to hold both payment instruments.

People will likewise compare the features that digital cash offers with the features currently offered by government-provided currency and chequing accounts available from depository institutions. As Table 16-2 indicates, the acceptability of digital cash is uncertain at present. Nonetheless, we are contemplating an environment with wide acceptability, and in such an environment, digital cash would be nearly as acceptable as government-provided currency. Digital cash held on smart cards without special security features such as personal identification numbers will be as susceptible to theft as government currency. Some digital cash, however, may be held on devices, such as laptop computers or even wristwatches. (Swiss watch manufacturers have already developed watches with microchips for storing digital cash), requiring an access code before a microchip containing digital cash can be accessed. Overall, therefore, digital cash is likely to be somewhat more secure than government-provided currency, though not as secure as cheque transactions.

Digital cash transactions are likely to be less costly to undertake, because people will not have to go to depository institution branches or automated teller machines to obtain digital cash (although they will be able to do this if they wish). They will also be able to access digital cash at home on their personal computers. In addition, they will be able to send digital cash from remote locations using the Internet, and digital cash transactions will be instantaneously final. Unlike transactions using currency, therefore, digital cash transactions need not be conducted face to face. Like currency transactions, however, most digital cash transfers will be anonymous.

In most respects, therefore, digital cash looks like a better means of payment than government-provided currency. Certainly, for some time to come, a number of items—canned beverages and candy in vending machines, for example—will be easiest to purchase using government-provided currency. Many economists, however, believe that widespread adoption of privately issued digital cash will ultimately tend to crowd out government-provided currency. On many college campuses, vending machines already accept store-value cards. Eventually, vending machines on street corners are likely to have smart card readers.

TABLE 16-2
Features of Alternative Forms of Money

Digital cash tends to overshadow government-issued currency.

Feature	Cheques	Currency	Digital Cash
Security	High	Low	High(?)
Per-Transfer Cost	High	Medium	Low
Payment Final, Face-to-face	No	Yes	Yes
Payment Final, Non-Face-to-Face	No	No	Yes
Anonymity	No	Yes	Yes
Acceptability	Restricted	Wide	Uncertain at present

Source: Aleksander Berentsen, *"Monetary Policy Implications of Digital Money,"* Kyklos, 51 (1998), p. 92.

Deregulating the Financial Services Industry

Concepts Applied: Regulation, deregulation

Deregulation of the financial services industry is paving the way for new kinds of banks in Canada. "VanCity had already achieved significant market penetration in British Columbia, and was looking for national growth opportunities for its business and mandate of corporate social responsibility," says Dave Mowat, CEO of VanCity Credit Union. "The trendlines in our market research at the time revealed that consumers were beginning to ask for electronic banking options. Since VanCity wasn't in a position to fund the establishment of a nationwide bricks and mortar branch system, the opportunity became clear: a national, electronic bank serving its members by telephone, fax, ATM, and the Internet."

Over the early years of this century, Canada created an array of regulations which constrained the behaviour of the financial services industry. Only banks could grant commercial mortgages, only licensed brokerage firms could sell stocks, only insurance companies could sell life insurance. But recently, the trend has been towards deregulation resulting in "one-stop shopping" for financial services.

Deregulation Step-by-Step

The first of a series of moves towards blurring the lines between financial intermediaries came in 1987 when chartered banks were given permission to acquire investment dealers. While the banks themselves could not sell stocks and bonds, their wholly-owned subsidiaries could.

In 1992, the insurance business was deregulated. Banks and trust and insurance companies are now allowed to carry out most of each other's business functions. For the banks, which previously could sell only mortgage insurance, this was a big step. They could now sell life insurance, property and accident insurance, and travel insurance, again through subsidiaries.

Consequently, in 1996, National Bank, which operates primarily in Quebec, joined forces with New York-based Metropolitan Life Insurance Co. to form National Bank Financial Services. Former bank employees now also sell insurance, while former insurance salespeople have added mortgages to their product lines.

Also in 1996, the Royal Bank of Canada teamed up with IBM and 60 US banks to offer its services via the Internet. This electronic network allows Royal Bank customers to transfer money, pay bills, purchase airline tickets, and trade stocks by computer from their homes.

In a futuristic application of electronic technology to banking, Vancouver City Savings Credit Union, one of Canada's largest, purchased Citizens Trust which it converted to a bank. However, this bank has no branches where customers talk over financial matters with their bankers. All business—from depositing and withdrawing money to applying for mortgages—is conducted electronically through the Internet or at ATMs.

More Changes to Come

The three largest banks in the world, Germany's Deutsche Bank, the United States' Citigroup, and France's BNP Paribas, all have loans outstanding (assets) of more than US$1 trillion. The Canadian banks, which used to be relatively large, have fallen behind. The Royal Bank with assets of $300 million now ranks No. 55.

After a long review and lobbying by the financial services industry, early in 2001 the federal government introduced long awaited legislation setting out a three-stage process for Canadian bank mergers. First they would begin with a detailed application to the Competition Bureau, the Superintendent of Financial Institutions and the Minister of Finance. Secondly, Senate and Commons committees would also hold public hearings. Finally, after all the reviews were completed, the Minister of Finance would make a final decision.

For Critical Analysis

1. The term "nonbank bank" has been used a lot recently. What do you think it means?

2. Would there be an increased moral hazard problem associated with deposit insurance if banks were allowed to do everything—sell insurance, stocks and bonds, and airline tickets, plus everything else a bank does?

372 PART 5 • Money, Monetary Policy, and Stabilization

CHAPTER SUMMARY

1. Chartered banks maintain reserves, which consist of deposits in the Bank of Canada plus vault cash. Other financial institutions maintain reserves of deposits, sometimes in the chartered banks, and vault cash.

2. When depository institutions have more reserves than are desired, they are said to have excess reserves.

3. The Bank of Canada can control the money supply through open market operations—by buying and selling Canadian government securities.

4. When the Bank of Canada buys a bond, it pays for the bond by writing a cheque on itself. This creates additional reserves for the banking system. The result will be an increase in the money supply that is a multiple of the value of the bond purchased. If the Bank of Canada sells a bond, it reduces reserves in the banking system. The result will be a decrease in the money supply that is a multiple of the value of the bond sold.

5. Single depository institutions that have no excess reserves cannot alter the money supply.

6. The banking system as a whole can change the money supply pursuant to a change in reserves brought about by a Bank of Canada purchase or sale of government bonds. The Bank of Canada can also change the money supply by undertaking drawdowns or redeposits, or by using moral suasion.

7. The maximum money multiplier is equal to the reciprocal of the desired reserve ratio.

8. The actual money multiplier will be less than the maximum because of leakages—currency drains and excess reserve holdings of some banks.

9. The Canadian Deposit Insurance Corporation was created in 1967 to insure deposits in federally incorporated depository institutions. Credit unions and *caisses populaires* have their own system of deposit insurance. Because of the existence of deposit insurance, the probability of a run on the banking system, even if a significant number of depository institutions were to fail, is quite small.

10. A major flaw in the deposit insurance system has been the relatively low price for the insurance irrespective of risk. Moral hazard under the current deposit insurance system has led to overly risky and fraudulent behaviour on the part of some depository institution managers.

DISCUSSION OF PREVIEW QUESTIONS

1. **What is a fractional reserve banking system?**

   A fractional reserve banking system is one in which the reserves kept by the depository institutions are only a fraction of total deposits owned by the public. In general, depository institutions accept funds from the public and offer their depositors interest or other services. In turn the depository institutions lend out some of these deposits and earn interest. Because at any given time new deposits are coming in while people are drawing down on old deposits, prudent banking does not require a 100 percent reserve-deposit ratio. Because Canadian depository institutions keep less than 100 percent of their total deposits in the form of reserves, we refer to our banking structure as a fractional reserve system.

2. **What happens to the money supply when a person deposits currency in a single depository institution?**

   Initially, nothing. The total money supply is unaffected. The composition of the money supply has changed but not the total money supply. Chequable deposits will have increased but currency in circulation outside the banks will have decreased by an equivalent amount. Currency held by a bank is not part of the money supply.

3. **What happens to the money supply when a bank makes a loan?**

   When a bank makes a loan, it creates a chequable deposit, which is money, and adds to the money supply. The bank has monetized a loan or IOU.

4. **What happens to the overall money supply when a person deposits currency in a single depository institution which is part of a banking system?**

   A process of multiple expansion is initiated. The new currency deposit creates excess reserves and the potential and incentive for the receiving bank to make new loans, thus creating money. As this new money cascades through the banking system, more, but increasingly smaller, excess reserves are created, more new loans are made, and more new money created. Ultimately the maximum potential expansion of the money supply is equal to the new excess reserves times 1 divided by the desired reserve ratio—the potential money multiplier.

5. **How does the existence of deposit insurance affect a financial institution's choice of risky versus nonrisky assets?**

The best way to answer this question is with an analogy. Assume that you are given $10,000 to gamble at the Windsor Casino. In situation 1, you share equally with your benefactor in losses and in gains. In situation 2, your benefactor lets you share in the gains (at less than 100 percent) but incurs all losses. Will your behaviour be any different in situation 1 than in situation 2 while you are gambling? The answer is, of course, yes. In situation 1, you will be much more careful—you will choose games of chance that offer less risk but lower potential payoffs. In situation 2, you might as well try to break

the bank. At the roulette wheel, rather than going for odd or even or red or black, you might as well bet your benefactor's money on single numbers or groups of numbers or zero or double zero because if you hit it, you stand to gain a lot, but if you don't, you stand to lose nothing. Situation 2 is analogous to that of today's managers in depository institutions—it is a situation that involves moral hazard. When times get tough and business is bad, they have had a tendency to "go for broke." They bought risky but high-yielding assets, such as dubious real estate loans, loans at high interest rates to developing countries, and oil development loans. For those whose bets don't pay off, the federal government may bail out all the depositors. The few whose bets do pay off look like heroes.

PROBLEMS

(Answers to the odd-numbered problems appear at the back of the book.)

16-1. Bank 1 has received a deposit of $1 million. Assuming that the banks retain no excess reserves, answer the following questions.

a. The desired reserve ratio is 25 percent. Fill in the blanks in the table below. What is the money multiplier?

b. Now the desired reserve ratio is 5 percent. Fill in the blanks in a similar table. What is the money multiplier?

Multiple Deposit Creation

Bank	Deposits	Reserves	Loans
Bank 1	$1,000,000	$_____	$_____
Bank 2	_____	_____	_____
Bank 3	_____	_____	_____
Bank 4	_____	_____	_____
Bank 5	_____	_____	_____
All other banks	_____	_____	_____
Totals	_____	_____	_____

16-2. Arrange the following items on the proper side of a bank's balance sheet.

a. Chequing deposits

b. Vault cash

c. Time deposits

d. Deposits with the Bank of Canada

e. Loans to private businesses

f. Loans to households

g. Holdings of Canadian government, provincial, and municipal bonds

h. Borrowings from other banks

Assets	Liabilities

16-3. If the desired reserve ratio is 10 percent, what will be the maximum change in the money supply in each of the following situations?

a. Theola Smith deposits in Bank 2 a cheque drawn on Bank 3.

b. Smith finds $1,000 in coins and paper currency buried in her backyard and deposits it in her chequing account.

c. Smith writes a $1,000 cheque on her own account and takes $1,000 in currency and buries it in her backyard.

16-4. Assume a desired reserve ratio of 8 percent. A cheque for $60,000 is drawn on an account in Bank B and deposited in a chequable deposit in Bank A.

   a. How much have the excess reserves of Bank A increased?

   b. How much in the form of new loans is Bank A now able to extend to borrowers?

   c. By how much have reserves of Bank B decreased?

   d. By how much have excess reserves of Bank B decreased?

   e. By how much has the money supply increased?

16-5. Examine the following balance sheet of Bank B.

Bank B

Assets		Liabilities	
Total reserves	$ 50	Chequable deposits	$200
Loans	100	Capital stock	200
Government securities	50		
Property	200		

Assume that the desired reserve ratio is 10 percent.

   a. Calculate the excess reserves of Bank B.

   b. How much money can Bank B lend out?

   c. If Bank B lends the money in part (b) of this problem, what are the new values for total reserves? For chequable deposits? For loans?

   d. What is the maximum expansion of the money supply if Bank B lends the amount suggested in part (b) of this problem?

16-6. It is the year 2310. Residents of an earth colony on Titan, the largest moon of the planet Saturn, use chequable deposits at financial institutions as the only form of money. Depository institutions on Titan wish to hold 10 percent of deposits as excess reserves at all times. There are no other deposits in the banking system. If the banking system on Titan has $300 million in reserves and the total quantity of money is $1.5 billion, what is the desired reserve ratio?

ECONOMICS ON THE NET

What is Deposit Insurance?

Internet URL: http://www.cdic.ca

Title: Deposit Insurance

Navigation: Begin at the homepage of the Canada Deposit Insurance Corporation (http://www.cdic.ca). Click on How Deposit Insurance Works.

Application: Perform the operations indicated above and answer the following questions:

   a. How much deposit insurance do you have?

   b. Is every account at a financial institution insured?

   c. Are all accounts insured at a financial institution? Is every Canadian financial institution a CDIC member?

THE BANK OF CANADA AND MONETARY POLICY

If you follow any of the news stories about the economic policies being made in Ottawa, you cannot fail to learn about what this nation's central bank, the Bank of Canada, is doing to stop a recession, cool down an overheated economy, or something else of that nature. Whatever the Bank of Canada does, some part of the press or the academic world is apt to "bash" it for doing the wrong thing. Whenever a vacancy occurs on its Board of Governors, speculation about the political leaning of the next appointee is rampant. Some analysts argue that even though the Bank of Canada is only a quasi-government agency, it is not really independent of the government's wishes. These commentators go further and argue that the Bank of Canada should become completely independent of the government. Is the Bank of Canada already independent? And if not, does it matter? To answer these questions, you need to know more about how monetary policy works.

PREVIEW QUESTIONS

1. What are the functions of the Bank of Canada?

2. What is the demand for money curve, and how is it related to the interest rate?

3. Why is the price of existing bonds inversely related to the interest rate?

4. What is a monetarist?

5. How do the supply of, and demand for, money determine the interest rate?

DID YOU KNOW THAT... the Governor of the Bank of Canada is often considered the second most important person politically and economically in the country after the prime minister? Why is the head of the Bank of Canada considered so important? Because the Governor of the Bank of Canada and the rest of the Bank's Governors determine monetary policy in Canada. A strongly worded public statement by the Governor of the Bank of Canada can cause instant reaction in our financial markets and sometimes in those in the rest of the world.

This chapter will deal with the Bank of Canada and monetary policy—the Bank of Canada's altering interest rates or changing the supply of money (or the rate at which it grows) in order to achieve national economic goals. When you were introduced to aggregate demand in Chapter 10, you discovered that the position of the aggregate demand curve is determined by the willingness of firms, individuals, governments, and foreigners to purchase domestically produced goods and services. Monetary policy works in a variety of ways to change this willingness, both directly and indirectly.

Think about monetary policy in an intuitive way: An increase in the money supply adds to the amount of money that firms and individuals have on hand and so increases the amount that they wish to spend. The result is an increase in aggregate demand. A decrease in the money supply reduces the amount of money that people have on hand to spend and so decreases aggregate demand. Integral to this process is the central bank.

Central Banks

The first central bank, which began operations in 1668, was Sweden's Sveriges Riksbank (called the Risens Standers Bank until 1867). In 1694, the British Parliament established the most historically famous of central banks, the Bank of England. It authorized the Bank of England to issue currency notes redeemable in silver, and initially the Bank of England's notes circulated alongside currency notes issued by the government and private finance companies. Until 1800, the Riksbank and the Bank of England were the only central banks. The number of central banks worldwide remained less than 10 as late as 1873. The number expanded considerably toward the end of the nineteenth century and again during the second half of the twentieth century, as shown in Figure 17.1.

FIGURE 17.1 The Number of Central Banking Institutions, 1670 to the Present

The twentieth century witnessed considerable growth in the number of central banks.

Source: Data from Forrest Capie, Charles Goodhart, and Nobert Schnadt, *"The Development of Central Banking,"* in Forrest Capie et al., *The Future of Central Banking: The Tercentenary Symposium of the Bank of England* (Cambridge: Cambridge University Press, 1994.)

Canada's Central Banking System

The Bank of Canada is Canada's central bank. It oversees the Canadian monetary system and as such is considered the country's monetary authority. The Bank of Canada was established with the *Bank of Canada Act* of 1934 and opened its doors for business in 1935. At first privately owned, by 1938 the federal government had nationalized it. According to the preamble to the *Bank of Canada Act* of 1934, the Bank of Canada was expected to:

> …regulate credit and currency in the best interest of the economic life of the nation, to control and protect the external value of the national monetary unit and to mitigate by its influence fluctuations in the general level of production, trade, prices and employment, so far as may be possible within the scope of monetary action, and generally to promote the economic and financial welfare of the Dominion.

ORGANIZATION OF THE BANK OF CANADA. The Bank of Canada is governed by a Board of Directors consisting of the Governor of the Bank of Canada, the Senior Deputy Governor, 12 directors from non-banking occupations, and the Deputy Minister of Finance, who is a non-voting member of the Board. The Governor is appointed by the Board, with Cabinet approval, for a seven-year term. Directors are appointed for three-year terms. Regional representation is a priority when appointing directors.

The Board of Directors must meet at least four times per year, but frequently meets more often. The day-to-day operations of the Bank are directed by an executive committee of the Board, consisting of the Governor, the Senior Deputy Governor, and two to four other directors who meet weekly. While the Bank of Canada is ultimately responsible to the federal government, it is an independent body charged with maintaining price stability and economic growth in Canada. Whether this independence is beneficial is the topic of the Issues and Applications section at the end of Chapter 17.

THE BANK OF CANADA'S CUSTOMERS. The Bank of Canada accepts deposits from the federal government and the chartered banks only. Almost all federal government transactions pass through the Bank of Canada, although the government also has accounts with the chartered banks.

The chartered banks hold deposits at the Bank of Canada for two reasons. First, the banks hold a large part of their reserve deposits in these accounts. Until 1992, they were required to hold reserves by law; however, the *Bank Act* of 1992 eliminated this requirement. Now they hold reserves at the Bank of Canada as part of prudent banking practice.

The second reason the chartered banks hold reserves at the Bank of Canada is to facilitate cheque clearing. When your employer pays you with a $200 cheque drawn on the Royal Bank and you deposit it in your account at the Bank of Nova Scotia, no money actually changes hands. All across Canada, similar transactions are taking place at financial institutions. At the end of the day, the **Canadian Payments Association** adds up all the money that each bank owes the other—for instance, the Royal Bank would owe the Bank of Nova Scotia $200 for your paycheque—and arrives at a net transfer of funds that should be made between banks. If the Toronto-Dominion Bank owes the Bank of Montreal $1.5 million, for example, while the Bank of Montreal owes the Toronto-Dominion Bank $1 million, the Canadian Payments Association would ask the Bank of Canada to transfer $500,000 out of the reserve deposits of the Toronto-Dominion Bank and into the deposits of the Bank of Montreal. Near banks maintain deposits with the chartered banks so that they may participate in the cheque-clearing process as well.

Canadian Payments Association (CPA)
A regulated organization that operates a national cheque-clearing and settlements system.

Functions of the Bank of Canada

The Bank of Canada serves four basic functions. It conducts monetary policy on behalf of the federal government, it acts as a lender of last resort to the financial community, it issues bank notes, and it is fiscal agent and financial advisor to the government. Let's examine each of these functions in more detail.

MONETARY POLICY. The Bank of Canada is charged with keeping inflation within a target band of 1 to 3 percent to facilitate economic growth. It does this primarily by varying the reserve deposits held by the chartered banks at the Bank of Canada.

LENDER OF LAST RESORT. Occasionally the chartered banks will feel their reserve deposits are lower than they would like. In these situations, the banks can ask the Bank of Canada for short-term loans to ensure that they do not run short of cash to satisfy withdrawals. This practice lends stability to the system. Should a bank not be able to meet demand for withdrawals, it could be forced into bankruptcy.

ISSUING BANK NOTES. From the opening of Canada's first chartered bank in 1871, the chartered banks issued their own bank notes. This practice declined when the Bank of Canada began issuing Canadian currency, and stopped completely in 1945. The Bank of Canada now is the only body which can issue legal bank notes in Canada. Read Example 17-1 for a discussion of another type of "currency"—Canadian Tire money.

FISCAL AGENT AND FINANCIAL ADVISOR. The Bank of Canada acts as the federal government's fiscal agent and financial advisor. In this capacity, it manages the government's debt by arranging payment of interest to debt-holders, and payment in full on maturing debt. It also holds government deposits, and provides advice with respect to issuing government securities. The Bank of Canada frequently intervenes in the foreign exchange market to support the external value of the Canadian dollar and to manage the government's holdings of foreign reserves. Chapter 20 looks at the foreign exchange market in more detail.

Try Preview Question 1:

What are the functions of the Bank of Canada?

Table 17.1 shows a consolidated balance sheet for the Bank of Canada. Its assets consist mainly of Government of Canada securities and Treasury bills. These securities form part of the public debt. The Bank's liabilities are mostly currency in circulation, with chartered bank reserve deposits the next largest component.

TABLE 17.1

Bank of Canada Consolidated Balance Sheet at December 31, 2000 (millions of dollars)

Source: Bank of Canada, *Annual Report 2000*, pp. 48-49.

Assets		Liabilities	
Treasury Bills of Canada	$9,234.7	Bank notes in circulation	$36,775.3
Other Government of Canada securities	26,503.3	Government of Canada deposits	16.1
Foreign currency deposits	746.9	Chartered bank deposits (reserves)	1,669.2
Advances to members of CPA	952.3	Other deposits	368.8
Other assets	1,910.9	Other liabilities and capital	718.7
Total assets	$39,348.1	Total liabilities	$39,548.1

EXAMPLE 17-1   Is Canadian Tire Money Real Money?

One of the functions of the Bank of Canada is to issue bank notes. Canadian Tire, however, issues its own "currency," which can be used to purchase goods and services at any Canadian Tire store. Every time you purchase with cash one dollar's worth of merchandise, you receive five cents in Canadian Tire money. Is this note "real" money?

If you said, no, Canadian Tire money is not real money, you would be right. However, in some instances it is used in place of real money. Consider the bartender who is given Canadian Tire notes as part of a tip. If that individual's car happens to need new tires, for example, then those notes are as good as money. If the bartender doesn't want anything from Canadian Tire, then they are worthless.

But what if the bartender had a friend who wanted to buy tires? The two could exchange the Canadian Tire money for Canadian currency, which is real money. However, one of the tests of Canadian legal tender is that it must be accepted in payment of debts in Canada. In this instance Canadian Tire money would not measure up.

For critical analysis: What conditions would have to exist for Canadian Tire money to act as real money in practice, if not in theory?

CONCEPTS IN BRIEF

- The Bank of Canada is Canada's central bank. It is run by a Board of Directors from non-banking occupations, as well as the Governor and Senior Deputy Governor of the Bank.
- The only customers of the Bank of Canada are the federal government and the chartered banks. The chartered banks hold reserve deposits at the Bank of Canada as a precaution in case of heavy withdrawals, and to facilitate cheque clearing.
- The Canadian Payments Association handles cheque clearing for the financial community.
- The Bank of Canada conducts monetary policy on behalf of the federal government, acts as a lender of last resort to the financial community, issues bank notes, and provides financial advice to the federal government.

The Money Supply and Tools of Monetary Policy

Monetary policy is one means of influencing the economy through regulating the money supply. This is done by changing the reserves in the banking system.

Why do we need a monetary policy? We need monetary policy to keep our economy growing at its potential. Too little money can hamper economic growth, and too much money can cause inflation. Canada's monetary policy is conducted by the Bank of Canada which, in general, faces one of two economic conditions: a recessionary gap or an inflationary gap in the economy.

If the Bank is confronted with a recessionary gap in the economy it will pursue easy money, that is, expansionary policy. Intuitively, this suggests increasing the money supply and lowering interest rates so as to increase aggregate demand, increase employment (thereby reducing unemployment), and increase real economic output to its full-employment potential.

If the Bank is confronted with an inflationary gap in the economy it will pursue tight money, that is, restrictive or contractionary policy. Intuitively, this suggests reducing the money supply and raising interest rates to cause excessive growth of aggregate demand to fall, thereby reducing GDP to close the inflationary gap.

In general, the Bank of Canada seeks to alter consumption, investment, and aggregate demand as a whole by altering the rate of growth of the money supply. To do this the Bank of Canada uses four tools as part of its policymaking action: open market operations, drawdowns and redeposits, setting the bank rate, and moral suasion.

Open Market Operations

Open market operations The purchase and sale of existing Canadian government securities (such as bonds) in the open private market by the Bank of Canada.

Open market operations are the purchase and sale of *existing* government securities in the open market (the private secondary Canadian securities market) by the Bank of Canada in order to change the money supply.

A Sample Transaction: Purchase of a $100,000 Canadian Government Security by the Bank of Canada

Assume that the Bank of Canada decides to purchase $100,000 worth of Canadian government securities. The Bank pays for these securities by writing a cheque on itself for $100,000. This cheque is given to the bond dealer in exchange for the $100,000 worth of bonds. The bond dealer deposits the $100,000 cheque in its chequing account at a bank, which then sends the $100,000 cheque back to the Bank of Canada. When the Bank of Canada receives the cheque, it adds $100,000 to the reserve account of the bank that sent it the cheque. The Bank of Canada has created $100,000 of reserves. It can create reserves because it has the ability to "write up" (add to) the reserve accounts of the chartered banks whenever it buys Canadian securities. When the Bank of Canada buys a government security in the open market, it initially expands total reserves and the money supply by the amount of the purchase.

USING BALANCE SHEETS. Consider the balance sheets of the Bank of Canada and of a chartered bank receiving the cheque. Balance Sheet 17.1 shows the results for the Bank of Canada after the bond purchase and for the bank after the bond dealer deposits the $100,000 cheque. The Bank of Canada's balance sheet (which here reflects only account *changes*) shows that after the purchase, its assets have increased by $100,000 in the form of Canadian government securities. Liabilities have also increased by $100,000 in the form of an increase in the reserve account of the bank. The balance sheet for the chartered bank shows an increase in assets of $100,000 in the form of reserves with the Bank of Canada. The bank also has an increase in its liabilities in the form of $100,000 in the chequing account of the bond dealer; this is an immediate $100,000 increase in the money supply.

BALANCE SHEET 17.1

Balance sheets for the Bank of Canada and a chartered bank when a Canadian government security is purchased by the Bank of Canada, showing changes in assets and liabilities.

The Bank of Canada		Chartered Bank	
Assets	Liabilities	Assets	Liabilities
+$100,000	+$100,000	+$100,000	+$100,000
Canadian government securities	chartered bank's reserves	reserves	chequing deposit owned by bond dealer

Effect on the Money Supply

The initial increase of the money supply of $100,000, assuming a desired reserve ratio of 10 percent, requires desired reserves of $10,000, and generates new excess reserves of $90,000. For the sake of simplicity, ignore the previous assets and liabilities in the banking system and concentrate only on the balance sheet *changes* resulting from this new deposit, as shown in Balance Sheet 17-2. A plus sign indicates that the entry has increased, and a minus sign indicates that the entry has decreased.

BALANCE SHEET 17.2

Banking System

Assets			Liabilities	
Total reserves		+$100,000	New chequable deposits	+$100,000
Desired reserves	$10,000			
Excess reserves	90,000			
Total		+$100,000	Total	+$100,000

Of course, excess reserves are not income producing. Consequently, the banking system will reduce them to zero by making loans. Given a money multiplier of 10 in this example, the loans will be $900,000, which will earn interest income for the banks. The banks will have also created deposits for borrowers equal to $900,000. The money supply has therefore further increased by $900,000. This is shown in Balance Sheet 17-3. If the banks wish to increase loans to the general public, interest rates typically have to be reduced. The overall effect of this increase in the money supply and reduction in interest rates will be expansionary.

BALANCE SHEET 17.3

Banking System

Assets			Liabilities	
Total reserves		+$100,000	Chequable deposits	$ 100,000
Desired reserves	$100,000			+ 900,000
Excess reserves	0			1,000,000
Loans		900,000		
Total		$1,000,000	Total	$1,000,000

Sale of a $100,000 Canadian Government Security by the Bank of Canada

The process is reversed when the Bank of Canada sells a Canadian government security from its portfolio. When the individual or institution buying the security from the Bank of Canada writes a cheque for $100,000, the Bank of Canada reduces the reserves of the chartered bank on which the cheque was written. The $100,000 sale of the Canadian government security leads to a reduction in reserves in the banking system.

Balance Sheet 17.4 shows the results for the sale of a Canadian government security by the Bank of Canada. When the $100,000 cheque goes to the Bank of Canada, it reduces by $100,000 the reserve account of the chartered bank on which the cheque is written. The Bank of Canada's assets are also reduced by $100,000 because it no longer owns the Canadian government security. The bank's liabilities are reduced by $100,000 when that amount is deducted from the account of the bond purchaser, and the money supply is thereby reduced by that amount. The chartered bank's assets are also reduced by $100,000 because the Bank of Canada has reduced its reserves by that amount.

As Balance Sheet 17-4 indicates, the reserves in the chartered banks decrease due to the sale of the securities. This implies a shortage of reserves and a reduction in lending. The scarcity of new loans will likely cause interest rates to increase. Bond purchases cause a contraction in the economy.

BALANCE SHEET 17.4

Balance sheets after the Bank of Canada has sold $100,000 of Canadian government securities, showing changes only.

The Bank of Canada		Chartered Bank	
Assets	Liabilities	Assets	Liabilities
−$100,000	−$100,000	−$100,000	−$100,000
Canadian government securities	chartered bank's reserves	reserves	chequing deposit owned by bond dealer

Concepts in Brief

- When reserves are increased by the Bank of Canada through a purchase of Canadian government securities, the result is a multiple expansion of deposits and therefore of the money supply.
- When the Bank of Canada reduces the banking system's reserves by selling Canadian government securities, the result is a multiple contraction of deposits and therefore of the money supply.

Drawdowns and Redeposits

Drawdown A movement of Government of Canada deposits from deposits of the chartered banks into the Bank of Canada's own government accounts.

Redeposit A movement of Government of Canada deposits from the Bank of Canada's own government accounts to the accounts of the chartered banks.

The Bank of Canada changes the amount of reserves in the system through the use of **drawdowns** and **redeposits**. When the Bank of Canada conducts a drawdown, it moves Government of Canada deposits from the accounts of the chartered banks held at the Bank of Canada, into the Bank's own government accounts. This has the effect of reducing the chartered banks' reserves, which induces the banks to call in loans to replenish their reserves. A drawdown has a contractionary effect on the money supply.

A redeposit occurs when the Bank of Canada moves government deposits into the accounts of the chartered banks, thus increasing their reserves. The banks then lend out their excess reserves thereby increasing the money supply.

CONTRACTIONARY MONETARY POLICY: EFFECTS ON AGGREGATE DEMAND, THE PRICE LEVEL AND REAL GDP. When the Bank of Canada engages in contractionary monetary policy, it conducts drawdowns. Remember that when it does so, the chartered banks will call in loans. There will be fewer reserves available for the chartered banks to lend out. The way they ration available money among potential borrowers is by raising the rate of interest they charge on loans. Some borrowers, deeming the new rate too high, will eliminate themselves from the market. Consequently, some borrowers who otherwise would have borrowed in order to spend no longer will do so at the higher rate of interest.

EXPANSIONARY MONETARY POLICY: EFFECT OF A REDEPOSIT. The Bank of Canada engages in expansionary monetary policy by conducting redeposits. Remember that a redeposit transfers Government of Canada deposits to the accounts of the chartered banks at the Bank of Canada. The chartered banks now have more reserves. Flush with excess reserves, the banks seek ways to lend them out. To induce customers to borrow more, the banks will cut interest rates even further. People who thought they were not going to be able to buy a new car, house, or whatever now find themselves able to do so. Their spending rises.

| EXAMPLE 17-2 | Determining the Price of Bonds |

A bond is an IOU from a government or a corporation that states how much they owe you (the principal) and how much interest will be paid to you for lending them money (also called the yield). Determining the selling price of a bond depends on how much those payments are worth and on an assessment of the risk associated with the likelihood that the promised interest payments and principal repayment will occur. For example, if the company is on the verge of bankruptcy, the bond is likely not worth much. Such *risk* is important in determining the price of a bond.

The second factor in determining the price of a bond is the prevailing interest rate in the economy. There is an inverse relationship between the price of existing bonds and the rate of interest. Assume that the average yield on bonds is 5 percent. You decide to purchase a bond. A local corporation agrees to sell you a bond that will pay you $50 a year forever. What is the price you are willing to pay for it? $1,000. Why? Because $50 divided by $1,000 equals 5 percent. You purchase the bond. The next year something happens in the economy. For whatever reason, you can go out and obtain bonds that have effective yields of 10 percent. That is to say, the prevailing interest rate in the economy is now 10 percent. What has happened to the market price of the existing bond that you own, the one you purchased the year before? It will have fallen. If you try to sell it for $1,000, you will discover that no investors will buy it from you. Why should they when they can obtain $50 a year from someone else by paying only $500? Indeed, unless you offer your bond for sale at a price of $500, no buyers will be forthcoming. Hence, an increase in the prevailing interest rate in the economy has caused the market value of your existing bond to fall.

The important point to understand is this:

The market price of existing bonds (and all fixed-income assets) is inversely related to the rate of interest prevailing in the economy.

Try Preview Question 2:
Why is the price of existing bonds inversely related to the interest rate?

For critical analysis: If the Bank of Canada was about to initiate an easy money policy or an expansionary monetary policy, how would this affect your assessment of an investment in a long-term bond?

Bank Rate

Bank Rate The Bank Rate is the rate of interest that the Bank of Canada charges chartered banks for loans it makes to them. Changes in the Bank Rate signal changes in monetary policy.

The banks now hold tiny reserves relative to their deposits. The reason they can do this is because the Bank of Canada stands ready to lend reserves to them to ensure that they can always meet any depositor's demands for currency. The **Bank Rate** is the rate of interest that the Bank of Canada charges any chartered bank for any reserves that it lends them.

Lending to the chartered banks occurs infrequently. The more important role of the Bank Rate is to communicate changes in monetary policy by announcing changes in the Bank Rate. When the Bank of Canada wants to signal its intent to pursue tight money, it will increase the Bank Rate. Private sector interest rates will typically increase in response to the Bank Rate. If the Bank of Canada implements easy money, the Bank Rate would be lowered, prompting decreases in private sector interest rates. Refer to Policy Example 17-1 on the next page for a discussion of how the Bank Rate is announced.

POLICY EXAMPLE 17-1

The Determination of the Bank Rate

Bank of Canada releases dates for announcing Bank Rate actions

OTTAWA—The Bank of Canada on October 30, 2000 made public the dates through the year 2001 on which it will announce any changes to the official interest rate it uses to implement monetary policy. Last month the Bank outlined its plan to adopt a new system of pre-set or "fixed" dates for announcing changes to the Bank Rate, which will replace the previous approach under which it could announce an adjustment on any business day in the year.

In releasing the dates, the Bank also confirmed that interest rate announcements will be made on Tuesdays at 9 a.m. (ET) eight times a year and announcement dates will be integrated with the Bank's other key monetary policy publications throughout the year to provide a more regular, frequent, and continuous process of public communication on monetary policy. The Bank would still have the option of acting between fixed dates, but would exercise this option only in extraordinary circumstances.

"We wish to thank all those who provided views on details of the Bank's proposed plan," said Bank Governor Gordon Thiessen. "With the benefit of these views, I am confident that the Bank's decision to implement pre-set announcement dates for Bank Rate changes will contribute to the improved functioning of financial markets, better public understanding of the factors affecting the Bank's decisions on interest rates, and more effective Canadian monetary policy."

An announcement on each fixed date

At 9 a.m. on each announcement date, the Bank will issue a press release indicating its decision either to change the Bank Rate or to leave it unchanged, together with a short explanation of the factors influencing the decision and the Bank's view of the risks in the period ahead.

For critical analysis: Why has the Bank of Canada chosen pre-set or "fixed" dates for announcing changes to the Bank Rate?

Moral Suasion

When the Bank of Canada wants to restrict the money supply, but doesn't want to conduct open market operations or drawdowns, another tool it can use is **moral suasion**. The Governor of the Bank of Canada might ask the presidents of the "Big Six" chartered banks for their assistance in tightening credit, for example. The banks are not commanded to do so, but to blatantly disobey could cause negative repercussions—such as fewer government deposits—for them.

Earlier in this century, this was a fairly effective and commonly used tool since there were only about 10 banks in Canada. However with the proliferation of other financial intermediaries who are all offering credit, this tool has lost much of its effectiveness. Even if the "Big Six" chartered banks cooperated with the Bank of Canada, credit unions, *caisses populaires*, trust companies, and insurance companies might well refuse to do so, thinking that their relative smallness would not affect the overall success of the plan.

The Supply of Money Curve

The Bank of Canada can direct the money supply by engaging in open market operations by buying and selling Government of Canada securities, by transferring Government of Canada deposits to and from the chartered banks, by setting the Bank Rate, and by moral suasion. If the monetary authorities and the financial institutions have provided the economy with a particular quantity of money, then the money supply is a vertical line relative

Moral suasion A formal or informal request by the Governor of the Bank of Canada to the CEOs of the chartered banks to voluntarily restrict or expand credit or other loans, in an effort to control the money supply.

FIGURE 17-2 The Supply of Money

The supply of money is a given at any point in time regardless of the interest rate. The money supply curve is a vertical line.

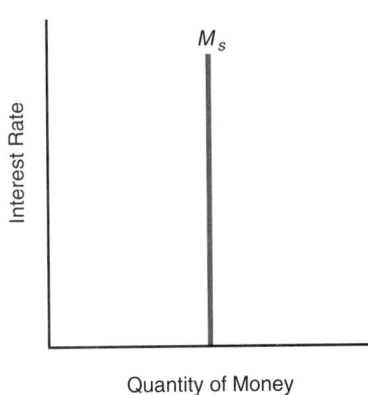

to interest rates. In other words, at any given point in time, the money supply is fixed by the tools of monetary policy regardless of interest rates as in Figure 17-2.

CONCEPTS IN BRIEF

- Monetary policy is one means of influencing the economy through regulating the money supply.
- The four tools of monetary policy are open market operations, drawdowns and redeposits, setting the Bank Rate, and moral suasion.
- The Bank of Canada can directly increase chartered banks' reserves by purchasing Canadian government securities in the open market; it can decrease chartered banks' reserves by selling Canadian government securities in the open market.
- The Bank of Canada can affect the money supply by moving Government of Canada deposits either to (redeposits) or from (drawdowns) the accounts of the chartered banks.
- The Bank of Canada can signal either a tight or an easy money policy in the changes it makes to the Bank Rate.
- The Bank of Canada can try to influence the direction of the chartered banks' lending posture by using moral suasion.
- The money supply at a point in time is a vertical curve.

The Demand for Money or What's So Special About Money?

By definition, monetary policy has to do, in the main, with money. But what is so special about money? Money is the product of a "social contract" in which we all agree to do two things:

1. Express all prices in terms of a common unit of account, which in Canada we call the dollar
2. Use a specific medium of exchange for market transactions

These two features of money distinguish it from all other goods in the economy. As a practical matter, money is involved on one side of every nonbarter transaction in the economy—and trillions of them occur every year. What this means is that something that changes the amount of money in circulation will have some effect on many transactions and thus on elements of GDP. If something affects the number of snowmobiles in existence, probably only the snowmobile market will be altered. But something that affects the amount of money in existence is going to affect *all* markets.

Holding Money

All of us engage in a flow of transactions. We buy and sell things all of our lives. But because we use money—dollars—as our medium of exchange, all *flows* of nonbarter transactions involve a *stock* of money. We can restate this as follows:

> To use money, one must hold money.

Given that everybody must hold money, we can now talk about the *demand* to hold it. People do not demand to hold money just to look at pictures of past prime ministers. They hold it to be able to use it to buy goods and services.

The Demand for Money: What People Wish to Hold

People have a certain motivation that makes them want to hold money balances. Individuals and firms could try to have zero non-interest-bearing money balances. But life is inconvenient without a ready supply of money balances. There is a demand for money by the public, motivated by several factors.

Transactions demand Holding money as a medium of exchange to make payments. The level varies directly with nominal national income.

THE TRANSACTIONS DEMAND. The main reason people hold money is that money can be used to purchase goods and services. People are paid at specific intervals (once a week, once a month, and so on), but they wish to make purchases more or less continuously. To free themselves from making expenditures on goods and services only on payday, people find it beneficial to hold money. The benefit they receive is convenience: They willingly forgo interest earnings in order to avoid the inconvenience and expense of cashing in such nonmoney assets as bonds every time they wish to make a purchase.

Thus people hold money to make regular, *expected* expenditures under the **transactions demand.** As national income rises, the community will want to hold more money. Suppose that national income rises due exclusively to price level increases. If people are making the same volume of physical purchases but the goods and services cost more due to higher prices, people will want to hold more money.

Precautionary demand Holding money to meet unplanned expenditures and emergencies.

THE PRECAUTIONARY DEMAND. The transactions demand involves money held to make *expected* expenditures; people hold money for the **precautionary demand** to make *unexpected* purchases or to meet emergencies. It is not unreasonable to maintain that as the price level or real national income rises, people will want to hold more money. In effect, when people hold money for the precautionary demand, they incur a cost in forgone interest earnings that is offset by the benefit that the precautionary balance provides. Nonetheless, the higher the rate of interest, the lower the money balances people wish to hold for the precautionary demand.

Asset demand Holding money as a store of value, instead of other assets such as certificates of deposit, corporate bonds, and stocks.

THE ASSET DEMAND. Remember that one of the functions of money is as a store of value. People can hold money balances as a store of value, or they can hold bonds or stocks or other interest-earning assets. The desire to hold money as a store of value leads to the **asset demand** for money. People choose to hold money rather than other assets for two reasons: its liquidity and the lack of risk. Moreover, if deflation is expected, holding money balances makes sense.

The disadvantage of holding money balances as an asset, of course, is the interest earnings forgone. Each individual or business decides how much money to hold as an asset by looking at the opportunity cost of holding money. The higher the interest rate—which is our proxy for the opportunity cost of holding money—the lower the money balances people will want to hold as assets. Conversely, the lower the interest rate offered on alternative assets, the higher the money balances people will want to hold as assets.

The Demand for Money Curve

Assume that the transactions demand for money is fixed, given a certain level of income. That leaves the precautionary and asset demands for money, both determined by the opportunity cost of holding money. If we assume that the interest rate represents the cost of holding money balances, we can graph the relationship between the interest rate and the quantity of money demanded. In Figure 17.3, the demand for money curve shows a familiar downward slope. The horizontal axis measures the quantity of money demanded, and the vertical axis is the interest rate. In this sense, the interest rate is the price of holding money. At a higher price, a lower quantity of money is demanded, and vice versa.

Imagine two scenarios. In the first one, you can earn 20 percent a year if you put your cash into purchases of government securities. In the other scenario, you can earn 1 percent if you put your cash into purchases of government securities. If you have $1,000 average cash balances in a non-interest-bearing chequing account, in the second scenario over a one-year period, your opportunity cost would be 1 percent of $1,000, or $10. In the first scenario, your opportunity cost would be 20 percent of $1,000, or $200. Under which scenario would you hold more cash?

Try Preview Question 3:

What is the demand for money curve, and how is it related to the interest rate?

FIGURE 17.3 The Demand for Money Curve

If we use the interest rate as a proxy for the opportunity cost of holding money balances, the demand for money curve, M_d, is downward-sloping, similar to other demand curves.

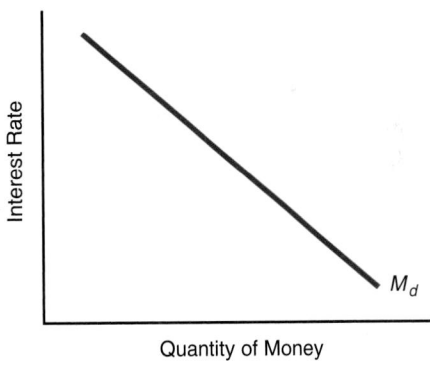

CONCEPTS IN BRIEF

- To use money, people must hold money. Therefore, they have a demand for money balances.
- The determinants of the demand for money balances are the transactions demand, the precautionary demand, and the asset demand.
- Because holding money carries with it an opportunity cost—the interest income forgone—the demand for money curve showing the relationship between money balances and the interest rate slopes downward.

The Choice Between Cash and Savings Accounts in Colombia

In countries with high inflation rates, nominal interest rates are also high. Remember from Chapter 7 that the nominal interest rate equals the real interest rate plus the expected rate of inflation. Colombia is one country that has consistently high rates of inflation. Consequently, its depository institutions usually offer high nominal interest rates to attract people's cash. In Ciudad, Bolívar, about an hour from Bogotá, the *Caja Social de Ahorros* (Social Savings Bank) services a low-income area of about a million people. This depository institution was started by a Jesuit priest and continues to be overseen by a board of directors appointed by the Jesuits. On passbook savings accounts, it pays 19 percent. This sounds high, but not compared to Colombia's 22 percent annual inflation. Thus its 10,000 depositors are willing to accept a *negative* real rate of interest of 3 percent. Why? In the first place, if they kept their cash as cash, they would suffer a 22 percent reduction in purchasing power every year. In the second place, the *Caja Social* keeps its low-income clients' money safe in a high-crime area.

For critical analysis: Why are nominal interest rates higher when a country experiences inflation?

Monetary Policy in Action: the Transmission Mechanism

Monetary policy, regulating the money supply, has both indirect and direct effects. The indirect effect occurs due to a change in interest rates. In the case of expansionary monetary policy, lower interest rates induce people and businesses to spend more than they otherwise would have spent. The direct effect is simply that an increase in the money supply causes people to have excess money balances. To get rid of these excess money balances, they increase expenditures.

The Keynesian Transmission Mechanism

One school of economists believes that the indirect effect of monetary policy is the more important. This group, typically called Keynesian because of its belief in Keynes' work, asserts that the main effect of monetary policy occurs through changes in the interest rate. The Keynesian money transmission mechanism is shown in Figure 17.4. There you see that the money supply changes the interest rate, which in turn changes the desired rate of investment. This transmission mechanism can be seen explicitly in Figure 17.5. In part (a), you see that an increase in the money supply reduces the interest rate. This reduction in the interest rate causes desired investment expenditures to increase from I_1

FIGURE 17.4 The Keynesian Money Transmission Mechanism

FIGURE 17.5 Adding Monetary Policy to the Keynesian Model

In part (a), we show a demand for money function, M_d. It slopes downward to show that at lower rates of interest, a larger quantity of money will be demanded. The money supply is given initially as M_s—the equilibrium rate of interest will be r_1. At this rate of interest, we see from the planned investment schedule given in part (b) that the quan- tity of planned investment demanded per year will be I_1. After the shift in the money supply to M'_s the resulting increase in investment from I_1 to I_2 shifts the aggregate demand curve in part (c) outward from AD_1 to AD_2. Equilibrium moves from E_1 to E_2, at $700 billion real GDP per year.

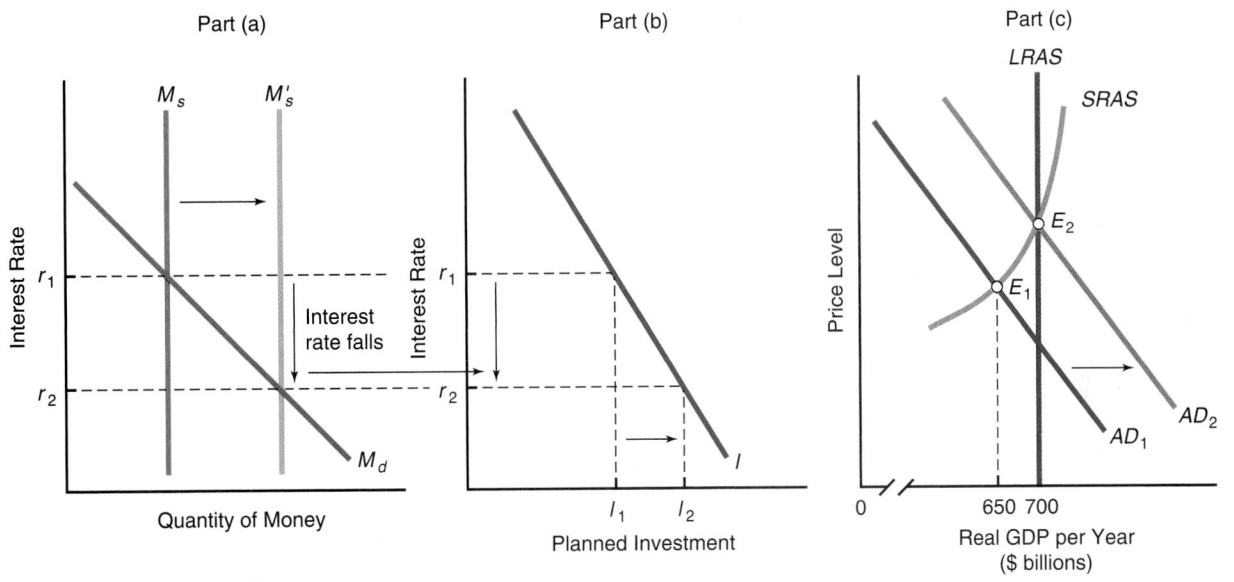

to I_2 in part (b). This increase in investment shifts aggregate demand outward from AD_1 to AD_2 in part (c).

CONCEPTS IN BRIEF

- The indirect effect of an increase in the money supply works through a lowering of interest rates which increases investment spending and consumption.
- The direct effect of an increase in the money supply arises because people desire to spend more on goods and services when they have excess money balances.
- In the Keynesian model, monetary transmission operates through a change in the interest rates, which changes investment, causing a multiple change in the equilibrium level of GDP.

Monetary Policy, Inflation, and Monetarists

Most theories of inflation relate to the short run. The price index in the short run can fluctuate because of events such as oil price shocks, labour union strikes, or discoveries of large amounts of new natural resources. In the long run, however, empirical studies show a relatively stable relationship between excessive growth in the money supply and inflation.

Simple supply and demand can explain why the price level rises when the money supply is increased. Suppose that a major oil discovery is made, and the supply of oil increases dramatically relative to the demand for oil. The relative price of oil will fall; now it will take more units of oil to exchange for specific quantities of non-oil products. Similarly, if the supply of money rises relative to the demand for money, it will take more units of money to purchase specific quantities of goods and services. That is merely another way of stating that the price level has increased or that the purchasing power of money has fallen. In fact, the classical economists referred to inflation as a situation in which more money is chasing the same quantity of goods and services.

The Equation of Exchange and the Quantity Theory

A simple way to show the relationship between changes in the quantity of money in circulation and the price level is through the **equation of exchange**, developed by Irving Fisher:

$$M_s V \equiv PQ$$

Equation of exchange The formula indicating that the number of monetary units times the number of times each unit is spent on final goods and services is identical to the price level times output (or nominal national income).

where

$M_s =$ actual money balances held by the nonbanking public
$V =$ **income velocity of money**, or the number of times, on average, each monetary unit is spent on final goods and services
$P =$ price level or price index
$Q =$ real national output (real GDP)

Income velocity of money The number of times per year a dollar is spent on final goods and services; equal to GDP divided by the money supply.

Consider a numerical example involving a one-commodity economy. Assume that in this economy the total money supply, M_s, is $100; the quantity of output, Q, is 50 units of a good; and the average price, P, of this output is $10 per unit. Using the equation of exchange,

$$M_s V \equiv PQ$$
$$\$100 V \equiv \$10 \times 50$$
$$\$100 V \equiv \$500$$
$$V \equiv 5$$

Thus each dollar is spent an average of five times a year.

THE EQUATION OF EXCHANGE AS AN IDENTITY. The equation of exchange must always be true—it is an *accounting identity*. The equation of exchange states that the total amount of money spent on final output, $M_s V$, is equal to the total amount of money *received* for final output, PQ. Thus a given flow of money can be seen from either the buyers' side or the producers' side. The value of goods purchased is equal to the value of goods sold.

If Q represents real national output and P is the price level, PQ equals the dollar value of national output, or nominal national income. Thus

$$M_s V \equiv PQ \equiv Y$$

THE CRUDE QUANTITY THEORY OF MONEY AND PRICES. If we now make some assumptions about different variables in the equation of exchange, we come up with the simplified theory of why prices change, called the **crude quantity theory of money and prices**. If you assume that the velocity of money, V, is constant and that real national output, Q, is basically stable, the simple equation of exchange tells you that a change in the money supply can lead only to a proportionate change in the price level. Continue with our numerical example. Q is 50 units of the good. V equals 5. If the money supply increases

Crude quantity theory of money and prices The belief that changes in the money supply lead to proportional changes in the price level.

to 200, the only thing that can happen is that the price index, P, has to go up from 10 to 20. Otherwise the equation is no longer in balance.

EMPIRICAL VERIFICATION. There is considerable evidence of the empirical validity of the relationship between excessive monetary growth and high rates of inflation. Look back at Figure 16.1. There you see the loose correspondence between money supply growth and the rate of inflation in Canada from 1960 to the present. International Example 17-2 shows the relationship between inflation and money growth internationally.

INTERNATIONAL EXAMPLE 17-2   Inflation and Money Growth Throughout the World

Is there much evidence that the rate of inflation is closely linked to the rate of monetary growth? The answer seems to be that in the long run there is a clear correlation between the two. Look at Figure 17.6. On the horizontal axis, in ratio form, is the rate of growth of the money supply. On the vertical axis is the annual rate of inflation (again, based on a ratio scale). As you can see, if you were to draw a line through the average of the points, it would slope upward: Faster monetary growth leads to a higher rate of inflation throughout different countries. This relationship appears to hold in Canada also. Decades of relatively high money supply growth are consistent with relatively higher rates of inflation and vice versa in Canada.

**FIGURE 17.6
International Relationship Between Money Supply Growth Rates and Rates of Inflation**

If we plot rates of inflation and rates of monetary growth for different countries, we come up with a scatter diagram that shows an obvious direct relationship. If you were to draw a line through the "average" of the points in this figure, it would be upward-sloping, showing that an increase in the rate of growth of the money supply leads to an increase in the rate of inflation.

Source: International Monetary Fund. Data are for latest available periods.

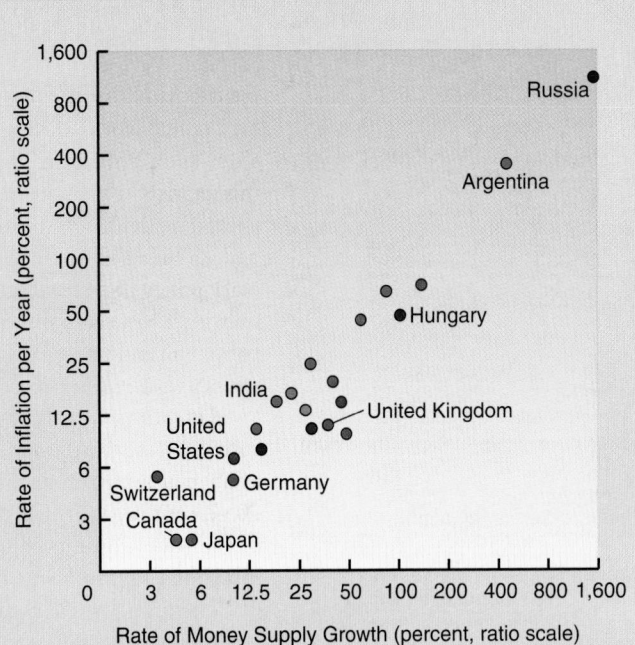

For critical analysis: Do the data shown in Figure 17.6 "prove" the crude quantity theory of money and prices?

Thinking Critically About the Media 17-1   Pity Those Poor Printing Presses

An examination of stories about hyperinflation throughout the world over the past several decades yields one common media statement: "Prices are increasing so fast that the money printing presses can't keep up with the inflation." What is wrong with this statement is that the order of causation is reversed. Hyperinflation is caused by an excessive growth in the money supply—hyperactive money printing presses, if you will. Countries that have experienced hyperinflation have typically had governments that resorted to printing excessive amounts of currency. Indeed, economists have hundreds of years of empirical evidence to validate such a statement, the media notwithstanding.

Monetarists Macroeconomists who believe that inflation is always caused by excessive monetary growth and that changes in the money supply affect aggregate demand both directly and indirectly.

THE MONETARISTS' VIEW OF MONEY SUPPLY CHANGES. **Monetarists**, economists who believe in a modern quantity theory of money and prices, contend that monetary policy works its way more directly into the economy. They believe that changes in the money supply lead to changes in nominal GDP in the same direction. An increase in the money supply because of expansionary open market operations (purchases of bonds) by the Bank of Canada, for example, leads the public to have larger money holdings than desired. This excess quantity of money demanded induces the public to buy more of everything, especially more durable goods such as cars, stereos, and houses. If the economy is starting out at its long-run equilibrium rate of output, there can only be a short-run increase in real GDP. Ultimately, though, the public cannot buy more of everything; it simply bids up prices so that the price level rises. This pattern is displayed in Figure 17.6.

MONETARISTS' CRITICISM OF MONETARY POLICY. The monetarists' belief that monetary policy works through changes in desired spending does not mean that they consider such policy an appropriate government stabilization tool. According to the monetarists, although monetary policy can affect real GDP (and employment) in the short run, the length of time required before money supply changes take effect is so long and variable that such policy is difficult to conduct. For example, an expansionary monetary policy to counteract a contractionary gap may not take effect for a year and a half, by which time inflation may be a problem. At that point, the expansionary monetary policy will end up making current inflation worse. Monetarists therefore see monetary policy as a *destabilizing* force in the economy.

Monetary rule A monetary policy that incorporates a rule specifying the annual rate of growth of some monetary aggregate.

According to the monetarists, therefore, policymakers should follow a **monetary rule:** Increase the money supply *smoothly* at a rate consistent with the economy's long-run average growth rate. *Smoothly* is an important word here. Increasing the money supply at 20 percent per year half the time and decreasing it at 17 percent per year the other half of the time would average out to about a 3 percent increase, but the results would be disastrous, say the monetarists. Instead of permitting the Bank of Canada to use its discretion in setting monetary policy, monetarists would force it to follow a rule such as "Increase the money supply smoothly at 3.5 percent per year" or "Abolish the Bank of Canada and replace it with a computer program allowing for a steady rise in the money supply."

Try Preview Question 4:

What is a monetarist?

FIGURE 17.7 **The Effects of Expansionary Monetary Policy**

If we start with equilibrium at E_1, an increase in the money supply will cause the aggregate demand curve to shift to AD_2. There is an excess quantity of real goods and services demanded. The price level increases so that we move to E_2 at an output rate of $725 billion per year and a price level of 130. But input owners revise their expectations of prices upward, and $SRAS_1$ shifts to $SRAS_2$. The new long-run equilibrium is at E_3 at the long-run aggregate supply of $700 billion of real GDP per year and a price level of 135.

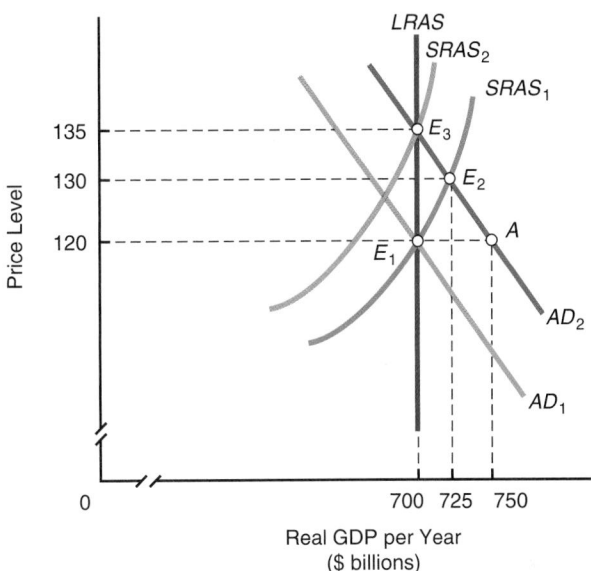

POLICY
EXAMPLE 17-2

Monetary Policy: Where Are We Now?

Monetary policy has come a long way since 1935. It is now directed towards a single long-run objective: the attainment and maintenance of price stability. Monetary authorities in Canada and elsewhere have realized that this is the best contribution that monetary policy can make to economic welfare and, indeed, the only one that they can deliver on an ongoing basis. There is no inherent conflict between price stability and most of the other objectives that are set out in the preamble to the *Bank of Canada Act*. Focusing on price stability helps us to guard against the sort of systematic errors that often occurred when we tried to aim directly at output and employment. Optimistic estimates of potential output and full employment in the early 1970s introduced a strong inflationary bias into the policy-formulation process and did not deliver any of the long-run improvements in the real economic performance that the Phillips-curve literature had promised.

Today's monetary policy differs from past approaches in yet another important way. It is conducted in a far more open and less-complicated manner. Secrecy and surprise are no longer critical elements of our modus operandi. The Bank tries to work with markets, rather than against them, to avoid surprising them with unexpected actions. Greater transparency facilitates the policy-transmission process by conditioning market expectations, and helps avoid unnecessary confusion about the reasons for our actions.

Various techniques for manipulating domestic credit conditions and the external value of the currency by means of direct controls, moral suasion, and active foreign exchange market intervention are no longer used. Globalization and market liberation have eliminated many of the barriers that used to separate different segments of the domestic financial system and have subjected them to increased international competition. As a result, these techniques became both less effective and more costly in terms of their impact on market efficiency. Monetary authorities now have a clearer understanding of the limitations of alternative policy measures, as well as more sympathy for indirect, market-based solutions.

Monetary policy is now implemented in a more straightforward manner. Today, policy adjustments are effected and signalled to the market mainly through announced changes in the Bank Rate and the target band for the overnight interest rate. Private agents are then free to determine how these changes will be transmitted through the rest of the financial system and the economy in general. The Bank simply issues a press release indicating what the new Bank Rate is, and this, in turn, anchors the short-term end of the yield curve.

Central bank independence and accountability have also been more clearly defined. ... the 1967 amendments to the *Bank of Canada* Act allow the Minister of Finance, acting on behalf of the government, to issue a directive to the Governor if serious differences arise on the conduct of monetary policy that cannot be resolved. The directive must indicate the specific policy changes that the Bank is supposed to undertake. Ultimate responsibility for monetary policy, therefore, rests where it should in a democratic society—with the elected government. But, because of the consequences of issuing a directive, it is likely to be used only in unusual circumstances. Thus, a high degree of operational independence has, nevertheless, been preserved to allow the Bank to maintain its medium-term focus for monetary policy without the short-term pressures that arise in the political process.

Moreover, the explicit targets for inflation control in Canada have been set jointly by the Bank and the Minister of Finance. It is then the Bank's responsibility to achieve the agreed target. An explicit objective, a clear assignment of responsibility for achieving it, as well as the appropriate instrument and independence of action to do what is required to meet the objective, are crucial ingredients in an effective process of accountability. That is what we now have in place in Canada for monetary policy.

For critical analysis: What is the current goal of Bank of Canada monetary policy and has it changed since 1935?

Lecture by Gordon Thiessen, Governor of the Bank of Canada, to the Faculty of Social Science, University of Western Ontario, October 17, 2000. For a detailed exposition of the evolution of monetary policy at the Bank of Canada, go to "Can a Bank Change? The Evolution of Monetary Policy at the Bank of Canada, 1935–2000" at www.bankofcanada.ca/pdf/thiessen-eng-book.pdf.

CONCEPTS IN BRIEF

- The equation of exchange states that the expenditures by some people will equal income receipts by others, or $M_s V \equiv PQ$ (money supply times velocity equals nominal national income).
- Viewed as an accounting identity, the equation of exchange is always correct, because the amount of money spent on final output must equal the total amount of money received for final output.
- The crude quantity theory of money and prices states that a change in the money supply will bring about an equi-proportional change in the price level.
- Monetarists believe that changes in the money supply lead to changes in nominal GDP in the same direction. The effect is both direct and indirect, however, as individuals spend their excess money balances on cars, stereos, houses, and a variety of many other things.
- Monetarists, among others, argue in favour of a monetary rule—increasing the money supply smoothly at a rate consistent with the economy's long-run average growth rate. Monetarists do not believe in discretionary monetary (or fiscal) policy.
- If we start out in long-run and short-run equilibrium, contractionary monetary policy first leads to a decrease in aggregate demand, resulting in a reduction in real GDP and in the price level. Eventually, though, the short-run aggregate supply curve shifts downward, and the new equilibrium is at *LRAS* but at an even lower price level. Expansionary monetary policy works the opposite way.

Effectiveness of Monetary Policy

So far we have discussed monetary policy in a closed economy. When we move to an open economy, in which there is international trade and the international purchase and sale of all assets including dollars and other currencies, monetary policy becomes more complex. Consider first the effect on exports of any type of monetary policy.

The Net Export Effect

When we examined fiscal policy, we pointed out that deficit financing can lead to higher interest rates. Higher (real, after-tax) interest rates do something in the foreign sector—they attract foreign financial investment. More people want to purchase Canadian government securities, for example. But to purchase Canadian assets, people first have to obtain Canadian dollars. This means that the demand for dollars goes up in foreign exchange markets. The international price of the dollar therefore rises. This is called an *appreciation* of the dollar, and it tends to reduce net exports because it makes our exports more expensive in terms of foreign currency and imports cheaper in terms of dollars. Foreigners demand fewer of our goods and services, and we demand more of theirs. In this way, expansionary fiscal policy that creates deficit spending financed by government borrowing can lead to a reduction in net exports.

But what about expansionary monetary policy? If expansionary monetary policy reduces real, after-tax Canadian interest rates, there will be a positive net export effect because foreigners will want fewer Canadian financial instruments, demanding fewer dollars and thereby causing the international price of the dollar to fall. This makes our exports cheaper for the rest of the world, which then demands a larger quantity of our exports. It also means that foreign goods and services are more expensive in Canada, so we therefore demand fewer imports. We come up with two conclusions:

1. Expansionary fiscal policy may cause international flows of financial capital (responding to interest rate *increases*) to offset its effectiveness to some extent. The net export effect is in the opposite direction of fiscal policy.
2. Expansionary monetary policy may cause interest rates to fall. Such a fall will induce international outflows of financial capital, thereby lowering the value of the dollar and making Canadian goods more attractive. The net export effect of expansionary monetary policy will be in the same direction as the monetary policy effect.

Now assume that the economy is experiencing inflation and the Bank of Canada wants to use contractionary monetary policy. In so doing, it may cause interest rates to rise. Rising interest rates will cause financial capital to flow into Canada. The demand for dollars will increase, and their international price will go up. Foreign goods will now look cheaper to Canadians, and imports will rise. Foreigners will not want our exports as much, and exports will fall. The result will be a deterioration in our international trade balance. Again, the international consequences reinforce the domestic consequences of monetary policy.

GLOBALIZATION OF INTERNATIONAL MONEY MARKETS. On a broader level, the Bank of Canada's ability to control the rate of growth of the money supply may be hampered as Canadian money markets become less isolated. With the push of a computer button, millions or even billions of dollars can change hands halfway around the world. In the world dollar market, the Bank of Canada finds an increasing number of dollars coming from *private* institutions. If the Bank of Canada reduces the growth of the money supply, individuals and firms in Canada can increasingly obtain dollars from other sources. People in Canada who want more liquidity can obtain their dollars from foreigners, or can even obtain foreign currencies and convert them into dollars in the world dollar market. Indeed, it is possible that as world markets become increasingly integrated, Canadian residents may someday conduct domestic transactions in *foreign* currencies.

Monetary Policy During Periods of Underutilized Resources

If the economy is operating at an equilibrium output level that is below that given by the long-run aggregate supply curve, monetary policy (like fiscal policy) can generate increases in the equilibrium level of real GDP per year up to a long-run equilibrium on *LRAS*. In Figure 17.8, you see initial aggregate demand as AD_1. It intersects *SRAS* at E_1, at an output rate of $650 billion of real GDP per year and a price level of 120. There is a contractionary gap of $50 billion. That is the difference between *LRAS* and the current equilibrium. The Bank of Canada can engage in expansionary monetary policy, the direct and indirect effects of which will cause AD_1 to shift to AD_2. The new equilibrium is at E_2, at an output rate of $700 billion of real GDP per year and a price level of 125. Note that expansionary monetary policy gets the economy to its *LRAS* sooner than otherwise.

FIGURE 17.8 Expansionary Monetary Policy with Underutilized Resources

If we start out with equilibrium at E_1, expansionary monetary policy will shift AD_1 to AD_2. The new equilibrium will be at E_2.

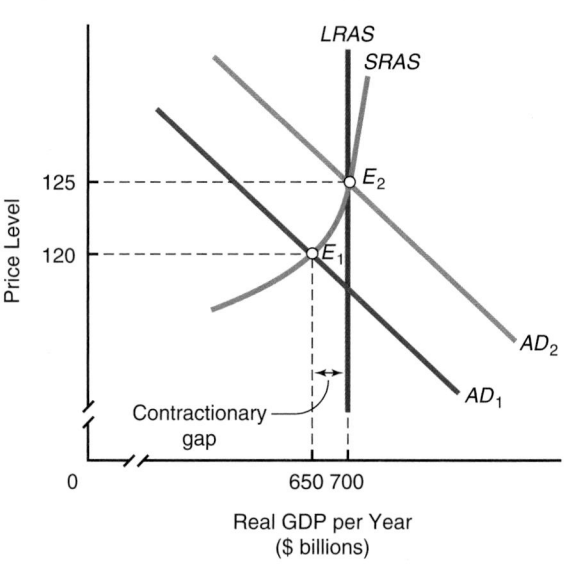

Bank of Canada Target Choice: Interest Rates or Money Supply?

Money supply and interest rate targets cannot be pursued simultaneously. Interest rate targets force the Bank of Canada to abandon control over the money supply; money stock growth targets force it to allow interest rates to fluctuate.

Figure 17.9 shows the relationship between the total demand for money and the supply of money. Note that in the short run (in the sense that nominal national income is fixed), the demand for money is constant; short-run money supply changes leave the demand for money curve unaltered. In the short run, the Bank of Canada can choose either a particular interest rate (r_e or r_1) or a particular money supply (M_s or M'_s).

FIGURE 17.9 **Choosing a Monetary Policy Target**

The Bank of Canada, in the short run, can select an interest rate or a money supply target, but not both. It cannot, for example, choose r_e and M'_s; if it selects r_e, it must accept M_s; if it selects M'_s, it must allow the interest rate to fall to r_1. The Bank of Canada can obtain point A or B. It cannot get to point C or D. It must therefore choose one target or the other.

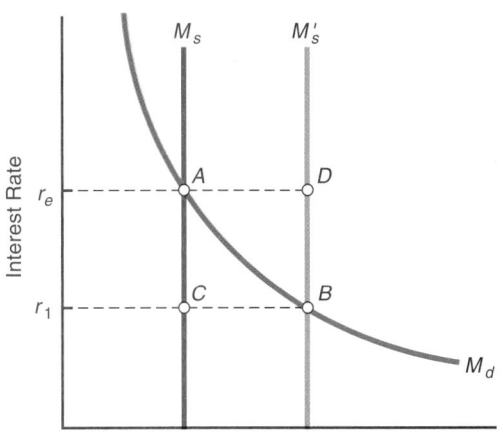

If the Bank of Canada wants interest rate r_e, it must select money supply M_s; if it desires a lower interest rate in the short run, it must increase the money supply. Thus by targeting an interest rate, the Bank of Canada must relinquish control of the money supply. Conversely, if it wants to target the money supply at, say, M'_s, it must allow the interest rate to fall to r_1.

Consider now the case in which the Bank of Canada wants to maintain the present level of interest rates. If actual market interest rates in the future rise persistently above the present (desired) rates, it will be continuously forced to increase the money supply. The initial increase in the money supply will only temporarily lower interest rates. The increased money stock eventually will induce inflation, and inflationary premiums will be included in nominal interest rates. To pursue its low-interest-rate policy, the Bank of Canada must *again* increase the money stock because interest rates are still rising. Note that to attempt to maintain an interest rate target (stable interest rates), the Bank of Canada must abandon an independent money stock target. Symmetrical reasoning indicates that by setting growth rate targets at M_s or M'_s, the Bank of Canada must allow short-run fluctuations in interest rates when the economy experiences a contraction or an expansion.

But which should the Bank of Canada target, interest rates or monetary aggregates? (And which interest rate or which money stock?) It is generally agreed that the answer depends on the source of instability in the economy. If the source of instability is variations in private or public spending, monetary aggregate (money supply) targets should be set and pursued. However, if the source of instability is an unstable demand for (or perhaps supply of) money, interest rate targets are preferred.

THE MONETARY CONDITIONS INDEX. From the early 1990s, the Bank of Canada has used the Monetary Conditions Index (MCI) as a rough measure of how tight monetary conditions in the economy are. The MCI is a weighted index made up of changes in short-term interest rates and changes in the foreign exchange value of the Canadian dollar.

The stated aim of the Bank of Canada is price stability. To this end, the Bank has promised to keep inflation between 1 percent and 3 percent through to the year 2002. We have seen that a decrease in interest rates or the exchange rate of the dollar will stimulate aggregate demand, leading to possible price increases although these increases take some time to occur due to lags in the economy. The Bank, however, can forecast future price increases through movements in the MCI.

For example, if the foreign exchange rate of the Canadian dollar fell consistently over a number of weeks, dragging the MCI down, there might be a risk of inflation recurring due to the net export effect. The Bank would estimate the seriousness of the risk, and act either to raise interest rates or to support the dollar to keep the MCI in the target range (currently −4.5 to −5.5), which should ensure price stability. Conversely, if the exchange rate of the dollar were climbing, pulling the MCI up out of the target range, this could lead to a dampening of aggregate demand and falling prices. The Bank could intervene to ease monetary conditions by increasing the money supply, thus reducing interest rates. This would result in a fall of the MCI back into the Bank's target range.

To add to the complexity of choosing a target, other events in the Canadian (or world) economy may force the Bank of Canada to pursue a policy it doesn't necessarily like, as shown in the example which follows.

Try Preview Question 5:

How do the supply of, and demand for, money determine the interest rate?

POLICY EXAMPLE 17-3   Political Uncertainty and Monetary Targeting

In November 1995, the government of Quebec held a referendum asking Quebeckers if they wished to separate from Canada, thus creating their own nation. Leading up to the referendum there was much speculation about how the vote would turn out, and what the consequences of a "Yes" vote would be.

At the same time, Canada's economy was not growing quickly, inflation was relatively low, and unemployment was relatively high. The preferred monetary policy would be one of interest rate reductions, to allow spending to pick up.

However, with the uncertainty in Quebec the Bank of Canada held interest rates high to keep foreign capital from leaving Canada. What was happening, in fact, was that the Bank of Canada was forced to add a risk premium to its bank rate due to the political uncertainty.

But Quebeckers voted "No." The "No" vote allowed the Bank of Canada to reduce interest rates over the course of 1996, which in turn led to some easing of the unemployment rate.

For critical analysis: What would have happened to interest rates if Quebeckers had voted "Yes"?

Other Considerations

The magnitude of expansionary and contractionary monetary policy is affected by the shapes or elasticity of the money-demand and the investment-demand curves. The steeper or more inelastic the M_d curve the larger the impact of any change in the money supply on the equilibrium interest rate. Moreover, changes in the interest rates will have a larger effect on investment spending and equilibrium GDP the flatter or more elastic the investment-demand curve. Monetary policy is most effective with a relatively inelastic money-demand curve and a relatively elastic investment-demand curve.

Another advantage of monetary policy is it can be quickly altered. Compared to fiscal policy which is forged in the political forum of Parliament, the Bank of Canada can and does buy and sell securities on a daily basis.

Finally, the governor and deputy governor of the Bank of Canada are appointed for seven-year terms and can be removed only by an act of Parliament. Thus, the Bank of Canada can take a longer-term view of the national economy. Furthermore, because monetary policy works subtly and with time lags, it is usually more politically acceptable.

CONCEPTS IN BRIEF

- Monetary policy in an open economy has repercussions for net exports.
- If expansionary monetary policy reduces Canadian interest rates, there is a positive net export effect because foreigners will demand fewer Canadian financial instruments, thereby demanding fewer dollars and hence causing the international price of the dollar to fall. This makes our exports cheaper for the rest of the world.
- Expansionary monetary policy during periods of underutilized resources can cause the equilibrium level of real GDP to increase (sooner than it otherwise would) to the rate of real output consistent with the vertical long-run aggregate supply curve.
- The Bank of Canada can choose to stabilize interest rates or to change the money supply, but not both.
- Monetary policy is most effective with a relatively inelastic money-demand curve and a relatively elastic investment-demand curve.
- Two other advantages of monetary policy are its speed and flexibility and its relative isolation from political pressures.

NETNOMICS

Will Digital Cash Weaken Monetary Policy?

In Chapter 16 you learned about digital cash, or e-money. In this chapter, you learned that monetary policy usually works through a process that involves changes in the money supply, which then affect interest rates and nationwide economic activity.

Whether money takes the form of coins, paper, or deposits makes little difference to officials who are charged with conducting monetary policy, as long as it does not interfere with their ability to control the total *quantity* of money in circulation. It is this issue that makes policymakers nervous about digital cash.

If the Bank of Canada and other central banks desire to control, or at least influence, the quantity of money in circulation, it is helpful for them to have direct or indirect oversight over the process by which money is placed into circulation.

It is conceivable that traditional banking institutions, such as commercial banks, savings institutions, and credit unions, may not be the only ones that choose to issue digital cash. To a central bank such as the Bank of Canada, this is the *fundamental* monetary policy issue posed by the development of e-money. Like banks and their customers, the Bank of Canada does not particularly care what form money takes. Nevertheless, it does have some reason to be concerned about who has the power to issue money.

In principle, anyone can issue digital cash accounts. Even if the government were to decide that only traditional banking institutions that fall under the Bank of Canada's regulatory umbrella can issue smart cards, what is to stop other firms from setting up e-money accounts over the Internet? That is, what is to stop firms that technically are not banks from issuing Internet-based digital chequing accounts that effectively function as money? Presumably, one answer is that Parliament could pass laws prohibiting such accounts, and the Bank of Canada and other bank regulators would have to police the Internet to ensure that only traditional banks issue such accounts.

Another possible answer, however, is that ultimately nothing may be able to stop a host of firms from pecking away at legal loopholes and eventually finding a way to enter the banking business by issuing e-money accounts. Balances stored in these digital cash accounts would be as much a part of the nation's quantity of circulating money as government currency and chequable deposits at traditional banks. As a result, the Fed's central-banking task of measuring and regulating this quantity would become much more complicated.

This is one way in which the new electronic banking systems have the potential to alter profoundly monetary affairs in Canada and worldwide. This potential development, more than any other, may be the *truly* fundamental change brought about by the use of digital cash.

ISSUES AND APPLICATIONS | Is the Bank of Canada Independent and, If Not, Does It Matter?

Concepts Applied: Monetary policy, inflation, money supply, central banking

The Bank of Canada manipulates the money supply as a way to control inflation. Evidence shows that central banks that are free of political pressure have more success in preventing inflation.

In principle, the Bank of Canada, although "owned" by the federal government, is an independent agency. Nonetheless, the prime minister appoints the Directors for three-year terms, subject to cabinet approval. The prime minister also appoints the Governor of the Bank of Canada, again with cabinet approval, for a seven-year term. Given the obvious relationship between the government of the day and the Bank of Canada, is the Bank of Canada really an independent policy-making body?

What Does the Evidence Show?

The Bank of Canada was created with a view to keeping it free both of private interference and political pressure. Over the early years, it was understood that the Bank would conduct day-to-day monetary policy, but ultimately the federal government would bear responsibility for its actions.

During the late 1950s, the then-governor of the Bank of Canada was pursuing restrictive monetary policy in spite of relatively high unemployment and slow growth. The Minister of Finance of first one government, and then of a newly elected government, declared that they would not take responsibility for the consequences of the Bank's policies. Academics also began to criticize the Bank, but its Governor, James Coyne, was resolute and did not change his course. Finally, the government moved to fire Coyne by introduc-ing legislation in Parliament declaring a less restrictive monetary policy and a vacancy in the position of the Governor of the Bank of Canada. While Parliament passed the legislation, the Senate defeated it. Eventually pressure was such that Coyne resigned. This event is now known as the *Coyne Affair*.

On taking office, the new Governor of the Bank of Canada, Louis Rasminsky, issued a statement that the Bank would be responsible for day-to-day conduct of monetary policy, but that if the government issued a written directive for a change in course and if the Governor could not agree, the Governor would have to resign. To this day, no such directive has been issued.

Does Independence Matter?

Whether the Bank of Canada is more or less independent of the government is not just an academic issue. Rather, there is now evidence to show that a central bank's degree of independence over time influences a country's long-term rate of inflation. The evidence indicates that at least since the 1950s, greater central bank independence tends to lessen a nation's inflation rate during periods of high worldwide inflation.

A Case in Point: New Zealand

The government in New Zealand decided to give its central bank one job: keeping the price level stable. It passed the Reserve Bank Act of 1989, setting desired price stability at inflation rates of zero to 2 percent. Only if New Zealand's central bank fails to achieve these goals can its governor be fired. Consequently, New Zealand's central bank no longer has to concern itself with short-term ups and downs in GDP growth rates. So far, its new independence and explicit mission have seemed to work: In 1989, the CPI increased by 5.7 percent; today, that increase is running at less than 1.5 percent per year.

For Critical Analysis

1. Since the government is ultimately responsible for the conduct of monetary policy, is the Bank of Canada really independent?

2. What would you expect to see happen to New Zealand's net exports after enactment of the Reserve Bank Act of 1989?

CHAPTER SUMMARY

1. Our central bank is the Bank of Canada. Its governing body is the Board of Directors.

2. The basic functions of the Bank of Canada are (a) conducting monetary policy, (b) acting as a lender of last resort, (c) issuing bank notes, and (d) advising the federal government on financial matters and acting as its fiscal agent.

3. The Bank of Canada regulates the money supply using four tools of monetary policy: open market operations, drawdowns and redeposits, setting the Bank Rate, and moral suasion.

4. The Bank of Canada can control the money supply through open market operations—by buying and selling Canadian government securities.

5. When the Bank of Canada buys a bond, it pays for the bond by writing a cheque on itself. This creates additional reserves for the banking system. The result will be an increase in the money supply that is a multiple of the value of the bond purchased. If the Bank of Canada sells a bond, it reduces reserves in the banking system. The result will be a decrease in the money supply that is a multiple of the value of the bond sold.

6. The banking system as a whole can change the money supply pursuant to a change in reserves brought about by a Bank of Canada purchase or sale of government bonds. The Bank of Canada can also change the money supply by undertaking drawdowns or redeposits, or by using moral suasion.

7. The Bank of Canada can signal changes in monetary policy by changing the Bank Rate. The money supply curve is a vertical curve.

8. The determinants of the demand for money balances are the transactions demand, the precautionary demand, and the asset demand.

9. Because holding money carries an opportunity cost—the interest income forgone—the demand for money curve showing the relationship between money balances and the interest rate slopes downward.

10. The direct effect of an increase in the money supply occurs through people desiring to spend more on real goods and services when they have excess money balances. The indirect effect of an increase in the money supply works through a lowering of the interest rate, thereby encouraging businesses to make new investments with the money loaned to them. Individuals will also engage in more consumption because of lower interest rates.

11. In the Keynesian model, monetary transmission operates through a change in the interest rates, which changes investment, causing a multiple change in national income.

12. The equation of exchange states that the expenditures by some people will equal income receipts by others: $M_sV \equiv PQ$ (money supply times velocity equals nominal national income). Viewed as an accounting identity, the equation of exchange is always correct because the amount of money spent on final output must equal the total amount of money received for final output.

13. The crude quantity theory of money and prices states that a change in the money supply will bring about a proportional change in the price level.

14. Monetarists believe that changes in the money supply lead to changes in nominal GDP in the same direction. The effect is direct and indirect because individuals have excess money balances that they spend on cars, stereos, houses, and other things. Monetarists, among others, argue in favour of a monetary rule—increasing the money supply smoothly at a rate consistent with the economy's long-run growth rate. Monetarists do not believe in discretionary monetary (or fiscal) policy.

15. If we start out in long-run and short-run equilibrium, contractionary monetary policy initially leads to a decrease in aggregate demand, resulting in a reduction in real GDP and in the price level. Eventually, though, the short-run aggregate supply curve shifts downward, and the new equilibrium is at *LRAS* but at an even lower price level. Expansionary monetary policy works the opposite way if we are starting out in both long-run and short-run equilibrium. The end result is simply a higher price level rather than a change in the equilibrium level of real GDP per year.

16. If expansionary monetary policy reduces Canadian interest rates, there is a positive net export effect because foreigners will demand fewer Canadian financial instruments, thereby demanding fewer dollars, causing the international price of the dollar to fall. This makes our exports cheaper for the rest of the world.

17. Expansionary monetary policy during periods of underutilized resources can cause the equilibrium level of real GDP to increase up to that rate of real output consistent with the vertical long-run aggregate supply curve.

DISCUSSION OF PREVIEW QUESTIONS

1. What are the functions of the Bank of Canada?

The Bank of Canada has four basic functions. It conducts monetary policy on behalf of the federal government. It acts as a lender of last resort to the financial community. It issues bank notes. Finally, the Bank of Canada acts as a fiscal agent and financial advisor to the federal government.

2. What is the demand for money curve, and how is it related to the interest rate?

Three types of demands—transactions, precautionary, and asset—motivate people to hold money, and each type provides benefits to money holders. Because people get paid at discrete intervals but want to make expenditures more or less continuously, they find it convenient to hold a stock of money (transactions demand); the benefit they receive is convenience. People also desire a pool of readily available purchasing power in order to meet emergencies (precautionary demand); the benefit is a measure of security. Finally, money is an asset; it is a means of storing value or wealth. At certain times money becomes a superior form of wealth—superior to other asset forms (bonds, stocks, real estate, and the like) that are risky. Asset demand money holders receive the benefit of liquidity. There is an opportunity cost to holding money (especially the narrow form of money, M1). The opportunity cost is forgone interest. The demand for money curve shows an inverse relationship between the interest rate and desired money holdings. As the interest rate falls, the opportunity cost of holding money falls concomitantly; people are more and more disposed to avail themselves of the benefits of holding money as the cost of doing so falls.

3. Why is the price of existing bonds inversely related to the interest rate?

Suppose that you know nothing about some faraway planet except that a bond (or an investment project) there yields $100 per year forever. Can you determine whether that bond or investment project will have a high price; that is, will it be "valuable"? No, you can't; you would have to know what the interest rate was on that planet. If interest rates are very, very low, say, one-thousandth of 1 percent, that bond or investment would be very valuable indeed. This is because the interest rate summarizes the opportunity cost for investment projects or bonds; if interest rates are very low, a given amount of money can

earn very little annually, but if interest rates are very high, a given amount of money can earn a great deal annually. Thus $100 per year looks good (high) or bad (low) depending on whether prevailing interest rates are low or high, respectively. The nature of a bond is such that it yields a given and known stream of revenues (nominal dollar amounts) over time. This given revenue stream will be priced relatively high if interest rates are relatively low and will command a low price if interest rates are high. In short, an inverse relationship exists between the price (market value) of an existing bond and the prevailing economy-wide interest rate.

4. What is a monetarist?

Monetarists are economists who maintain that changes in the money supply are the primary influence on the levels of employment, output, and prices. They maintain that there is little theoretical or empirical evidence to indicate the effectiveness of fiscal policy. Moreover, they maintain that monetary policy is not desirable either. This is because the time lag between changes in the money supply and changes in these macroeconomic variables is too long and imprecise, and that control of the money supply is not independent of politics. Consequently, present-day monetarists suggest that the government get out of the stabilization business; governments should use neither fiscal nor monetary policy. Instead, monetarists say governments should raise taxes and make expenditures only for pressing social matters (national defence, welfare, and so on), and monetary authorities should be commanded to increase the money supply at some constant and predetermined rate, which is related to the long-run growth potential of the economy.

5. How do the supply of, and demand for, money determine the interest rate?

The accompanying graph depicts the total supply of and demand for money in an economy. To demonstrate that given these supply and demand schedules for money, the equilibrium interest rate will eventually be established at i_e, we must rule out all other possible interest rates. Thus let i_2 represent any interest rates below i_e. At i_2, the group wants to hold more money than is actually available ($M_d = 300 > M_s = 200$), and a shortage of liquidity exists. People become more liquid (hold more cash) by selling bonds (converting bonds, which are non-money, into money). As many people try to become more liquid, they attempt to sell many bonds. This forces bond prices down and interest rates up. These same conditions exist at all interest rates below i_e. Similarly, at all interest rates above i_e (i_1 in particular), $M_s > M_d$, and the group will be holding more money than it wants to hold to meet the three money-holding motives demands. Hence many people will buy bonds (to rid themselves of the opportunity cost of holding money), forcing bond prices up—and interest rates down towards i_e. At i_e, M_d = M_s = 200, and the group is voluntarily holding the available money supply.

PROBLEMS

(Answers to the odd-numbered problems appear at the back of the book.)

17-1. Assume that the desired reserve ratio is 15 percent and that the Bank of Canada sells $3 million worth of government securities to a customer who pays with a cheque drawn on the Toronto-Dominion Bank.

    a. The excess reserves of the Toronto-Dominion Bank have changed by how much?

    b. By how much has the money supply changed?

    c. What is the maximum change in the money supply that can result from this sale?

17-2. The Bank of Canada purchases a $1 million government security from Gulwinder Mann, who deposits the proceeds in Bank 1. Use balance sheets to show the immediate effects of this transaction on the Bank of Canada and on Bank 1.

17-3. Continuing the example from Problem 17-2:

    a. Indicate Bank 1's position more precisely if desired reserves equal 5 percent of chequable deposits.

    b. By how much can Bank 1 increase its lending?

17-4. Assume a 5 percent desired reserve ratio, zero excess reserves, no currency leakage, and a ready loan demand. The Bank of Canada buys a $1 million Treasury bill from a depository institution.

    a. What is the maximum money multiplier?

    b. By how much will total deposits rise?

17-5. Briefly outline the Keynesian monetary transmission mechanism.

17-6. The equation that indicates the value (price) right now of a nonmaturing bond (called a consol) is $V = R/i$, where V is the present value, R is the annual net income generated from the bond, and i is the going interest rate.

    a. Assume that a bond promises the holder $1,000 per year forever. If the interest rate is 10 percent, what is the bond worth now (V)?

    b. Continuing part (a), what happens to the value of the bond (V) if interest rates rise to 20 percent? What if they fall to 5 percent?

    c. Suppose that there were an indestructible machine that was expected to generate $2,000 per year in revenues but costs $1,000 per year to maintain—forever. How would that machine be priced relative to the bond described in part (a)?

17-7. Show in the form of a chart the processes by which the Bank of Canada can reduce inflationary pressures by conducting drawdowns.

17-8. Assume that M = $30 billion, P = $1.72, and Q = 90 billion units per year. What is the income velocity of money?

17-9. Briefly outline expansionary monetary policy according to a monetarist.

ECONOMICS ON THE NET

What is the Bank of Canada's Monetary Policy?

Internet URL: http://www.bankofcanada.ca

Title: Monetary Policy

Navigation: Begin at the homepage of the Bank of Canada (http://www.bankofcanada.ca). Click on English, then on Search, and then type in *thiessen-eng-book*. Your search should take you to The Thiessen Lectures. Find the lecture "Can a Bank Change? The Evolution of Monetary Policy at the Bank of Canada 1935-2000."

Application: Perform the operations indicated above and answer the following questions:

a. Compare the Bank of Canada's monetary policy from 1971 to 1981 (during stagflation and monetarism) to inflation targets during the 1991 to 2000 period.

b. For the most recently published review of the Bank of Canada's monetary policy and strategies, go to the Bank's homepage, then to Monetary Policy, then to Monetary Policy Report and/or Monetary Policy Report Update. According to the report, what economic events played the most important role in shaping recent monetary policy actions? What are the Bank of Canada's current monetary policy goals?

For another source of current Bank of Canada thinking, go to the Bank's homepage, then to Publications and Research, then to Speeches and statements by the Governor.

APPENDIX D

MONETARY POLICY: A KEYNESIAN PERSPECTIVE

According to the traditional Keynesian approach to monetary policy, changes in the money supply can affect the level of aggregate demand only through their effect on interest rates. Moreover, interest rate changes act on aggregate demand solely by changing the level of investment spending. Finally, the traditional Keynesian approach argues that there exist plausible circumstances under which monetary policy may have little or no effect on aggregate demand.

Figure D-1 measures real national income along the horizontal axis and total planned expenditures (aggregate demand) along the vertical axis. The components of aggregate demand are consumption (C), investment (I), government spending (G), and net exports (X). The height of the schedule labelled $C + I + G + X$ shows total planned expenditures (aggregate demand) as a function of income. This schedule slopes upward because consumption depends positively on income. Everywhere along the line labelled $Y = C + I + G + X$, planned spending equals income. At point Y^*, where the $C + I + G + X$ line intersects this 45-degree reference line, planned spending is consistent with income. At any income less than Y^*, spending exceeds income, so income and thus spending will

FIGURE D-1 An Increase in the Money Supply

An increase in the money supply increases income by lowering interest rates and thus increasing investment from I to I'.

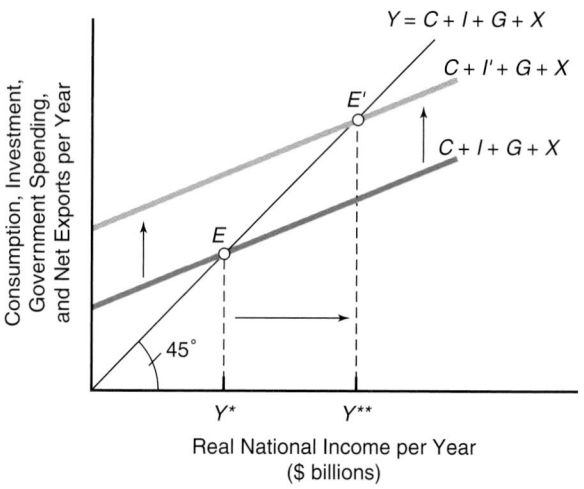

tend to rise. At any level of income greater than Y^*, planned spending is less than income, so income and thus spending will tend to decline. Given the determinants of C, I, G, and X, total spending (aggregate demand) will be Y^*.

Increasing the Money Supply

According to the Keynesian approach, an increase in the money supply pushes interest rates down. This reduces the cost of borrowing and thus induces firms to increase the level of investment spending from I to I'. As a result, the $C + I + G + X$ line shifts upward in Figure D-1 by the full amount of the rise in investment spending, thus yielding the line $C + I' + G + X$. The rise in investment spending causes income to rise, which in turn causes consumption spending to rise, which further increases income. Ultimately, aggregate demand rises to Y^{**}, where spending again equals income. A key conclusion of the Keynesian analysis is that total spending rises by *more* than the original rise in investment spending because consumption spending depends positively on income.

Decreasing the Money Supply

Not surprisingly, contractionary monetary policy works in exactly the reverse manner. A reduction in the money supply pushes interest rates up, which increases the cost of borrowing. Firms respond by reducing their investment spending, and this starts income downward. Consumers react to the lower income by scaling back on their consumption spending, which further depresses income. Thus the ultimate decline in income is larger than the initial drop in investment spending. Indeed, because the change in income is a multiple of the change in investment, Keynesians note that changes in investment spending (similar to changes in government spending) have a *multiplier* effect on the economy.

Arguments Against Monetary Policy

It might be thought that this multiplier effect would make monetary policy a potent tool in the Keynesian arsenal, particularly when it comes to getting the economy out of a recession. In fact, however, many traditional Keynesians argue that monetary policy is likely to be relatively ineffective as a recession fighter. According to their line of reasoning, although monetary policy has the potential to reduce interest rates, changes in the money supply have little actual impact on interest rates. Instead, during recessions, people try to build up as much as they can in liquid assets to protect themselves from risks of unemployment and other losses of income. When the monetary authorities increase the money supply, individuals are willing to allow most of it to accumulate in their bank accounts. This desire for increased liquidity thus prevents interest rates from falling very much, which in turn means that there will be virtually no change in investment spending and thus little change in aggregate demand.

PROBLEM

D-1. Assume that the following conditions exist:

a. All banks are fully loaned up—there are no excess reserves, and desired excess reserves are always zero.

b. The money multiplier is 3.

c. The planned investment schedule is such that at a 10 percent rate of interest, investment is $200 billion; at 9 percent, investment is $225 billion.

d. The investment multiplier is 3.

e. The initial equilibrium level of national income is $2 billion.

f. The equilibrium rate of interest is 10 percent.

Now the Bank of Canada engages in expansionary monetary policy. It buys $1 million worth of bonds, which increases the money supply, which in turn lowers the market rate of interest by 1 percent. Indicate by how much the money supply increased, and then trace out the numerical consequences of the associated reduction in interest rates on all the other variables mentioned.

ISSUES IN STABILIZATION POLICY

The 1960s was an extended period of uninterrupted growth in Canada. The 1970s and 1980s were difficult times for many Canadians, as both inflation and unemployment continued to grow to double digits. We had increasing government deficits as unemployment reduced tax revenues, and inflation added to the cost of maintaining programs for the unemployed. Clearly, the government needed to implement a focused economic policy to turn this trend around. So, it charged the Bank of Canada with the responsibility of using contractionary monetary policy to beat inflation. Was this the best policy the government could have chosen? To answer this question, you need to know more about how various economists view the economy, about its fluctuations in the short run and in the long run, and about certain issues pertaining to stabilization policies.

PREVIEW QUESTIONS

1. Why might the actual unemployment rate depart from the natural rate of unemployment?
2. What is the Phillips Curve?
3. How do expectations affect the actual relationship between the inflation rate and the unemployment rate?
4. What is new classical theory and the implications for economic policymaking?
5. What are the central features and predictions of real business cycle theory?
6. What is supply-side economics?
7. What are the alternative new Keynesian views of business fluctuations?

Active (discretionary) policymaking All actions on the part of monetary and fiscal policymakers that are undertaken in response to or in anticipation of some change in the overall economy.

Passive (nondiscretionary) policymaking Policymaking that is carried out in response to a rule. It is therefore not in response to an actual or potential change in overall economic activity.

DID YOU KNOW THAT... since the Great Depression of the 1930s until today, the federal government has passed dozens of bills aimed at fighting recession by means of fiscal policy? In the mid-1990s, in one 17-month period, the Bank of Canada decreased short-term interest rates 20 times. And over a longer period, the Bank of Canada has even changed its basic operating targets.

Active Versus Passive Policymaking

All of these actions constitute part of what is called **active (discretionary) policymaking.** At the other extreme is **passive (nondiscretionary) policymaking,** in which there is no deliberate stabilization policy at all. You have already been introduced to one nondiscretionary policymaking idea in Chapter 17—the *monetary rule,* by which the money supply is allowed to increase at a fixed rate per year. In the fiscal arena, passive (nondiscretionary) policy might simply consist of balancing the federal budget over the business cycle. Recall from Chapter 13 that there are numerous time lags between the time that the economy enters a recession or a boom and when that event becomes known, acted on, and sensed by the economy. Proponents of passive policy argue strongly that such time lags often render short-term stabilization policy ineffective, or worse, procyclical.

To take a stand on this debate concerning active versus passive policymaking, you first need to know the potential trade-offs that policymakers believe they face. Then you need to see what the data actually show. The most important policy trade-off appears to be between price stability and unemployment. Before exploring that trade-off, we need first to look at the economy's natural, or long-run, rate of unemployment.

The Natural Rate of Unemployment

Recall from Chapter 7 that there are different types of unemployment: frictional, cyclical, seasonal, and structural. Frictional unemployment arises because individuals take the time to search for the best job opportunities. Except when the economy is in a recession or a depression, much unemployment is of this type.

There are a number of aspects to frictional unemployment during normal times. Frictional unemployment can be made worse by a variety of "rigidities" throughout the economy. As a result of factors such as the following, frictional unemployment can be increased:

1. Union activity that sets wages above the equilibrium level and also restricts the mobility of labour
2. Government-imposed licensing arrangements that restrict entry into specific occupations or professions
3. Government-imposed minimum wage laws and other laws that require all workers to be paid union wage rates on government contract jobs
4. Welfare and Employment Insurance benefits that reduce incentives to work
5. Changes in technology that make current workers' skills obsolete

In each case, these factors reduce individuals' abilities or incentives to choose employment rather than unemployment.

Consider the effect of Employment Insurance benefits on the probability of an unemployed person finding a job. When unemployment benefits run out, according to economists Lawrence Katz and Bruce Meyer, the probability of an unemployed person finding a job doubles. The conclusion is that unemployed workers are more serious about finding a job when they are no longer receiving such benefits.

FIGURE 18.1 Estimated Natural Rate of Unemployment

As you can see in this figure, the actual rate of unemployment has varied widely in Canada in the second half of the twentieth century. If we estimate the natural rate of unemployment by averaging unemployment rates from five years earlier to five years later at each point in time, we get the heavy solid line so labelled. It rose from the 1950s until the early 1990s and seems to be trending down since then. (Post-1996 natural rate is approximated.)

Sources: Statistics Canada, CANSIM University Base, Series D76783, Matrix 3472, and M.C. Urquhart and K.A.H. Buckley, Historical Statistics of Canada.

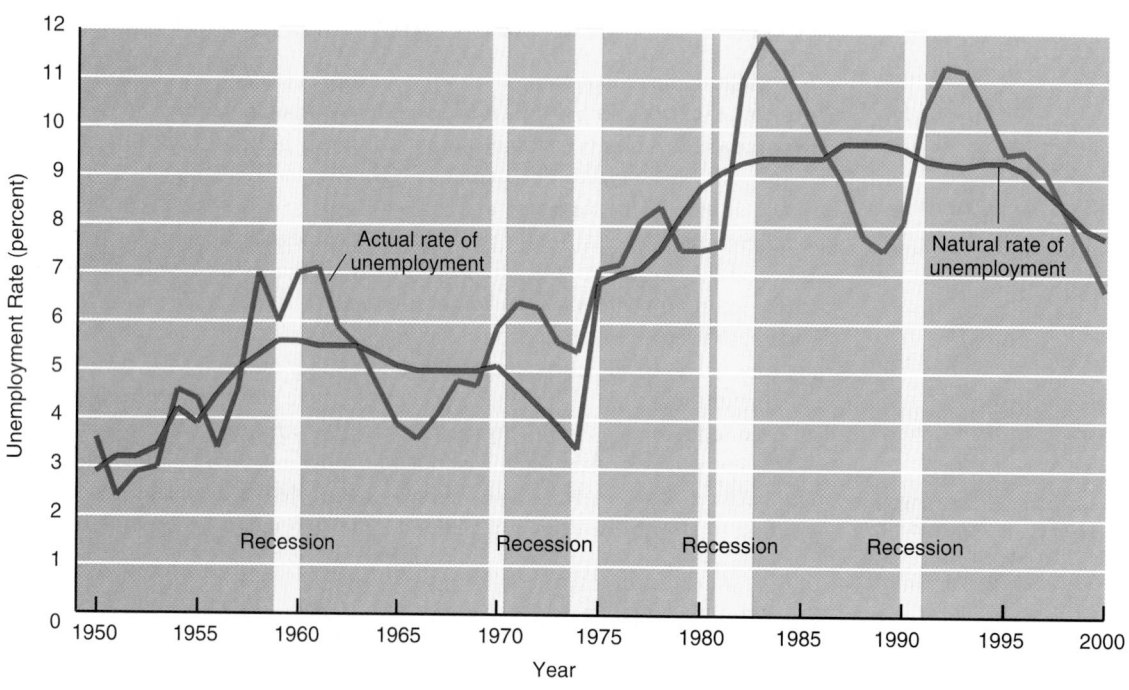

EXAMPLE 18-1   Canada's Natural Rate of Unemployment

In 1945, at the end of World War II, the unemployment rate was below 4 percent. By the early 1990s, it was above 10 percent. These two endpoints for half a century of unemployment rates prove nothing by themselves. But look at Figure 18.1. There you see not only what has happened to the unemployment rate over that same time period, but also an estimate of the natural rate of unemployment. The solid line labelled "Natural rate of unemployment" is estimated by averaging unemployment rates from five years earlier to five years later at each point in time. This computation reveals that until about 1990, the natural rate of unemployment was rising. But since then, the natural rate of unemployment held steady, and then began trending down.

For critical analysis: Of the factors listed on page 409 that create frictional unemployment, which do you think may explain the trend upward in the natural rate of unemployment since World War II?

Frictional unemployment exists even when the economy is in long-run equilibrium—it is a natural consequence of costly information (the need to conduct a job search) and the existence of rigidities such as those noted. Because frictional unemployment is a natural consequence of imperfect information and rigidities, it is related to what economists call the **natural rate of unemployment.** It is defined as the rate of unemployment that would exist in the long run after everyone in the economy fully adjusted to any changes that have occurred. Recall that national output tends to return to the level implied by the long-run aggregate supply curve (*LRAS*). Thus whatever rate of unemployment the economy tends to return to can be called the natural rate of unemployment. See Figure 18-1 on page 410 for an estimate of Canada's natural rate of unemployment.

Natural rate of unemployment The rate of unemployment that is estimated to prevail in long-run macroeconomic equilibrium, when all workers and employers have fully adjusted to any changes in the economy.

Departures from the Natural Rate of Unemployment

Even though the unemployment rate has a strong tendency to stay at and return to the natural rate, it is possible for fiscal and monetary policy to move the actual unemployment rate away from the natural rate, at least in the short run. Deviations of the actual unemployment rate from the natural rate are called *cyclical unemployment* because they are observed over the course of nationwide business fluctuations. During recessions, the overall unemployment rate exceeds the natural rate; cyclical unemployment is positive. During periods of economic booms, the overall unemployment rate can go below the natural rate; at such times, cyclical unemployment is in essence negative.

To see how departures from the natural rate of unemployment can occur, let's consider two examples. Referring to Figure 18.2, we begin in equilibrium at point E_1 with the associated price level P_1 and real GDP per year of level Y_1.

THE IMPACT OF EXPANSIONARY POLICY. Now imagine that the government decides to use fiscal or monetary policy to stimulate the economy. Further suppose that this policy surprises decision makers throughout the economy in the sense that they did not anticipate that the policy would occur. The aggregate demand curve shifts from AD_1 to AD_2 in Figure 18.2, so both the price level and real GDP rise to P_2 and Y_2, respectively. In the labour market, individuals will find that conditions have improved markedly relative to what they expected. Firms seeking to expand output will want to hire more workers. To accomplish this, they will recruit more actively and possibly ask workers to work overtime, so that individuals in the labour market will find more job openings and more possible

FIGURE 18.2 Impact of an Increase in Aggregate Demand on Output and Unemployment

If the economy is operating at E_1, it is in both short-run and long-run equilibrium. Here the actual rate of unemployment is equal to the natural rate of unemployment. Subsequent to expansionary monetary or fiscal policy, the aggregate demand curve shifts outward to AD_2. The price level rises to P_2; real GDP per year increases to Y_2. The new short-run equilibrium is at E_2. The unemployment rate is now below the natural rate of unemployment. We are at a temporary equilibrium at E_2. In the long run, expectations of input owners are revised. The short-run aggregate supply curve shifts from $SRAS_1$ to $SRAS_2$ because of higher prices and higher resource costs. Real GDP returns to the *LRAS* level of Y_1 per year. The price level has increased to P_3.

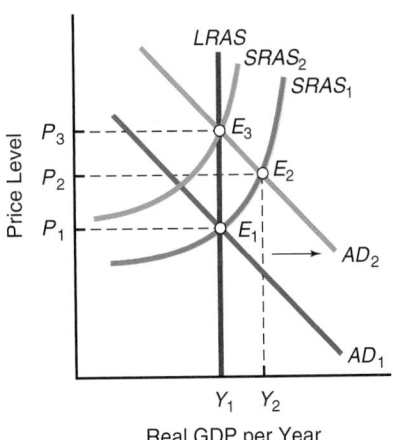

hours they can work. Consequently, as you learned in Chapter 7, the average duration of unemployment will fall and the unemployment rate falls. This unexpected increase in aggregate demand simultaneously causes the price level to rise to P_2 and the unemployment rate to fall. The *SRAS* curve will not stay at $SRAS_1$, however. A change in the expectations of input owners, such as workers and owners of capital and raw materials, will be revised. The short-run aggregate supply curve shifts to $SRAS_2$, as input prices rise. We find ourselves at a new equilibrium at E_3, which is on the *LRAS*. Long-run real GDP per year is Y_1 again, but at a higher price level, P_3.

Try Preview Question 1:

Why might the actual unemployment rate depart from the natural rate of unemployment?

THE CONSEQUENCES OF CONTRACTIONARY POLICY. Instead of expansionary policy, the government could have decided to engage in contractionary (or deflationary) policy. As shown in Figure 18.3, the sequence of events would have been in the opposite direction of those in Figure 18.2. Again, beginning from an initial equilibrium E_1, an unanticipated reduction in aggregate demand puts downward pressure on both prices and real GDP; the price level falls to P_2, and real GDP declines to Y_2. Fewer firms will be hiring, and those that are hiring will offer fewer overtime possibilities. Individuals looking for jobs will find that it takes longer than predicted. As a result, unemployed individuals will remain unemployed longer. The average duration of unemployment will rise, and so, too, will the rate of unemployment. The unexpected decrease in aggregate demand simultaneously causes the price level to fall to P_2 and the unemployment rate to rise. This is a short-run situation only at E_2. $SRAS_1$ will shift to $SRAS_2$ with a change in the expectations of input owners about future prices, and input prices fall. The new equilibrium will be at E_3, which is on the long-run aggregate supply curve, *LRAS*. The price level will have fallen to P_3.

The Phillips Curve: The Trade-Off?

Let's recap what we have just observed. An *unexpected* increase in aggregate demand causes the price level to rise and the unemployment rate to fall. Conversely, an *unexpected* decrease in aggregate demand causes the price level to fall and the unemployment rate to rise. Moreover, although not shown explicitly in either diagram, two additional points are true:

FIGURE 18.3 Impact of a Decline in Aggregate Demand on Output and Unemployment

Starting from equilibrium at E_1, a decline in aggregate demand to AD_2 leads to a lower price level, P_2, and real GDP declines to Y_2. The unemployment rate will rise above the natural rate of unemployment. Equilibrium at E_2 is temporary, however. At the lower price level, the expectations of input owners will be revised. $SRAS_1$ will shift to $SRAS_2$. The new equilibrium will be at E_3, with real GDP equal to Y_1 and a price level of P_3.

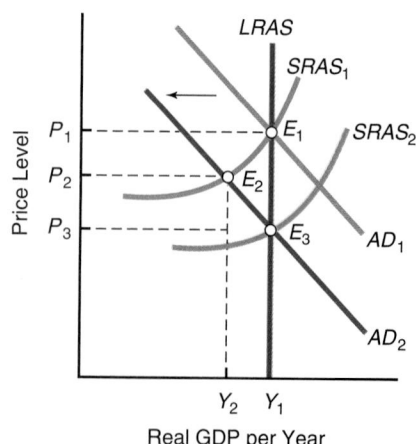

1. The greater the unexpected increase in aggregate demand, the greater the amount of inflation that results, and the lower the unemployment rate.
2. The greater the unexpected decrease in aggregate demand, the greater the deflation that results, and the higher the unemployment rate.

THE NEGATIVE RELATIONSHIP BETWEEN INFLATION AND UNEMPLOYMENT. Figure 18.4 summarizes these findings. The inflation rate (*not* the price level) is measured along the vertical axis, and the unemployment rate is measured along the horizontal axis. Point *A* shows an initial starting point, with the unemployment rate at the natural rate, U^*. Note that as a matter of convenience, we are starting from an equilibrium in which the price level is stable (the inflation rate is zero). Unexpected increases in aggregate demand cause the price level to rise—the inflation rate becomes positive—and cause the unemployment rate to fall. Thus the economy moves up to the left from *A* to *B*. Conversely, unexpected decreases in aggregate demand cause the price level to fall and the unemployment rate to rise above the natural rate—the economy moves from point *A* to point *C*. If we look at both increases and decreases in aggregate demand, we see that high inflation rates tend to be associated with low unemployment rates (as at *B*) and that low (or negative) inflation rates tend to be accompanied by high unemployment rates (as at *C*).

Phillips curve A curve showing the relationship between unemployment and changes in wages or prices. It was long thought to reflect a trade-off between unemployment and inflation.

IS THERE A TRADE-OFF? The apparent negative relationship between the inflation rate and the unemployment rate shown in Figure 18.4 has come to be called the **Phillips curve**, after A. W. Phillips, who discovered that a similar relationship existed historically in the United Kingdom. Although Phillips presented his findings only as an empirical regularity, economists quickly came to view the relationship as representing a *trade-off* between inflation and unemployment. In particular, policymakers believed they could choose alternative combinations of unemployment and inflation (or worse, that the trade-off was inevitable because you could not get more of one without giving up the other). Thus it seemed that a government which disliked unemployment could select a point like *B* in Figure 18.4, with a positive inflation rate but a relatively low unemployment rate. Conversely, a government that feared inflation could choose a stable price level at *A*, but only at the expense of a higher associated unemployment rate. Indeed, the Phillips curve seemed to suggest that it was possible for policymakers to fine-tune the economy by selecting the policies that would produce the exact mix of unemployment and inflation that suited current government objectives. As it turned out, matters are not so simple.

Try Preview Question 2:

What is the Phillips curve?

FIGURE 18.4 The Phillips Curve

Unanticipated changes in aggregate demand produce a negative relationship between the inflation rate and unemployment rate. U^* is the natural rate of unemployment.

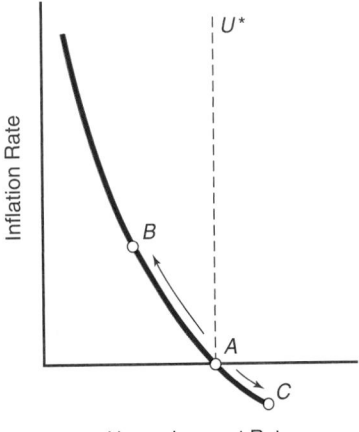

Nonaccelerating inflation rate of unemployment (NAIRU) The rate of unemployment below which the rate of inflation tends to rise and above which the rate of inflation tends to fall.

THE NAIRU. If we accept that a trade-off exists between the rate of inflation and the rate of unemployment, then the notion of "noninflationary" rates of unemployment seems appropriate. In fact, some economists have proposed what they call the **nonaccelerating inflation rate of unemployment (NAIRU).** If the Phillips curve trade-off exists and if the NAIRU can be estimated, that estimate will define the short-run trade-off between the rate of unemployment and the rate of inflation. Economists who have estimated the NAIRU for the world's 24 richest industrial countries claim that it has been steadily rising since the 1960s. Critics of the NAIRU concept argue that inflationary expectations must be taken into account.

The Importance of Expectations

The reduction in unemployment that takes place as the economy moves from A to B in Figure 18.4 occurs because the wage offers encountered by unemployed workers are unexpectedly high. As far as the workers are concerned, these higher *nominal* wages appear, at least initially, to be increases in *real* wages; it is this fact that induces them to reduce their duration of search. This is a sensible way for the workers to view the world if aggregate demand fluctuates up and down at random, with no systematic or predictable variation one way or another. But if policymakers attempt to exploit the apparent trade-off in the Phillips curve, according to some macroeconomists, aggregate demand will no longer move up and down in an *unpredictable* way.

THE EFFECTS OF AN UNANTICIPATED POLICY. Consider Figure 18.5, for example. If the Bank of Canada attempts to reduce the unemployment rate to U_1, it must increase the money supply enough to produce an inflation rate of π_1. If this is a one-shot affair in which the money supply is first increased and then held constant, the inflation rate will temporarily rise to π_1 and the unemployment rate will temporarily fall to U_1; but as soon as the money supply stops growing, the inflation rate will return to zero and unemployment will return to U^*, its natural rate. Thus a one-shot increase in the money supply

FIGURE 18.5 A Shift in the Phillips Curve

When there is a change in the expected inflation rate, the Phillips curve (*PC*) shifts to incorporate the new expectations. PC_0 shows expectations of zero inflation; PC_5 reflects an expected inflation rate of 5 percent.

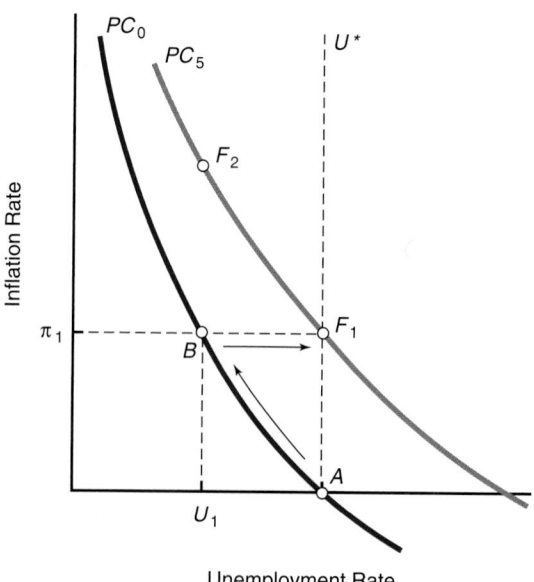

will move the economy from point A to point B, and the economy will move of its own accord back to A.

If the authorities wish to prevent the unemployment rate from returning to U^*, some macroeconomists argue that the Bank of Canada must keep the money supply growing fast enough to keep the inflation rate up at π_1. But if the Bank of Canada does this, all of the economic participants in the economy—workers and job seekers included—will come to *expect* that inflation rate to continue. This, in turn, will change their expectations about wages. For example, suppose that π_1 equals 5 percent per year. When the expected inflation rate was zero, a 5 percent rise in nominal wages meant a 5 percent expected rise in real wages, and this was sufficient to induce some individuals to take jobs rather than remain unemployed. It was this perception of a rise in real wages that reduced search duration and caused the unemployment rate to drop from U^* to U_1. But if the expected inflation rate becomes 5 percent, a 5 percent rise in nominal wages means *no* rise in *real* wages. Once workers come to expect the higher inflation rate, rising nominal wages will no longer be sufficient to entice them out of unemployment. As a result, as the *expected* inflation rate moves up from 0 percent to 5 percent, the unemployment rate will move up also.

THE ROLE OF EXPECTED INFLATION. In terms of Figure 18.5, as authorities initially increase aggregate demand, the economy moves from point A to point B. If the authorities continue the stimulus in an effort to keep the unemployment rate down, workers' expectations will adjust, causing the unemployment rate to rise. In this second stage, the economy moves from B to point F_1: The unemployment rate returns to the natural rate, U^*, but the inflation rate is now π_1 instead of zero. Once the adjustment of expectations has taken place, any further changes in policy will have to take place along a curve such as PC_5, say, a movement from F_1 to F_2. This new schedule is also a Phillips curve, differing from the first, PC_0, in that the actual inflation rate consistent with any given unemployment rate is higher because the expected inflation rate is higher.

Not surprisingly, when economic policymakers found that economic participants engaged in such adjustment behaviour, they were both surprised and dismayed. If decision makers can adjust their expectations to conform with fiscal and monetary policies, then policymakers cannot choose a permanently lower unemployment rate of U_1, even if they are willing to tolerate an inflation rate of π_1. Instead, the policymakers would end up with an unchanged unemployment rate in the long run, at the expense of a permanently higher inflation rate.

Initially, however, there did seem to be a small consolation, for it appeared that in the short run—before expectations adjusted—the unemployment rate could be *temporarily* reduced from U^* to U_1, even though eventually it would return to the natural rate. If an important federal election were approaching, it might be possible to stimulate the economy long enough to get the unemployment rate low enough to assure re-election. However, policymakers came to learn that not even this was likely to be a sure thing.

The Canadian Experience with the Phillips Curve

In separate articles in 1968, economists Milton Friedman and E. S. Phelps published pioneering studies suggesting that the apparent trade-off suggested by the Phillips curve could not be exploited by policymakers. Friedman and Phelps both argued that any attempt to reduce unemployment by inflating the economy would soon be thwarted by economic participants' incorporating the new higher inflation rate into their expectations. The Friedman-Phelps research thus implies that for any given unemployment rate, any inflation rate is possible, depending on the actions of policymakers. As reflected in Figure 18.6, the propositions of Friedman and Phelps were to prove remarkably accurate.

When we examine the data for unemployment and inflation in Canada over the past half century, we see virtually no clear relationship between them. Although there seemed

FIGURE 18.6 The Phillips Curve: Theory Versus Data

If you plot points representing the rate of inflation and the rate of unemployment for Canada from 1950 to the present, there does not appear to be any Phillips curve trade-off between the two variables.

Sources: Statistics Canada, CANSIM Database, Series P200000, D31252, D31253, D984954; *Historical Statistics of Canada,* Catalogue No. 11-516-XIE, Series D129, D132, D233.

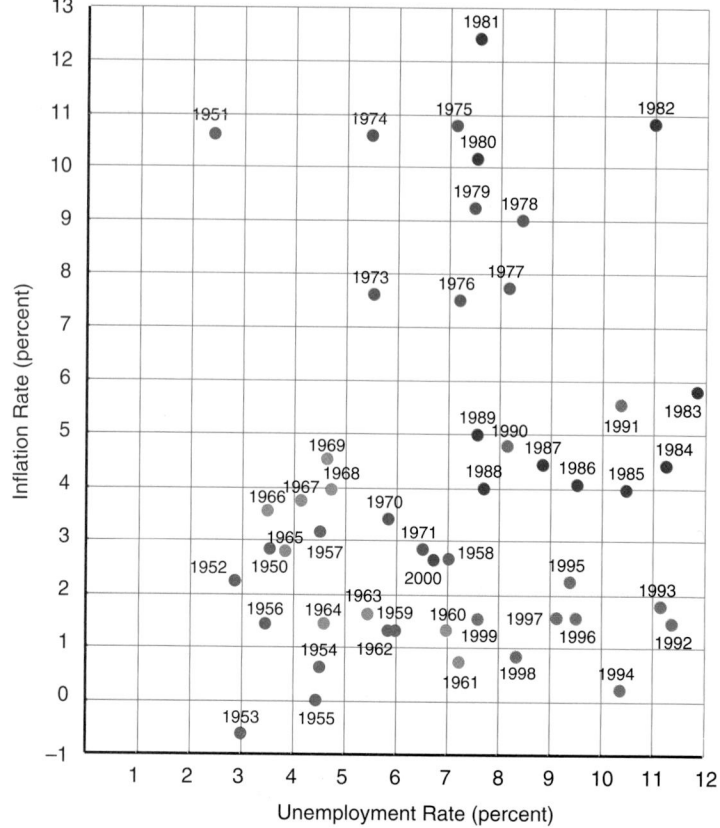

to have been a Phillips curve trade-off between unemployment and inflation from the mid-1950s to the mid-1960s, apparently once people in the economy realized what was happening, they started revising their forecasts accordingly. So, once policymakers attempted to exploit the Phillips curve, the apparent trade-off between unemployment and inflation disappeared.

INTERNATIONAL EXAMPLE 18-1

Can European Policymakers Exploit the Phillips Curve?

Although the data for Canada seem clear—policymakers cannot exploit the Phillips curve trade-off—is the same true in Europe? It appears that European policymakers cannot exploit the trade-off either. As Figure 18.7 shows, the unemployment rate in Europe remained almost constant from 1967 to 1974 in spite of a skyrocketing inflation rate.

If one believes in the Phillips curve analysis, there seems to be little hope today for European policymakers to reduce their double-digit unemployment rates. More complete research was conducted in 1994 by two British economists, David Blanchflower and Andrew Oswald, who spent five years analysing numerous data points across 12 countries. Their conclusion was that there is no relationship between inflation and unemployment.

FIGURE 18.7 Relationship Between Inflation and Unemployment in Europe

If we examine the so-called Phillips curve trade-off in Europe since 1967, there does not appear to be any long-run stable relationship between the rate of inflation and the rate of unemployment.

Source: David Blanchflower and Andrew Oswald.

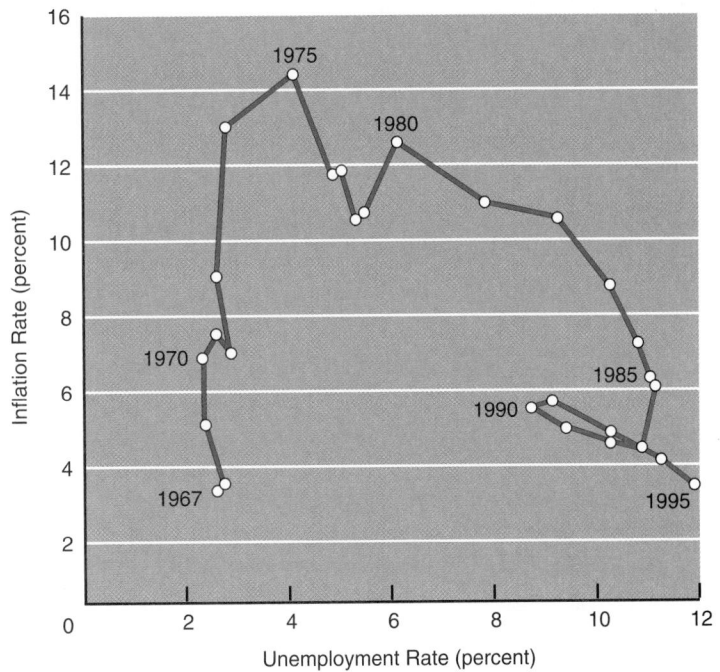

For critical analysis: How do the data in Figure 18.6 and Figure 18.7 support the proponents of a monetary rule?

CONCEPTS IN BRIEF

- The natural rate of unemployment is the rate that exists in long-run equilibrium, when workers' expectations are consistent with actual conditions.
- Departures from the natural rate of unemployment can occur when individuals encounter unanticipated changes in fiscal or monetary policy; an unexpected rise in aggregate demand will reduce unemployment below the natural rate, whereas an unanticipated decrease in aggregate demand will push unemployment above the natural rate.
- The Phillips curve exhibits a negative relationship between the inflation rate and the unemployment rate that can be observed when there are *unanticipated* changes in aggregate demand.
- It was originally believed that the Phillips curve represented a trade-off between inflation and unemployment. In fact, no trade-off exists because workers' expectations adjust to any systematic attempts to reduce unemployment below the natural rate.

Rational Expectations and the New Classical Model

You already know that economists assume that economic participants act *as though* they were rational and calculating. We think of firms that rationally maximize profits when they choose today's rate of output, and consumers who rationally maximize utility when they choose how much of what goods to consume today. One of the pivotal features of current macro policy research is the assumption that rationality also applies to the way that economic participants think about the future as well as the present. This relationship was developed by Robert Lucas, who won the Nobel Prize in 1995 for his work. In particular, there is widespread agreement among a growing group of macroeconomics researchers that the **rational expectations hypothesis** extends our understanding of the behaviour of the macroeconomy. There are two key elements to this hypothesis:

Rational expectations hypothesis A theory stating that people combine the effects of past policy changes on important economic variables with their own judgment about the future effects of current and future policy changes.

1. Individuals base their forecasts (or expectations) about the future values of economic variables on all available past and current information.
2. These expectations incorporate individuals' understanding about how the economy operates, including the operation of monetary and fiscal policy.

In essence, the rational expectations hypothesis assumes the old saying is correct: "It is true that you may fool all the people some of the time; you can even fool some of the people all of the time; but you can't fool *all* of the people *all* of the time."

If we further assume that there is pure competition in all markets and that all prices and wages are flexible, we obtain the **new classical model** (referred to in Chapter 13 when discussing the Ricardian equivalence theorem). To see how rational expectations operate within the context of this model, let's take a simple example of the economy's response to a change in monetary policy.

New classical model A modern version of the classical model in which wages and prices are flexible, there is pure competition in all markets, and the rational expectations hypothesis is assumed to be working.

The New Classical Model

Consider Figure 18.8, which shows the long-run aggregate supply curve (*LRAS*) for the economy, as well as the initial aggregate demand curve (*AD₁*) and the short-run aggregate supply curve (*SRAS₁*). The money supply is initially given by $M = M_1$, and the price level and real GDP are shown by P_1 and Q_1, respectively. Thus point A represents the initial equilibrium.

Suppose now that the money supply is unexpectedly increased to M_2, thereby causing the aggregate demand curve to shift outward to AD_2. Given the location of the short-run aggregate supply curve, this increase in aggregate demand will cause output and the

FIGURE 18.8 Response to an Unanticipated Rise in Aggregate Demand

Unanticipated changes in aggregate demand have real effects. In this case, the rise in demand causes real output to rise from Q_1 to Q_2.

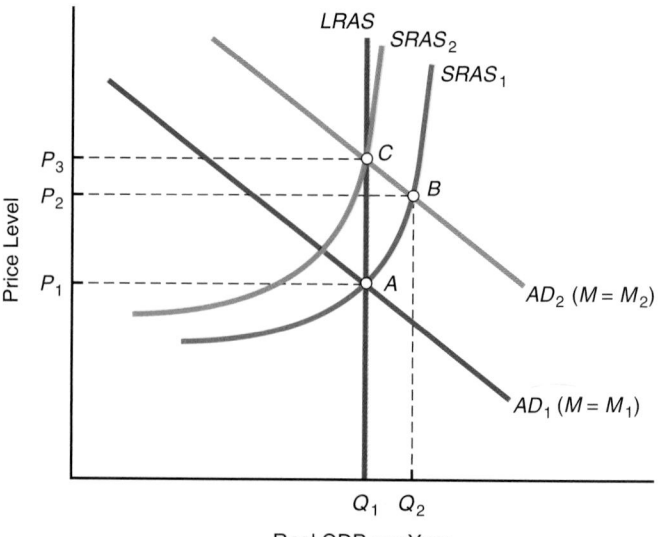

price level to rise to Q_2 and P_2, respectively. The new short-run equilibrium is at B. Because output is *above* the long-run equilibrium level of Q_1, unemployment must be below long-run levels (the natural rate), and so workers will soon respond to the higher price level by demanding higher nominal wages. This will cause the short-run aggregate supply curve to shift upward vertically (to the left), moving the economy to the new long-run equilibrium at C. The price level thus continues its rise to P_3, even as real GDP declines back down to Q_1 (and unemployment returns to the natural rate). So as we have seen before, even though an increase in the money supply can raise output and lower unemployment in the short run, it has no effect on either variable in the long run.

THE RESPONSE TO ANTICIPATED POLICY. Now let's look at this disturbance with the perspective given by the rational expectations hypothesis, as it is embedded in the new classical model. Suppose that workers (and other input owners) know ahead of time that this increase in the money supply is about to take place. Assume also that they know when it is going to occur and understand that its ultimate effect will be to push the price level from P_1 to P_3. Will workers wait until after the price level has increased to insist that their nominal wages go up? The rational expectations hypothesis says that they will not. Instead, they will go to employers and insist on nominal wages that move upward in step with the higher prices. From the workers' perspective, this is the only way to protect their real wages from declining due to the anticipated increase in the money supply.

THE POLICY IRRELEVANCE PROPOSITION. As long as economic participants behave in this manner, when we draw the *SRAS* curve, we must be explicit about the nature of their expectations. This we have done in Figure 18.9. In the initial equilibrium, the short-run aggregate supply curve is labelled to show that the expected money supply (Me) and the actual money supply (M_1) are equal ($Me = M_1$). Similarly, when the money supply changes in a way that is anticipated by economic participants, the aggregate supply curve shifts to reflect this expected change in the money supply. The new short-run aggregate

Try Preview Question 3:

How do expectations affect the actual relationship between the inflation rate and the unemployment rate?

FIGURE 18.9 Effects of an Anticipated Rise in Aggregate Demand

When policy is fully anticipated, a rise in the money supply causes a rise in the price level from P_1 to P_3, with no change in real output.

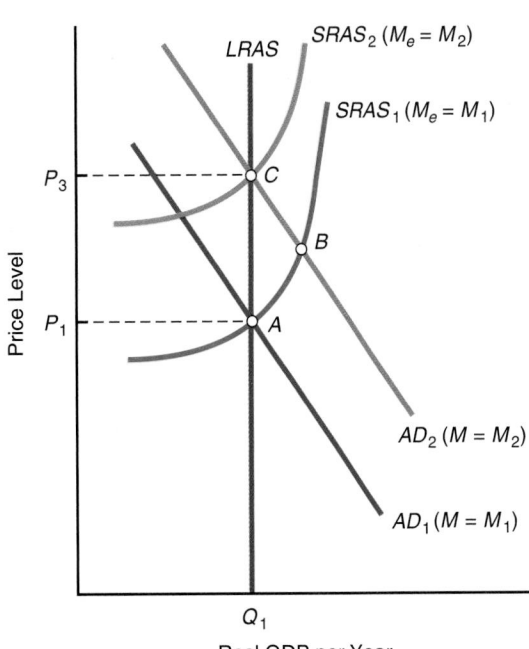

Try Preview Question 4:

What is new classical theory and the implications for economic policymaking?

Policy irrelevance proposition The new classical and rational expectations conclusion that policy actions have no real effects in the short run if the policy actions are anticipated and none in the long run even if the policy actions are unanticipated.

supply curve is labelled ($Me = M_2$) to reveal this. According to the rational expectations hypothesis, the short-run aggregate supply will shift upward *simultaneously* with the rise in aggregate demand. As a result, the economy will move directly from point *A* to point *C* in Figure 18.9 without passing through *B*: The *only* response to the rise in the money supply is a rise in the price level from P_1 to P_3; neither output nor unemployment changes at all. This conclusion—that fully anticipated monetary policy is irrelevant in determining the levels of real variables—is called the **policy irrelevance proposition**:

> Under the assumption of rational expectations on the part of decision makers in the economy, anticipated monetary policy cannot alter either the rate of unemployment or the level of real GDP. Regardless of the nature of the anticipated policy, the unemployment rate will equal the natural rate, and real GDP will be determined solely by the economy's long-run aggregate supply curve.

Thinking Critically About the Media 18-1   Higher Interest Rates and "Tight" Monetary Policy

The media often report changes in interest rates to indicate changes in monetary policy, whether they are referring to Canada or any other country. The problem with such analyses is that they fail to distinguish between real and nominal interest rates. Normally, a high interest rate is evidence that a country's central bank has been pursuing loose monetary policy in the past rather than tight monetary policy now. Why? Because in the long run, consistent increases in the rate of growth of the money supply lead to a higher rate of inflation. A higher rate of inflation normally leads to expectations of inflation and therefore higher nominal interest rates. After all, the nominal interest rate is equal to the real rate of interest plus the expected rate of inflation. In the long run, evidence shows that monetary authorities have little effect on an economy's real rate of interest.

WHAT MUST PEOPLE KNOW? There are two important matters to keep in mind when considering this proposition. First, our discussion has assumed that economic participants know in advance exactly what the change in monetary policy is going to be and precisely when it is going to occur. In fact, the Bank of Canada does not announce exactly what the future course of monetary policy (down to the last dollar) is going to be. Instead, the Bank of Canada announces only in general terms what policy actions are intended for the future. It is tempting to conclude that because the Bank of Canada's intended policies are not freely available, they are not available at all. But such a conclusion is wrong. Economic participants have great incentives to learn how to predict the future behaviour of the monetary authorities, just as businesses try to forecast consumer behaviour and college students do their best to forecast what their next economics exam will look like. Even if the economic participants are not perfect at forecasting the course of policy, they are likely to come a lot closer than they would in total ignorance. The policy irrelevance proposition really assumes only that *people don't persistently make the same mistakes in forecasting the future.*

WHAT HAPPENS IF PEOPLE DON'T KNOW EVERYTHING? This brings us to our second point. Once we accept the fact that people are not perfect in their ability to predict the future, the possibility emerges that some policy actions will have systematic effects that look much like the movements *A* to *B* to *C* in Figure 18.8. For example, just as other economic participants sometimes make mistakes, it is likely that the Bank of Canada sometimes makes mistakes—meaning that the money supply may change in ways that even the Bank of Canada does not predict. And even if the Bank of Canada always accomplished every policy action it intended, there is no guarantee that other economic participants would fully forecast those actions. What happens if the Bank of Canada makes a mistake or if firms and workers misjudge the future course of policy? Matters will look much as they do in part (a) of Figure 18.10, which shows the effects of an unanticipated increase in the money supply. Economic participants expect the money supply to be M_0, but the actual money supply turns out to be M_1. Because $M_1 > M_0$, aggregate demand shifts relative to aggregate supply. The result is a rise in real output (real GDP) in the short run from Q_1 to Q_2; corresponding to this rise in real output will be an increase in employment and hence a fall in the unemployment rate. So even under the rational expectations hypothesis, monetary policy can have an effect on real variables in the short run, but only if the policy is unsystematic and therefore unanticipated.

In the long run, this effect on real variables will disappear because people will figure out that the Bank of Canada either accidentally increased the money supply or intentionally increased it in a way that somehow fooled individuals. Either way, people's expectations will soon be revised so that the short-run aggregate supply curve will shift upward. As shown in part (b) of Figure 18.10, real GDP will return to long-run levels, meaning that so will the employment and unemployment rates.

The Policy Dilemma

Perhaps the most striking and disturbing feature of the new classical model is that it seems to suggest that only mistakes can have real effects. If the Bank of Canada always does what it intends to do, and if other economic participants always correctly anticipate the Bank of Canada's actions, monetary policy will affect only the price level and nominal input prices. It appears that only if the Bank of Canada makes a mistake in executing monetary policy or people err in anticipating that policy will changes in the money supply cause fluctuations in real output and employment. If this reasoning is correct, the Bank of Canada is effectively precluded from using monetary policy in any rational way to lower the unemployment rate or to raise the level of real GDP. This is because fully

FIGURE 18.10 Effects of an Unanticipated Rise in Aggregate Demand

Even with rational expectations, an unanticipated change in demand can affect output in the short run.

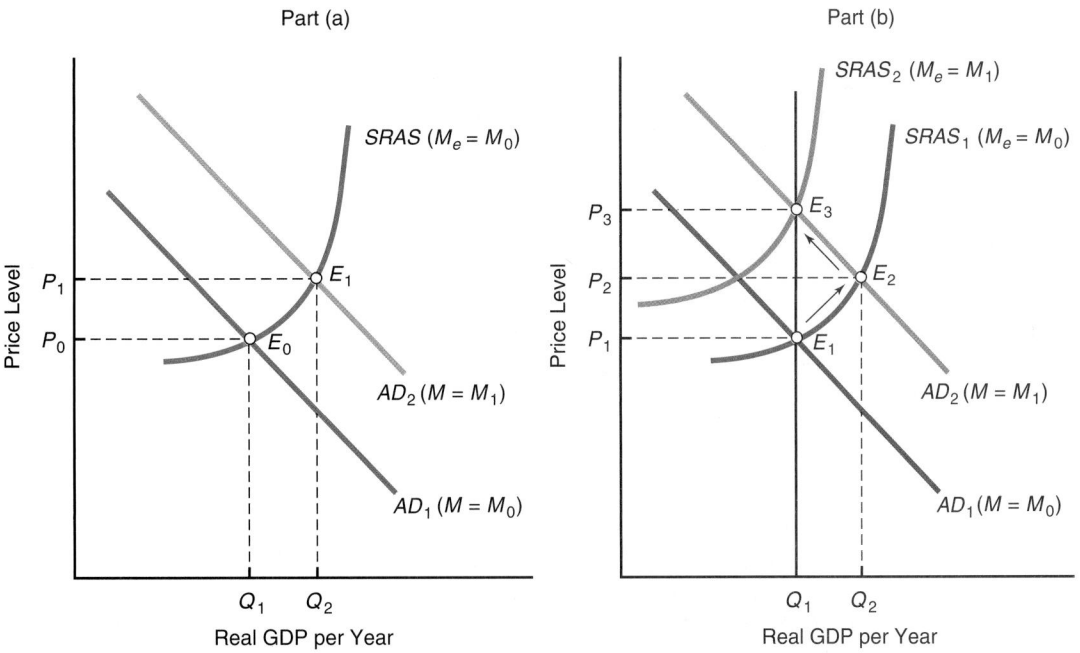

anticipated changes in the money supply will lead to exactly offsetting changes in prices and hence no real effects. Many economists were disturbed at the prospect that if the economy happened to enter a recessionary period, policymakers would be powerless to push real GDP and unemployment back to long-run levels. As a result, they asked the question, "In light of the rational expectations hypothesis, is it ever possible for systematic policy to have predictable real effects on the economy?" The answer has led to even more developments in the way we think about macroeconomics.

CONCEPTS IN BRIEF

- The rational expectations hypothesis assumes that individuals' forecasts incorporate all available information, including an understanding of government policy and its effects on the economy.
- The new classical economics assumes that the rational expectations hypothesis is valid, and also that there is pure competition and that all prices and wages are flexible.
- The policy irrelevance proposition says that under the assumptions of the new classical model, fully anticipated monetary policy cannot alter either the rate of unemployment or the level of real GDP.
- The new classical model implies that policies can alter real economic variables only if the policies are unsystematic and therefore unanticipated, otherwise people learn and defeat the desired policy goals.

Real Business Cycle Theory

The modern extension of new classical theory involves re-examining the first principles that assume fully flexible prices.

The Distinction Between Real and Monetary Shocks

The research of the new business cycle theorists differs importantly from that of new classical theorists in that business cycle theorists seek to determine whether real, as opposed to purely monetary, forces might help explain aggregate economic fluctuations. An important stimulus for the development of **real business cycle theory**, as it has come to be known, was the economic turmoil of the 1970s. During that decade, world economies were staggered by two major disruptions to the supply of oil. The first occurred in 1973, the second in 1979. In both episodes, members of the Organization of Petroleum Exporting Countries (OPEC) reduced the amount of oil they were willing to supply and raised the price at which they offered it for sale. Each time, the price level rose sharply in Canada, and real GDP declined. Thus each episode produced a period of "stagflation"—real economic stagnation combined with high inflation. Figure 18.11 illustrates the pattern of events.

We begin at point E_1 with the economy in both short- and long-run equilibrium, with the associated supply curves, $SRAS_1$ and $LRAS_1$. Initially, the level of real GDP is Q_1, and the price level is P_1. Because the economy is in long-run equilibrium, the unemployment rate must be at the natural rate.

A reduction in the supply of oil, as occurred in 1973 and 1979, causes the $SRAS$ curve to shift to the left to $SRAS_2$ because fewer goods will be available for sale due to the reduced supplies. If the reduction in oil supplies is (or is believed to be) permanent, the $LRAS$ shifts to the left also. This assumption is reflected in Figure 18.11, where $LRAS_2$ shows the new long-run aggregate supply curve associated with the lowered output of oil.

Real business cycle theory An extension and modification of the theories of the new classical economists of the 1970s and 1980s, in which money is neutral and only real, supply-side factors matter in influencing labour employment and real output.

FIGURE 18.11 Effects of a Reduction in the Supply of Resources

The position of the *LRAS* depends on our endowments of all types of resources. Hence a reduction in the supply of one of those resources, such as oil, causes a reduction—an inward shift—in the aggregate supply curve. In addition, there is a rise in the equilibrium price level and a fall in the equilibrium rate of real GDP per year (output).

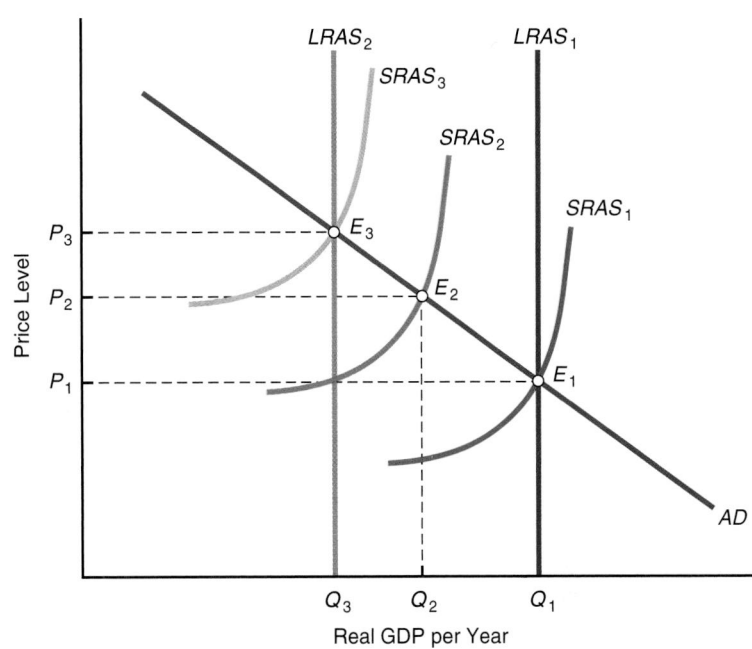

In the short run, two adjustments begin to occur simultaneously. First, the prices of oil and petroleum-based products begin to rise, so that the overall price level rises to P_2. Second, the higher costs of production occasioned by the rise in oil prices induce firms to cut back production, so total output falls to Q_2 in the short run. The new temporary short-run equilibrium occurs at E_2, with a higher price level (P_2) and a lower level of real GDP (Q_2).

Impact on the Labour Market

If we were to focus on the labour market while this adjustment from E_1 to E_2 was taking place, we would find two developments occurring. The rise in the price level pushes the real wage rate downward, even as the scaled-back production plans of firms induce them to reduce the amount of labour inputs they are using. So not only does the real wage rate fall, but the level of employment declines as well. On both counts, workers are made worse off due to the reduction in the supply of oil.

Now this is not the full story, because owners of non-oil inputs (such as labour) who are willing to put up with reduced real payments in the short run simply will not tolerate them in the long run. Thus, for example, some workers who were willing to continue working at lower wages in the short run will eventually decide to retire, switch from full-time to part-time employment, or drop out of the labour force altogether. In effect, there is a reduction in the supply of non-oil inputs, reflected in an upward shift in the *SRAS* from $SRAS_2$ to $SRAS_3$. This puts additional upward pressure on the price level and exerts a downward force on real GDP. The final long-run equilibrium thus occurs at point E_3, with the price level at P_3 and real GDP at Q_3. (In principle, because the oil supply shock has had no long-term effect on labour markets, the natural rate of unemployment does not change when equilibrium moves from E_1 to E_3.)

Generalizing the Theory

Naturally, the focus of real business cycle theory goes well beyond the simple "oil shock" that we have discussed here, for it encompasses all types of real disturbances, including technological changes and shifts in the composition of the labour force. Moreover, a complete treatment of real shocks to the economy is typically much more complex than we have allowed for in our discussion. For example, an oil shock such as is shown in Figure 18.11 would likely also have effects on the real wealth of Canadians, causing a reduction in aggregate demand as well as aggregate supply. Nevertheless, our simple example still manages to capture the flavour of the theory.

It is clear that real business cycle theory has improved our understanding of the economy's behaviour, but there is also agreement among economists that it alone is incapable of explaining all of the facets of business cycles that we observe. For example, it is difficult to imagine a real disturbance that could possibly account for the Great Depression in this country, when real income fell 30 percent and the unemployment rate rose to 20 percent. Moreover, real business cycle theory continues to assume that prices are perfectly flexible and so fails to explain a great deal of the apparent rigidity of prices throughout the economy.

Try Preview Question 5:
What are the central features and predictions of real business cycle theory?

Supply-Side Economics

The supply-side shocks of the 1970s, especially the reduction in the supply of oil, resulted in the worst combination of economic outcomes—high inflation, stagnation in economic output, and increasingly higher unemployment or "stagflation". But this shock caused some economists to take note that virtually all attention in mainstream macroeconomic theory was focused on aggregate demand. This is focusing on only half the model.

Let us revisit the aggregate supply shock illustrated in Figure 18-11. If we could stimulate an increase in aggregate supply, could we not achieve the reverse of what had been observed? Instead of the worst combination of economic outcomes, could we not achieve the best possible combination of outcomes—low inflation, increasing real economic output, and lower unemployment? This is shown in Figure 18-12.

Supply-side economists argued that all the attention paid to demand-oriented theories distracted attention from the real problems of the economy. The real problems, according to the supply-siders, was that increasing levels of taxation and regulation were reducing incentives to work, save, and invest. What was needed were policies that would better stimulate aggregate supply, not aggregate demand. They advocated reducing marginal income tax rates, business taxes, and other business costs.

Advocates for such changes argue that lower tax rates will lead to an increase in productivity because individuals will work harder and longer, save more, and invest more; thus, increased productivity will lead to more economic growth which will lead to higher real GDP. The government, by applying lower marginal tax rates, will not necessarily lose tax revenues, since the lower marginal taxes will be applied to a growing tax base because of economic growth. After all, tax revenues are the product of a tax rate times a tax base.

This relationship is sometimes called the Laffer Curve, named after economist Arthur Laffer, who developed it in front of some journalists and politicians in 1974. It is reproduced in Figure 18-13. On the horizontal axis are tax revenues, and on the vertical axis is the marginal tax rate. As you can see, total tax revenues rise as tax rates increase and then eventually fall after some unspecified tax-revenue-maximizing rate.

People who support the notion that reducing taxes does not necessarily lead to reduced tax revenues are called supply-side economists. **Supply-side economics** involves chang-

Supply-side economics The notion that creating incentives for individuals and firms to increase productivity will cause the aggregate supply curve to shift outward.

FIGURE 18.12 **Effects of an Increase in the Supply of Resources**

The position of the *LRAS* depends on our endowments of all types of natural and man-made resources. Hence an increase in the supply of one of these resources, such as the Internet, causes an increase—an outward shift—in the aggregate supply curve. In addition, there is a decline in the equilibrium price level and a rise in the rate of real GDP per year (output).

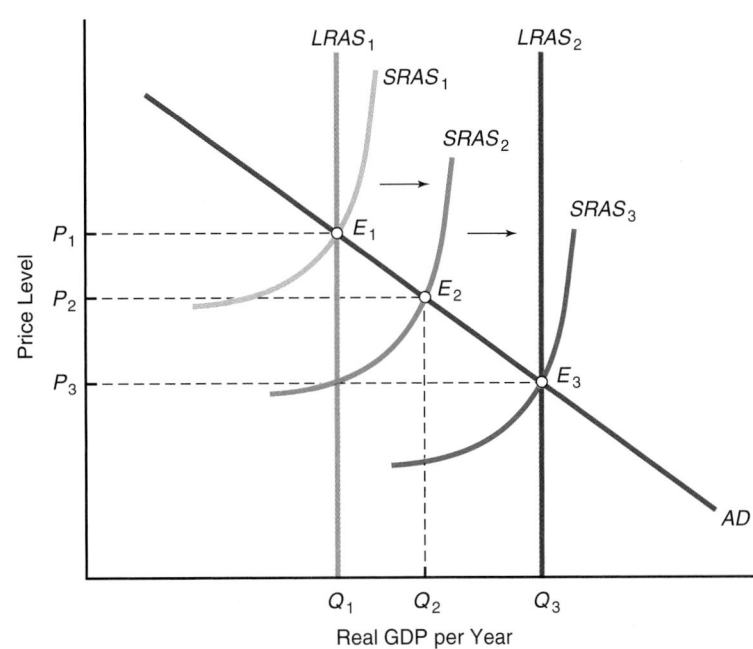

FIGURE 18.13 **Laffer Curve**

The Laffer Curve indicates that tax revenues initially increase with a higher tax rate. Eventually, however, tax revenues decline as the tax rate increases.

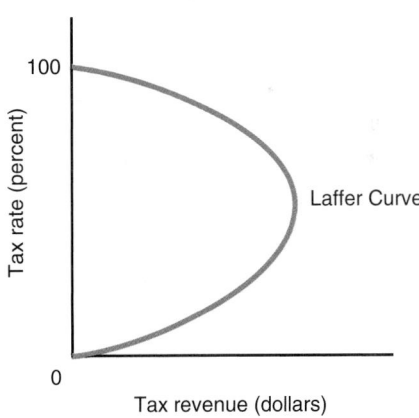

ing the tax structure to create incentives to increase productivity. Due to a shift in the aggregate supply curve to the right, there can be greater output without upward pressure on the price level. Refer to International Example 18-2 on the following page for a historical view of supply-side economics.

Criticisms of Supply-Side Economics

The supply-siders view and the Laffer Curve have been controversial.

A fundamental criticism has to do with timing and time lags. Investment does not occur overnight. Skeptics say that it is unlikely that a tax cut would have a very large impact on incentives; it would be of uncertain direction and slow to emerge. They are of small magnitude and, at best, long-term effects. In fact, most economists believe that the demand-side effects would be more immediate and overwhelm the supply-side effects.

Equally, a supply-side program is likely to have only a limited effect on inflation. Furthermore, if such policies were implemented when the economy was near or at the full-employment level, then the likely outcome would be inflationary.

In addition, there is a different problem. Most supply-side incentives and initiatives would increase income inequality.

The supply-siders claimed that President Reagan's substantial tax cuts in 1981 could, because of the Laffer Curve effect, maintain expenditures (even increasing defence spending) and balance the budget. These excessive promises proved false. In the decade after 1982, the US federal government ran huge record deficits, adding about 2 trillion dollars to the national debt and turning the US from the largest creditor nation in the world to the largest debtor nation in the world.

Somewhere between levels of taxation of 0 percent and 100 percent, there will be a point of maximum tax revenue. This is a logical proposition. The policy issue is where a particular economy is located on its Laffer Curve.

On balance, supply-side policies are not a substitute for short-run stabilization policy but, rather, could be approached as a way to enhance slightly faster long-run economic growth.

Try Preview Question 6:
What is supply-side economics?

INTERNATIONAL EXAMPLE 18-2

Islam and Supply-Side Economics

Supply-side economics has a long history, dating back to at least the fourteenth century. The greatest of medieval Islamic historians, Abu Zayd Abd-ar-Rahman Ibn Khaldun (1332–1406), included an Islamic view of supply-side economics in his monumental book *The Muqaddimah* (1377). He pointed out that "when tax assessments … upon the subjects are low, the latter have the energy and desire to do things. Cultural enterprises grow and increase …. [Therefore] the number of individual imposts [taxes] and assessments mounts." If taxes are increased both in size and rates, "the result is that the interest of subjects in cultural enterprises disappears, because when they compare expenditures and taxes with their income and gain and see little profit they make, they lose all hope." Ibn Khaldun concluded that "at the beginning of a dynasty, taxation yields a large revenue from small assessments. At the end of a dynasty, taxation yields a small revenue from large assessments."

For critical analysis: How do this Islamic scholar's economic theories apply to the modern world?

New Keynesian Economics

New Keynesian economics Economic models based on the idea that demand creates its own supply as a result of various possible government fiscal and monetary coordination failures.

Although the new classical and real business cycle theories both incorporate pure competition and flexible prices, a body of research called the **new Keynesian economics** drops both of these assumptions. The new Keynesian economists do not believe that market-clearing models of the economy can explain business cycles. Consequently, they argue that macroeconomics models must contain the "sticky" wages and prices assumption that Keynes outlined in his major work. Thus the new Keynesian research has as its goal a refinement of the theory of aggregate supply that explains how wages and prices behave in the short run. There are several such theories. The first one relates to the cost of changing prices.

Small-Menu Cost Theory

Small-menu cost theory A hypothesis that it is costly for firms to change prices in response to demand changes because of the cost of renegotiating contracts, printing price lists, and so on.

If prices do not respond to demand changes, two conditions must be true: Someone must be consciously deciding not to change prices, and that decision must be in the decision maker's self-interest. One combination of facts that is consistent with this scenario is the **small-menu cost theory**, which supposes that much of the economy is characterized by imperfect competition and that it is costly for firms to change their prices in response to changes in demand. The costs associated with changing prices are called *menu costs*, and they include the costs of renegotiating contracts, printing price lists (such as menus), and informing customers of price changes.

Many such costs may not be very large in magnitude; that is why they are called *small-menu costs*. Some of the costs of changing prices, however, such as those incurred in bringing together business managers from points around the country or the world for meetings on price changes, or renegotiating deals with customers, may be significant.

Firms in different industries have different cost structures. Such differences explain diverse small-menu costs. Therefore, the extent to which firms hold their prices constant in the face of changes in demand for their products will vary across industries. Not all prices will be rigid. Nonetheless, new Keynesian theorists argue that many—even most—firms' prices are sticky for relatively long time intervals. As a result, the aggregate level of prices could be very nearly rigid because of small-menu costs.

Although most economists agree that such costs exist, there is considerably less agreement on whether they are sufficient to explain the extent of price rigidity that is observed.

Efficiency Wage Theory

Efficiency wage theory The hypothesis that the productivity of workers depends on the level of the real wage rate.

An alternative approach within the new Keynesian framework is called the **efficiency wage theory**. It proposes that worker productivity actually *depends on* the wages that workers are paid, rather than being independent of wages, as is assumed in other theories (see International Example 18-3 on the following page). According to this theory, higher real wages encourage workers to work harder, improve their efficiency, increase morale, and raise their loyalty to the firm. Across the board, then, higher wages tend to increase workers' productivity, which in turn discourages firms from cutting real wages because of the damaging effect that such an action would have on productivity and profitability. Under highly competitive conditions, there will generally be an optimal wage—called the *efficiency wage*—that the firm should continue paying, even in the face of large fluctuations in the demand for its output.

The efficiency wage theory model is a rather simple idea, but it is somewhat revolutionary. All of the models of the labour market adopted by traditional classical, traditional Keynesian, monetarist, new classical, and new Keynesian theorists alike do not consider such real-wage effects on worker productivity.

There are significant, valid elements in the efficiency wage theory, but its importance in understanding national business fluctuations remains uncertain. For example, although the theory explains rigid real wages, it does not explain rigid prices. Moreover, the theory ignores the fact that firms can (and apparently do) rely on a host of incentives other than wages to encourage their workers to be loyal, efficient, and productive.

Try Preview Question 7:

What are the alternative new Keynesian views of business fluctuations?

| INTERNATIONAL EXAMPLE 18-3 | Henry Ford and the Efficiency Wage Model |

One of the most clear-cut examples of the efficiency wage model involved the Ford Motor Company in the United States. When nominal wage rates were about US$2 to US$3 a day in 1914 (about US$30 in today's dollars and with no benefits such as health insurance), Henry Ford ordered his managers to start paying workers US$5 a day. Ford later argued that the increase in wages was a "cost-cutting" move. The evidence bears him out. Absenteeism dropped by over 70 percent. Moreover, labour turnover virtually disappeared. Consequently, Ford's managers had to spend less time training new workers.

For critical analysis: What alternative ways do managers have to provide incentives to their workers to become more efficient?

Effect of Aggregate Demand Changes on Output and Employment in the Long Run

Some new Keynesian economists argue that a reduction in aggregate demand that causes a recession may affect output and employment even in the long run. They point out that workers who are fired or laid off may lose job skills during their period of unemployment. Consequently, they will have a more difficult time finding new employment later. Furthermore, those who remain unemployed over long periods of time may change their attitudes towards work. They may even have a reduced desire to find employment later on. For these reasons and others, a recession could permanently raise the amount of frictional unemployment.

As yet, little research has been done to quantify this theory.

Macroeconomic Models and Their Implications for Stabilization Policy

Although it is impossible to compare accurately and completely every single detail of the various macroeconomic approaches we have examined, it is useful to summarize and contrast some of their key aspects. Table 18.1 presents features of our five key models: traditional classical, traditional Keynesian, new (modern) classical, new (modern) Keynesian, and modern monetarist. Realize when examining the table that we are painting with a broad brush.

TABLE 18.1

A Comparison of
Macroeconomic Models

Issue	Macroeconomic Model				
	Traditional Classical	Traditional Keynesian	New Classical	New Keynesian	Modern Monetarist
Stability of capitalism	Yes	No	Yes	Yes, but can be enhanced by policy	Yes
Price-wage flexibility	Yes	No	Yes	Yes, but imperfect	Yes, but some restraints
Belief in natural rate of employment hypothesis	Yes	No	Yes	Yes	Yes
Factors sensitive to interest rate	Saving, consumption, investment	Demand for money	Saving, consumption, investment	Saving, consumption, investment	Saving, consumption, investment
View of the velocity of money	Stable	Unstable	No consensus	No consensus	Stable
Effect of changes in money supply on economy	Changes aggregate demand	Changes interest rates, which change investment and real output	No effect on real variables if anticipated	Changes aggregate demand	Directly changes aggregate demand
Effects of fiscal policy on the economy	Not applicable	Multiplier changes in aggregate demand and output	Generally ineffective*	Changes aggregate demand	Ineffective unless money supply changes also
Causes of inflation	Excess money growth	Excess real aggregate demand	Excess money growth	Excess money growth	Excess money growth
Stabilization policy	Unnecessary	Fiscal policy necessary and effective; monetary policy ineffective	Too difficult to conduct	Both fiscal and monetary policy may be useful	Too difficult to conduct

*Some fiscal policies affect relative prices (interest rates) and so many have real effects on economy.

Stabilization Policy and the New Growth Theorists

Recall from Chapter 9 that there is a group of economists who support what is now called new growth theory. In this theory, real wealth creation comes from innovation, which is part of new technology. New growth theorists repeatedly point out that small differences in annual rates of growth over a few decades make a tremendous difference in the standard of living of each individual. Indeed, they argue that short-run monetary and fiscal stabilization policies are in fact beside the point. To them, the Keynesian emphasis on the business cycle appears to be a strange fixation.

If what really matters is the underlying growth rate rather than the business cycle around it, then any efforts to fine-tune the economy are perhaps misguided. Actually, according to the new growth theorists, one of the processes underlying the business cycle is that of discovery and innovation. This process generates long-run improvements in the standard of living. It determines in large part how steep the slope is over a long-run upward trend. The little wiggles—business cycles—take on less importance. The federal government should not be concerned with them.

Does that mean that government policy has no place in our economy? The answer from the new growth theorists is that the government does have a place, but it has little to do with discretionary changes in taxes or spending or monetary growth rates. Rather, it has to do with speeding up the pace of innovation. It also has to do with government's devising policies that promote new technology. One of these policies might be to strengthen patent protection. In any event, the new growth theorists would probably agree with economists who argue in favour of passive nondiscretionary stabilization policy.

In sum, stabilization policy analysis is really about the costs and benefits of getting the economy to where it *eventually* will go anyway—to its long-run aggregate supply curve (*LRAS*). According to the new growth theorists, the costs outweigh the benefits so that short-run stabilization policy should not be the main macroeconomic activity of the federal government. It is economic growth that shifts *LRAS* rightward. Government macroeconomic policy should focus, according to the new growth theorists, solely on this issue.

CONCEPTS IN BRIEF

- Real business cycle theory holds that even if all prices and wages are perfectly flexible, real shocks to the economy (such as technological change and changes in the supplies of factors of production) can cause national business fluctuations.
- Supply-side economics is the notion that creating incentives for individuals and firms will increase productivity, cause the aggregate supply curve to shift outward, and increase tax revenues.
- The new Keynesian economics explains why various features of the economy, such as small-menu costs and wage rates that affect productivity, make it possible for monetary shocks to cause real effects.
- Although there remain significant differences between the classical and Keynesian branches of macroeconomics, the rivalry between them is an important source of innovation that helps improve our understanding of the economy.
- New growth theorists in general reject the effectiveness of short-run discretionary stabilization policies and argue, in contrast, that the federal government should focus its policy efforts on fostering a climate that will generate higher economic growth rates.

New Keynesian Economics, Sticky Prices, and the Internet

You have read about new Keynesian economics in this chapter. You discovered that new Keynesian economists support the supposition that prices are "sticky." One resulting model is the small menu cost theory. It supposes that much of the economy is characterized by imperfect competition because it is costly for firms to change their prices and respond to changes in demand. Today, many economists believe that the Internet will reduce such supposed price stickiness.

Prices change only when the cost of *not* changing them is greater than the expense of adjusting them. We know that there is virtually no stickiness in prices in financial markets—stocks, bonds, foreign currencies, and so on—because the cost of such price stickiness can be dramatic. The same is true for anyone selling perishable goods. If prices are not reduced downward to eliminate excess quantities supplied, financial losses can be quite great. The existence of the Internet will not change these markets much. Before the Internet, we saw quick movements in prices in response to changing supply and demand in these markets.

No so elsewhere. Electronic price tags are relatively costless to change. Thus anything that is sold over the Internet can have its price changed instantaneously at the click of a mouse. A travel agency, for example, selling holiday excursions can alter its vacation package prices digitally without any reprinting. Notice also that comparison shopping has become a major activity on the Internet. Any retailer who does not change prices downward in response to an excess quantity supplied will be driven out of the marketplace very quickly. Comparison shopping on the Internet for hotel rooms, airline tickets, CDs, books, and other commodities should cause prices to be far less sticky than just a few years ago. Thus in a sense, the Internet is making competition more intense. Prices will adjust more quickly, thereby undermining macro models that rely on the assumption of price stickiness.

ISSUES AND APPLICATIONS
The Bank of Canada's High Interest Rate Policy

Concepts Applied: Nominal and real interest rates, unemployment, economic growth

Gordon Thiessen, formerly the Governor of the Bank of Canada, supported the use of relatively high interest rates to dampen inflation and stabilize the economy. Critics claimed his plan kept real interest rates high and encouraged financial rather than productive investment in Canada.

A debate rages among economists about whether the Bank of Canada's interest rate policy is helping or harming the economy. In 1991, the Bank of Canada made a formal commitment to the federal government to keep inflation between 1 and 3 percent through to 1998. The Bank has used high interest rates as its policy tool in pursuit of this goal. High interest rates discourage consumer and business spending, dampen aggregate demand, and thus keep prices from rising.

The former Governor of the Bank of Canada, Gordon Thiessen, asserted that his high interest rate policy allows businesses to make "smarter" decisions since they can plan on a relatively stable price level into the future. This in turn makes Canada more conducive to expanding business activity. Further, low inflation rates contribute to lower nominal interest payments on the federal debt since nominal interest rates are the sum of real rates plus a premium for expected inflation. The combination of low debt service payments and expanding business activity will result in a lower debt-to-GDP ratio. A lower debt-to-GDP ratio makes Canada a more attractive place for investment, which will induce economic growth. Overall, Mr. Thiessen's plan was one of short-term pain—continuing high unemployment—for long-term gain—economic growth which will lead to job creation in the future.

Critics of Mr. Thiessen's plan argued that the Bank of Canada has more than one mandate: the 1934 charter of the Bank also included a directive that it should promote trade, production, and employment in Canada. By following a high interest rate policy, the Bank of Canada has kept real interest rates high. Inflation has indeed been falling, but nominal interest rates are lagging. See Figure 18.14 for a history of real interest rates. High real interest rates, argued the Bank of Canada's critics, encourage passive investment—the purchase of financial instruments in order to earn a hefty return. Low real interest rates encourage active investment—investment in capital equipment and job-creating businesses because the cost of borrowing is low. With active investment the tax base increases, raising government revenues and reducing the need for costly social programs, thus making a reduction of the debt-to-GDP ratio possible.

What should students of economics make of this debate? Is it time to turn from fighting inflation to job creation? The natural rate of unemployment in Canada is thought to be about 8 percent (look back at Figure 18.1). The unemployment rate in 2000 was 6.8 percent, with inflation at about 2.7 percent. Has the natural rate fallen, suggesting that unemployment could be further reduced without risking renewed inflation?

For Critical Analysis

1. What different effects do you think passive and active investment have on the Canadian economy?

2. According to the policy irrelevance proposition, would unemployment have been affected by former Governor Thiessen's high interest rate policy?

FIGURE 18.14 Real Interest Rates Since World War II

Real interest rates in Canada have varied from a low of minus 10 percent just after World War II to a high of about 8 percent in 1980, in the wake of the OPEC oil price hikes. Real interest rates peaked again in the late 1980s.

Source: Statistics Canada, CANSIM Database, Matrix 02560, Series B14020.

CHAPTER SUMMARY

1. The natural rate of unemployment is the rate that exists in long-run equilibrium, when workers' expectations are consistent with actual conditions. Departures from the natural rate of unemployment can occur when individuals are surprised by unanticipated changes in fiscal or monetary policy.

2. The Phillips curve shows a negative relationship between the inflation rate and the unemployment rate that can be observed when there are unanticipated changes in aggregate demand. It was originally believed that the Phillips curve represented a trade-off between inflation and unemployment. In fact, no trade-off exists because workers' expectations adjust to systematic attempts to reduce unemployment below its natural rate.

3. The rational expectations hypothesis assumes that individuals' forecasts incorporate all available information, including an understanding of government policy and its effects on the economy. The new classical economics assumes that the rational expectations hypothesis is valid and also that there is pure competition and that all prices and wages are flexible.

4. The policy irrelevance proposition says that under the assumptions of the new classical model, anticipated monetary policy cannot alter either the rate of unemployment or the level of real GDP. Thus according to the new classical model, policies can alter real economic variables only if the policies are unsystematic and therefore unanticipated; such policies cannot affect output and employment systematically.

5. Real business cycle theory holds that even if all prices and wages are perfectly flexible, real shocks to the economy (such as technological change and changes in the supplies of factors of production) can cause national business fluctuations.

6. Supply-side economics is the notion that creating incentives for individuals and firms will increase productivity, cause the aggregate supply curve to shift outward, and increase tax revenues.

7. The new Keynesian economics explains why various features of the economy, such as small-menu costs and wage rates that affect productivity, make it possible for monetary shocks to cause real effects.

DISCUSSION OF PREVIEW QUESTIONS

1. **Why might the actual unemployment rate depart from the natural rate of unemployment?**

   According to the basic theory of aggregate demand and short- and long-run aggregate supply, an unexpected increase in aggregate demand can cause real GDP to rise in the short run, which results in a reduction in the unemployment rate. Consequently, for a time the actual unemployment rate can fall below the natural rate of unemployment. Likewise, an unanticipated reduction in aggregate demand can push down real GDP in the short run, thereby causing the actual unemployment rate to rise above the natural unemployment rate.

2. **What is the Phillips Curve?**

   An unexpected increase in aggregate demand that causes a drop in the unemployment rate also induces a rise in the equilibrium price level and, consequently, inflation. Thus the basic aggregate demand-aggregate supply model indicates that, other things being equal, there should be an inverse relationship between the inflation rate and the unemployment rate. This downward-sloping relationship is called the Phillips curve, and it implies that there may be a short-run trade-off between inflation and unemployment.

3. **How do expectations affect the actual relationship between the inflation rate and the unemployment rate?**

   Theory only predicts that there will be a Phillips curve relationship when another important factor, expectations, is held unchanged. If people are able to anticipate efforts of policymakers to exploit the Phillips curve trade-off by engaging in inflationary policies to push down the unemployment rate, then basic theory also suggests that input prices such as nominal wages will adjust more rapidly to an increase in the price level. As a result, the Phillips curve will shift outward, and the economy will adjust more speedily toward the natural rate of unemployment. When plotted on a chart, therefore, the actual relationship between the inflation rate and the unemployment rate will not be a smooth, downward-sloping Phillips curve.

4. **What is new classical theory and the implications for economic policymaking?**

A key innovation of the new classical approach was the rational expectations hypothesis. According to this hypothesis, people form expectations of future economic variables, such as inflation, using all available past and current information based on their understanding of how the economy functions. A fundamental implication of the new classical theory is that the only unanticipated actions can induce even short-run changes in real GDP. If people completely anticipate the actions of policymakers, wages and the other input prices adjust immediately, so that real GDP remains unaffected. Thus a key implication of new classical theory is the policy irrelevance proposition, which states that the unemployment rate is unaffected by fully anticipated policy actions.

5. **What are the central features and predictions of real business cycle theory?**

The key emphasis of real business cycle theory is on the importance of technological changes and labour market shocks such as variations in the composition of the labour force as factors that can induce business fluctuations. Therefore, this theory focuses on how shifts in aggregate supply curves can cause real GDP to vary over time.

6. **What is supply-side economics?**

Supply-side economics is the notion that creating incentives by reducing marginal tax rates for individuals and firms will increase productivity, cause the aggregate supply curve to shift outward, and increase tax revenues.

7. **What are the alternative new Keynesian views of business fluctuations?**

New Keynesian approaches to understanding the sources of business fluctuations highlight wage and price stickiness. Small-menu cost theory proposes that imperfectly competitive firms that face costs of adjusting their prices may be slow to change prices in the face of variations in demand, so that real GDP may exhibit greater short-run variability than it otherwise would. Another new Keynesian approach, efficiency wage theory, proposes that worker productivity depends on real wages that workers earn, which dissuades firms from reducing real wages and thereby leads to widespread wage stickiness. Finally, some new Keynesian theorists propose that short-term downturns in economic activity can affect the natural unemployment rate because people who lose their jobs in the short run also lose the opportunities to develop skills while unemployed or may change their attitudes toward work.

PROBLEMS

(Answers to the odd-numbered problems appear at the back of the book.)

18-1. Answer the following questions based on the accompanying graph.

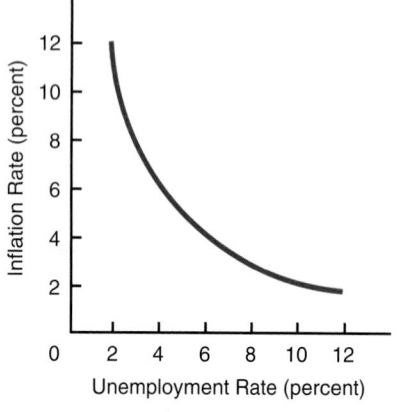

a. If we regard this curve as showing a trade-off between inflation and unemployment, how much unemployment will it "cost" to reduce inflation to 2 percent per year?

b. What might cause this curve to shift upward?

c. Why do economists argue that there is generally no useable trade-off between unemployment and inflation?

18-2. The natural rate of unemployment is a function of a variety of factors, including wage and price rigidities and interferences with labour mobility. Give some examples of such rigidities and interferences.

18-3. How does the existence of contracts, small-menu costs, and efficiency wages affect the amount of discretion available to policymakers?

18-4. Explain how the average duration of unemployment may be different for a given rate of unemployment.

18-5. What effect does the average duration of unemployment have on the rate of unemployment if we hold constant the variables you used to explain Problem 18-4?

18-6. What is meant by an optimal duration of unemployment? What may affect such an optimal duration of unemployment?

18-7. If both employers and workers incorrectly perceive the rate of inflation to the same extent, would the Phillips curve still be expected to be negatively sloped?

18-8. Unemployment is arbitrarily defined. What differences do different definitions have with respect to policy?

ECONOMICS ON THE NET

The Inflation-Unemployment Relationship

Internet URL: http://www.statcan.ca

Title: Economic conditions—inflation and unemployment—Canada

Navigation: Begin at the homepage of Statistics Canada (http://www.statcan.ca). Then click on English, followed by Canadian statistics.

Application: Perform the indicated operations, and answer the following questions:

1. Under The Economy, click on Economic conditions, then Prices, then on Consumer Price Index, 1996 classification, annual average all-items indexes, historical summary. What has the trend been for prices in the last 5 years?

2. Under The Economy, click on Economic conditions, then Labour market, then on Labour force, employment and unemployment. What has the trend been for unemployment in the last five years? Is there an inverse relationship between the unemployment rate and inflation during this time period?

COMPARATIVE ADVANTAGE AND THE OPEN ECONOMY

If you are a consumer of milk, chicken, and eggs, then you are almost certainly consuming Canadian products. You are also almost certainly paying twice the world price for milk, and at least 20 percent more than the world price for the chicken and eggs. Yet, just across the border in the United States, consumers pay prices which are much closer to world prices. Why do Canadians have to pay high prices while Americans do not? In order to understand this issue, you have to know about international trade, comparative advantage, and protectionism.

PREVIEW QUESTIONS

1. Is international trade important to Canada?

2. What is the difference between comparative advantage and absolute advantage?

3. Why can nations gain from specializing in production and engaging in international trade?

4. What is the relationship between imports and exports?

5. What are some arguments against free trade?

6. How can nations restrict foreign trade?

7. What is the ultimate effect of a restriction on imports?

Try Preview Question 1:

Is international trade important to Canada?

Did You Know That... Bombardier Inc.'s Global Express, a long-range, high-speed business jet, is made near Toronto, but many of its parts come from other countries, including Japan, Germany, the United States, and the United Kingdom?

The story of the Global Express is repeated in the automobile industry. Parts from literally all over the world end up in cars that are "made in Canada." The running shoes you buy, the sheets you sleep on, and the clothes you put on your back are often wholly or partly produced outside Canada. Clearly, international trade today affects you whether you are aware of it or not. We are entering an age of a truly global economy. Learning about international trade is simply learning about everyday life.

The Worldwide Importance of International Trade

Look at part (a) of Figure 19.1. Since the end of World War II, world output of goods and services (world gross domestic product, or GDP) has increased almost every year until the present, when it is almost six times what it used to be. Look at the top line in part (a). World trade has increased to almost 13 times what it was in 1950.

Canada figured prominently in this expansion of world trade. In part (b) of Figure 19.1, you see imports and exports expressed as a percentage of total annual yearly income (GDP). While international trade was always important to Canada, with imports plus exports adding up to almost 50 percent of annual national income in 1950, today it accounts for over 85 percent of GDP.

FIGURE 19.1 The Growth of World Trade

In part (a), you can see the growth in world trade in relative terms because we use an index of 100 to represent real world trade in 1950. By the early 2000s, that index had increased to over 1,700. At the same time, the index of world GDP (annual world income) had gone up to only around 700. World trade is clearly on the rise: Both imports and exports, ex-

pressed as a percentage of annual national income (GDP) in part (b), have been rising.

Sources: Part (a) Steven Husted and Michael Melvin, *International Economics, 3d ed.* (New York: HarperCollins, 1995), p. 11, used with permission; World Trade Organization; Federal Reserve System; U.S. Department of Commerce; Part (b) Statistics Canada <www.statcan.ca/english/Pgdb/Economy/Economic/econ05.htm>, accessed on March 10, 2001.

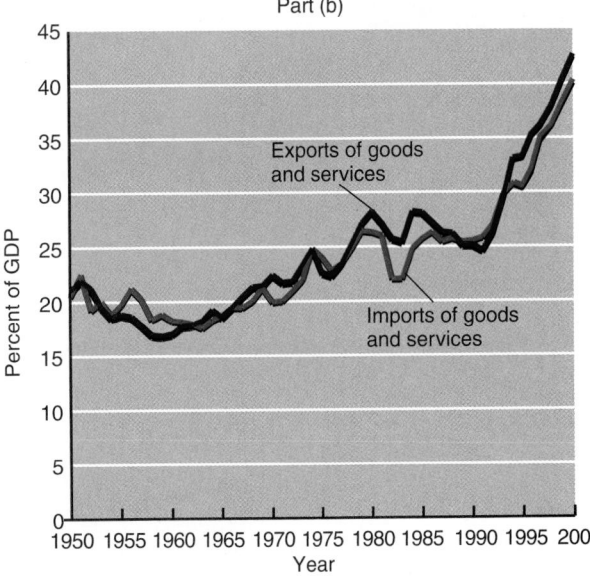

INTERNATIONAL EXAMPLE 19-1

The Importance of International Trade in Various Countries

While imports and exports each account for more than 30 percent of total annual national income in Canada, in some countries the figure is much higher. In others it is much less, as you can see in Table 19.1. Another way to understand the worldwide importance of international trade is to look at trade flows on the world map in Figure 19.2.

TABLE 19.1
Importance of Imports in Selected Countries

Country	Imports as a Percentage of Annual National Income
Luxembourg	95.0
Netherlands	58.0
Canada	35.0
Norway	30.0
Germany	23.0
United Kingdom	21.0
China	19.0
France	18.4
United States	12.8
Japan	6.8

Source: International Monetary Fund.

FIGURE 19.2 World Trade Flows

International merchandise trade amounts to over US$3 trillion worldwide. The percentage figures show the proportion of trade flowing in the various directions.

Source: World Trade Organization (data are for 2000).

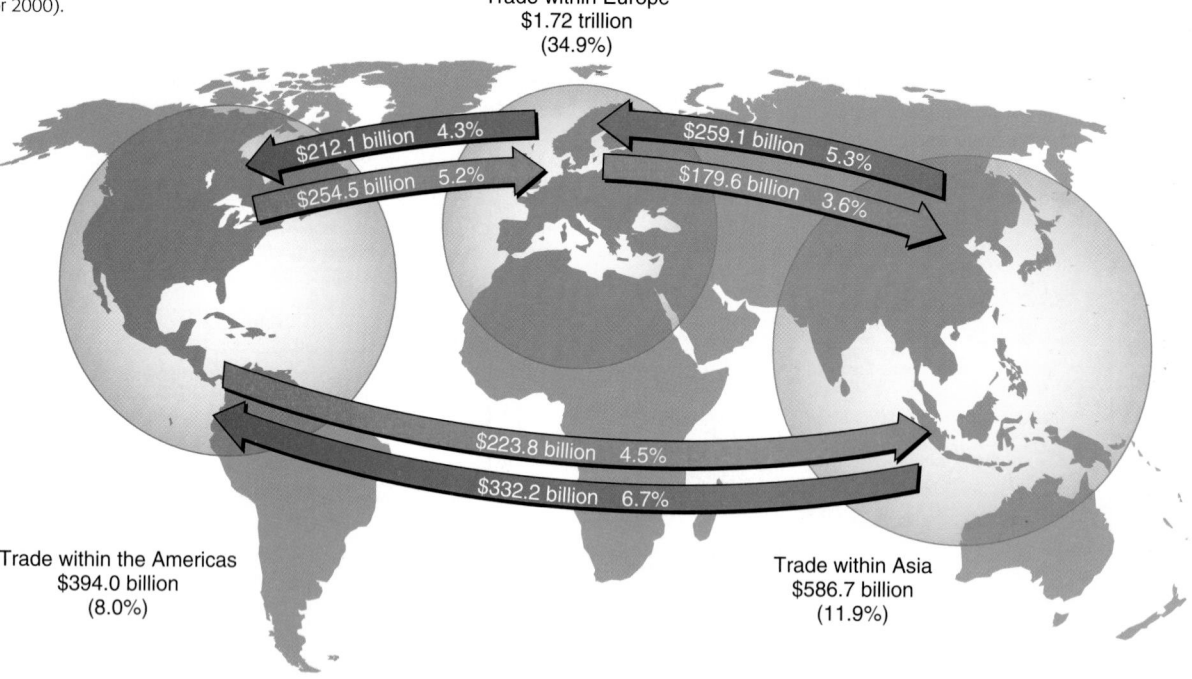

Trade within Europe
$1.72 trillion
(34.9%)

$212.1 billion   4.3%
$254.5 billion   5.2%

$259.1 billion   5.3%
$179.6 billion   3.6%

$223.8 billion   4.5%
$332.2 billion   6.7%

Trade within the Americas
$394.0 billion
(8.0%)

Trade within Asia
$586.7 billion
(11.9%)

For critical analysis: The yearly volume of imports in Hong Kong is almost twice Hong Kong's total national income. How is that possible? (Hint: Is there another reason to import a good besides wanting to consume it?)

The pattern of Canada's merchandise trade in goods with the rest of the world is shown in the 2000 data in Figure 19-3. There it can be seen that the United States is far and away both Canada's largest customer at $359.6 millions representing 86.1 percent of total exports, and the largest source of imports at $267.6 millions representing 73.7 percent of total imports. Canada's next largest trading partners are the European Union and Japan.

The composition of Canadian merchandise exports and imports by type is shown in Figure 19-4. Imports of manufactured goods—machinery and equipment, automotive products, and industrial and agricultural machinery—make up about 55 percent of imports. On the export side, manufactured goods—automotive products and machinery

**FIGURE 19.3
Canadian
Merchandise
Trade by
Geographic Area,
2000**

Source: Based on information from Statistics Canada Web site <www.statcan.ca/english/Pgdb/Economy/International/gblec02a.htm>, accessed on February 28, 2001.

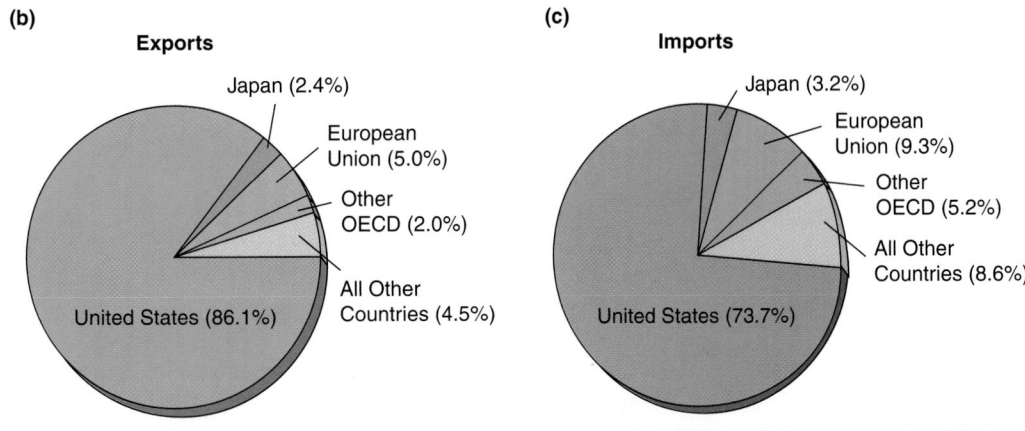

FIGURE 19.4 Distribution of Merchandise Exports and Imports for Canada by Broad Commodity Groups, 2000

Source: Based on information from Statistics Canada Web site <www.statcan.ca/english/Pgdb/Economy/International/gblec04.htm> and <www.statcan.ca/english/Pgdb/Economy/Economic/econ05.htm>, accessed on February 28, 2001.

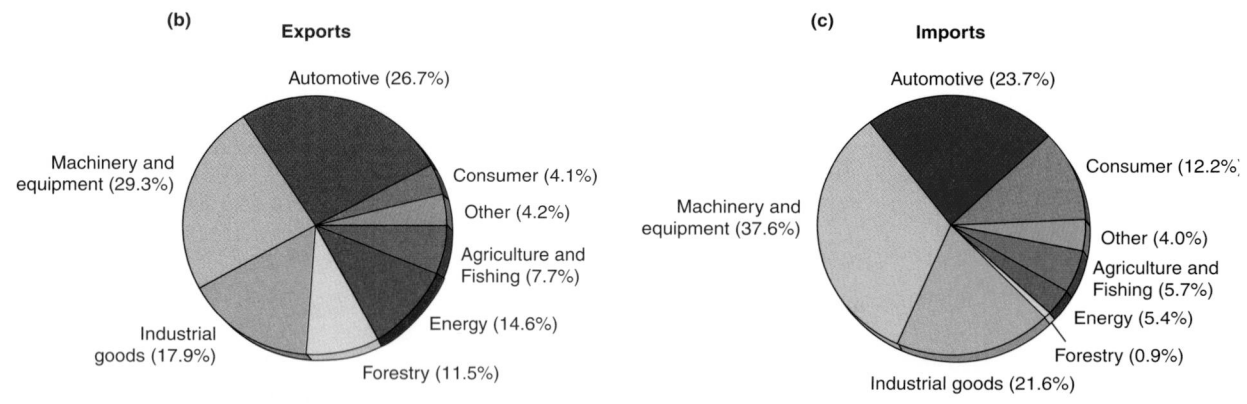

and equipment—account for about 44 percent of all exports. About 45 percent of exports are made up of industrial goods, and forestry, energy, agricultural, and fishing products.

The preceding discussion focused on Canada's merchandise trade in goods. Canada also trades in services—non-merchandise trade—such as insurance services, banking services, consulting services, and so forth. In 2000, Canada imported $62.8 millions and exported $56.2 millions in services.

Why We Trade: Comparative Advantage and Exhausting Mutual Gains from Exchange

You have already been introduced to the concepts of specialization and mutual gains from trade in Chapter 2. These ideas are worth repeating because they are essential to understanding why the world is better off because of more international trade. The best way to understand the gains from trade among nations is first to understand the output gains from specialization between individuals.

The Output Gains from Specialization

Suppose that a creative advertising specialist can generate two pages of ad copy (written words) or one computerized art rendering per hour. At the same time, a computer artist can write one page of ad copy or complete one computerized art rendering per hour. Here the ad specialist can come up with more pages of ad copy per hour than the computer specialist, and seemingly is just as good as the computer specialist at computerized art renderings. Is there any reason for the creative specialist and the computer specialist to "trade"? The answer is yes, because such trading will lead to higher output.

Consider the scenario of no trading. Assume that during each eight-hour day, the ad specialist and the computer whiz devote half of their day to writing ad copy and half to computerized art rendering. The ad specialist would create eight pages of ad copy (4 hours × 2) and four computerized art renderings (4 × 1). During that same period, the computer specialist would create four pages of ad copy (4 × 1) and four computerized art renderings (4 × 1). Each day, the combined output for the ad specialist and the computer specialist would be 12 pages of ad copy and eight computerized art renderings.

If the ad specialist specialized only in writing ad copy and the computer artist specialized only in creating computerized art renderings, their combined output would rise to 16 pages of ad copy (8 × 2) and eight computerized art renderings (8 × 1). Overall, production would increase by four pages of ad copy per day.

The creative advertising employee has a comparative advantage in writing ad copy, and the computer specialist has a comparative advantage in doing computerized art renderings. **Comparative advantage** involves the ability to produce something at a lower opportunity cost compared to other producers, as we pointed out in Chapter 2.

Comparative advantage The ability to produce a good or service at a lower opportunity cost compared to other producers.

Specialization Among Nations

To demonstrate the concept of comparative advantage for nations, let's take the example of France and Canada. In Table 19.2, we show the comparative costs of production of wine and beer in terms of worker-days. This is a simple two-country, two-commodity world in which we assume that labour is the only factor of production. As you can see from the table, in Canada, it takes one worker-day to produce 1 litre of wine, and the same is true for 1 litre of beer. In France, it takes one worker-day to produce 1 litre of wine but two worker-days for 1 litre of beer. In this sense, Canadians appear to be just as good at producing wine as the French and actually have an **absolute advantage** in producing beer.

Absolute advantage The ability to produce more output from given inputs of resources than other producers can.

TABLE 19.2
Comparative Costs of Production

Product	Canada	France
Wine (1 litre)	1 worker-day	1 worker-day
Beer (1 litre)	1 worker-day	2 worker-days

Trade will still take place, however, which may seem paradoxical. How can trade take place if Canada is able to produce both goods at least as cheaply as the French can? Why don't we just produce both ourselves? To understand why, let's assume first that there is no trade and no specialization and that the workforce in each country consists of 200 workers. These 200 workers are divided equally in the production of wine and beer. We see in Table 19.3 that 100 litres of wine and 100 litres of beer are produced per day in Canada. In France, 100 litres of wine and 50 litres of beer are produced per day. The total daily world production in our two-country world is 200 litres of wine and 150 litres of beer.

TABLE 19.3

Daily World Output Before Specialization

It is assumed that 200 workers are available in each country.

Product	Canada Workers	Canada Output (litres)	France Workers	France Output (litres)	World Output (litres)
Wine	100	100	100	100	200
Beer	100	100	100	50	150

Now the countries specialize. What can France produce more cheaply? Look at the comparative costs of production expressed in worker-days in Table 19.2. What is the cost of producing 1 litre more of wine? One worker-day. What is the cost of producing 1 litre more of beer? Two worker-days. We can say, then, that in France the opportunity cost of producing wine is less than that of producing beer. France will specialize in the activity that has the lower opportunity cost. In other words, France will specialize in its comparative advantage, which is the production of wine.

Try Preview Question 2:

What is the difference between comparative advantage and absolute advantage?

TABLE 19.4

Daily World Output After Specialization

It is assumed that 200 workers are available in each country.

Product	Canada Workers	Canada Output (litres)	France Workers	France Output (litres)	World Output (litres)
Wine	—	—	200	200	200
Beer	200	200	—	—	200

According to Table 19.4, after specialization, Canada produces 200 litres of beer and France produces 200 litres of wine. Notice that the total world production per day has gone up from 200 litres of wine and 150 litres of beer to 200 litres of wine and 200 litres of beer per day. This was done without any increased use of resources. The gain, 50 "free" litres of beer, results from a more efficient allocation of resources worldwide. World output is greater when countries specialize in producing the goods in which they have a comparative advantage and then engage in foreign trade. Another way of looking at this is to consider the choice between two ways of producing a good. Obviously, each country would choose the less costly production process. One way of "producing" a good is to import it, so if in fact the imported good is cheaper than the domestically produced good, we will "produce" it by importing it.

Gains from Trade

Trade is the means by which consumers in these two countries can consume both wine and beer.

Because 1 beer = 1 wine in Canada, if trade is to occur, Canada would expect to get more than 1 wine for every beer it sells; otherwise why specialize and engage in trade?

Similarly, because 1 wine = 0.5 beer in France, France would expect to get more than 0.5 beer for every wine.

Suppose the terms of trade falls somewhere in between these two cost conditions, say 1 wine = 0.75 beer (alternatively 1 beer = 1.33 wine) and 100 wine is exchanged for 75 beer. The gains from trade after specialization based upon comparative advantage in this situation are 25 beer for Canada and 25 beer for France. This equals the overall gain in global output of 50 beer. This result is shown in Table 19-5.

TABLE 19-5

International Specialization Based on Comparative Advantage and the Gains from Trade

Country	(1) Outputs before Specialization	(2) Outputs after Specialization	(3) Trade Exports (−) Imports (+)	(4) Outputs after Trade	(5) = (4) − (1) Gains from Specialization and Trade
Canada					
Wine	100	0	+100	100	0
Beer	100	200	−75	75	+25
France					
Wine	100	200	−100	100	0
Beer	50	0	+75	75	+25

How the overall gains from international specialization and trade are divided will depend on the actual terms of trade or exchange ratio. This ratio will be determined by world supply and demand conditions.

Not everybody, of course, is better off when free trade occurs. In our example, Canadian wine makers and French beer makers are worse off because those two *domestic* industries have disappeared. Beer customers in the importing country, France, get lower-priced beer and more beer. In Canada, which has comparative advantage in beer production, customers will get more beer but they will be paying more, the world price, for that beer.

Some people are worried that Canada (or any other country, for that matter) might someday "run out of exports" because of overaggressive foreign competition. The analysis of comparative advantage tells us the opposite. No matter how much other countries compete for our business, Canada (or any other country) will always have a comparative advantage in something that it can export. In 10 or 20 years, that something may not be what we export today, but it will be exportable nonetheless because we will have a comparative advantage in producing it.

As a result of specialization based on comparative advantage and trade, countries benefit. The effect of such specialization is to improve global efficiencies and to move the respective possibilities curves outward.

Try Preview Question 3:

Why can nations gain from specializing in production and engaging in international trade?

Other Benefits from International Trade: The Transmission of Ideas

Beyond the fact that comparative advantage generally results in an overall increase in the output of goods produced and consumed, there is another benefit to internationa trade—the international transmission of ideas. According to economic historiar international trade has been the principal means by which new goods, services, a processes have spread around the world. For example, coffee was initially grown in Ar near the Red Sea. Around 675 AD, it began to be roasted and consumed as a beve Eventually, it was exported to other parts of the world, and the Dutch started cultiv it in their colonies during the seventeenth century and the French in the eigh

century. The lowly potato is native to the Peruvian Andes. In the sixteenth
was brought to Europe by Spanish explorers. Thereafter, its cultivation and c
tion spread rapidly. The alphabet was spread through international trade, as d.
in International Example 19-2.

All of the *intellectual property* that has been introduced throughout the world is
sult of international trade. This includes new music, such as rock and roll in the 1950s
hip-hop and grunge in the 1990s. It includes the software applications that are commc
for computer users everywhere.

New processes have been transmitted through international trade. One of those involves the Japanese manufacturing innovation which emphasized redesigning the system rather than running the existing system in the best possible way. Inventories were
reduced to just-in-time levels by re-engineering machine setup methods. Just-in-time
inventory control is now common in Canadian factories.

**INTERNATIONAL
EXAMPLE 19-2**

International Trade and the Alphabet

Even the alphabetic system of writing that appears to be the source of most alphabets
in the world today was spread through international trade. According to some schol-
ars, the Phoenicians, who lived on the long, narrow strip of Mediterranean coast north of Israel
from the ninth century B.C. to around 300 B.C., created the first true alphabet. Presumably, they developed the alphabet to keep international trading records on their ships rather than having to take
along highly trained scribes.

For critical analysis: Before alphabets were used, how might have people communicated in written form?

The Relationship Between Imports and Exports

The basic proposition in understanding all of international trade is this:

> In the long run, imports are paid for by exports.[1]

The reason that imports are ultimately paid for by exports is that foreigners want something in exchange for the goods that are shipped to Canada. For the most part, they
want goods made in Canada. From this truism comes a remarkable corollary:

> Any restriction of imports ultimately reduces exports.

This is a shocking revelation to many people who want to restrict foreign competition in order to protect domestic jobs. Although it is possible to protect certain Canadian
jobs by restricting foreign competition, it is impossible to make *everyone* better off by
imposing import restrictions. Why? Because ultimately such restrictions lead to a reduction in employment in the export industries of the nation.

Think of exports as simply another way of producing goods. International trade is
merely an economic activity like all others; it is a production process that transforms exports into imports.

Try Preview Question 4:

What is the relationship between imports
and exports?

---

[1] We have to modify this rule by adding that in the short run, imports can also be paid for by the sale (or export) of real and financial assets, such as land, stocks, and bonds, or through an extension of credit from other
countries.

INTERNATIONAL EXAMPLE 19-3	The Importation of Priests into Spain

Imports affect not only goods but also services and the movement of labour. In Spain, some 3,000 priests retire each year, but barely 250 young men are ordained to replace them. Over 70 percent of the priests in Spain are now over the age of 50. The Spanish church estimates that by 2005, the number of priests will have fallen to half the 20,441 who were active in Spain in 1990. The Spanish church has had to seek young seminarians from Latin America under what it calls "Operation Moses." It is currently subsidizing the travel and training of an increasing number of young Latin Americans to take over where native Spaniards have been before.

For critical analysis: How might the Spanish church induce more native Spaniards to become priests?

Thinking Critically About the Media 19-1 | Foreigners' Productivity

With so much emphasis on Canada's competitiveness in the global economy, the media fail to understand a basic tenet: International trade is not a zero-sum game. If other countries in the world increase their productivity faster than Canada, so be it. A more productive Germany will of course have more products to sell in Canada. At the same time, though, Germany will represent a bigger market for Canada's exports. In other words, a successful European economy can become successful without that success being at our expense. In fact, such successful economies are likely to help us by providing us with larger markets (and by selling us their own goods of higher quality at lower prices).

International Competitiveness

"Canada is falling behind." "We need to stay competitive internationally." These and similar statements are often heard in government circles when the subject of international trade comes up. There are two problems with this issue. The first has to do with a simple definition. What does "global competitiveness" really mean? When one company competes against another, it is in competition. Is Canada like one big corporation, in competition with other countries? Certainly not. The standard of living in each country is almost solely a function of how well the economy functions within that *country*, not how it functions relative to other countries.

Another problem arises with respect to the real world. According to the International Institute for Management Development in Lausanne, Switzerland, Canada has been *improving* its world competitive position. In 1994, Canada was ranked 20th in the world; by 1997, Canada was ranked 10th. According to the report, Canada's improved ranking is due to better government, improving technology and a highly productive labour force. Other factors include Canada's sophisticated financial system and better management of the private sector.

> ## CONCEPTS IN BRIEF
>
> - Countries can be better off materially if they specialize in producing goods for which they have a comparative advantage.
> - It is important to distinguish between absolute and comparative advantage; the former refers to the ability to produce a unit of output with fewer physical units of input; the latter refers to producing output that has the lowest opportunity cost for a nation.
> - Different nations will always have different comparative advantages because of differing opportunity costs due to different resource mixes.

Arguments Against Free Trade

Numerous arguments are raised against free trade. They mainly point out the costs of trade; they do not consider the benefits, or the possible alternatives for reducing the costs of free trade while still reaping benefits.

The Infant Industry Argument

A country may feel that if a particular industry were allowed to develop domestically, it could eventually become efficient enough to compete effectively in the world market. Therefore, if some restrictions were placed on imports, domestic producers would be given the time needed to develop their efficiency to the point where they would be able to compete in the domestic market without any restrictions on imports. In graphic terminology, we would expect that if the protected industry truly does experience improvements in production techniques or technological breakthroughs towards greater efficiency in the future, the supply curve will shift outward to the right so that the domestic industry can produce larger quantities at each and every price. This **infant industry argument** has some merit in the short run and has been used to protect a number of industries in their infancy around the world. Such a policy can be abused, however. Often the protective import-restricting arrangements remain even after the infant has matured. If other countries can still produce more cheaply, the people who benefit from this type of situation are obviously the shareholders (and specialized factors of production that will earn economic rents) in the industry that is still being protected from world competition. The people who lose out are the consumers, who must pay a price higher than the world price for the product in question. In any event, it is very difficult to know beforehand which industries will eventually survive. In other words, we cannot predict very well the specific infant industries that should be protected. Note that when we talk about which industry "should be" protected, we are in the realm of normative economics. We are making a value judgment, a subjective statement of what *ought to be*.

Infant industry argument The contention that tariffs should be imposed to protect from import competition an industry that is trying to get started. Presumably, after the industry becomes technologically efficient, the tariff can be lifted.

Countering Foreign Subsidies and Dumping

Another strong argument against unrestricted foreign trade concerns countering other nations' subsidies to their own producers. When a foreign government subsidizes its producers, our producers claim that they cannot compete fairly with these subsidized foreigners. To the extent that such subsidies fluctuate, it can be argued that unrestricted free trade will seriously disrupt domestic producers. They will not know when foreign governments are going to subsidize their producers and when they are not. Our competing industries will be expanding and contracting too frequently.

The phenomenon called *dumping* is also used as an argument against unrestricted trade. **Dumping** occurs when a producer sells its products abroad at a price below its cost of production or below the price that is charged in the home market (see Example

Dumping Selling a good or a service abroad at a price below its cost of production or below the price charged in the home market.

1901 and International Policy Example 19-1). Although cries of dumping are often heard against foreign producers, they typically occur only when the foreign nation is in the throes of a serious recession. The foreign producer does not want to slow down its production at home. Because it anticipates an end to the recession and doesn't want to hold large inventories, it dumps its products abroad at prices below its costs. This does, in fact, disrupt international trade. It also creates instability in domestic production and therefore may impair commercial well-being at home.

EXAMPLE 19-1   Dumping Chinese Garlic

In 1996, Canadian garlic growers complained to the Canadian International Trade Tribunal (CITT) that, between 1992 and 1996, growers from mainland China had been dumping fresh garlic on the Canadian market, thus suppressing price and causing profits to decline. The domestic producers claimed that over this period Canadian demand for garlic had increased by 8 million kilograms, and at the same time the market share filled by Chinese garlic had grown from 29 percent to 68 percent.

The CITT investigated the garlic growers' complaint. It determined that the "normal" price of garlic in China, that is the price which reflects the producers' costs, would be $1.91 per kilogram. (Since China does not have a free market in garlic, the CITT determined this price by looking at prices in other garlic-growing countries such as Mexico.) However, Chinese garlic was selling in Canada for 58 cents per kilogram, a price reduction of 70 percent.

The CITT concluded that Chinese garlic growers had dumped 6 million kilograms of garlic on the Canadian market between 1992 and 1996. As a result, importers of Chinese garlic must pay a countervailing duty sufficient to bring its selling price to $1.91 per kilogram, in line with Canadian prices.

For critical analysis: Since consumers benefit from the low prices of dumping, why might they be in favour of countervailing duties?

INTERNATIONAL POLICY EXAMPLE 19-1   Who's Dumping on Whom?

Claims of dumping are handled on a case-by-case basis under international rules. Only a few firms in an industry have to lodge a claim to justify a dumping investigation. Under international law, antidumping rules permit governments to impose *duties*—special taxes on imported goods—on the products sold by firms of offending nations. Take a look at Figure 19-5. As you can see, in the early 1990s, developed nations filed an increasing number of claims seeking antidumping relief. The biggest filer of dumping claims during this period was the United States, which launched cases mainly against companies based in South America and Asia. The United States began to cut back on dumping claims beginning in the mid-1990s. Nevertheless, dumping claims by emerging economies—notably Argentina, Brazil, Mexico, and South Africa—rose precipitously. Whom did these emerging economies accuse of dumping? Firms in the United States, of course.

FIGURE 19.5 Claims to the World Trade Organization for Antidumping Relief

In recent years, developing nations have filed at least as many claims seeking antidumping relief as the number filed by developed nations.

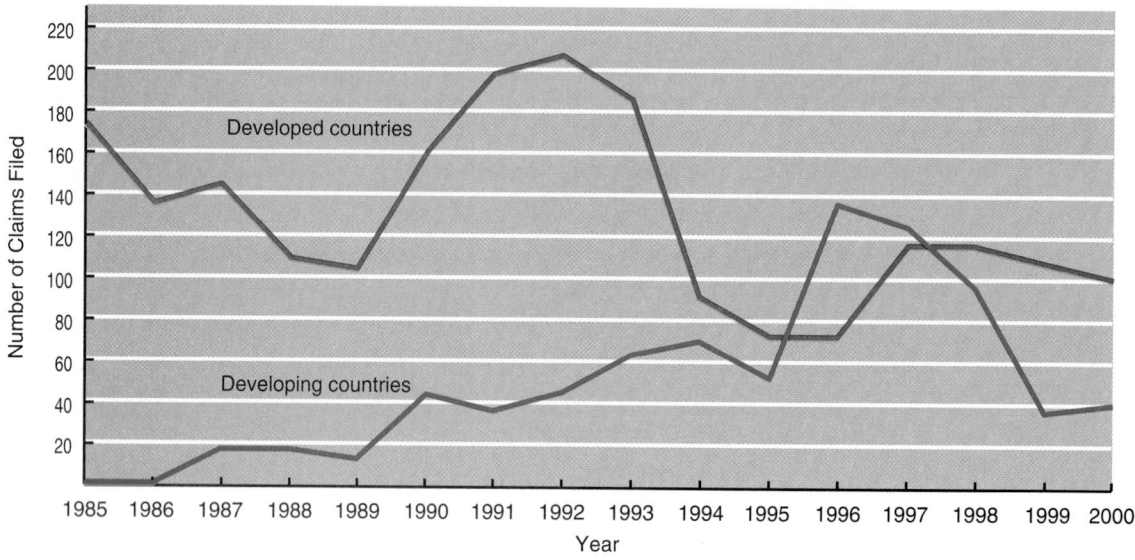

Source: World Trade Organization.

For critical analysis: Why did dumping claims by emerging nations fall as their economies expanded after the early 1990s?

Protecting Canadian Jobs

Perhaps the argument used most often against free trade is that unrestrained competition from other countries will eliminate Canadian jobs because other countries have lower-cost labour than we do. (Less restrictive environmental standards in other countries might also lower their costs relative to ours.) This is a compelling argument, particularly for politicians from areas that might be threatened by foreign competition. For example, a Member of Parliament from an area with shoe factories would certainly be upset about the possibility of constituents' losing their jobs because of competition from lower-priced shoe manufacturers in Brazil and Italy. But of course this argument against free trade is equally applicable to trade between the provinces.

Economists David Gould, G. L. Woodbridge, and Roy Ruffin examined the data on the relationship between increases in imports and the rate of unemployment. Their conclusion was that there is no causal link between the two. Indeed, in half the cases they studied, when imports increased, unemployment fell.

Another issue has to do with the cost of protecting Canadian jobs by restricting international trade. Several years ago, the North-South Institute examined the cost of protection in the Canadian textile and clothing industries. It found that consumers were paying about $36,000 per year in taxes and higher prices to protect each textile and clothing industry job which at the time paid about $10,000 per year to the average worker.

In the long run, the industries that have had the most protection—textiles, clothing, and iron and steel—have seen the most dramatic reductions in employment in Canada.

Try Preview Question 5:

What are some arguments against free trade?

CONCEPTS IN BRIEF

- The infant industry argument against free trade contends that new industries should be protected against world competition so that they can become technologically efficient in the long run.
- Unrestricted foreign trade may allow foreign governments to subsidize exports or foreign producers to engage in dumping—selling products in other countries below their cost of production. To the extent that foreign export subsidies and dumping create more instability in domestic production, they may impair our well-being.

Ways to Restrict Foreign Trade

There are many ways in which international trade can be stopped or at least stifled. These include quotas and taxes (the latter are usually called *tariffs* when applied to internationally traded items). Let's talk first about quotas.

Quotas

Quota system A government-imposed restriction on the quantity of a specific good that another country is allowed to sell in Canada. In other words, quotas are restrictions on imports. These restrictions are usually applied to one or several specific countries.

Under the **quota system**, individual countries or groups of foreign producers are restricted to a certain amount of trade. An import quota specifies the maximum amount of a commodity that may be imported during a specified period of time. For example, the government might not allow more than 50 million barrels of foreign crude oil to enter Canada in a particular year.

Consider the example of quotas on textiles. Figure 19.6 presents the demand and the supply curves for imported textiles. In an unrestricted import market, the equilibrium quantity imported is 90 million metres at a price of $1 per metre (expressed in constant-quality units). When an import quota is imposed, the supply curve is no longer S. Rather, the supply curve becomes vertical at some amount less than the equilibrium quantity—here, 80 million metres per year. The price to the Canadian consumer increases from $1.00 to $1.50. The domestic suppliers of textiles obviously benefit by an increase in revenues because they can now charge a higher price.

Voluntary export restraint agreement (VER) An official agreement with another country that "voluntarily" restricts the quantity of its exports to Canada.

VOLUNTARY QUOTAS. Quotas do not have to be explicit and defined by law. They can be "voluntary." Such a quota is called a **voluntary export restraint agreement (VER).** In the early 1980s, the Canadian government asked Japan voluntarily to restrain its automobile

FIGURE 19.6 The Effect of Quotas on Textile Imports

Without restrictions, 90 million metres of textiles would be imported each year into Canada at the world price of $1.00 per metre. If the federal government imposes a quota of only 80 million metres, the effective supply curve becomes vertical at that quantity. It intersects the demand curve at the new equilibrium price of $1.50 per metre.

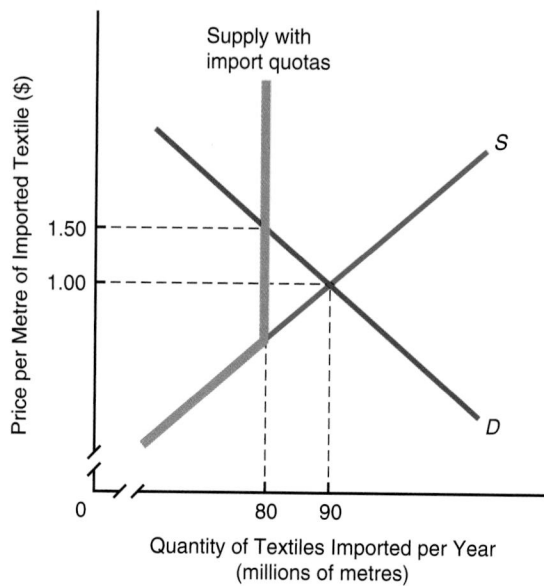

exports to Canada for a period of three years. The Japanese government did so, and even now continues to limit its automobile exports to the west.

Tariffs

We can analyse tariffs by using standard supply and demand diagrams. Let's use as our example computer software, some of which is made in the United States and some of which is made domestically. In part (a) of Figure 19.7, you see the demand and supply of US software. The equilibrium price is $100 per constant-quality unit, and the equilibrium quantity is 10 million per year. In part (b), you see the same equilibrium price of $100, and the *domestic* equilibrium quantity is 5 million units per year.

Now a tariff of $50 is imposed on all imported American software. The supply curve shifts upward by $50 to S_2. For purchasers of American software, the price increases to $125. The quantity demanded falls to 8 million per year. In part (b), you see that at the higher price of imported American software, the demand curve for Canadian-made software shifts outward to the right to D_2. The equilibrium price increases to $125, and the equilibrium quantity increases to 6.5 million units per year. So the tariff benefits domestic software producers because it increases the demand for their products due to the higher price of a close substitute, American software. This causes a redistribution of income from Canadian consumers of software to Canadian producers of software.

TARIFFS IN CANADA. In Figure 19.8 we see that tariffs on all imported goods have varied widely, but in general have been falling since the mid-1930s. The highest rates since Confederation occurred as part of Sir John A. Macdonald's National Policy of 1879.

CURRENT TARIFF LAWS. Canada has always depended to a large extent on trade, first with England and now with the United States. About one in three jobs in Canada depends on our exports; about 11,000 jobs are either created or sustained by each $1 billion in new exports.

Try Preview Question 6:
How can nations restrict foreign trade?

Try Preview Question 7:
What is the ultimate effect of a restriction on imports?

FIGURE 19.7 The Effect of a Tariff on American-made Computer Software

Without a tariff, Canada buys units of American software per year at an average price of $100, as shown in part (a). Canadian producers sell 5 million units of domestically made software, also at $100 each, as shown in part (b). A $50-per-unit tariff will shift the American import sup- ply curve to S_2 in part (a), so that the new equilibrium is at E_2, with price $125 and quantity sold reduced to 8 million per year. The de- mand curve for Canadian-made software (for which there is no tariff) shifts to D_2 in part (b). Sales increase to 6.5 million per year.

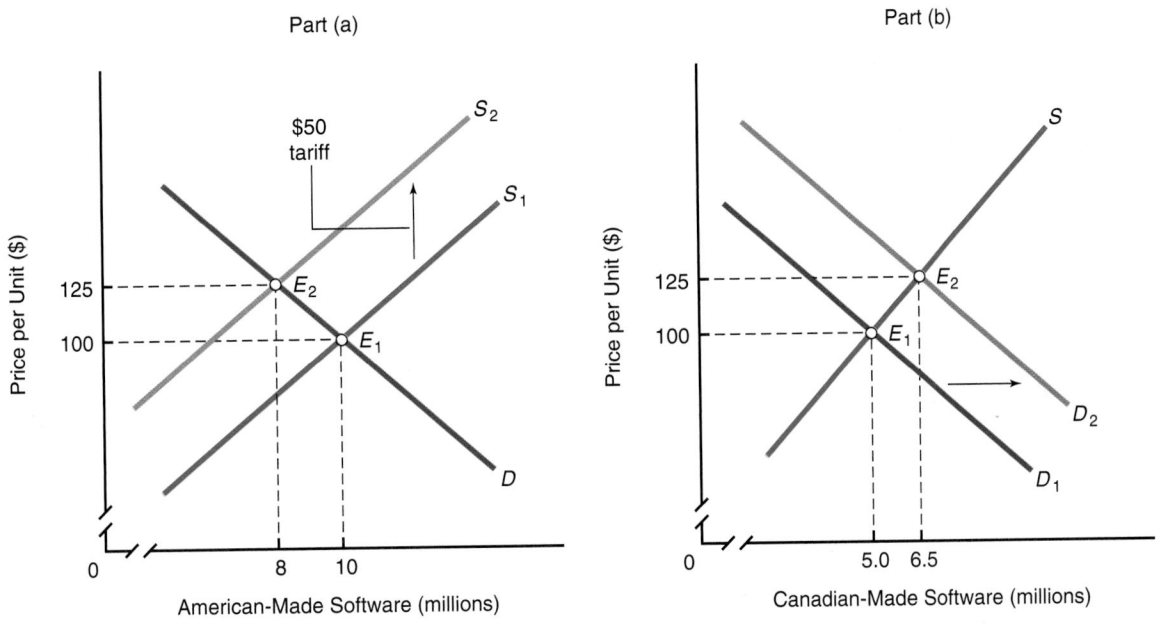

Part (a)

Part (b)

Not surprisingly, the federal government in recent years has emphasized the impor- tance of expanded trade for Canada. In 1985, Canada signed a free trade agreement with the United States; in 1994, Canada and the United States included Mexico in the **North American Free Trade Agreement (NAFTA)**. This remains Canada's most significant trade agreement, covering more than 80 percent of our exports. In 1997, Canada signed a separate free trade agreement with Chile.

Canada was also a signatory of the **General Agreement on Tariffs and Trade (GATT)** which was signed in 1947. The 127 member nations of GATT account for more than 85 percent of world trade. As you can see in Figure 19.8, there have been a number of rounds of negotiations to reduce tariffs since the early 1960s. The latest round was called the "Uruguay Round" because that is where the initial meetings were held.

The World Trade Organization (WTO)

The Uruguay Round of the General Agreement on Tariffs and Trade (GATT) was rat- ified by 117 nations at the end of 1993. A year later the entire treaty was ratified. As of January 1, 1995, the new **World Trade Organization (WTO)** replaced GATT.

The ratification of GATT will result in a cut of roughly 40 percent in tariffs world- wide. Agricultural subsidies will be reduced and perhaps eventually eliminated. Protection for patents will be extended worldwide. The WTO will have arbitration boards to settle international disputes over trade issues. No country has a veto. A country that loses a WTO ruling has to comply or face trade sanctions by the country that wins arbitration.

In short, the passage of GATT and the creation of the WTO constitute the fur- thest-reaching global trade agreement in history. Advanced technologies in particular

North American Free Trade Agreement (NAFTA) A free trade agreement between Canada, the United States, and Mexico, which covers about 80 percent of our exports.

General Agreement on Tariffs and Trade (GATT) An international agreement established in 1947 to further world trade by reducing barriers and tariffs.

World Trade Organization (WTO) The successor organization to GATT, it handles all trade disputes among its 117 member nations.

will benefit from the worldwide extension of the protection of patents. Copyrights on books and recordings will be protected from piracy better than ever before. Protectionist rules, such as "local content" requirements that force foreign firms to use locally produced inputs, will be eliminated. Also, other countries will have to treat Canadian service suppliers no less favourably than they treat their own service suppliers.

FIGURE 19.8 Tariff Rates in Canada Since 1867

Tariff rates in Canada have varied widely; indeed, in Parliament, tariffs are a political football. Import-competing industries prefer high tariffs. In the twentieth century, the highest single tariff we had was the Bennett Retaliatory Tariff (1933), which was imposed in retaliation against the United States' Smoot-Hawley Tariff of 1930.

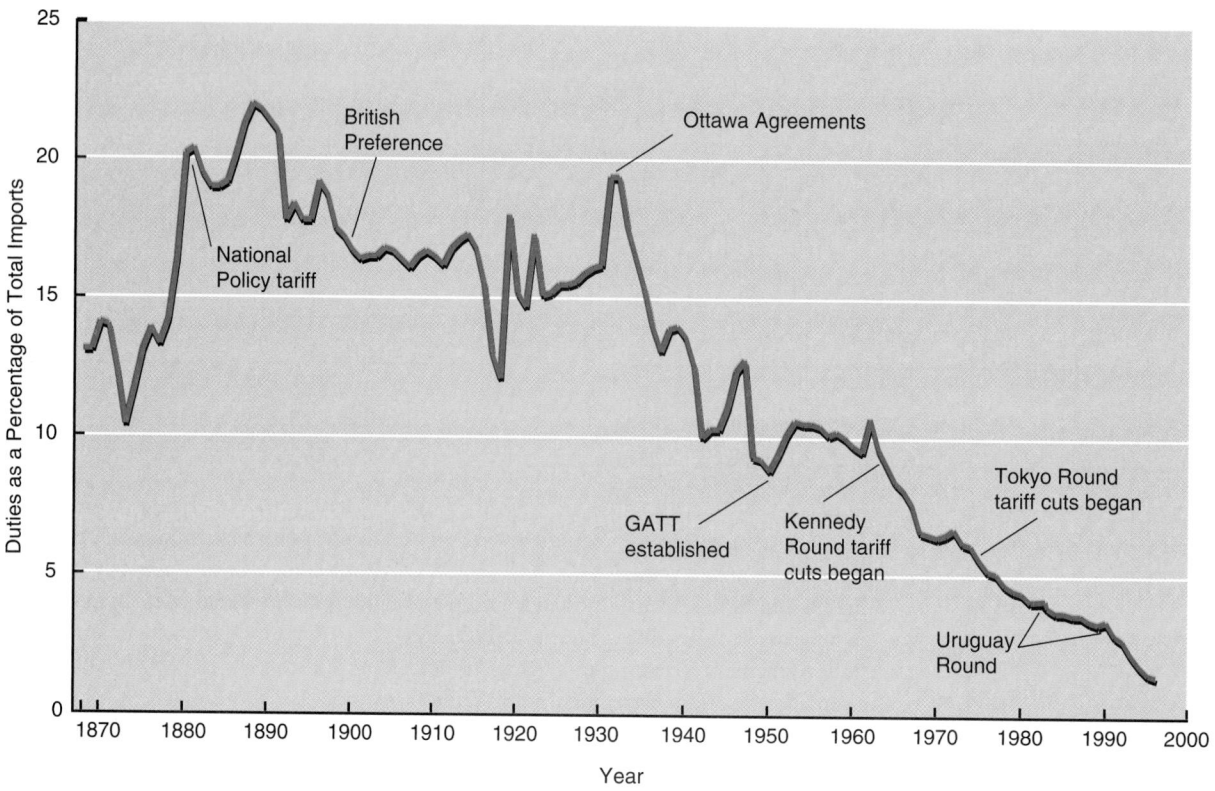

Source: Statistics Canada, *Historical Statistics of Canada,* Series G485 and Stat Can: CANSIM Disc, March 1999.

POLICY EXAMPLE 19-1   Should Culture Be Excluded from Free Trade Agreements?

For the past 60 years, Canada has aggressively protected its magazine industry by placing tariffs on imported American magazines, by not allowing foreign-controlled magazines produced in Canada to claim advertising as a tax-deductible cost, and by giving postal subsidies to all-Canadian magazines. The federal government went further in 1995, putting an 80 percent tariff on "split-run" editions of magazines such as *Time* and *Sports Illustrated*—those magazines with American content financed by Canadian advertising. The federal government was trying to direct Canadian advertising revenue to Canadian publications so that our 1,400 consumer and trade magazines can preserve Canadian culture.

In 1997, the WTO ruled against three of the four protective measures, allowing for the time being only the postal subsidies for Canadian magazines to continue. The publishing industry fears that with no protection, Canadian titles will start to die off within a few months, down to perhaps two or three survivors within five years. As Figure 19.9 shows, the health of the Canadian magazine industry is directly related to the amount of available advertising revenue.

American magazine publishers claim the publishing business is just another business. The Canadian position is that Canadian magazines preserve our culture against the already large onslaught of American media today. Whether culture should be protected from free trade, and whether the WTO is the appropriate body to make that decision is still a matter for debate.

FIGURE 19.9 The Health of the Canadian Magazine Industry

Since 1990, the number of different Canadian magazines has risen and fallen with the amount of advertising revenue available to the Canadian magazine publishing industry.

Source: Maclean's, June 2, 1997.

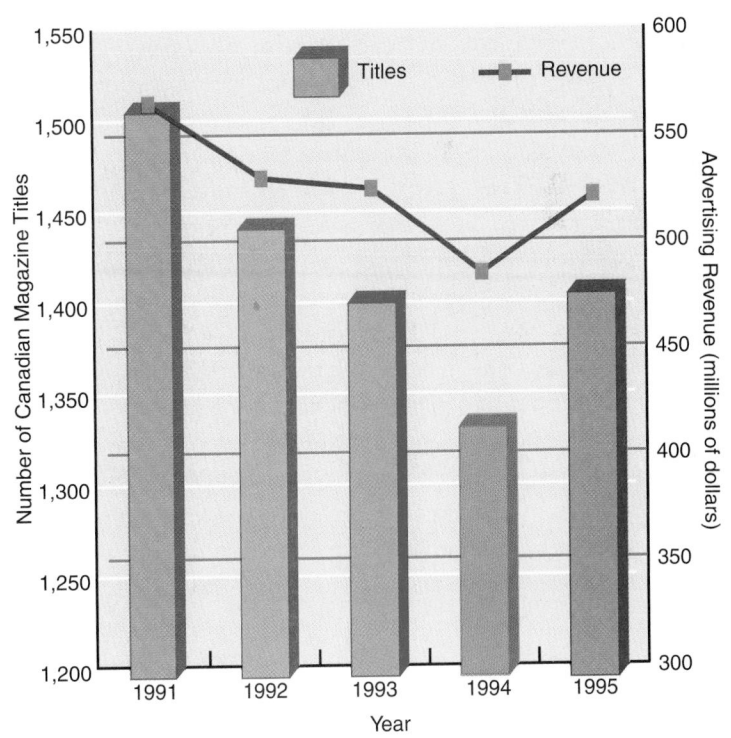

For critical analysis: Why do Canadian magazines need government protection to ensure they attract Canadian advertising revenue?

CONCEPTS IN BRIEF

- One means of restricting foreign trade is a quota system. Beneficiaries of quotas are the importers who get the quota rights and the domestic producers of the restricted good.
- Another means of restricting imports is a tariff, which is a tax on imports only. An import tariff benefits import-competing industries and harms consumers by raising prices.
- Canada's most significant trade agreement is the North American Free Trade Agreement between Canada, the United States, and Mexico.
- The other important international institution created to improve trade among nations is the General Agreement on Tariffs and Trade (GATT). The latest round of trade talks under GATT, the Uruguay Round, led to the creation of the World Trade Organization (WTO).

NETNOMICS

WTO: "Wired Trade Organization"?

Across the span of human history, technological change has helped advance international trade. Speedier transoceanic transport fed the growth of cross-border trade inthe eighteenth and nineteenth centuries. Air transport played a key role in spurring trade among nations in the twentieth century.

Likewise, the telecommunications revolution promises to provide a big boost in the twenty-first century. Books and compact discs are easier to locate and purchase from afar using the Internet. In addition to increasing cross-border trade in such physical goods, however, the Internet also promises to be an avenue for increased trade in services. Anything that is tradable in digital form is fair game. Examples include architectural designs, information about new medical treatments and surgical techniques, and banking, insurance, and brokerage services.

Electronic commerce is emerging as a big problem for the WTO. WTO rules work differently for tariffs versus quotas. In most nations, goods are subjected to tariffs. By contrast, many nations have chosen to apply quotas to services by placing restrictions on access to national markets.

The Internet and digital technology are blurring the distinctions between traded goods and traded services, however. Under current interpretation, a recording by a top rap artist that crosses a national border while resident on a CD is a good subject to tariffs. Is the same recording send over the Internet in digital form a service under WTO rules? Or is it no different from a CD and thus subject to the WTO's tariff guidelines? Likewise, if an architectural firm ships detailed drawings to a customer in another country, the drawings are treated as goods, and tariffs apply. But what if the firm sends the drawings to its client in the form of an e-mail attachment?

These examples illustrate how WTO rules concerning how to define goods and services might exert significant effects on the choice between physical and digital methods of trade. National authorities are already having trouble keeping track of the proliferation of Internet-based service offerings. If quotas on cross-border Internet services are difficult for national authorities to enforce, people will have a strong incentive to shift even more trade to the Internet.

ISSUES AND APPLICATIONS
Playing Chicken with the United States

Concepts Applied: Comparative advantage, competitiveness, quotas, tariffs, benefits from trade

Canadian chicken and dairy farmers claim that the cost of farming in Canada is higher than in the US because of our more severe climate. They welcome high import duties to protect them from lower-cost US imports, but these high duties raise the cost of their products to Canadian consumers.

Canada's dairy, egg, and poultry producers won a major battle with their American counterparts in 1996. In spite of our free trade agreement with the Americans, which prohibits any new tariffs between Canada and the US, a NAFTA dispute settlement board declared that Canada could retain its tariff rate quotas (TRQs) placed on dairy and poultry products under WTO auspices. But have consumers also won this war?

Supply-Management at Work

In the late 1960s, dairy and poultry farmers opted to take part in a supply-management system designed to smooth the often wild fluctuations in farm prices and farm incomes. The supply-management system consists of production quotas which restrict output and keep prices stable and high enough for farmers to make a living. Since imports of competing products increase supply and reduce market price, the Canadian government also devised a system of import quotas on American dairy and poultry products.

In 1995, member countries of the WTO (which includes Canada and the United States) removed agricultural import quotas and replaced them with tariffs offering equivalent protection. It was agreed that these tariffs will be substantially reduced over the next 10 years. Table 19.6 shows some of the Canadian TRQs on dairy and poultry products which the United States complained were unduly high.

The United States appealed under the NAFTA, but because the US had not voiced concerns during the WTO talks, the dispute settlement board ruled in favour of Canada.

Winners and Losers with Restricted Trade

Dairy and poultry farmers and the federal and provincial governments were indeed pleased. As a 1996 *Informetrica* study showed, they had a lot to lose with completely open borders: over the period 1996 to 2000, farmers could have lost up to $16 billion in income, and the federal and provincial governments up to $18.1 billion in revenues if the TRQs were declared illegal. Canadian farm workers could have lost upwards of 28,000 person-hours of employment.

Canadian consumers, however, would have gained from open borders. With the removal of the TRQs, the Consumer Price Index could have dropped about 1.5 percent. Americans

TABLE 19.6	Product	1993 Duty (%)	1995 Duty (%)
Canadian Duties on Imports of Selected American Products	Frozen whole chicken	6.2	273.4
	Fluid milk (1%–6% butter fat)	8.7	276.7
The 1993 duty was in effect prior to the WTO agreement to remove import quotas.	Ice cream and ice milk	7.7	307.2
	Yogurt	7.5	272.5

Source: The Financial Post, August 22, 1996.

could have gained from open borders too. One estimate predicts that US exports to Canada of dairy products alone would rise from under $100 million to $1 billion.

What's the Problem?

Why can't Canada's 36,000 dairy and poultry producers compete with their American counterparts without government protection? Are they so inefficient that they need both production quotas and TRQs to survive?

Supporters of the supply-management system have answers to these questions. They say that the Americans have a comparative advantage in producing dairy and poultry products. The costs of doing business in Canada are high, they suggest, because of our difficult weather. Americans don't have to heat their barns and henhouses to protect their animals and, in addition, they have access to cheaper feed, so their overall costs are lower. Supporters also point out that, especially in poultry, Americans experience large economies of scale as huge "agribusinesses" operate giant farms. By contrast, the supply-management system has allowed Canada to retain the family farm, which typically is smaller and less cost-efficient. But proponents are also quick to mention that the supply-management system is justified not only because of maintenance of the family farm, but also because the output of the family farm is more wholesome than that of an agribusiness.

However, Canadian beef farmers disagree. Back in the 1960s, they decided not to take part in a supply-management system. Since that time they have become very competitive, exporting almost half of their production in spite of Canada's position as one of the world's largest importers of beef.

For Critical Analysis

1. If the TRQs on dairy and poultry are eventually removed, but Canada's supply-management system is not dismantled, what will be the effect on Canadian dairy and poultry farmers?

2. Can you think of any reason that Canadian beef farmers can be competitive in a world market but dairy and poultry farmers cannot?

CHAPTER SUMMARY

1. It is important to distinguish between absolute and comparative advantage. A person or country that can do everything "better" (with higher labour productivity) than every other person or country has an absolute advantage in everything. Nevertheless, trade will still be advantageous if people specialize in the things that they do relatively best, exploiting their respective comparative advantage.

2. Along with the gains, there are costs from trade. Certain industries and their employees may be hurt if trade is opened up.

3. An import quota restricts the quantity of imports coming into the country. It therefore raises the price. Consumers always lose.

4. When governments impose "voluntary" quotas, they are called voluntary export restraints (VERs).

5. An import tariff raises the domestic price of foreign produced goods. It therefore allows domestic producers to raise their own prices. The result is a higher price to consumers, a lower quantity of imports, and a lower volume of international trade.

6. Canada's most important trade agreement is the North American Free Trade Agreement (NAFTA), signed by Canada, the United States, and Mexico. The NAFTA covers about 80 percent of Canada's exports.

7. The other main international institution created to improve trade among nations was the General Agreement on Tariffs and Trade (GATT), replaced in 1995 by the World Trade Organization (WTO).

DISCUSSION OF PREVIEW QUESTIONS

1. Is international trade important to Canada?

The direct impact of international trade on Canada, as measured by the ratio of exports to GDP, is relatively large compared with many other nations. It is hard to imagine what life would be like without international trade. Initially, many prices would rise rapidly, but eventually domestic production would begin on many goods we presently import. However, consider life without imports of coffee, tea, bananas, and foreign wines, motorcycles, automobiles, televisions, VCRs, and hundreds of other goods from food and clothing to electronics—not to mention vital imports such as bauxite, chromium, cobalt, nickel, platinum, and tin.

2. What is the difference between comparative advantage and absolute advantage?

A nation has a comparative advantage in producing a good when it can produce the good at lower opportunity cost relative to the opportunity cost of producing the good in another nation. A nation has an absolute advantage when it can produce more output with a given set of inputs than can be produced in the other country. Nevertheless, trade can still take place if both nations have a comparative advantage in producing goods that they can agree to exchange. The reason is that it can still benefit the nation with an absolute advantage to specialize in production.

3. Why can nations gain from specializing in production and engaging in international trade?

A country has a comparative advantage in producing a good if it can produce that good at a lower opportunity cost, in terms of foregone production of a second good, than another nation. If the other nation has a comparative advantage in producing the second good, both nations can gain by specializing in producing the goods in which they have a comparative advantage and engaging in international trade. Together they can then produce and consume more than they would have produced and consumed in the absence of specialization and trade.

4. What is the relationship between imports and exports?

Because foreigners eventually want real goods and services as payment for the real goods and services they export to other countries, ultimately each country pays for its imports with its exports. Hence on a worldwide basis, the value of imports must equal the value of exports.

5. What are some arguments against free trade?

The infant industry argument maintains that new industries developing domestically need protection from foreign competitors until they are mature enough themselves to compete with foreigners, at which time protection will be removed. One problem with this argument is that it is difficult to tell when maturity has been reached, and domestic industries will fight against weaning. Moreover, this argument is hardly relevant to most Canadian industries. It is also alleged (and is true to a large extent) that free trade leads to instability for specific domestic industries as comparative advantage changes in a dynamic world. Countries that have traditionally held a comparative advantage in the production of some goods occasionally lose that advantage (while gaining others). Regional hardships are a result, and protection of domestic jobs is demanded.

6. How can nations restrict foreign trade?

One way to restrict trade is to impose a quota, or a limit on imports of a good. This action restricts the supply of the good in the domestic market, thereby pushing up the equilibrium price of the good. Another way to reduce trade is to place a tariff on imported goods. This reduces the supply of foreign-made goods and increases the demand for domestically produced goods, which brings about a rise in the price of the goods.

7. What is the ultimate effect of a restriction on imports?

Because each country must pay for its imports with its exports, any restriction on imports must ultimately lead to a reduction in exports. So even though restrictions on imports because of tariffs or quotas may benefit workers and business owners in the protected domestic industry, such protection will harm workers and business owners in the export sector in general.

PROBLEMS

(Answers to the odd-numbered problems appear at the back of the book.)

19-1. Examine the hypothetical table of worker-hours required to produce caviar and wheat in Canada and in Russia.

Product	Canada	Russia
Caviar (kilogram)	6 worker-hours	9 worker-hours
Wheat (bushel)	3 worker-hours	6 worker-hours

a. What is the opportunity cost to Canada of producing one kilogram of caviar per time period? What is the opportunity cost to Canada of producing one bushel of wheat?

b. What is the opportunity cost to Russia of producing one kilogram of caviar per time period? What is the opportunity cost to Russia of producing one bushel of wheat?

c. Canada has a comparative advantage in what? Russia has a comparative advantage in what?

19-2. Study the hypothetical table of worker-hours required to produce coffee and beans in Colombia and Turkey.

Product	Colombia	Turkey
Coffee (kilogram)	2 worker-hours	1 worker-hour
Beans (kilogram)	6 worker-hours	2 worker-hours

a. What is the opportunity cost to Colombia of producing one kilogram of coffee? One kilogram of beans?

b. What is the opportunity cost to Turkey of producing one kilogram of coffee? One kilogram of beans?

c. Colombia has a comparative advantage in what? Turkey has a comparative advantage in what?

19-3. Assume that Canada can produce *everything* with fewer worker-hours than any other country on earth. Even under this extreme assumption, why would Canada still trade with other countries?

19-4. Examine the hypothetical table of worker-hours required to produce cheese and cloth in two countries, A and B.

Product	Country A	Country B
Cheese (kilogram)	2/3 worker-hours	2 worker-hours
Cloth (metre)	1/2 worker-hours	1 worker-hour

a. What is the opportunity cost to country A of producing one kilogram of cheese? One metre of cloth?

b. What is the opportunity cost to country B of producing one kilogram of cheese? One metre of cloth?

c. Country A has a comparative advantage in what?

d. Country B has a comparative advantage in what?

19-5. The use of tariffs and quotas to restrict imports results in higher prices and is successful in reducing imports. In what way is using a tariff different from using a quota?

19-6. Two countries, Austral Land and Boreal Land, have the following production opportunities shown in the graphs.

Austral Land

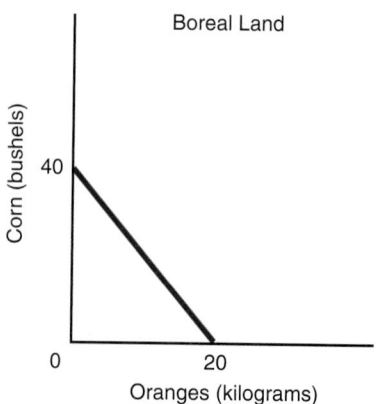

Boreal Land

a. Who has an absolute advantage in corn? In oranges?

b. Who has a comparative advantage in corn? In oranges?

c. Should Boreal Land export at all? If so, which good should it export?

d. What is Austral Land's opportunity cost of oranges in terms of corn? What is Boreal Land's opportunity cost of corn in terms of oranges?

19-7. The accompanying graph gives the supply and demand for peaches. *S* and *D* are Canada's supply and demand curves, respectively. Assume that the world price of peaches is 50 cents per kilogram.

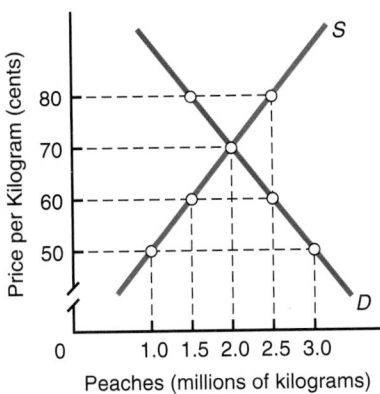

a. How many kilograms are produced domestically? How many kilograms are imported?

b. Suppose that Canada imposes a 10-cent-per-kilogram tariff. How many kilograms would now be produced domestically? How many kilograms would be imported? What are the federal government's revenues?

c. Suppose now that the government imposes a 20-cent-per-kilogram tariff. What price can domestic growers now receive for their peaches? How many kilograms will domestic growers produce? How many kilograms will be imported? What are government revenues?

19-8. Explain why an increase in taxes on imports (tariffs) will reduce exports.

19-9. Assume that a country with whom Canada is trading imposes restrictions on Canadian-made imports into that country. Will Canada be better off by simultaneously imposing restrictions on the other country's imports into Canada? Why or why not?

19-10. Look at the *Canadian Trade Review* on the Department of Foreign Affairs and International Trade Web site at: http:// www.infoexport.gc.ca/ section4/revue-e.asp

a. What three types of products does Canada export the most?

b. What three countries does Canada sell the most goods and services to?

c. Which trade agreement—the GATT or the NAFTA—would be most important for Canada? Why? (Hint: Think about your answer to part b.)

ECONOMICS ON THE NET

How Does the World Trade Organization Settle Trade Disputes?

Internet URL: www.wto.org

Title: The World Trade Organization: Settling Trade Disputes

Navigation: Begin at the WTO's homepage (http://www.wto.org). Click on Dispute Settlement, then on How Does the WTO Settle Disputes?

Application: Read the article, which can be scrolled by clicking the right arrow at the bottom of the page. Answer the following questions:

a. As the article discusses, settling trade disputes often takes at least a year. What aspects of the WTO's dispute settlement process take the longest times?

b. Does the WTO actually "punish" a country it finds has broken international trading agreements? If not, who imposes sanctions?

EXCHANGE RATES AND THE BALANCE OF PAYMENTS

If you talk to Canadians who travelled to Europe in the mid-1980s, they will probably tell you how cheap their trip was. If you go to Europe today, the stories will be quite different. What difference does a decade make? Well, when you are talking about the dollar, a lot. Today, in some countries such as Germany and Japan the dollar buys barely half what it did in 1985. Should we be worrying about a weaker dollar? To answer this question, you need to know about international financial transactions and the determinants of foreign exchange rates.

PREVIEW QUESTIONS

1. What is the difference between the balance of trade and the balance of payments?

2. What is a foreign exchange rate?

3. What is a flexible exchange rate?

4. What factors can induce changes in equilibrium exchange rates?

5. How can policymakers attempt to keep exchange rates fixed?

6. What are alternative approaches to limiting exchange rate variability?

DID YOU KNOW THAT... every day, around the clock, over $1 trillion of foreign currencies are traded? Along with that trading come news headlines, such as "The dollar weakened today," "The dollar under attack," and "The Bank of Canada intervened in money markets today to halt the dollar's slide." If you are confused by such newspaper headlines, join the crowd. Surprisingly, though, if you regard the dollar, the pound sterling, the deutsche mark, the yen, and the franc as assets that are subject to the laws of supply and demand, the world of international finance becomes much clearer. Perhaps the first step is to examine the meaning of the terms used with respect to Canada's international financial transactions during any one-year period.

The Balance of Payments and International Capital Movements

Governments typically keep track of each year's economic activities by calculating the gross domestic product—the total of expenditures on all newly produced final domestic goods and services—and its components. In the world of international trade also, a summary information system has been developed. It relates to the balance of trade and the balance of payments. The **balance of trade** refers specifically to exports and imports of *goods and services* as discussed in Chapter 19. When international trade is in balance, the value of exports equals the value of imports.

The **balance of payments** is a more general concept that expresses the total of all economic transactions between two countries, usually for a period of one year. Each country's balance of payments summarizes information about that country's exports, imports, earnings by domestic residents on assets located abroad, earnings on domestic assets owned by foreign residents, international capital movements, and official transactions by central banks and governments. In essence, then, the balance of payments is a record of all the transactions between households, firms, and government of one country and the rest of the world. Any transaction that leads to a *payment* by a country's residents (or government) is a deficit item, identified by a negative sign (–) when we examine the actual numbers that might be in Table 20.1. Any transaction that leads to a *receipt* by a country's residents (or government) is a surplus item and is identified by a plus sign (+) when actual numbers are considered. Table 20.1 gives a listing of the surplus and deficit items on international accounts.

Balance of trade The value of goods and services bought and sold in the world market.

Balance of payments A summary record of a country's economic transactions with foreign residents and governments over a year.

TABLE 20.1
Surplus (+) and Deficit (–) Items on the International Accounts

Surplus Items (+)	Deficit Items (–)
Exports of merchandise	Imports of merchandise
Private and governmental gifts from foreigners	Private and governmental gifts to foreigners
Foreign use of domestically owned transportation	Use of foreign-owned transportation
Foreign tourists' expenditures in this country	Tourism expenditures abroad
Foreign military spending in this country	Military spending abroad
Interest and dividend receipts from foreigners	Interest and dividends paid to foreigners
Sales of domestic assets to foreigners	Purchases of foreign assets
Funds deposited in this country by foreigners	Funds placed in foreign depository institutions
Sales of gold to foreigners	Purchases of gold from foreigners
Sales of domestic currency to foreigners	Purchases of foreign currency

Accounting Identities

Accounting identities Statements that certain numerical measurements are equal by accepted definition (for example, "assets equal liabilities plus stockholders' equity").

Accounting identities—definitions of equivalent values—exist for financial institutions and other businesses. We begin with simple accounting identities that must hold for families, and then go on to describe international accounting identities.

If a family unit is spending more than its current income, such a situation necessarily implies that the family unit must be doing one of the following:

1. Drawing down its wealth. The family must reduce its money holdings, or it must sell stocks, bonds, or other assets.
2. Borrowing.
3. Receiving gifts from friends or relatives.
4. Receiving public transfers from a government, which obtained the funds by taxing others. (A transfer is a payment, in money or in goods or services, made without receiving goods or services in return.)

In effect, we can use this information to derive an identity: If a family unit is currently spending more than it is earning, it must draw on previously acquired wealth, borrow, or receive either private or public aid. Similarly, an identity exists for a family unit that is currently spending less than it is earning: It must increase its wealth by increasing its money holdings or by lending and acquiring other financial assets, or it must pay taxes or bestow gifts on others. When we consider businesses and governments, each unit in each group faces its own identities or constraints; thus, net lending by households must equal net borrowing by businesses and governments.

Even though our individual family unit's accounts must balance, in the sense that the identity discussed previously must hold, sometimes the item that brings about the balance cannot continue indefinitely. *If family expenditures exceed family income and this situation is financed by borrowing, the household may be considered to be in disequilibrium because such a situation cannot continue indefinitely.* If such a deficit is financed by drawing on previously accumulated assets, the family may also be in disequilibrium because it cannot continue indefinitely to draw on its wealth; eventually, it will become impossible for that family to continue such a lifestyle. (Of course, if the family members are retired, they may well be in equilibrium by drawing on previously acquired assets to finance current deficits; this example illustrates that it is necessary to understand circumstances fully before pronouncing an economic unit in disequilibrium.)

Individual households, businesses, and governments, as well as the entire group of households, businesses, and governments, must eventually reach equilibrium. Certain economic adjustment mechanisms have evolved to ensure equilibrium. Deficit households must eventually increase their incomes or decrease their expenditures. They will find that they have to pay higher interest rates if they wish to borrow to finance their deficits. Eventually their credit sources will dry up, and they will be forced into equilibrium. Businesses, on occasion, must lower costs and/or prices—or go bankrupt—to reach equilibrium.

When countries trade or interact, certain identities or constraints must also hold. Countries buy goods from people in other countries; they also lend to and present gifts to people in other countries. If a country interacts with others, an accounting identity ensures a balance (but not an equilibrium, as will soon become clear). Let's look at the three categories of balance of payments transactions: current account transactions, capital account transactions, and official settlements account transactions.

Current Account Transactions

During any designated period, all payments and gifts that are related to the purchase or sale of both goods and services constitute the current account in international trade. The three major types of current account transactions are the exchange of merchandise goods, the exchange of services, and transfers.

TABLE 20.2

Canada's Balance of International Payments, 2000 (in Billions of Dollars)

Current Account	Exports(+)	Imports(−)	Balance
Merchandise	417.7	363.2	54.5
Services	56.2	62.8	−6.6
Trade Balance			47.9
Investment Income	37.9	68.1	−30.2
Transfers	5.7	4.5	1.2
Total Current Account balance			**18.9**
Capital Account			
Net Capital Flows [capital outflow (−)]	116.2	127.4	−11.2
Capital Account balance			**−11.2**
Official Financing Account			
Statistical Discrepancy*			−2.3
Official International Reserves = −(18.9 − 11.2 − 2.3) [increases (−)]			−5.4
Official Financing balance			**−7.7**
Balance of Payments = (18.9 − 11.2 − 7.7)			**0.0**

Source: Based on information from Statistics Canada Web site <www.statcan.ca/english/Pgdb/Economy/Economic/econ01a.htm> and <www.statcan.ca/english/Pgdb/Economy/Economic/econ01b.htm>, accessed on March 25, 2001.

*The statistical discrepancy compensates for the inability to account for some items, probably unaccounted capital outflows, many of which relate to the underground economy.

MERCHANDISE TRADE TRANSACTIONS. The largest portion of any country's balance of payments current account is typically the importing and exporting of merchandise goods. During 2000, for example, as can be seen in Table 20.2, Canada exported $447.7 billion of merchandise and imported $363.2 billion. The balance of merchandise trade is defined as the difference between the value of merchandise exports and the value of merchandise imports. For 2000, Canada had a balance of merchandise trade surplus because the value of its merchandise exports exceeded the value of its merchandise imports. This surplus amounted to $54.5 billion.

Thinking Critically About the Media 20-1 | Perhaps the Trade Situation Isn't So Bad After All

Virtually every month, there appears a spate of articles and TV sound bites about Canada's current account deficit. The official numbers may be in error, however, for they ignore the multinational nature of modern firms. Canadian international trade figures exclude sales in other countries for subsidiaries of Canadian-owned companies. Because of a host of other problems, some government economists believe that they are underestimating the value of Canadian exports by as much as 10 percent. Economist Paul Krugman agrees. When he added up the value of world exports and compared it with the value of world imports, he found that the planet Earth had a trade deficit of $100 billion! Perhaps we are trading with aliens and don't know it.

SERVICE EXPORTS AND IMPORTS. The balance of (merchandise) trade has to do with tangible items—you can feel them, touch them, and see them. Service exports and imports have to do with invisible or intangible items that are bought and sold, such as shipping, insurance, tourist expenditures, and banking services. As can be seen in Table 20.2, in 2000, service exports were $56.2 billion and service imports were $62.8 billion. Thus the balance of services was in deficit about $6.6 billion in 2000. Exports constitute receipts or inflows into Canada and are positive; imports constitute payments abroad or outflows of money and are negative.

When we combine the balance of merchandise trade with the balance of services, we obtain a trade balance on goods and services equal to $47.9 billion in 2000.

INVESTMENT INCOME. Canadians earn investment income on assets they own in foreign countries. These earnings represent an inflow into Canada. Conversely, when Canadians pay income to foreigners who own assets in Canada, those earnings represent an outflow from Canada. You can see that net investment income for 2000 was −$30.2 billion. The fact that there is a negative sign before the number for investment income means that Canadians paid out more earnings on domestic assets owned by foreigners than they earned on assets owned in other countries.

TRANSFERS. Canadians give gifts to relatives and others abroad. The federal government grants gifts to foreign countries. Foreigners give gifts to Canadians, and some foreign governments have granted money to the Canadian government. In the current account, we see that net transfers—the total amount of gifts given by Canadians minus the total amount received by Canadians from abroad—came to $1.2 billion in 2000.

BALANCING THE CURRENT ACCOUNT. The balance on current account tracks the value of a country's exports of goods and services, earnings on investments abroad and transfer payments (private and government) relative to the value of that country's import of goods and services, earnings on investments in Canada, and transfer payments (private and government). In 2000, it was a $18.9 billion.

If exports exceed imports, a current account surplus is said to exist; if imports exceed exports, a current account deficit is said to exist. A current account surplus means that we are exporting more than we are importing. Such a surplus must be offset by the import of money or money equivalent, which means (in the absence of central bank intervention) a capital account deficit.

Capital Account Transactions

In world markets, it is possible to buy and sell not only goods and services but also real and financial assets. This is what the capital accounts are concerned with in international transactions. Capital account transactions occur because of foreign investments—either foreigners investing in Canada or Canadians investing in other countries. The purchase of shares of stock on the London stock exchange by a Canadian causes an outflow of funds. The building of a Japanese automobile factory in Canada causes an inflow of funds. Any time foreigners buy Canadian government securities, there is an inflow of funds. Any time Canadians buy foreign government securities, there is an outflow of funds. Loans to and from foreigners cause outflows and inflows.

Table 20.2 indicates that in 2000, the value of private and government capital going out of Canada was −$127.4 billion, and the value of private and government capital coming into Canada (including a statistical discrepancy) was +$116.2 billion. Canadian capital going abroad constitutes payments or outflows and is therefore negative. Foreign capital coming into Canada constitutes receipts or inflows and is therefore positive. Thus there was a negative net capital movement of –$11.2 billion out of Canada. This is also called the balance on capital account.

There is a relationship between the current account and the capital account, assuming no interventions by the central banks of countries. *The current account and the capital account must sum to zero. In other words, the current account deficit equals the capital account surplus. Any country experiencing a current account surplus, such as Canada, should also be running a capital account deficit.*

EXAMPLE 20-1   Does Canada's Frequent Current Account Deficit Mean It Has a Weak Economy?

In recent years, the current account in Canada has been in deficit more than it has been in surplus. This is not something new. During the second half of the nineteenth century, Canada had many years of current account deficits. They were equally matched by capital account surpluses, as the rest of the world sent capital to Canada to finance the building of the railroads and the development of Canada's industrial economy. By the end of World War I, Canadians had repaid all their external debt and had become a net creditor. However, this condition was short-lived, and by 1950 Canada was once again experiencing current account deficits. This can be seen in Figure 20.1. Whenever Canada is in deficit in its current account, it is in surplus in its capital account.

FIGURE 20.1 The Relationship Between the Current Account and the Capital Account

To some extent, the capital account is the mirror image of the current account. We can see this in the years since 1976. When the current account was in surplus, the capital account was in deficit. When the current account was in deficit, the capital account was in surplus. Indeed, virtually the only time foreigners can invest in Canada is when the current account is in deficit.

Source: Statistics Canada, CANSIM Database, Matrix 02360, Series D58032, D58049.

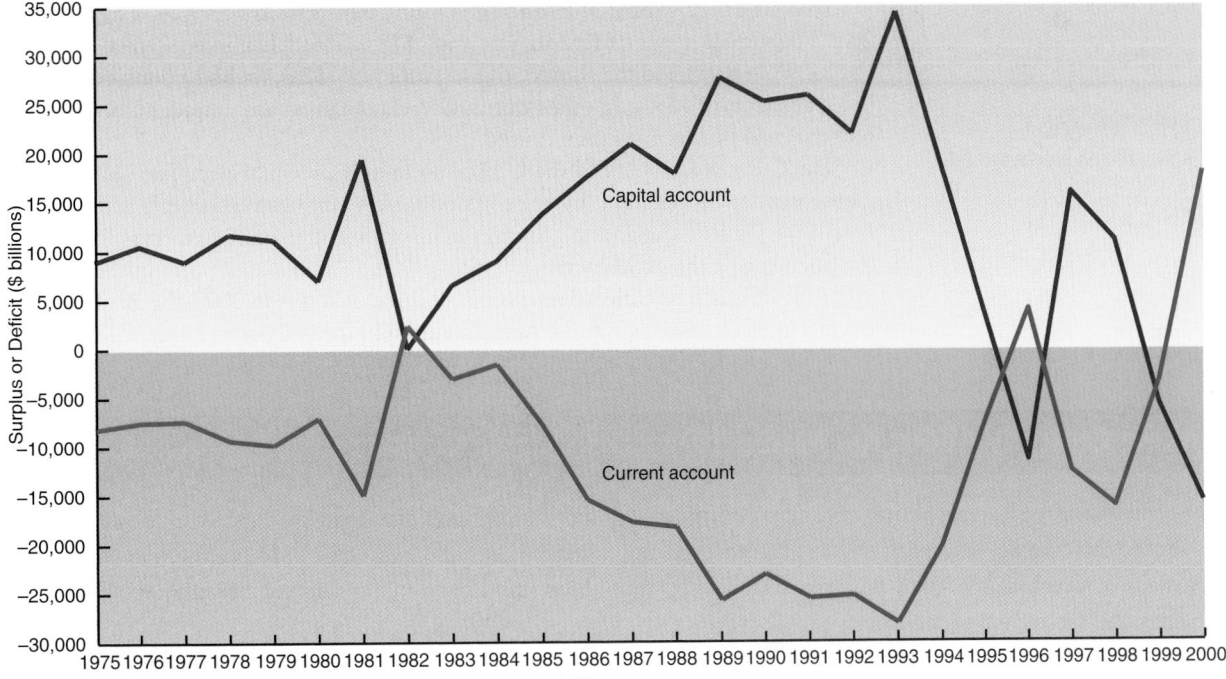

Contrary to popular belief, Canada does not necessarily have a current account deficit because it is a weak economy and cannot compete in world markets. Rather, Canada appears to be a good place to invest capital because there are strong prospects for growth and investment opportunities. So long as foreigners wish to invest more in Canada than Canadians wish to invest abroad, there will always be a deficit in our current account balance. Canadians are the beneficiaries of international capital flows.

For critical analysis: Why are politicians, nonetheless, so worried about the current account deficit?

Official Financing Account Transactions

The final section in the balance of payments concerns the statistical discrepancy and transactions in the official reserve assets of the Bank of Canada. This is referred to as the official financing account or the official settlements account.

The statistical discrepancy compensates for the inability to account for some items, probably unaccounted capital outflows, many of which relate to the underground economy.

The Bank of Canada's official reserve assets consist of the following:

1. Foreign currencies
2. Gold
3. **Special drawing rights (SDRs),** which are reserve assets that the International Monetary Fund created to be used by countries to settle international payment obligations
4. The reserve position in the International Monetary Fund
5. Financial assets held by an official agency, such as the Bank of Canada.

To consider how official financing account transactions occur, look again at Table 20.2. The surplus in our current account was +$18.9. The deficit in our capital account was −$11.2. When you add the statistical discrepancy of −$2.3, we had a deficit on the combined accounts of −$5.4. In other words, Canada obtained less in foreign money in all its international transactions than it used.

The Current account and the Capital account must equal zero. The balance of payments must equal zero, as it must be with double-entry bookkeeping. It is the intervention of the Bank of Canada and changes in its official international reserves that represent the financing of the deficiency.

If the official international reserves is *negative,* as it was in 2000, the Bank of Canada has increased its reserves because of intervention in the foreign exchange market; this is a

Special drawing rights (SDRs) Reserve assets created by the International Monetary Fund that countries can use to settle international payments.

Try Preview Question 1:
What is the difference between the balance of trade and the balance of payments?

Thinking Critically About the Media 20-2   Developing Countries Are Getting All the Capital

Many developing countries are growing more rapidly than the developed countries. Several reports have been commented on by the media in recent years in which it is argued that developing economies are "sucking up" all the world's capital. Let's put the numbers in context. About US$60 billion a year of capital moves from advanced to developing countries. All of the countries in the world, in contrast, invest over US$4 trillion a year. So such capital flows represent only 1.5 percent of total world investment. What's to worry?

balance of payments surplus. When the Bank of Canada is a net purchaser of foreign exchange and a seller of Canadian dollars, this puts *downward pressure on the Canadian dollar.*

If the official international reserves is *positive*, the Bank of Canada has decreased its reserves because of intervention in the foreign exchange market; this is a *balance of payments deficit.* When the Bank of Canada is a net seller of foreign exchange and a buyer of Canadian dollars, this puts *upward pressure on the Canadian dollar.*

What Affects the Balance of Payments?

A major factor affecting our balance of payments is our rate of inflation relative to that of our trading partners. Assume that the rates of inflation in Canada and in the United States are equal. All of a sudden, our inflation rate increases. The Americans will find that Canadian products are becoming more expensive, and we will export fewer of them to the United States. Canadians will find American products relatively cheaper, and we will import more. The converse will occur if our rate of inflation suddenly falls relative to that of the United States. All other things held constant, whenever our rate of inflation exceeds that of our trading partners, we expect to see a "worsening" of our balance of trade and payments. Conversely, when our rate of inflation is less than that of our trading partners, other things being constant, we expect to see an "improvement" in our balance of trade and payments.

Another important factor that sometimes influences our balance of payments is our relative political stability. Political instability causes *capital flight:* Owners of capital in countries anticipating or experiencing political instability will often move assets to countries that are politically stable, such as Canada. Hence our balance of payments is likely to worsen whenever the threat of separation looms in Quebec.

CONCEPTS IN BRIEF

- The balance of payments reflects the value of all transactions in international trade, including goods, services, financial assets, and gifts.
- The merchandise trade balance gives us the difference between exports and imports of tangible items. Merchandise trade transactions are represented by exports and imports of tangible items.
- Service exports and imports relate to the trade of intangible items, such as shipping, insurance, and tourist expenditures.
- Investment income includes income earned by foreigners on Canadian investments and income earned by Canadians on foreign investments.
- Transfers involve international private gifts and federal government grants or gifts to foreign nations.
- When we add the balance of merchandise trade plus the balance of services and take account of net transfers, we come up with the balance on current account, which is a summary statistic taking into account the three transactions that form the current account transactions.
- There are also capital account transactions that relate to the buying and selling of financial and real assets. Foreign capital is always entering Canada, and Canadian capital is always flowing abroad. The difference is called the balance on capital account.
- Another type of balance of payments transaction concerns the official settlement assets of individual countries, or what is often simply called official transactions. By standard accounting convention, official transactions are exactly equal, but opposite in sign, to the balance of payments of Canada.
- Our balance of trade can be affected by our relative rate of inflation and by political instability elsewhere compared to the stability that exists in Canada.

Determining Foreign Exchange Rates

When you buy foreign products, such as French wine, you have dollars with which to pay the French winemaker. The French winemaker, however, cannot pay workers in dollars. The workers are French, they live in France, and they must have francs to buy goods and services in that country. There must therefore be some way of exchanging dollars for the francs that the winemaker will accept. That exchange occurs in a **foreign exchange market**, which in this case specializes in exchanging francs and dollars. (When you obtain foreign currencies at a bank or an airport currency exchange, you are participating in the foreign exchange market.)

Foreign exchange market The market for buying and selling foreign currencies.

The particular exchange rate between francs and dollars that would prevail depends on the current demand for and supply of francs and dollars. In a sense, then, our analysis of the exchange rate between dollars and francs will be familiar, for we have used supply and demand throughout this book. If it costs you 20 cents to buy one franc, that is the **foreign exchange rate** determined by the current demand for and supply of francs in the foreign exchange market. The French person going to the foreign exchange market would need five francs to buy one dollar. (Our numbers are, of course, hypothetical.)

Foreign exchange rate The price of one currency in terms of another.

We will continue our example in which the only two countries in the world are France and Canada. Now let's consider what determines the demand for and supply of foreign currency in the foreign exchange market.

Try Preview Question 2:

What is a foreign exchange rate?

Demand for and Supply of Foreign Currency

You wish to buy some French Bordeaux wine. To do so, you must have French francs. You go to the foreign exchange market (or your Canadian bank). Your desire to buy the French wine therefore causes you to offer (supply) dollars to the foreign exchange market. Your demand for French francs is equivalent to your supply of Canadian dollars to the foreign exchange market. Indeed:

> Every Canadian transaction concerning the importation of foreign goods constitutes a supply of dollars and a demand for some foreign currency, and the opposite is true for export transactions.

In this case, this import transaction constitutes a demand for French francs.

In our example, we will assume that only two goods are being traded, French wine and Canadian jeans. The Canadian demand for French wine creates a supply of dollars and a demand for francs in the foreign exchange market. Similarly, the French demand for Canadian jeans creates a supply of francs and a demand for dollars in the foreign exchange market. In the situation of **flexible exchange rates**, the supply of and demand for dollars and francs in the foreign exchange market will determine the equilibrium foreign exchange rate. The equilibrium exchange rate will tell us how many francs a dollar can be exchanged for—that is, the dollar price of francs—or how many dollars (or fractions of a dollar) a franc can be exchanged for—the franc price of dollars.

Flexible exchange rates Exchange rates that are allowed to fluctuate in the open market in response to changes in supply and demand. Sometimes called *floating exchange rates.*

The Equilibrium Foreign Exchange Rate

To determine the equilibrium foreign exchange rate, we have to find out what determines the demand for and supply of foreign exchange. We will ignore for the moment any speculative aspect of buying foreign exchange; that is, we assume that there are no individuals who wish to buy francs simply because they think that their price will go up in the future.

The idea of an exchange rate is no different from the idea of paying a certain price for something you want to buy. If you like coffee, you know you have to pay about $1.00 a cup. If the price went up to $2.50, you would probably buy fewer cups. If the price went down to 5 cents, you might buy more. In other words, the demand curve for cups of coffee, expressed in terms of dollars, slopes downward following the law of demand. The demand curve for francs slopes downward also, and we will see why.

DEMAND SCHEDULE FOR FRENCH FRANCS.   Let's think more closely about the demand schedule for francs. Let's say that it costs you 20 cents to purchase one franc; that is the exchange rate between dollars and francs. If tomorrow you had to pay 25 cents for the same franc, the exchange rate would have changed. Looking at such an increase with respect to the franc, we would say that there has been an **appreciation** in the value of the franc in the foreign exchange market. But this increase in the value of the franc means that there has been a **depreciation** in the value of the dollar in the foreign exchange market. The dollar used to buy five francs; tomorrow, the dollar will be able to buy only four francs at a price of 25 cents per franc. If the dollar price of francs rises, you will probably demand fewer francs. Why? The answer lies in looking at the reason you demand francs in the first place.

> **Appreciation** An increase in the value of a currency in terms of other currencies.
>
> **Depreciation** A decrease in the value of a currency in terms of other currencies.

You demand francs in order to buy French wine. Your demand curve for French wine, we will assume, follows the law of demand and therefore slopes downward. If it costs you more Canadian dollars to buy the same quantity of French wine, presumably you will not buy the same quantity; your quantity demanded will be less. We say that your demand for French francs is *derived* from your demand for French wine. In part (a) of Figure 20.2, we present the hypothetical demand schedule for French wine in Canada by a representative wine drinker. In part (b), we show graphically the Canadian demand curve for French wine in terms of Canadian dollars taken from part (a).

Let us assume that the price per litre of French wine in France is 20 francs. Given that price, we can find the number of francs required to purchase up to four litres of French wine. That information is given in part (c) of Figure 20.2. If one litre requires 20 francs, four litres require 80 francs. Now we have enough information to determine the derived demand curve for French francs. If one franc costs 20 cents, a bottle of wine would cost $4 (20 francs per bottle × 20 cents per franc = $4 per bottle). At $4 per bottle, the typical representative Canadian wine drinker would, we see from part (a) of Figure 20.2, demand four litres. From part (c) we see that 80 francs would be demanded to buy the four litres of wine. We show this quantity demanded in part (d). In part (e), we draw the derived demand curve for francs. Now consider what happens if the price of francs goes up to 30 cents. A bottle of French wine costing 20 francs in France would now cost $6. From part (a) we see that at $6 per litre, three litres will be imported from France into Canada by our representative domestic wine drinker. From part (c) we see that three litres would require 60 francs to be purchased; thus in parts (d) and (e) we see that at a price of one franc per 30 cents, the quantity demanded will be 60 francs. We continue similar calculations all the way up to a price of 50 cents per franc. At that price a bottle of French wine costing 20 francs in France would cost $10, and our representative wine drinker would import only one bottle.

DOWNWARD-SLOPING DERIVED DEMAND.   As can be expected, as the price of francs falls, the quantity demanded will rise. The only difference here from the standard demand analysis developed in Chapter 4 and used throughout this text is that the demand for francs is derived from the demand for a final product—French wine in our example.

SUPPLY OF FRENCH FRANCS.   The supply of French francs is a derived supply in that it is derived from a French person's demand for Canadian jeans. We could go through an example similar to the one for wine to come up with a supply schedule of French francs in France. It slopes upward. Obviously, the French want dollars in order to purchase Canadian goods. In principle, the French will be willing to supply more francs when the dollar price of francs goes up because they can then buy more Canadian goods with the same quantity of francs; that is, the franc would be worth more in exchange for Canadian

Part (a)
Demand Schedule for French Wine in Canada per Week

Price per Litre	Quantity Demanded (litres)
$10	1
8	2
6	3
4	4

Part (b)
Canadian Demand Curve for French Wine

Part (c)
Francs Required to Purchase Quantity Demanded (at P = 20 francs per litre)

Quantity Demanded (litres)	Francs Required
1	20
2	40
3	60
4	80

Part (d)
Derived Demand Schedule for Francs in Canada with Which to Pay for Imports of Wine

Dollar Price of One Franc	Dollar Price of Wine	Quantity of Wine Demanded (litres)	Quantity of Francs Demanded per Week
$ .50	$10	1	20
.40	8	2	40
.30	6	3	60
.20	4	4	80

FIGURE 20.2 Deriving the Demand for French Francs

In part (a), we show the demand schedule for French wine in Canada, expressed in terms of dollars per litre. In part (b), we show the demand curve, D, which slopes downward. In part (c), we show the number of francs required to purchase up to four litres of wine. If the price per litre of wine in France is 20 francs, we can now find the quantity of francs needed to pay for the various quantities demanded. In part (d), we see the derived demand for francs in Canada in order to purchase the various quantities of wine given in part (a). The resultant demand curve, D_1, is shown in part (e). It is the Canadian derived demand for francs.

Part (e)
Canadian Derived Demand for Francs

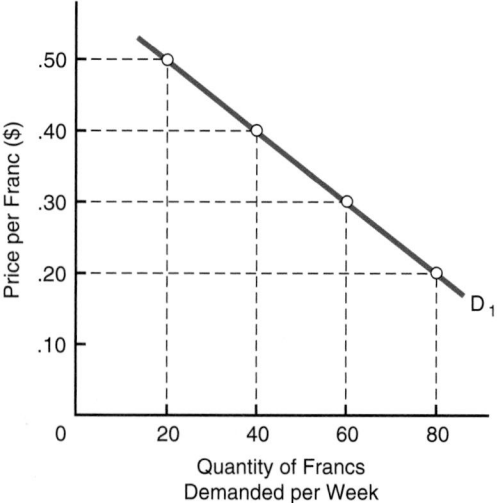

goods than when the dollar price for francs was lower. Let's take an example. Suppose a pair of jeans in Canada costs $10. If the exchange rate is 25 cents for one franc, the French have to come up with 40 francs ($10 at 25 cents per franc) to buy one pair of jeans. If, however, the exchange rate goes up to 50 cents for one franc, the French must come up with only 20 francs ($10 at 50 cents per franc) to buy a pair of Canadian jeans. At a lower price (in francs) of Canadian jeans, the French will demand a larger quantity. In other words, as the price of French francs goes up in terms of dollars, the quantity of Canadian jeans demanded will go up, and hence the quantity of French francs supplied will go up. Therefore, the supply schedule of foreign currency (francs) will slope upward.[1]

We could easily work through a detailed numerical example to show that the supply curve of French francs slopes upward. Rather than do that, we will simply draw it as upward-sloping in Figure 20.3. In our hypothetical example, assuming that there is only one wine drinker in Canada and one demander of jeans in France, the equilibrium exchange rate will be set at 20 cents per franc, or five francs to one dollar. Let us now look at the aggregate demand for and supply of French francs. We take all demanders of French wine and all demanders of Canadian jeans and put their demands for and supplies of francs together into one diagram. Thus we are showing an aggregate version of the demand for and supply of French francs. The horizontal axis in Figure 20.4 represents a quantity of foreign exchange—the number of francs per year. The vertical axis represents the exchange rate—the price of foreign currency (francs) expressed in dollars (per franc). Thus at the foreign currency price of 25 cents per franc, you know that it will cost you 25 cents to buy one franc. At the foreign currency price of 20 cents per franc, you know that it will cost you 20 cents to buy one franc. The equilibrium is again established at 20 cents for one franc. This equilibrium is not established because Canadians like to buy francs or because the French like to buy dollars. Rather, the equilibrium exchange rate depends on how many pairs of

FIGURE 20.3 The Equilibrium Exchange Rate for Two Individuals

The derived demand curve for French francs is taken from part (e) of Figure 20.2. The derived supply curve, S, results from the representative French purchaser of Canadian jeans, who supplies francs to the foreign exchange market when demanding Canadian dollars in order to buy Canadian jeans. D_1 and S intersect at E. The equilibrium exchange rate is 20 cents per franc.

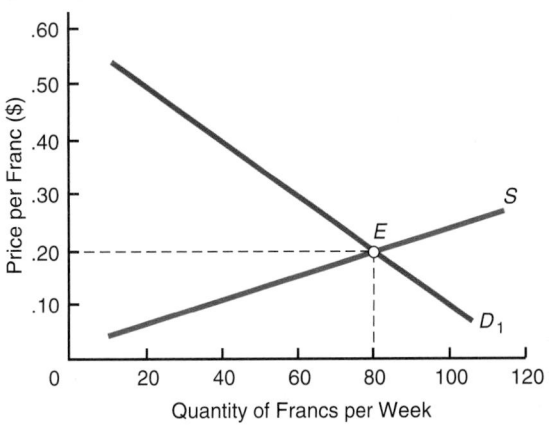

---

[1] Actually, the supply schedule of foreign currency will be upward-sloping if we assume that the demand for Canadian imported jeans on the part of the French is price-elastic. If the demand schedule for jeans is price-inelastic, the supply schedule will be negatively sloped. In the case of unit elasticity of demand, the supply schedule for francs will be a vertical line. Throughout the rest of this chapter, we will assume that demand is price-elastic. Remember that the price elasticity of demand tells us whether or not total expenditures by jeans purchasers in France will rise or fall when the French franc drops in value. In the long run, it is quite realistic to think that the price elasticity of demand for imports is numerically greater than 1 anyway.

FIGURE 20.4 Aggregate Demand for and Supply of French Francs

The aggregate supply curve for French francs results from the total French demand for Canadian jeans. The demand curve, D, slopes downward like most demand curves, and the supply curve, S, slopes upward. The foreign exchange price, or the Canadian dollar price of francs, is given on the vertical axis. The number of francs, in millions, is represented on the horizontal axis. If the foreign exchange rate is 25 cents—that is, if it takes 25 cents to buy one franc—Canadians will demand 80 million francs. The equilibrium exchange rate is at the intersection of D and S. The equilibrium exchange rate is 20 cents. At this point, 100 million French francs are both demanded and supplied each year.

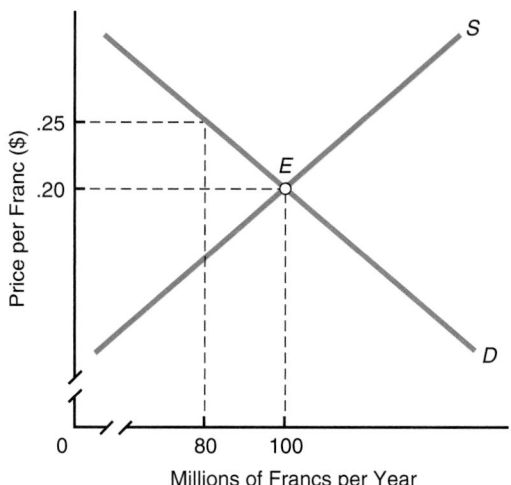

jeans the French want and how much French wine the Canadians want (given their respective incomes, their tastes, and the relative price of wine and jeans).[2]

A SHIFT IN DEMAND. Assume that a successful advertising campaign by Canadian wine importers has caused the Canadian demand (curve) for French wine to double. Canadians demand twice as much wine at all prices. Their demand curve for French wine has shifted outward to the right.

The increased demand for French wine can be translated into an increased demand for francs. All Canadians clamouring for bottles of French wine will supply more dollars to the foreign exchange market while demanding more French francs to pay for the wine. Figure 20.5 presents a new demand schedule, D_2, for French francs; this demand schedule is to the right of and outward from the original demand schedule. If the French do not change their desire for Canadian jeans, the supply schedule for French francs will remain stable. A new equilibrium will be established at a higher exchange rate. In our particular example, the new equilibrium is established at an exchange rate of 30 cents per franc. It now takes 30 cents to buy one French franc, whereas it took 20 cents before. This is translated as an increase in the price of French wine to Canadians and as a decrease in the price of Canadian jeans to the French. (Otherwise stated, there has been a decline in the foreign exchange value of the dollar.)

A SHIFT IN SUPPLY. We just assumed that Canadians' preference for French wine had shifted. Because the demand for French francs is a derived demand by Canadians for French wine, it has caused a shift in the demand curve for francs. Alternatively, assume that the supply curve of French francs shifts outward to the right. This may occur for many reasons, the most probable one being a relative rise in the French price level. For example, if the price of all French-made clothes went up 100 percent in francs, Canadian jeans would become relatively cheaper. That would mean that French people would want

---

[2] Remember that we are dealing with a two-country world in which we are considering only the exchange of Canadian jeans and French wine. In the real world, more than just goods and services are exchanged among countries. Some Canadians buy French financial assets; some French buy Canadian financial assets. We are ignoring such transactions for the moment.

FIGURE 20.5 A Shift in the Demand Schedule

The demand schedule for French wine shifts to the right, causing the derived demand schedule for francs to shift to the right also. We have shown this as a shift from D_1 to D_2. We have assumed that the French supply schedule for francs has remained stable—that is, French demand for Canadian jeans has remained constant. The old equilibrium foreign exchange rate was 20 cents. The new equilibrium exchange rate will be E_2; it will now cost 30 cents to buy one franc. The higher price of francs will be translated into a higher Canadian dollar price for French wine and a lower French franc price for Canadian jeans.

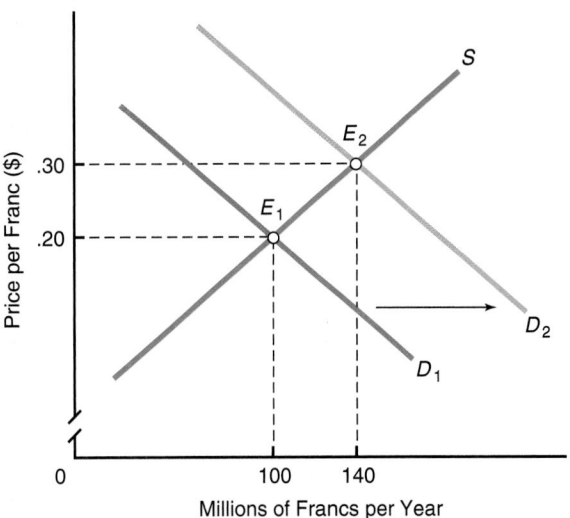

to buy more Canadian jeans. But remember that when they want to buy more Canadian jeans, they supply more francs to the foreign exchange market. Thus we see in Figure 20.6 that the supply curve of French francs moves from S to S_1. In the absence of restrictions—that is, in a system of flexible exchange rates—the new equilibrium exchange rate will be one franc equals 10 cents, or $1 equals 10 francs. The quantity of francs demanded and supplied will increase from 100 million per year to 200 million per year. We say, then, that in a flexible international exchange rate system, shifts in the demand for and supply of foreign currencies will cause changes in the equilibrium foreign exchange rates. Those rates will remain in effect until supply or demand shifts.

Try Preview Question 3:

What is a flexible exchange rate?

Market Determinants of Exchange Rates

The foreign exchange market is affected by many other changes in market variables in addition to changes in relative price levels, including these:

FIGURE 20.6 A Shift in the Supply of French Francs

There has been a shift in the supply curve for French francs. The new equilibrium will occur at E_1, meaning that 10 cents, rather than 20 cents, will now buy one franc. After the exchange rate adjustment, the amount of francs demanded and supplied will increase to 200 million per year.

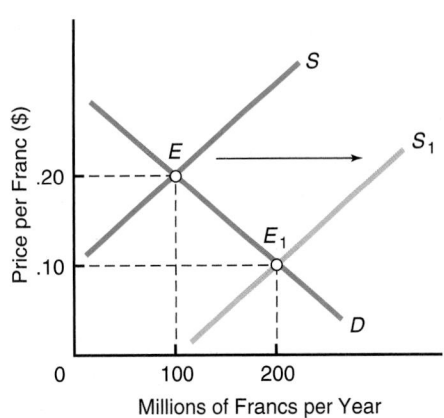

1. *Changes in real interest rates.* If Canada's interest rate, corrected for people's expectations of inflation, abruptly increases relative to the rest of the world, international investors elsewhere will increase their demand for dollar-denominated assets, thereby increasing the demand for dollars in foreign exchange markets. An increased demand for dollars in foreign exchange markets, other things held constant, will cause the dollar to appreciate and other currencies to depreciate.

2. *Changes in productivity.* Whenever one country's productivity increases relative to another's, the former country will become more price competitive in world markets. The demand for its exports will increase, and so, too, will the demand for its currency.

3. *Changes in product preferences.* If Germany's citizens suddenly develop a taste for Canadian-made automobiles, this will increase the derived demand for Canadian dollars in foreign exchange markets.

4. *Perceptions of economic stability.* As already mentioned, if Canada looks economically and politically more stable relative to other countries, more foreigners will want to put their savings into Canadian assets than into their own domestic assets. This will increase the demand for dollars.

Try Preview Question 4:
What factors can induce changes in equilibrium exchange rates?

CONCEPTS IN BRIEF

- The foreign exchange rate is the rate at which one country's currency can be exchanged for another's.
- The demand for foreign exchange is a derived demand; it is derived from the demand for foreign goods and services (and financial assets). The supply of foreign exchange is derived from foreigners' demands for our goods and services.
- In general, the demand curve of foreign exchange slopes downward and the supply curve of foreign exchange slopes upward. The equilibrium foreign exchange rate occurs at the intersection of the demand and supply curves for a currency.
- A shift in the demand for foreign goods will result in a shift in the demand for foreign exchange. The equilibrium foreign exchange rate will change. A shift in the supply of foreign currency will also cause a change in the equilibrium exchange rate.

The Gold Standard and the International Monetary Fund

The current system of more or less freely floating exchange rates is a recent development. We have had, in the past, periods of a gold standard, fixed exchange rates under the International Monetary Fund, and variants of these two.

The Gold Standard

Gold standard An international monetary system in which countries fix their exchange rates in terms of gold. All currencies are fixed in terms of all others, and any balance of payments deficits or surpluses can be made up by shipments of gold.

Until the 1930s, many countries were on a **gold standard**. The values of their currencies were tied directly to gold.[3] Countries operating under this gold standard agreed to redeem their currencies for a fixed amount of gold at the request of any holder of that currency. Although gold was not necessarily the means of exchange for world trade, it was the unit to which all currencies under the gold standard were pegged. And because all currencies in the system were linked to gold, exchange rates between those currencies were fixed. Indeed, the gold standard has been offered as the prototype of a fixed exchange rate sys-

---

[3] This is a simplification. Most countries were on a *specie metal standard* using gold, silver, copper, and other precious metals as money. Countries operating under this standard agreed to redeem their currencies for a fixed exchange rate.

tem. The heyday of the gold standard was from about 1870 to 1914. England had been on such a standard as far back as the 1820s. See Policy Example 20-1, on the following page, and determine whether Canada should return to the gold standard.

There turns out to be a relationship between the balance of payments and changes in domestic money supplies throughout the world. Under a gold standard, the international financial market reached equilibrium through the effect of gold flows on each country's money supply. When a country suffered a deficit in its balance of payments, more gold would flow out than in. Because the domestic money supply was based on gold, an outflow of gold to foreigners caused an automatic reduction in the domestic money supply. This caused several things to happen. Interest rates rose, thereby attracting foreign capital and improving the balance of payments. At the same time, the reduction in the money supply was equivalent to a restrictive monetary policy, which caused national output and prices to fall. Imports were discouraged and exports were encouraged, thereby again improving the balance of payments.

Two problems that plagued the gold standard were that no country had control of its domestic monetary policy and that the world's commerce was at the mercy of gold discoveries.

POLICY EXAMPLE 20-1

Should We Go Back to the Gold Standard?

In the past several decades, Canada has regularly run a current account deficit. The dollar has become weaker. We have had inflation. We have had recessions. Some economists and politicians argue that we should return to the gold standard. Canada operated under a gold standard from 1879 to 1931, except for a period during World War I. During this time, the dollar was defined as 23.22 grains of gold. During that time period, general prices more than doubled during World War I, there was a major recession in 1920–1921, and the Great Depression occurred.

Clearly, a gold standard is not a guarantee of either stable prices or economic stability.

For critical analysis: Why does no country today operate on a gold standard?

Bretton Woods and the International Monetary Fund

International Monetary Fund (IMF) An institution set up, in 1945, under the Bretton Woods agreement to manage the international monetary system. It established fixed exchange rates for the world's currencies.

In 1944, as World War II was ending, representatives from the world's capitalist countries met in Bretton Woods, New Hampshire, to create a new international payment system to replace the gold standard, which had collapsed during the 1930s. The Bretton Woods agreement created the **International Monetary Fund (IMF)**, to administer the agreement and to lend to member countries in balance of payments deficit. The arrangements thus provided are now called the old IMF system or the Bretton Woods system.

Each member country was assigned an IMF contribution quota determined by its international trade volume and national income. Twenty-five percent of the quota was contributed in gold or US dollars and 75 percent in its own currency. At the time, the IMF therefore consisted of a pool of gold, dollars, and other major currencies.

Par value The legally established value of the monetary unit of one country in terms of that of another.

Member governments were then obligated to intervene to maintain the values of their currencies in foreign exchange markets within 1 percent of the declared **par value**— the officially determined value. Except for a transitional arrangement permitting a one-time adjustment of up to 10 percent in par value, members could alter exchange rates thereafter only with the approval of the IMF. The agreement stated that such approval would be given only if the country's balance of payments was in *fundamental disequilibrium*, a term that has never been officially defined.

SPECIAL DRAWING RIGHTS. In 1967, the IMF created a new type of international money, *special drawing rights (SDRs)*. SDRs are exchanged only between monetary authorities (central banks). Their existence temporarily changed the IMF into a world central bank. The IMF creates SDRs the same way that the Bank of Canada can create dollars. The IMF allocates SDRs to member countries in accordance with their quotas. Currently, the SDR's value is determined by making one SDR equal to a bundle of currencies. In reality, the SDR rises or falls in terms of the American dollar.

END OF THE OLD IMF. In 1970, Canada moved away from the IMF peg and allowed the dollar to float. In 1971, the United States' government suspended the convertibility of the US dollar into gold. Finally, in March 1973, the finance ministers of the European Economic Community (now the European Union, or EU) announced that they would let their currencies float against the US dollar, something Japan had already begun doing with its yen. Since 1973, Canada and most other trading countries have had either freely floating exchange rates or managed ("dirty") floating exchange rates.

Fixed Versus Floating Exchange Rates

Canada went off the Bretton Woods system of fixed exchange rates in 1970. As Figure 20.7 indicates, many other nations of the world have been less willing to permit the values of their currencies to vary in the foreign exchange markets.

FIGURE 20.7 Current Foreign Exchange Rate Arrangements

Currently, 56 percent of the member nations of the International Monetary Fund have an independent float or managed float exchange rate agreement. Among countries with a fixed exchange rate, nearly one in three uses a fixed US dollar exchange rate. Fixing the exchange rate relative to a composite or basket of currencies is the next most common arrangement.

Source: International Monetary Fund.

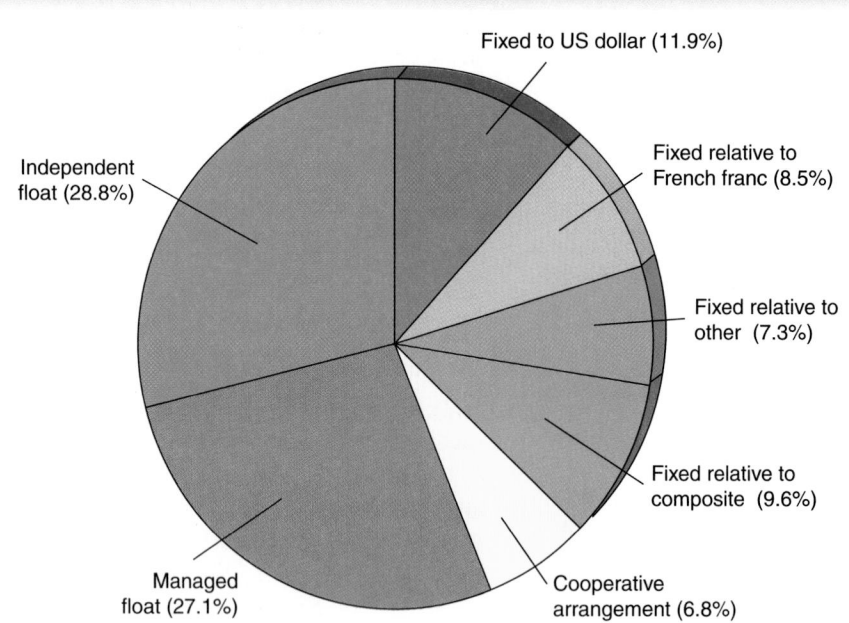

Fixed to US dollar (11.9%)

Fixed relative to French franc (8.5%)

Fixed relative to other (7.3%)

Fixed relative to composite (9.6%)

Cooperative arrangement (6.8%)

Managed float (27.1%)

Independent float (28.8%)

Fixing the Exchange Rate

How did nations fix their exchange rates in years past? How do many countries accomplish this today in a world in which the United States dollar is the international reserve currency? Figure 20.8 on the next page shows the market for baht, the currency of Thailand. At the initial equilibrium point E_1, US residents had to give up $0.40 to obtain 1 baht. Suppose now that there is an increase in the supply of baht for dollars, per-

FIGURE 20.8 A Fixed Exchange Rate

This figure illustrates how the Bank of Thailand could fix the dollar-baht exchange rate in the face of an increase in the supply of baht caused by a rise in the demand for US goods by Thai residents. In the absence of any action by the Bank of Thailand, the result would be a movement from point E_1 to point E_2. The dollar value of the baht would fall from $0.40 to $0.30. The Bank of Thailand can prevent this exchange rate change by purchasing baht with dollars in the foreign exchange market, thereby raising the demand for baht. At the new equilibrium point E_3, the baht's value remains at $0.40.

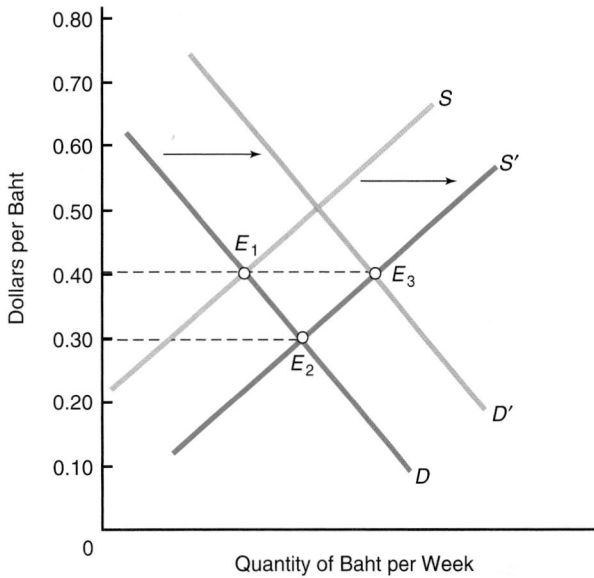

haps because Thai residents wish to buy more US goods. Other things being equal, the result would be a movement to point E_2 in Figure 20.8. The dollar value of the baht would fall to $0.30.

To prevent baht depreciation from occurring, however, the Bank of Thailand, the central bank, could increase the demand for baht in the foreign exchange market by purchasing baht with dollars. The Bank of Thailand can do this using dollars that it had on hand as part of its *foreign exchange reserves*. All central banks hold reserves of foreign currencies. Because the US dollar is a key international currency, the Bank of Thailand and other central banks typically hold billions of dollars in reserve so that they can, if they wish, make transactions such as the one in this example. Note that a sufficiently large purchase of baht could, as shown in Figure 20-8, cause the demand curve to shift rightward to achieve the new equilibrium point E_3, at which the baht's value remains at $0.40. Provided that it has enough dollar reserves on hand, the Bank of Thailand could maintain—effectively fix—the exchange rate in the face of the sudden fall in the demand for baht.

This is the manner in which the Bank of Thailand fixed the dollar-baht exchange rate until 1997. This basic approach—varying the amount of the national currency demanded at any given exchange rate in foreign exchange markets when necessary—is also the way that *any* central bank seeks to keep its nation's currency value unchanged in light of changing market forces.

> Central banks can keep exchange rates fixed as long as they have enough foreign exchange reserves available to deal with potentially long-lasting changes in the demand for or supply of their nation's currency.

Try Preview Question 5:
How can policymakers attempt to keep exchange rates fixed?

Can Foreign Exchange Rates Be Fixed Forever?

Trying to keep the exchange rate fixed in the face of foreign exchange market volatility can be a difficult policy to pursue. Consider Thailand's experience. At the beginning of 1997, the Bank of Thailand was holding $40 billion in foreign exchange reserves. Within 10 months, those reserves had fallen to $3 billion. Whatever the Bank of Thailand promised about not devaluing, it no longer had credibility. Not surprisingly, the baht's value relative to the dollar fell by more than 25 percent in July 1997 alone.

The Thai experience was repeated on a larger scale throughout Southeast Asia in 1997 and 1998 as efforts by the central banks of Indonesia, Malaysia, South Korea, and Vietnam to fix exchange rates ultimately collapsed, leading to sizable devaluations. Even the previously stalwart exchange rate arrangements of Singapore, Taiwan, and Hong Kong became increasingly less credible. These nations learned an old lesson: Trying to protect residents from foreign exchange risks works only as long as foreign exchange market traders believe that central banks have the financial wherewithal to keep exchange rates unchanged. Otherwise, a fixed exchange rate policy can ultimately prove unsustainable.

For critical analysis: Why do you think governments attempt to maintain the foreign exchange value of their domestic currencies?

Pros and Cons of a Fixed Exchange Rate

Why might a nation such as Thailand wish to keep the value of its currency from fluctuating? One reason is that changes in the exchange rate can affect the market value of assets that are denominated in foreign currencies. This can increase the financial risks that a nation's residents face, thereby forcing them to incur costs to avoid these risks.

FOREIGN EXCHANGE RISK. The possibility that variations in the market value of assets can take place as a result of changes in the value of a nation's currency is called the **foreign exchange risk** that residents of a country face because their nation's currency value can vary. For instance, if companies in Thailand had many loans denominated in dollars but earned nearly all their revenues in baht from sales within Thailand, a decline in the dollar value of the baht would mean that Thai companies would have to allocate a larger portion of their earnings to make the same *dollar* loan payments as before. Thus a fall in the baht's value would increase the operating costs of these companies, thereby reducing their profitability and raising the likelihood of eventual bankruptcy.

Limiting foreign exchange risk is a classic rationale for adopting a fixed exchange rate. Nevertheless, a country's residents are not defenseless against foreign exchange risk. They can **hedge** against such risk, meaning that they can adopt strategies intended to offset the risk arising from exchange rate variations. For example, a company in Thailand that has significant euro earnings from sales in Germany but sizable loans from US investors could arrange to convert its euro earnings into dollars via special types of foreign exchange contracts called *currency swaps*. The Thai company could thereby avoid holdings of baht and shield itself—*hedge*—against variations in the baht's value.

THE EXCHANGE RATE AS A SHOCK ABSORBER. If fixing the exchange rate limits foreign exchange risk, why do so many nations allow the exchange rates to float? The answer must be that there are potential drawbacks associated with fixing exchange rates. One is that exchange rate variations can actually perform a valuable service for a nation's econ-

Foreign exchange risk The possibility that changes in the value of a nation's currency will result in variations in market values of assets.

Hedge A financial strategy that reduces the chance of suffering losses arising from foreign exchange risk.

omy. Consider a situation in which residents of a nation speak only their own nation's language, which is so difficult that hardly anyone else in the world takes the trouble to learn it. As a result, the country's residents are very *immobile*: They cannot trade their labour skills outside of their own nation's borders.

Now think about what happens if this nation chooses to fix its exchange rate. Imagine a situation in which other countries begin to sell products that are close substitutes for the products its people specialize in producing, causing a sizable drop in worldwide demand for the nation's goods. Over a short-run period in which prices and wages cannot adjust, the result will be a sharp decline in production of goods and services, a fall-off in national income, and higher unemployment. Contrast this situation with one in which the exchange rate floats. In this case, a sizable decline in outside demand for the nation's products will cause it to experience a trade deficit, which will lead to a significant drop in the demand for the nation's currency. As a result, the nation's currency will experience a sizable depreciation, making the goods that the nation offers to sell abroad much less expensive in other countries. People abroad who continue to consume the nation's products will increase their purchases, and the nation's exports will increase. Its production will begin to recover somewhat, as will its residents' incomes. Unemployment will begin to fall.

This example illustrates how exchange rate variations can be beneficial, especially if a nation's residents are relatively immobile. It can be much more difficult, for example, for a Polish resident who has never studied Portuguese to make a move to Lisbon, even if she is highly qualified for available jobs there. If many residents of Poland face similar linguistic or cultural barriers, Poland could be better off with a floating exchange rate even if its residents must incur significant costs hedging against foreign exchange risk as a result.

Splitting the Difference: Dirty Floats and Target Zones

In recent years, national policymakers have tried to soften the choice of either adopting a fixed exchange rate or allowing exchange rates full flexibility in the foreign exchange markets by "splitting the difference" between the two extremes.

A DIRTY FLOAT.   One way to split the difference is to let exchange rates float most of the time but "manage" exchange rate movements part of the time. Canada went off the Bretton Woods system in 1970, but it has nonetheless tried to keep certain elements of that system in play. We have occasionally engaged in what is called a **dirty float**, or management of flexible exchange rates. The management of flexible exchange rates has usually come about through international policy cooperation. For example, the Group of Seven (G-7) nations—Canada, France, Germany, Italy, Japan, the United Kingdom, and the United States—have for some time shared information on their policy objectives and procedures. They do this through regular meetings between economic policy secretaries, ministers, and staff members. One of their principal objectives has been to "smooth out" foreign exchange rates.

Is it possible for these groups to "manage" foreign exchange rates? Some economists do not think so. For example, economists Michael Bordo and Anna Schwartz studied the foreign exchange intervention actions coordinated by the Federal Reserve and the United States' Treasury for the second half of the 1980s. Besides showing that such interventions were sporadic and variable, Bordo and Schwartz came to an even more compelling conclusion: Exchange rate interventions were trivial relative to the total trading of foreign exchange on a daily basis. Thus their conclusion is that neither the Canadian central bank nor the central banks of the other G-7 nations can influence exchange rates in the long run.

CRAWLING PEGS.   Another approach to splitting the difference between fixed and floating exchange rates is called a **crawling peg**. This is an automatically adjusting target for

Dirty float A system between flexible and fixed exchange rates in which central banks occasionally enter foreign exchange markets to influence rates.

Crawling peg An exchange rate arrangement in which a country pegs the value of its currency to the exchange value of another nation's currency but allows the par value to change at regular intervals.

the value of a nation's currency. For instance, a central bank might announce that it wants the value of its currency relative to the US dollar to decline at an annual rate of 5 percent, a rate of depreciation that it feels is consistent with long-run market forces. The central bank would then try to buy or sell foreign exchange reserves in sufficient quantities to be sure that the currency depreciation takes place gradually, thereby reducing the foreign exchange risk faced by the nation's residents.

In this way, a crawling peg functions like a floating exchange rate in the sense that the exchange rate can change over time. But it is like a fixed exchange rate in the sense that the central bank always tries to keep the exchange rate close to a target value. In this way, a crawling peg has elements of both kinds of exchange rate systems.

TARGET ZONES. A third way to try to split the difference between fixed and floating exchange rates is to adopt an exchange rate **target zone**. Under this policy, a central bank announces that there are specific upper and lower *bands*, or limits, for permissible values for the exchange rate. Within those limits, which define the exchange rate target zone, the central bank permits the exchange rate to move flexibly. The central bank commits itself, however, to intervene in the foreign exchange markets to ensure that its nation's currency value will not rise above the upper band or fall below the lower band. For instance, if the exchange rate approaches the upper band, the central bank must sell foreign exchange reserves in sufficient amounts of foreign exchange reserves to halt any further currency appreciation.

Starting in 1999, officials from the European Union attempted to get the United States, Japan, and several other countries' governments to agree to target zones for the exchange rate between the newly created euro and the dollar, yen, and some other currencies. Officials in the United States were not in favour. So far no target zones have been created, and the euro has floated freely—mostly downward.

Target zone A range of permitted exchange rate variations between upper and lower exchange rate bands that a central bank defends by selling or buying foreign exchange reserves.

Try Preview Question 6:
What are alternative approaches to limiting exchange rate variability?

CONCEPTS IN BRIEF

- The International Monetary Fund was developed after World War II as an institution to maintain fixed exchange rates in the world. Since 1973, however, fixed exchange rates have disappeared in most major trading countries. For these nations, exchange rates are largely determined by the forces of demand and supply in foreign exchange markets.
- Many other nations, however, have tried to fix their exchange rates, with varying degrees of success. Although fixing the exchange rate helps protect a nation's residents from foreign exchange risk, this policy makes less mobile residents susceptible to greater volatility in income and employment. It can also expose the central bank to sporadic currency crises arising from unpredictable changes in world capital flows.
- Countries have experimented with exchange rate systems between the extremes of fixed and floating exchange rates. Under a dirty float, a central bank permits the value of its nation's currency to float in the foreign exchange markets but intervenes from time to time to influence the exchange rate. Under a crawling peg, a central bank tries to push its nation's currency value in a desired direction. Pursuing a target zone policy, a central bank aims to keep the exchange rate between upper and lower bands, intervening only when the exchange rate approaches either limit.

Making Foreign Exchange Markets More Efficient

The buying and selling of foreign exchange can involve considerable transaction costs. This is particularly true for companies that do not engage in large orders. The Internet has allowed for increased efficiency in this market, at least measured by real-time access and lower implicit commission rates for such transactions.

Back in 1993, a company called E-FOREX was founded to take advantage of Internet technology to develop a new marketplace for foreign exchange. In October 1995, E-FOREX completed its first Internet-based foreign exchange trade. Initially, E-FOREX was conceived as an online brokerage company, similar to E*Trade for stocks. Starting in 1996, though, E-FOREX began to license its Internet platforms to other financial institutions. Banks, brokers, and asset managers, for companies, pension plans, and governments, are using E-FOREX to trade today.

Consider a client that wishes to convert US dollars to pay a 13 million yen invoice from its Japanese parts supplier. Even though a foreign exchange trading company would charge only a $50 commission on such a trade, it would also impose a large "spread" between the buying and selling price of yen. E-FOREX charges no commission but makes its profit on a small spread. In this transactions, the savings would be over $500 to the client. Throughout a year's worth of transactions, these savings might become considerable.

With large quantities of dollars, yen, euros, baht, and other currencies being traded over the Internet, security is a major issue. E-FOREX incorporates the latest 128-bit encryption technology and uses digital certificates from Versign as well as firewalls, which prevent outsiders from entering the secure system.

To avoid disaster, if one computer system fails, E-FOREX, similar to other Internet-based brokerage companies, operates two or more systems for routers and database servers. In addition, a remote backup data centre supports those systems redundantly. In the event of a service interruption at any facility, no data are lost.

Finally, E-FOREZX provides so-called 100 percent double-blind dealing. The party who takes the other side of a client's trade does not know who the client is, and vice versa. This increases foreign exchange efficiency because no clients can guess at the direction of trades and skew rates to earn trading profits in excess of a normal profit. ●

ISSUES AND APPLICATIONS

Should We Worry About the Weak Dollar?

Concepts Applied: Flexible exchange rates, current account deficit, depreciation

The dollar became relatively weaker against the yen and deutsche mark in 1984. However, the dollar has held its value when weighted against the currencies of all Canadian trading partners.

The course of history has seen various countries emerge at different times to dominate world trade. Rome's currency was the world's strongest for a period of 400 years, but then it lost its attractiveness in world trade. The United Kingdom saw its currency, the pound sterling, lose its world dominance over a period of 50 years. Now the United States' currency is on top. Do we need to worry because not only has Canada's currency never dominated world currency markets, it now also seems to be becoming weaker relative to those of our major trading partners?

The Dwindling Value of the Dollar

The dollar definitely does not seem to buy as much as it used to. Figure 20.9 shows what has happened to dollar exchange rates with respect to the yen and the deutsche mark. The value of the dollar against those two currencies has been falling steadily since 1984. There are several reasons the yen and the mark have become so strong and the dollar so weak. Until 1997, both Japan and Germany had lower rates of inflation than Canada. Also, at least in Germany, investors have earned higher rates of return.

FIGURE 20.9 The Dollar Relative to the Deutsche Mark and the Yen

From the mid-1980s to the late 1990s, the value of the Canadian dollar in terms of the German (deutsche) mark and the Japanese yen tended to decline.

Source: Bank of Canada Review.

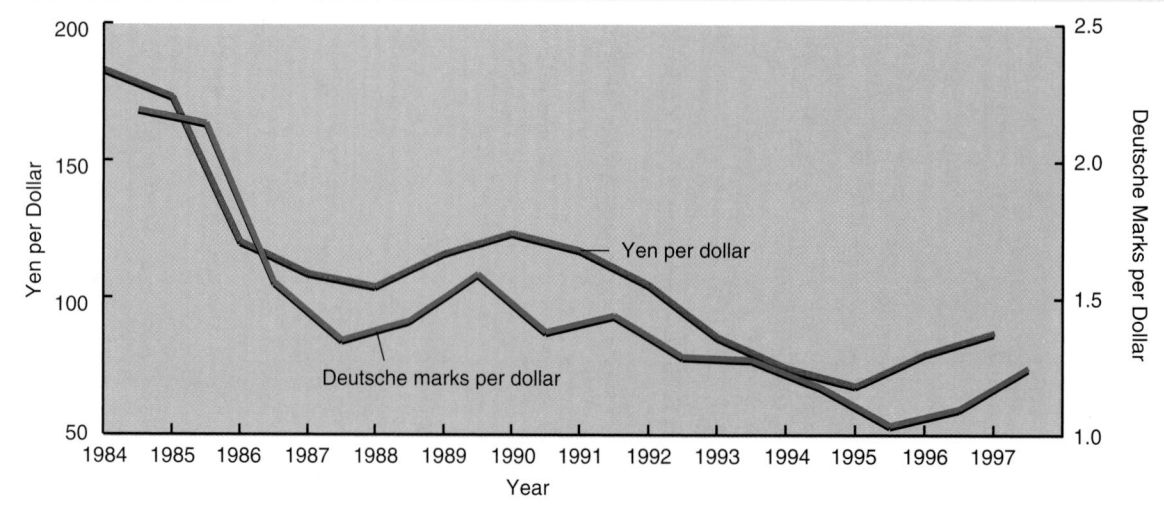

FIGURE 20.10 The Dollar Relative to an Index of 45 Currencies

If we look at the dollar relative to a basket of 45 of the world's currencies, it has held more or less firm since 1994.

Sources: J. P. Morgan Company.

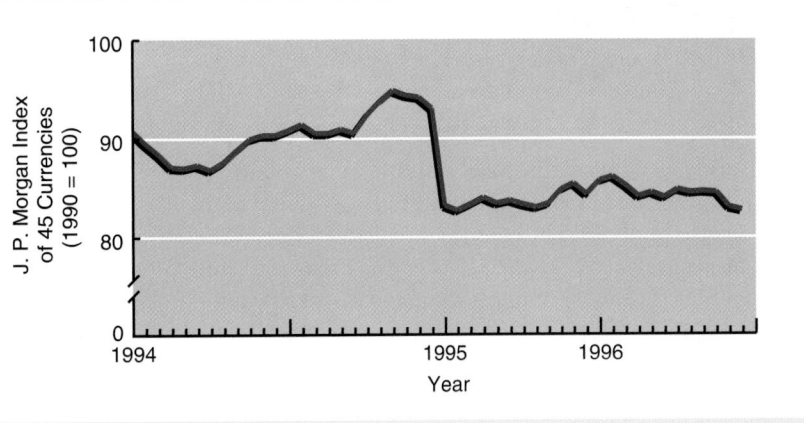

Who Is Hurt by the Falling Dollar?

Besides the outraged Canadian tourist in Germany, France, Switzerland, and Japan, who else is hurt by the weak dollar? The weaker dollar translates into higher prices for imported goods, such as BMWs, Mercedes, Toyotas, NEC computers, and Nintendo videogames. So Canadians who purchase imported goods from countries whose currencies are stronger relative to the dollar must now pay more than they did before. But there is a flip side to this equation. Foreigners now find our products cheaper, so employees and shareholders in Canadian companies that export find themselves better off.

Is the Dollar Really So Weak?

The dollar is indisputably changing relative to the yen, the deutsche mark, the Swiss franc, the French franc, the American dollar, and a few other currencies. But as you can see in Figure 20.10, the dollar has actually held its own since early 1995. Weighted against the currencies of all of Canada's trading partners, the dollar has been relatively stable since 1990.

The Dollar Is Still in Demand

Even though our dollar does not dominate money markets, millions of dollars of Canadian currency are held overseas. To obtain these dollar bills, foreigners have had to give up something of value, such as oil, computers, and tomatoes. In return, we were kind enough to give them pieces of paper money that cost us virtually nothing to produce. As long as they hold on to those pieces of paper, we are obtaining an interest-free loan which is repaid when foreigners buy goods and services from us.

For Critical Analysis

1. Why would a lower rate of inflation in Germany lead to a weaker dollar?

2. Why would foreigners agree to hold dollar bills instead of their own currencies?

CHAPTER SUMMARY

1. The balance of merchandise trade is defined as the value of goods bought and sold in the world market, usually during the period of one year. The balance of payments is a more inclusive concept that includes the value of all transactions in the world market.

2. Canadians purchase financial assets in other countries, and foreigners purchase Canadian financial assets, such as stocks or bonds. The buying and selling of foreign financial assets has the same effect on the balance of payments as the buying and selling of goods and services.

3. Our balance of trade and payments can be affected by our relative rate of inflation and by political instability elsewhere compared to the stability that exists in Canada.

4. Market determinants of exchange rates are changes in real interest rates (interest rates corrected for inflation), changes in productivity, changes in product preferences, and perceptions of economic stability.

5. To transact business internationally, it is necessary to convert domestic currencies into other currencies. This is done via the foreign exchange market. If we were trading with France only, French producers would want to be paid in francs because they must pay their workers in francs. Canadian producers would want to be paid in dollars because Canadian workers are paid in dollars.

6. A Canadian's desire for French wine is expressed in terms of a supply of dollars, which is in turn a demand for French francs in the foreign exchange market. The opposite situation arises when the French wish to buy Canadian jeans. Their demand for jeans creates a demand for Canadian dollars and a supply of French francs.

We put the demand and supply schedules together to find the equilibrium foreign exchange rate. The demand schedule for foreign exchange is a derived demand—it is derived from Canadians' demand for foreign products.

7. With no government intervention, a market-clearing equilibrium foreign exchange rate will emerge. After a shift in demand or supply, the exchange rate will change so that it will again clear the market.

8. If Canadians increase their demand for French wine, the demand curve for French wine shifts to the right. The derived demand for francs also shifts to the right. The supply schedule of francs, however, remains stable because the French demand for Canadian jeans has remained constant. The shifted demand schedule intersects the stable supply schedule at a higher price (the foreign exchange rate increases). This is an appreciation of the value of the French franc (a depreciation of the value of the dollar against the franc).

9. In a managed exchange rate system (a "dirty float"), central banks occasionally intervene in foreign exchange markets to influence exchange rates.

10. Under a gold standard, movement of gold across countries changes domestic money supplies, causing price levels to change and to correct balance of payments imbalances.

11. In 1945, the International Monetary Fund (IMF) was created to maintain fixed exchange rates throughout the world. The Bretton Woods system was abandoned by the major signatories by 1973.

DISCUSSION OF PREVIEW QUESTIONS

1. What is the difference between the balance of trade and the balance of payments?

The balance of trade is defined as the difference between the value of exports and the value of imports. If the value of exports exceeds the value of imports, a trade surplus exists; if the value of exports is less than the value of imports, a trade deficit exists; if export and import values are equal, we refer to this situation as a trade balance. The balance of payments is more general and takes into account the value of *all* international transactions. Thus the balance of payments identifies not only goods and services transactions among countries but also investments (financial and nonfinancial) and gifts (private and public). When the value of all these transactions is such that one country is sending more to other countries than it is receiving in return, a balance of payments deficit exists. A payments surplus and payments balance are self-explanatory.

2. What is a foreign exchange rate?

We know that countries trade with one another; they buy and sell goods, make and receive financial and nonfinancial investments, and give and receive gifts. However, countries have different currencies. People who sell to, invest in, or receive gifts from Canada ultimately want their own currency so that they can use the money domestically. Similarly, Canadian residents who sell to, invest in, or receive gifts from people in other countries ultimately want Canadian dollars to spend in Canada. Because most people want to end up with their own currencies, foreign exchange markets have evolved to enable people to sell one currency for other currencies. A foreign exchange rate, then, is the rate at which one country's currency can be exchanged for another's. For example, the exchange rate between the United Kingdom (UK) and Canada might dictate that one pound sterling is equivalent to $2.50; alternately stated, the Canadian dollar is worth 0.40 pounds sterling.

3. What is a flexible exchange rate system?

A flexible exchange rate system is an international monetary system in which foreign exchange rates are allowed to fluctuate to reflect changes in the supply of and demand for international currencies. Say that Canada and the UK are in payments balance at the exchange rate of one pound sterling to Canadian $2.50. The Canadian demand for sterling is derived from private and government desires to buy British goods, to invest in the UK, or to send gifts to the British people and is *inversely* related to the number of dollars it takes to buy one pound. Conversely, the supply of sterling is derived from the UK's private and governmental desires to buy Canadian goods and services, to invest in Canada, and to send gifts to Canadian residents. The supply of sterling is *directly* related to the number of dollars one pound is worth. The intersection of the supply and demand curves for sterling determines the market foreign exchange rate of dollars per pound. In a system of flexible exchange rates, shifts in the supply or demand curves will lead to changes in the foreign exchange rates between countries.

4. What factors can induce changes in equilibrium exchange rates?

The equilibrium exchange rate changes in response to changes in the demand for or supply of another nation's currency. Changes in desired flows of exports or imports, real interest rates, productivity in one nation relative to productivity in another nation, tastes and preferences of consumers, and perceptions of economic stability are key factors that can affect the positions of the demand and supply curves in foreign exchange markets. Thus, changes in these factors can induce variations in equilibrium exchange rates.

5. How can policymakers attempt to keep exchange rates fixed?

If the current price of another nation's currency in terms of the home currency starts to fall below the level where the home country wants it to remain, the home country's central bank can use reserves of the other nation's currency to purchase the home currency in foreign exchange markets. This raises the demand for the home currency and thereby pushes up the currency's value in terms of the other nation's currency. In this way, the home country can keep the exchange rate fixed at a desired value, as long as it has sufficient reserves of the other currency to use for this purpose.

6. What are alternative approaches to limiting exchange rate variability?

Today, many nations permit their exchange rates to vary in foreign exchange markets. Others pursue policies that limit the variability of exchange rates. Some engage in a dirty float, in which they mange exchange rates, often in cooperation with other nations. Some establish crawling pegs, in which the target value of the exchange rate is adjusted automatically over time. And some establish target zones, with upper and lower limits on the extent to which exchange rates are allowed to vary.

PROBLEMS

(Answers to the odd-numbered problems appear at the back of the book.)

20-1. In the graph, what can be said about the shift from D to D_1?

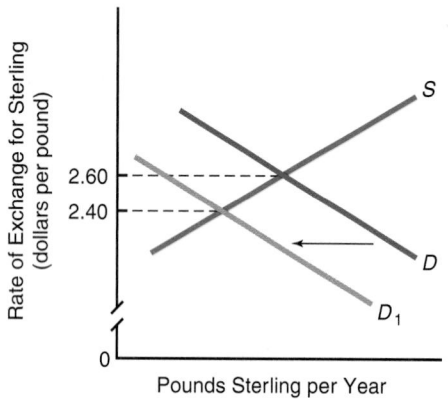

Pounds Sterling per Year

a. It could be caused by the British demanding fewer Canadian products.

b. It is a result of increased Canadian demand for British goods.

c. It causes an appreciation of the dollar relative to the pound.

d. It causes an appreciation of the pound relative to the dollar.

20-2. If the rate of exchange between the pound and the dollar is $2.00 for one pound, and Canada then experiences severe inflation, we would expect the exchange rate (under a flexible rate system) to change. What would be the new rate?

a. More than $2.00 for one pound

b. Less than $2.00 for one pound

c. More than one pound for $2.00

d. None of the above

20-3. The dollar, the pound sterling, and the deutsche mark are the currency units of Canada, the United Kingdom, and Germany, respectively. Suppose that these countries decide to go on a gold standard and define the value of their currencies in terms of gold as follows: $400 = 1 ounce of gold; 160 pounds sterling = 1 ounce of gold; and 475 marks = 1 ounce of gold. What would the exchange rate be between the dollar and the pound? Between the dollar and the mark? Between the mark and the pound?

20-4. Examine the following hypothetical data for Canadian international transactions, in billions of dollars.

Exports: goods, 165.8; services, 130.5
Imports: goods, –250.7; services, –99.3
Net investment: –20.0
Net transfers: –20.0

a. What is the balance of trade?

b. What is the balance on goods and services?

c. What is the balance on current account?

20-5. Maintenance of a fixed exchange rate system requires government intervention to keep exchange rates stable. What is the policy implication of this fact? (Hint: Think in terms of the money supply.)

20-6. Suppose that we have the following demand schedule for German beer in Canada per week:

Price per Case	Quantity Demanded (cases)
$40	2
32	4
24	6
16	8
8	10

a. If the price is 30 deutsche marks per case, how many marks are required to purchase each quantity demanded?

b. Now derive the demand schedule for marks per week in Canada to pay for German beer.

c. At a price of 80 cents per mark, how many cases of beer would be imported from Germany per week?

20-7. The graph on the next page shows the supply of and demand for pounds sterling.

a. Assuming that the demand for sterling is represented by D, what is the dollar price of pounds? What is the equilibrium quantity?

b. Suppose that there is general inflation in Canada. Starting at D, which demand curve could represent this situation? If exchange rates are allowed to float freely, what would be the new dollar price of one pound sterling? What would be the equilibrium quantity?

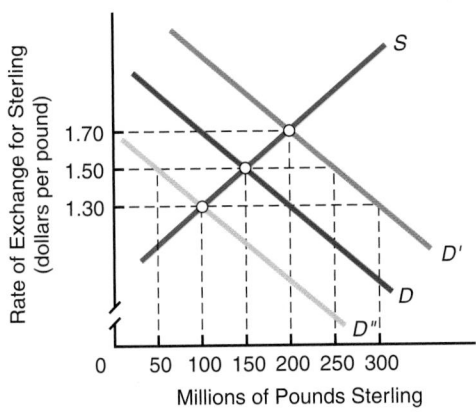

c. Suppose that the inflation in part (b) occurs and Canada has the dollar price of one pound sterling fixed at $1.50. How would the Bank of Canada be able to accomplish this?

d. Now suppose that instead of inflation, there was general deflation in Canada. Which demand curve could represent this situation? How could Canada maintain a fixed price of $1.50 per pound sterling in this situation?

20-8. Which of the following will cause the yen to appreciate? Explain.

a. Canadian real incomes increase relative to Japanese real incomes.

b. It is expected that in the future the yen will depreciate relative to the dollar.

c. The Canadian inflation rate rises relative to the Japanese inflation rate.

d. The after-tax, risk-adjusted real interest rate in Canada rises relative to that in Japan.

e. Canadian tastes change in favour of Japanese-made goods.

ECONOMICS ON THE NET

What Are Canadian Exchange Rates?

Internet URL: http://www.bankofcanada.ca

Title: Canadian Exchange Rates

Navigation: Begin at the homepage of the Bank of Canada (http://www.bankofcanada.ca). Click on English, then on Currency, then on Currency Converter and, finally, Nominal Noon Exchange Rates.

Application: Perform the operations indicated above and answer the following questions:

a. The Canadian dollar converts into how many US dollars? The U.S. dollar converts into how many Canadian dollars?

b. For each day during a given week, track the value of the Canadian dollar relative to the US dollar. Based on your tabulations, try to predict the value of the currency at the end of the next week, following your data collections.

DEVELOPMENT: ECONOMIC GROWTH AROUND THE WORLD

Children in Canada have gathered money in boxes for the United Nations Children's Fund (UNICEF) at Hallowe'en for many years. This money is used by the organization to help developing nations with aid and development programs especially aimed at children.

In its recent report, "State of the World's Children 2001," UNICEF makes the argument that economic development is greatly helped by programs that aid children. Investing in basic education and nutrition, and in the education of their mothers, makes a decisive difference in the long-run economic health of a nation.

In this chapter, we'll look at many of the issues that surround international development.

PREVIEW QUESTIONS

1. What is a developing country?

2. Must developing countries develop by industrializing?

3. Can developing countries create their own capital stock?

4. Does a lack of protected property rights hinder a developing country's development?

Did You Know That... a 1967 best-selling business book called *The American Challenge* predicted that by 1985, the world's economies would be owned and run by a dozen huge American multinationals, producing over 90 percent of the world's manufactured goods? Of course, nothing could be further from the truth today. American companies remain important in the world economy, but they do not dominate. Since that prediction was made, Germany, Japan, South Korea, Hong Kong, Singapore, and Taiwan grew to become economic powerhouses. Today, there are indeed many "rich" countries, including, of course, Canada. But this country was not always rich. In fact, it was quite poor 200 years ago. If you go back far enough, every country was poor and undeveloped. Why do some countries develop faster than others? In other words, what causes economic development? Although there are no easy answers to this important question, economists now have enough data to know what conditions favour economic growth in the developing world.

Putting World Poverty in Perspective

It is difficult to comprehend the reality of poverty in the world today. At least one-half, if not two-thirds, of the world's population lives at subsistence level, with just enough to eat for survival. The official poverty level in Canada exceeds the average income in at least half the world. That is not to say that we should ignore problems at home with the poor and homeless simply because they are living better than many people elsewhere in the world. Rather, it is necessary for Canadians to keep their perspective on what are considered problems for this country relative to what are considered problems elsewhere.

What Is Development Economics?

How did developed countries travel the path from extreme poverty to relative riches? In part, the answer is the same as the answers we looked at in Chapter 10 on long-run growth. However, because of the differences between the developed nations, who took many years to reach their current state of economic development and the desire to speed up the process, there are substantial differences in the approach needed. That is the essential issue of development economics. It is the study of why some countries develop and others do not. Further, it is the study of changes in policies that might help developing countries get richer. It is not good enough simply to say that people in diverse countries are different and therefore that is why some countries are rich while some are poor. Economists do not deny that different cultures create different work ethics, but they are unwilling to accept such a pat and fatalistic answer.

Look at any world map. About four-fifths of the countries you will see on that map are considered relatively poor. The goal of students of development economics is to help the more than four billion people with low living standards today join the billion or so who have relatively high living standards.

Industrially Advanced Economies

Any system of defining poor countries and rich countries, developing countries and developed countries, is, of course, arbitrary. Nonetheless, it is instructive to examine some figures on the difference between **industrially advanced countries (IACs)** and so-called developing countries. There are 19 IACs. (Excluded from this classification are countries whose economies are based on a single resource, such as oil, but whose industrial development in other fields is minimal.) The latest data available on the IACs (1995) show an estimated per capita income of $16,341, an annual growth rate of about 2.2 percent,

Industrially advanced countries (IACs) Canada, Japan, the United States, and the countries of Western Europe, all of which have market economies based on a large skilled labour force and a large technically advanced stock of capital goods.

and a population growth of about 0.6 percent. At the other end of the scale, the more than 100 developing countries have a per capita income of $980, an annual growth rate of almost 3 percent, and a population growth rate of 2 percent per year, more than three times that of the IACs.

To be sure, we must be careful about accepting such data at face value. There is a tremendous disparity in incomes among the developing countries, and the data are notoriously inaccurate. Nonetheless, it is certain that a tremendous gap exists between average incomes in the IACs and in the developing countries. See Thinking Critically About the Media 21-1 for further illumination.

Thinking Critically About the Media 21-1   The Gap Between the Rich and the Poor

Contrary to what we are often told by the media, government statisticians, and politicians, the rich countries are not leaving the poor countries in the dust. The International Monetary Fund revised its estimates of relative size of economies a few years ago and came up with this startling conclusion: The share of world output produced by the rich industrial economies is only 54 percent rather than the 75 percent formerly reported. Because the majority of countries in the developing world are growing faster than those in the developed world, the world's rich countries will dominate the world economy less and less in the future.

Newly Industrialized Economies

Not all developing countries are stuck in abject poverty. The developing countries vary greatly in their ability to experience economic growth, but one group of recently industrialized economies achieved annual growth rates two and three times that of Canada. These newly industrialized economies are the so-called Four Tigers—Singapore, Hong Kong, Taiwan, and South Korea—all on the Pacific Rim. From 1960 to 1995, per capita income in these economies grew sixfold. One of the reasons the newly industrialized countries have grown so rapidly is that a huge increase in world trade and in international communications has allowed technology to be disseminated much more quickly today than in the past. Indeed, these countries have advanced so quickly that three of the four now have a higher per capita income than Spain, the United Kingdom, and Italy. Yet during the same 35-year period, a number of sub-Saharan African countries experienced a *fall* in real per capita income.

Try Preview Question 1:

What is a developing country?

CONCEPTS IN BRIEF

- Any definition of developing countries or industrially advanced countries (IACs) is arbitrary. Nonetheless, we have identified 19 IACs and over 100 developing countries.
- The IACs have per capita incomes that are roughly 17 times the per capita incomes in the developing countries. Population in developing countries is growing more than three times as fast as in the IACs.
- Four newly industrialized countries on the Pacific Rim—Singapore, Taiwan, South Korea, and Hong Kong—have increased their real per capita incomes sixfold since 1960.

Economic Development: Industry Versus Agriculture

One of the most widely discussed theories of development concerns the need for balanced growth, with industry and agriculture given equal importance. One characteristic of many developed countries is their high degree of industrialization, although there are clearly exceptions—Hong Kong, for example. In general, countries with relatively high standards of living are more industrialized than countries with low standards of living. The policy prescription then seems obvious: less-developed countries in which a large percentage of the total resources are devoted to agricultural pursuits should attempt to obtain more balanced growth by industrializing (Refer to International Example 21-1).

Although the theory is fairly acceptable at first glance, it leads to some absurd results. We find that in many developing countries with steel factories and automobile plants the people are actually worse off because of this attempted industrialization. Most developing countries currently cannot profitably produce steel or automobiles because they lack the necessary domestic human and physical capital. They can engage in such industrial activities only with heavy government subsidization of the industry itself. Import restrictions abound, preventing the purchase of foreign, mostly cheaper substitutes for the industrial products that the country itself produces. Also, in general, the existence of subsidies leads to a misallocation of resources and a lower economic welfare for the country as a whole.

INTERNATIONAL EXAMPLE 21-1

Industrialized Poverty

Amazingly, some of the poorest countries in the world today have some of the highest rates of industrialization. Industry's share of gross output is greater in sub-Saharan Africa than in Denmark, is greater in Zimbabwe, Botswana, and Trinidad and Tobago than in Japan, and is greater in Argentina than in every country in the European Union!

Agriculture represents a relatively low share of gross output in some of the world's poorest countries. For example, agriculture represents a greater share of national output in Denmark than it does in Trinidad and Tobago. The same is true in Spain relative to Botswana, and in Portugal relative to Gabon. It is clear that industrialization does not necessarily lead to high standards of living.

For critical analysis: If industry represents a large share of gross output in extremely poor countries, what does this tell you about the rate of return on investment in industry in those countries?

The Stages of Development: Agriculture to Industry to Services

If we analyze the development of modern rich countries, we find that they went through three stages. First is the agricultural stage, when most of the population is involved in agriculture. Then comes the manufacturing stage, when much of the population becomes involved in the industrialized sector of the economy. And finally there is a shift towards services. That is exactly what happened in Canada: The so-called tertiary, or service, sector of the economy continues to grow, whereas the manufacturing sector (and its share of employment) is declining in relative importance.

However, it is important to understand the need for early specialization in a country's comparative advantage. We have repeatedly referred to the doctrine of comparative advantage, and it is even more appropriate for the developing countries of the world. If trading is allowed among countries, a country is normally best off if it produces what it has a comparative advantage at producing and imports the rest (see Chapter 19). This means that many developing countries should continue to specialize in agricultural production or in labour-intensive manufactured goods.

Try Preview Question 2:

Must developing countries develop by industrializing?

How Subsidized Agriculture Affects Developing Countries

Modern Western countries have continually subsidized their own agricultural sectors to allow them to compete more easily with the developing countries in this area. If we lived in a world of no subsidization, we would probably see less food being produced in the highly developed Western world (except for Canada, the United States, and Australia) and much more being produced in the developing countries of the rest of the world. They would trade food for manufactured goods. It would seem, then, that one of the most detrimental aspects of our economic policy for the developing countries has been the continued subsidization of the Canadian farmer. Canada, of course, is not alone; virtually the entire European Union does exactly the same thing.

Even with this situation, however, a policy of using higher taxes on imported goods or domestic manufacturing subsidies in order to increase industrialization in the developing countries may do more harm than good. Industrialization is generally beneficial only if it comes about naturally, when the market conditions are such that the countries' entrepreneurs freely decide to build factories instead of increasing farm output because it is profitable to do so.

CONCEPTS IN BRIEF

- A balanced-growth theory predicts that industry and agriculture must grow together in order for a country to experience growth.
- For many developing countries, balanced growth requires subsidization of manufacturing firms.
- Historically, there are three stages of economic development: the agricultural stage, the manufacturing stage, and the service-sector stage, when a large part of the workforce is employed in providing services.

Natural Resources and Economic Development

One theory of development states that for a country to develop, it must have a large natural resource base. The theory continues to assert that much of the world is running out of natural resources, thereby limiting economic growth and development. We must point out that only the narrowest definition of a natural resource could lead to such an opinion. In broader terms, a natural resource is something scarce occurring in nature that we can use for our own purposes. Natural resources therefore include knowledge of the use of something. The natural resources that we could define several hundred years ago did not, for example, include hydroelectric power—no one knew that such a natural resource existed or, indeed, how to make it exist.

In any event, it is difficult to find a strong correlation between the natural resources of a country and its stage of development. Japan has virtually no crude oil and must import most of the natural resources that it uses as inputs for its industrial production. Brazil has huge amounts of natural resources, including fertile soil and abundant minerals, yet Brazil has a much lower per capita income than Japan. Only when we include the human element of natural resources can we say that natural resources determine economic development.

Natural resources by themselves are not particularly useful for economic development. They must be transformed into something usable for either investment or consumption. This leads us to another aspect of development, the trade-off between investment and consumption. The normal way this subject is analyzed is by dealing with investment simply as capital accumulation.

Capital Accumulation

It is often asserted that a necessary prerequisite for economic development is a large capital stock—machines and other durable goods that can be used to aid in the production of consumption goods and more capital goods in the future. It is true that industrially advanced countries indeed have larger capital stocks per capita than developing countries. It is also true that the larger the capital stock for any given population, the higher the possible rate of economic growth (assuming that the population makes good use of the capital goods). This is basically one of the foundations for many of the foreign aid programs in which Canada and other countries have engaged. We and other countries have attempted to give developing countries capital so that they, too, might grow. However, the amount of capital that we have actually given to other countries is quite small: a hydroelectric dam here, a factory there.

Thinking Critically About the Media 21-2   The Dark Side of the PC Revolution

According to more than a handful of articles, the "PC revolution" will increase the gap between the rich and the poor. According to one "expert," technology can only be afforded by the rich, and furthermore, computers displace "hordes of workers." Nothing could be further from the truth. The country that has the most computers in place per capita is the United States, and its unemployment rate has not varied much in the past two decades. Moreover, even if computers are essential to the success of a business, their prices are dropping every month. And what is to prevent several businesses in less-developed countries from sharing a PC if the price is too high?

Domestic Capital Formation

How does a developing country accumulate capital? The answer is that it must save, and invest those accumulated savings profitably. Saving, of course, means not consuming. Resources must be released from consumer goods production in order to be used for investment.

SAVING AND THE POOR. It is often stated that people in developing countries cannot save because they are barely subsisting. This is not actually true. Many anthropological studies—of villages in India, for example—have revealed that saving is in fact going on, but it takes forms that we don't recognize in our money economy; for example, saving may involve storing dried onions that can later be traded for other goods. Some researchers speculate that much saving in developing countries takes the form of rearing children who then feel a moral obligation to support their parents during the latter's retirement. In any event, saving does take place even in the most poverty-stricken areas. In general, there is no pronounced relationship between the *percentage* of income saved and the level of income (over the long run).

Basically, then, saving is a method by which individuals can realize an optimal consumption stream throughout their expected lifetimes. The word *optimal* here does not mean adequate or necessary or decent; it means most desirable from the individual's point of view (given that individual's resources).

Try Preview Question 3:

Can developing countries create their own capital stock?

EVIDENCE OF SAVING IN DEVELOPING COUNTRIES. Savings in developing countries do not necessarily flow into what we might consider productive capital formation projects. We do see the results of literally centuries of saving in the form of religious monuments such as cathedrals, and in government buildings. Indeed, one major problem in developing countries is that much of the saving that occurs does not get channelled into productive capital formation. This is also true of much of the foreign aid that has been sent to developing countries. These countries could productively use more factories and a better infrastructure—roads and communications—rather than more government buildings and fancy stadiums built exclusively for merrymaking and sports.

Property Rights and Economic Development

If you were in a country in which bank accounts and businesses were periodically expropriated by the government, how willing would you be to leave your money in a savings account or to invest in a business? Certainly, you would be less willing than if such things never occurred. Periodic expropriation of private property rarely occurs in developed countries. It *has* occurred in numerous developing countries, however. For example, private property was once nationalized in Chile and still is in Cuba. In some cases, former owners are compensated, but rarely for the full value of the property taken over by the state.

Empirically, we have seen that, other things being equal, the more certain private property rights are, the more private capital accumulation there will be. People are more willing to invest their savings in endeavours that will increase their wealth in future years. They have property rights in their wealth that are sanctioned and enforced by the government. In fact, some economic historians have attempted to show that it was the development of well-defined private property rights that allowed Western Europe to increase its growth rate after many centuries of stagnation. The degree of certainty with which one can reap the gains from investing also determines the extent to which businesspeople in *other* countries will invest capital in developing countries. The threat of nationalization in some countries may scare away foreign investment that would allow these countries to become more developed.

In a sentence, economic development depends more on individuals who are able to perceive opportunities and then take advantage of those opportunities than it does on capital or natural resources.[1] Risks will not be taken, though, if the risk takers cannot expect a reward. The political institutions must be such that risk takers are rewarded. That requires well-established property rights, lack of the threat of expropriation of profits, and no fear of government nationalization of businesses.

Try Preview Question 4:

Does a lack of protected property rights hinder a developing country's development?

CONCEPTS IN BRIEF

- Some policymakers believe that a large capital stock is a prerequisite for economic growth and development. They therefore suggest that developing countries need more capital.
- The human element, however, is vital; the labour force must be capable of using any capital that the developing country acquires. This requires training and education.
- Saving is a prerequisite for capital formation.
- Saving goes on even in poor developing countries, although not necessarily in the same form as in rich developed countries.
- Saving and individual capital accumulation will be greater the more certain individuals are about the safety of their wealth.

---

[1] The member countries of OPEC might be considered exceptions to this generalization.

The Importance of an Open Economy

The data are conclusive: Open economies experience faster economic development than economies closed to international trade. That is to say, the less government protects the domestic economy by imposing trade barriers, the faster that economy will experience economic development. According to a study by economists Nouriel Roubini and Xavier Sala-i-Martin, when a country goes from being relatively open to relatively closed via government-enacted trade barriers, it will have a 2.5 percentage point decrease in its growth rate.

Open economies accomplish several things. For one, individuals and businesses end up specializing in those endeavours in which they have a comparative advantage. International trade encourages individuals and businesses to discover ways to specialize so that they can become more productive and earn higher incomes. Increased productivity and the subsequent increase in the rate of economic development are the results. Open economies also allow the importation of already developed technology. For instance, no developing country today needs to spend years to figure out how to make computers or how to use them; that has already been done elsewhere.

The True Cost of Protectionism

A statistical study of the cost of trade barriers might give the impression that taxes on imported goods simply raise their price to domestic consumers. But there is another cost that is normally hidden. Statisticians call it a *Type II error*—the cost of omission. It is the cost of what would have been had there not been tariff barriers. The best example of a Type II error is the cost of overregulating the pharmaceutical industry. If it causes fewer life-saving drugs to be introduced, it is a Type II error. When trade is restricted in a developing country, that country's people are deprived of a potential larger range of new goods and production processes. Such new foreign products could spur local support businesses, which in turn would cause other businesses to be created. Developing countries that have restricted the entry of computer products have clearly slowed down the development of their own software industry. Trade barriers sometimes guarantee that new goods and services never appear in protected countries. According to economist Paul Romer, because of protectionism, many developing countries do not simply cut back on their consumption of the entire range of goods available to rich countries; rather, they use a smaller quantity of a much smaller range of goods. He calculates that the cumulative forgone benefits from new economic activity blocked by an across-the-board 10 percent tariff in a developing country might be as high as 20 percent of annual national income.

The Importance of an Educated Population

Both theoretically and empirically, we know that a more educated workforce aids economic development because it allows individuals to build on the ideas of others. According to economists David Gould and Roy Ruffin, increasing the rate of enrolment in secondary schools by only two percentage points, from eight to 10 percent, raises the average rate of economic growth by half a percent per year. Thus we must conclude that developing countries can advance more rapidly if they invest more heavily in secondary education. Or stated in the negative, economic development cannot be sustained if a country allows a sizable portion of its population to avoid education. After all, education allows young people who grew up poor to acquire skills that enable them to avoid poverty as adults. Read International Policy Example 21-1, on the next page, for further discussion.

Some of the fastest-growing countries in the world, including the Four Tigers, virtually eliminated illiteracy very early on.

Should School Tuition Vouchers Be Used in Developing Countries?

Nobel Prize–winning economist Gary Becker has argued in favour of a school voucher system in developing countries. According to his scheme, low-income parents would receive the vouchers, which could then be used at any approved school in their country. The participating schools would also have to provide meals for their students. According to Becker, such vouchers would stimulate competition among private and public schools in developing countries. There is a problem for very poor families, however. They want their children to work to provide income. Becker suggests that such families be given a bonus that offsets the income loss while their children are going to school.

For critical analysis: Do parents in developed countries have to be compensated for sending their children to school? Explain.

Letting Companies Disappear: Creative Destruction

Economist Joseph Schumpeter (1883–1950) championed the concept of *creative destruction*. He pointed out that new technologies and successful new businesses end up destroying old jobs, old companies, and old industries. Change is painful and costly, but it is necessary for economic advancement. Nowhere is this more important than in developing countries, where the principle is often ignored.

Developing countries have had a history of supporting current companies and industries by preventing new technologies and new companies from entering the marketplace. The process of creative destruction has not been allowed to work its magic.

One key element in providing the most favourable condition for economic development is allowing businesses to fail. A corollary to this principle is that governments should not consistently use their taxpayers' money to subsidize or even own businesses. It does little good (and normally a lot of harm) for governments in developing countries to own banks, phone companies, electric companies, car companies, or airlines. There are few historical examples of state-owned companies doing other than one thing—draining the public coffers.

Do not get the impression that government-owned and -operated businesses are run by individuals who are somehow less competent than those in the private sector. Rather, the incentive structure for managers in private businesses is different from that for managers in state-owned businesses.

The Relationship Between Population Growth and Economic Development

World population is growing at the rate of 2.8 people each and every second. That turns out to be 242,000 a day, or 88.3 million a year. Today, there are about 5.8 billion people on earth. By the year 2030, according to the United Nations, there will be 8.5 billion. Look at Figure 21.1 to see which countries are growing the most.

Now look at Figure 21.2. There you see that virtually all of the growth in population comes from developing countries. Some countries, such as Germany, are expected to lose population over the next several decades.

FIGURE 21.1 Expected Growth in World Population by 2030

Asia and Africa are expected to gain the most in population by the year 2030.

Source: United Nations.

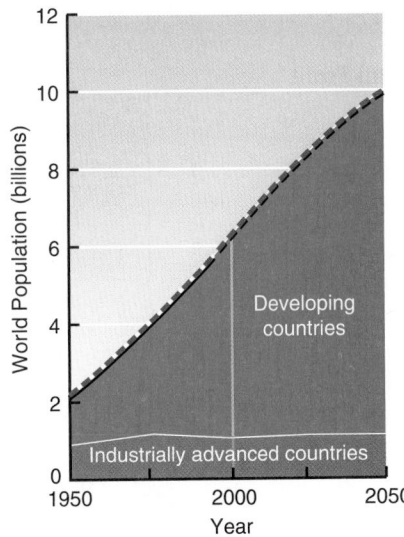

Europe:
741,707,000
9% of world population
+1.5%
(includes all of Russia)

Russia
+1.5%

Canada
+20%

United States
+25%

Brazil
+43%

Americas:
1,082,702,000
13% of world population
+41%

Nigeria
+110%

Zaire
+144%

China
+25%

India
+53%

Asia:
5,053,974,000
60% of world population
+47%

Africa:
1,556,723,000
18% of world population
+116%

Australia:
22,824,000
0.3% of world population
+25%

FIGURE 21.2 Population Growth by 2050

Population will increase dramatically in the developing countries. The industrially advanced countries will grow very little in population over the next half century.

Source: United States Population Reference Bureau.

Developing
countries

Industrially advanced countries

World Population (billions)

Year

The Conventional Wisdom

Ever since the Reverend Thomas Robert Malthus wrote his essay *The Principle of Population* in 1798, excessive population growth has been a concern. Modern-day Malthusians are able to generate just as much enthusiasm for the concept that population growth is bad. We are told that rapid population growth threatens economic development and the quality of life. This message was made loud and clear by numerous participants in the United Nations' International Conference on Population and Development held in Cairo, Egypt, in the fall of 1994.

WHAT THE DATA SHOW. First of all, according to economist Nicholas Eberstadt, Malthus's prediction that population would outstrip food supplies has never held true for the entire world. Figure 21.3 shows how population has grown over the past 35 years. At the same time, the food supply, measured by calories per person, has also increased somewhat steadily.

Also, the price of food, corrected for inflation, has been falling steadily for over a century. That means that the supply of food is expanding faster than the demand caused by increased population.

POPULATION DENSITY AND ECONOMIC DEVELOPMENT. There is no consistent relationship between population density and economic development. Japan, for example, has a higher per capita income than many Western European countries, yet it has more people per square kilometre than India, one of the poorest countries. Hong Kong is the most densely populated country. Fifty years ago it was one of the poorest, but today its per capita income exceeds that in France and the United Kingdom. (Hong Kong has almost no natural resources either—it has to import even its drinking water.) As a general proposition, some of the richest countries in the world today are the most densely populated— South Korea, Taiwan, Belgium, the Netherlands, England, Germany, and Japan.

THE RELATIONSHIP BETWEEN POPULATION GROWTH RATES AND ECONOMIC DEVELOPMENT. Again there seems to be little relationship between economic development and rapid population growth. Consider Malaysia, which grew from a sparsely populated country of villages in the 1890s to a country of cities in the 1930s. During this period, its population increased from 1.5 million to 6 million, but its standard of living also increased, by about

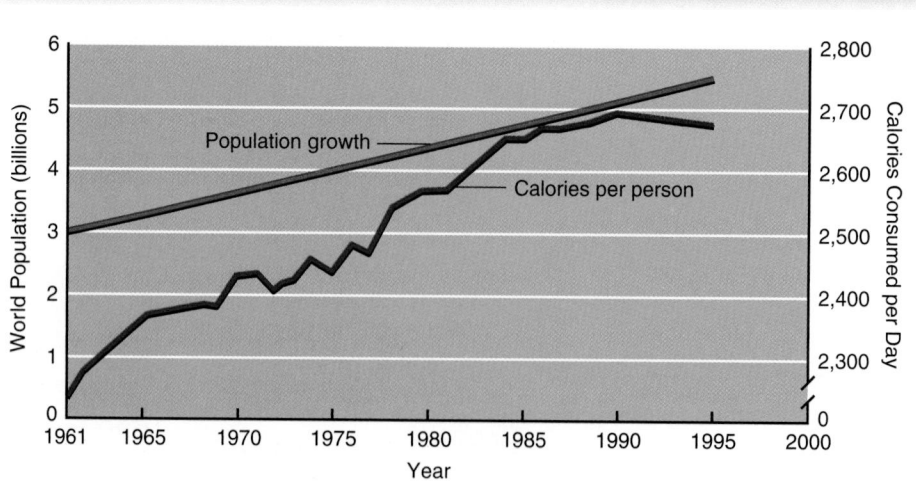

FIGURE 21.3
Population and Food Supplies

Malthus has been proved wrong: Population has not outstripped the world's food supply. In fact, for at least the past half century, calories consumed per person have been increasing at a rate even faster than the increase in population.

Source: United States Department of Agriculture.

140 percent. Historically, the largest increases in Western living standards took place during the period when the Western population was growing faster than it is in today's developing countries. Also, in spite of relatively high population growth rates, per capita incomes in many, if not most, developing countries are much higher today than they were four decades ago. Much of the population growth in developing countries has occurred because both adults and children live longer than they used to, not necessarily because families are having more children. There are just fewer deaths caused by malnutrition and contagious diseases than there used to be.

The Relationship Between Average Family Income and Size

One thing that economists know for sure is that over the past century, as countries became richer, the average family size fell. Otherwise stated, the more economic development occurs, the slower the population growth rate. Predictions of birthrates in developing countries have often turned out to be overstated if those countries experience rapid economic growth. This was the case in Hong Kong, Mexico, Taiwan, and Colombia.

Recent research on population and economic development has revealed that social and economic modernization has been accompanied by what might be called a fertility revolution—the spread of deliberate family size limitation within marriage and a decline in childbearing. Modernization reduces infant mortality, which in turn reduces the incentive for couples to have many children to make sure that enough will survive to satisfy each couple's demand. Also, modernization lowers the demand for children for a variety of reasons, not least being that couples in more developed countries do not need to rely on their children to take care of them in old age.

Population and Productivity

Recall the discussion of comparative advantage and specialization in Chapter 19. Specialization turns out to be a function of the size of the market, which is, of course, a function of population. Thus a growing population can help improve the quality of life because it allows individuals to devote their talents to what they are best suited to do—whatever their comparative advantage is. Individuals don't "exhaust" the earth's resources. People create wealth through imagination and innovation. It was not all that long ago that oil was considered useless. So was sand; today, it is used to make silicone and glass from which computer chips and fibre optics are manufactured.

Three hundred years ago, there were one-tenth the number of humans who now live. Yet the world is incredibly more wealthy than it was three centuries ago. Today, there are six times as many Canadians as there were 100 years ago. Yet today we live longer and are about seven times richer per capita.

Foreign Aid

Many countries, including Canada, extend assistance to developing countries. A number of reasons are given to justify this assistance, which can be in the form of grants, low-interest loans, food, or technical expertise. Although the humanitarian argument in support of foreign aid is often given, security and economics also enter into the discussion. During the Cold War, many Western nations gave foreign aid to developing countries in order to support noncommunist régimes or to prevent communist takeovers. Canada also extends foreign aid to help develop foreign markets for the output of Canadian firms. This is particularly true when foreign aid is tied to the purchase of Canadian products. Tied foreign aid requires that the recipient spend all or part of the sum extended as foreign aid on Canadian-produced goods.

The Results of Foreign Aid

Since the end of World War II, the developed world has transferred about $2.4 trillion (in today's dollars) to developing countries. The results have been mixed. According to one study by economist Peter Bauer, there is little correlation between the level of foreign aid received and changes in living standards. He also found that foreign aid did not necessarily reduce infant mortality rates. His conclusion was that foreign aid simply raised the standard of living of the recipient countries' richest people.

Consider Tanzania. Between 1970 and 1988, this African country received $8.6 billion in aid, four times that country's 1988 gross domestic product. This is the equivalent of someone giving Canada around $3 trillion. During the same period, Sudan was given $9.6 billion, an amount equal to one year's output. Zaire, Togo, Zambia, Mozambique, and Niger each received around $6 billion during the same period. What happened to these billions of dollars? In all of these countries, gross output actually fell. Critics of foreign aid point out that much of the money went into new government centres, showy airports, and grand conference halls. Some of it also went into government officials' Swiss bank accounts. According to economist George Ayittey, Zaire ex-president Mobutu Sese Seko was worth $10 billion at his death, and Zambia's Kenneth Kaunda is currently worth $6 billion.

INTERNATIONAL EXAMPLE 21-2

The World Bank and the Development of Poor Countries (or Lack Thereof)

The International Bank for Reconstruction and Development, known as the World Bank, was established in 1944. To date it has lent over $300 billion, mostly to poor countries. However, its accomplishments have recently been questioned. For example, since 1951, India has received $55 billion—more foreign aid than any other country on earth—yet over 40 percent of India's population still lives in poverty. In sub-Saharan Africa, massive amounts of money have gone into development planning, yet that region has a lower per capita income than it did before it received aid.

Another criticism of the World Bank is that its lending policies during the 1970s encouraged large-scale, capital-intensive technology, which helped governments in less-developed countries to plunder their natural resources. These large-scale projects displaced millions of poor and tribal peoples. In India, World Bank development projects uprooted over 20 million people. Throughout the world, dam projects have altered natural ecologies. Indeed, a mid-1990's internal review of the bank's lending portfolio found that almost 40 percent of recently evaluated projects did not adhere to established environmental and social policies.

The major problem with the World Bank's lending activities is that they help government bureaucracies flourish with funds that could be used to help individuals in the host countries.

For critical analysis: How does lending to governments in less-developed countries hinder market reforms?

CONCEPTS IN BRIEF

- The openness of an economy can determine its rate, or lack thereof, of economic development. Open economies allow, among other things, the importation of technology from the rest of the world.
- The more educated the workforce, the greater the chance of successful economic development, so enrolment in secondary schools is a key determinant of economic growth.
- While many believe population growth hinders economic development, there is little historic relationship between either population density or growth rates and economic growth rates.
- Critics of foreign aid point out that foreign aid will not increase the rate of economic growth unless a well-functioning capital base and infrastructure are in place.

NETNOMICS

The PC Revolution in the Developing World

The PC revolution is showing up in the world's developing countries, sometimes at a faster pace than in Canada. In its wake is a quickly narrowing competitive gap between the more advanced and the less advanced economies. There are several reasons the PC may be at the heart of improved economies in developing countries.

Low-Price Accessibility

Even in the developed countries, the PC revolution would never have happened without dramatic improvements in microprocessors, memory chips, and software, all occurring while prices continue to drop. Computer technology is now economically viable for most businesses except in the extremely poor countries, according to Eduardo Talero, information technology specialist at the World Bank.

"Necessity: The Mother of Invention"

Another reason PC technology has taken off in some countries is simply that it was needed. The advanced home-banking system in Brazil referred to at the beginning of this chapter did depend on cheap technology and software. Also, high inflation rates in Brazil have meant that people who did not deposit their earnings immediately would see the real value of their wealth drop through inflation. Home banking allows for instantaneous transfers of earnings. Necessity is the mother of invention.

The Benefit of Being a Latecomer

Perhaps just as important for developing countries, the fact that they are latecomers has helped them tremendously. Developing countries by definition have had low levels of technology in their business infrastructure. Consequently, they have not invested large amounts in old systems, such as IBM mainframe computers. When the PC revolution came along, they were able to take advantage of it without waiting for their old equipment to wear out. Economic theory predicts that late starters—developing countries—can benefit from new technology at a much faster rate than the already developed countries. And that is what has been happening.

Bringing Down the Trade Barriers

The developing countries that have reduced their trade barriers fastest have seen technology circulate the most freely and have experienced the greatest benefits. Many Latin American countries are leading the way by allowing unfettered imports of computer equipment and software. The PC market in Latin America is growing at a rate of almost 25 percent a year. Sales in Eastern Europe are growing at 15 percent a year. Software sales are growing even faster.

ISSUES AND APPLICATIONS

International Development and Basic Education

Concepts Applied: Investment, growth, economic development

The money these children are collecting for UNICEF will go towards programs to enhance the lives of children in many third world nations. Evidence shows that breaking the cycle of poverty early is the best way to develop third world countries.

The development of an economy rests in part upon the development of the most fundamental of resources, its people. In its 2001 report, *State of the World's Children,* UNICEF presents a number of arguments that support the premise that intervention early in life will help break the cycle of poverty that exists in many countries.

Their report calls for three basic outcomes for children. First, infants need good nutrition and nurturing. This will enhance their long-term abilities as adults. Second, a good basic education is important for the transformation of societies. This means that literacy must become universal. Children should not be exploited for their labour in the early years of their lives. Girls are particularly vulnerable to being left behind because of cultural prejudices against education for females. Third, adolescents need to given opportunity to reach their full potential. This means protecting their rights for dignity, for basic health programs to fight against AIDS/HIV, and for a life free from war and conflict.

In order to achieve these goals, UNICEF is first asking that international aid be used differently, with a larger proportion (20 percent) going to fund basic social services. It also notes that much of the debt of these developing nations is creating a terrific burden through interest repayments, a burden which is felt most heavily by children. Canada has also been involved in seeking forgiveness of loans for the most heavily indebted nations, many of whom will not be able to repay these loans. Finally, it notes, as many researchers have found, that education and empowerment for women helps tremendously in encouraging development and reducing birth rates in developing countries.

For Critical Analysis

1. What basic investment does Canada put into its children through government programs?

2. Why does international development lead to a better life for Canadians?

CHAPTER SUMMARY

1. The 19 industrially advanced countries (IACs)— Canada, the United States, Japan, and the countries of Western Europe—have market economies based on a large skilled labour force and a large technically advanced stock of capital goods.

2. One of the major characteristics of developing countries is a high rate of population growth. However, high population growth does not necessarily prevent or retard economic development.

3. Some authorities contend that balanced development of industry and agriculture is necessary for growth in the developing countries. There are, however, exceptions to this rule; Hong Kong is one.

4. Industrialization in many developing countries has involved subsidization of manufacturing. Such subsidization leads to a misallocation of resources and to a lower per capita standard of living for the population even though the country may become more highly industrialized.

5. Capital accumulation is an important determinant of economic development. However, massive transfers of capital to developing countries do not guarantee economic development. Appropriately trained personnel must be available to use the capital given to these countries.

6. Domestic capital formation requires saving—nonconsumption of current income. Even the poorest countries' citizens do some saving. In fact, there is no pronounced relationship between percentage of income saved and level of income.

7. Saving in the developing countries may take on different forms than in more developed countries. For example, having children is a form of saving if those children feel an obligation to support their parents during retirement.

8. The more certain private property rights are, the more private capital accumulation there will be, other things being equal.

DISCUSSION OF PREVIEW QUESTIONS

1. What is a developing country?

Developing countries are arbitrarily defined as those with very low per capita incomes. Relative to developed countries, people in developing countries have lower incomes, life expectancies, literacy rates, and daily caloric intake, and higher infant mortality rates.

2. Must developing countries develop by industrializing?

Proponents of the balanced-growth theory point out that the industrially advanced countries (IACs) are highly industrialized and the developing countries are mostly agrarian. They feel that balanced growth requires that the developing countries expand the manufacturing sector; labourers and other resources should be reallocated to promote industrialization. It is often suggested that the developing countries restrict imports of nonagricultural goods to help industrialization. It is alleged that these countries must industrialize even if their comparative advantage lies in the production of agricultural goods because they can't compete with the subsidized agricultural sectors of the IACs. Yet it is easy to oversell the pro-industrialization balanced-growth approach.

Numerous examples of gross inefficiency can be cited when the developing countries attempted to develop steel and automobile industries. Moreover, when the developing countries restrict the imports of manufactured goods, they lower living standards and promote inefficiency. It would seem that the time to develop the industrial sector would be when it is profitable for businesses to do so.

3. Can developing countries create their own capital stock?

It is often asserted that a large capital stock is necessary for economic development, the developing countries are too poor to save sufficient amounts to develop domestic capital formation, and the IACs should therefore give capital to the developing countries. Experts disagree about the validity of each contention. The question under discussion here deals with the second proposition. A good deal of evidence exists to support the notion that the developing countries do save—although in forms that are not easily observed or cannot be readily converted into capital. Even people with extremely low incomes are forced by economic circumstances to provide for future consumption; they often store dried or cured food. On a nationwide scale, much evidence of capital formation exists: cathedrals, pyramids, great walls, fortresses, government buildings, and so on. Of course, the problem is to get savings into forms that can be used to produce goods or services.

4. Does a lack of protected property rights hinder a developing country's development?

Yes. When individuals fear that their property rights will not be protected, they invest in ways that reflect this risk. Thus people in politically and economically unstable countries prefer to accumulate diamonds, gold, silver, and currency in foreign banks rather than invest in factories, equipment, and savings in domestic bank accounts. Similarly, a country that expropriates property or nationalizes industry discourages investment by foreign businesses. Many developing countries could be aided to a great extent by attracting foreign investment—but foreign investors will require property rights guarantees.

PROBLEMS

(Answers to the odd-numbered problems appear at the back of the book.)

21-1. List five developing countries and five industrially advanced countries.

21-2. What problems are associated with advancements in medicine and health that are made available to developing countries?

21-3. Outline a typical pattern of economic development.

21-4. Suppose that you are shown the following data for two countries, known only as country X and country Z:

Country	GDP	Population
X	$ 81 billion	9 million
Z	$135 billion	90 million

a. From this information, which country would you expect to be classified as a developing country? Why?

b. Now suppose that you were also given the following data:

Country	Life Expectancy at Birth (years)	Infant Mortality per 1,000 Live Births	Literacy (%)
X	70	15	60
Z	58	50	70

Are these figures consistent with your answer to part (a)?

c. Should we expect the developing country identified in part (a) to have a much greater population density than the other country?

21-5. Would unrestricted labour immigration end up helping or hurting developing countries? Explain.

21-6. Many countries in Africa have extremely large potential stocks of natural resources. Nonetheless, those natural resources often remain unexploited. Give reasons why this situation continues to exist.

21-7. Sketch a scenario in which population growth causes an increase in income per capita.

21-8. Visit the Organisation for Economic Cooperation and Development (OECD) development indicators Web site at http://www.oecd.org/dac/Indicators/htm/list.htm.

a. What indicators of general development does the OECD use?

b. Now open the general development indicators table. List four of the poorest countries according to per capita GDP. (For example, countries with per capita GDP less than US$500.) What is the life expectancy in these countries?

c. List four of the richer countries according to per capita GDP (countries with per capita GDP greater than US$10,000). What is the life expectancy in these countries?

d. What conclusions can you draw about life expectancy and economic wealth as represented by per capita GDP? Which set of countries would you expect to experience more rapid economic development? Why?

ECONOMICS ON THE NET

International Development

Internet URL: http://www.countrywatch.com

Navigation: Start at the site above, and click on the map of the world. Click first on the region, and then on the country. On the left is a menu of choices of information about the country of your choice.

Application: Look at countries of your choice and see how their economy is doing. What changes are mentioned that indicate how the country has been doing economically over the past few years?

ANSWERS TO ODD-NUMBERED PROBLEMS

Chapter 1
The Nature of Economics

1-1.
   a. Macroeconomic, as the unemployment rate is national or economy-wide.
   b. Microeconomic, as wage increases of specific occupations like nurses and doctors relate to specific parts of the economy.
   c. Microeconomic, as prices of a specific part of the economy—cigarettes—is being studied.
   d. Macroeconomic, as the inflation rate tracks the average price of all goods, which is an economy-wide measure.
   e. Macroeconomic, as the nation's total annual production is an economy-wide measure.
   f. Microeconomic, as an individual firm's situation, such as Eaton's bankruptcy, focuses on a specific part of the economy.

1-3. The decision based on availability of funds is not a rational one. In order to allocate resources in a manner which maximizes the satisfaction of the city's wants, the council should compare the marginal (extra) benefit of constructing the city hall with the marginal (extra) cost including alternatives sacrificed. If the extra benefit to the city of constructing the city hall is less than the value of some other alternative that has to be sacrificed, such as paving of city roads, the council's decision is not rational.

1-5.
   a. We should observe younger drivers to be more frequently involved in traffic accidents than older persons.
   b. Slower monetary expansion should be associated with less inflation.
   c. Professional basketball players receiving smaller salaries should be observed to have done less well in their high school studies.
   d. Employees being promoted rapidly should have lower rates of absenteeism than those being promoted more slowly.

1-7.
   a. Positive, for it is a statement that can be tested by the facts.
   b. Normative, involving a value judgment about what should be.
   c. Normative, involving a value judgment about what should be.
   d. Positive, for it is a statement that can be tested by the facts.

Chapter 2
Scarcity and the World of Trade-Offs

2-1. The plot of the product possibility curve is displayed in the graph below.

The PPC exhibits constant opportunity costs. That is, the cost of earning an additional mark in Economics is always the same, in terms of additional Biology marks sacrificed. In this case, the PPC is a straight line with the opportunity cost of earning an additional mark in Economics always being 1 mark in Biology.

2.3 The plot of the product possibility curve is displayed in the graph below.

The bowed-out PPC described above illustrates an increasing opportunity costs situation. The opportunity cost of increasing the Economics grade from 60 to 70 is a loss of 8 Biology marks; from 90 to 100 is a loss of 20 Biology marks.

2-5.

a.

b.

c.

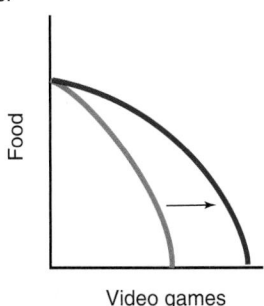

d.

2-7.   If we assume that a two-year college diploma consists of four 15-week semesters, this amounts to committing 60 weeks to college studies. The opportunity cost is: 60 wks × 35 h × $7.00 = $14,700.00. The incentive of incurring this cost is that, upon graduating, you will be earning a significant amount in excess of $7.00 per hour. You are sacrificing current consumption to obtain a greater amount of future consumption.

2-9.   Yes, you and your roommate should specialize. Since your opportunity cost of completing a basket of laundry (2 meals) is lower than your roommate (3 meals) you should specialize in the laundry completion while your roommate should specialize in the meal preparation. As an example, if you complete an extra basket of laundry, you give up only 2 meals. However, you free up an additional 3 hours of your roommate's time, which allows your roommate to produce an additional 3 meals. Overall, one extra meal is gained.

Appendix A
Reading and Working with Graphs

A-1.   a.   Price is independent.
       b.   Work-study hours is independent.
       c.   Hours studied is independent and grade is independent.

A-3.

y	x
12	4
9	3
6	2
3	1
0	0
−3	−1
−6	−2
−9	−3
−12	−4

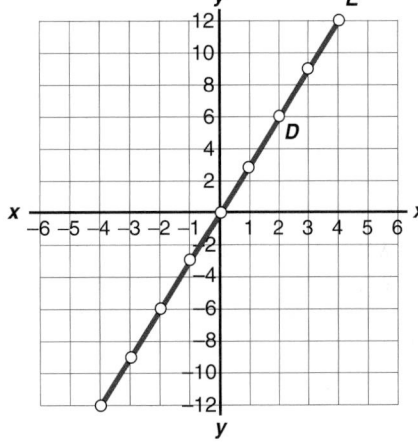

A-5.   If you move along the line in Problem A-3 from point D to point E, the slope equals the change in the y-values divided by the change in the x-values is:

$$(12 − 6)/(4 − 2) = 6/2 = 3.$$

A-7.   For the ordered pair (4,16) the tangent line is upward-sloping, slope is positive.
       For the ordered pair (0,0) the tangent line is horizontal, slope is zero.
       For the ordered pair (−4,16) the tangent line is downward-sloping, slope is negative.

Chapter 3
Economies in Transition

3-1.   On the supply side, all of the industries responsible for automobile inputs would have to be considered. This would include steel (and coke and coal), glass, tires (and rubber), plastics, railroads (and thus steel again), aluminum (and electricity), and manufacturers of stereos, hubcaps, and air conditioners, to name a few. On the demand side, you would have to take into account industries involving complements (such as oil, gasoline, concrete, and asphalt) and substitutes (including bicycles, motorcycles, buses, and walking shoes). Moreover, resource allocation decisions regarding labour and the other inputs, complements, and substitutes for these goods must also be made.

3-3. a. Profit equals total revenue minus total cost. Because revenue is fixed (at $172), if the firm wishes to maximize profit, this is equivalent to minimizing costs. To find total costs, simply multiply the price of each input by the amount of the input that must be used for each technique.

Costs of A = ($10)(7) + ($2)(6) + ($15)(2) + ($8)(1)
= $120
Costs of B = ($10)(4) + ($2)(7) + ($15)(6) + ($8)(3)
= $168
Costs of C = ($10)(1) + ($2)(18) + ($15)(3) + ($8)(2)
= $107

Because C has the lowest costs, it yields the highest profits, and thus it will be used.
b. Profit equals $172 – $107 = $65.
c. Each technique's costs rise by the increase in the price of labour multiplied by the amount of labour used by that technique. Because technique A uses the least amount of labour, its costs rise the least, and it thus becomes the lowest-cost technique at $132. (The new cost of B is $182, and the new cost of C is $143.) Hence technique A will be used, resulting in profits of $172 – $132 = $40.

3-5. a. In the market system, the techniques that yield the highest (positive) profits will be used.
b. Profit equals total revenue minus total cost. Because revenue from 100 units is fixed (at $100), if the firm wishes to maximize profit, this is equivalent to minimizing costs. To find total costs, simply multiply the price of each input by the amount of the input that must be used for each technique.

Costs of A = ($10)(6) + ($8)(5) = $100
Costs of B = ($10)(5) + ($8)(6) = $98
Costs of C = ($10)(4) + ($8)(7) = $96

Because technique C has the lowest costs, it also yields the highest profits ($100 – $96 = $4).
c. Following the same methods yields these costs: A = $98, B = $100, and C = $102. Technique A will be used because it is the most profitable.
d. The profits from using technique A to produce 100 units of X are $100 – $98 = $2.

Chapter 4
Demand and Supply

4.1. a. P_e = $11 and Q_e = 80 million CDs.
b. At a price of $13 there would be a surplus equal to (120 – 60) = 60 million CDs. The surplus will drive down the price.
c. At a price of $10 there would be a shortage equal to (90 – 60) = 30 million CDs. The shortage will drive up the price.

4.3.

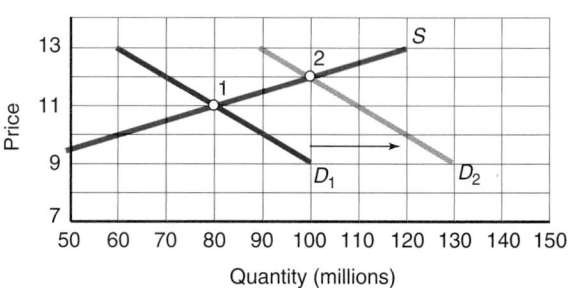

The graph above illustrates a shift to the right in the demand curve which indicates an *increase in demand*. The new equilibrium price and quantity is $12 and 100 million CDs. A change in any factor other than the price of CDs will cause an increase in demand, such as an increase in income or an increase in the popularity of rock music.

4-5. a. Increase in demand
b. Increase in demand
c. Increase in demand
d. Increase in demand
e. Decrease in demand

4-7. a. At a price of $1.40, there would be a surplus equal to (5 – 3) or 2,000 dozen eggs. This will drive down the price.
b. At a price of $0.80, there would be a shortage equal to (6 – 2) or 4,000 dozen eggs. This will drive up the price.
c. The equilibrium price and quantity is $1.20 and 4,000 dozen eggs.
d. i. Increase in demand, $P_e \uparrow, Q_e \uparrow$
   ii. Decrease in supply, $P_e \uparrow, Q_e \downarrow$
   iii. Decrease in demand, $P_e \downarrow, Q_e \downarrow$
   iv. Increase in supply, $P_e \downarrow, Q_e \uparrow$

4-9. a. The equilibrium rent and quantity is $400 and 4,000 units per month.
b. There will be a shortage equal to (6 – 2) or 4,000 units per month.
c. In the short run, by keeping the price of a substitute (one-bedroom units) lower, there will

be a decrease in demand for two-bedroom units, causing a decrease in equilibrium rent and quantity of two-bedroom units. In the longer run, due to the shortage of one-bedroom units, there will be an increase in demand for two-bedroom units causing equilibrium price and quantity to increase.

4-11.   a.   Increase in demand and increase in supply. While the equilibrium quantity will increase, the combined effect on equilibrium price is indeterminate.

b.   Decrease in supply and increase in demand. While the equilibrium price will increase, the combined effect on equilibrium quantity is indeterminate.

c.   Increase in supply and decrease in demand. While the equilibrium price will decrease, the combined effect on equilibrium quantity is indeterminate.

Chapter 5
Elasticity

5-1.   a.

Quantity Demanded per Week (kilograms)	Price per Kilogram	Elasticity
1,000	$ 5	
		$\frac{1}{3}$, or .33
800	10	
		$\frac{5}{7}$, or .714
600	15	
		$\frac{7}{5}$, or 1.4
400	20	
		$\frac{9}{3}$, or 3
200	25	

b.   There are several ways to explain why elasticity is greater at higher prices on a linear curve. At higher prices, a given price change will result in a smaller percentage price change. The smaller resulting denominator of the elasticity ratio leads to a larger overall ratio. Similarly, as prices rise, quantities fall, thereby implying greater percentage quantity changes for a given absolute quantity change, and a larger numerator. Alternatively, the sizes of total revenue changes first increase and then decrease as price is lowered throughout a linear demand curve, thus implying declining elasticity.

5-3.   a.   Using averages in the elasticity equation, the income elasticity of demand for VCRs is $0.6666 \div 0.2857 = 2.33$. It is income-elastic.

b.   It is presumably a luxury good.

5-5.   The problem is with the denominator, percentage change in P. Because the initial price was zero, any increase in price is of infinite percentage. However, if we take the average elasticity over a segment, there will be no problem. P will become the average of P_1 ($=0$) and P_2 ($=10$), or $(P_1 + P_2)/2 = 5$.

5-7.   a. $E_p = 0.80$

b.   Demand is price-inelastic.

c. $E_s = 1.067$

d.   Supply is price-elastic (but only slightly so).

5-9.   In each case, "before" is before the development of an acceptable substitute for the good in question, and "after" is after the development of that substitute. For example, between 1840 and 1880, the railroad emerged as a good substitute for canal transportation. In general, the better the substitutes for a good, the greater the price elasticity of demand for that good. Thus in each case we would expect the price elasticity of demand to be higher after the emergence of the substitute.

Chapter 6
The Public Sector

6-1.   The marginal tax rate on the first $3,000 of taxable income is 0 percent because no taxes are imposed until $5,000 is earned. The marginal rate on $10,000 is 20 percent, as it is on $100,000 and all other amounts above the $5,000 level, because for each additional dollar earned after $5,000, 20 cents will be taxed away. The average tax rate, which is the tax amount divided by the pretax income, is 0 for $3,000, 10 percent for $10,000, and 19 percent for $100,000. The average tax rate will approach a maximum of 20 percent as income increases. It cannot reach exactly 20 percent because of the untaxed $5,000 at the beginning. Such is the nature of a degressive tax system.

6-3.   Mr. Smith pays nothing on his first $1,500 of income, 14 percent ($70) on the $500 of earnings between $1,500 and $2,000, and 20 percent ($100) on the $500 that he earns above $2,000. Thus Mr. Smith has a total tax bill of $170 on an income of $2,500; his average tax rate is 6.8 percent, and his marginal tax rate is 20 percent.

6-5. Market failure means that the unrestrained operation of a market leads to either too few or too many resources being used in that activity.

6-7. a. If you give and everyone else does also, you account for 1 percent. If you are the only one who gives, you account for 100 percent. If you give nothing, you account for 0 percent, regardless of what others give.

b. In principle, your contribution matters whatever the level of participation. But as a practical matter, if participation is near 100 percent, the absence of your contribution may have little effect.

c. There is no free ride. If you do not make your contribution, total contributions will be lower, and the quality of the services provided will be lower.

6-9. The existence of these costs implies the notion of rational ignorance, so that individuals choose not to be informed about certain issues because the cost of being informed is high relative to any benefit forthcoming from the state of the issue. This also contributes to the growth of special-interest groups because individuals have no strong economic incentive to act against them.

Chapter 7
The Macroeconomy: Unemployment and Inflation

7-1. Event **a.** will result in a measured unemployment rate that is lower than what actually occurs because these people will not be counted in the labour force survey. These workers are called **discouraged workers** and form part of the "hidden unemployed." Event **b.** will result in a measured unemployment rate that is higher than what actually occurs because these people will be doing work at home and are not making themselves available to the labour market. This assumes that they still declare to the survey that they are looking for employment.

7-3. a. 5 percent
b. One month
c. 5 percent
d. 10 percent
e. In this example, the unemployment rate doubled, but it is not obvious that the economy has become sicker or that workers are worse off.

7-5. a. The consumer price index for 2001 is calculated as follows:

Commodity	Quantity	1999 Price	1999 Cost	2001 Price	2001 Cost
Pop	10	$1	$10	$1	$10
Chocolate Bars	30	$2	$60	$4	$120
Indigestion Pills	20	$5	$100	$6	$120
			$170		$250

The consumer price index is therefore

$$\frac{\$250}{\$170} \times 100 = 147.06$$

b. The rate of inflation between 1999 and 2001 is calculated as:

$$\frac{147.06 - 100}{100} \times 100\% = 47.06\%$$

c. The GDP deflator is calculated as follows:

Commodity	1999 Quantity	1999 Price	1999 GDP	2001 Quantity	2001 Price	2001 GDP
Pop	10	$1	$10	15	$1	$15
Chocolate Bars	30	$2	$60	35	$4	$140
Indigestion Pills	20	$5	$100	20	$6	$120
			$170			$275

Therefore, the GDP deflator is calculated as:

$$\frac{\$275}{\$170} \times 100 = 161.76$$

The GDP deflator is higher than the CPI because of the increases in quantities sold in 2001 over the quantities sold in 1999.

7-7. a. The nominal rate of interest is composed of the real rate of interest plus the anticipated rate of inflation. If the current rate of inflation is zero and people anticipate that there will continue to be no inflation, the real rate of interest equals the nominal rate of interest—in this example, 12 percent.

b. If the nominal rate of interest stays at 12 percent while the rate of inflation goes to 13 percent, and if that rate is anticipated to last, the real rate of interest drops to a *negative* 1 percent! Lending money at 12 percent would not normally be advisable in such a situation.

7-9. a. 10, 9, 8, 7, 6, 5, 4, 3
b. 8.0, 8.3, 9.4, 10.9, 12.0, 13.8, 16.0

Chapter 8
Measuring the Economy's Performance

8-1.   a.   GDP = $950; NDP = $900; NI = $875
       b.   GDP = $825
       c.   The value of depreciation exceeding gross private investment implies that the total capital stock of the country is declining. This would likely decrease future productivity because capital is a productive resource.

8-3.   a.   Coal; $2
       b. $3. Auto manufacturers took something worth $5 and transformed it into an auto that they sold for $8.
       c. $9, because intermediate goods are not counted.
       d. $9, resulting from adding the value added at each stage. Note that in this economy, which produces only autos, the earnings and the income approaches both yield a GDP estimate of $9.

8-5.   a.   GDP falls.
       b.   GDP is unchanged because illegal transactions are not measured anyway.
       c.   GDP rises.

8-7.   a.   Nominal GDP for 1992 = ($4)(10) + ($12)(20) + ($6)(5) + ($25)(10) = $560. Nominal GDP for 2000 = ($8)(12) + ($36)(15) + ($10)(15) + ($30)(12) = $1,146.
       b.   Real GDP for 1992 = $560. Real GDP for 2000 = ($4)(12) + ($12)(15) + ($6)(15) + ($25)(12) = $618.

Chapter 9
Economic Growth: Technology, Research and Development, and Knowledge

9-1.   Point B is associated with the highest feasible growth rate. Capital goods implicitly represent future consumption, and point B has the highest feasible ratio of capital goods to current consumption (and thus the highest ratio of future consumption to current consumption).

9-3.   a.   J
       b.   M

9-5.   The answer to this question will vary depending upon which region of the country you inhabit. In most parts of the country, there have been technological changes in most industries.

Chapter 10
Modelling the Economy: Aggregate Demand and Aggregate Supply

10-1. At P_1, the quantity of AS exceeds the quantity of AD; therefore, a surplus of real national income (output) exists. At that price level, suppliers are willing to produce more than buyers want to purchase; in this surplus situation, producers find their inventories rising involuntarily, and they find it profitable to reduce prices and output. At P_2, the quantity of AD exceeds the quantity of AS, and a shortage exists. At that price level, buyers want more than producers are willing to produce, and buyers, competing for goods and services, will bid the price level upward. A higher price level induces an increase in the quantity of AS and a decrease in the quantity of AD. Only at P_e does the quantity of AS equal the quantity of AD; at P_e, equilibrium exists.

10-3. The long-run aggregate supply curve is vertical at the point representing the maximum potential output possible. Prices can vary, but output cannot. In the short run, some increase in the level of output is possible with prices rising. This is possible because of the existence of some excess capacity, as well as flexibility in the nature and intensity of work. Therefore, the positively sloped portion of the aggregate supply curve constitutes the short-run aggregate supply curve.

10-5. a.   The price level increases.
       b.   National output decreases.

10-7. In answering this question, assume that the economy is starting at full employment. This is shown at the intersection of the $SRAS_0$ and AD_0. The decline in aggregate demand to AD_1 is due to the loss of exports to the European Community. Europeans will buy fewer imports as their economy falls into recession, and thus a recession is also created in Canada, as shown by the contractionary gap between actual real GDP (680 billion) and full employment GDP (700 billion).

The recession in the European Community will reduce real GDP, lower the price level, and create a recession in Canada.

10-9. a. This will result in a reduction in our net exports, as Canadian goods will become relatively more expensive for foreigners to purchase, and foreign goods will become relatively cheaper for Canadians to buy. Aggregate demand will therefore decrease as illustrated below. Real GDP and the price level will decline.

Input costs will also decline if businesses purchase significant amounts of their inputs from other countries. This will encourage aggregate supply, as shown in the diagram below. Note that it does not affect long-run aggregate supply. Note that these effects work in opposite directions on real GDP, so it is not possible to determine how real GDP will be affected without knowing how much each will move. It is likely, however, that aggregate demand changes will be larger than the aggregate supply changes.

b. Assuming the value of the Canadian dollar is unchanged, rising interest rates will primarily affect the investment component of aggregate demand. (It may also affect the value of the Canadian dollar and net exports depending on whether interest rates rise in other countries as well). Rising interest rates will mean a decline in investment spending, and a reduction in aggregate demand. The illustration is the same as in a. above.

c. A decrease in taxes will increase aggregate demand through the consumption expenditure because of the increase in disposable income that results. It will also increase both short run and long run aggregate supply because of the greater incentive business has to invest in new production. Profitability of companies will increase because of the lowered tax rates. These shifts are illustrated below.

With the shift of both the *AD* and the *AS* curves, it is not possible to determine whether prices will rise or fall, because it depends on the relative amounts that each curve shifts. Aggregate demand shifts, however, will likely occur much more quickly than *AS* shifts, because of the greater time lag involved in creating new businesses or expanding existing ones. There will definitely be an increase in real GDP in both the short term and the long term.

In the illustration below, aggregate demand shifts more than aggregate supply, so the price level will rise.

d. A rise in incomes of Americans will increase our net exports, and shift aggregate demand as shown below. Americans will purchase more of all products as their incomes rise, and that includes products purchased from Canada.

e. Investment expenditure on technology will affect both aggregate demand and aggregate supply. The immediate effect of increased investment spending will be to increase aggregate demand. The increased use of technology will also shift out both the aggregate supply and aggregate demand curves. The net effect on the price level depends on the relative shifts of these two curves, while real GDP will rise. The illustration is the same as in c. above.

Chapter 11
Classical and Keynesian Macro Analyses

11-1. If the interest rate is higher than equilibrium, desired saving exceeds desired investment. Those who desire investment funds from savers will offer to pay lower rates of interest. Savers, in competition with each other, will be willing to accept lower rates of interest. The interest rate will be bid down, which will simultaneously decrease the quantity of saving desired and increase the quantity of investment desired.

11-3. Equilibrium starts out at E_1 with the price level at 100 and equilibrium real GDP at Q_0. When AD_1 shifts to AD_2, the end result is that the equilibrium is at E_1 with the same equilibrium level of real GDP per year but a price level of only 90. The equilibrium level of real GDP is supply-determined.

11-5. With a plunge in confidence, both consumers and businesses will react by reducing their spending. Consumers will be less likely to purchase expensive items such as cars and houses because they expect to have greater difficulty paying for those items (as they are often purchased over time). As well, they may want to increase savings to help them through any unemployment they might experience.

Businesses are also likely to reduce their investment spending, and to cut back on their capacity as confidence declines. If they expect sales to decline, then their existing capacity will probably be sufficient to meet their demand, and they would cut back on planned investment spending.

This reduction in aggregate demand will result (in the short run) in a reduction in both real GDP and a lower price level, as illustrated below.

Chapter 12
Consumption, Income, and the Multiplier

12-1. a.

Disposable Income	Consumption	Saving
$ 500	$510	$−10
600	600	0
700	690	10
800	780	20
900	870	30
1,000	960	40

a.

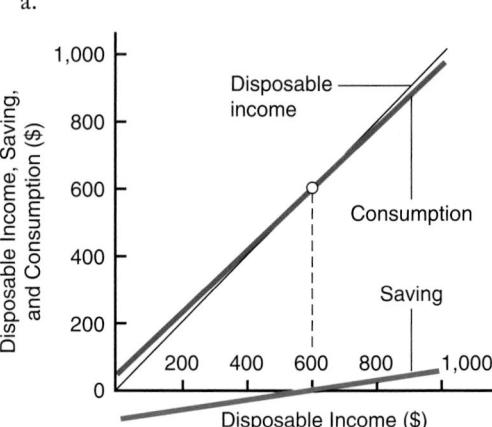

b. The marginal propensity to consume is 0.9; the marginal propensity to save is 0.1.

c.

Disposable Income	Average Propensity to Consume	Average Propensity to Save
$ 500	1.0200	−.0200
600	1.0000	0
700	.9857	.0143
800	.9750	.0250
900	.9667	.0333
1,000	.9600	.0400

12-3. Stock: a, c; Flow: b, d, e, f, g

Real National Income	Consumption Expenditures	Saving	Investment	APC	APS	MPC	MPS
$1,000	$1,100	$−100	$100	1.1	−.1	.9	.1
2,000	2,000	0	100	1.0	.0	.9	.1
3,000	2,900	100	100	.967	.033	.9	.1
4,000	3,800	200	100	.950	.050	.9	.1
5,000	4,700	300	100	.940	.060	.9	.1
6,000	5,600	400	100	.933	.067	.9	.1

12-5. a.

b.

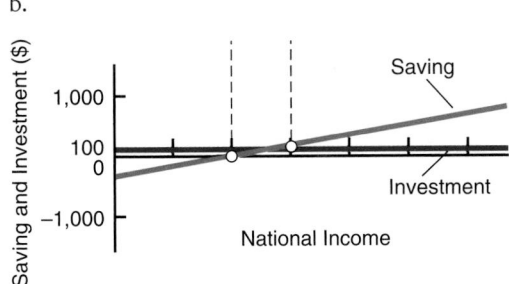

c. The multiplier effect from the inclusion of investment is to raise equilibrium national income by $1,000 over the equilibrium level it would otherwise have reached.

d. The value of the multiplier is 10.

e. The equilibrium level of national income without investment is $2,000; with investment, it is $3,000.

f. Equilibrium income will rise by $1,000.

g. Equilibrium income will again rise by $1,000 to $4,000.

12-7. This question is a bit harder than it looks. You must first remember that the MPC and MPS values are calculated out of *disposable* income, not out of national income. The multiplier process is calculated on the basis of *national* income, so we must first find the proportion of savings that come out of national income.

In general, the proportion of savings that leaks out of each round, with a tax rate that is proportional to national income, is $(1 - t) \times \text{MPS}$, where t is the marginal tax rate.

a. Since 10 percent of income is taken away by the government, that leaves 90 percent of income for households to spend. They spend 90% of the remainder, or 81% of their gross income. This leaves 9% for savings.

Thus, the proportion of leakages is 9% (savings) + 20% (imports) + 10% (taxes) = 39%. The multiplier is therefore 1/0.39 = 2.56

b. Savings out of national income is
$$\text{MPS} \times (1 - t) = 0.2 \times (1 - .3) = 0.14$$
The proportion of leakages is calculated as 14% (savings) + 30% (taxes) = 42%
The multiplier is therefore 1/0.42 = 2.38

c. The proportion of leakages is calculated as 8% (savings) + 40% (imports) + 20% (taxes) = 68% The multiplier is therefore 1/0.68 = 1.47

12-9. Net exports will decline as a result of the ban. This will reduce net exports, and shift the total planned expenditures curve down. Total planned expenditures will decline, and this change will be magnified by the multiplier into a larger change in real GDP. This change is illustrated below.

Chapter 13
Fiscal Policy

13-1. Discretionary fiscal policy is policy in which the levels of government spending and taxes change as a result of a deliberate decision by the government. *Example:* A change in the structure of tax rates, or a change in government expenditures not associated with a change in government revenues. Automatic stabilizers cause the level of government spending or taxes to change as a result of endogenous changes in a variable such as income, other than changes due to deliberate decisions of the government. *Example:* Government revenues increasing from taxes during an economic expansion.

13-3. Consumers must not regard current budget deficits as equivalent to higher future taxes and current budget surpluses as equivalent to lower future taxes. For example, if consumers regard a $1 million deficit as imposing an equivalent amount of new taxes on them in the future, they will increase current saving so as to be in a position to pay the higher future taxes. As a result, current consumption will decline, and at least some, and possibly all, of the stabilizing effect of the deficit will be wiped out.

13-5. Answers to the question will vary depending on the years you are considering and the province you reside in.

13-7. The choices for eliminating an inflationary gap are through a reduction in spending, an increase in taxes, or some combination of the two. The effect of any of these policies is to eliminate the inflationary gap by reducing aggregate demand. This is illustrated below.

Appendix C
Fiscal Policy: A Keynesian Perspective

C-1. a. The marginal propensity to consume is equal to $1 - MPS$, or $\frac{6}{7}$.

b. Investment or government spending must increase by $20 billion.

c. The government would have to cut taxes by $23.33 billion.

C-3. a. Aggregate demand will shift downward by $500; therefore, national income will fall by $5,000.

b. Aggregate demand will shift upward by $0.9(\$500) = \$450$; therefore, national income will rise by $4,500.

Chapter 14
Deficit Spending and the Public Debt

14-1. The federal budget balance is the difference between federal spending and federal taxes—in this case, a deficit of $30 billion.

14-3. Ultimately, all government debt must be repaid by means of taxation. (The government cannot forever "repay" its debt by issuing more debt because ultimately the public debt would exceed the wealth of the entire country!) Thus when the government adds to the debt, it is simultaneously adding to future taxes that must be equivalent in present value to the added debt.

14-5. Some observers say that the true burden of government is the real value of the resources it uses. Changing the way the books are kept leaves this burden unchanged. Moreover, neither current nor future taxes would be affected by this accounting change, so no one's tax liability would be altered. In brief, the change will have no real consequences. The net public debt equals the gross public debt minus the portion held by government agencies (what the government owes to itself).

14-7. Answers to the question will vary depending on the year you are considering and the province you reside in.

Chapter 15
Money and the Banking System

15-1.
a. The painting by Renoir would have the greatest advantage as a store of value, for works of art have generally appreciated over time. As a medium of exchange or a unit of account, it would be deficient because of its high, and sometimes variable, value and the limited market for its exchange.

b. A 90-day treasury bill also has a good store of value; it is guaranteed by the government and it will pay some interest. Of course, to the extent that the money to be returned for the matured bill is an imperfect store of value, so will be the bill. A 90-day bill will not vary much in value over its life because the redemption date is not far off and there is a ready market for its exchange; thus it is a serviceable medium of exchange and unit of account. But the large denominations in which these bills are issued detract from the latter functions.

c. It is important to distinguish between the balances in a notice deposit account and the account itself. The account is a relationship between depositor and bank. The money in the account will have the attributes of money, qualified by the increased return that interest pays, the "notice" risk of withdrawal, and the solvency of the trust company in St. John's.

d. There are significant transactions costs in exchanging one share of IBM stock, and its value can be volatile in the short run, making it an imperfect medium of exchange and unit of account. Its qualities as a store of value depend on the health of the company and the economy in which it operates.

e. A $50 Bank of Canada note is cash, and its qualities will correspond accordingly. Of course, its denomination is a multiple of the common unit of our account, which is $1.

f. A MasterCard, like the notice account, indicates the existence of a relationship. Its transferability is severely limited, and its value depends on the terms of the credit agreement. (There is probably an illegal market for MasterCards, in which they assume an independent value for exchange, although they probably lack most of the advantages of a store of value or unit of account.)

g. Because it is negotiable, a chequing account could be a useful medium of exchange, as long as its size does not restrict the available market too strongly. The only limits on its qualities as a store of value are the reliability of the credit union and the value of the money into which it can be converted. Because the value is determined by the size of an anticipated transaction, there is no real independent unit of account to be measured by the chequing account.

h. Assuming that the pass is for the lifetime of the Expos and not for an owner who could not trade the pass, the ticket would be like many other nonmoney goods. Its money qualities would depend on the market available for its exchange and the value taken on by the good in the market. The fortunes of the Expos, the Montreal consumers' taste for baseball, and other demand determinants would affect the three monetary qualities of a lifetime pass.

15-3. M2 consists of the values of M1 plus balances in personal savings accounts and non-personal notice deposits.

15-5.
a. V
b. A
c. V
d. E

15-7. If there are n goods, the number of exchange rates will be $n(n-1)/2$. In this case, $n = 10$, so the number of exchange rates will be $10(10-1)/2 = 90/2 = 45$.

Chapter 16
Money Creation and Deposit Insurance

16-1. a. Multiple Deposit Creation

Bank	Deposits	Reserves	Loans
Bank 1	$1,000,000	$ 250,000	$ 750,000
Bank 2	750,000	187,500	562,500
Bank 3	562,500	140,625	421,875
Bank 4	421,875	105,469	316,406
Bank 5	316,406	79,102	237,304
All other banks	949,219	237,304	711,915
Totals	4,000,000	1,000,000	3,000,000

The money multiplier is 4.

b. Multiple Deposit Creation

Bank	Deposits	Reserves	Loans
Bank 1	$ 1,000,000	$ 50,000	$ 950,000
Bank 2	950,000	47,500	902,500
Bank 3	902,500	45,125	857,375
Bank 4	857,375	42,869	814,506
Bank 5	814,506	40,725	773,781
All other banks	15,475,619	773,781	14,701,838
Totals	20,000,000	1,000,000	19,000,000

The money multiplier is 20.

16-3. a. No change.

b. This is a little tricky. If the Bank of Canada had been "keeping track" of currency, the $1,000 currency buried in Smith's backyard is accounted for; therefore, the money supply will rise by $9,000 because the Bank of Canada did not have to "create" the $1,000 already in existence.

c. The money supply will decrease by $9,000; see (b).

16-5. a. The excess reserves of Bank B are $30.

b. Bank B can lend out $30. A single bank can lend out up to but not exceeding its excess reserves.

c. After the maximum loan is made, loans have increased by $30 to $130, chequable deposits have increased by $30 to $230, and there has been no change in the total reserves.

d. The maximum expansion of the money supply that can occur if Bank B loans $30, thereby creating money, is $30.

Chapter 17
The Bank of Canada and Monetary Policy

17-1. a. The bank's excess reserves have decreased by $2,550,000.

b. The money supply has decreased by $3 million.

c. The money supply can decrease by as much as $20 million.

17-3. a.

Assets		Liabilities	
Total reserves	+$1,000,000	Demand deposits	+$1,000,000
Required reserves ($50,000) + excess reserves ($950,000)			
Total	+$1,000,000	Total	+$1,000,000

b. Bank 1 can increase its lending by $950,000.

17-5. A change in monetary policy leads to a change in interest rates, which leads to a change in investment. This, then, through the multiplier process, leads to a change in income.

17-7.

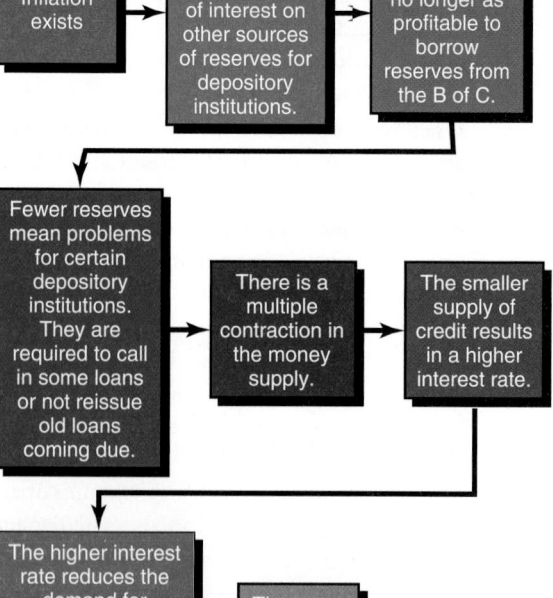

17-9. An expansionary open-market operation (purchase of bonds), for example, means that the public has larger money holdings than desired. This excess quantity of money demanded induces the public to buy more of everything, especially more durable goods. So if the economy is starting out at its long-run equilibrium rate of output, there can only be a short-run increase in real GDP. Ultimately, the public cannot buy more of everything, so it simply bids up prices, such that the price level rises.

Appendix D
Monetary Policy: A Keynesian Perspective

D-1. By its purchase of $100 million in bonds, the Bank of Canada increased excess reserves by $100 million. This ultimately caused a $300 million increase in the money supply after full multiple expansion. The 1 percent drop in the interest rate, from 10 to 9 percent, caused investment to rise by $2.5 billion, from $20 billion to $22.5 billion. An investment multiplier of 3 indicates that equilibrium national income rose by $7.5 billion to $207.5 billion.

Chapter 18
Issues in Stabilization Policy

18-1.   a. 10 percent
   b. A rise in the expected rate of inflation will cause the curve to shift upward by the amount of the rise in expectations.
   c. They argue thus because the systematic policies that attempt to exploit the seeming trade-off will be incorporated into workers' and firms' expectations. As a result, the expected inflation rate will move in lockstep with the actual rate (excepting random errors), so that the unemployment rate will not change when the inflation rate changes.

18-3. The existence of contracts, small-menu costs, and efficiency wages will increase the amount of discretion available to policymakers because all of these will tend to slow the adjustment of wages to changes in expectations.

18-5. A rise in the duration of unemployment will tend to raise the average unemployment rate because each unemployed person will be counted as unemployed more times over any given time period.

18-7. Yes. It is precisely the fact that both employers and workers incorrectly perceive a change in nominal demand as a change in real demand which generates the negatively sloping Phillips curve.

Chapter 19
Comparative Advantage and the Open Economy

19-1.   a. The opportunity cost to Canada of producing one kilogram of caviar is two bushels of wheat. The six hours that were needed to make the caviar could have been used to grow two bushels of wheat. The opportunity cost of producing one bushel of wheat is 0.5 kilogram of caviar.
   b. The opportunity cost to Russia of producing one kilogram of caviar is 0.67 bushels of wheat. The opportunity cost of producing a bushel of wheat in Russia is 1.5 kilograms of caviar.
   c. Canada has a comparative advantage in wheat because it has a lower opportunity cost in terms of caviar. Russia has a comparative advantage in caviar. Less wheat is forgone to produce a kilogram of caviar in Russia.

19-3. The assumption given in the question is equivalent to Canada's having an absolute advantage in the production of all goods and services. But the basis of world trade lies in differences in comparative advantage. As long as other countries have a lower opportunity cost in producing some goods and services, Canada will benefit from international trade.

19-5. Tariffs yield government revenues; quotas do not.

19-7.   a. One million kilograms are produced and 2 million kilograms are imported.
   b. With a 10 cent tariff, 1.5 million kilograms would be produced and 1 million kilograms would be imported. Government revenues would amount to ($2.5 million − $1.5 million) × $.10 = $100,000.
   c. With a 20 cent tariff, domestic growers can receive 70 cents per kilogram. They will produce 2 million kilograms, and no peaches will be imported, in which case government revenues are zero.

19-9. In general, trade restrictions are harmful both to a nation's trading partners and to the nation itself. There may, however, be an exception. If Canada were to impose a tariff in response to other countries' restrictions, that may discourage other countries from imposing restrictions as often as they otherwise would.

Chapter 20
Exchange Rates and the Balance of Payments

20-1. The answer is (c). A declining dollar price of the pound implies an increasing pound price of the dollar—appreciation of the dollar. (a) is incorrect because an increase in demand for Canadian products would affect the supply of pounds and the demand for dollars, whereas here we are dealing with the demand for pounds. (b) explains a phenomenon that would have just the opposite result as that shown in the graph: An increased Canadian demand for British goods would lead to an increase in the demand for the pound, not a decrease as shown. (d) is incorrect because the pound depreciates.

20-3. One pound equals $3.50; $1 equals 0.2857 pound. One mark equals 35 cents; $1 equals 2.857 marks. One mark equals 0.1 pound; one pound equals 10 marks.

20-5. To maintain the exchange rate, domestic policy variables such as the money supply are also affected. Suppose that the government plans an expansive monetary policy to encourage output growth. A balance of payments deficit leads the government to buy up dollars, which in turn leads to a contraction in the domestic money supply. Therefore, in order to maintain the expansionary monetary policy, the government would have to expand the money supply in larger magnitudes than it would without the balance of payments deficits with a fixed exchange rate system.

20-7. a. The dollar price of pounds is $1.50. The equilibrium quantity is 150 million pounds.
b. Curve D' describes this situation. The new dollar price of pounds would be $1.70, and the equilibrium quantity would be 200 million.
c. At a price of $1.50 per pound, 250 million pounds sterling would be demanded and only 150 million would be supplied, so the Bank of Canada would have to supply an extra 100 million pounds to Canadian buyers of British goods or British exporters.
d. Curve D'' describes this situation. 150 million pounds sterling would be supplied at a price of

$1.50, but only 50 million pounds would be demanded. Therefore, the Bank of Canada would have to buy up 100 million pounds sterling.

Chapter 21
Development: Economic Growth Around the World

21-1. The following countries may be considered developing countries: Burkina Faso, Bangladesh, Afghanistan, India, and China; there are many others. The following are considered industrially advanced countries: Canada, Australia, Germany, France, and the United States; there are many others.

21-3. Initially, there is an agricultural stage where most of the population is involved in agriculture. Many developing countries are still in this stage. Then comes the manufacturing stage. Industry dominates the economy, and gains from the division of labour lead to rapid increases in output. In the final stage, the service sector becomes prominent in the economy. Canada and other industrially advanced countries are in this stage.

21-5. Economic development depends greatly on individuals who are able to perceive and take advantage of opportunities. Immigrants who possessed attributes such as these started Canada on the road to our present affluence. In general, voluntary exchange is mutually beneficial. If the potential immigrants are willing and able to offer their services at prices (wages) that existing residents are willing to pay, and to purchase the goods and services offered for sale by existing residents, the immigrants' arrival is likely to benefit existing residents as well as themselves.

21-7. It is important to remember that all resources are owned by human beings, and that in general there is an optimal (wealth-maximizing) mix of land, labour, and capital. So even though population growth (relative to growth in capital or land) would be expected to lower wages, it would also be expected to raise the earnings of capital and land. On balance, if the population growth moved the country closer to the optimal mix of land, labour, and capital, the added income accruing to the owners of land and capital would more than offset the reduced earnings of labour, producing an overall rise in per capita income.

ANSWERS TO CRITICAL ANALYSIS QUESTIONS

Chapter 1
The Nature of Economics

Issues and Applications: Does Money Buy Happiness?

1. In answering this question it is important to note that pursuing one's self-interest does not mean just spending additional income on oneself. It can also include spending income in ways that help loved ones, help others in need, help establish one's prestige in the community, and so forth. This realization may help you appreciate why it is rational for individuals to prefer higher income over lower income even if the additional money does not buy personal happiness.

2. a. The politician can use this model to consider proposing tax cuts which provide voters with higher after-tax income.

   b. Hospital management can use this model to devise a policy of offering above-average wages to those nurses who decide to live in its remote region.

   c. The newly established bank can use this model to devise a strategy of offering interest rates that exceed the rates offered by the new bank's competition.

Chapter 2
Scarcity and the World of Trade-Offs

Issues and Applications: The Costs of Raising a Child

1. One factor that causes the costs of raising a child to decline at age six and again at age 12 is daycare expenses. At age six, the parent can reduce costs by replacing full-time daycare costs with part-time, after-school, daycare costs. When a child becomes 12 years of age, many parents likely eliminate all the child's daycare expenses.

2. According to the current discussion, the cost of raising a child includes forgone wages, as well as explicit costs. In lower-income countries, parents who stay at home raising their children do not sacrifice as much in wages as parents who live in higher-income countries. Hence, it is not surprising to observe higher birth rates in lower-income countries.

Chapter 3
Economies in Transition

Issues and Applications: For-Profit Health Care in Canada?

1. Since the Canadian patient does not pay an additional charge for each additional visit to a physician, there is a danger that the limited Health care resources do not get allocated to the highest-valued uses. Also, since government budgets play a major role in the total amount of resources devoted to health care, there is a concern that the supply of health care services will not keep up with the increased demand for these services due to the aging population and new technology.

2. In cases where privately owned HMOs hire health care resources in the US, the profit motive can serve as a strong incentive to keep the costs of providing a given quality of health care to a minimum, thereby promoting productive efficiency.

3. In those situations where patients must pay a significant co-payment for each hospital or physical visit, the health care services will be less accessible to lower-income patients, despite the fact that these patients might have a greater need to use the health care services. Also, the existence of experience ratings severely penalizes those who are chronically ill (through no fault of their own).

4. The data described in Tables 3.4 and 3.5 may be explained by the fact that the more competitive US health care system results in an excessive duplication of administrative expenses. That is, compared to the US, for every dollar that Canadians spend on health care, a greater portion of that dollar goes to serving the patient and not the owners and managers of private health care corporations.

Chapter 4
Demand and Supply

Issues and Applications: Online Auctions: Reaching Equilibrium Price on the Web

1. In a typical auction, the supply of the item being auctioned is fixed, which means that the supply curve is a fixed vertical line. In this case, it is the buyers who must

compete with each other by bidding up the price until an equilibrium price is reached. The advantage of letting the equilibrium price prevail (the highest bidder wins) is that the product offered for sale ends up in the hands of the buyer(s) who place the highest value on the product.

2. The successful bid for a particular product in one auction can be an important factor affecting the equilibrium price for other auctions of the same product, assuming that there has been no significant shift in demand or supply in these other auctions. If there was a significant difference between the price of the same product offered at different auctions, middlemen could make a profit by buying the auctioned item where it is offered at a low price and then immediately reselling this item in auctions where buyers are willing to pay high prices. This is called "arbitrage." These arbitrage activities will tend to increase the demand for the auctioned items in markets where the item is "underpriced." Thus, arbitrage tends to equalize the equilibrium price for an item sold at different auctions.

Chapter 5
Elasticity

Issues and Applications: The Y2K Energy Crisis

1. Between 1997 and 1998, while the supply of oil significantly increased, the demand decreased due to the economic slowdown in the Asian economies. As a result, the price of a barrel of oil fell to record low levels.

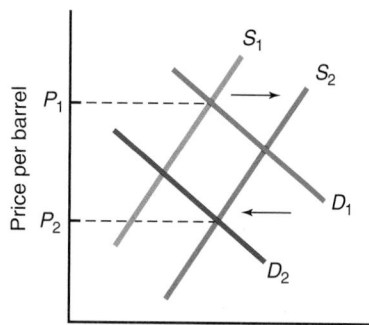

Quantity of barrels

2. The percentage change in quantity = $(25.65 - 23.77)/24.71 = 0.076$ or 7.6%

The percentage change in price = $(26.21 - 11.08)/18.65 = 0.811$ or 81.1%

The elasticity of demand = 7.6/81.1 = 0.094 or inelastic.

The daily total revenue increased from (11.08×25.65) = \$284.20 million to (26.21×23.77) = \$623.01 million.

This is consistent with the theory of elasticity which suggests that when demand is inelastic, an increase in price will increase total revenue.

3. Demand factors included an increase in the growth rate of the global economy and the anticipation of increased heating requirements for the cold winter months. Supply factors included OPEC suppliers producing at near capacity, reduction in capacity of the world tanker fleet, and potential conflict between Iraq and Kuwait.

4. The Liberal government believed that the demand was inelastic. This is because a tax would increase the price of gasoline and therefore reduce the quantity demanded for gasoline. However, since the government expected government revenue to increase, they believed that the percentage decrease in quantity would be less than the percentage increase in price—inelastic demand.

5. A decrease in the gasoline tax would increase the supply of gasoline and therefore decrease the equilibrium price of gasoline. The decrease in gasoline prices would increase the profitability and supply in other markets such as taxi services, trucking services, and courier services.

6. A decrease in taxes would increase the supply and equilibrium quantity of gasoline usage. This would only add to the global concerns surrounding the "greenhouse effect."

Chapter 6
The Public Sector

Issues and Applications: Should We Switch to a Flat Tax?

1. Employees at Revenue Canada might well be against a flat-tax system. Advocates of a flat tax claim that one of the benefits would be a significantly downsized Revenue Canada, implying that many Revenue Canada employees might lose their jobs. We know from Chapter 1 that the rationality assumption tells us that people usually don't make decisions that reduce their well-being. It is likely that Revenue Canada employees would want to keep their jobs to maintain their well-being, and would thus oppose a flat-tax system.

2. A flat-tax system is more efficient than a progressive tax system because the method of calculation of tax owing is much simpler: there is only one calculation to make, rather than the many calculations required in a progressive system. There would be efficiencies realized by taxpayers who could complete their tax returns easily, and by Revenue Canada employees who could check the calculation as simply. The opportunity cost of the yearly

tax return would fall, leaving resources free to pursue more productive activities.

Chapter 7
The Macroeconomy: Unemployment and Inflation

Issues and Applications: Do We Need to Worry About Deflation?

1. In order to protect yourself against deflation you need to have an asset that is fixed in value, and won't change in value as prices rise and fall. Most of our assets will tend to change in value over time with the general rate of change in prices. Houses, stocks and commodities such as gold all fluctuate in value. However, some assets don't fluctuate, such as bonds and cash. These will hold their value regardless of the decline in the price level since their value is fixed. You can protect yourself against deflation, therefore, by keeping your assets in cash and bonds, which will gain purchasing power as prices fall.

2. Deflation means most businesses across the country are actually lowering their prices as part of a long-term trend. Businesses would be reluctant to do this because lower prices usually mean lower profits. Remember that they pay their expenses before they can sell their product, so they have paid for these products before they get to market with (relatively expensive) money. In order for businesses to undertake this behaviour, we would expect that it would only happen if there were a major recession occurring at the same time, which would mean a rising rate of unemployment.

Chapter 8
Measuring the Economy's Performance

Issues and Applications: The Worldwide Underground Economy

1. Revenue Canada is overestimating the lost tax revenue because its estimate of "off-the-books" income is too high. If all underground activities were declared, those relating to drug trafficking, illegal gambling, and prostitution would decrease as authorities put an end to them. The size of the underground economy would shrink, and the lost tax revenue would decline as well.

2. If the government declared many transactions which are now part of the underground economy free of tax, the incentive to avoid federal and sales tax would disappear. For example, if street vendors did not have to pay sales tax on their sales, there would be no reason for them not to declare their income.

Chapter 9
Economic Growth: Technology, Research and Development, and Knowledge

Issues and Applications: Setting Goals for a Nation: What Do We Aim For?

1. Measured GDP growth will be bigger than would be indicated by the GPI because the GPI calculation would deduct a value for the pollution created by the oil project, the consumption of the oil products themselves, and the depletion of the resources used in the oil projects from measured economic activity.

2. The answer to this question will depend upon your individual values.

3. With many activities moving from the "unmeasured" economy to the "measured" economy, you would naturally see an increase in measured GDP, without a corresponding increase in the standard of living. Simply because childcare is now provided by a daycare instead of a "stay-at-home" parent, doesn't mean we are better off economically. Indeed, many people feel that having two working parents in a family is creating tremendous stress and difficulty for family life.

   However, this must also be measured against the increase in satisfaction that is felt be people who now have careers that weren't possible a couple of generations ago. Indeed, much of the change brought about by the feminist movement was not about economics, but about choices for women that they didn't have before. With the increase in opportunity for women, there is likely to be a greater sense of self-worth and satisfaction, which is not measured in GDP.

Chapter 10
Modelling the Economy: Aggregate Demand and Aggregate Supply

Issues and Applications: What If ...?

1. Both aggregate demand and aggregate supply will shift to the left. Aggregate demand will decrease because of a drop in investment spending and a reduction in consumption expenditure. Consumption expenditure will decline because of the higher cost of borrowing for many consumption goods (such as automobiles). Because of the reduced expectations about the future, Canadians will likely increase their savings today.

   Foreigners and Canadians will also be less likely to invest in Canada because of the political uncertainty associated with the breakup of Canada. This will result in a reduction in investment expenditure (affecting aggregate demand) and will result in a reduced short-run and long-run aggregate supply (because of a reduced ability to produce).

The decline in the value of the Canadian dollar will offset some of the effect on the aggregate demand side of the economy because of the increased costs of purchasing imports, and make our exports cheaper. It will, however, increase the costs of inputs that are purchased abroad.

According to the BMO forecast, the declines in aggregate demand and supply are likely to substantially decrease real GDP, both in the short run with a recession, and affect the long-run potential output of the Canadian economy.

2. Forecasting is important for businesses because they will be making decisions today that are dependent upon economic conditions in the future. It may take several years for new equipment to be available for use in production. The ability to accurately forecast the demand for the production will make a difference as to whether or not the business will be willing to undertake that investment. Investment is one of the most variable of the components of GDP, and this is a result of this uncertainty about the future that always exists.

Chapter 11
Classical and Keynesian Macro Analyses

Issues and Applications: The Impact of the Great Depression

1. There exist a number of income-replacement programs that give money to people when they are not working. These include:

   • Employment Insurance (formerly called Unemployment Insurance) This program gives individuals a portion of their income earned while working during periods of unemployment, typically up to a year. This program is federally administered and funded by premiums paid by people when they are employed.

   • Canada Assistance Plan. This program is sometimes called "welfare." It provides a minimal level of income to people who otherwise have no available income. This program is funded jointly by the federal and provincial governments.

   • Worker's Compensation. This program compensates employees who are injured in the workplace. The program provides income, training and some medical services to injured workers, and enforces safety regulations. This provincial government program is funded through premiums charged to employers.

   • Old Age Security and Guaranteed Income Supplement. Old Age Security (OAS) and the Guaranteed Income Supplement provide basic income security for low- and middle-income seniors. The program is funded through federal government revenues.

   • Canada Pension Plan. This program is designed to ensure that working people who retire have sufficient income to make ends meet. It is funded through payroll deduction by both employers and employees while working. It is federally administered, except in Quebec.

   • Tax credits and deductions. Various tax credits and deductions are available to all Canadians, but many are aimed at particular groups. There are currently child tax credits and GST credits available to low-income Canadians. and various deductions available to anyone earning income that will reduce taxes owing to the government.

   All of these programs provide income to people when they are unemployed, and most are "income tested," that is, they are only payable when income is low. When recessions occur, and people lose their jobs, they become eligible to receive payments from these various programs. The payments ensure that they can continue to consume and spend (albeit at a lower level) than if there were no program. This keeps the economy from falling as far into a recession as it otherwise would if these people had no income.

2. The Second World War brought Canada out of recession because of the huge increase in government spending associated with being at war. The government itself hired hundreds of thousands of people directly for the war effort, and purchased many more billions of goods and services from private industry than it would otherwise have purchased. This had the effect of greatly reducing unemployment and pushed the economy to full employment.

Chapter 12
Consumption, Income, and the Multiplier

Issues and Applications: Can Stock Market Crashes Affect the Economy?

1. Declining business confidence means that businesses will require a greater return on their investments in order to undertake that investment. This would shift the planned investment schedule to the left, as illustrated below.

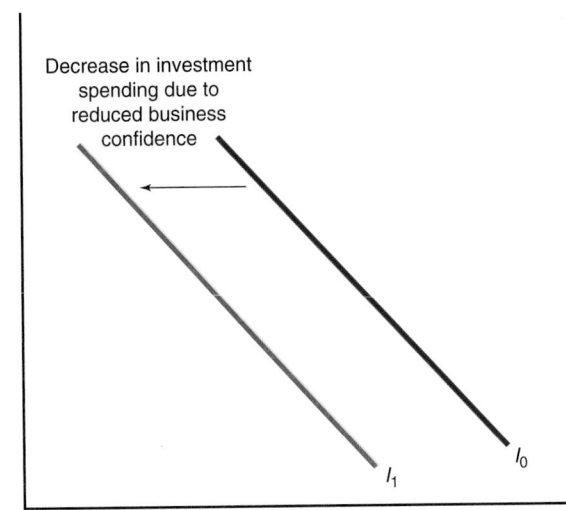

Decrease in investment spending due to reduced business confidence

Rate of Interest (y-axis)

I_1 I_0

Planned Investment per Year ($ billion)

2. A decline in consumer confidence would mean a decline in consumer spending. This could result in both a reduction in autonomous spending which would shift the consumption function down in figure 12.3, and a reduction in the MPC, which would mean the consumption function was flatter. With a decline in the MPC, the proportion of disposable income going to savings would increase, and thus reduce the value of the multiplier.

Chapter 13
Fiscal Policy

Issues and Applications: Employment Insurance and the Deficit

1. If the employee's share of the EI payroll tax were reduced, employees would have more disposable income. With more disposable income, consumption (and saving) would increase. Businesses would experience inventory decreases and would increase their rate of production, employing more workers in the process. With more people employed, unemployment would fall, tax revenues would increase, and payments out of the EI fund would decrease. The deficit would fall.

2. Raising the GST instead of using payroll taxes to raise money would mean that the disincentive to hire new employees would be lessened. It would mean that employers have fewer expenses when hiring employees, and therefore they would likely hire more of them. With the GST, the cost of the taxes would be much more broadly based, and have a smaller effect on the economy.

    Any policy the government has to reduce the deficit during a recession will likely deepen and lengthen the recession. Increasing taxes and/or reducing spending will have a fiscal "drag" on the economy as it recovers from any recession. While this is appropriate when the economy is experiencing a boom, it will worsen a recession. While dealing with the deficit, the trade-off is that any recession would be exacerbated.

Chapter 14
Deficit Spending and the Public Debt

Issues and Applications: The Baby Boom Generation Moves into Retirement Years

1. Unanticipated lifespan increases mean that the Canada Pension Plan must pay out more to retirees than it had anticipated. This would mean that the rate paid by contributors would be too low during their contributing years, and that the difference would have to be made up by the government or by current contributors.

2. The Registered Retirement Savings Plan program is a tax-deferral plan whereby money can be saved today for withdrawal at a later date, usually after retirement. The government will collect taxes from these savings at the time of the withdrawal; no taxes are paid today. The other benefit for the government is that fewer people will receive benefits under the income-supplement programs that are available to elderly people. The RRSP funds also provide a pool of savings for investment, thus helping today's economy as well as we learned in chapter 9.

Chapter 15
Money and the Banking System

Issues and Applications: The Dollarization Movement: Is the US Fed Destined to be a Multinational Central Bank?

1. The advantage of dollarizing an economy would be increased faith in the currency (acceptability) and reduced transactions costs associated with currency conversion in international commerce. The increased transparency and predictability in prices should encourage more investment and trade. This will result in improved efficiency and increased welfare from the reduced uncertainty and better resource allocation.

2. If actual US currency had to be acquired by issuing bonds to the US government, then there would be payments to the United States out of Canadian and Argentine tax collections every year. If the US Fed raised US interest rates, then Canadian and Argentine citizens would have to pay higher taxes to the United States.

Chapter 16
Money Creation and Deposit Insurance

Issues and Applications: Deregulating the Financial Services Industry

1. A bank is a business that holds funds for customers and grants loans to customers who qualify. A nonbank bank is a business that does the above but is not a bank. An example of a nonbank bank would be an insurance company, or a trust company such as Canada Trust.

2. There could be an increased moral hazard problem as banks diversify their services. With deposit insurance, banks already have an incentive to take on riskier investments than may be prudent. The additional profits the bank could earn from the sale of insurance or airline tickets would act as an increased incentive to sell to high-risk customers, or to grant credit to less-than-creditworthy customers for air travel. Because of the existence of deposit insurance, customers would still lack the incentive to monitor the bank's decisions closely.

Chapter 17
The Bank of Canada and Monetary Policy

Issues and Applications: Is the Bank of Canada Independent, and If Not, Does It Matter?

1. Following the *Coyne Affair*, the Bank of Canada Act was amended in 1967. The Act now allows the Government of Canada to issue a directive to the Bank in the event of a serious disagreement over the conduct of monetary policy. However, former Governor G. Thiessen said: "... because of the consequences of issuing a directive, it is likely to be used only in unusual circumstances. Thus, a high degree of operational independence has ... been preserved." (See page 393.)

2. We would expect to see New Zealand's net exports increase. The nominal interest rate is the real interest rate plus a premium for expected inflation. If inflation decreases, interest rates decrease. When interest rates decrease, foreigners wish to hold fewer financial instruments denominated in the New Zealand currency. Therefore there is a decrease in the demand for the currency, and its exchange rate depreciates. With a relatively less valuable currency, imports fall and exports rise, thus increasing net exports.

Chapter 18
Issues in Stabilization Policy

Issues and Applications: The Bank of Canada's High Interest Rate Policy

1. Passive investment in financial instruments to earn a hefty return will result in a reduction in interest rates. As we learned in Chapter 17, as bond prices rise, interest rates fall. With lower interest rates, investors will be tempted to turn to active investing in technology and businesses. Active investment in businesses and technology will stimulate aggregate demand. Depending on the output gap, the result in the economy will be inflation if the economy is at full employment, or economic growth if the economy is not.

2. The policy irrelevance proposition states that no real variables can be affected by anticipated policy. Since former Governor Theissen announced his plan to keep interest rates relatively high to combat inflation, players in the economy are informed, and will not act to decrease unemployment.

Chapter 19
Comparative Advantage and the Open Economy

Issues and Applications: Playing Chicken with the United States

1. If the TRQs on dairy and poultry are eventually removed, imports from the United States will be much cheaper in Canadian markets. Canadian dairy and poultry farmers will have to compete with the imports—which means working to reduce their costs. Some producers will probably go out of business, but, as the beef producers have shown, others should be able to become competitive with US producers.

2. Canada has a comparative advantage in producing beef, but not dairy products or poultry. Dairy and poultry farmers argue that the Canadian climate drives up their costs. Beef farmers do not face those same costs, as beef cattle remain outside in all but the most inclement weather. Also, beef cattle can graze on open fields in the summer, while dairy cows must be milked, and poultry fed purchased feed. Since comparative advantage derives from having a lower cost of production that other countries, Canadian beef farmers have an advantage over dairy and poultry producers.

Chapter 20
Exchange Rates and the Balance of Payments

Issues and Applications: Should We Worry About the Weak Dollar?

1. A lower rate of inflation in Germany would lead to a weaker Canadian dollar because of the change in relative prices. Lower inflation in Germany means that German goods and services will now be relatively less expensive. Consumers will substitute the relatively cheaper German products for Canadian products. The demand for the Deutsche mark will increase, the Deutsche mark will appreciate, and the Canadian dollar will depreciate. Figure 20-5 depicts this scenario.

2. Foreigners will agree to hold Canadian dollars instead of their own currencies if they anticipate consuming Canadian goods and services. Everything from clothing and produce, to Canadian stocks and bonds, to tourism, must be paid for in Canadian dollars—which foreigners must obtain somehow. Another reason foreigners might hold Canadian dollars is for speculative purposes. In 1998 the Canadian dollar reached all-time lows vis-à-vis the US dollar. A speculator may purchase Canadian dollars when the value is low, hold them until the value rises in the currency market, and then sell them to make a capital gain.

Chapter 21
Development: Economic Growth Around the World

Issues and Applications: International Development and Basic Education

1. Canada invests heavily in its children through a number of different programs. All children receive their basic education for free, and post-secondary education is heavily subsidized. As well, children receive free medical care as part of the health care system, and there are various income supplements and tax credits for families with children that have low incomes. The federal government has also considered spending more money on subsidized day care for children. All of these investments ensure that most children in Canada will grow up to become healthy contributors to Canadian society.

2. International development helps Canadians in many ways. First, as foreign incomes grow, Canadians are able to sell more exports, and thus development and the associated trade provides Canadians with jobs. Second, international development is usually associated with greater peace and thus we are able enjoy a safer world. Third, a growth in income also means there will be less population growth, and thus less strain on the environment in the long run.

INDEX